www.wadsworth.com

wadsworth.com is the World Wide Web site for Wadsworth and is your direct source to dozens of online resources.

At *wadsworth.com* you can find out about supplements, demonstration software, and student resources. You can also send email to many of our authors and preview new publications and exciting new technologies.

wadsworth.com
Changing the way the world lea

Statistics and
Data Interpretation
for the Helping Professions

James A. Rosenthal
University of Oklahoma, Norman

BROOKS/COLE

THOMSON LEARNING ™

Australia • Canada • Mexico • Singapore • Spain • United Kingdom • United States

BROOKS/COLE

THOMSON LEARNING

Social Work Executive Editor: Lisa Gebo
Assistant Editor: Susan Wilson
Editorial Assistant: Sheila Walsh
Marketing Manager: Caroline Concilla
Marketing Assistant: Jessica McFadden
Project Editor: Teri Hyde
Print Buyer: Barbara Britton
Permissions Editor: Bob Kauser

Production Service: Penmarin Books
Copy Editor: Anita Wagner
Illustrator: PRD Group
Cover Designer: Cuttriss & Hambleton
Cover Image: Courtesy of PhotoDisc
Cover Printer: R.R. Donnelley, Crawfordsville
Compositor: PRD Group
Printer: R.R. Donnelley, Crawfordsville

Wadsworth/Thomson Learning
10 Davis Drive
Belmont, CA 94002-3098
USA

For more information about our products, contact us:
Thomson Learning Academic Resource Center
1-800-423-0563
http://www.wadsworth.com

International Headquarters
Thomson Learning
International Division
290 Harbor Drive, 2nd Floor
Stamford, CT 06902-7477
USA

UK/Europe/Middle East/South Africa
Thomson Learning
Berkshire House
168-173 High Holborn
London WC1V 7AA
United Kingdom

Asia
Thomson Learning
60 Albert Street, #15-01
Albert Complex
Singapore 189969

Canada
Nelson Thomson Learning
1120 Birchmount Road
Toronto, Ontario M1K 5G4
Canada

Library of Congress Cataloging-in-Publication Data

Rosenthal, James A.
    Statistics and data interpretation for the helping professions /
James A. Rosenthal.
        p. cm.
    Includes bibliographical references and index.
    ISBN 0-8304-1509-2
        1. Social sciences—Statistical methods. 2. Social service—
Statistical methods. 3. Statistics. I. Title.

HA29 .R795 2000
001.4'22—dc21   00-043975

Grateful acknowledgement is given for permission to adapt excerpts from the following article(s):

Rosenthal, J. A. (1997). Pragmatic concepts and tools for data interpretation: A balanced model. *Journal of Teaching in Social Work, 15*(1/2), 113–130).

Rosenthal, J. A. (1996). Qualitative descriptors of strength of association and effect size. *Journal of Social Service Research, 21*(4), 37–59.

Contents

Chapter 5

Shape of Distribution and Important Distributions   **73**

Part Three

ASSOCIATION BETWEEN TWO VARIABLES   **97**

Chapter 6

The Concept of Relationship and Relationship Between Categorical Variables   **98**

Part Four

CAUSAL AND NONCAUSAL RELATIONSHIPS   173

Chapter 10

The Assessment of Causality   174

Chapter 11

Controlling for Confounding Variables   194

Part Five

INFERENTIAL STATISTICS: BEGINNING APPLICATIONS   213

Chapter 12

An Introduction to Inferential Statistics   215

Chapter 13

Confidence Intervals for Means and Proportions   233

Chapter 14

The Logic of Statistical Significance Tests   249

Chapter 15

The Large Sample Test of the Mean and New Concepts   267

Chapter 16

Statistical Power and Selected Topics   297

Part Six

SELECTED SIGNIFICANCE TESTS AND A DATA INTERPRETATION MODEL   317

Chapter 17

The t Distribution and One-Sample Procedures for Means   318

Chapter 18

Independent Samples t Test and Dependent Samples t Test   337

Chapter 19

Single Sample Tests of Proportions   360

Chapter 20

The Chi-Square Test of Independence   376

Chapter 21

Analysis of Variance   391

Chapter 22

Selected Statistical Tests   407

Chapter 23

Generalizability, Importance, and a
Data Interpretation Model   427

Appendix A

Tables   447

Appendix B

Review of Basic Math   455

Appendix C

Introductory Computer Exercise for SPSS for Windows 10.0   463

Appendix D

Description of Variables in Data Set for End-of-Chapter
Computer Exercises   477

Appendix E

Appropriate Measures for Different Situations   479

Appendix F

Answers to End-of-Chapter Problems and Questions   482

Preface

GETTING STARTED

Statistics involves the use of numbers to summarize data and research study findings. I sometimes come away from reading journal articles thinking that the fundamental goal of statistics is to mystify: If one can say something in a complicated, abstract way that most cannot understand, they must, by definition, be saying something important. Furthermore, although many articles present sophisticated statistical methods, authors often forget the fundamentals, the straightforward and commonsense side of things. Several years ago, I resolved to write a straightforward statistics text that emphasized fundamentals and common sense.

But as I wrote this text, I increasingly realized that statistics is not easy, that is, that the fundamentals require rigorous and critical thinking. This text seeks to fill a middle ground. On the one hand, many texts are complicated, mathematical, and difficult. At the other extreme, particularly in the helping professions, some texts are so simplified that they do not sufficiently prepare one for the tasks ahead—understanding the professional literature and carrying out basic research studies.

CHARACTERISTICS OF THE TEXT

What are some key characteristics of *Statistics and Data Interpretation for the Helping Professions?* First, it gives careful attention to fundamentals. The length of the text reflects its in-depth coverage of basics rather than the inclusion of advanced material. Second, extensive end-of-chapter exercises include both simple hand-calculation problems and computer-based applications. The chapter exercises are of sufficient depth and scope so that a separate workbook is not needed. These text-based computer materials are built assuming the use of SPSS for Windows program, Version 10.0, and include a 90-minute exercise that introduces the program. The text has enough material to get the student started in SPSS without a separate book dedicated to SPSS. A third distinguishing feature is that examples are based on human services settings and agencies.

A fourth characteristic—and what most differentiates this text from others—is that it moves the student beyond statistical procedures into data interpretation. The text teaches one how to decide whether study results do one or more of the following:

- May simply reflect *chance* (the "luck of the draw")
- Demonstrate that one factor (variable) *causes* another
- *Generalize* from the study setting to some other setting
- Convey *important* information

A considerable amount of the text material is on the cusp between statistics and research and thus provides a segue into content that courses in research methods typically cover in greater depth.

The text seeks to ground students in the concepts and tools of statistics and data interpretation. Its examples are geared toward social work (my discipline), the human services, and counseling. Many examples are also pertinent to allied fields such as criminal justice, geriatrics, public administration, public health, and education. A psychology or sociology professor with a pragmatic bent might like this book. It is appropriate for both undergraduate and masters students. The text is supported by a Website, http://helpingprofs.wadsworth.com/resources/rosenthal/rosenthal.html, which includes a data set for the computer exercises.

FOR FACULTY

This section is for potential instructors (so others may skip ahead). *Statistics and Data Interpretation for the Helping Profession* is designed to be used in a one-semester dedicated statistics course or in a two-semester sequence that combines statistics and research. It provides a brief review of basic math, and the text includes a moderate amount of hand (calculator) calculation, most often with conceptual formulas that help students understand the procedure. It is accompanied by an instructor's manual.

The text emphasizes size, or strength, of association much more than most texts in the field do. In particular, it presents qualitative descriptors for interpreting size of association for assorted combinations of variables at different levels of measurement. Though strength of association is presented in relationship to percentage of shared variance, the emphasis is on tools that are more straightforward and intuitive. For instance, discussion of a difference between means interprets this difference in terms of standard deviation units (in essence, effect size). The text emphasizes measures that are straightforward and, as much as possible, part of everyday life. For instance, the percentage difference and the odds ratio rather than phi are emphasized for assessing relationship between dichotomous variables. The text conveys some of the usually unspoken realities of human services research, for instance, that researchers often conduct significance tests with non-random samples.

Multivariate analysis is not covered, with the exception that contingency table examples demonstrate control for confounding variables and multiple regression is briefly discussed. The final chapter presents a five-part data interpretation model that emphasizes statistical significance (or lack thereof), size of association, causality, generalizability, and importance.

SUMMING UP

Kennth D. Hopkins, my statistics professor at the University of Colorado School of Education, and Larry E. Toothaker, David Ross Boyd Professor of Psychology at the University of Oklahoma, consulted generously with me on a variety of questions. At the University of Oklahoma School of Social Work, Julia M. Norlin, former director of the school, supported the project enthusiastically, Elaine Waters created numerous figures, and Carla Jennings and Wendy Nelson helped with many tasks. I also thank my reviewers: J. M. Gold, University of South Carolina; Richard W. Greenlee, Ohio University; Rob Lawson, Western Washington University; Christine Marlow, New Mexico State University; Bill Nugent, University of Tennessee, Knoxville; Cathy Pike, University of South Carolina, Columbia; Roosevelt Wright, Jr., University of Missouri, St. Louis. At Brooks/Cole, Susan Wilson, assistant editor for the helping professions, encouraged me through several rewrites. Anita Wagner's editing enhanced both readability and organization. Hal Lockwood of Penmarin Books helped guide the text to its final format. Thanks also to Teri Hyde at Wadsworth. And biggest thanks of all to my family—Cindy, Catie, Aaron, Mom, Dad, and faithful basset/beagle Rainbow.

I trust that you will find *Statistics and Data Interpretation for the Helping Professions* to be a solid, pragmatic book that helps data make sense. A good foundation in statistics and data interpretation can help you as you help people and communities.

Jim Rosenthal
University of Oklahoma School of Social Work
Norman, Oklahoma

INTRODUCTION AND THE PRESENTATION OF DATA

Part One introduces basic concepts that will give you a solid footing in the field of statistics and discusses how you can present data. Chapters 1 and 2 both present concepts, and Chapter 1 also gives an overview of the key topics in this text. Chapter 2 goes on to focus on how to present data via tables and figures.

INTRODUCTION AND OVERVIEW

1.1 CHAPTER OVERVIEW

Although some parts of statistics are complex, you will find it much easier once you understand basic concepts that underlie the field. Chapter 1 presents some of these concepts and gives an overview of what this book will cover. We begin with a discussion of how the field of *statistics*° fits within the broader fields of research and science. Next we focus on *variables* and different *levels of measurement*. The concept of *relationship* and the distinction between *univariate, bivariate,* and *multivariate* statistical procedures are covered. We take a first look at how to assess whether one variable *causes* another, and we consider the distinction between *surveys* and *experiments* and also between *random* and *nonrandom* samples. The chapter presents the two major branches of statistics, *descriptive statistics* and *inferential statistics*. But as the chapter emphasizes, we need to keep in mind that importance cannot be determined by statistical tools alone.

1.2 PHILOSOPHICAL FOUNDATIONS AND BACKGROUND

People learn about the world around them from many different sources, including tradition, experience, common sense, intuition, and trial and error. No approach to learning is perfect. Common sense, for instance, is sometimes dead wrong, and any approach may be flawed by human mistakes. Science attempts to develop *objective* knowledge, less prone to human error than knowledge gained in other ways. Most people would agree that although it's not perfect, science has succeeded at least to some degree with this task.

°In the introduction to each chapter, selected key terms and concepts to be presented in the chapter are italicized. Definitions are provided within the chapter, pointed out by the same term in bold.

Science has two sides, a theoretical side based on theory, concepts, and ideas and an applied side built on real-world observations. The theoretical side is termed **theory.** The gathering of real-world observations is termed **research.** The observations that are gathered are one's **data.** Social science research involves **measurement,** that is, the process of assigning numbers or classifications to observations/data.

Broadly speaking, human services research uses two basic methods, qualitative and quantitative. **Quantitative research methods** are characterized by objective measurement, usually involving numbers. The two basic quantitative research designs are the experiment and the survey, both of which are discussed later in this chapter. **Qualitative methods** "emphasize depth of understanding and the deeper meanings of human experience" (Rubin and Babbie, 1997, Glossary p. 7). Important qualitative methods include field research and in-depth interviewing. Though the procedures presented in this text are sometimes used in qualitative studies, its predominant focus is on the analysis and interpretation of data as gathered in quantitative research studies.

This chapter seeks to build a "vocabulary," as we've already begun to do. As stated above, the data are the measurements that have been made and recorded. If, for instance, you record the gender and height of each person in your current class, these measurements are your data. Broadly speaking, a **statistic** is a numerical summary of data (Toothaker and Miller, 1996, p. 7). For instance, if 72% of students in your class are female, then "72%" is a statistic; it provides a numerical summary of data. Similarly, if the average height is 5 feet $7\frac{1}{2}$ inches, then "5 feet $7\frac{1}{2}$ inches" is a statistic.

The field of **statistics** can be defined as the study of ways to summarize data. As used in this text, "data analysis" and "statistics" have the same meaning. This book's title, *Statistics and Data Interpretation for the Helping Professions,* uses the term "data interpretation." The dictionary defines *interpret* as "to explain the meaning of." This text seeks to teach not only statistical analysis but also how to understand what one's data "mean."

1.3 MEASUREMENT IN SOCIAL RESEARCH

Measurements are recorded for individual units, and each unit is a **case.** In social research, cases are typically individual people. In the example above, you recorded the gender and height of each person in your class, and each person represents a different case. Thus, if your class consists of 30 individuals (and presuming that you took measurements on all of them) your data consist of 30 cases. Cases are not always persons. For instance, a research study might examine the rate of child abuse reporting in each of the 50 states of the United States. In such a study, each state represents a different case. (Or, one could equally well say, each case represents a different state.)

The different kinds of measurements that are made for each case are referred to as variables. For instance, the classroom data have two variables, these being gender and height.

In a general sense, a variable is a characteristic of a case. In our example, each case in the classroom data has two characteristics, sex and height. The more specific and formal meaning of **variable** is something that takes on different values. For instance, sex takes on two different values, female and male. Height may take on many different values, for instance, 5 feet $4\frac{1}{2}$ inches, 5 feet $7\frac{1}{4}$ inches, and 6 feet 2 inches. Given that they take on different values, gender and height meet the formal definition and thus are variables.

A definition of **value** (*attribute*) is the different numbers or classifications that a variable assumes or takes on. Variables and values are sometimes confused. Thus, for instance, female and male are values that the variable sex may take on or assume. Similarly, the different heights of your classmates are the values of the variable height. **Score** is a synonym for numeric value. For instance, if someone is 67 inches tall, the score on the height variable is "67 inches."

Variables can be distinguished from constants. **Constants** take on only one value. Pi (π, the ratio of a circle's circumference to its diameter), for instance, is a constant. It *always* equals 3.14159. If all the students in your class are of the same sex, then in your data, sex is not a variable but a constant.

Variables should also be distinguished from concepts. **Concepts** are "something conceived in the mind" and are the ingredients of scientific *theory*. In a nutshell, social science theory seeks to understand the effects that some concepts have on others. For instance, one could theorize about how "conflicting job expectations" (one concept) contribute to "burnout" (a second concept) among child welfare workers. Variables, in contrast, are the ingredients of *research*, science's applied side. A concept "becomes" a variable when the procedure for measuring it is specified. Thus the concept of burnout becomes the variable of burnout when one states how to measure it. For instance, a researcher might measure the variable burnout using a scale consisting of, say, 20 items, all probing different aspects of burnout. Clear, specific definitions of variables are critical to effective research.

1.4 DIFFERENT KINDS OF VARIABLES

There are two major types of variables. **Quantitative variables** (*numeric variables*) take on numeric values. Height is such a variable. So is the number of children in a family. **Qualitative variables** are nonnumeric. Their values represent (nonnumeric) categories. Sex and political party affiliation (Democratic, Republican, etc.) are both qualitative variables. So is the degree of agreement with the statement "Most women who are abused by their partner are 'asking for it' " where participants choose between the responses "strongly agree," "agree," "disagree," and "strongly disagree."[1] A term synonymous with *qualitative variable* is **categorical variable.** A categorical variable with exactly two categories is a **dichotomous variable.** For instance, sex may take on only two values, female and male. As such, it is a dichotomous variable.

Variables may be classified as discrete or continuous. A **discrete variable** can take on only a limited number of values. All categorical variables are discrete. A variable that can take on an unlimited number of values between any two selected values is a **continuous variable** (Toothaker and Miller, 1996, p. 41). Some quantitative variables are continuous. For instance, height can take on an infinite number of values between say, 5 feet 2 inches and 5 feet 3 inches—5.21736, 5.28189, 5.25554, and so on. The number of children in a family, on the other hand, is discrete (one cannot have, for instance, 1.5 children). In actual research, few variables formally meet the definition of continuous because one's measurement tool limits the number of possible values. If a yardstick, for instance, can measure only to the nearest 1/32 inch, then height cannot take on an infinite number of values between any two selected values.

Consider another example, in which students rate how much they enjoy a given class on a scale of 1 to 100. Presume that all ratings are whole numbers (fractions and decimals are not permitted). Such a variable does not meet the definition of continuous and thus, technically, is discrete. The vocabulary of research contains no word that conveys that a variable can take on a great many different values. For instance, the just-described rating scale can take on 100 values and as such differs distinctly from a categorical variable with, say, five categories. Discrete variables with many values generally call for the same statistical procedures used for continuous variables.

In this text, whenever a variable can assume about 20 or more values we refer to it as being "almost continuous." That helps to distinguish such variables from the majority of categorical variables, which typically have six or seven values at most.

1.5   LEVELS OF MEASUREMENT

1.5.1   Overview

In social science research, variables are typically measured at one of four different **levels of measurement.** These may be ordered from low to high. As one moves from lower to higher levels, greater precision is gained and new kinds of conclusions can be drawn. A variable's level of measurement has important implications for the statistical procedure(s) that may be used. Some statistical procedures may be used appropriately with variables measured at different levels of measurement. Others are valid only for variables at one particular level. Ordered from low to high, the levels of measurement are nominal, ordinal, interval, and ratio, as detailed next.

1.5.2   The Nominal Level

At the **nominal level** of measurement, a variable's values are classified into discrete and separate categories, but these cannot be ordered. Eye color (blue, brown, hazel, or green), political party affiliation (Democratic, Republican, Libertarian, Socialist Workers Party, etc.), and sex (male, female) are nominal-level variables. For each, values can be classified but not ordered. For instance, "Which is higher, blue, brown, hazel, or green eyes?" Such a question is nonsensical and asks for an ordering that is neither possible nor logical.

1.5.3   The Ordinal Level

Variables measured at the **ordinal level** possess a quality that nominal-level variables do not. In addition to being able to classify values, one may *order* values from low to high (or from high to low if one prefers). For instance, suppose that a question asks participants to choose which of the responses "happy," "neutral," or "sad" best describes how they feel. These responses (values) can be ordered. "Happy" represents a more positive mood than "neutral," which in turn represents a more positive mood than "sad."

Many variables that require subjective judgment are at the ordinal level of measurement. For instance, a question asking one to assess the "overall quality of counseling services" as "excellent," "good," "fair," or "poor" represents ordinal-level measurement. Similarly, most questions probing level of agreement ("strongly agree," "agree," "disagree," and "strongly disagree") are at the ordinal level of measurement. Social class status rated as "lower-class," "middle-class," or "upper-class" also represents ordinal-level measurement.

All rank orderings are at the ordinal level. In a **rank ordering,** subjects are ordered on some characteristic from highest to lowest. A subject's position in that ordering is its **rank.**

For example, in discussing the height of persons in your class earlier in the chapter, we assumed that a yardstick or similar tool was used to measure height. Perhaps, however, no such tool was available. An alternative would be to rank order persons by height. To do so, students could arrange themselves in a line with the tallest person at one end, the second tallest in the next position, and so on to the shortest person at the other end of the line. The tallest person would be assigned the rank of "1," the second tallest would be assigned the rank of "2," and so on. For a class with 30 persons, the shortest person would be assigned rank 30.[2]

When variables are measured at the ordinal level, the "difference" between two values cannot be determined. How much more positive feeling do those who are "happy" have than those who are "neutral"? How much taller is rank order 2 than rank order 5? Does the difference between "strongly agree" and "agree" represent a larger or smaller difference than that between "agree" and "disagree"? The ordinal level of measurement does not provide the necessary precision to answer such questions. Stated in terms of arithmetic operations, subtraction is not meaningful. For instance, one cannot subtract "agree" from "strongly disagree." At the ordinal level, statements about the size of differences between values don't make sense.

1.5.4   The Interval Level

The difference between two values is termed an **interval.** At the **interval level,** values may be classified and ordered and, in addition, intervals can be measured and statements about them make sense.[3]

Temperature measured in degrees Fahrenheit is an interval-level variable. As such, statements about intervals make sense. For instance, 70 degrees is precisely 10 degrees hotter than 60 degrees. Similarly, the difference between 80 and 60 degrees represents a greater amount of heat (20 degrees) than the difference between 50 and 40 degrees (10 degrees). In contrast to the ordinal level, addition and subtraction can be carried out. For instance, one can subtract 10 degrees from 30 degrees to get an accurate answer, 20 degrees.

For a variable measured at the interval level, the "zero point" on the measurement scale is arbitrary and does not convey the absence of what is being measured. Zero degrees Fahrenheit does not, for instance, convey the absence of heat. Because the zero point is arbitrary, statements about ratios are neither accurate nor meaningful. For instance, 6 degrees Fahrenheit is not twice as hot as 3 degrees Fahrenheit.[4]

Shoe size as measured in the United States represents the interval-level measurement. For instance, according to my local shoe store, there is indeed a size zero children's shoe. It is about three inches long. As the zero point on the children's shoe size scale does not represent "the absence of foot length," ratios are not meaningful. A size 4 shoe, for instance, is not twice as long as a size 2.

1.5.5 *The Ratio Level*

Variables measured at the ratio level possess all the characteristics mentioned so far. Thus, values may be classified and ordered and intervals may be measured. In addition, at the **ratio level** ratios are meaningful and accurate. This is so because the zero point on the measurement scale does indeed indicate the absence of what is being measured. The zero point thus is a true zero rather than an arbitrary one.

A count of the number of articles published by faculty illustrates the ratio level of measurement. If Dr. X has published zero articles, a count would record 0 as the value for Dr. X. This zero is not arbitrary but instead conveys the absence of publication. As just stated, ratios make sense. For instance, if Dr. Z has published 10 articles and Dr. Q has published 5, then Dr. Z has indeed published twice as many articles as has Dr. Q.

It is easy to think of variables that can be measured at the ratio level. All counts are at the ratio level. Physical characteristics (height, weight, distance, etc.) are almost always measured at this level.

1.6 MEASUREMENT ISSUES AND CONTROVERSIES

Notice that for certain variables, the nature of the variable limits the level of measurement. For instance, no matter how hard one tries, eye color cannot be measured at the ordinal level. There is simply no way to order eye color. Many variables, however, can be measured at different levels. For instance, height measured via a yardstick illustrates ratio-level measurement. Measured via a rank ordering, height is at the ordinal level.

As a rule, one should measure at the highest possible level of measurement. For instance, more detailed information is gained by measuring height at the ratio level than by measuring it at the ordinal level. When height is measured only at the ordinal level, information has been lost. Similarly, one could have respondents indicate their age (to the nearest year) rather than simply mark an age category (21 to 30, 31 to 40, etc.). By so doing, the researcher would gain more precise data and open the way for statistical procedures that could not otherwise be used.

As stated earlier, the level of measurement has important implications for the statistical procedures that will be used. Many statistical procedures are appropriate only for variables at particular levels of measurement. From a pragmatic perspective, the distinction between interval- and ratio-level measurement is less important than are the other distinctions. With only minor exceptions, the same statistical procedures are used with variables at the interval level as are used with those at the ratio level. In most subsequent descriptions, this text groups these two levels into a single level termed the interval/ratio level.

Earlier we mentioned two major types of variables, categorical (qualitative) and quantitative (numeric). Most categorical variables are measured at either the nominal level (such as gender, political party affiliation) or the ordinal level (such as the subjective judgments "strongly agree," "agree," "disagree," "strongly disagree"). Most quantitative variables (counts, etc.) represent the interval/ratio level of measurement. Similarly, most variables that are continuous or nearly so are at the interval/ratio level.

Counts and measurements of physical quantities are unambiguously at the interval/ratio level of measurement. Yet social research often involves the measurement of abstract, subjective concepts such as self-esteem, prejudice, and assertiveness. Often these concepts are measured by multi-item scales. For instance, the Index of Self-Esteem (Hudson, 1992) is a scale with 25 "items," each pertaining to some aspect of self-esteem. Responses to each item generate points, which are summed to yield a total self-esteem score that may range from 0 to 100. Consider temperature measured in degrees Fahrenheit. How much heat is represented by the difference between 31 and 30 degrees? The answer, of course, is 1 degree ($31 - 30 = 1$). Is the amount of heat represented by the difference between 31 and 30 degrees the same as that represented by the difference between 71 and 70 degrees? Yes, both differences represent the same amount of heat, 1 degree. Regardless of location on the temperature scale, one unit (i.e., 1 degree) always represents the same amount of heat. Now let's ask a parallel question for the Index of Self-Esteem. Is the amount of self-esteem that is represented by the difference between 31 and 30 points the same as the amount of self-esteem represented by the difference between 71 and 70 points?

Further, does a difference of 1 point on the self-esteem scale always represent the same actual amount of self-esteem? In general, questions such as this do not arise when physical quantities are being measured. We correctly take it for granted that an inch is always an inch; a pound is always a pound. Given the subjectivity of self-esteem—one can't simply take a ruler and measure it—these questions are difficult to answer. If the answer is yes, then the Index of Self-Esteem meets the basic requirement of interval-level measurement. If it is no, the level of measurement is only ordinal.

Social science has no easy answer to the just-posed questions. Scholars disagree on whether variables measured by multi-item attitudinal scales formally meet the requirements of the interval level of measurement. However, almost all concur that such scales come very close to doing so. Further, they concur that statistical procedures designed for use with the interval/ratio level of measurement may be appropriately used with such scales. For clarity of discussion, this text characterizes variables measured via multi-item scales as being "almost at the interval/ratio level." Procedures designed for variables at the interval/ratio level may indeed be used with such scales.

1.7 UNIVARIATE, BIVARIATE, AND MULTIVARIATE STATISTICS AND THE CONCEPT OF RELATIONSHIP

Now that we have covered that background information, the rest of this chapter looks forward, providing an overview of the material covered in this text.

Statistical procedures may be classified by the number of variables that are involved. **Univariate statistics** summarize data for a single variable. As typically used, percentages are univariate statistics. For instance, the "72%" mentioned earlier pertained to a single variable, that being the sex of students. Part Two of this text (Chapters 3 to 5) presents selected univariate statistical concepts and procedures.

Bivariate statistics summarize the degree of relationship between two variables. Two variables have a **relationship,** that is, they are **related,** when the values observed for one variable vary, differ, or change according to those of the other. As an example, sex and height are related because height varies by sex (men tend to be taller than women, or stated differently, women tend to be shorter than men). A synonym for *relationship* is **association;** one for *related* is **associated.**

The text gives considerable attention to size of association. **Size of association** (also termed **strength of association**) concerns the degree to which the values of one variable vary, differ, or change according to changes in the values of the other. The assessment of relationship is a central goal of many research studies in the human services. Part Three (Chapters 6 to 9) presents a variety of bivariate statistical concepts and procedures for assessing size of relationship.

Multivariate statistics summarize relationships involving three or more variables. Multivariate approaches are sometimes used to address whether a relationship between two variables is a causal relationship. In a **causal relationship,** one variable affects another. Consider, for instance, smoking and lung cancer. As numerous studies document that smokers are more likely to contract lung cancer than are nonsmokers, these variables are clearly related. Some persons, notably representatives of tobacco companies, have contended that this relationship is not causal but instead reflects the influences of confounding variables. **Confounding variables** are variables that affect the pattern of association between two other variables. For instance, a tobacco representative might contend that (1) smokers are more likely than nonsmokers to have numerous poor health habits and (2) one or more of these habits, not the fact of smoking, explains why smokers are more likely to develop lung cancer. In this example, the poor health habits are confounding variables. Chapters 10 and 11 present the logic that researchers use to assess whether relationships are causal. Often the limitations of one's data and research procedures make this assessment difficult or impossible. Multivariate procedures are introduced briefly in Chapter 22.

Researchers often classify variables as independent or dependent. **Independent variables** are presumed to affect or *cause* dependent variables. In turn, **dependent variables** are presumed to be affected by (caused by) independent variables. To classify variables as independent or dependent, one must have two variables. For instance, presented by itself, one cannot classify gender as independent or dependent. When two variables are presented together such a classification can often be made. For instance, given the variables gender and self-esteem, one would classify gender as the independent variable and self-esteem as the dependent. Sometimes it is difficult to classify variables as independent or dependent. When this is the case or when such classification is not pertinent to the study's purpose, one need not do so.

1.8   TWO QUANTITATIVE RESEARCH DESIGNS

The two basic quantitative research designs are experiments and surveys. In **experiments,** researchers *manipulate* the environment via an intervention. The **intervention** (also called the **treatment,** or *treatment stimulus*) is what is done to the study participant. For instance, for clients with an irrational fear of snakes, a researcher might implement a procedure (intervention) designed to help the clients become desensitized to snakes. In experiments, the intervention is the key independent variable and that which the intervention seeks to influence (in this study, fear of snakes) is the dependent variable. In **surveys,** researchers *do not* manipulate the environment. They simply take measurements.

1.9   SAMPLES AND POPULATIONS

A **population** may be defined as *all* of the objects that possess a specified set of characteristics. In most research studies in human services, populations are composed of people. Yet this need not be the case. One could have a population of rocks, case records, old movies, or child abuse reports. Populations come in different sizes. For some statistical procedures, populations of infinite size are postulated. Such populations are discussed in Chapter 5. Presume again that there are 30 students in your current class. This being the case, the population of students in your class numbers 30 and consists of those 30 students. The population of authors of *Statistics and Data Interpretation for the Helping Professions* consists of *one* person, that being me.

A **sample** consists of *some but not all* of the objects in a population. Just as with populations, samples in human services research are usually but not always composed of people. The students who sit in the front row of your class are a sample of students from the population of students in your class. Likewise, if your professor puts the names of all students in your class in a hat and draws out seven names at random, these seven students are a sample of the population of students in your class.

Sample is used in two related but different ways. Its formal, precise meaning has already been given: some but not all of the objects in a population. *Sample* is also used in a general way to refer to the participants in a research study. For instance, suppose that a researcher studies all 150 clients discharged from a given psychiatric hospital in the prior year. As these clients represent *all* objects possessing a characteristic (they represent all of the discharges in a year) they would be considered to be a population rather than a sample. But with the general, more relaxed use of the term, they are also a sample, the participants in the research study. To reduce confusion, this text typically uses *sample* to indicate some but not all of the objects in a population and *study sample* to indicate the participants (cases) in a research study. The term *study population* is often used to mean the population from which the study sample was selected.

1.10   RANDOM AND NONRANDOM SAMPLES

Samples may be selected from populations in two basic ways. When researchers use methods of chance to select a sample, they are using **random sampling (probability sampling)** methods and the resulting sample is a **random sample (probability sample).** When methods of chance are not used, the sampling methodology is termed **nonprobability sampling** (or, one may say, nonrandom sampling) and the sample is a **nonrandom sample (nonprobability sample).**

Picking names randomly from a hat selects cases via chance and thus illustrates a random sampling method. For instance, when your professor drew seven names from a hat, the resulting sample was a random one. By contrast, passing out class evaluations only to those who sit in the front row does not use methods of chance and thus illustrates nonprobability (nonrandom) sampling. In this instance, the resulting sample is a nonprobability (nonrandom) sample.

1.11   SAMPLING METHOD AND APPROPRIATE STATISTICAL PROCEDURES

The implications of the sampling method are covered in depth in Chapter 12, but let's consider some basics here. Often, the researchers' interest is not in the sample per se. Instead, they study the sample to learn about a larger group, typically the population from which the sample was selected. Whenever nonrandom sampling methods have been used, **bias** is a concern. A sample is **biased** if its characteristics differ *systematically* from those of the population about which one seeks to make inferences. For instance, suppose that only those who sit in the first row fill out a student evaluation. My best guess is that their evaluations will tend to be more positive than those of typical students. Stated differently, these results may well be biased in a positive direction.

In the recently provided example of random sampling, the instructor randomly drew the names of seven students from a hat. Presume that these students also evaluate their instructor. Given the random sampling process, only the luck of the draw differentiates those in the sample from other students. As such, there is no reason to suspect bias.

This does not mean the opinions of those in the sample will be exactly the same as those of persons in the full class. Due to the luck of the draw they will, almost assuredly, differ to some degree. The key point is that, given random sampling, *systematic* bias is not a concern.

When random samples are small in size, such as in the current example, just by luck, the opinions (characteristics) of those in the sample may differ considerably from those in the population. Suppose, for the moment, that in the full population of students in the course, most students have positive opinions regarding the course and instructor. Even so, just by luck, the instructor could randomly draw the names of seven students, each of whom has a decisively negative attitude. As sample size gets larger, the luck of the draw tends to get smaller (to "even out"), and thus the opinions and characteristics of those in the sample become increasingly similar to those in the population.

1.12   DESCRIPTIVE AND INFERENTIAL STATISTICS

The two major branches of the field of statistics are descriptive statistics and inferential statistics.

1.12.1   Descriptive Statistics

Descriptive statistics describe a study sample (the participants or cases in the study). The examples of statistics presented earlier in the chapter were examples of descriptive statistics. For instance, if one reports that 72% of students in a class are female and that the class members' average height is 5 feet $7\frac{1}{2}$ inches, they are describing the study sample and thus are engaging in descriptive statistics.

Descriptive statistical procedures summarize *only* the study sample. Suppose that in a large random sample of, say, 1000 persons selected from across the United States, 64% of respondents favor a raise in the minimum wage. Given that this sample is both random and large, one may deduce that the percentage of persons in the United States who support a raise in the minimum wage is fairly close to 64%. In this example, one uses the study sample to draw conclusions pertaining to *another group,* that group being the population from which the study sample was drawn. Although such reasoning is logically correct, it is not part of the field of descriptive statistics. As stated above, descriptive statistics confines itself to the task of describing and summarizing the study sample.

1.12.2   Inferential Statistics

According to the dictionary, when one makes an *inference,* one derives a conclusion from facts or premises. **Inferential statistics** (inferential statistical procedures) are used to draw conclusions (inferences) about a population based on a random sample selected from that population. When one's sample is not random, statistical inferences about the population may not be made. For instance, a researcher may not select a sample of students in the front row (a nonrandom sample) and, based on this sample, use inferential statistical procedures to draw conclusions about the full class.

1.13   TWO KINDS OF INFERENCES

Using inferential statistical tools, researchers make two kinds of inferences about populations based on randomly selected samples from those populations: estimates and decisions (Toothaker, 1986, p. 18).

1.13.1   *Estimates*

The earlier example pertaining to minimum wage illustrates estimation. Based on the conditions in the sample, the researcher estimated those in the population. The researcher concluded that the percentage favoring a minimum wage increase is reasonably close to 64%. Using procedures presented in Chapters 12 and 13, you will be able to make much more precise estimates than this. For instance, you will be able to make statements such as, "I am 95% confident that the percentage in the population is between 60% and 68%."

1.13.2   *Decisions*

The second use of inferential statistics is for making decisions. For instance, suppose that two interventions are developed to teach parents and youth better communication skills. Let's say that you design an experiment to see which one—Intervention A or Intervention B—would be a better choice at the high school where you are a social worker. You select a random sample of 20 families from the 1000 families at the school and ask them whether they will participate. All agree. You put the 20 family names in a hat and randomly select 10 families to receive Intervention A and 10 to receive B. This is an example of random assignment. **Random assignment (randomization)** is the use of methods of chance to assign participants to groups. The term **group** indicates cases that have the same value on a study's key independent variable. For instance, the participants assigned to Intervention A may be referred to as the Intervention A Group or Group A.

Not all experiments use random assignment. For instance, in most studies of smoking, those who smoke compose one group and those who do not compose the other. In such studies, assignment is nonrandom. (In essence, study participants made their own decision to smoke or not to smoke and, by so doing, "chose" their own group.) In the absence of random assignment, confounding variables can bias comparisons. For instance, in the earlier smoking example, it was postulated that poor health habits, not smoking per se, caused the higher lung cancer rate among smokers.

Research designs with random assignment are preferred for drawing causal conclusions. With random assignment, potential confounding variables are *randomly* (rather than systematically) distributed between the groups. As such, they cannot introduce bias. For instance, in the high school example, there is no reason to suspect that Intervention Group A is more motivated to improve communication skills than is Group B.

Following intervention, presume that (1) families fill out a scale that assesses communication, (2) you score the scale (the higher the score, the better the communication), and (3) the average score is higher in Group B than in Group A. Because of the random assignment, you may indeed conclude that the difference in scores is not due to systematic bias introduced by confounding variables. Thus study results seem to suggest that B is the more effective intervention.

Yet just as random sampling does not result in a sample that precisely matches the population, random assignment typically creates *approximately* (rather than precisely) equal groups. Perhaps, just by the luck of the random assignment process, those who received Intervention B were more motivated than were those who received A. Or perhaps the explanation is simpler still. Perhaps, just by luck, those in B simply had more effective communication skills to begin with. How can one be *sure* that luck (the luck of the draw) is not the explanation for a study result? Based on only a *sample* of observations, the level of certainty can never be *100%*.

Researchers assess the role of chance—luck and chance are one and the same—via the statistical significance test. A **statistical significance test** is an inferential statistical procedure conducted to determine the likelihood that a study result is due to chance. In the current example, the appropriate significance test could tell you whether chance (the luck of the random assignment process) is a likely or an unlikely explanation for the difference in average scores. One should conclude that Intervention B is more effective than A only if chance is an *unlikely* explanation. However, if chance is a plausible (reasonably likely or, at a minimum, not an unlikely) explanation, one should reason that study results do not merit the conclusion that B is more effective.

In sum, significance tests reveal whether chance is a likely or unlikely explanation for the study result. Only when chance is an unlikely explanation do researchers conclude that a given result reflects a *real* difference. Chapters 14 to 22 deal with significance testing. (The just-presented discussion has been brief, so don't expect to fully grasp significance testing at this time.)

1.14 GENERALIZABILITY

Researchers use inferential statistical procedures to make inferences about the population from which the study sample(s) was randomly selected. Yet sometimes researchers (and others) seek to draw conclusions about different populations. For instance, perhaps you have read about an intervention to prevent pregnancy that was effective with a predominantly white population in a rural midwestern state. How could you assess whether that same intervention would be effective with your urban northeastern and predominantly African American clients? This question addresses the **generalizability** of a study result, that is, the degree to which a similar result is expected in a different setting or context. Chapter 23 presents tools for assessing generalizability. These tools are largely *nonstatistical.* The key consideration is the **degree of similarity** between the research study setting and the setting to which one seeks to generalize. In the just-mentioned pregnancy prevention example, one would expect fairly low generalizability because the two settings differ considerably.

1.15   OTHER TOPICS IN THIS BOOK

Most of the major topics to be covered in this text have been mentioned in the course of this chapter, but we have not yet touched on some content of the next chapter and the final chapter. Chapter 2 presents some straightforward, though sometimes misused, statistics (percentages, percentiles, ratios, and others) and various ways to present data. In Chapter 23 we build a model for analyzing and interpreting data. This five-part model, integrating previously presented tools and concepts, calls for a balanced approach to data interpretation. The chapter points out many common misinterpretations of study results and emphasizes that the **importance,** that is, the real-world meaning of a study's result, cannot be determined by statistical analysis alone.

1.16   CHAPTER SUMMARY

The theoretical side of science is termed *theory.* The gathering of real-world observations is termed *research,* and the observations that are gathered are termed *data.* Qualitative research methods emphasize understanding and meaning. Quantitative methods involve objective measurement, usually with numbers. A statistic is a numerical summary of data.

Each unit on which measurements are recorded is a case. A variable takes on different values, but constants take on only one value. Quantitative (numeric) variables take on numeric values. Qualitative (categorical) variables are nonnumeric. A dichotomous variable has exactly two categories. Discrete variables take on only a limited number of values. A continuous variable can take on an unlimited number of values between any two selected values.

Ordered from low to high, the levels of measurement are nominal, ordinal, interval, ratio. At the nominal level, one may only classify. At the ordinal level, one may classify and order. (All rank orderings are at the ordinal level.) At the interval level, one may classify, order, and determine differences between values. The ratio level possesses the qualities already mentioned and also has a zero point that is true rather than arbitrary, so that ratios are meaningful.

As a rule, one should measure at the highest possible level of measurement. Almost all statisticians concur that procedures designed for interval/ratio-level variables may be used with multi-item scales.

Univariate statistics summarize data for a single variable. Bivariate statistics summarize the degree of relationship (association) between two variables. Two variables are related (associated) when the values observed for one variable vary, differ, or change according to those of the other. Size of association (strength of association) concerns the degree to which this is the case.

In a causal relationship one variable causes or affects another. Confounding variables affect the association between two other variables and can make the assessment of causality problematic. Independent variables affect or cause dependent variables. In turn, dependent variables are affected by (caused by) by independent variables.

In experiments, researchers manipulate the environment. In surveys, they simply take measurements. Experiments are better suited for drawing causal conclusions than are surveys.

A population consists of all of the objects possessing a specified set of characteristics. A sample consists of some but not all of these objects. In random sampling, methods of chance are used to select the sample. In nonrandom sampling, they are not. Whenever sampling is nonrandom, one is concerned about bias. Random sampling methods eliminate systematic bias.

Descriptive statistics describe a study sample. Inferential statistical procedures are used to draw inferences about a population based on a sample randomly selected from that population.

Researchers use inferential statistics to make (1) estimates and (2) decisions. Random assignment, the use of random methods to assign participants to groups, eliminates bias due to confounding variables. Research designs with random assignment are best suited for drawing causal conclusions. Randomization creates approximately equal rather than precisely equal groups.

Statistical significance tests reveal the likelihood that a study result is due to chance. One should conclude that a study result (difference) is real only when chance is an unlikely explanation.

The generalizability of a study result concerns the degree to which a similar result would be expected in a different setting. The importance of a study result cannot be determined by statistical analysis alone.

Problems and Questions

Section 1.2

1. The theoretical side of science is termed _____ and the applied/observational side is termed _____.
2. The observations that one gathers are termed _____.
3. The two basic social science research methods are _____ methods and _____ methods.
4. Broadly speaking, a statistic is a(n) _____ _____ of data.
5. (T or F) Quantitative, statistically based reasoning is sufficient for deriving the *meaning* of one's study result.

Section 1.3

6. Each unit on which measurements are recorded is termed a(n) _____.
7. The different kinds of measurements or observations that are made for each case are termed _____.
8. A variable is something that takes on different _____.
9. What are the values of the variable gender?
10. _____ take on only one value.
11. _____ are the ingredients of theory. _____ are the ingredients of research.

Section 1.4

12. _____ variables are numeric. _____ variables are nonnumeric.

13. Is the variable height (as it is most often measured) a quantitative or a qualitative variable?

14. Is the variable gender qualitative or quantitative?

15. A term synonymous with *qualitative variable* is _____ variable.

16. A(n) _____ variable can take on only a limited number of values.

17. A variable that can take on an unlimited number of values between any two values is a(n) _____ variable.

18. Indicate whether the following variables are discrete or continuous. (If the only reason that the variable would not be considered continuous pertains to limitations of the measuring device, consider it to be continuous.)
    a. Weight
    b. Undergraduate academic classification (freshman, sophomore, junior, senior)
    c. Number of children in a family
    d. Number of arrests
    e. Time in 100-meter run

19. A variable that takes on precisely two values is termed a(n) _____ variable.

Section 1.5

20. Ordered from low to high, the four levels of measurement are _____, _____, _____, and _____.

21. When variables are at the nominal level, one may _____ responses into categories. At the ordinal level, one may also _____ responses or categories. At the interval level, one may speak meaningfully about the _____ between values. At the ratio level, _____ become meaningful.

22. All rank orderings are at the _____ level of measurement.

23. At the ratio level of measurement, 0 may be regarded as a(n) _____ zero rather than an arbitrary zero. Zero on a scale at the ratio level conveys the _____ of the quantity being measured.

24. In your own words, explain why it doesn't make sense to say that 10 degrees Fahrenheit is twice as hot as 5 degrees.

25. Indicate the level of measurement for each of the following:
    a. Shoe size as measured in the United States
    b. Social class (lower, middle, upper)
    c. Weight measured with a scale
    d. Political party (Republican, Democratic, etc.)
    e. Students rank order themselves according to the amount of time that they spent studying
    f. Religion (Christian, Hindu, Buddhist, Native American Church, other)

Section 1.6

26. As a rule, one should measure at the _____ possible level of measurement.

27. (T or F) Some statistical procedures are appropriate only for variables at particular levels of measurement.

28. (T or F) Whether a variable is at the interval level versus the ratio level typically has important implications for the statistical procedures that may be used.

29. (T or F) Abstract concepts, when measured by multi-item scales, are clearly and unequivocally at the interval level of measurement.

30. (T or F) Most social scientists think that multi-item scales that assess abstract concepts come close enough to the interval/ratio level of measurement that statistical procedures designed for this level may be used.

Section 1.7

31. _____ procedures summarize data for a single variable, _____ procedures convey relationship between two variables, and _____ procedures convey relationships involving three or more variables.

32. Two variables have a relationship when the values observed for one variable _____, _____, or _____ according to those of the other.

33. A synonym for *relationship* is _____. A synonym for *related is* _____.

34. _____ of association, also termed _____ of association, concerns the degree to which the values of one variable vary, differ, or change according to those of the other.

35. In a(n) _____ relationship, one variable cause affects the other.
36. _____ variables affect the pattern of association between two other variables.
37. Can you give an example of a relationship in the human services field that may be due to a confounding variable?

Section 1.8

38. In _____, researchers manipulate the environment. In _____, they simply take measurements.
39. In experiments, the "environmental manipulation" is often termed the _____.

Section 1.9

40. A(n) _____ consists of all of the objects possessing a specified set of characteristics. A(n) _____ consists of _____ but not _____ of the objects in a population.

Section 1.10

41. In _____ sampling, methods of chance are used. In _____ sampling, these methods are not used.
42. Another name for a probability sample is a(n) _____ sample.
43. Indicate whether each of the following is a probability sample or a nonprobability sample.
    a. A computer program generates a random list of clients who will participate in a follow-up study.
    b. Social workers, working from memory, provide a list of clients who they believe would want to participate in a follow-up study.
    c. Clients who keep their appointments participate in a study. (Those who do not keep the appointment do not participate.)

Section 1.11

44. Indicate the likely bias in situation b in the prior problem.
45. A sample study is _____ if its characteristics differ systematically from those of the population from which it was selected.
46. When sample size is _____, just by luck ("the luck of the draw") the characteristics of

those in the sample may differ greatly from characteristics of those in the population.

Section 1.12

47. _____ statistics describe the study sample. _____ statistics are used to draw inferences about the population from which the study sample has been randomly sampled.

Section 1.13

48. Researchers make two kinds of inferences about the population from which the study sample was randomly selected, these being _____ and _____.
49. _____ _____ is the use of methods of chance to assign participants to groups.
50. (T or F) Research designs with random assignment are generally acknowledged to be the best designs for drawing causal conclusions.
51. (T or F) Most often, random assignment creates *precisely* equal groups.
52. (T or F) In studies with random assignment, the "luck of the draw" rarely has any effect on study results.
53. (T or F) In designs with random assignment, confounding variables do not introduce systematic bias.
54. In your own words, explain what the results of statistical significance tests show.
55. (T or F) One should conclude that a study result is due to something *real* (something other than chance) only when chance is an unlikely explanation for that result.

Section 1.14

56. Define generalizability.

NOTES

1. Note that quantitative studies regularly have both qualitative (categorical) and quantitative variables. The term *qualitative variable* does not indicate a qualitative method of research.

2. In the example here the tallest person was assigned the lowest rank, that is, 1. But we could have assigned the highest rank to the case with the highest value. For in-

stance, we might have assigned the tallest person the rank of 30, the next tallest 29, and so on to the shortest person, who would be assigned the rank 1.

3. Only occasionally do researchers actually classify the values of interval-level variables. The text simply makes the point that this may be done. For instance, as will be demonstrated shortly, shoe size in the United States is at the interval level of measurement. Shoe sizes 0 to 3, for instance, could be placed in one category, 4 to 6 in another, 7 to 9 in another, and so on.

4. If you recall the facts of physics, you know that zero on the Kelvin scale does indeed indicate the absence of heat. This temperature is known as "absolute zero" and equals -273 degrees on the Celsius scale.

More Basics and the Presentation of Data

2.1 Chapter Overview

We begin Chapter 2 with more essential information for statistics, defining *sample size* and *frequency* and considering the formulas for *proportions, percentages,* and *ratios.* We look at *distributions* and the distinction between *empirical* and *theoretical distributions.* Next, the focus shifts to the presentation of data via *tables* and *figures.* To fit different kinds of data and information needs, there are *frequency distribution tables, grouped frequency distribution tables,* and *stem and leaf displays.* Important figures include *bar charts, histograms, frequency polygons,* and *pie charts.* We conclude with a discussion of how to present data in ways that do not mislead the reader.

2.2 Sample Size and Frequency

The total number of cases in the study sample is the **sample size,** symbolized by N. Thus, if there are 42 persons in your sample, the sample size is 42, symbolized by $N = 42$. The number of cases with the same value is the **frequency** of that value, symbolized by f. If 28 of the 42 persons in your sample are women, the frequency of women is 28, that is, $f = 28$. If three persons are 5 feet 6 inches tall, then $f = 3$ for that height. A synonym for frequency is **count.** Hence, the count of persons who are 5 feet 6 inches tall is three.

Recall from Chapter 1 (Section 1.13) that a *group* consists of cases having the same value on a key independent variable. For instance, if gender is a key independent variable, then women make up one group and men the other. The symbol n indicates the number (frequency) in a group. Hence, if there are 28 women in your study, this may be symbolized as $n = 28$. The symbol n is an alternative to f when a group is involved, because either symbol is appropriate in this situation.

2.3 PROPORTIONS, PERCENTAGES, AND RATIOS

2.3.1 Proportions

A **proportion** is calculated by dividing the number of objects with a given characteristic by the total number of objects. Hence, if one has 10 marbles, 6 of which are red, then the proportion of red marbles is $6/10 = .60$. Proportions may range from 0.00 to 1.00. If none of the 10 marbles were red, then the proportion of red marbles would be $0/10 = 0.00$. If all 10 marbles were red, the proportion would be $10/10 = 1.00$. The symbol for proportion is p. A general formula is:

$$p = \frac{\text{number with a given characteristic}}{\text{total number}} \tag{2.1}$$

In research studies, proportions are typically calculated by dividing the frequency of cases with a given value by the sample size. For instance, if 28 of 42 participants in a study are women, the proportion of women is $28/42 = .67$. Using our recently defined terms and symbols, another formula for proportion is:

$$p = \frac{\text{frequency}}{\text{sample size}} = \frac{f}{N} \tag{2.2}$$

2.3.2 Percentages

Percentages convey *exactly* the same information as proportions. The percentage of objects with a given characteristic is calculated by multiplying the proportion by 100. For instance, suppose that 15 of 75 youth offenders are arrested at least once within a year of discharge from a treatment program. What percentage were arrested? First, calculate the proportion: $15/75 = .20$. Next, multiply by 100: $.20 \times 100 = 20\%$. Percentages may range from 0% to 100%. A general formula is:

$$\% = \frac{\text{number with a given characteristic}}{\text{total number}} \times 100 \tag{2.3}$$

Using the terms already presented, we have:

$$\% = \frac{\text{frequency}}{\text{sample size}} \times 100 = \frac{f}{N} \times 100 \tag{2.4}$$

This text sometimes presents information via proportions and sometimes via percentages. An advantage of percentages over proportions is that they are more familiar to audiences with limited statistical knowledge. Also, oral communication is easier; it is more natural to say, "Twenty percent of youth were arrested" than to say, "The proportion of youth who were arrested was .20." The main advantages of using proportions are that calculation is quicker, and they are a more standard form in statistical formulas than percentages are.

The easiest way to misinterpret percentages and proportions is to mix up (thinking back to English composition class) subjects and objects. On a bicycle trip, a rider in my group stated: "Eighty-five percent of serious injuries sustained by cyclists are head injuries." The next day another rider from my group relayed that to another group as, "Eighty-five percent of cyclists sustain serious head injuries." In the first statement, the subject is injuries. In the second, it is cyclists. Thus the second statement did not convey the original meaning. So think carefully about subjects and objects as you communicate about percentages. (Saying that 90% who heed this advice will communicate accurately is not the same as saying that 90% will heed it.)

2.3.3 Ratios

Ratios are calculated by dividing the frequency (number of cases) in a first group by that in a second. Suppose that in a human services class of 45 graduate students, 35 choose a concentration in direct practice with individuals and small groups and 10 choose a concentration in community practice. The ratio of direct practice students (first group) to community practice students (second) is $35/10 = 3.5$. Ratios are often expressed using the number 1 and the word *to*. In those terms, the ratio of direct practice to community practice students is 3.5 to 1. Another common method of expression is to reduce the ratio (fraction) to its lowest common denominator. In this case, $35/10 = 7/2$; hence the ratio of direct practice to community practice students is 7 to 2.

   Note that the ratio of community practice students to direct practice students is *not* the same as the ratio of direct practice students to community practice students. The ratio of community practice students (this is now the first group) to direct practice students (second group) is $10/35 = .29$. This ratio may also be stated as .29 to 1, as 2 to 7 ($10/35 = 2/7$), and as 1 to 3.5. Generally, ratios that are greater than 1 are easier to grasp and understand than are those that are less than 1. Hence, in calculating ratios one should generally divide the number in the larger group by that in the smaller. Don't make the mistake of dividing the number (frequency) in a group by the total number (sample size). For instance, the ratio of direct practice students to community practice students is *not* $35/45 = .78$. A general formula is:

$$\text{Ratio} = \frac{\text{number (frequency) in first group}}{\text{number (frequency) in second group}} \tag{2.5}$$

2.4 DISTRIBUTIONS

2.4.1 Empirical and Theoretical Distributions

A **distribution** is a group of values that have been organized in some way (Toothaker and Miller, 1996, p. 23). Researchers deal with two major classifications of distributions, empirical distributions and theoretical distributions. *Empirical* means "based on observation." **Empirical distributions** are composed of real-world (actual) data, typically gathered in research studies. **Theoretical distributions** are composed of assumed (hypothetical) values rather than real data and are encountered predominantly in inferential statistics. The best known theoretical distribution is the normal (bell-shaped) distribution, which is first presented in Chapter 5 (Section 5.7). For now, our focus is on empirical distributions.

2.4.2 Frequency Distributions

Table 2.1 presents 20 measurements of the sex of persons in a given class. As presented in Table 2.1, these measurements do not compose a distribution, because they have not been "organized." A **frequency distribution** organizes by grouping together cases with the same values. In addition, it indicates the frequency of each value. Table 2.2 presents the frequency distribution of sex of students in a hypothetical classroom. A table that presents a frequency distribution is termed a **frequency distribution table.** Hence, Table 2.2 is a frequency distribution table. In addition to reporting frequencies, frequency distribution tables typically present percentages. Table 2.2 indicates that the frequency of women is 11 and that the percentage of women is 55%. This percentage was calculated by dividing the frequency of women by the sample size and multiplying by 100: $11/20 = .55 \times 100 = 55\%$.

When values may be ordered, frequency distribution tables present them in order, almost always with lower values presented first. For instance, Table 2.3[1] presents the age of sexual abuse perpetrators at a child protective services agency in this way. (These data are hypothetical.) When values can be ordered, cumulative frequencies and cumulative percentages are typically presented. The **cumulative frequency** for a given value is the number of cases having that value or a lower value. For instance, in the sexual abuse data, the cumulative frequency of perpetrators age 17 and below is five. Two perpetrators were 14, one was 15, and two were 17: $2 + 1 + 2 = 5$. The **cumulative percentage** for a given value is the percentage of cases having that value or a lower value. It may be calculated in two

TABLE 2.1	SEX OF PERSONS IN A HYPOTHETICAL CLASS

Female, male, male, male, female, male, female, female, female, male, female, male, female, male, female, male, male, female, female, female

TABLE 2.2	FREQUENCY DISTRIBUTION TABLE FOR SEX OF CLASS MEMBERS

Value	Frequency	Percentage
Female	11	55
Male	9	45

Note: Data are hypothetical. $N = 20$.

TABLE 2.3   AGES OF SEXUAL ABUSE PERPETRATORS

Age	Frequency	Percentage	Cumulative Frequency	Cumulative Percentage
14	2	10	2	10
15	1	5	3	15
17	2	10	5	25
21	2	10	7	35
23	1	5	8	40
26	1	5	9	45
32	1	5	10	50
37	1	5	11	55
38	1	5	12	60
42	1	5	13	65
44	1	5	14	70
55	3	15	17	85
63	1	5	18	90
67	1	5	19	95
77	1	5	20	100

Note: Hypothetical data for a child protective services agency. $N = 20$.

ways. The easiest is to divide the cumulative frequency by the sample size and then multiply by 100, in this case, $5/20 = .25 \times 100 = 25\%$. The formula is:

$$\text{Cumulative percentage} = \frac{\text{cumulative frequency}}{\text{sample size}} \times 100 \tag{2.6}$$

Alternatively, one may sum the percentages for the given value and all lower values: 10% (percentage age 14) + 5% (percentage age 15) + 10% (percentage age 17) = 25%.

Table 2.4 is a frequency distribution table generated by a software program called SPSS for Windows (Version 7.5). This program is specifically designed for analyzing social science and related data research. Output from SPSS is presented throughout this text.[2]

The data in Table 2.4 are from a study on special-needs adoption by this author and Victor Groze (Rosenthal and Groze, 1992). Examples from this study are used frequently in this text. Special needs are characteristics of children that may delay or prevent their timely adoption. Important special needs include older ages, developmental delays or disabilities, emotional/behavioral problems, a sibling group in need of placement, and minority ethnicity. The cohesion scale is a 10-item scale that measures "the degree of emotional bonding that family members have toward one another" (Olson, McCubbin, Larsen, Muxen, and Wilson, 1985, p. 3). The higher the score on this scale, the greater the level of cohesion. The highest possible score is 50 points and the lowest is 10 points.

Some explanation regarding Table 2.4 should prove helpful. First, FCOH is an example of a *variable name*. In SPSS for Windows, all variables have variable names that are eight or fewer characters in length and start with a letter. For each variable, the user may create a *variable label*, a short description of the variable

TABLE 2.4   FCOH FACES Cohesion Scores in Special-Needs Adoption Study

		Frequency	Percent	Valid Percent	Cumulative Percent
Valid	15.00	1	.1	.1	.1
	17.00	1	.1	.1	.3
	20.00	1	.1	.1	.4
	23.00	2	.3	.3	.7
	24.00	1	.1	.1	.8
	25.00	4	.5	.5	1.3
	26.00	2	.3	.3	1.6
	27.00	6	.8	.8	2.4
	28.00	5	.6	.7	3.1
	29.00	7	.9	.9	4.0
	30.00	10	1.3	1.3	5.4
	31.00	12	1.5	1.6	7.0
	32.00	13	1.6	1.8	8.8
	33.00	12	1.5	1.6	10.4
	34.00	28	3.5	3.8	14.2
	35.00	19	2.4	2.6	16.7
	36.00	33	4.1	4.4	21.2
	37.00	36	4.5	4.9	26.0
	38.00	42	5.3	5.7	31.7
	39.00	55	6.9	7.4	39.1
	40.00	57	7.1	7.7	46.8
	41.00	49	6.1	6.6	53.4
	42.00	74	9.3	10.0	63.3
	43.00	54	6.8	7.3	70.6
	44.00	49	6.1	6.6	77.2
	45.00	55	6.9	7.4	84.6
	46.00	37	4.6	5.0	89.6
	47.00	41	5.1	5.5	95.1
	48.00	15	1.9	2.0	97.2
	49.00	14	1.8	1.9	99.1
	50.00	7	.9	.9	100.0
	Total	742	92.9	100.0	
Missing	System Missing	57	7.1		
	Total	57	7.1		
Total		799	100.0		

Note: FCOH = FACES Cohesion Scale; FACES stands for Family Adaptability and Cohesion Evaluation Scale, but the name FACES is more commonly used.

that communicates more about the variable than its name does. The variable label for the variable FCOH is "FACES Cohesion Scale."

Notice the term *System Missing* near the bottom. *Missing* refers to situations in which a case does not have a valid value for the variable in question. In survey research, the most common reason for a missing value is that the respondent chooses not to answer a question. Other reasons include these: (1) an interviewer forgets to ask a question, and (2) a question does not apply (for instance, for a male respondent, the question "Have you ever given birth?" would be skipped). For the cohesion score, a total of 57 cases did not have valid values. Such cases are often termed *missing cases.*

A *valid case* is a nonmissing case, that is, any case on which data have been gathered. Thus, as Table 2.4 indicates, 742 persons responded to the questions on the cohesion scale. Notice that the percentages in the Valid Percent column are based on valid cases only. For instance, the valid percentage of those scoring 40 on scale is 7.7. This percentage is determined by dividing the frequency of the score 40 (57) by the number of valid cases (742) and then multiplying by 100: $57/742 = .077 \times 100 = 7.7\%$. Observe that percentages in the Percent column are based on *all* (both valid and missing) cases. For instance, the percentage of those scoring 40 is $57/799 = .071 \times 100 = 7.1\%$. Finally, observe that Table 2.4 does not have a Cumulative Frequency column. Some frequency distribution tables simply do not present cumulative frequencies. Cumulative percentages are presented in the Cumulative Percent column and are based on valid cases.

2.4.3   *Grouped Frequency Distributions*

In a **grouped frequency distribution,** cases with similar values are grouped together to form categories. This is typically done to make data easier to manage and interpret. Table 2.5 presents a grouped frequency distribution table for cohesion scores created by the SPSS for Windows program.

2.4.4   *Stem and Leaf Displays*

An alternative to a grouped frequency distribution is a **stem and leaf** display. In the simplest stem and leaf display, the **stem** for a given score consists of all digits that compose that score except for the last digit. The **leaf** for that score is its last digit. For instance, for the score 26 the stem is 2 and the leaf is 6. In this example, the stem (2) conveys that the score is in the 20s (somewhere between 20 and 29) and the 6 conveys that the last digit of the score is a 6. Following this logic, a stem and leaf display may be developed for a distribution.

TABLE 2.5   A GROUPED FREQUENCY DISTRIBUTION TABLE FOR FAMILY COHESION

		Frequency	Percent	Valid Percent	Cumulative Percent
Valid	30 or below	40	5.0	5.4	5.4
	31 to 35	84	10.5	11.3	16.7
	36 to 40	223	27.9	30.1	46.8
	41 to 45	281	35.2	37.9	84.6
	46 to 50	114	14.3	15.4	100.0
	Total	742	92.9	100.0	
Missing	System Missing	57	7.1		
	Total	57	7.1		
Total		799	100.0		

	FAMILY COHESION SCORES: A STEM AND LEAF DISPLAY WITH FREQUENCIES	
TABLE 2.6		
Frequency	**Stem**	**Leaf**
1	1	7
2	2	29
24	3	024455556666677777799999
39	4	000001111122222223335555555666677777778
1	5	0

Table 2.6 presents a stem and leaf display for family cohesion scores for a randomly selected sample of 67 cases in the special-needs adoption study (Rosenthal and Groze, 1992). The first row of data lists a stem of 1 and a single leaf of 7. Putting the stem and leaf together tells us that there is one score in the 10s (between 10 and 19) and that this is 17. The second data row consists of the stem 2 (conveying the 20s) and two leaves, 2 and 9. Hence, it conveys that there are two scores in the 20s, 22 and 29. The stem for the third row is 3, which corresponds to the 30s. As there are 24 leaves in the third row, this indicates a total, or a frequency, of 24 scores in the 30s. Note that within each row, leaves are ordered from low to high.

A stem and leaf display has two advantages over a grouped frequency distribution. First, it conveys frequencies visually. The longer the row, the greater the frequency. For instance, in Table 2.6, the fourth row (scores in the 40s) is the longest and therefore has the highest frequency. Second, the stem and leaf display provides greater detail. A grouped frequency distribution table conveys only the frequency in a given category. The stem and leaf display conveys this frequency (though in some displays one must count leaves) and also allows determination of exact scores. (To do so, put each leaf with its stem.)

Stem and leaf displays are readily produced by most statistical software packages. See Tukey (1977, pp. 1–25) for an in-depth treatment or some less specialized statistics texts for more details (e.g., Toothaker and Miller, 1996, pp. 78–81; Moore and McCabe, 1996, pp. 6–10).

2.5 PERCENTILE RANK

A case's **percentile rank** equals the percentage of cases with values lower than or equal to the case's value. Thus, if Sally's score on her statistics test is equal to or higher than that of 79% of students in the class, her percentile rank on the test is 79. In such a situation, we may also say that Sally's score is in (or at) the 79th **percentile.**

Obviously, one may not compute percentile ranks for a variable that is at the nominal level of measurement, because those values cannot be ordered.

Though percentiles may be calculated with ordinal-level variables, their primary application is with variables at or "almost at" the interval/ratio level. A general formula is:

$$\text{Percentile rank} = \frac{\text{number of cases with equal or lower values}}{\text{total number of cases}} \times 100 \qquad (2.7)$$

The number of cases with equal or lower values equals the cumulative frequency. Hence, another formula[3] is:

$$\text{Percentile rank} = \frac{\text{cumulative frequency}}{\text{sample size}} \times 100 \qquad (2.8)$$

The just-presented formula (2.8) is identical to the formula for cumulative percentage (2.6). Cumulative percentage and percentile rank have essentially identical meanings. Indeed, in a frequency distribution, the percentile rank of a score equals the cumulative percentage of that score. When one has access to a frequency distribution, the easiest way to "calculate" a percentile rank is simply to note the cumulative percentage. For instance, suppose that the cohesion score (see Table 2.4) for the Jones family was 43. What is their percentile rank? The cumulative percentage for a score of 43 is 70.6% and, hence, this is the percentile rank. Percentile ranks are typically rounded to whole numbers. Hence, we would round to 71 and state either: "The Jones family's percentile rank is 71" or "The Jones family's score is at the 71st percentile."

It may be helpful to work through an example in which one does not have access to a frequency distribution table. Suppose that 227 students take a test, on which 166 students score lower than Sally and 60 score higher. Note that 166 + 60 = 226, that is, one less than 227. Sally's score is the "missing score": 166 + 60 + 1 (Sally's score) = 227. The cumulative frequency of scores *equal to* or lower than Sally's score is 166 + 1 (Sally's score) = 167. This example illustrates that the trick to calculating a case's percentile rank is to include that case in the calculation. Using formula 2.8, Sally's percentile rank is (167/227) × 100 = 73.6, which rounds to 74. Sally's score then is at the 74th percentile.[4]

A different problem from determining the percentile rank of a given score is determining the score that corresponds to a given percentile. To do so, find the first value in the frequency distribution with a cumulative percentage greater than or equal to the stated percentile (Norusis, 1997, p. 44). For instance, what cohesion score is at the 25th percentile? The cumulative percentage of a score of 37 is 26.0%. This is the first value with a cumulative percentage greater than 25. Hence, the score corresponding to the 25th percentile is 37. (However, this method is not appropriate for grouped frequency distributions.)

Percentile rank is easily computed by statistical software packages and spreadsheets. Percentile ranks calculated by these may differ very slightly from those derived from the formula presented in this chapter. (This chapter's formulas should be regarded as very close approximations of percentile rank.)

2.6 FIGURES FOR PRESENTING DATA FOR A SINGLE VARIABLE

2.6.1 Introduction

This section focuses on figures. It is useful to distinguish figures from tables. **Tables** do not include "pictures" or graphics. With the exception of horizontal and vertical lines, they are composed of numbers, letters, and (sometimes) statistical notation. In contrast, when pictures or graphics are used, one has a **figure.** Thus, Tables 2.1 to 2.7 in this chapter are designated as tables because they do not contain pictures or graphics. Figures 2.1 to 2.7 are designated as figures because they do.

There are many different types of figures. Figures with columns or bars are **bar graphs.** Those with lines are **line graphs.** The following discussion presents four types of figures, each of which presents frequencies or percentages. Because they make use of bars, the bar chart and the histogram are classified as bar graphs. The frequency polygon is a line graph. The final figure is the pie chart.

2.6.2 Bar Charts

Bar charts display frequencies of nominal-level variables. A variable's values are typically displayed on the horizontal axis. The height of each bar (column) conveys frequency. To estimate the frequency, "trace" from the top of the bar to the vertical axis.

Figure 2.1 presents a bar chart for the variable "family ethnicity" from the special-needs adoption study (Rosenthal and Groze, 1992). Adoptive families fall into one of three family ethnicity groups (values): (1) minority, inracial, that is, minority (nonwhite) parents who adopt a child of the same race as at least one parent; (2) white, inracial: white parents who adopt a white child; and (3) transracial: white parents who adopt a minority child. Tracing over to the vertical axis from the top of the highest bar reveals that about 470 white, inracial families participated in the study.

Note that the bars in a bar chart do not touch other bars. A nominal-level variable's values cannot be ordered, so the order of values in a bar chart is arbitrary. The values represented by adjacent bars have no greater similarity than do those represented by bars that are not adjacent. By keeping the bars separate (not touching), the bar chart's appearance reinforces the separateness of the values that each bar conveys.

2.6.3 Histograms

Histograms convey information in the same way as bar charts: the height of each bar (column) represents frequency. The major difference is that the bars in a histogram touch or nearly do so. Histograms are used with variables at the ordinal and

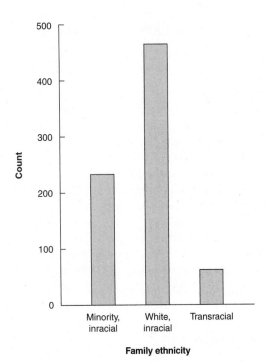

FIGURE 2.1

BAR CHART OF FAMILY ETHNICITY

interval/ratio levels of measurement, when values can be ordered. The ordering of bars on the histogram is not arbitrary but rather is in accord with the ordering of the values. The frequency of the lowest value is presented first (the leftmost bar); then the next lowest, and so on up to the highest value (the rightmost bar). The fact that the bars touch (or nearly do so) signifies that adjacent bars stand for adjacent values and that the values represented by a first bar lead in ordered fashion to those represented by the next. In a histogram, values represented by bars that are located physically close together are indeed more similar than are those represented by bars that are physically distant. Having the bars touch reinforces this point.

Figure 2.2 is a histogram showing the age in years of children in the special-needs adoption study at the time that they first entered their adoptive homes. The bars in this histogram represent one-year intervals. The "tallest" bar (highest frequency) pertains to age 0, which represents the first year of life (prior to the first birthday). About 110 children entered their adoptive home at this age.

2.6.4   Frequency Polygons

Frequency polygons, also used with variables at the ordinal and interval/ratio levels, represent with lines the same information as do histograms via bars. Frequency is conveyed by the height of the line. Figure 2.3 presents the data pertaining to age at entry into the home as a frequency polygon.

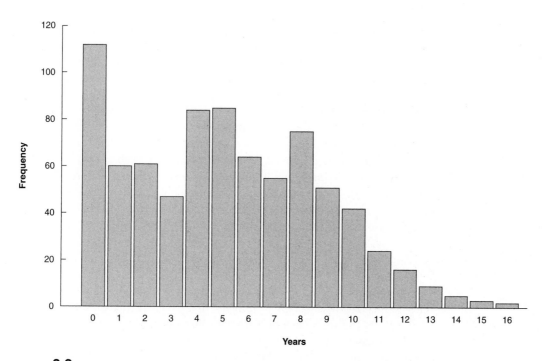

FIGURE **2.2**

HISTOGRAM OF AGE AT ENTRY INTO ADOPTIVE HOME

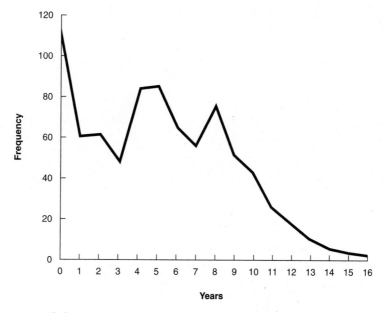

FIGURE **2.3**

FREQUENCY POLYGON OF AGE AT ENTRY INTO ADOPTIVE HOME

The line that defines frequencies in a frequency polygon is termed a **frequency distribution curve.** When actual, real-world (rather than theoretical) data are depicted, the term *curve* is a misnomer. As in most frequency polygons that depict real data, the frequency distribution curve in Figure 2.3 jags and turns rather than curves.[5]

Both histograms and frequency polygons can be used with variables at the ordinal and interval/ratio level and both convey frequencies. The only difference between these two is in physical appearance. When one's data are at the ordinal level, the histogram is usually preferred over the frequency polygon. For data at the interval/ratio level, the histogram is generally preferred when there are relatively few values (say, seven or fewer) and the frequency polygon when there is a greater number. These are recommendations only. The choice between the two ultimately reflects the researcher's preference and the particular situation.

2.6.5   Pie Charts

Pie charts provide still another way to present frequencies. Figure 2.4 is a pie chart presenting the categories of family ethnicity. In a pie chart, the size of a "slice" is proportionate to the frequency of cases with that value. Hence, a value that has twice as many cases as a second value will be represented by a piece of pie that is twice as large. Similarly, suppose that a given slice of pie represents about one-half of the total area of the pie. This being the case, one may conclude that about one-half of cases have the value that corresponds to that slice. In Figure 2.4, the slice of pie representing white, inracial families is about 60% of the pie. Hence, one

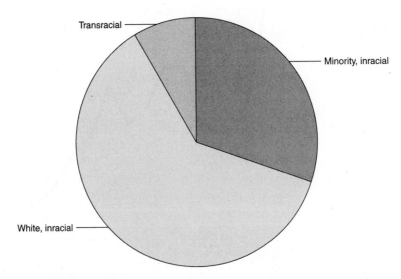

FIGURE 2.4

PIE CHART OF FAMILY ETHNICITY

may conclude that about 60% of all families in the study were white, inracial families.

2.7 BIVARIATE TABLES AND FIGURES

All the tables and figures so far have presented information for only one variable, making them univariate. Bivariate tables and figures allow us to examine the relationship between two variables. Let's look at some examples. In the special-needs adoption study, a substantial percentage of adoptions were by single parents. Table 2.7 allows a comparison between responses of these parents and those in two-parent families to the question, "How do you and your child get along?" The table presents frequency distributions on this question for the two groups of respondents. Examination of Table 2.7 reveals that 71% of parents in single-parent homes versus 64% of those in two-parent homes selected the response "very well." Thus, the table does reveal a modest relationship between family structure and "getting along" with one's child—single parents, taken as a group, seem to get along somewhat better with their child than do parents in two-parent families. (Part Three of this text, Chapters 6 to 9, covers in depth how to assess and interpret relationships.)

Other data from the special-needs adoption study provide an example of a bivariate figure. A question in this study queried: "Overall, was the impact of this child's adoption on your family . . . 'very positive,' 'mostly positive,' 'mixed,' 'mostly negative,' or 'very negative'?" Figure 2.5 presents the percentage of families in each category of family ethnicity who selected the "very positive" response. This figure reveals a relationship between family ethnicity and assessment of the adoption's impact. There is a relationship because, in the three groups, respondents were not equally likely to choose the "very positive" category. Respondents in the minority, inracial group were most likely to respond "very positive" (their percentage is 58%), those in the transracial group were next most likely (53%), and those in the white, inracial group were least likely (41%).

TABLE 2.7 ASSOCIATION BETWEEN FAMILY STRUCTURE AND HOW PARENT AND CHILD "GET ALONG"

	ONE-PARENT FAMILIES		TWO-PARENT FAMILIES	
Response	**Frequency**	**Percentage**	**Frequency**	**Percentage**
Very well	115	71.4	401	64.1
Fairly well	43	26.7	197	31.5
Not so well	3	1.9	21	3.4
Very poorly	0	0.0	7	0.9

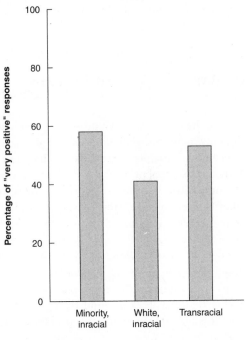

FIGURE 2.5

FAMILY ETHNICITY AND PERCENTAGE OF "VERY POSITIVE" RESPONSES

Family ethnicity is related to how likely respondents were to assess the effect of adoption on their family as "very positive."

2.8   MISLEADING WITH FIGURES

It is fairly easy to create misleading graphs. One simple way is to change the scaling of the vertical axis. Note that in Figure 2.5, the vertical axis covers the full range of percentages from 0 to 100%. Figure 2.6 presents the same data but with the vertical axis scaled from 30 to 60%. Note how much more pronounced the differences between the three groups appear to be in Figure 2.6 than in Figure 2.5. Whereas Figure 2.5 gives the impression of medium-sized differences, in Figure 2.6 the differences appear extremely large. Figure 2.6 could lead an unwary reader to conclude that the real size of the differences is correspondingly large.

Another way to affect impressions is to tinker with the relative lengths of the axes. For instance, differences between the three groups appear larger still in Figure 2.7. In this figure, the vertical axis has been lengthened relative to the horizontal axis. To still further accentuate differences, the scaling of the vertical axis in Figure 2.7 ranges from 40 to 60% rather than from 30 to 60%.

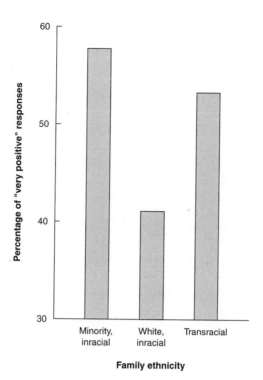

FIGURE **2.6**

BAR CHART WITH RESCALED VERTICAL AXIS

One should display data in straightforward ways that do not mislead. Usually, the horizontal axis should be slightly longer than the vertical axis. A ratio of 4 to 3 presents a visually pleasing, straightforward figure. For instance, when the horizontal axis is 4 inches, the vertical axis should usually be about 3 inches. This is not a hard-and-fast rule and you may deviate where doing so improves appearance or clarity. For instance, a bar chart with 15 columns may need to be wider than one with 3 columns.

Choosing how to scale the vertical axis can be tricky. In most circumstances in which frequencies are displayed (as in bar charts, histograms, and frequency polygons), 0 should be at the bottom of the vertical axis and a number slightly higher than the greatest frequency should be at the top. When percentages are involved (as in Figures 2.5 to 2.7), the safest choice—the one with the least possibility to mislead—is to scale the vertical axis with 0% at the bottom and 100% at the top. Sometimes, however, such scaling makes it difficult to discern small differences, such as a difference of 3%. When the vertical axis is scaled in this way and differences are small, all bars will be about the same height, creating the visual impression of "no difference." If your data have small differences and you believe these differences to be important, you may choose to scale the vertical axis differently. Using computer software to create figures enables you to readily experiment with different ways to scale the axes.

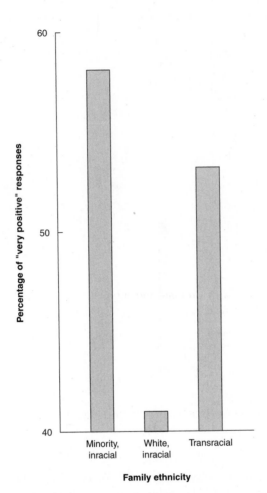

FIGURE **2.7**

BAR CHART WITH ELONGATED VERTICAL AXIS

2.9   CHAPTER SUMMARY

Sample size refers to the number of cases and is symbolized by N. Frequency (or count), symbolized most often by f, refers to the number of cases having a given value. The symbol n is an alternative to f for conveying the number in a group.

Proportions are calculated by dividing the number of objects with a given characteristic by the total number of objects. Percentages and proportions convey identical information. To calculate a percentage, multiply the proportion by 100. Ratios are calculated by dividing the number in one group by that in another.

A distribution is a group of values that have been organized in some way. Empirical distributions are composed of actual data gathered in research. Theoretical distributions are composed of assumed (hypothetical) values and are encountered mostly in inferential statistical applications.

Grouping cases with the same values gives a frequency distribution. Such a distribution is presented in a frequency distribution table, reporting frequencies and sometimes percentages. The cumulative frequency for a given value is the number of cases having that value or a lower one. The cumulative percentage for a given value is the percentage of cases having that value or a lower one. The percentile rank of a case equals the percentage of cases with values lower than or equal to the case's value. Percentile rank and cumulative percentage have identical formulas and are basically synonymous.

In a grouped frequency distribution, cases with similar values are grouped together to form categories. This distribution is presented in a grouped frequency distribution table or in a stem and leaf display, which offers increased detail and provides a visual sense of data.

The use of pictures or graphics indicates a figure rather than a table. Figures come in several types: Bar charts use bars to display frequencies of nominal-level variables. Histograms also use bars but require variables at the ordinal or interval/ratio level. Typically, the columns of the bar chart do not touch, but those of the histogram do (or nearly do). Frequency polygons use lines rather than bars and are used with ordinal- and interval/ratio-level variables. The line in a frequency polygon is termed a *frequency distribution curve*. The easiest way to mislead with figures is by changing the scale of one or both axes.

PROBLEMS AND QUESTIONS

Sections 2.2 and 2.3

1. For a graduate class of social work students, the areas of concentration and the number of students choosing each area are as follows: children and family services, 25; mental health services, 40; health services, 20; community development, 35. What is the value for each of the following?
   a. *N*·
   b. *f* for mental health services
   c. *n* for mental health services
   d. *p* for mental health services
   e. % for mental health services
   f. The ratio of those choosing mental health services to those choosing children and family services
   g. The ratio of those choosing children and family services to those choosing mental health services

Section 2.4

2. A _____ is a group of values that have been organized. _____ distributions are com-

posed of real-world data, whereas _____ distributions are composed of hypothetical values.
3. Create a frequency distribution table for the data provided in problem 1.
4. Cover the last two columns in Table 2.3 with a sheet of paper and compute the following:
   a. The cumulative frequency for age 26 or below
   b. The cumulative percentage for age 26 or below
   c. The cumulative frequency for age 38 or below
   d. The cumulative percentage for age 38 or below
5. What is a missing case?
6. In Table 2.4, listing FACES cohesion scores, why do the percentages in the Percentage column differ from those in the Valid Percentage column?
7. Develop a stem and leaf display for the following observations: 42, 44, 44, 48, 51, 52, 55, 55, 55, 56, 64, 68, 69, 71, 72

Section 2.5

8. In Table 2.4,
   a. What is the cumulative percentage of a score of 33?

b. What is the percentile rank of a score of 33?

c. At what percentile is a score of 33?

d. In calculating cumulative percentages for Table 2.4, should the denominator of the formula (formula 2.7 and/or formula 2.8) be 742 or 799?

9. In a group of 75 persons who take a job readiness exam, 28 score higher than Bill and 46 score lower. What is Bill's percentile rank?

10. What cohesion score is at the following percentiles in Table 2.4?

a. 25

b. 50

c. 75

Section 2.6

11. _____ do not include pictures or graphics whereas _____ do include them.

12. Figures that use lines are termed _____ graphs; those that use columns or bars are termed _____ graphs.

13. Among clients at a mental health center, 33 receive individual therapy, 72 receive group therapy, and 22 receive an innovative service called computer-assisted therapy. For these data,

a. What is the level of measurement?

b. Is a histogram or a bar chart the better choice?

c. Should the columns of the chart "touch"? Why or why not?

d. Draw a bar chart.

14. Refer to Table 2.5, the grouped frequency distribution for family cohesion. For this distribution,

a. What is the level of measurement?

b. Is a histogram or a bar chart the best choice?

c. Should the columns of the chart "touch"? Why or why not?

d. Draw a histogram.

15. Draw a frequency polygon to depict cohesion scores in Table 2.4. To save time, present only those scores in the range (inclusive) from 30 to 40.

16. (T or F) Frequency polygons and histograms present the same information in different ways.

17. In your own words, when is a histogram preferred? When is a frequency polygon preferred?

18. In a sample of 90 clients at a family support agency, 25 participate in a job-search skills program, 45 in a basic skills training program, and 20 in a mentor program. For these data,

a. What are the percentages for the three programs?

b. In a pie chart, what percentage of the pie area should the slice representing the job-search skills program represent?

c. Draw a pie chart.

Section 2.7

19. (This example expands on the data presented in problem 1.) Among the 80 women who are graduate students at a school of social work, the number selecting each concentration is as follows: children and family services, 20; mental health services, 25; health services, 15; community development, 20. Among the 40 men, these numbers are 5, 15, 5, 15, respectively. For these data,

a. Create a table that presents the data. The table should include both frequencies and percentages. (You may want to model your table after Table 2.7.)

b. Are women and men equally likely to select the different concentrations?

c. (Advanced question on relationship, jumps ahead to Chapter 6 topic.) Are gender and choice of concentration related?

Section 2.8

20. What are two ways to create misleading impressions with a bar graph?

21. (T or F) In a bar chart, information is *always* presented most effectively with percentages scaled from 0 to 100.

22. Give an example of when using percentages other than 0 and 100 might present information more effectively.

23. The text suggests a horizontal-to-vertical axis ratio of _____ to _____ .

Introduction to End-of-Chapter Computer Exercises

The computer exercises at the end of each chapter make use of the data set on special-needs adoption that is in the SPSS for Windows (Version 10.0) data file named "Special Needs Adoption SPSS Data File." If you have not yet downloaded this file, you should do so. It is located at the web address http://helpingprofs.wadsworth.com/resources/rosenthal/data_set. If you want to use the SPSS program with a Mac computer[6] or another statistical package[7] see the appropriate endnote cited here. It is presumed that most students will do these exercises using SPSS, so most of the exercises guide you through the needed SPSS procedures.

The data set for the exercises consists of 28 variables and 799 cases. See Appendix D for descriptions of the variables, and Section 23.5 for discussion of the study sample and research design.

Appendix C is a 90-minute SPSS-based exercise. You will find it useful to complete this exercise prior to beginning the end-of-chapter computer exercises. (Appendix C also recommends sections of the SPSS tutorial to complete.) However, as the end-of-chapter exercises guide you step-by-step through most procedures, completing Appendix C is not a necessity. The following conventions are used in all end-of-chapter computer exercises:

Anything to be typed is in **bold and underlined.**

Anything to be chosen or clicked is in *italics*. For instance: *OK* signals you to click the button entitled OK.

When multiple menu choices should be made sequentially, the "greater than" symbol (>) indicates this. For instance:

Analyze > Descriptive Statistics > Frequencies

instructs you to choose/click "Analyze," then "Descriptive Statistics," and then "Frequencies."

SPSS variable names appear in capital letters.

To open SPSS 10.0 for Windows, find it in your Programs list (located via the Start button in Windows) and click. (This assumes that SPSS is installed on your computer.) (If SPSS prompts you with a "What do you want to do?" box, click on the "type in data" button and click *OK*.) The SPSS exercises will be easier if you do the following (if you have completed the Appendix C exercises, you have likely already done this): from the menus at the top of SPSS, click/choose *Edit > Options*. If it is not already selected, select the "General" tab by clicking it. In the upper right part of the dialog box in the "Variable lists" area, check whether the "Display names" and "Alphabetical" buttons are marked. If so, click *OK*. If not: (1) Click/mark both of these. (2) Click *OK*. (3) If you clicked the buttons, observe that the program informs you that each of the changes takes effect the next time a data file is opened, and (4) click *OK* to both messages.

To open the adoption data set from the SPSS menus, click/choose *File > Open* and then browse your way to the directory where the data have been downloaded and click the file. (At the website, the file was named "Special Needs Adoption SPSS Data File.")

 # Computer Exercises

1. Create frequency distribution tables for the variables GENDER (adopted child's gender), AGEHOMYT (child's age when he or she entered the adoptive home, rounded back to prior birthday), CHIETH (child's ethnicity), and RELSCALE (scale measuring closeness/quality of the parent-child relationship). [In SPSS, *Analyze > Descriptive Statistics > Frequencies*, highlight the variables and using the arrow in the center, click the variables over to the right side, and click *OK*.]

A question to think about: Do cumulative frequencies and percentages make sense for the variables GENDER and CHIETH? (You can check your answer in the following paragraph.)

Cumulative frequencies don't convey meaningful information for GENDER and CHIETH, because these variables are at the nominal level of measurement and cumulative statistics presume that a variable is at least ordinal (that is, that values can be ordered).

2. Create the following graphs:

   a. A frequency polygon for AGEHOMYT [In SPSS, *Graphs > Line*, click box next to "Simple," *Define*, click AGEHOMYT over to "Category Axis" (making sure the line represents "<u>N</u> of cases"), *OK*.]

   b. A histogram for AGEHOMYT [In SPSS, *Graphs > Bar*, click box next to "Simple," *Define*, click AGEHOMYT over to "Category Axis" (making sure the line represents "<u>N</u> of cases"), *Options*, click box next to "Display groups defined by missing values" so that it is not checked, *Continue, OK*.]

   c. A bar chart for CHIETH [In SPSS, *Graphs > Bar*, click box next to "Simple," *Define*, click AGEHOMYT back to the box at the left, click CHIETH over to "Category Axis" (making sure the line represents "<u>N</u> of cases"), *OK*.]

   d. A pie chart for ENJOYSCH (parental report of child's enjoyment of school) [In SPSS, *Graphs > Pie Chart, Define*, click ENJOYSCH over into the "Define slices" box, *OK*.]

      Note: In SPSS, *Analyze > Descriptive Statistics > Frequencies* and clicking the "Charts" box also generates frequency polygons, histograms, bar charts, and pie charts.

3. Create a stem and leaf display for FCOH (family closeness/cohesion scale). [In SPSS, *Analyze > Descriptive Statistics > Explore*, click FCOH over into "Dependent List," *Plots*, click box next to "Stem-and-leaf," *Continue, OK*.]

4. Create a frequency distribution table for FEEL-CLOS (how "close" parent feels to child). Also, create a histogram. (Hint: A histogram can be created within the Frequencies procedure. See the note for 2.d above.) Run the Frequencies procedure a second time but create a bar chart this time to see how it differs from a histogram.

5. For some practice entering and defining data, close the adoption data set and get ready to enter a new data set using the following informa-

tion: Twelve mental health professionals attend a workshop. Seven rate it as excellent, three as good, two as fair, and none as poor. To create a new Data Entry Window, click or choose *File > New > Data*. The data set will have one variable, the rating. Name the variable. Give it a variable label. Enter numeric codes (excellent = 4, good = 3, fair = 2, poor = 1) and provide value labels for these. Finally, set decimal places to 0. Create a frequency distribution table. (The section of the SPSS tutorial entitled "Using the Data Editor" can help you with this. Or see "Background and Defining of Data" in Appendix C.) You need not save either the adoption data set or the data set created for this question.

NOTES

1. This table conforms reasonably well to the style required by many academic journals. For instance, academic-style tables do not have any vertical lines. See the *Publication Manual of the American Psychological Association* (1994) for further information.

2. SPSS for Windows is best learned by using it. The program has an on-screen tutorial for new users. Appendix C in this text is an SPSS-based exercise that builds on the tutorial. Additional SPSS exercises are found at the end of most chapters. (Appendix D documents the data and variables for these exercises.) Resources for in-depth learning about SPSS include: *SPSS Base 10.0 User's Guide* (SPSS, 1999), *SPSS 10.0 Guide to Data Analysis* (Norusis, 2000), *Using SPSS for Windows: Analyzing and Understanding Data* (Green, Salkind, and Akey, 2000), *Adventures in Social Research: Data Analysis Using SPSS for Windows 95/98* (Babbie, Halley, and Zaino, 2000), and *SPSS for Beginners* (Gupta, 1999; see www.spss.org). Other titles may be found at the websites www.spss.com and www.prenticehall.com. Students may purchase the SPSS software via either the *SPSS Graduate Pack 10.0 for Windows* (1999, complete version of the basic software package at a reduced price) or via the *SPSS Student Version 10.0 for Windows* (2000, a reduced capability version of the basic package at an even greater price reduction).

3. Formulas 2.7 and 2.8 should be regarded as extremely close approximations of percentile rank. Also, these formulas are not appropriate for grouped fre-

quency distributions (that is, when cases with similar values have been combined into categories). For a formula for grouped frequency distributions, see most statistics books (for instance, Toothaker and Miller, 1996, p. 155).

4. Glass and Hopkins (1996, p. 26) suggest an alternative method when precision is needed: count one-half of an individual's case as being above his or her score and one-half as below. For instance, Sally's score is higher than 166 cases, lower than 60 cases, and equal (obviously) to her own score. Her score could be considered higher than $166\frac{1}{2}$ cases and lower than $60\frac{1}{2}$ cases. Then her percentile rank computes to $(166.5/227) \times 100 = 73.34$, which rounds to 73.

5. Sometimes the area between the frequency distribution curve of a frequency polygon and the horizontal axis is shaded. Such a figure is often called an area graph.

6. If you have an Apple Macintosh computer, it is recommended that you download the file "Special Needs Adoption SPSS Portable Mac File." (As this book is being written the latest version of SPSS for the Macintosh is not fully compatible with the exercises in the book, which are designed for SPSS for Windows Version 10.0.

The Macintosh-based SPSS program may be released in a new version by the time you read this and thus may become compatible.) To open the file, highlight the "SPSS Portable File" choice (.por) in the SPSS open file dialog box. The present (as of June 2000) Macintosh-based version of SPSS is highly similar to Version 6.1.4 of SPSS for Windows. The end-of-chapter exercises should work well for Macintosh if you (1) click the *Statistics* menu choice whenever the exercises direct you to click *Analyze* and (2) after having clicked *Statistics*, click *Summarize* whenever the exercises direct you to click *Descriptive Statistics*. The Appendix C exercises have too many inconsistencies with the present Macintosh-based version to be useful with this program. None of the exercises in this book have been formally tested for the Macintosh.

7. If you do the exercises with a statistical package other than SPSS, you can find the same data in a Microsoft Excel (spreadsheet) file named "Special Needs Adoption Excel File." (If you are doing the exercise with SPSS, be sure to use the SPSS file, because what SPSS terms "Variable Labels" and "Value Labels" are not included in the Excel file.)

DESCRIPTIVE PROCEDURES FOR ONE VARIABLE

Part Two focuses on statistical procedures you can use to describe a single variable. (A variable is something that takes on different values. For instance, the variable sex takes on the values female and male.) Chapter 3 presents measures of central tendency, which are tools for assessing what the "typical" and most common value in your data is. Chapter 4 presents measures of variability, that is, measures of the degree to which values are dispersed and spread out. Chapter 5 examines shape of distribution, that is, the particular pattern of dispersion in your data, and presents the most important distribution in statistics, the normal distribution.

CENTRAL TENDENCY

3.1 CHAPTER OVERVIEW

In Chapter 3 we introduce *central tendency* along with *variability* and *shape of distribution*. In this chapter we focus on the first of these, central tendency, and discuss its three key measures—the *mode*, the *median*, and the *mean*. The chapter presents situations in which each measure is appropriately used, and compares the relative advantages and disadvantages of each. Finally, we consider how *outliers* make the mean a misleading measure.

3.2 KEY CONCEPTS IN UNIVARIATE DESCRIPTIVE STATISTICS

Univariate descriptive statistical procedures describe the three general characteristics of variables. The first, **central tendency,** refers to a variable's typical and most common value(s), and, generally, to the value(s) around which most values tend to cluster or converge. The three primary measures of central tendency are the mode, the median, and the mean. The second characteristic, **variability,** refers to the degree to which values are dispersed or "spread out" around some central value. Chapter 4 presents five measures of variability: the range, the interquartile range, the mean deviation, the standard deviation, and the variance; of those, the standard deviation is most important. The third characteristic, **shape of distribution,** refers to the particular way (the pattern) in which values vary. Chapter 5 presents several different shapes of distributions—or, one may simply say, distributions—the most important of which is the normal distribution. This chapter addresses central tendency.

3.3 THREE MEASURES OF CENTRAL TENDENCY

Measures of central tendency inform one about the "typical," the "common," the "middle," the "everyday"—if you will, the "run of the mill." There are three key measures of central tendency:

- The **mode** is the value with the greatest frequency. Stated differently, it is the most commonly occurring value.
- The **median** is the value with the same number of values higher than and lower than it.
- The **mean** is the sum of the values of all cases divided by the number of cases.

Consider the values 5, 8, 5, 10, 9, 11, 43. Perhaps these represent the number of books read by the seven members of the first-grade Chickadees reading group.

The mode is 5 because it occurs twice, more than any other value.

To determine the median, order the values from low to high: 5, 5, 8, 9, 10, 11, 43. The median is 9 as there are three lower values and an equal number (three) of higher values.

The mean is 13: $(5 + 8 + 5 + 10 + 9 + 11 + 43)/7 = 13$.

The next three sections discuss these measures. They direct particular attention to how a variable's level of measurement influences choice of measure. All three measures are univariate, that is, they pertain to only a single variable (rather than to the relationship between two or more variables). Statistical packages and spreadsheets readily calculate these measures.

3.4 THE MODE

The mode is appropriate for variables at all levels of measurement. For a variable at the nominal or ordinal level, the mode will ordinarily be a nonnumeric value. Thus, if there are 28 women and 14 men in your classroom, the mode for sex is female. (Don't confuse a value with its frequency. The mode for sex is not 28; 28 is the frequency of women.) Suppose that 27 people evaluate a workshop as excellent, 42 as good, 17 as fair, and 1 as poor. In this example, the mode—or, one may say, the modal response—is the value "good." At the interval/ratio level, the mode is numeric, as demonstrated in the example of the Chickadees reading group. Some variables have more than one mode. For instance, consider a variable whose values are the scores 1, 3, 4, 3, 5, 4, 2, 6. This variable is **bimodal,** that is, it has two modes, 3 and 4, both of which occur twice, which is more than any other value.

3.5 THE MEDIAN

3.5.1 Calculation and Formulas

The median requires measurement at the ordinal level or above. For instance, it makes sense to think about the modal sex of a sample. If the majority (more than 50%) in the sample are female, then female is the mode. However, it is nonsensical to think of a median sex. Calculation of the median requires that values be ordered from low to high. Sex is a nominal-level variable, so such an ordering cannot be carried out.

The median was defined as the value with the same number of cases with values above and below it. In essence, it is the middle value in the ordering of values. In the Chickadees reading example, the number of cases was odd ($N = 7$). If the number of cases is even, no single value has the same number of values above and below it. Stated differently, there is no single middle value. For instance, consider the following values, which have already been ordered from low to high: 2, 4, 5, 7, 8, 9, 12, 13.

Four values are higher than 7 and three are lower. Three values are higher than 8 and four are lower. If the number of cases is equal, the median is defined as the mean of the two middlemost values.[1] The two middlemost values in the just-presented distribution are 7 and 8. Hence, the median is $(7 + 8)/2 = 7.5$.

The major mistake that students make in calculating the median is to forget to order values. For instance, asked to find the median of 0, 4, 1, 2, 3, they respond (incorrectly) 1, as this is the middle value presented. Values must be ordered from low to high prior to finding the median: 0, 1, 2, 3, 4. Hence, the correct median is 2.

The median has already been defined as the value with the same number of values higher than and lower than it. An alternative definition is the value at the 50th percentile.

In the examples presented so far, we have not dealt with distributions in which several or more cases have the same values. These are commonly encountered. For instance, consider Table 3.1, a frequency distribution table that presents responses to the question: "Overall, has the impact of this child's adoption on your family been . . . ?" This question is taken from the special-needs adoption study introduced in Chapter 2 (Rosenthal and Groze, 1992).

When several or more cases have the same values, the just-provided definition of the median as the score at the 50th percentile can be used to find the median.

TABLE 3.1	IMPACT OF ADOPTION ON FAMILY			
Value	Frequency	Cumulative Frequency	Percentage	Cumulative Percentage
Very negative	10	10	1	1
Mostly negative	24	34	3	4
Mixed . . .	163	197	21	25
Mostly positive	218	415	28	53
Very positive	365	780	47	100

Note: $N = 780$.

Chapter 2 (Section 2.5) provides a method for finding the score that corresponds to a stated percentile. That score is the first score with a cumulative percentage greater than the stated percentile. Reading down the cumulative percentage column in Table 3.1, the first cumulative percentage greater than or equal to 50 is 53. This cumulative percentage corresponds to "mostly positive." Thus "mostly positive" is the median.[2] This method for finding the median is valid in frequency distributions in which several cases have the same values but is *not* valid for *grouped* frequency distributions.[3]

3.5.2 Values Differ Less from the Median Than from Any Other Point

We need to note one other characteristic of the median. A case's **deviation score** equals the value for that case minus some other value. That other value is typically a measure of central tendency. For instance, to determine a case's deviation score from the median, one subtracts the median from the case's value. So, if a case has a value of 7 and the median is 10, the case's deviation score from the median is $7 - 10 = -3$. Suppose that for all cases in a distribution you did the following: (1) calculated deviation scores from some given value, (2) converted these scores to absolute values (in other words, changed all negatives to positives), and (3) summed the absolute values. This sum has its lowest possible value when calculated from the median. Stated formally, the median minimizes the sum of the absolute values of deviation scores (Toothaker and Miller, 1996, p. 111). Stated intuitively, scores differ less from the median than from any other value.[4] This is clearly an attractive characteristic for a measure of central tendency. Figure 3.1 presents visually how the median minimizes the sum of the absolute value of deviation scores. In Figure 3.1 this sum is lower from 5, the median, than from any other point. In Figure 3.1, the sum of absolute values of deviation scores from the median is 12. This calculation follows. (Recall that the symbol for absolute value is | |.)

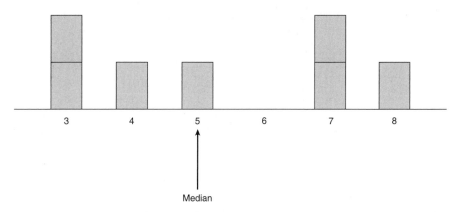

FIGURE **3.1**

THE MEDIAN: THE POINT FROM WHICH OTHER SCORES DIFFER LEAST

$$|(3 - 5)| + |(3 - 5)| + |(4 - 5)| + |(5 - 5)| + |(7 - 5)|$$
$$+ |(7 - 5)| + |(8 - 5)|$$
$$= |-2| + |-2| + |-1| + |0| + |2| + |2| + |3|$$
$$= 2 + 2 + 1 + 0 + 2 + 2 + 3 = 12$$

3.6   THE MEAN

3.6.1   *Formula*

The mean is by far the most commonly used measure of central tendency. The mean corresponds with the commonsense notion of the "average" that most of us learned in elementary or high school. It may be used appropriately with variables at or almost at the interval/ratio level. (See Chapter 1, Section 1.6, for a discussion of almost-interval measurement.) Unlike the mode and the median, the mean is easily expressed with a formula:

$$\overline{X} = \frac{\Sigma X}{N} \tag{3.1}$$

where $\overline{X}$ is the mean, X represents the value of an individual case, and N is the number of cases (sample size). The summation sign, Σ, instructs one to sum together *all* the X's, that is, the values of all cases. Thus the formula directs one to (1) sum the individual values and then (2) divide by the sample size. An alternate symbol for the mean is M.

3.6.2   *The Mean and Level of Measurement*

Most people grasp intuitively that a mean may not be computed for a nominal-level variable. For instance, it is nonsensical to attempt to add up eye colors (blue, brown, green, etc.) and divide by the sample size to determine mean eye color. Similarly, it is intuitive that one may not add up qualitative values such as strongly agree, agree, disagree, and strongly disagree to compute a mean level of agreement.

Confusion can develop when numbers (numeric codes) are used to record qualitative values. Social scientists have long used such codes, and computer methods have encouraged more use of codes. For instance, consider the question from the special-needs adoption study that asked parents to evaluate the impact that adopting a child with special needs had on their family (see Table 3.1). In responding, parents choose from the following: "very positive," "mostly positive," "mixed . . . ," "mostly negative," "very negative." These responses were then entered into a computerized data file. If the response was "very positive," the number 5 was entered; for "positive," 4 was entered; for "mixed," 3 was entered; for "negative," 2 was entered; and for "very negative," 1 was entered. With numbers entered, a computer software program can indeed calculate a mean. Summing together the numbers for all the responses and dividing by sample size ($N = 780$),

SPSS for Windows would calculate the mean to be 4.16. This value is between 4 (mostly positive) and 5 (very positive), though it is much closer to 4. Can't one conclude the mean is 4.16 and that this represents a response modestly more positive than "mostly positive"? Formally, the answer is no. Pragmatically, researchers disagree.

Addressing the issue formally, the numbers 1, 2, 3, 4, and 5 were basically selected at the researcher's whim. They are codes for keeping track of responses and have little meaning beyond that. Another set of numeric codes could also have been selected—perhaps 0, 23, 47, 68, and 103.[5] Each different set of codes would yield a different mean. From this perspective, the mean of 4.16 is "meaningless."

Yet the numbers 1, 2, 3, 4, and 5 seem to be sensible, straightforward choices. The same issues arise here as in the Chapter 1 (Section 1.6) discussion of whether self-esteem could be measured at the interval level. The numbers 1, 2, 3, 4, and 5 represent equal intervals (differences), that interval being 1; for instance, $2 - 1 = 1$; $3 - 2 = 1$. These numbers represent responses. For this representation to be accurate, the intervals between responses should also be equal. (There are four such intervals: "very negative" to "mostly negative"; "mostly negative" to "mixed"; "mixed" to "mostly positive"; and "mostly positive" to "very positive.") Yet, given that measurement is at the ordinal level, one cannot determine whether this is the case. (For instance, one does not know whether the interval from "mixed" to "mostly positive" represents the same difference as the interval from "mostly positive" to "very positive.") Given that one does not know whether the numbers represent responses accurately, the accuracy, or validity, of the mean is suspect.

Thus we see that, formally, ordinal-level measurement does not permit calculation of the mean. Operating from a pragmatic perspective rather than a formal one, however, many researchers believe that straightforward numeric codes typically do a good job of representing responses. As such, they hold that (given straightforward and reasonable numeric codes) the mean is a useful and appropriate measure for ordinal-level data. As a matter of practice, you will do well either to (1) *not* calculate means for ordinal-level data or to (2) do so cautiously with appropriate recognition of limitations. (Though many researchers recommend that the mean should not be calculated for ordinal-level data, almost all concur that one may indeed use the mean for almost-interval-level data, such as multi-item attitudinal scales; see Section 1.6.)

3.6.3   Two Characteristics of the Mean

Before closing this discussion, we should note two characteristics of the mean. First, the mean represents the "balance point" (Toothaker and Miller, 1996, p. 113) of a distribution. Figure 3.2 portrays this graphically. If any of the "weights" (measurements) were moved to a new position on the "see-saw," the balance point would change. This illustrates that changing any individual score always changes the value of the mean. This is not necessarily the case for the mode and the median.

Second, suppose that you do the following: (1) calculate deviation scores from some given value, (2) square these scores (recall that squaring a negative number results in a positive), and (3) sum these squares. This sum is smaller for deviations

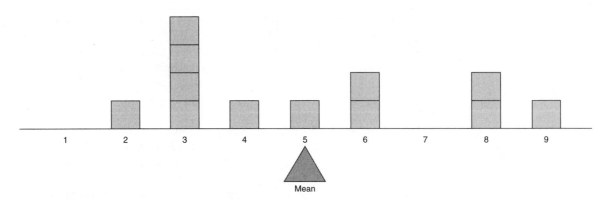

FIGURE **3.2**

THE MEAN AS THE BALANCE POINT OF A DISTRIBUTION SEE-SAW

from the mean than from any other value. Stated formally, the mean minimizes the sum of squared deviation scores.

3.7 ADVANTAGES AND DISADVANTAGES OF THE MEASURES OF CENTRAL TENDENCY

Table 3.2 summarizes the required level of measurement for the three measures of central tendency. An X indicates that the measure may be appropriately used at a given level of measurement. Note that the mode may be used with variables at all levels of measurement. The median may only be used when the level of measurement is ordinal or interval/ratio. Finally, from a formal perspective, use of the mean requires interval/ratio measurement.

A different question from when a given measure may be used is, Which measure is the *best* measure? The answer depends on the situation. The following discussion presumes measurement at the interval/ratio level.

MEASURES OF CENTRAL TENDENCY APPROPRIATE AT THE DIFFERENT LEVELS OF MEASUREMENT

TABLE 3.2

Level of Measurement	MEASURE		
	Mode	Median	Mean
Nominal	X		
Ordinal	X	X	
Interval/ratio	X	X	X

The mean is clearly the workhorse—the most commonly used measure. One advantage is its stability. Suppose you were to gather data for a variable in not one but many different random samples from a population and for each sample calculate the mean, the median, and the mode. In the long run, the mean would fluctuate less from sample to sample than the other measures. A second advantage is that the mean appears in many different statistical formulas. For instance, the formula for the standard deviation, the key measure of variability, makes use of the mean. Given data at the interval/ratio level, the mean is *usually* the preferred measure.

The mean, however, is not preferred if outliers substantially affect its value. An **outlier** (or **extreme value**) is an *extremely* high or *extremely* low value, a value that is markedly different from other values. For instance, consider the number of books read by the Chickadees as presented earlier in the chapter: 5, 8, 5, 10, 9, 11, 43. The 43 differs markedly from other values and thus is an outlier. Outliers can greatly influence the mean. For instance, largely due to the 43, the mean number of books read computed to 13, a value higher than all other measures. Measures of central tendency seek to convey the typical, commonplace score. The mean for Chickadee readers, 13, does not convey this. Instead, it creates the misleading impression that the "average," "typical" Chickadee read 13 books. Outliers pull the mean in their direction. **Positive outliers,** values much higher than other values, pull the mean upward, that is, in a positive direction. **Negative outliers,** values much lower than others, pull the mean downward, that is, in a negative direction. The value 43 is a positive outlier.

If an outlier (or outliers) substantially affects the mean, the median is ordinarily the preferred measure. The median is simply the middle value. As such, it is not affected by how extreme the highest or lowest value may be. For instance, consider the following scores: 5, 8, 5, 10, 9, 11, 15. These scores are identical to those of the Chickadees with the exception that the last score has been changed from 43 to 15. The median for these scores is 9, identical to that of the Chickadees. But the change in the highest score does indeed affect the mean, which now computes to 9 rather than 13: $(5 + 8 + 5 + 10 + 9 + 11 + 15)/7 = 9$.[6] The fact that the median is unaffected by the values of extreme cases is a distinct advantage.

As a second example of how outliers "pull" the mean, consider that household income in the United States is ordinarily summarized by the median rather than by the mean. This is so because the astronomically high incomes of a few households (for instance, that of Microsoft founder Bill Gates) pull the mean household income substantially upward. Therefore, mean income does not effectively convey common, typical income. Median household income, considerably lower than mean household income, provides the better measure of central tendency.

Many are surprised that the median is not the generally preferred measure of central tendency. Clearly, the score at the 50th percentile—exactly in the middle of the distribution—is an intuitively pleasing definition of central tendency. The primary reason why the mean is preferred is its applicability to many other statistical procedures. For instance, as mentioned earlier, it is used in calculating the standard deviation. The median, in contrast, has very limited applicability to other procedures. It is essentially an end in itself.

The mode is usually the least preferred measure of central tendency. In small samples, luck influences the mode. For instance, two Chickadee readers read 5 books, whereas only one read each other value. As such, 5 is the mode. Yet it was presumably just a coincidence (luck) that two Chickadees happened to read 5 books. Two Chickadees might just as easily have read 9 books (or 8 or 7), not 5, and the mode would then have shifted accordingly. In sum, with small samples the mode tends to be unstable; it jumps around largely because of luck. The mode's major advantage is ease of interpretation. The most commonly occurring value is an easy concept for all to grasp.

3.8   CHAPTER SUMMARY

Univariate statistical procedures describe the characteristics of a single variable. Central tendency refers to a variable's typical, common values. Variability refers to the degree to which values are dispersed, or spread out, around some central value. Shape of distribution refers to the particular way (pattern) in which values vary.

The mode is the most commonly occurring value. The median is the value with the same number of values higher than and lower than it. The mean is the sum of all values divided by the number of cases.

The mode may be used at all levels of measurement. Its key advantages are simplicity and straightforward meaning. It fluctuates considerably, particularly when sample size is small. A variable with two modes is bimodal.

The median may also be defined as the value at the 50th percentile. Calculation of the median requires measurement at the ordinal level or above. The median minimizes the sum of the absolute values of deviation scores. It is usually preferred to the mean when outliers are present. It has limited applicability to other statistical procedures. If the number of values is even, the median is the mean of the two middlemost values.

The mean, the arithmetic average, is the most commonly used measure. It requires measurement at the interval/ratio level. The mean represents the balance point of a distribution and also minimizes the sum of squared deviation scores. It has applicability to a variety of statistical procedures, an important reason for its popularity. Outliers can pull the mean and, by so doing, make it a misleading measure.

PROBLEMS AND QUESTIONS

Section 3.2

1. Three key characteristics of variables are: _____ _____, _____, and _____ _____ _____.

Section 3.3

2. Central tendency refers to the _____, common values, those around which values tend to _____. Variability refers to the degree to which values are _____ around some central value. Shape of distribution refers to the particular way in which values vary, that is, to the _____ of variability.

3. The three major measures of central tendency are the _____, the _____, and the _____.

4. The mode is the value with the greatest (highest) _____. The median is the value that has the same number of values _____ than and _____ than its value. The mean is the _____ of the values of all cases divided by the _____ of cases.

5. Consider these values: 2, 6, 1, 2, 5, 4, 29. Regarding these values:
   a. The mode is _____.
   b. The median is _____.
   c. The mean is _____.

Section 3.4

6. What special term describes the following variable and its distribution?

   4, 5, 5, 6, 7, 7, 9

7. The mode "makes sense" (is appropriate) for variables at what levels of measurement?

Section 3.5

8. Calculation of the median requires measurement at the _____ level or above.
9. In a state legislature, there are 22 Democrats, 19 Republicans, and 2 Independents. What is the median?
10. Consider the following observations: 9, 4, 7, 6, 8.
    a. Order the observations from low to high.
    b. What is the value of the middle case in the ordering of cases?
    c. What is the median?
11. Consider the following observations: 14, 11, 8, 16, 9, 15.
    a. Order the observations from low to high.
    b. What are the two middlemost values?
    c. What is the mean of the two middlemost cases?
    d. What is the median?
12. Consider Table 2.4 in Chapter 2, which presents cohesion scores.
    a. What is the first cumulative percentage that is greater than or equal to 50?
    b. What value or score is associated with the just-determined percentage?
    c. What is the median?
13. The frequencies of responses regarding the effectiveness of a workshop on sexual harassment are: "poor," 18; "fair," 42; "good," 86; "excellent," 54.
    a. What is the cumulative percentage for each response?
    b. What is the first cumulative percentage greater than or equal to 50?
    c. What response corresponds to the just-determined percentage?
    d. What is the median response?
14. The median of a given distribution is 10. What is the deviation score from the median for each of the following values?
    a. 8
    b. 13
    c. 10
    d. 12.5
15. The median minimizes the _____ of the _____ values of deviation scores.

Section 3.6

16. The most commonly used measure of central tendency is the _____.
17. (T or F) Strictly and formally, the mean is a valid and appropriate measure for variables at the ordinal level of measurement.
18. Strictly and formally, the mean is a valid and appropriate measure of central tendency only for variables at the _____ / _____ level of measurement.
19. The _____ is the balance point of a distribution.
20. The mean minimizes the sum of _____ deviation scores.
21. What is the mean of the following observations? 18, 22, 38, 17, 12

Section 3.7

22. Which measure of central tendency is most stable, that is, tends to fluctuate least from one random sample to the next?
23. Consider the following distribution: 8, 10, 11, 12, 14, 83.
    a. What term describes the value 83?
    b. Is the median or the mean preferred?
    c. What is the median?
    d. The outlier 83 pulls the mean in a(n) _____ direction.
    e. In your own words, why is the mean ($\overline{X} = 23$) a misleading measure of central tendency?
24. (T or F) Typically, the median is affected less by outliers than is the mean.
25. Indicate one major advantage of the mode.

26. Indicate a disadvantage of the mode.
27. Positive outliers pull the mean _____; negative outliers pull it _____.

 # COMPUTER EXERCISES

For general instructions on computer exercises, see the note in Chapter 2.

1. Find the mean, median, and mode of the variables AGEHOMEY (age at entry into home), CHIETH (ethnicity of child), and RELSCALE (scale measuring closeness of parent/child relationship). [In SPSS, *Analyze > Descriptive Statistics > Frequencies;* click over desired variables; *Statistics,* click boxes next to "Mean," "Median," and "Mode"; *Continue, OK.*]

   Question to think about: Do the median and mean "make sense" for CHIETH?

   Check your answers: For AGEHOMEY, the mean, median, and mode in years are 5.52, 5.33, and 0.08, respectively. (0.08 conveys one-twelfth of a year, that is, one month.) For RELSCALE, these are expressed as points on a scale: 3.34, 3.40, and 4.00, respectively. The median and mean do not make sense for CHIETH because the level of measurement (nominal) is not appropriate for these statistics. The mode for CHIETH is white.

2. Find the mean, median, and mode for BEHAVTOT (score on a behavior problem checklist) and also the scores at the 25th and 75th percentiles. [In SPSS, *Analyze > Descriptive Statistics > Frequencies* (after clearing variables from the prior problem by using *Reset* or by highlighting them and clicking (the arrow), click over BEHAVTOT, *Statistics* (if boxes next to "Mean," "Median," and "Mode," are not checked, click these to check them), click small box to left of "Percentile (s)," type **25** into space to right of "Percentile (s)," *Add,* type **75** into space to right of "Percentile (s)," *Add, Continue, OK.*]

   Check your answers: For BEHAVTOT: mean = 36.65, median = 32, mode = 32, 25th percentile = 17, 75th percentile = 51.

3. Find the mean, median, and mode for AGECHIY (child's age at time of the survey). Also, find the ages at the 25th and 75th percentiles.

   Check your answers: For AGECHIY: mean = 10.83, median = 11.00, mode = 8.25, 25th percentile = 8.25, 75th percentile = 13.67. Note that the mode is not particularly helpful. As age is calculated to the nearest month, frequencies at any given month are quite low. (In a situation like this, the mode can jump around due to luck.)

NOTES

1. The middlemost values are those that divide the distribution into upper and lower halves. The lower middlemost value is the highest value in the lower half. The higher middlemost value is the lowest value in the upper half. For instance, the distribution 2, 4, 5, 7, 8, 9, 12, 13 has eight values. Half of eight is four. The highest of the lower four values is 7. The lowest of the upper four is 8. Hence, 7 and 8 are the two middlemost values.

2. Though this example demonstrates calculation with an ordinal-level variable, the median is used more often with interval/ratio-level variables. At the ordinal level, some characteristics of the median do not apply. For instance, one can't calculate the mean of the two middlemost values where the variable is ordinal. In most texts, the median is presented as a numeric value rather than a qualitative one. For instance, in the special-needs adoption example, the numeric code 4 signifies the response "mostly positive." According to one interpretation, the correct median is 4, not "mostly positive." In my view, qualitative values describe the median more effectively for categorical variables and thus are preferred.

3. For a grouped frequency distribution, the median is computed via the grouped frequency distribution formula for percentile rank with the rank 50 entered into the formula. Such a formula is in Toothaker and Miller (1996, p. 156) or other statistics books.

4. In some distributions, the sum of absolute values of deviation scores may be equally low from some value(s) other than the median. However, this sum will never be lower from any other value than from the median. The characteristic of minimizing the sum of absolute deviation scores only holds for variables measured at the interval/ratio level. (At the ordinal level, addition and subtraction do not make sense.)

5. The only constraint on the numbers used to represent responses is that their ordering should be the same as that of the responses. For instance, the highest code (in our example, 103) should correspond to the highest response ("very positive"), the next highest code (68) to the next highest response, and so on.

6. If an outlier greatly influences the value of the mean, researchers sometimes exclude the outlier in calculating the mean. Another strategy is to include the outlying case but to reset its value closer to the rest of the values. For instance, one could set a positive outlier to the value of the next highest case. SPSS for Windows can calculate a "5% trimmed mean," which eliminates the highest and lowest 5% of cases to provide a measure of central tendency not influenced by these. (Choose *Analyze > Descriptive Statistics > Explore* and then run the Explore procedure to compute a trimmed mean.) If you follow one of these strategies, be sure to report this as you write up your research.

VARIABILITY

4.1 CHAPTER OVERVIEW

In this chapter we focus on the concept of *variability*. The chapter demonstrates how to assess variability for variables at the nominal level of measurement and then at the ordinal level. We consider five measures of variability for interval/ratio-level variables. These include the *range*, the *interquartile range*, the *mean deviation*, the *standard deviation*, and the *variance*. We conclude with two tools for summarizing distributions, the *five-number summary* and the *box-and-whisker plot*.

4.2 THE CONCEPT OF VARIABILITY

Variability concerns the degree to which values of a variable are dispersed, that is, "spread out" around a common or "typical" value. That common value is almost always a measure of central tendency. Hence, **variability** assesses the degree of dispersion around a measure of central tendency. If most values are tightly clustered, variability is low. If values are widely dispersed, variability is high. Consider the following two distributions:

Distribution 1: 5, 6, 7, 7, 7, 8, 9
Distribution 2: 0, 5, 7, 8, 9, 11, 16

The mean of both distributions is 7:

$$(1 + 5 + 6 + 7 + 7 + 7 + 8 + 9)/7 = 7$$
$$(0 + 5 + 7 + 8 + 9 + 11 + 16)/7 = 7$$

Scores in the second distribution are more dispersed (spread out) than those in the first. Therefore, the second has greater variability.

4.3 ASSESSING VARIABILITY AT THE NOMINAL LEVEL

Pragmatically speaking, there are no widely known, commonly used measures of variability for nominal-level variables.[1] As such, this section describes the assessment of variability for nominal-level variables but presents no measures. Consider the three distributions for the variable of eye color presented in Table 4.1.

In Distribution 1, everyone has blue eyes. When all cases have the same value, as in Distribution 1, there is *no* variability. In fact, in Distribution 1, eye color is not a variable but a constant, because it takes on only one value.

In Distribution 2, an extremely high percentage (92%) of participants have blue eyes. When an extremely high percentage of cases have the same value, a variable has low or limited variability. Percentages rather than frequencies are key to the assessment of variability. Consider the following distribution, which is identical to Distribution 2 with respect to percentages but 1000 times larger in terms of frequencies: blue eyes 46,000 (92%); brown eyes 2000 (4%); green eyes 2000 (4%). Even though the frequencies of people with brown and green eyes are reasonably large (2000), the variable of eye color still has low, limited variability. This is because an extremely high *percentage* of people (92%) have the same color eyes (blue). As already stated, this text does not provide measures of variability for nominal-level variables. Yet, Distribution 2 and the just-presented distribution clearly have the same amount of variability, because the pattern of values as indicated by the percentages is identical.

In Distribution 3, cases are fairly equally distributed between the three eye colors. Though this may be seen by examination of the frequencies, which are very nearly equal (17, 17, 16), in the interest of consistency, we will continue to focus on the percentages, which likewise are nearly equal (34, 34, 32). When the percentages for the different values of a nominal variable are reasonably equal—in other words, when cases are distributed fairly equally among the different values—then that variable has high or considerable variability.

In the absence of a formal measure, here is a rough guideline for qualitative assessment of variability of nominal variables: If 90% or more of cases have the same value, a nominal-level variable has low variability. A guideline for high variability is impractical, but in general, the more equal the percentages, the greater the variability.

TABLE 4.1 DIFFERING VARIABILITY IN EYE COLOR

Eye Color	DISTRIBUTION 1		DISTRIBUTION 2		DISTRIBUTION 3	
	Frequency	Percentage	Frequency	Percentage	Frequency	Percentage
Blue	50	100	46	92	17	34
Brown	0	0	2	4	17	34
Green	0	0	2	4	16	32

4.4 ASSESSING VARIABILITY AT THE ORDINAL LEVEL

There are no widely used measures of variability at the ordinal level of measurement, so we again discuss variability in a general way, emphasizing concepts. As with nominal-level variables, if most cases have the same value, an ordinal-level variable clearly has limited variability.

In assessing the variability of an ordinal-level variable, we pay attention to the order of the categories. For instance, consider Table 4.2, which presents two hypothetical sets of assessments regarding the quality of a workshop. In both distributions, 10% of responses are in each of two categories and 40% of responses are in each of two other categories. In Distribution 1, responses are concentrated in the "fair" and "good" categories. In Distribution 2, they are concentrated in the "poor" and "excellent" categories.

With an ordinal variable, one cannot make accurate statements about differences between values. Even so, adjacent values in the ordering tend to convey reasonably similar responses and nonadjacent values tend to convey dissimilar ones. For instance, in the current example, "fair" and "good" (adjacent values) convey reasonably similar (not greatly differing) opinions regarding the workshop, and "poor" and "excellent" convey divergent ones.

A concentration of responses in adjacent (similar) values conveys less variability than a concentration in nonadjacent ones. Hence, even though the distributions of percentages in the Distributions 1 and 2 have some similarity (each has 40% in two response categories and 10% in two others), Distribution 2 conveys greater variability. In Distribution 1, 80% of responses convey the reasonably similar opinions "fair" and "good." In Distribution 2, 80% of respondents have greatly differing perceptions—40% responded "excellent" and 40% "poor." Distribution 2 thus indicates considerable variability of opinion. Distribution 1 indicates much less.

Lacking a widely used measure of variability for ordinal variables, the best tactic is to examine percentages and also to observe whether responses tend to be in similar or dissimilar categories. The just-recommended 90% guideline for nominal-level variables may be extended to ordinal-level variables. If 90% or more of responses are in a single category, variability is clearly low. As we have noted,

TABLE 4.2	EVALUATIONS OF WORKSHOP QUALITY: TWO HYPOTHETICAL SETS OF RESPONSES	
Evaluation	Distribution 1 (%)	Distribution 2 (%)
Excellent	10	40
Good	40	10
Fair	40	10
Poor	10	40

there is no truly valid way to assign numbers to ordinal-level variables. But if the assigned numbers are straightforward and appear to do a good job of representing responses, some (not all) researchers use measures designed for interval/ratio variables to assess the variability of ordinal ones. If you choose to do so, be cautious. (The same points brought up with respect to the mean in Chapter 3, Section 3.6.2, apply.)

4.5 THE RANGE

The first measure of variability we discuss for interval/ratio-level variables is the range. The **range** is equal to the highest score minus the lowest score. Consider the scores 3, 5, 6, 7, 7, 8, 9. The highest score is 9 and the lowest is 3. Hence, the range is $9 - 3 = 6$. The formula is:

$$\text{Range} = X_{\text{highest}} - X_{\text{lowest}} \tag{4.1}$$

where X_{highest} is the highest score and X_{lowest} is the lowest.

Why is the interval/ratio level of measurement (or almost so) required to calculate the range? With a nominal-level variable, scores cannot be ordered, so there is no highest or lowest score. At the ordinal level, highest and lowest scores may be determined, but the formula for the range also requires subtraction, which ordinal-level measurement does not permit. (For instance, one may not subtract "poor" from "excellent.")

Although the range is formally defined as the highest score minus the lowest, it is usually conveyed with specific mention of these scores. Suppose that the youngest participant in a therapy group was 21 years old and the oldest was 41. The statement, "The range in age was 20 years" is technically correct: $41 - 21 = 20$. However, it communicates less information than does the statement, "The range in age was from 21 years of age to 41 years," which better informs the reader about participants' ages.

The major advantages of the range are its ease of calculation and its easily understood meaning. Reporting the range helps the reader get a "feel" for the data. One disadvantage is that a single case can greatly influence the range. Consider, for instance, the ages of participants in a therapy group: 32, 34, 34, 35, 36, 38, 88. Your research report might state correctly, "The range in age was from 32 years to 88 years." This statement may create the misleading impression of substantial variability in age when actually six of the seven members had very similar ages.

The range is influenced by sample size. As sample size increases, there is increased opportunity that an outlier—for instance, a very old or very young person in the therapy group—will be included, thereby increasing the range. The fact that the range tends to increase as sample size increases is a distinct disadvantage. One would prefer a measure of variability that is unaffected by sample size. Even with this disadvantage, the range is a commonly used and useful tool.

4.6   THE INTERQUARTILE RANGE

The **interquartile range** (*IQR*, also known as the **midrange**) is defined as the score at the 75th percentile minus the score at the 25th percentile. Like the range, it is designed for use with interval/ratio-level (or almost so) variables. Its formula is:

$$IQR = X_{75\%} - X_{25\%} \qquad (4.2)$$

where $X_{75\%}$ is the score at the 75th percentile and $X_{25\%}$ is that at the 25th.

The discussion of percentiles in Chapter 2, Section 2.5, provides a method for determining the value that corresponds to a given percentile: To find the value that corresponds to a given percentile, find the *first* value with a cumulative percentage greater than or equal to the stated percentile. Let's make use of the frequency distribution table for cohesion from the special-needs adoption study presented as Table 2.4 in Section 2.4. Referring to the cumulative percentage column, a score of 37 corresponds to the 25th percentile and a score of 44 corresponds to the 75th percentile. Hence, the *IQR* is 44 − 37 = 7 points.

The interquartile range is encountered occasionally in human services research reports, though less often than the most common measures of variability, the range and the yet-to-be-discussed standard deviation. Given that it is defined by the 75th and 25th percentiles, the *IQR* conveys the amount of spread for the middle 50% of scores.

4.7   THE MEAN DEVIATION

The **mean deviation** measures the degree to which observations vary around the mean. It requires measurement at the interval/ratio level or almost so. Its formula is:

$$MD = \frac{\Sigma |X - \overline{X}|}{N} \qquad (4.3)$$

where *MD* is the mean deviation, $\overline{X}$ is the mean, *X* is the score of an individual case, and *N* is the sample size. The two vertical bars, | |, indicate absolute value. The Σ symbol is the summation sign.

Recall from Chapter 3 (Section 3.5.2) that when you subtract some value, usually a measure of central tendency, from a case's value, you have calculated a deviation score. To calculate the mean deviation:

1. Find the mean.
2. For each case, subtract the mean from the case's score to determine the case's deviation score from the mean.
3. Find the absolute value of each deviation score.
4. Sum these absolute values.
5. Divide this sum by the sample size (*N*).

Consider the scores 1, 4, 5, 6, 9. Carrying out the five steps:

1. The mean is: $(1 + 4 + 5 + 6 + 9)/5 = 5$.
2. The deviation scores from the mean are:

   $1 - 5 = -4, 4 - 5 = -1, 5 - 5 = 0, 6 - 5 = 1, 9 - 5 = 4$

3. The absolute values of the deviation scores are:

   $|-4| = 4, |-1| = 1, |0| = 0, |1| = 1, |4| = 4$

4. The sum of the absolute values is:

   $4 + 1 + 0 + 1 + 4 = 10$

5. N is 5; dividing the sum in step 4 by N yields the MD:

   $MD = 10/5 = 2$

A major advantage of the mean deviation is simplicity. The more the scores differ from the mean, the greater the MD. The mean deviation may be interpreted as the average of the absolute values of deviation scores. With small samples, it may be calculated easily by hand.[2] The mean deviation is seldom used in actual research, which is its major disadvantage. Many statistics books do not cover it. The standard deviation, to be discussed next, is much more widely used.

4.8 THE STANDARD DEVIATION

4.8.1 Formula and Basics

The standard deviation is the most used and most useful measure of variability. Just as the mean is the workhorse measure of central tendency, the standard deviation is the workhorse measure of variability. In this chapter, we study the standard deviation's use as a descriptive measure of variability. The standard deviation is also integral to (1) the normal distribution, the most important distribution in statistics; and (2) many common applications of inferential statistics. It requires measurement at the interval/ratio level or almost so. The best formula for gaining an understanding of the standard deviation is the following:

$$s_{\text{samp}} = \sqrt{\frac{\Sigma(X - \overline{X})^2}{N}} \tag{4.4}$$

where s_{samp} is the standard deviation of a sample, $\overline{X}$ is the mean, X is the score of an individual case, N is the sample size, and Σ is the summation sign. This formula directs you to:

1. Find the mean.
2. For each case, subtract the mean from the case's score to determine the case's deviation score from the mean.
3. Square each deviation score.
4. Sum the squared deviation scores.
5. Divide the sum of the squared deviation scores by the sample size (N).
6. Take the square root.

Before we calculate a standard deviation, let me pose three questions that I had when I first encountered the standard deviation: "Why is the formula so complex?" "In particular, why go to the trouble of *squaring* deviations from the mean?" and "Why not use the much simpler mean deviation?" Unfortunately, answers to these questions are ultimately complex, abstract, mathematical, and beyond our scope.[3] Simply put, the standard deviation is the preferred measure of variability because it is useful in so many ways. My advice is to not concern yourself with the just-posed questions but to study the standard deviation well. That attention will be rewarded as you come to appreciate its many uses in a wide diversity of situations.

Let's calculate a standard deviation. Suppose a study finds that seven residents in a shelter for the homeless spent the following numbers of nights "on the street" in the prior month: 19, 24, 7, 22, 14, 29, 11. What is the standard deviation of nights on the street? The first step is to calculate the mean:

$$19 + 24 + 7 + 22 + 14 + 29 + 11 = 126 \text{ nights}$$
$$\overline{X} = 126/7 = 18 \text{ nights}$$

At this point, calculations are made easier by a grid with columns, as shown in Table 4.3.

The grid's first column lists individual scores and its second lists the mean. The second step calculates deviation scores from the mean. This is accomplished by subtracting values in the second column from those in the first. The resulting deviation scores are presented in the third column. The third step is to square each deviation score. Hence, values in the third column are squared and the resulting squared deviation scores are presented in the fourth column. The fourth step is to sum the squared deviation scores. This sum is calculated at the bottom of the fourth column. The fifth step is to divide by the sample size: $360/7 = 51.4$. The sixth and last step is to take the square root: $\sqrt{51.4} = 7.2$. Hence, the standard deviation of nights on the street is 7.2 nights: $s_{samp} = 7.2$. When calculated using formula 4.4, the standard deviation (s_{samp}) may be expressed in words as follows: the square root of the average squared deviation score from the mean.

TABLE 4.3   **CALCULATION OF THE SUM OF SQUARED DEVIATION SCORES**

X	$\overline{X}$	$X - \overline{X}$	$(X - \overline{X})^2$
19	18	1	1
24	18	6	36
7	18	−11	121
22	18	4	16
14	18	−4	16
29	18	11	121
11	18	−7	49
			360

The just-presented formula has an important drawback. Discussion of this drawback detours us to the realm of inferential statistics. Researchers often use characteristics of a random sample to estimate characteristics of the population from which that sample was selected. For instance, the sample mean is used to estimate the population mean. Similarly, the sample standard deviation is used to estimate the population standard deviation. When calculated via formula 4.4, the standard deviation of a randomly selected sample tends to be slightly smaller than that of the population from which it was selected. This is an undesirable trait. One wants a sample characteristic to provide an **unbiased** estimate of that same characteristic in the population, an estimate that is neither too high or too low. When calculated via formula 4.4, the sample standard deviation of a random sample provides a biased estimate of that in the population; it is slightly low. A **biased** estimate tends to be systematically too high or too low.

A simple adjustment to formula 4.4 makes the standard deviation of a sample a much better estimator of that in the population. Even with this adjustment, the slightest amount of bias remains. The remaining bias is so negligible that, for practical purposes, it may be ignored. A second formula for the standard deviation of a sample, one that provides an almost unbiased estimate of the standard deviation in the population from which the sample was randomly selected, is:

$$s = \sqrt{\frac{\Sigma(X - \bar{X})^2}{N - 1}} \tag{4.5}$$

Notice that the standard deviation in this formula is symbolized by s rather than s_{samp}. The only other change from formula 4.4 is that the denominator is $N - 1$ rather than N. The difference between the standard deviations that result from the two formulas is typically very small. The change in formula affects the fifth listed step in calculations, which may be restated as:

5. Divide the sum of the squared deviation scores by $(N - 1)$.

The new formula may be applied to the nights-on-the-street data. The sum of the squared deviations was 360. Dividing 360 by 6 ($N - 1 = 7 - 1 = 6$) rather than 7 yields $360/6 = 60.0$. The final step is to take the square root: $\sqrt{60} = 7.7$ Suppose that the sample of seven homeless persons is indeed a random sample from a much larger population. If so, 7.7 nights provides an estimate of the standard deviation in that population that has so little bias that, pragmatically speaking, we may regard it as the best possible estimate.[4]

With two formulas for the standard deviation, things have become more confusing. Which formula should be used? The formula with $N - 1$ is used more often and, in the opinion of many, is the better of the two. From here on, we use this formula exclusively.[5]

One final point should be made regarding formulas 4.4 and 4.5. These formulas are preferred for *understanding* the standard deviation. They demonstrate that the greater the squared deviations around the mean, the greater the value of the standard deviation. They are not, however, preferred for hand calculations.[6] The easiest way to calculate the standard deviation is with statistical software.

4.8.2 *Characteristics of the Standard Deviation*

One advantage of the standard deviation is that its value is influenced hardly at all by sample size. For instance, suppose that you had a large population and that you chose ten random samples of varying sizes—say, 10, 20, 30, 40, 50, 60, 70, 80, 90, and 100—from that population. The standard deviations of these samples would not be identical. By the luck of the draw, some samples would have larger standard deviations than would others. The key point is that the size of the standard deviation varies hardly at all as sample size changes.[7] One would not, for instance, expect to see the standard deviation increase steadily as sample size increased. This contrasts with the range, which does tend to get larger as sample size increases.

The standard deviation measures variability around the mean of a sample. If a constant (that is, the same number) is added to or subtracted from *each* case, the standard deviation does not change. For instance, suppose that, measured in their bare feet, the mean height of a group of people was 5 feet 6 inches with a standard deviation of 4 inches. Now suppose that all in the group put on identical pairs of shoes that make them exactly 2 inches taller. Their mean height will, therefore, increase to 5 feet 8 inches. Assuming accurate measurement, the standard deviation of height will be unaffected. It will continue to be 4 inches. However, if one multiplies or divides scores by a constant, the standard deviation will change proportionately. For instance, consider the following scores: 0, 3, 5, 7, 8. Their standard deviation is 3.2. If we multiplied each score by, say, 3, the scores would become 0, 9, 15, 21, 24. Given that the scores were multiplied by 3, the standard deviation of the new scores will be three times greater: $s = 3.2 \times 3 = 9.6$.

Just as the mean is the primary measure of central tendency, the standard deviation is the primary measure of variability. These two statistics are typically presented together to describe data. One may have two groups with similar means but very different standard deviations. For instance, suppose that the following are the reading scores for two groups of elementary school students who have been randomly assigned to one of two interventions, A or B, designed to improve reading skills:

> Intervention A: 60, 70, 75, 78, 80, 80, 82, 85, 90, 100
> Intervention B: 70, 75, 78, 79, 80, 80, 81, 82, 85, 90

Using SPSS for Windows to compare means and standard deviations in Table 4.4, we find the mean reading test score in both intervention groups is 80.00. As a visual inspection indicates, variability in scores is greater for those who received A ($s = 10.8$) than for those who received B ($s = 5.3$). These results may suggest that some "ingredient" in Intervention B promotes fairly equal levels of reading achievement among students. The much greater variability of scores for Intervention A may suggest that this intervention helps some kids a great deal but others much less.

| TABLE | **EXAMPLE OF SIMILAR MEANS BUT DIFFERENT STANDARD DEVIATIONS** |

Report

READING   Reading Score

	INTERVEN Intervention		
	Intervention A	Intervention B	Total
Mean	80.0000	80.0000	80.0000
N	10	10	20
Std. Deviation	10.8423	5.3748	8.3288

Note: SPSS for Windows output.

4.9   THE VARIANCE

The formula for the variance, like that for the standard deviation, makes use of squared deviations around the sample mean. As stated earlier, when calculated via the formula (4.4) with N in the denominator, the standard deviation, s_{samp}, is the square root of the average squared deviation score. The variance, s^2_{samp}, *is* the average squared deviation score. The standard deviation, then, is the square root of the variance. In turn, the variance is the square of the standard deviation. The first formula we have for the variance of a sample is:

$$s^2_{\text{samp}} = \frac{\Sigma(X - \overline{X})^2}{N} \tag{4.6}$$

where s^2_{samp} is the symbol for the variance of a sample.

The just-stated formula suffers from the same problem as formula 4.4 for the standard deviation. When calculated via formula 4.6, the variance of a random sample provides a biased estimate of the variance in the population from which it was selected. (It is too low.) But if $N - 1$ rather than N is used in the denominator, the variance of a random sample provides an *unbiased* estimate of the variance in the population from which it was selected.[8] This formula is:

$$s^2 = \frac{\Sigma(X - \overline{X})^2}{N - 1} \tag{4.7}$$

Observe that formula 4.7 uses the symbol s^2 rather than s^2_{samp} to convey the variance. Formula 4.7 is more commonly used than formula 4.6 and is acknowledged by many to be the better of the two. For the same reasons discussed earlier for the standard deviation, all subsequent references to the variance will symbolize it using s^2 and calculate it using formula 4.7, which provides an unbiased estimate of the population variance.[9]

Calculation of the variance follows the same steps as the standard deviation except that the last step, taking the square root, is omitted. The variance of nights on the street for the homelessness data was computed previously. It was simply the result obtained upon completion of the fifth step. When the $N - 1$ formula was used, following formula 4.5, the variance was 60.0.

One disadvantage of the variance is that, formally speaking, it is composed of squared units. For instance, the variance of 60.0 in the homelessness data represents 60.0 "*square* nights" (or, one could say, 60.0 nights squared). It is impossible to make intuitive sense out of squared units. What, for instance, is a *square* night? The fact that the variance has no straightforward, intuitive meaning is its great disadvantage. Even if the variance formally consists of squared units, it is typical practice not to state this. For instance, a research report would say that $s^2 = 60.0$ rather than that $s^2 = 60.0$ square nights.

In calculating the standard deviation, one *squares* deviation scores in step 3 but then returns to the original unit of measurement by taking a square root in step 6, an advantage the standard deviation has compared to the variance. For instance, the standard deviation of nights on the street was 7.7 *nights*, certainly an easier concept to grasp than 60 square nights.

In sum, do not attempt to make intuitive sense of the variance. It is simply a mathematical concept. As one progresses into inferential statistics and into more advanced applications, one encounters an increasing number of procedures that use the variance.

4.10   FIVE-NUMBER SUMMARIES AND BOX PLOTS

4.10.1   Five-Number Summary

Univariate statistics summarize a variable's distribution. For instance, providing both a measure of central tendency (often the mean) and a measure of variability (often the standard deviation) helps the reader to see where values tend to cluster and also the degree to which values are dispersed. Tukey (1977) proposed a **five-number summary.** These five numbers, ordered from lowest to highest, are (1) the score of the lowest case, (2) the score that is approximately at the 25th percentile, (3) the median (which is at the 50th percentile), (4) the score that is approximately at the 75th percentile, and (5) the score of the highest case.[10]

The special-needs adoption study measured to the nearest month children's ages at entry into their adoptive homes. The five-number summary for age in months is 0.0, 28.5, 64.0, 100.0, and 195.0. Hence, the youngest child was 0 months old (entered at birth), the age at (approximately) the 25th percentile was 28.5 months, the median age was 64 months, the age at (approximately) the 75th percentile was 100 months, and the oldest child was 195 months old. The five-number summary is used more than occasionally and is a useful tool.

4.10.2   Box Plots

The five-number summary may be portrayed graphically in a **box-and-whisker plot (box plot)** (Tukey, 1977, pp. 39–56). Figure 4.1 presents a box-and-whisker plot for the just-presented data pertaining to children's age in months at entry into their adop-

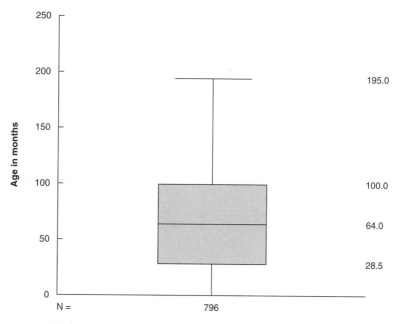

Age in months

250 —

200 — ⌐————————————195.0

150 —

100 — ┌─────────────┐ 100.0

50 — │   │ 64.0

│   │ 28.5

0 —

N =   796

FIGURE **4.1**

Box-and-Whisker Plot of Age in Months at Entry into the Home

tive home. A box plot's vertical axis conveys values. The lower and upper edges of the shaded box convey the second and fourth numbers of the five-number summary (approximately the 25th and 75th percentiles), and the horizontal line through the box conveys the median. The vertical lines extending from the edges of the box are the **whiskers.** In the simplest box plots, such as in Figure 4.1, whiskers end at the first and fifth numbers of the summary, that is, at the lowest and highest values.[11]

Box plots portray variability in a straightforward, intuitive way. For instance, in Figure 4.1, the lower edge of the box is located at about 25 months and the upper edge at about 100 months, conveying that the middle half of children entered their adoptive homes within this age range. One can see that the upper whisker extends all the way to about 195 months, representing the oldest age at entry. (Obviously the lower whisker cannot extend past 0 months, which represents birth.) Many statistical packages including SPSS produce box plots. See Toothaker and Miller (1996, pp. 128–129) or Tukey (1977, pp. 39–56) for more information on box-and-whisker plots.

4.11   A Comment on Variability and Relationship

When a variable has very limited variability, it is typically quite difficult to study its association to other variables. For instance, suppose that you want to study factors associated with recidivism (return to the hospital) among previously discharged patients in a psychiatric hospital. Perhaps your particular interest is in whether gender is associated, that is, whether women or men are more likely to recidivate. Suppose that almost all persons in your study sample do not recidivate. (They cope well enough in their home setting so that they do not need to be rehospitalized.) Your human side would welcome such fine results, yet your researcher side would be vaguely sad. If almost all subjects remain at home, variability is limited, making it difficult to examine the possible association between gender and recidivism.

When variability is extremely limited, a variable becomes almost a constant, in effect. One cannot investigate the association of a constant with anything else. (Stated differently, something that does not vary cannot be associated with something else.) For instance, if no one recidivates, the question of what factors predict recidivism is a meaningless one. Generally speaking, researchers "root for" considerable variability. In most circumstances, this enhances opportunities for finding and examining relationships. In the current example, your researcher side would root for half of the cases to recidivate and half not to.

4.12   CHAPTER SUMMARY

Variability concerns the degree to which values are dispersed around a measure of central tendency. The greater the dispersion, the greater the variability.

There are no widely used measures of variability for variables at the nominal and ordinal levels. At those levels, variability is assessed primarily by percentages. If a high percentage of cases have the same value, variability is limited. If cases are distributed reasonably equally across values, variability is greater.

At the interval/ratio level, we examined five measures of variability:

- The range is calculated by subtracting the lowest value from the highest. An important advantage is simplicity, but a disadvantage is that the range tends to increase as sample size increases.
- The interquartile range (midrange) is calculated by subtracting the score at the 25th percentile from that at the 75th percentile.
- The mean deviation, the "average" of the absolute values of deviation scores from the mean, is rarely encountered in actual research studies.
- The standard deviation is the most common measure of tendency. When calculated with N in the denominator (formula 4.4), it may be interpreted as the square root of the average squared deviation from the mean. Calculated in this way, it provides a biased estimate of the population variance. When calculated with $N-1$ in the denominator, the degree of bias becomes negligible, making that the preferred formula: $s = \sqrt{\Sigma(X - \overline{X})^2 > (N - 1)}$ (formula 4.5). Adding or subtracting a constant from all scores does not affect the standard deviation. Multiplying or dividing all scores by a constant affects it proportionately. The standard deviation varies hardly at all by sample size, an important advantage.

- The variance is the square of the standard deviation. In turn, the standard deviation is the square root of the variance. When calculated via the formula with N in the denominator (formula 4.6), the variance, s_{samp}, may be interpreted as the average squared deviation from the mean. The preferred formula for the variance (formula 4.7) uses $N - 1$ in the denominator. Via this formula, the variance in a random sample, s^2, provides an unbiased estimate of the population variance. It is difficult to make intuitive sense of the variance.

The five-number summary includes the lowest score, the score at (approximately) the 25th percentile, the median score, the score at (approximately) the 75th percentile, and the highest score. A simple box-and-whisker plot presents the five-number summary graphically.

If a variable has limited variability, it can be difficult to assess its association to other variables. Researchers generally hope for considerable variability.

PROBLEMS AND QUESTIONS

Section 4.2

1. The greater the _____ of observations, the greater the variability.
2. Variability concerns the degree to which observations are dispersed around a measure of _____ _____.

3. Which set of observations has greater variability?
   a. 2, 6, 9, 11, 12, 13, 15, 18, 22
   b. 7, 9, 10, 11, 12, 13, 14, 15, 17

Section 4.3

4. (T or F) There are many widely accepted, commonly used measures of variability for nominal-level variables.
5. In Sample A, 50% of cases are women and 50% are men. In Sample B, 95% are women and 5% are men. In which sample does gender have greater variability?
6. Sample A has 50 men (50%) and 50 women (50%). Sample B has 100 men (50%) and 100 women (50%). In which sample is the variability of gender greater?
7. (T or F) In general, the more that cases are concentrated around a single value, the greater the variability.

Section 4.4

8. In Sample A, 45% respond "agree," 10% respond "neutral," and 45% respond "disagree." In

Sample B, 10% respond "agree," 45% respond "neutral," and 45% respond "disagree." In which sample is the variability in responses greater?

Section 4.5

9. In your own words, what is the definition of range?
10. Consider the observations 6, 4, 7, 2, 9, 5. What is the range?
11. As sample size increases, the value of the range tends to _____.
12. (T or F) The fact that the range tends to increase as sample size increases is an important *advantage* of this measure of variability.

Section 4.6

13. In your own words, what is the definition of interquartile range?

Section 4.7

14. In your own words, describe how to calculate the mean deviation.
15. Consider the observations 7, 9, 5, 10, 2, 3. What is the mean deviation?
16. (T or F) The mean deviation is a commonly used measure of variability.

Section 4.8

17. (T or F) The standard deviation is a commonly used measure of variability.
18. In your own words, describe how to calculate the standard deviation.

19. When calculated via the formula $\sqrt{\Sigma(X - \overline{X})^2/N}$, the standard deviation in a sample tends to . . .
    a. Slightly underestimate the standard deviation in the population from which the sample was randomly selected
    b. Neither overestimate nor underestimate the standard deviation in the just-mentioned population
    c. Slightly overestimate the standard deviation in the just-mentioned population

20. When calculated by the formula $\sqrt{\Sigma(X - \overline{X})^2/N}$, the standard deviation in a sample provides a(n) _____ estimate of that in the population from which the sample was randomly selected.

21. Using the formula $\sqrt{\Sigma(X - \overline{X})^2/N}$, calculate the standard deviation of the following observations: 2, 3, 3, 5, 6, 11.

22. Using the formula $\sqrt{\Sigma(X - \overline{X})^2/(N - 1)}$, calculate the standard deviation of the observations in the prior question.

23. Which formula for the standard deviation provides the more accurate (less biased) estimate of the standard deviation in the population from which the sample was randomly selected?

24. For purposes of estimating the standard deviation in the population from which the sample was randomly selected, how much bias is in the formula $\sqrt{\Sigma(X - \overline{X})^2/(N - 1)}$?
    a. No bias
    b. Considerable bias
    c. Very small (negligible) bias

25. Suppose that one has a set of observations and adds the same amount—that is, adds a constant—to each observation. What effect, if any, does this have on the standard deviation?

26. Using the formula with $N - 1$ in the denominator, what is the standard deviation of the observations 5, 6, 7, 8, 9?

27. Using the formula with $N - 1$ in the denominator, what is the standard deviation of the observations 4, 5, 6, 7, 8? (Hint: Compare observations in this question to those in prior question.)

28. Suppose that one multiplies each observation listed in the prior question by 4 and thus obtains the following observations: 16, 20, 24, 28,

32. What is the standard deviation of the observations? (Use $N - 1$ in the denominator.)

29. Consider again the initial observations, 5, 6, 7, 8, 9. If you first add the constant 17 to each observation and then divide that result by 2, what is the standard deviation of the resulting observations? (Use $N - 1$ in the denominator.)

30. For the observations 2, 4, 5, 6, 6, 6, 7, 8, 10, and using the $N - 1$ formula, compute the standard deviation.

Section 4.9

31. In your own words, what is the basic definition of the variance?

32. The standard deviation is equal to the _____ _____ of the variance.

33. The variance equals the standard deviation _____.

34. When calculated via the formula $\Sigma(X - \overline{X})^2/N$, the variance in a sample tends to (slightly) _____ the variance in the population from which the sample was randomly selected.

35. When calculated by the formula $\Sigma(X - \overline{X})^2/N - 1$, the variance in a sample provides a(n) _____ estimate of that in the population from which the sample was randomly selected.

36. What is the variance of the observations 5, 6, 7, 8, 9? (Hint: You computed the standard deviation of these in problem 26. Use the formula with $N - 1$ in the denominator.)

37. What is the variance of the following observations?

    2, 4, 5, 6, 6, 6, 7, 8, 10

    (Hint: You computed the standard deviation of these in problem 30. Use the $N - 1$ formula.)

38. Consider the four symbols s_{samp}^2, s^2, s_{samp}, s. Match each symbol with its definition.
    a. Standard deviation of a sample but not the preferred estimate of standard deviation of the population from which the sample was randomly selected
    b. Standard deviation of a sample and the preferred estimate of standard deviation of the population

c. Variance of a sample but not the preferred estimate of variance of the population

d. Variance of a sample and the preferred (and unbiased) estimate of variance of the population

39. (T or F) Most people with limited statistical knowledge find interpretation of the standard deviation to be (at least somewhat) easier than interpretation of the variance.

Section 4.10

40. A five-number summary is composed of what scores?

41. Draw a simple box plot that corresponds to the following five-number summary: 5, 20, 25, 33, 50.

42. The vertical lines that are connected to the box in a box plot are known as the _____.

Section 4.11

43. (T or F) In general, low variability in a dependent variable facilitates the study of relationships involving that variable.

 COMPUTER EXERCISES

For general instructions on computer exercises, see the note in Chapter 2.

1. Find the standard deviation and variance for AGEHOMEY (child's age at entry into home) and BEHAVTOT (score on behavior problem checklist). [In SPSS, *Analyze > Descriptive Statistics > Frequencies* (if necessary click back any unwanted variables from prior problems), click over AGEHOMEY and BEHAVTOT, *Statistics*, click boxes next to "Std. deviation" and "Variance," *Continue, OK.*]

Check your answers: For AGEHOMEY, $s = 3.70$, $s^2 = 13.66$. For BEHAVTOT, $s = 26.12$, $s^2 = 683.29$. In SPSS, in addition to *Frequencies*, the *Descriptives* procedure (*Analyze > Descriptive Statistics > Descriptives*) calculates means and standard deviations.

2. Construct a box plot for RELSCALE (scale assessing closeness of parent-child relationship).

[In SPSS, *Analyze > Descriptive Statistics > Explore*, click RELSCALE over to "Dependent List," *Plots*, verify that the box next to "stem-and-leaf" is checked (if not, do so), *Continue, OK.*] Look at the box plot to answer the following questions: What is the approximate value of the median? Of the scores at the 25th and 75th percentiles?

Check your answers: The median for RELSCALE, conveyed by the thick horizontal line near the center of the box, is about 3.4. The 25th percentile, conveyed by the line at the box's bottom, is about 3.0. The 75th percentile is about 3.8. [All of these estimates are made by tracing from the lines on the box over to the Y (vertical) axis.] Note that the circles toward the bottom of the plot highlight negative outliers, cases with extremely low levels of closeness. [In SPSS, *Graphs > Boxplot* also produces box plots.]

3. Youths who have been missing school attend a workshop designed to encourage attendance. In the semester following the workshop, the number of unexcused absences for each youth is 7, 6, 4, 0, 4, 5, 9, 1, 11, 3, 2, 8. Create a new data set and find the mean, median, mode, and standard deviation of unexcused absences.

Check your answers: For unexcused absences, mean = 5.00, median = 4.50, mode = 4.00, standard deviation = 3.33.

NOTES

1. See Pilcher, 1990, pp. 155–156, for a discussion of the index of dispersion and the index of qualitative variation, two measures used occasionally. Researchers sometimes do calculate the standard deviation of dichotomous variables, particularly those coded with 0s and 1s. Coded in this way, the standard deviation of a dichotomous variable is $s_{dich} = \sqrt{p(1-p)}$ where p is the proportion coded with 1s. The mean of such a variable equals the proportion of 1s.

2. Some researchers recommend computing the mean deviation using deviations from the median rather than from the mean (e.g., Toothaker and Miller, 1996, p. 119). But the mean deviation is used so rarely that it hardly matters whether deviations are calculated from the mean or the median.

3. One mathematical problem is that for some distributions no one *single* point minimizes the sum of the absolute values of deviation scores. On the other hand, *one* point (the mean) always minimizes the sum of squared deviations. The standard deviation is based on squared deviations, and mathematically, this helps a great deal.

4. Although 7.7 provides, pragmatically speaking, the best possible estimate, it is not necessarily a close estimate. If the population from which cases were randomly selected is quite large, seven cases is not enough for an accurate estimate, so the standard deviation in the population may differ considerably from 7.7. Still, this estimate is basically the best we can make given the small sample size. As mentioned in the text, when calculated via formula 4.5 with $N - 1$, the sample standard deviation has an extremely small amount of bias. (It underestimates the population standard deviation by a negligible amount.) For an unbiased formula, see Glass and Hopkins (1996, p. 244).

5. A technically correct rather than pragmatic recommendation would be (1) if your interest is in the sample only (that is, if you have no interest in the standard deviation in the population), use formula 4.4 (with N in the denominator) and (2) if your interest is in the population, use formula 4.5 (with $N - 1$ in the denominator). The small difference between the two formulas does not justify the confusion that would result from continuing to use both through the rest of the text.

6. An excellent computational formula that is mathematically equivalent to formula 4.5 is:

$$s = \sqrt{\frac{\sum X^2 - \dfrac{(\sum X)^2}{N}}{N - 1}}$$

This formula directs you to (1) square each score and then sum these squared scores together, (2) sum the scores, square this sum, and divide by N, (3) subtract results of step 2 from results of step 1, (4) divide by $N - 1$, and (5) compute the square root.

7. Even when $N - 1$ is used in the denominator, the size of the standard deviation (s) does vary to an *extremely* small degree with sample size. Specifically, as sample size increases, s tends to increase by an extremely small and inconsequential amount.

8. Notice that the estimate of the population variance is unbiased when $N - 1$ is used in the denominator. In contrast, the estimate of the population standard deviation (formula 4.5) has some bias even with $N - 1$ in the denominator.

9. If you want to be technically correct, (1) use the variance formula (4.6) with N in the denominator when your interest is in the sample and (2) use the formula (4.7) with $N - 1$ in the denominator when your interest is in the population. My recommendation, and the most common practice, is to always use the formula (4.7) with $N - 1$. For hand calculation of the variance (s^2), use the formula presented in note 6 for the standard deviation (s), but do not compute the square root.

10. The scores at approximately the 25th and 75th percentiles are known as the "hinges." See Tukey (1977, pp. 32–39) or Toothaker and Miller (1996, pp. 118–119) for the exact method for calculating hinges.

11. Box plots are often more complex than shown in Figure 4.1. In more complex plots, whiskers may end at horizontal lines known as fences, which "fence off" outliers, cases that meet some criterion for being sufficiently distant from the edges of the box. Often these outliers are plotted and labeled.

SHAPE OF DISTRIBUTION AND IMPORTANT DISTRIBUTIONS

5.1 CHAPTER OVERVIEW

As you study distributions, you will see that different distributions have different *shapes*. The key distribution in statistics is the bell-shaped *normal distribution*. Other distributions include *positively* and *negatively skewed* distributions and those with different degrees of *kurtosis*. In closing, the chapter shows how to use *z scores* and how to calculate percentages of cases located in various regions of the normal distribution.

5.2 INTRODUCTION

The variability of a frequency distribution refers to the degree to which scores vary around a measure of central tendency. The **shape** of a frequency distribution refers to the *pattern* of the distribution of scores, that is, to *how* scores are distributed.

Let's consider some common patterns. In some distributions, many cases cluster around some "middle" value and proportionately fewer cases are found as one moves to lower or higher values. In others, many cases cluster at low values with a few cases spread over a wide range of higher values. Or the pattern may be reversed, with the great majority of cases having fairly high values and only a few having low values. Some distributions have two sets of values where scores tend to cluster. Perhaps, for instance, people taking a statistics test tend to do either very poorly or very well, but not in between. A frequency polygon depicting this distribution would show two "hills," one corresponding to low scores and the other to high scores. Each of these four examples describes a distribution with a different shape.

An unlimited number of shapes of distributions are possible. Just as no two individuals are alike, each different variable tends to be distributed in a different way. This chapter covers the most common distributions encountered in human services research. The single most important distribution is the normal distribution.

5.3   THE NORMAL DISTRIBUTION

The best-known distribution, the **normal distribution,** is not an empirical distribution, one of actual scores, but instead is a theoretical distribution, one defined mathematically. No variable in real-world research *exactly* conforms to the normal distribution. On the other hand, many approximate it. For instance, the shapes of frequency distributions of physical characteristics such as height and weight often correspond reasonably well with a normal distribution. The normal distribution shape resembles a bell, as shown in Figure 5.1. As it is a theoretical distribution, the line that defines it is not jagged, reflecting the ups and downs of a real-world sample, but instead is smooth. As such it contrasts with, for instance, the line in the frequency polygon in Figure 2.3 that shows the distribution of age at entry into the home in the special-needs adoption study. The line defining the normal distribution in Figure 5.1 is better described as a curve. As its shape resembles a bell, it is termed the **bell-shaped curve,** or, more formally, the **normal curve.**

The vertical axis in Figure 5.1 depicts frequency; the higher the curve, the greater the frequency.[1] The horizontal axis presents values (scores). Lower values are to the left and higher ones to the right. In a normal distribution, frequency is greatest in the "middle" of the distribution and tapers off in both the negative (left) and positive (right) directions, as shown by the curve in Figure 5.1. The normal distribution has an infinite number of cases and extends *infinitely* in both directions. These aspects of the theoretical normal distribution cannot be depicted accurately in a frequency distribution figure such as Figure 5.1.

The normal distribution has three defining features:

1. Its mean, median, and mode all have the same value. For instance, if variable X is normally distributed with a mean of 100 points, then its median and mode are also 100 points.
2. Approximately 68% (68.26%), or about two-thirds, of cases have values located within one standard deviation of the mean.
3. It is **symmetrical,** that is, each side is a mirror image of the other. (The left is a mirror image of the right and the right is a mirror image of the left.)

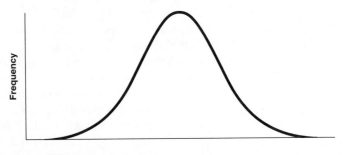

FIGURE 5.1

THE NORMAL DISTRIBUTION

Point 1 is illustrated by Figure 5.2, which presents the mode, median, and mean of a normal distribution. As stated earlier, the curve's height conveys frequency. Thus any distribution curve is highest at the mode, which is the value with the greatest frequency. A vertical line passing through the high point of the curve, as in Figure 5.2, indicates the value of the mode. By definition of the normal distribution, its mode and median have the same value, so the vertical line also indicates the median. Recall that the median is located at the 50th percentile. Thus exactly 50% of cases are located to the left of the vertical line and exactly 50% to the right. The mean of the normal distribution also has the same value as the mode and median, so the vertical line also conveys the mean. Therefore 50% of cases have values greater than the mean and 50% have lower values. We make frequent use of this fact later in the chapter.

To illustrate Point 2, suppose that the height of women is normally distributed with a mean of 5 feet 6 inches and a standard deviation of 3 inches. Given this information, one can infer that about 68% of women are between 5 feet 3 inches (the mean minus one standard deviation: 5 feet 6 inches − 3 inches = 5 feet 3 inches) and 5 feet 9 inches (the mean plus one standard deviation: 5 feet 6 inches + 3 inches = 5 feet 9 inches).

Furthermore, in a normal distribution about 95% of cases (95.44%) are located within two standard deviations of the mean. Given that the height of women is normally distributed with a mean of 5 feet 6 inches and a standard deviation of 3 inches, we know that about 95% of women are between 5 feet 0 inches and 6 feet 0 inches: 5 feet 6 inches − 2(3 inches) = 5 feet 0 inches, and 5 feet 6 inches + 2(3 inches) = 6 feet 0 inches.

Almost all cases (99.74%) in a normal distribution have values within three standard deviations of the mean. Hence (assuming $\overline{X}$ = 5 feet 6 inches, s = 3 inches, and a normal distribution) almost all women are between 4 feet 9 inches and 6 feet 3 inches. Figure 5.3 presents the percentages of cases within one, two, and three standard deviations in a normal distribution.

The space between the normal curve and the horizontal axis may be thought of as an area. Different areas under the normal curve correspond to the just-presented percentages. Thus about 68% of the area under the curve is located

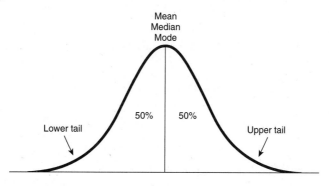

FIGURE 5.2

MEASURES OF CENTRAL TENDENCY AND TAILS FOR THE NORMAL DISTRIBUTION

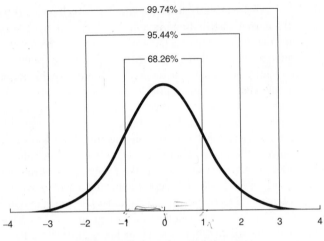

Standard deviations above or below mean

FIGURE **5.3**

THE NORMAL DISTRIBUTION AND STANDARD DEVIATIONS

The percentage of cases within one, two, and three standard deviations of the mean are shown for the normal distribution.

within one standard deviation of the mean; about 95% is within two standard deviations of the mean; and almost all is within three standard deviations.

As already mentioned, the normal distribution is a theoretical ideal. No variable in a real (rather than theoretical) population or sample will ever be distributed *exactly* as a normal distribution. Stated differently, no real variable will ever have a precisely normal shape.

Though some variables may have nearly normal distributional shapes, others depart markedly from normality. In statistical jargon, **normality** means "has a normal shape." Hence, when a variable departs markedly from normality, its shape differs greatly from that of the normal distribution.

5.4   TAILS OF A DISTRIBUTION

Before considering distributions with shapes other than normal, we need to define the tails of a distribution. The **tails** are the areas in the far (extreme) left and right of the distribution. The extreme left area is the **lower tail** (*negative tail, left tail*). The extreme right area is the **upper tail** (*positive tail, right tail*). The arrows in Figure 5.2 point to the tails of a normal distribution. As mentioned before, the normal curve stretches infinitely in both negative and positive directions. Another way to say this is that both the lower and upper tails extend infinitely.

As different distributions are described, you will see that some distributions have long, stretched-out tails and others have short, stubby tails. Sometimes one tail is short and stubby, and the other is long and stretched out.

5.5   Skewed Distributions

5.5.1   *Characteristics*

A common pattern for a distribution is to be **skewed,** or, one may say, to have a skewed shape. **Skewness** is the degree to which a distribution departs from symmetry (Toothaker and Miller, 1996, p. 90). The greater that departure, the greater the skewness. The normal distribution is symmetrical, so it is not a skewed distribution. Any distribution in which the left and right sides are mirror images is not skewed.

Some variables (distributions) are positively skewed. In a **positively skewed** distribution, scores tend to concentrate in the lower end (the left, negative side) of the distribution. Stated differently, frequencies tend to be higher on the left side than on the right (positive) side. The lower tail of a positively skewed distribution tends to be stubby and short, and the upper tail tends to be long and stretched out. Figure 5.4 presents four examples of positively skewed distributions. One may speak of the degree, or amount, of skewness in a distribution. Social science has no formal terms for characterizing the precise degree of skewness, but the descriptions attached to the distributions provide some informal guidelines. For instance, the first figure is described as having a "modest" positive skew, because it departs hardly at all from symmetry. The last figure has an "extreme" positive skew because it is highly asymmetrical.

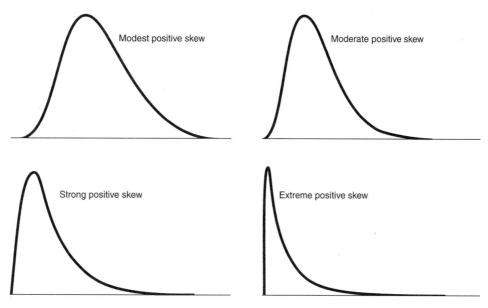

Modest positive skew

Moderate positive skew

Strong positive skew

Extreme positive skew

FIGURE 5.4

DIFFERING DEGREES OF POSITIVE SKEWNESS

The frequency polygon in Figure 2.3 demonstrates that in the special-needs adoption study, age at entry into the adoptive home is positively skewed. Thus this variable's distribution tends to be higher on the left side than on the right side, conveying the greater frequencies of younger rather than older ages. The upper tail of this distribution is elongated and extends much farther from the distribution's center than the lower tail does. The upper tail shows that, even though frequencies of older ages are low, some children entered their homes near the end of childhood (e.g., at 16, 17, or 18 years).

It is easy to think of variables whose distributions are positively skewed. A common example is family income in the United States, a variable also used in Chapter 3 to demonstrate how extreme values can "pull" the value of the mean in their direction. Figure 5.5 presents the distribution of family income (the data are hypothetical). Most families in the United States have moderate or somewhat low incomes; hence, the frequency distribution is higher on the left side of the figure. A smaller number have high incomes; hence, the distribution is lower on the right side. A few have what might be described as astronomical incomes. For instance, it is not unusual for CEOs of large corporations to earn millions of dollars in a year. Those with such incomes form the cases of the upper tail. Those with the very highest incomes (like Bill Gates) cause the tail to stretch extremely far to the right.

Another example of a positively skewed variable is the number of chin-ups people can do. Most people can do only a few (or no) chin-ups. This makes the left side of the distribution higher than the right. A few people can do many chin-ups (say, 20 or more). As such, the upper tail is elongated.

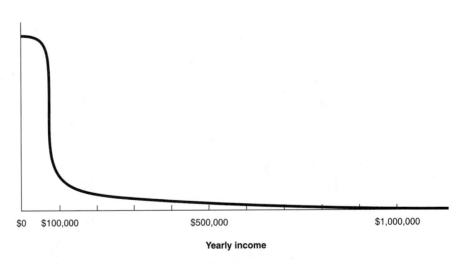

Yearly income

FIGURE 5.5

FAMILY INCOME IN THE UNITED STATES (HYPOTHETICAL DATA)

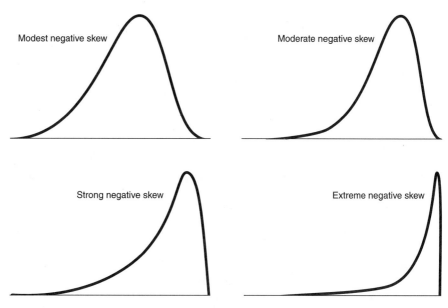

FIGURE **5.6**

DIFFERING DEGREES OF NEGATIVE SKEWNESS

In **negatively skewed** distributions, the lower (left) tail is elongated and the upper (right) tail is shorter. Cases in a negatively skewed distribution tend to concentrate in the right (positive) side of the distribution; in other words, frequencies are greater on this side. Figure 5.6 presents four negatively skewed distributions, each skewed to a different degree.

Examples of negatively skewed variables are usually harder to think of than positively skewed ones. One good example is length of gestation (time from conception to birth) of infants born in the United States. To simplify discussion, we will include only infants who survive birth. The modal gestational time is about 9 months. As such, the frequency distribution curve will be highest at this value. In the United States, it is exceptionally rare for gestational time to exceed 10 months. If a mother has carried her baby that long, almost always the baby will be delivered via cesarean section or labor will be induced. Thus the frequency of births at 10 months is markedly lower than that at 9 months, and virtually no babies' gestational time exceeds 11 months. Hence, the upper tail of the distribution ends by 11 months. The left side of the frequency distribution curve declines much more slowly, however. For instance, many more babies are born at 8 months than at 10 months. Indeed, some babies survive who are born at 5 months or even earlier. Thus the lower tail stretches out more than the upper tail. Figure 5.7 presents a hypothetical frequency distribution curve for length of gestation.

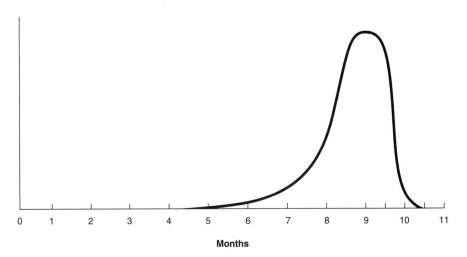

FIGURE **5.7**

LENGTH OF GESTATION IN MONTHS (HYPOTHETICAL DATA)

Students sometimes mix up negatively and positively skewed distributions; they can't remember which is which. The confusion stems from the fact that a negatively skewed distribution appears to "tip" to the right, that is, to the positive side (see Figures 5.6 and 5.7), and conversely, a positively skewed distribution appears to tip to the left, that is, to the negative side (see Figures 5.4 and 5.5). To avoid confusing the two, remember this saying: "The tail tells the tale." In other words, a distribution's correct name corresponds to the location of the elongated tail. In a negatively skewed distribution, the lower (negative) tail is elongated. In a positively skewed distribution, the upper (positive) tail is elongated.

5.5.2 Skewness and Measures of Central Tendency

As stated in Chapter 3, Section 3.7, an outlier is an *extremely* high or *extremely* low value. Saying that a distribution has outliers on the positive (right) side of the distribution is like saying that distribution is positively skewed. Thus, if a variable's distribution is positively skewed, most of its outliers are located in the upper (positive) tail. Family income in the United States is a good example; the outliers have incomes in the far end of the upper tail. By the same line of reasoning, if a distribution is negatively skewed, most outliers will be located in the lower (negative) tail.

The degree of skewness of a distribution exerts predictable effects on the measures of central tendency. Skewness ordinarily exerts no (or only a small) effect on the mode. For instance, the long stretch of the upper tail in the distribution of family income does not affect the mode, which is simply the most frequently occurring value. Similarly, the degree of stretch of the tail does not affect the median. Each case in the tail, whatever its value, simply counts as one more case in locating the case at the 50th percentile.

However, skewness can greatly affect the mean. The value of the mean is pulled in the direction of the elongated tail. The greater the skewness—that is, the more stretched out and elongated the tail—the greater the effect on the mean. If the degree of skewness is large enough, the mean can be pulled so much that it becomes a misleading measure of central tendency. In such situations, the median is ordinarily preferred to the mean as a measure of central tendency. There is no hard-and-fast point at which the mean is pulled enough so that the median is preferred, but the degree of skew in the strongly and extremely skewed distributions in Figures 5.4 and 5.6 is sufficient for the median to be preferred. When in doubt about whether to use the median or the mean, an effective solution is to simply present both measures.

In a normal distribution, the three measures of central tendency all have the same value. In a skewed distribution, they almost always have different values. Figure 5.8 presents a positively skewed distribution and a negatively skewed distribution. Each figure has three vertical lines, corresponding to the mode, the

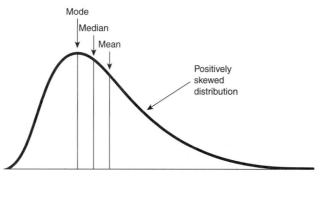

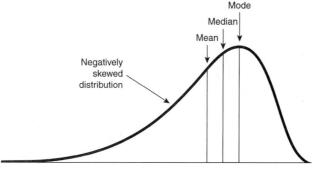

FIGURE **5.8**

MEASURES OF CENTRAL TENDENCY IN SKEWED DISTRIBUTIONS

mean, and the median. Suppose, for the moment, that the vertical lines in Figure 5.8 were not labeled. One could logically reason which line represents which measure. Consider the positively skewed distribution. The tallest line represents the mode, because the mode is defined as the value with the greatest frequency. The rightmost line is the mean, because the value of the mean is pulled toward the elongated tail. By the process of elimination, the remaining line (the middle line) represents the median. In the negatively skewed distribution in Figure 5.8, the right line represents the mode, the left line the mean, and the middle line the median.

Chapter 4 noted that researchers frequently present the mean and the standard deviation as they describe data for their readers. If a distribution is strongly skewed, this too is frequently communicated. Thus a researcher might state, "The mean income of clients in the study was $12,000 per year with a standard deviation of $5,000. The distribution of income was positively skewed." Degree of skewness is best communicated visually via a histogram or frequency polygon. Skewness is an important concept, one that often bears on which statistical procedures are appropriate.

The value for skewness can be determined with statistical software, but the precise number is rarely reported. If a distribution is symmetrical, its skewness is 0.00. If a distribution is positively skewed, its skewness is greater than 0.00 (i.e., a positive number). If a distribution is negatively skewed, its skewness is less than 0.00 (i.e., a negative number).

5.6   KURTOSIS

One of the two major characteristics of shape of distribution is skewness, the degree of departure from symmetry. The second is **kurtosis,** the degree of "peakedness" of a distribution relative to that of the normal distribution (Toothaker and Miller, 1996, p. 90). A distribution with high kurtosis has, relative to a normal distribution, a higher proportion of cases in the very center of the distribution. This gives the distribution its peaked shape. Distributions with high kurtosis also have, relative to the normal distribution, a higher proportion of cases in the tails. Thus these distributions have heavy-looking tails, thick and elongated. In contrast, a distribution with low kurtosis has, relative to the normal distribution, a flatter shape. The center of the distribution has a broadly rounded (almost flat) shape and the tails are usually thin and stubby.

Distributions that are more peaked than the normal distribution (those with high kurtosis), are termed **leptokurtic distributions.** Those that are flatter than the normal distribution (those with low kurtosis) are termed **platykurtic distributions.** A degree of peakedness approximately equal to that of the normal distribution is a **mesokurtic distribution.** Figure 5.9 presents a leptokurtic distribution, a platykurtic distribution, and a mesokurtic distribution. The mesokurtic distribution presented is simply the normal distribution.[2]

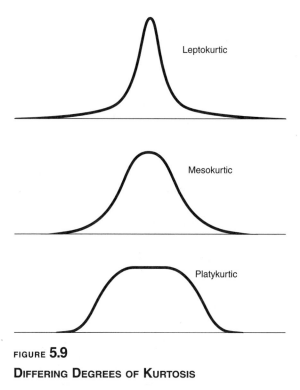

FIGURE **5.9**

DIFFERING DEGREES OF KURTOSIS

Although the degree of skewness can have important implications for the appropriateness or lack thereof of a given statistical procedure, the degree of kurtosis rarely does. Its main use is simply in describing the distributional shape, and in practice it is seldom mentioned.

A mistake sometimes made in assessing kurtosis is to think of it as the ratio of a distribution's height to its width. This ratio is determined predominantly by the scaling of the vertical and horizontal axes, and changes in scaling do not affect kurtosis. For instance, Figure 5.10 presents the normal distribution in three different ways. The shape of distribution is the same in each. All that has been altered is the ratio of height to width. Each of the three distributions in Figure 5.10 is a normal distribution and each has the same kurtosis, that is, the same degree of peakedness.

5.7   FLAT AND BIMODAL DISTRIBUTIONS

If each value of a variable has the same frequency, that variable has a **flat distribution** (also called a *rectangular* distribution).[3] Figure 5.11 presents a distribution with a shape that is very close to flat.

Figure 5.12 presents a bimodal distribution. In a technical sense a **bimodal distribution** has two modes, each with exactly the same frequency. In practical usage, the term *bimodal distribution* describes any distribution where cases tend

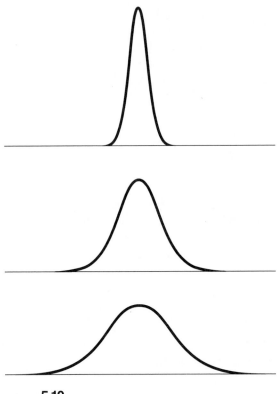

FIGURE **5.10**

THREE NORMAL DISTRIBUTIONS WITH DIFFERENTLY SCALED AXES

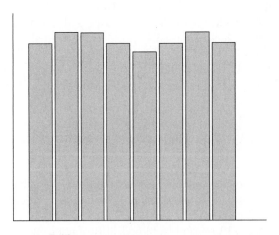

FIGURE **5.11**

A NEARLY FLAT DISTRIBUTION

FIGURE 5.12

A BIMODAL DISTRIBUTION

to cluster around two distinct values. Thus, practically speaking, this term is used even when frequencies of the two "modes" are not precisely equal.

5.8 PERCENTAGES AND THE NORMAL DISTRIBUTION

5.8.1 Percentages Above and Below the Mean

Recall that in a normal distribution, 68.26% of cases are within one standard deviation of the mean, 95.44% are within two standard deviations of the mean, and 99.74% are within three standard deviations of the mean. Recall also that the mean is located at the 50th percentile and the distribution is symmetrical. Putting these points together, we may deduce that in a normal distribution:

> 34.13% of cases (68.26%/2 = 34.13%) are located between the mean and one standard deviation above the mean, and 34.13% are located between the mean and one standard deviation below the mean.

> 47.72% of cases (95.44%/2 = 47.72%) are located between the mean and two standard deviations above the mean, and 47.72% are located between the mean and one standard deviation below the mean.

> 49.87% of cases (99.74%/2 = 49.87%) are located between the mean and three standard deviations above the mean, and 49.87% are located between the mean and three standard deviations below the mean.

Recall that one may conceptualize the normal distribution in terms of areas between the curve and the horizontal axis. The just-mentioned percentages describe areas. For instance, 34.13% of the area of the normal curve is located between the mean and one standard deviation above the mean. Figure 5.13 presents the percentage of cases in each of the just-mentioned areas.

5.8.2 Percentile Ranks

Our knowledge of the normal distribution may be used to calculate percentile ranks. Recall that the percentile rank of a score equals the percentage of cases with equal or lower scores. Recall also that the mean of a normal distribution is at the 50th percentile.

Suppose that in a normal distribution a score is two standard deviations above the mean. What is its percentile rank? To answer: (1) Recall that 50% of scores are equal to or below the mean. (2) Recall that 47.72% of scores are located between

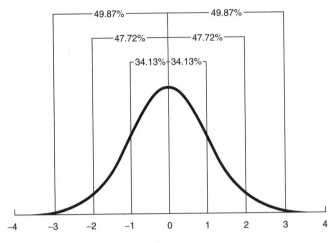

Standard deviations above or below mean

FIGURE **5.13**

AREAS ABOVE AND BELOW THE MEAN IN A NORMAL DISTRIBUTION

Percentage of cases between the mean and one, two, and three standard deviations above and below the mean are shown for the normal distribution.

the mean and two standard deviations above the mean (see Figure 5.13). (3) Add these two percentages together to determine the percentage of cases with scores that are lower than or equal to a score two standard deviations above the mean: 50.00% + 47.72% = 97.72%. Hence, the percentile rank is 97.72, which may be rounded to 98. Figure 5.14 presents this percentile rank visually.

The problem above called for finding the percentile rank for a case located above the mean. As such, it called for addition. When the percentile rank pertains to a case below the mean, subtraction is called for. For instance, in a normal distribution, what is the percentile rank of a case that is located one (1.00) standard deviation below the mean? To answer: (1) Recall that 50% of cases have scores at or below the mean. (2) Recall that 34.13% of cases are located between the mean and one standard deviation below the mean (see Figure 5.13). (3) *Subtract* the second percentage (34.13%) from the first (50%): 50.00% − 34.13% = 15.87%. Hence, given a normal distribution, a score one standard deviation below the mean is at about the 16th percentile.

5.8.3   *Percentages That Differ from the Mean by More Than a Given Amount*

Particularly in inferential statistics, researchers often focus on the percentage of cases with scores that differ from the mean by more than some given amount. If their interest is in scores that differ in *either* direction (in scores on both sides of

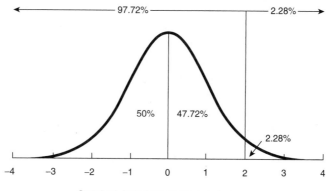

FIGURE **5.14**

PERCENTILE RANK AND STANDARD DEVIATIONS IN A NORMAL DISTRIBUTION

The percentile rank of a score two standard deviations above the mean can be found on the normal curve.

the distribution), they may subtract the percentage of scores within a given distance from 100%. For instance, given that 95.44% of cases have scores within two standard deviations of the mean, one may subtract this percentage from 100% to determine the percentage of cases with scores that differ from the mean by more than two standard deviations: 100% − 95.44% = 4.56%. Thus slightly less than 5% of cases have scores located more than two standard deviations from the mean.

Sometimes, one's interest is only in cases that differ by more than a given amount in *one particular* (rather than in either) direction. Given that the normal distribution is symmetrical, one may simply divide by 2 the percentage that differ in either direction. Suppose that the question is posed: "What percentage of cases in a normal distribution have scores that are more than two standard deviations above the mean?" As just calculated, 4.56% of cases differ in both directions, and 4.56%/2 = 2.28%. Hence, slightly more than 2% of cases have scores that are more than two standard deviations above the mean.

A more direct calculation method is to subtract the percentage of cases between the mean and the given score from 50%. For instance: (1) 50% of cases in a normal distribution have scores greater than the mean, and (2) 47.72% of cases have scores between the mean and two standard deviations above the mean. (3) Subtract the second percentage from the first: 50.00% − 47.72% = 2.28%. (Note that the two methods yield the same result.)

The same logic may be applied to find the percentage of cases that differ by more than some given amount in the opposite (negative) direction. For instance: "What percentage of cases in a normal distribution have scores that are more than one (1.00) standard deviation below the mean?" To solve: (1) Recall that 50% of cases are located below the mean. (2) Recall that 34.13% of cases are located between the mean and one standard deviation below the mean. (3) Subtract:

$50.00\% - 34.13\% = 15.87\%$. Questions concerning the percentage of cases located more than some given amount below the mean are, in essence, questions about percentile rank. Hence the question, "What percentage of cases are more than one standard deviation below the mean?" is basically asking for the percentile rank of a case at this location. Thus, for a normal distribution, the percentile rank of a case one standard deviation below the mean is 15.87.

5.8.4   *When Do Conclusions About Percentages Apply?*

All the various conclusions about percentages that have just been drawn apply *only* to the normal distribution. For instance, if a distribution is positively skewed or has any other nonnormal shape, these conclusions are not valid. Suppose that the following situation is described on your statistics test: "Juanita scored one standard deviation above the mean on her counseling theories test. Scores on the test were positively skewed." Now suppose that the test asks you the following: "(a) What is Juanita's percentile rank? (b) What percentage of students obtained scores between Juanita's and the mean?" The correct response to these questions—and to any others that might pertain to percentages—would be "cannot be determined." This is so because the percentages we have discussed apply only to the normal distribution; you have no percentage information about this skewed distribution.

5.9   INTRODUCTION TO Z SCORES

5.9.1   *Calculation*

The **z score** of a case (also called the **standard score**) indicates the number of standard deviation units that the value (score) of that case is above or below the mean. For instance, if Alice's score on a self-esteem scale is two standard deviations below the mean, her z score is -2.00. If Shawn's score is one-half of a standard deviation above the mean on the same scale, his z score is $+0.50$ (or, simply, 0.50). To compute a case's z score, subtract the mean from the score and divide by the standard deviation, as follows:

$$z = \frac{X - \overline{X}}{s} \tag{5.1}$$

where z is the z score for a case, X is the score for that case, $\overline{X}$ is the mean score, and s is the standard deviation.

Suppose, for instance, that the mean score on a self-esteem scale is 25 points with a standard deviation of 10 points and that Ann's score is 17 points. Her z score is:

$$z = \frac{17 - 25}{10} = \frac{-8}{10} = -0.80$$

Thus Ann's score is 0.80 standard deviations (or one could say, 0.80 standard deviation units) below the mean. Suppose that Rosa scored 37 on this scale. Her z score is $(37 - 25)/10 = 12/10 = 1.20$. Hence, she scored 1.2 standard deviations above the mean.

A score that has not been converted into a z score, that is, a score expressed in its original unit of measurement, is often termed a **raw score**. In the current example Ann's raw score is 17 and her z score is -0.80. Figure 5.15 displays Ann's and Rosa's raw scores and z scores.

5.9.2 *Basics of* z *Scores*

For *all* variables: (1) All scores below the mean have negative z scores; (2) all scores above the mean have positive z scores; and (3) scores exactly at the mean have a z score of 0.00. Furthermore, if one calculates (with formula 5.1) the z score for all cases in a sample or population, the mean of these z scores will be 0.00 and the standard deviation will be 1.00. This is so for *all* variables. For instance, suppose that an elementary school teacher gives five tests: a spelling test, a math test, a history test, a reading test, and a science test. Presumably each test has a different mean and a different standard deviation. If the teacher converts scores on each test to z scores, the mean score on each test (that is, the mean z score on each test) will be 0.00 and the standard deviation on each test (that is, the standard deviation of the z scores on each test) will be 1.00. In sum, for any distribution of z scores, (1) the mean is always 0.00 and (2) the standard deviation is always 1.00.

Although converting all scores in a distribution to z scores affects the mean and the standard deviation (it changes these to 0.00 and 1.00 respectively), it does not affect shape of distribution. For instance, if one converts all scores in a positively skewed distribution to z scores, these z scores will also be positively distributed.

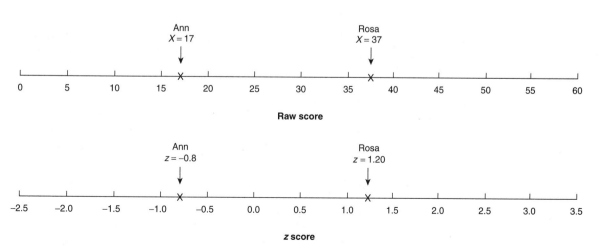

FIGURE 5.15

RAW SCORES COMPARED TO z SCORES

5.9.3   Uses of z Scores

Social scientists use z scores to assess a case's relative standing on different variables. For instance, suppose that Sally scored 75% on a math test and 85% on a history test. Which test did she do better on? The obvious answer seems to be the history test, because her percentage of correct answers was higher. But perhaps the history test was easy compared to the math test. Let's say, for instance, that the mean score on the history test was 90% and that on the math test was 70%. If so, then Sally's score was above the mean in math but below the mean in history. Thus, using her peers for comparison, Sally actually did better in math than in history.

Our example so far lacks information on standard deviations. Let's say that the standard deviation on the math test was 10% and that on the history test was 5%. Given that both means and standard deviations have been provided, z scores may be calculated. Sally's z score in math is $(75 - 70)/10 = 0.50$. Her z score in history is $(85 - 90)/5 = -1.00$. Hence, Sally scored one-half of a standard deviation above the mean in math and one standard deviation below the mean in history. Given that Sally's z score is higher in math ($z = 0.50$) than in history ($z = -1.00$), compared to her peers, she did better in math than in history. (The term "higher" can be misinterpreted. For z scores, "higher" conveys a higher relative standing, not a higher absolute value; for instance, a z score of -0.50 is higher than one of -1.00.)

In effect, z scores put all variables on a common metric and by so doing allow comparisons of "apples and oranges." Some students mistakenly believe that z scores may be used only for variables that are normally distributed. This is not the case. They may be calculated and used for all variables that are measured at the interval/ratio level or almost at this level.

5.10   z Scores and the Normal Distribution

Although z scores may be calculated for any interval/ratio-level variable, they are particularly useful for a variable that is normally distributed or almost so.[4] The prior section on the normal distribution demonstrated how to determine various percentages when scores are precisely 1.00, 2.00, or 3.00 standard deviations above or below the mean. Using Table A.1 in Appendix A, one may determine percentages in other situations as well. Table A.1 lists z scores in the first column. The second column lists the proportion of cases between the mean and the listed z score. Suppose you want to know the proportion of cases between the mean and a z score of $+1.26$. You could simply (1) go down the first column to find 1.26 and (2) go over to the second column to find that this proportion is .396 (39.6%). The second column lists proportions for both negative and positive z scores. Thus the proportion of cases between the mean and a z score of -1.26 is also .396 (39.6%).

To conserve space, Table A.1 lists z scores only to the nearest even hundredth. For instance, 1.25 is not listed. For all problems involving Table A.1, we will use the closest listed z score. If two listings are precisely equidistant, we will use the z score with the higher absolute value.

The third column of Table A.1 lists the proportion of cases with z scores that differ from the mean by more than does the z score listed in column 1. For positive z scores (z, those greater than 0.00), it lists the proportion of cases with z scores more positive than (greater than) the z score. For negative z scores ($-z$, those less than 0.00) it lists the proportion of cases with z scores more negative than (less than) the z score. So, if you want to know the proportion of cases with scores that are more than 1.26 standard deviations above the mean, you could (1) go down the first column to locate 1.26 and (2) go over to the third column to locate the proportion, .104 (10.4%). The same method yields the proportion of cases that are more than 1.26 standard deviations *below* the mean; this proportion is also .104 (10.4%). Figure 5.16 presents the proportion of cases between the mean and z scores of 1.26 and -1.26 as well as the proportion of cases that are more extreme.

Table A.1 may be used to find percentile ranks. For positive z scores, one determines percentile rank by adding .500 to the proportion in the second column and then multiplying by 100. For instance, to find the percentile rank for a z score of 0.80, (1) go down the first column to locate 0.80, (2) find the proportion in the second column (.288), (3) add .500 (.288 + .500 = .788), and (4) multiply by 100 (.788 × 100 = 78.8). Hence, a z score of 0.80 is at approximately the 79th percentile. To determine percentile rank for negative z scores, multiply the proportion in the third column by 100. The percentile rank for a z score of -0.80 is .212 × 100 = 21.2, which rounds to 21.

As mentioned earlier, a score expressed in its original unit of measurement is termed a raw score. To find the percentile rank of a raw score: (1) convert the score to a z score via formula 5.1 and (2) use Table A.1.

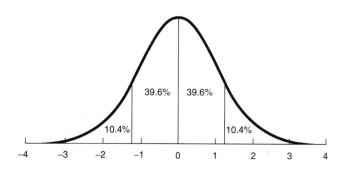

FIGURE 5.16

PERCENTAGES BETWEEN THE MEAN AND Z SCORES OF ±1.26

For the normal distribution, the figure indicates percentages of cases between the mean and **z** scores of -1.26 and $+1.26$, and percentages that are more extreme.

For instance, suppose that the mean score on a self-esteem test is 20 points with a standard deviation of 5 points and that scores are normally distributed. Jane scores 27. What is her percentile rank?

First, determine the z score:

$$z = \frac{27 - 20}{5} = \frac{7}{5} = 1.40$$

Second, refer to Table A.1: The proportion of cases located between the mean and a z score of 1.40 is .419. Add .500 and then multiply by 100: .419 + .500 = .919 × 100 = 91.9. Hence, Jane's score is at approximately the 92nd percentile.

5.11   COMMENTS ON Z SCORES

As noted earlier, z scores allow comparisons of a case's relative standing on two different variables. In addition, z scores convey relative standing or performance on a single variable. For instance, which statement communicates more information? (1) Jane scored 27 on a self-esteem scale, or (2) Jane's z score on a self-esteem scale is 1.40. Consider the first statement. Does 27 represent good or poor self-esteem? With only the raw score (27), one has no way to know. With statement 2, knowing that Jane's z score was 1.40, one could reason that a z score of 1.40 is well above the mean, so Jane's score is well above the mean, meaning that relative to her peers, Jane has good self-esteem.

Furthermore, if the shape of the distribution of self-esteem is close to normal (one could assess this via a frequency polygon), one could reason as follows: (1) Given a normal distribution, a z score of 1.00 is at the 84th percentile. (2) Jane's z score is higher than this, so (3) Jane's score is at the 84th percentile or even higher. (4) Relative to her peers, Jane has excellent self-esteem. In sum, given a nearly normal distribution, knowledge of a case's z score lets one estimate relative standing via percentile rank. Even for nonnormal distributions, knowledge of a case's z score permits assessment of whether that score is above or below the mean.

Interpreting abstract variables, such as scores on a self-esteem test, is made easier with z scores. For instance, a raw score of 27 by itself has no meaning. By comparison, variables measured in tangible, physical units usually make sense without z scores. For instance, the data that a given newborn weighs 3 pounds 7 ounces makes sense to us as we are familiar with pounds and ounces.

Yet, even for a tangible variable, knowing a z score adds useful information. For instance, knowing that a newborn's z score for birthweight is −1.50 indicates a weight below the mean and helps to convey the infant's weight relative to that of its peers.

5.12   CHAPTER SUMMARY

The shape of a frequency distribution refers to the pattern of the distribution of scores, that is, to how scores are distributed.

The normal distribution is a theoretical distribution. No real-world variable has a *precisely* normal shape. In a normal distribution: (1) the mean, median, and mode all have the same value, (2) about 68% of cases have values that are within one standard deviation of the mean, (3) the left and right sides are mirror images (i.e., distribution is symmetrical). Also, about 95% of cases have values within two standard deviations of the mean and about 99¾% have values within three standard deviations.

The tails of a distribution are its extreme left (negative) and extreme right (positive) areas. The normal distribution's lower (negative) and upper (positive) tails extend infinitely.

Skewness refers to the degree to which a distribution departs from symmetry. In a positively skewed distribution, cases tend to cluster in the left (negative) side of the distribution and the upper tail is elongated. In a negatively skewed distribution, cases tend to cluster in the right (positive) side and the lower tail is elongated. Though skewness exerts little influence on the mode or median, it can greatly affect the mean.

Kurtosis refers to degree of peakedness. Leptokurtic distributions are highly peaked. Platykurtic distributions are flat or broadly rounded. Mesokurtic distributions are about as peaked as the normal distribution.

A z score conveys how many standard deviations above or below the mean a given score is. For all variables, z scores have a mean of 0.00 and a standard deviation of 1.00. Converting scores to z scores does not affect shape of distribution. The z score formula (formula 5.1) is $z = (X - \overline{X})/s$. z scores allow comparisons of relative standing. Scores expressed in their original units of measurement are termed raw scores.

If variables are normally distributed, z scores may be used to calculate percentages of cases at specific locations. If they are not, such percentages may not be calculated. z scores are particularly helpful in interpreting abstract, intangible variables.

PROBLEMS AND QUESTIONS

Section 5.2

1. The shape of a distribution refers to the _____ of the distribution of scores.
2. (T or F) All frequency distributions have similar shapes.

Section 5.3

3. (T or F) The normal distribution is a theoretical distribution rather than an empirical one.
4. (T or F) Many real-world distributions conform *precisely* to the normal distribution.
5. The normal curve is sometimes called the _____-shaped curve.

6. (T or F) The normal distribution has a fixed (limited) number of cases.
7. (T or F) In a (precisely) normal distribution, the mean, median, and mode have similar but not identical values.
8. In a normal distribution, _____ % of cases are located within one standard deviation of the mean.
9. The normal curve is _____, that is, each side is a "mirror image" of the other.
10. In a normal distribution, about _____% of cases are located within two standard deviations of the mean.
11. About what percentage of cases in a normal distribution are located more than three standard deviations from the mean?

12. Suppose that the mean height of seventh-grade girls is 60 inches, with a standard deviation of 3 inches, and that the shape of this distribution is normal. About what percentage of these girls are between 54 and 66 inches tall?
13. The term _____ means "has a normal shape."

Section 5.4

14. The areas located in the extreme right and left sides of a distribution are termed the distribution's _____.
15. The area in the extreme left of a distribution is termed the _____ tail.

Section 5.5

16. Skewness is defined as the degree to which a distribution departs from _____.
17. Where a distribution is negatively skewed, scores tend to concentrate in the _____ side/area of the distribution.
    a. Lower (negative)
    b. Upper (positive)
    c. Middle
18. When a distribution is positively skewed, the tail that is stretched out and elongated is on the _____ side of the distribution.
19. (T or F) A negatively skewed distribution appears to "tip" to the positive (upper) side, that is, to the right.
20. The age of students at your college or university is, most likely, _____ skewed.
21. The number of months of gestation for babies born in the United States most likely has a(n) _____ skew.
22. A(n) _____ is a case with an extremely high or extremely low value.
23. The measure of central tendency on which skewness exerts the largest effect is the _____.
24. (T or F) If a distribution is positively skewed, the mean, the mode, and the median all have the same values.
25. If a distribution is negatively skewed, the mean is pulled in a(n) _____ direction.
26. (T or F) When a distribution is strongly skewed, the median is usually preferred to the mean as a measure of central tendency.

Section 5.6

27. Kurtosis refers to the degree of _____.
28. (T or F) When kurtosis is high, distributions tend to have thick, elongated tails.
29. A flat, nonpeaked distribution with short and stubby tails is termed a . . . .
    a. Leptokurtic distribution
    b. Platykurtic distribution
    c. Mesokurtic distribution
30. (T or F) In general, a distribution's skewness has greater implications for which statistical procedures may be used appropriately than does its kurtosis.
31. What shape do you think the distribution of the age of students at an elementary school (grades K to 6) might have?
    a. Very peaked (leptokurtic)
    b. Quite flat/rectangular (platykurtic)
    c. Normal (mesokurtic)
32. Give an example of a variable that you think might have a bimodal distribution.
33. Indicate the percentage of cases in a normal distribution in each of the following areas:
    a. Between the mean and one standard deviation above the mean
    b. Between the mean and one standard deviation below the mean
    c. Between the mean and two standard deviations above the mean
    d. Between the mean and three standard deviations below the mean
34. In a normal distribution, what is the percentile rank of each of the following cases?
    a. A case one standard deviation below the mean
    b. A case one standard deviation above the mean
    c. A case two standard deviations below the mean
    d. A case three standard deviations above the mean
35. What percentage of cases in a normal distribution have values that are greater than (in a positive direction only from) the following cases?
    a. A case one standard deviation below the mean
    b. A case one standard deviation above the mean

c. A case two standard deviations above the mean

36. What percentage of cases in a normal distribution are more extreme than—that is, differ from the mean in *either* direction by more than—the following cases?
   a. A case two standard deviations above the mean
   b. A case one standard deviation below the mean
   c. A case three standard deviations below the mean

37. A distribution is positively skewed. What percentage of cases are located between the mean and one standard deviation above the mean? (Might be a trick question.)

Section 5.9

38. Another name for a z score is a(n) _____ score.

39. In your own words, what does a z score indicate?

40. In your own words, describe how to calculate a z score.

41. Fred's z score is 1.5 standard deviations below the mean. What is his z score?

42. (T or F) All scores greater than the mean have positive z scores.

43. When a variable is expressed in terms of z scores, its mean is _____.

44. When a variable is expressed in terms of z scores, its standard deviation is _____.

45. The mean on a spelling test is 80, with a standard deviation of 10 points. Ann scored 83. What is her z score?

46. In a sample of children, the mean number of months in foster care is 30 with a standard deviation of 12 months. Determine the z score for each of the following children.
   a. Ann, 54 months
   b. Shawn, 30 months
   c. Ramon, 34 months
   d. Alice, 21 months

47. A score expressed in its original unit of measure is often referred to as a(n) _____ score.

48. (T or F) When raw scores are converted to z scores, the shape of the distribution changes.

49. Test 1: $\overline{X} = 88$, $s = 8$; Test 2: $\overline{X} = 75$, $s = 10$. Sondra scored 84 on Test 1 and 77 on Test 2. Relative to her classmates, on which test did she do better?

50. In reference to the prior problem, what was Sondra's z score on each test?

51. (T or F) z scores may be calculated only on normally distributed variables.

Section 5.10

52. In a normal distribution, what proportion of cases are between the mean and the following z scores?
   a. 0.36
   b. −1.18
   c. 1.76

53. Given a normal distribution, what is the percentile rank of the following z scores?
   a. 0.00
   b. 2.30
   c. −0.80

54. Given a normal distribution, what proportion of scores are more negative than a z score of −0.80?

55. Given a normal distribution, what proportion of scores are more extreme in either direction—that is, differ by more from the mean—than a z score of −0.80?

Section 5.11

56. If a distribution is nonnormal, a z score of −0.12 is located . . .
   a. Below the mean
   b. Above the mean
   c. Cannot be determined

57. In your own words, why are z scores particularly helpful in interpreting intangible, abstract variables (as contrasted to tangible variables that are encountered in everyday life)?

COMPUTER EXERCISES

For general instructions on computer exercises, see the note in Chapter 2.

1. For AGEHOMEY (child's age at entry into home), compute the mean, standard deviation,

and skew. Also create a histogram. [In SPSS, *Analyze > Descriptive Statistics > Frequencies* (click back any prior variables), click over AGEHOMEY, *Statistics*, click boxes next to "Mean," "Std. deviation," and "Skewness" (so that each is checked), *Continue, Charts*, click button next to "Histograms," *Continue, OK*.]

Check your answers: For AGEHOMEY, $\overline{X} = 5.52$, $s = 3.70$. Skewness computes to 0.302, a positive value. This is consistent with visual inspection of the histogram, which reveals that the tail is elongated in the positive direction. (Skewness greater than 0.00 conveys positive skewness; less than 0.00 conveys negative skewness. The precise numerical skewness value is seldom included in research reports.)

2. Create a frequency polygon for BEHAVTOT (score on behavior problem checklist) and comment on the skewness. [In SPSS, *Graphs > Line,* verify that "Summaries for groups of cases" is marked (if not, do so), click on the graphic next to "Simple," *Define,* make sure "N of cases" is checked, click BEHAVTOT over to the space below "Category Axis," *Options,* make sure "Display groups defined by missing values" is *not* marked, *Continue, OK*.]

Check your graph: The frequency polygon for BEHAVTOT reveals a positive skew.

3. Create a new variable in which each raw score on BEHAVTOT is converted to a z score. [In SPSS, *Analyze > Descriptive Statistics > Descriptives,* click over BEHAVTOT, click to check the box entitled "Save standardized values as variables," *OK*. Click the spreadsheet logo at top of Viewer window to return to the Data Editor window. Scroll over to the right of the variables in this window and observe that a new variable titled ZBEHAVTO has been created and added to the data set. This variable is composed of scores on BEHAVTOT converted to z scores. When you exit SPSS you will be prompted as to whether you wish to save the data file. Clicking "Yes" saves the new variable ZBEHAVTO with the file. Clicking "No" leaves the file as it was prior to the creation of ZBEHAVTO. My recommendation is to click "No," as the exercises make no further use of this variable.]

4. The new variable that you just created is named ZBEHAVTO. Calculate the mean and standard deviation of this new variable (which represents BEHAVTOT expressed as z scores).

Check your answers: The mean of the new variable is 0.00 and the standard deviation is 1.00. It is possible that the mean is expressed in scientific notation. This format is often used to express numbers with values very close to 0.00 or with extremely large values (see Appendix B: Review of Basic Math, Section B.5).

5. For AGECHIY (child's age at time of survey) use the "Frequencies" procedure to:
   a. Find the mean, standard deviation, and skewness.
   b. Create a histogram.
   c. Superimpose a normal curve on the histogram. (This can be accomplished by checking the "With normal curve" box within the "Charts" option within "Frequencies.")

Check your answers: For AGECHIY, $\overline{X} = 10.83$, $s = 3.79$, skewness $= -0.172$. Particularly with the help of the superimposed normal curve, one can see a very slight negative skewness.

NOTES

1. Formally speaking, the height of the normal curve depicts density rather than frequency. The normal curve cannot depict frequency because the normal distribution is a theoretical distribution with an infinite number of cases. Density refers to how many cases are located within a given range of the horizontal axis. Density and frequency are directly proportionate. As density increases or decreases, frequency does so by the same amount.

2. If a distribution has the same degree of peakedness as the normal distribution, its kurtosis equals 0.00. If a distribution is more peaked than normal, its kurtosis will be greater than 0.00 (i.e., a positive number). If a distribution is flatter than the normal distribution, its kurtosis will be less than 0.00 (i.e., a negative number).

3. A flat distribution may be thought of as a special case of a platykurtic distribution. (All flat distributions are platykurtic but not all platykurtic distributions are flat.)

4. A normally shaped distribution with a mean of 0.00 and a standard deviation of 1.00, that is, a normally shaped distribution of z scores, is termed a *standard normal distribution.*

ASSOCIATION BETWEEN TWO VARIABLES

An essential goal of research is to determine whether relationships exist between variables, and in Part Three we begin to explore how statistics can reveal relationship, or association. Two variables are related (associated) when the values observed for one variable vary, differ, or change according to those observed for the other. For instance, amount of time spent studying for a test and grade earned on that test are related because (in most cases) those who study longer earn higher grades. Chapter 6 presents underlying concepts. Chapters 6 through 9 present different tools for measuring the size of association between different kinds of variables. Key procedures examined include the difference in percentages (Chapter 6), the odds ratio (Chapter 7), correlation and regression (Chapter 8), and the standardized difference between means (Chapter 9).

THE CONCEPT OF RELATIONSHIP AND RELATIONSHIP BETWEEN CATEGORICAL VARIABLES

6.1 CHAPTER OVERVIEW

We explore the concept of *relationship* to begin this chapter, and go on to study some tools for assessing relationship between categorical variables, particularly those at the nominal level of measurement. This discussion introduces *contingency tables* and their interpretation. Two everyday tools for assessing association are presented, the *difference in percentages* and the *ratio of percentages*. The chapter introduces and defines the concept of *size* (or *strength*) *of association* and provides qualitative (nonnumeric) descriptors for interpreting size of association.

6.2 THE MEANING OF RELATIONSHIP

Chapter 1 presented this definition of relationship: Two variables are **related** when the values observed for one variable vary, differ, or change according to those of the other. Take, for instance, the following two variables: political party affiliation of state legislators (Democratic or Republican), and vote on Legislation X (yes or no). Let's say that 70% of Democrats vote yes and 30% vote no. In contrast, among Republicans, let's say that 20% vote yes and 80% vote no. Vote on Legislation X does indeed differ according to party affiliation. Stated differently, Democrats and Republicans do not have identical voting patterns. Democrats are more likely to vote yes than are Republicans. (And by the same token, Republicans are more likely to vote no than are Democrats.) In this example, vote on Legislation X and party affiliation are related. Stated differently, there is a relationship between these variables.

When variables are related, given values of one variable tend to "go with" given values of another, that is, the variables tend to "vary together." Stated still differently, "some values of one variable tend to occur more often with some values of the second variable than with other values of that variable" (Moore, 1997, p. 285).

Take shoe size and height. Those who are tall tend to have big feet. Those who are short tend to have small feet. Being tall and having big feet tend to go together.

Similarly, being short and having small feet also go together. Because their values tend to vary together, height and shoe size are related.

Take another two variables, score on a statistics test and eye color. A best guess is that those with blue, brown, green, and other eye colors are equally likely to get high, medium, or low scores on the statistics test. Presumably we won't find a pattern in which, for instance, those with blue eyes tend to get certain scores and those with brown eyes tend to get other scores. In this example, given values of one variable do not tend to go with given values of another. The likelihood of getting a high, medium, or low score does not vary by eye color. Thus these variables are not related.

Similarly, suppose that on Legislation Y, the same voting patterns are observed for Democrats and Republicans. Among Democrats 60% vote yes and 40% vote no, and among Republicans 60% vote yes and 40% vote no. In this example, vote on Y does not change or vary according to party affiliation. Hence, vote and party affiliation are not related.

Several terms have meanings similar or identical to *relationship* and *related*. **Association** is a synonym for relationship, and **associated** is a synonym for related. Similarly, saying that two variables are **unassociated** (not associated) is the same as saying that they are **unrelated** (not related). Sometimes *correlation* refers to a particular statistical procedure for assessing relationship, but when used in a more general way, **correlation** is synonymous with relationship. Similarly, saying that two variables are **correlated** says that they are related. A final term is **independent:** If two variables are independent, they are unrelated.

6.3   COMMENTS ON RELATIONSHIP

It takes two to tango. Similarly, it takes *two* variables to form a relationship. A trick exam question would be "On Legislation Z, 44% of Republicans voted yes and 56% voted no. Are political party affiliation and vote on Legislation Z associated?" This question presents only one variable, vote on Z. Political party affiliation takes on only one value, Republican, and, as such, is a constant rather than a variable. The question is nonsensical: One can't assess the presence or absence of association unless two variables are present.

Suppose that the question had instead been "66% of Democrats and 44% of Republicans voted yes on Z. Are political party and vote on Z related?" Now two variables are involved and the question makes sense. Given that Democrats and Republicans demonstrate different voting patterns, vote on Z and party affiliation are associated.

The fact of relationship between variables demonstrates only a pattern. In a recent class discussion, I remarked that there is a relationship between smoking and cancer. A student stated that this was not true because both of her parents had smoked heavily since their teens and neither had developed cancer. But pointing out a relationship or association only identifies the general pattern; exceptions almost always occur. So to say that smoking and cancer are associated (related) does not say that all smokers develop cancer or that all nonsmokers do not. It says only that smokers and nonsmokers are not equally likely to develop cancer.

A common mistake is to assume that because two variables are related, one variable causes the other, that is, that the relationship is causal. Sometimes relationships are indeed causal, but other times they are not. Because of limitations in research design or knowledge, researchers often cannot reach a definitive conclusion on causality. The presence of a relationship between two variables informs us that their values vary together but does not speak to what causes this to be the case. The presence (or absence) of relationship and the reason for that relationship are distinct issues. Chapters 10 and 11 focus on how to assess whether a relationship is causal.

In the discussion of statistical significance tests in Chapter 1 (Section 1.13) we introduced the notion that relationships in samples sometimes occur simply due to chance (the luck of the draw). For now, hold this notion in the back of your mind. It is not germane to this chapter's key points, but we return to the role of chance beginning in Chapter 12.

This chapter and the next three present the key tools of descriptive statistics for assessing relationship. This chapter focuses on nominal-level variables, in particular on dichotomous variables (those with exactly two categories).

6.4 RELATIONSHIP BETWEEN CATEGORICAL VARIABLES

6.4.1 Contingency Tables

A key tool for assessing relationship between categorical variables is **contingency table analysis** *(crosstabulation, crosstabs)*. Contingency table analysis is appropriate for both nominal- and ordinal-level variables. This chapter's primary focus is on nominal-level data, and Chapter 9 presents additional procedures designed for ordinal-level data.

Table 6.1 is a **contingency table** *(crosstabs table)* with hypothetical data pertaining to special-needs adoption. The **row variable,** the variable defining the rows, is type of adoption and takes on two values: (1) adoption by parents who were not previously foster parents to the child, labeled "New home adoption," and (2) adoption by a child's prior foster parents, labeled "Foster family adoption." Type of adoption is the independent variable. The **column variable** (and dependent variable) is adoption outcome, which also takes on two values: (1) "Disrupted," meaning the adoption ends and the child returns to the care of the social service agency, and (2) "Stable," meaning the child continues to reside with the adoptive family, that is, the adoption remains intact.

In Table 6.1, the independent variable is the row variable. There is no firm convention on this, so the independent variable could be the column variable instead. Sometimes variables cannot be classified as independent or dependent.

This contingency table is a two-by-two (2 × 2) table because it has two rows and two columns. The number of rows and columns corresponds to the number of categories (values) of the variables. Here both variables have two categories. The first number in the table description indicates the number of rows and the

TABLE 6.1	ABSENCE OF RELATIONSHIP BETWEEN VARIABLES		
	Disrupted	**Stable**	
New home adoption	10	90	100
	10%	90%	67%
	67%	67%	
Foster family adoption	5	45	50
	10%	90%	33%
	33%	33%	
	15	135	150
	10%	90%	100%

Note: Data are hypothetical.

second indicates the number of columns. A 3 × 4 table, for instance, has three rows and four columns.

Let's further decipher Table 6.1. The number 150 in the lower right-hand corner conveys the total number of cases, that is, *N*. The areas just to the right of and just below the table's boxed-in area are the **margins.** The number 100 in the right margin conveys the total number (frequency) of new home adoptions. The number 50 in the right margin conveys the total number (frequency) of adoptions by foster families. These numbers are the **row totals.** The number 15 in the bottom margin conveys the total number (frequency) of disrupted placements. The number 135 in the bottom margin conveys the total number (frequency) of stable placements. These are the **column totals.** The row totals (100 + 50 = 150) and also the column totals (15 + 135 = 150) sum to the total number of cases (150). In the upper left box, or **cell,** 10 is the number (frequency) of new home adoptions that ended in disruption. In the lower left cell, 5 is the number of foster family adoptions that ended in disruption. These are examples of **cell frequencies.** So are the 90 and 45 in the right-hand cells, conveying the number of stable adoptions in new homes and foster families, respectively. Note that cell frequencies sum down the columns to column totals (10 + 5 = 15; 90 + 45 = 135) and across the rows to row totals (10 + 90 = 100; 5 + 45 = 50).

The entry 10% in the bottom margin below the left column conveys the percentage of all adoptions, new family or foster family, that were disrupted (15 of 150, or 15/150, equals 10%). The percentage 90% in the bottom margin conveys the percentage of all adoptions that were stable (135/150 = 90%). The percentages in the right margin convey that (1) 67% of adoptions (100/150) were by new parents and (2) 33% (50/150) were by foster parents.

The percentages in the cells are **cell percentages.** The upper percentage in each cell is the **row percentage,** the percentage of a row's cases that are in that cell. For instance, the 10% in the top left cell conveys that 10% (10/100 = 10%) of new family placements ended in disruption. Similarly, the 90% in the top right cell conveys that 90% (90/100 = 90%) of new family placements were stable. Row percentages sum to 100 *across* the row. For instance, in the top row

10% and 90% sum to 100%. The lower percentage (bottom number) in each cell is the **column percentage,** the percentage of a column's cases that are in that cell. For instance, the 67% in the upper left cell indicates that 67% (10/15 = 67%) of disruptions were in new adoptive placements. Column percentages sum to 100 *down* the column. For instance, in the first column: 67% + 33% = 100%.

Some crosstab tables present only cell frequencies. Others present only row or only column percentages. Others, such as Table 6.1, present both sets of percentages. To determine whether percentages are row or column percentages, find the direction in which they sum to 100. If they do so across rows, they are row percentages. If they do so down columns, they are column percentages.

6.4.2   *Assessing Relationship Using a Contingency Table*

Cell *percentages* rather than cell frequencies are the key to assessing the presence or absence of relationship in a contingency table. The following guideline is recommended:

> When the independent variable is the row variable, compare row percentages.
>
> When the independent variable is the column variable, compare column percentages. (Norusis, 1993, p. 203)

This guideline facilitates contingency table analysis, and for the most part, this text follows it. However, both sets of percentages can be informative, regardless of the location of the independent variable. And sometimes variables cannot be classified as independent or dependent. Hence, this text occasionally presents comparisons that run counter to the guideline. Putting the guideline into action: In Table 6.1, the independent variable, type of adoption, is the row variable. Hence, initial attention is directed to the row percentages, the upper percentage in each cell.

In Table 6.1, row percentages are identical for the two rows. For new home adoptions, 10% disrupt and 90% are stable. For foster family adoptions, again, 10% disrupt and 90% are stable. Adoption outcomes do not differ according to type of adoption. Instead, the same pattern of outcomes is observed for new home and foster family adoptions. (In both, 10% disrupt and 90% are stable.) The data in Table 6.1 do not meet the definition of relationship: Type of adoption and adoptive outcome are unassociated (unrelated).

Whenever row percentages are identical, so are column percentages. For instance in Table 6.1, 67% of disruptions were new home adoptions and 33% were foster family adoptions. Similarly, 67% of stable placements were new home adoptions and 33% were foster family adoptions. Also, whenever row percentages are identical (and therefore column percentages are identical), percentages in the margins match those in the cells. For instance, the percentages in the right margin, 67% and 33%, match the column percentages. Similarly, the percentages in the bottom margin, 10% and 90%, match the row percentages. In sum, when variables in a contingency table are not related, row percentages are identical, column percentages are identical, and margin percentages match cell percentages.

Table 6.2 presents a different hypothetical situation using the same two variables. Again, we focus initially on row percentages.

In Table 6.2, row percentages differ in the two rows. For new home adoptions, 20% disrupt and 80% are stable. For foster family adoptions, 10% disrupt and 90% are stable. Adoption outcomes do indeed differ according to type of placement. (For instance, a higher percentage of new home adoptions than foster family adoptions end in disruption.) The data in Table 6.2 meet the definition of relationship. In Table 6.2, type of adoption and adoptive outcome are related.

Whenever row percentages in a contingency table differ, so do column percentages. For instance, in Table 6.2, column percentages for disrupted adoptions are 80% for new home adoptions and 20% for foster family adoptions. For stable adoptions these are 64% for new home adoptions and 36% for foster family adoptions.

To summarize, variables in a crosstab table are unassociated when the following occur:

- The row percentages are the same in every row.
- The column percentages are the same in every column.

Whenever one set of percentages is the same, so is the other (i.e., if row percentages are the same, so are column percentages, and vice versa).

Variables are related when the following occur:

- The row percentages differ (i.e., are not the same in every row).
- The column percentages differ (i.e., are not the same in every column).

Whenever one set of percentages differs, so does the other (if row percentages differ, so will column percentages and vice versa). We may further shorten these summaries and say simply that (1) whenever percentages are the same, variables are unrelated, and (2) whenever they differ, variables are related.

TABLE 6.2   A RELATIONSHIP BETWEEN VARIABLES

	Disrupted	Stable	
New home adoption	20	80	100
	20%	80%	67%
	80%	64%	
Foster family adoption	5	45	50
	10%	90%	33%
	20%	36%	
	25	125	150
	17%	83%	100%

Note: Data are hypothetical.

6.4.3   *Communicating About Relationship*

In a 2 × 2 table, one can typically describe relationship in eight different ways. For instance, with reference to Table 6.2:

1. New home adoptions are more likely to disrupt than are foster family adoptions.
2. New home adoptions are less likely to be stable than are foster family adoptions.
3. Foster family adoptions are more likely to be stable than new home adoptions.
4. Foster family adoptions are less likely to disrupt than are new home adoptions.
5. A higher percentage of disrupted adoptions than of stable adoptions are new home adoptions.
6. A lower percentage of disrupted adoptions than of stable adoptions are foster family adoptions.
7. A higher percentage of stable adoptions than of disrupted adoptions are foster family adoptions.
8. A lower percentage of stable adoptions than of disrupted adoptions are new home adoptions.

Each of these descriptions of the relationship between type of adoption and adoptive outcome is correct. Each is simply a different way to describe that relationship. The first four descriptions, based on row percentages, are in accord with the guideline to compare row percentages when the independent variable is the row variable. Descriptions 5 to 8, based on column percentages, run counter to this guideline. Even if all eight descriptions are correct, the first four are more straightforward and easier to understand. In sum, following the guideline communicates the gist of the relationship more effectively.

6.4.4   *Tips for Developing Contingency Tables*

As mentioned earlier, not all contingency tables present both row and column percentages. In practice, most present only one set. The key to developing a straightforward table is to select the "correct" percentages. Adapting the guideline to meet this goal: (1) When the independent variable is the column variable, one should present column percentages, and (2) when the independent variable is the row variable, one should present row percentages.

   As mentioned earlier, social science has not developed a firm convention regarding which variable (the independent or the dependent) should be the column variable and which the row variable. However, a trend may be observed: The independent variable is more often the column variable, leaving the dependent variable to be the row variable. Stated differently, the categories of the independent variable are more often listed across the top of the table and those of the dependent variable down the left side. This text usually follows this pattern, though it sometimes deviates.

You will do well to adopt this pattern. If you always place categories of the independent variable across the top and those of the dependent variable down the side, you will develop a routine that you can follow. In such a table, column percentages are preferred.

Tables 6.1 and 6.2 break with the recommended locations for variables. In both, the independent variable (type of adoption) is the row variable and the dependent variable (adoption outcome) is the column variable. Table 6.3 presents the same data as does Table 6.2 but follows the recommendation to make the independent variable the column variable and the dependent variable the row variable. As also recommended, Table 6.3 presents only one set of percentages, these being column percentages.

One more tip may help you to compare and present percentages: Preferred percentages sum to 100 *within* categories of the independent variable. For instance, the percentages in Table 6.3 sum to 100 within the categories of type of adoptive placement (within the new home adoption category and within the foster family adoption category). (This tip simply states the guideline in a different way.)

Although contingency tables have facilitated our discussion of relationship, one doesn't need a table to determine whether categorical variables are related. For instance, suppose you read that 33% of male students but only 18% of female students in the human services field pursue careers in administration. This information is sufficient for concluding that gender and career path are associated. Comparison of percentages is the key. When percentages differ, categorical variables are associated. When percentages are the same, they are not.

6.4.5 Additional Points

Tables 6.1, 6.2, and 6.3 present 2 × 2 tables, tables with two rows and two columns. The principle of relationship is the same with larger tables: If column or row percentages are identical, variables are unrelated; if percentages differ, they are related. Suppose a researcher studying voting behavior of college students constructs

TABLE 6.3	INDEPENDENT VARIABLE AS COLUMN VARIABLE		
	New Home Adoption	**Foster Family Adoption**	
Disrupted	20	5	25
	20%	10%	17%
Stable	80	45	125
	80%	90%	83%
	100	50	150
	67%	33%	100%

Note: Data are hypothetical.

a 3 × 4 table with the categories of political party affiliation (three values: Democratic, Republican, Other) composing the rows and those of class level (four values: freshman, sophomore, junior, senior) composing the columns. These variables would be unassociated only if the percentages of students registered as Democratic, Republican, and Other were the same for each class. If percentages differ by even 1% (or formally, by any amount, even 0.0001%) the variables are related.

Let's examine more closely the statement that whenever percentages differ, variables are related. Intuitively, one knows that differences of one or two percentage points are very small. If researchers found that 17% of adoptions into new homes but only 16% of adoptions into prior foster homes ended in disruption, they would obviously not trumpet the finding: "FOSTER FAMILY ADOPTIONS MORE SUCCESSFUL." Instead, they would correctly recognize (through common sense) that the pattern of outcomes was very nearly the same for the two types of adoption. By definition, there is a relationship. Yet it is obviously a weak one. How does one assess *size* or *strength* of relationship? Do the values of the variables "go together" in a strong, compelling pattern, or is the pattern one that can barely be discerned?

6.5   SIZE OF ASSOCIATION

Four terms, all with essentially the same meaning—**size of association, strength of association, size of relationship,** and **strength of relationship**—refer to the degree to which values of variables go together, or more formally, to the degree to which the values observed for one variable vary, differ, or change according to the values of the other. When their values vary together in a compelling pattern, the relationship between two variables may be characterized as "strong" or "large." When the degree to which the variables vary together is barely discernible, the relationship may be characterized as "weak" or "small."

All four just-presented terms are in common use, and hence one may use any of the four.[1] Two other terms that are nearly synonymous with these are *magnitude of association* and *effect size*. Note that when one refers to the *size* of an association, descriptors that convey size (small, medium, large, etc.) are appropriate. When one refers to the *strength* of an association, descriptors that convey strength (weak, moderate, strong, etc.) should be used.

6.6   DIFFERENCE IN PERCENTAGES

6.6.1   Basics and Computation

The most straightforward measure of size of association between categorical variables is the **difference in percentages** (or **percentage difference**). The difference in percentages is not a formal statistical measure but a tool for approximating ("getting a feel for") strength of association. It is a workhorse in the statistical tool set; social scientists examine differences in percentages almost by habit. Interpretation is straightforward: The larger the difference in percentages, the larger (or stronger) the relationship. For now, let's stick to 2 × 2 tables as we examine the difference in percentages. The formula for the difference in percentages is:

$$D\% = \%_1 - \%_2 \tag{6.1}$$

where $D\%$ is the difference in percentages, $\%_1$ is the percentage in the first designated category or group, and $\%_2$ is that in the second.

For a calculation example, we can use the Table 6.2 data that 20% of adoptions in new homes versus 10% of adoptions in prior foster homes end in disruption. $D\%$ (with new homes designated as the first group and foster homes as the second) is:

$$20\% - 10\% = 10\%$$

Formally, $D\%$ may calculate to a negative number. This occurs when the percentage in the first designated category is less than that in the second. For instance, had foster homes been designated as the first group and new homes as the second, $D\%$ would have been:

$$10\% - 20\% = -10\%$$

Negative differences are counterintuitive. From this point forward, this text always designates the category with the larger percentage as the first category and that with the smaller as the second. By so doing, $D\%$ is always a positive number.

The just-presented calculations focus on disruptions. We may equally well focus on stable placements. According to Table 6.2, 90% of prior foster family adoptions versus 80% of new home adoptions resulted in stability. $D\%$ (with foster homes designated as the first category and new homes as the second) is:

$$90\% - 80\% = 10\%$$

Both computations so far involve row percentages. In a 2 × 2 table (assuming that the category with the larger percentage is designated as the first category), the choice of which row percentages to compare does not affect the value of $D\%$. For instance, for Table 6.2 the comparison involving disruption (the first calculation above) and that involving stability (the most recent) both had the same result, $D\% = 10\%$.

The just-completed examples focus on the row percentages in Table 6.2. If we instead focus on the column percentages in Table 6.2, we might compare the percentages for new parents of 80% of disrupted adoptions versus 64% of stable adoptions. This $D\%$ computes to:

$$80\% - 64\% = 16\%$$

Conversely, we might have directed our attention to the fact that 20% of disrupted adoptions versus 36% of stable adoptions were adoptions by prior foster parents. This $D\%$ is:

$$36\% - 20\% = 16\%$$

(Note that in both of these calculations, the category with the larger percentage was treated as the first category and that with the smaller as the second.) Observe that both comparisons of column percentages lead to the same result, 16%. This demonstrates that in a 2×2 table, the choice of which column percentages to compare does not affect $D\%$.

6.6.2   A Disadvantage

A disadvantage of $D\%$ is that its value can differ depending on whether column or row percentages are used. Thus, for Table 6.2, $D\%$ computed to 10% when row percentages were used and to 16% when column percentages were used. How should one deal with this disadvantage?

When variables cannot be classified as independent or dependent, the best course is to calculate $D\%$ for both row and column percentages. Often the difference between results is quite small (less than the 6% difference in Table 6.2) and will have little effect on any conclusions that might be drawn.

When variables can be classified as independent and dependent, $D\%$ should always be calculated in accord with the recommendation for comparing percentages in contingency tables. The recommendation calls for row percentages if the independent variable is the row variable and column percentages if it is the column variable. Calculating $D\%$ in the other direction creates a less useful and sometimes misleading measure of size of association. In the current example (being sure to focus on Table 6.2 rather than 6.3) row percentages are preferred. Thus one could compare the percentage of disruptions in foster family placements (10%) with that in new home placements (20%). The appropriate $D\%$ to calculate, then, is $20\% - 10\% = 10\%$. (One could equally well have compared the percentage of stable placements: $D\% = 90\% - 80\% = 10\%$.)

6.7   QUALITATIVE DESCRIPTORS OF SIZE OF ASSOCIATION

We know that a larger difference in percentage represents a larger relationship than does a smaller difference. But to this point, this text has not provided guidelines for categorizing various differences as indicative of small, medium, or large associations. Should such guidelines be provided? Researchers disagree. Some take the position that qualitative descriptors (such as small, medium, or large) should not be used to describe relationships because they believe that numbers "speak for themselves" and that description in words confuses matters. Others oppose the use of descriptors for a different reason: They contend that what is a small, medium, or large relationship varies greatly by substantive area. For instance, they might consider a 10% difference in percentages to represent a strong relationship in the area of pregnancy prevention but a weak one in treatment of math anxiety.

However, some researchers, including this author, believe that qualitative descriptors are helpful. In this vein, Table 6.4 provides qualitative descriptors for assessing size and strength of association for the difference in percentages. Two cautions regarding this table are in order. First, it interprets size of association within

TABLE 6.4	DESCRIPTORS OF ASSOCIATION FOR DIFFERENCE IN PERCENTAGES	
Difference in Percentages	**Size of Association**	**Strength of Association**
About 7% (or about −7%)	Small	Weak
About 18% (or about −18%)	Medium	Moderate
About 30% (or about −30%)	Large	Strong
About 45% (or about −45%)	Very large	Very strong

Note: If any percentages involved in the comparison are less than 10 or greater than 90, this table should not be used.

the general context of social science rather than in a strict mathematical sense. For instance, a difference of 45 percentage points is very large in the context of relationships commonly encountered in social science. Second, what is "large" or "small" does vary by content area. Therefore, view Table 6.4 as a starting point for assessment. Don't just slap labels (strong, weak, etc.) on relationships. This won't help you to understand data. Instead, use the table to guide your thinking.

6.8 A CAUTION IN INTERPRETING THE DIFFERENCE IN PERCENTAGES

One final caution should be mentioned. The difference in percentages measures size of association effectively only when both compared percentages are within the range of about 10 to 90%. In particular, when one or both percentages are not in this range, the descriptors in Table 6.4 underestimate the size of association and should not be used. Stated differently, the actual size of association is greater than the descriptors convey.

An example can help one make intuitive sense of this. Suppose that 8% of people who take vaccine A develop a serious illness compared with 1% of those who take B. This difference of 7% (8% − 1% = 7%) represents, according to Table 6.4, a weak association. Yet common sense suggests something amiss in this characterization. Those taking vaccine A are *eight times more likely* to develop the illness than are those who take B. Common sense correctly informs us that in this situation a difference of 7% conveys a quite strong relationship between type of vaccine and risk for the illness.

6.9 RATIO OF PERCENTAGES

6.9.1 Basics and Computation

When one or both percentages are less than 10% or greater than 90%, the ratio of percentages is usually a better tool for assessing size of association than is the difference in percentages. The **ratio of percentages** is calculated by dividing the percentage in one group who experience a given outcome by the percentage in a second group who do so:

$$R\% = \frac{\%_1}{\%_2} \tag{6.2}$$

In formula 6.2, $R\%$ is the ratio of percentages, $\%_1$ is the percentage in Group 1 that experiences a given event or outcome, and $\%_2$ is the percentage in Group 2 that does so.

Using formula 6.2, the ratio of percentages in the vaccine example is $8\%/1\% = 8.0$, or, stated differently, 8 to 1.[2] As already stated, those who took vaccine A are eight times more likely to develop the illness than are those who took B. When the percentages in the formula refer to undesirable outcomes—illness, unsuccessful treatment outcome, undesired pregnancy—the ratio of percentages may be interpreted in terms of risk. For instance, in this example, those who took vaccine A are at eight times greater risk for developing the illness than are those who took vaccine B.

Because ratios that are greater than 1.0 are easier for most people to understand than are ratios of less than 1.0, one should usually divide the larger percentage by the smaller percentage. For instance, had we treated those who received vaccine B as Group 1 (the group in the numerator), the ratio of percentages would have computed as $1\%/8\% = 0.125$, or 1 to 8. This ratio is correct but not so easily communicated as the ratio 8.0 (8 to 1).

6.9.2   *Cautions Regarding Use*

Some cautions apply to the ratio of percentages. First, always calculate the ratio using those percentages that are close to 0% rather than those that are close to 100%. For instance, in the current example, we could have calculated the ratio of percentages using the percentages of persons who did *not* develop the illness. Thus, 99% of those who received B and 92% of those who received A did not develop the illness. Treating those who received B as Group 1 (the group in the numerator) yields the ratio $99\%/92\% = 1.08$. Thus, those who received B were 1.08 times more likely to stay well than were those who received A. This statement is correct but highly misleading. This ratio, so close to 1.0, suggests a very small association between type of vaccine and health status. Thus the ratio of percentages assesses size of association effectively only when one uses those percentages that are closest to 0%. All applications of the ratio of percentages from this point forward presume that these percentages are used. A final recommendation is that one should not use $R\%$ if one or more compared percentages are greater than about 30. For a table with qualitative descriptors for $R\%$, see Table 7.2.

6.10   DIFFERENCE IN PERCENTAGES VERSUS RATIO OF PERCENTAGES

On balance, the difference in percentages is used more often than the ratio of percentages. A good recommendation is to use the difference in percentages whenever it may be used appropriately (whenever both percentages are between 10%

and 90%, and to use the ratio of percentages as a backup tool for other situations. In general, $R\%$ is used when percentages are quite close to 0 and $D\%$ is used when this is not the case.

So far, two measures of size of association have been provided. Taken as a pair, these allow one to assess strength of association in most situations involving 2×2 tables. Yet it would be handy to have a single "best measure" that could be applied across almost all situations. The odds ratio is that measure and is presented in the next chapter.

6.11 CHAPTER SUMMARY

Two variables are related when the values observed for one variable vary, differ, or change according to those of the other. Association and relationship are synonymous terms. Relationship between variables demonstrates only a pattern; typically some cases are exceptions to the pattern. Some relationships are causal. Others are not.

In contingency table analysis, cell percentages rather than cell frequencies are the key to assessing the presence or absence of relationship. In general, one should compare row percentages when the independent variable is the row variable and column percentages when it is the column variable.

Variables are unrelated when the row percentages are the same for each row or the column percentages are the same for each column. (Whenever one set of percentages is the same, so necessarily is the other.) Variables are related when the row percentages differ between rows, or the column percentages differ between columns. (Whenever one set differs, so does the other.) Though there is no firm convention, the independent variable is typically the column variable. Formally, variables are associated even when percentages differ by an extremely small amount.

Size of association refers to the degree to which the values for one variable vary, differ, or change according to those of the other. When values vary together in a compelling pattern, the relationship may be characterized as "strong" or "large." Terms synonymous with size of association are strength of association, size of relationship, and strength of relationship.

The most straightforward measure of size of association between categorical variables is the difference in percentages, $D\%$. To compute $D\%$, subtract the percentage for a second group or category from that for a first: $D\% = \%_1 - \%_2$ (formula 6.1).

A disadvantage of $D\%$ is that its value usually differs according to whether row or column percentages are used. $D\%$ should be calculated in accord with the recommendation for comparing and presenting percentages.

Qualitative descriptors provide a starting point for assessing size of association. According to Table 6.4, a difference of about 7% indicates a small association, whereas one of about 30% indicates a large one. The descriptors in Table 6.4 should be used only when both compared percentages are between about 10 and 90%.

To calculate the ratio of percentages ($R\%$) divide the percentage in one group by that in the other: $R\% = \%_1/\%_2$ (formula 6.2). Percentages closer to 0% rather than to 100% should always be used. $R\%$ should not be used when either percentage exceeds about 30%.

PROBLEMS AND QUESTIONS

Section 6.2

1. Two variables are _____ when the values observed for one variable vary, differ, or change according to the values of the other.
2. For each of the following examples, mark R if the variables are related/associated, U if they are unrelated/unassociated, or I if the given information is insufficient for making a decision.
   a. 70% of women and 40% of men drink diet soft drinks.
   b. 80% of women and 60% of men choose the direct (clinical) practice track for the second year of their social work master's degree.
   c. The mean batting average for baseball players in the American League is .287 whereas that in the National League is .272 (hypothetical data).
   d. The mean grade point average (GPA) for men is 3.22. The mean GPA for women is 3.22.
   e. The greater the number of compliments given, the greater the number of chores completed.
   f. 80% of social work students choose direct practice and 20% choose community practice.
   g. In a sample of left-handed college students from the southern United States, 38% prefer burgers and 62% prefer salads.
   h. The greater the number of visits by family members, the lower the rate of depression among nursing home clients.
   i. 15% of women in Program 1 for pregnancy prevention become pregnant within one year. 15% in Program 2 become pregnant within one year.
   j. The longer you study, the sleepier you get.

3. (T or F) When two variables are independent, they are unassociated.

Section 6.3

4. (T or F) If at least one case runs counter to the overall pattern, two variables are unassociated.
5. (T or F) When two variables are related, one may safely conclude that one variable causes (influences) the other.

Section 6.4

The next series of questions (as well as several later questions) refer to Table 6PQ.1, a contingency table.
6. The row variable is _____.
7. The column variable is _____.
8. The independent variable is _____.
9. The total number of cases is _____.
10. The (total) number in Program 1 is _____.
11. The (total) number readmitted is _____.
12. The boxes of the table are termed _____.
13. The areas to the right of and below the cells of the table are known as the _____.
14. The number of clients in Program 2 who were readmitted is _____.
15. (T or F) The cells of the table present column percentages.
16. The percentage of clients in Program 2 who were readmitted is _____.

TABLE 6.PQ.1   **READMISSION TO PSYCHIATRIC HOSPITAL BY PROGRAM**

	Mental Health Program 1	Mental Health Program 2	
Readmitted to hospital	40 / 40%	20 / 33%	60 / 37.5%
Not readmitted to hospital	60 / 60%	40 / 67%	100 / 62.5%
	100 / 67%	60 / 33%	160 / 100%

17. The percentage of clients in Program 1 who were readmitted is _____.
18. (T or F) Clients in Programs 1 and 2 are equally likely to be readmitted.
19. (T or F) Clients in Program 1 are more likely to be readmitted than those in Program 2.
20. (T or F) The column percentages differ.
21. (T or F) The variables are unrelated.
22. (T or F) Table 6PQ.1 follows the text's suggestion to make the independent variable the column variable and the dependent variable the row variable.
23. Describe the relationship in the table in several different ways.
24. (T or F) The column percentages sum to 100 within categories of the independent variable.
25. (T or F) Had row rather than column percentages been calculated, the variables might not have been associated.
26. (T or F) When the independent variable is the column variable, the text recommends comparing row (rather than column) percentages.
27. (T or F) Whenever row percentages differ in a contingency table, so do column percentages.

Section 6.5

28. Define size/strength of relationship/association in your own words.

Section 6.6

29. 27% of Republicans and 52% of Democrats vote for Legislation Z. What is the difference in percentages? (Calculate so that $D\%$ computes to a positive percentage.)
30. (T or F) Use of row versus column percentages never affects the value of $D\%$.
31. (T or F) In calculating $D\%$, one should use the percentages that sum to 100 within categories of the independent variable rather than within categories of the dependent variable.
32. What is the value of $D\%$ in Table 6PQ.1? (Calculate so that $D\%$ computes to a positive percentage.)
33. (T or F) In general, the larger $D\%$, the larger the relationship between two variables.
34. Twenty-four months after the beginning of services designed to reduce parent-child conflict, 86% of youth who were served in their own home versus 55% of those served in out-of-home placement services reside in their own homes. What is $D\%$? (Calculate so that $D\%$ computes to a positive percentage.)

Section 6.7

35. (T or F) All researchers concur that qualitative (nonmathematical) description of size of association is an appropriate undertaking.
36. (T or F) The qualitative descriptors of size/strength of association in Table 6.4 interpret size of association within the context of social science rather than in a strict mathematical sense.
37. (T or F) According to the text, the qualitative descriptors in Table 6.4 do not need to be adjusted to take into account the particular content or substantive area.
38. Most would characterize the size/strength of association in Table 6PQ.1 as . . .
    a. Small/weak
    b. Medium/moderate
    c. Large/strong
    d. Very large/very strong
39. (T or F) A difference in percentages of 50% represents a fairly weak (to moderate) association.

Section 6.8

40. (T or F) In general, the difference in percentages is not a preferred tool when both percentages are very close to 0 or to 100.

Section 6.9

41. 12% in Program A versus 3% in Program B experience an unsuccessful treatment outcome. What is the ratio of percentages? (Presume that Program A is designated as the first group.)
42. 30% of boys versus 12% of girls engage in aggressive behavior during recess according to a behavioral observation tool. What is $R\%$? (Consider boys to be designated as the first group.)
43. (T or F) The ratio of percentages is typically the preferred measure of size of association where all percentages are very close to 50%.
44. Is the ratio of percentages preferred to the difference in percentages for assessing the association in Table 6PQ.1? Why or why not?

45. 96% in Program A and 92% in Program B experience a successful outcome. Is dividing 96% by 92% the best way to calculate $R\%$? Why or why not?

46. For the prior question, what is the ratio of percentages for the percentage of unsuccessful outcomes? (Assume that all outcomes that were not successful were unsuccessful.) Carry out your computation so that $R\%$ will be greater than 1.0.

47. (T or F) The ratio calculated in question 46 is preferred to that suggested in question 45.

 # COMPUTER EXERCISES

For general instructions on computer exercises, see the note in Chapter 2.

1. Create a contingency table where FOSTER (adoption by foster parents, the independent variable) is the column variable and IMPACTD (dichotomous variable measuring impact of adoption) is the row variable. Make sure that the table has column percentages. Use the information in the table to do a hand calculation of $D\%$. (SPSS does not calculate $D\%$ because it is largely an informal measure.) Comment on the size of the association. [In SPSS, *Analyze > Descriptive Statistics > Crosstabs*, click over FOSTER to "Column(s)" and IMPACTD to "Row(s)," *Cells*, click box next to "Column," *Continue, OK.*]

    Check your answer: $D\%$ for the FOSTER/IMPACTD example computes to 51.1% − 43.3% = 7.8%, indicative of a weak association.

2. Create a contingency table with the column variable GENDER (child's gender) and the row variable BEHCLIN (behavior problem score sufficiently severe to be regarded as "clinical"). The table should have column percentages. Calculate and interpret $D\%$. [In SPSS, *Analyze > Descriptive Statistics > Crosstabs* (click back unwanted variables), click over GENDER to "Column(s)" and BEHCLIN to "Row(s)," *Cells,* click box next to "Column" (if it is not already checked), *Continue, OK.*]

    Check your answers: The difference in percentages in the GENDER/BEHCLIN example computes to less than 1%: 41.2% − 40.3% = 0.9%. The association between gender and a behavior score in the clinical range is of trivial magnitude. Note that the precise cutoff score used to classify a score as in the clinical range differed for children in different age and gender groups.

3. Develop a contingency table of GENDER (column variable) by HANDICAP (row variable; does child have a handicap?). Also, find the difference in percentages and interpet it. (Use column percentages.)

    Check your answer: $D\% = 21.9\% - 18.6\% = 3.3\%$. The association between GENDER and HANDICAP is extremely weak, essentially of trivial magnitude.

NOTES

1. Some researchers do not view size of association and strength of association as synonymous terms. For instance, Toothaker and Miller (1996, p. 175) and many others define strength of association as the percentage of explained variance (see also Chapter 8, Section 8.8, in this text).

2. Instead of the ratio of percentages, one could equally well calculate a ratio of proportions by dividing the proportion in Group 1 by the proportion in Group 2. This ratio would always be the same as the ratio of percentages. For instance, regarding the vaccine example: .8/1 = 8.0, or 8 to 1. Another name for this statistic is the *rate ratio* (Fleiss, 1994, p. 247; see this source for discussion of pros and cons).

The Odds Ratio and Other Measures for Nominal-Level Variables

7.1 Chapter Overview

The preferred measure of size of association between dichotomous variables is the *odds ratio*, our first topic in this chapter. This discussion introduces *odds*, presents formulas for odds and the odds ratio, and interprets size of association. We move on to variables with more than two categories and get an overview of measures and methods for assessing association in those situations. Finally, we discuss *directional* versus *nondirectional relationship*.

7.2 Odds Ratio: Basics and Formula

The odds ratio is the preferred measure for assessing size of association between variables with two categories, that is, between dichotomous variables. As its name suggests, an **odds ratio** is a ratio of odds. The **odds** of an event are calculated by dividing the number that experience the event by the number that do not:

$$\text{Odds} = \frac{\text{number that experience event}}{\text{number that do not experience it}} = \frac{n_e}{n_{ne}} \tag{7.1}$$

An equally good alternative formula is:

$$\text{Odds} = \frac{\text{proportion that experience event}}{\text{proportion that do not experience event}} = \frac{p_e}{p_{ne}} \tag{7.2}$$

The contingency table in Table 7.1 presents support for a proposed child welfare services bill by political party affiliation of state legislators. We will designate supporting the legislation as the "event." Using formula 7.1, we can calculate the odds that a Democratic legislator will support the legislation: 30 (number supporting) divided by 20 (number against), or 30/20, which reduces to 3/2. Odds are commonly expressed using the word *to*. Thus the odds are "3 to 2." Carrying out the division, we see that 3/2 = 1.5. The odds may also be expressed as 1.5 or as 1.5 to

115

TABLE 7.1	CHILD WELFARE SUPPORT BY POLITICAL PARTY AFFILIATION		
	Democratic	**Republican**	
Supports	30 60%	15 43%	45 53%
Does not support	20 40%	20 57%	40 47%
	50 59%	35 41%	85 100%

Note: Data are hypothetical.

1. These odds inform us that Democratic senators are 1.5 times more likely to support the bill than to be against it.

Odds may be calculated with the alternative outcome designated as the event. For instance, in our example, the odds that a Democratic legislator will be against the bill are 20/30 = 2/3, or 2 to 3, or 0.67. Interpreting odds that are less than 1.00 can be tricky. In the current example, one could say, "Democrats are two-thirds as likely to reject the bill as to support it" or "Democrats are 0.67 times as likely to reject the bill as to support it."

Odds may vary from 0.00 to positive infinity. (There is no such thing as "negative" odds, that is, of odds less than 0.00.) When odds are greater than 1.00, the odds that the event will occur are greater than those that it will not. When odds are less than 1.00, the odds that the event will occur are less than those that it will not. When odds equal precisely 1.00, the odds that the event will occur and those that it will not are equal.

Our primary interest is not in the odds for each group but rather in the odds ratio. To calculate the odds ratio we need to establish odds for both Democrats and Republicans. The odds that a Republican will support the legislation are 15/20 = 3/4 = 3 to 4 = 0.75. As its name indicates, the odds ratio is a ratio of odds. Its formula is:

$$OR = \frac{\text{odds for first group}}{\text{odds for second group}} = \frac{\text{odds}_1}{\text{odds}_2} \tag{7.3}$$

In our example, Democrats are the first group and Republicans the second. Their respective odds of supporting the legislation are 1.5 and 0.75. The odds ratio, then, is 1.5/0.75 = 2.0, or 2 to 1. This odds ratio conveys that the odds that a Democrat will support the child welfare bill are twice the odds that a Republican will do so. Our designation of Democratic as the first group was arbitrary. Instead, we might have made Republican the first group. In this case, the odds ratio computes to 0.75/1.5 = 0.50, or 1 to 2. Hence, the odds that a Republican will support the legislation are one-half (0.5) those for a Democrat. Odds ratios may be calculated making direct use of the numbers in the cells in the table:

$$\frac{30}{20} \div \frac{15}{20} = \frac{30}{20} \times \frac{20}{15} = \frac{600}{300} = 2.00$$

In this calculation, 30/20 are the odds that Democrats will support the bill and 15/20 are the odds that Republicans will do so.[1]

Note that the odds ratios differed depending on whether Democratic or Republican was designated as the first group. The two odds ratios, 2.0 and 0.5, are reciprocals. Numbers are reciprocals when multiplication of one by the other results in 1.0. For instance: $2.0 \times 0.5 = 1.0$. In a 2×2 table, the odds ratio obtained with one group designated as the first group is always the reciprocal of that obtained with the other so designated. Hence, to find out what an odds ratio would have been had the groups been designated differently, calculate a reciprocal. To find a number's reciprocal, divide 1.00 by that number. For instance, if an odds ratio is 5.0 with Group A designated as the first group, it will be 0.20 with Group B so designated: $1.00 \div 5 = 0.20$. To give one more example, suppose that the odds that people in Group Q will experience Event X are 0.4 times those that people in Group R will. What is the odds ratio with Group R designated as the first group? To find this out, divide 1.00 by the odds ratio: $1 \div 0.40 = 2.5$. Hence, the odds that people in R will experience Event X are 2.5 times higher than those that people in Q will.

7.3 INTERPRETATION OF THE ODDS RATIO

7.3.1 Basics

Just as odds may vary from 0.00 to positive infinity, so may the odds ratio. An odds ratio of 1.00 conveys independence, the lack of association between two variables. When an odds ratio is greater than 1.00, the odds of the event are greater for the first group than for the second. When it is less than 1.00, the odds are lower for the first group than for the second.

As already mentioned, students (and professors) sometimes have difficulty interpreting odds ratios that are less than 1.00. Thus, when it is convenient to do so, one should designate groups so that the odds ratio computes to a number greater than 1.00. This is accomplished by designating the group with the larger odds as the first group (the numerator) and that with the smaller odds as the second (the denominator).

Odds ratios that are reciprocals convey the same size of association. For instance, an odds ratio of 2.0 and one of 0.50 convey the same size of association. Some other pairs of odds ratios that convey the same size of association are 10.00 and 0.10, 3.00 and 0.33, 1.33 and 0.75, and 6.0 and 0.167.

7.3.2 Predicting Likelihood and Risk

Suppose that 50% of those in Program A for school dropout prevention and 30% of those in Program B drop out. With A designated as the first group, the odds ratio for dropping out is $(50/50) / (30/70) = 2.33$.[2] Hence, the odds that those in A will drop out are 2.33 times greater than are the odds for those in B.

Many researchers interpret odds using the word *likely*. They would say that those in A are 2.33 times more likely to drop out than are those in B.[3] Similarly, odds ratios are often interpreted using the notion of risk, so one could say, "The risk of dropout is 2.33 times greater for those in A than for those in B."

The event predicted by the odds ratio may be either a "negative" (as in the most recent example, dropout) or a "positive" (as in the prior example, support for child welfare legislation, a positive in the opinion of most human services professionals). One can predict a negative event rather than a positive simply by changing the category that is designated as the "event" in formulas 7.1 and 7.2. For instance, rather than having predicted dropout, we could have focused instead on staying in school.

Changing the category designated as the event changes the odds ratio to its reciprocal, just as changing the group designated as the first group did. For instance, the odds ratio for the event of dropout (with Program A designated as the first group) calculated to 2.33. The odds ratio for the event of staying in school (with A still designated as the first group) is (50/50)/(70/30) = 0.43. These two odds ratios are reciprocals: 0.43 × 2.33 = 1.00. Changing the category that is defined as the event does not genuinely alter the size of the odds ratio but instead is a shift in emphasis, a shift in whether the positive or the negative is emphasized. It is often good strategy to focus on the positive. For instance, one could state: "Those in Program B were 2.33 times more likely to stay in school than were those in A." This statement (1) uses an odds ratio larger than 1.00 and thus facilitates interpretation, and (2) emphasizes the positive (given the choice, most human services professionals prefer this emphasis).

7.4 QUALITATIVE DESCRIPTORS FOR THE ODDS RATIO

Table 6.4 presents descriptors that characterize values of the difference in percentages as small, medium, large, or very large. Table 7.2 does the same for the odds ratio. Using these descriptors, the recently discussed odds ratio of 2.33 conveys an association of medium size. Hence, one could say that there is a moderate association between the use of Program A versus B and whether a youth remains in or drops out of school.

TABLE 7.2 DESCRIPTORS OF ASSOCIATION FOR THE ODDS RATIO		
Odds Ratio	**Size of Association**	**Strength of Association**
1.5 to 1 = 1.5 (or 1 to 1.5 = 0.67)	Small	Weak
2.5 to 1 = 2.5 (or 1 to 2.5 = 0.40)	Medium	Moderate
4 to 1 = 4 (or 1 to 4 = 0.25)	Large	Strong
10 to 1 = 10 (or 1 to 10 = 0.10)	Very large	Very strong

Note: The descriptors are appropriate for the odds ratio when both compared percentages are between 1 and 99. They are appropriate for the ratio of percentages when both percentages are less than about 30.

Chapter 6 recommends not using the difference in percentages when either percentage is less than 10% or greater than 90%, and not using the ratio of percentages when either percentage is greater than 30%. The great advantage of the odds ratio is that it may be used to assess the size of almost any relationship between dichotomous variables. The only situation in which one should hesitate to apply the descriptors in Table 7.2 is when the percentage for one or both of the compared variables is less than 1% or greater than 99%. For other advantages of the odds ratio see Fleiss (1994, pp. 251–258).

7.5 MEASURES FOR NOMINAL-LEVEL VARIABLES IN TABLES LARGER THAN 2 × 2

7.5.1 Computing an Average Difference in Percentages

So far we have primarily studied relationship in 2 × 2 contingency tables, that is, between dichotomous variables. How does one assess relationship in larger tables?

To get a feel for relationship in larger tables, let's use Table 7.3, a 2 × 3 table that presents data from the adoption study. The independent variable (the column variable) is termed family ethnicity and (as presented previously in Chapter 2, Section 2.6) consists of three groups of adoptive families: (1) minority, inracial, that is, minority (nonwhite) parents who adopt a child of the same race as at least one parent; (2) white, inracial: white parents who adopt a white child; and (3) transracial: white parents who adopt a minority child. The dependent variable is termed child behavior problems and is the row variable. All children who scored higher than a "cutting-point" score on a behavior checklist (Achenbach, 1991) are considered to have serious behavior problems, whereas children below this point are considered not to have such problems. The percentages in the contingency table are column percentages and sum to 100 within categories of the independent variable (family ethnicity). They convey the percentage of children with and without serious behavior problems.

A quick overview of percentages reveals that these do indeed differ and that the variables are, therefore, associated. The percentage of children with behavior problems is highest in the white, inracial group, "in the middle" in the transracial group, and lowest in the minority, inracial group. Recall that there are eight dif-

TABLE 7.3 TYPE OF ADOPTION BY SEVERITY OF BEHAVIORAL PROBLEMS

	Minority, Inracial	White, Inracial	Transracial
Child has serious behavior problems	59 29.4%	194 46.6%	20 37.0%
Child does not have serious behavior problems	142 70.6%	222 53.4%	34 63.0%

ferent ways to describe association in a 2×2 table, as presented in Chapter 6, Section 6.4.3. Each description, however, focuses on only a single comparison.

With a table larger than 2×2, a single comparison cannot describe relationship adequately. For instance, for Table 7.3, we need three comparisons to fully describe the association of family ethnicity to serious behavior problems: (1) the minority, inracial group versus the white, inracial group, (2) the minority, inracial group versus the transracial group, and (3) the white, inracial group versus the transracial group. One may use the qualitative descriptors to help interpret comparisons. For instance, comparing minority, inracial adoptions with white, inracial adoptions, the difference in percentages with respect to serious behavior problems is $46.6\% - 29.4\% = 17.2\%$. The table of descriptors for the difference in percentages (Table 6.4) characterizes such a difference as "medium." One should not, based on this comparison, conclude that the overall relationship between family ethnicity and behavior problems is of medium size, because the comparison represents only one of three that are possible. For the minority, inracial versus transracial comparison, $D\% = 37.0\% - 29.4\% = 7.6\%$. For the white, inracial versus transracial comparison: $D\% = 46.6\% - 37.0\% = 9.6\%$. Using the qualitative descriptors, each of the just-calculated differences would be characterized as "small."

In sum, assessment of relationship in tables larger than 2×2 requires more than one comparison. As all three measures presented to this point (the $D\%$, the $R\%$, the odds ratio) assess a single comparison, none of these can convey the overall size relationship for a table larger than 2×2.

One way to get a feel for the size of association in tables larger than 2×2 is to compute average differences between categories. For instance, an informal measure that we may term the "average difference in percentages" between categories has appeal. For the three comparisons in Table 7.3, the differences in percentages were 17.2%, 7.6%, and 9.6%. The average difference for Table 7.3 thus computes to 11.5%: $(17.2\% + 7.6\% + 9.6\%)/3 = 11.5\%$.[4] Using the qualitative descriptors for the $D\%$, the overall size of association is intermediate between medium and small.

The greatest problem with such an "average" difference measure is that the number of possible comparisons goes up rapidly as table size increases. For instance, a 4×4 table has 24 possible comparisons. Furthermore, such a measure is highly informal. It is not in common usage and is not computed by statistical programs.

On the other hand, the advantage of our average difference in percentages measure is that the process of calculating it helps convey how researchers begin to assess association in larger tables. Many peruse and "sift" through various percentages in the table. In particular, as we did for Table 7.3, they focus on the differences in percentages for the different groups (categories) that compose the table. When these differences tend to be small, they come to the informal conclusion that the overall relationship is a weak or small one. Conversely, predominantly large differences convey a large relationship.

7.5.2   Collapsing Categories

Before we examine formal measures of association for large tables, note that researchers sometimes "collapse" categories to simplify larger tables. When they **collapse** two (or more) categories, they combine them into one. The combined categories ordinarily have similar values. For instance, presume that the response categories for a question are "excellent," "good," "fair," "poor," and "very poor." To simplify the table, the "poor" and "very poor" categories could be combined, or collapsed, into a single one that would perhaps be titled "poor or very poor." Categories are often collapsed when the frequency of responses in one or both categories is very low. For instance, if only two respondents responded "very poor," this would likely lead the researcher to combine (collapse) categories.

7.5.3 *Measures of Association*

Although one may compute the informal measure of average difference in percentages, a measure that would convey the overall size of association in a larger table is preferred. The best overall measure of size of association for variables at the nominal level of measurement when one or both variables have more than two categories is **Cramer's V** (or simply **V**). V varies from 0.00, indicating no association between variables, to 1.00, indicating the strongest possible association. For a formula and further discussion, see Blalock (1979, pp. 305–306, 315) or Norusis (1999, pp. 353–354).

A close cousin to Cramer's V is **phi** (pronounced with a long *i* as in "five"). Phi and Cramer's V compute to the same value in all tables where at least one variable has two categories. In all such tables, phi has a maximum possible value of 1.00 and a minimum of 0.00. In other tables, its maximum shifts according to the number of rows and columns, so it should not be used. Phi is an excellent alternative to the odds ratio in 2 × 2 tables, and this is its most frequent use. (For 2 × 2 tables, it is customary to report phi rather than Cramer's V.)

For Table 7.3, both phi and Cramer's V compute to .16. The qualitative descriptors in Table 8.1, designed for the correlation coefficient, can provide some guidance in interpreting size of association for phi and Cramer's V. The value .16 is intermediate between "small" and "medium," so we would interpret the size of association between family ethnicity and behavioral problems accordingly.[5] Some other measures of association used in larger tables include lambda and the uncertainty coefficient. See Blalock (1979, pp. 279–334) or Norusis (1999, pp. 349–368) for discussion of these and related measures.

7.6 USE OF JUST-PRESENTED MEASURES WITH ORDINAL-LEVEL VARIABLES

The prior section recommended Cramer's V as the preferred measure of size of association when one or both nominal-level variables have more than two categories, that is, in contingency tables that are larger than 2 × 2. Consider now relationships between ordinal-level variables. Table 7.4 presents two examples involving the variables age group and level of motivation of graduate students. In some situations, Cramer's V and the other measures mentioned in the prior section are well suited for assessing the size of relationship between ordinal variables.

TABLE 7.4   EXAMPLES: ASSOCIATION BETWEEN ORDINAL-LEVEL VARIABLES

Age of Graduate Student	LEVEL OF MOTIVATION			
	Highly (%)	Somewhat (%)	Not Very (%)	Unmotivated (%)
Example 1				
35 and older	50	25	15	10
26 to 34	40	20	20	20
25 and younger	30	20	25	25
Example 2				
35 and older	50	25	15	10
26 to 34	30	20	25	25
25 and younger	50	20	25	5

In other situations, they are less so. This section describes their suitability by introducing the concept of direction of relationship. A relationship between two variables has **direction** if, as one variable increases or decreases, the other also increases or decreases. Such a relationship is termed a **directional relationship (directional association).**

With one exception, for variables to be involved in directional relationships they must be measured at the ordinal level or higher. For instance, one cannot order values of eye color (blue, brown, green, etc.), and thus eye color (a nominal-level variable) cannot take on directional relationships with other variables. The exception involves dichotomous variables, those with two categories. These are typically classified at the nominal level. Section 8.13 in Chapter 8 demonstrates that the values of such variables may be ordered, even if arbitrarily, so they may be involved in directional relationships. The special case of dichotomous variables is not key to the discussion here.

The guideline for assessing the presence or absence of relationship between ordinal-level variables is the same as for nominal-level variables: If percentages (row or column percentages) are the same, there is no relationship; if percentages differ, there is. The percentages in Table 7.4 sum to 100 across the rows, and thus are row percentages. In each example in Table 7.4, the row percentages differ, so age group and level of motivation are related.

Example 1 illustrates a directional relationship. The relationship is directional because, as age of students increases, so also does level of motivation. To discern this pattern, examine the percentages. For instance, the percentage of "highly motivated" students increases as age increases from "25 and younger" (30% are highly motivated), to "26 to 34" (40%), to "35 and older" (50%). Similarly, as age increases, the percentage "unmotivated" declines from 25% to 20% to 10%. Direction may be characterized as positive or negative. In a **positive relationship (positive association),** both variables change in the *same* direction—as one increases, so does the other (which is the same as saying that as one decreases, so does the other). In a **negative relationship (negative association),** the variables change in *opposite* directions—as one increases, the other decreases (or, to be redundant, as one decreases, the other increases). Both variables in Example 1 in Table 7.4 change in the same direction, demonstrating a positive relationship.

Example 2 demonstrates a **nondirectional relationship (nondirectional association).** Although percentages differ (therefore the variables are related), there is no directional pattern. For instance, the middle-aged group (26 to 34) is less motivated than both those who are older and those who are younger.

Cramer's V and measures designed for nominal-level data do not assess size of directional relationship. Instead they assess the overall size of relationship without regard to direction. (Stated differently, they assess the size of nondirectional association.) Another set of measures, to be presented in Chapter 9, are specifically designed to assess size of directional association between ordinal-level variables. But even when a relationship has direction, Cramer's V and other measures designed for nominal-level data may be used to provide some sense of overall size of association. However, as stated above, they do not effectively assess the size of directional relationship.[6]

7.7 CHAPTER SUMMARY

When both variables are dichotomous, the odds ratio is the preferred measure of size of association. As its name suggests, an odds ratio is a ratio of odds. Odds may be defined as the number that experience an event divided by the number that do not. The formula (7.3) for the odds ratio is $OR = \text{odds}_1/\text{odds}_2$.

The odds ratio may vary from 0.00 to positive infinity. Odds ratios greater than 1.00 indicate that the odds for an event are greater for the first designated group than for the second. Odds ratios less than 1.00 convey lower odds for the first group than for the second. Most find it easier to understand ratios greater than 1.00, in which the larger odds are divided by the smaller rather than vice versa. To find the odds ratio that would have resulted if the other category had been designated as the first category, compute a reciprocal.

Table 7.2 presents qualitative descriptors for the odds ratio. An odds ratio of about 1.5 (or 0.67) is characterized as a small (weak) association, whereas one of about 4.0 (or 0.25) is characterized as large (strong). Assuming that both variables are dichotomous, the odds ratio is an effective measure of size of association for almost all situations. In contrast, the difference in percentages and the ratio of percentages should be used only when particular conditions are met.

For tables larger than 2×2, Cramer's V is typically the preferred measure of size of association. It may vary from 0.00 (no association) to 1.00 (largest possible association). Phi is closely related to Cramer's V and is a good alternative to the odds ratio for 2×2 tables.

A relationship between two variables has direction if, as one variable increases or decreases, the other also increases or decreases. Direction of relationship may be either positive (both variables change in the same direction) or negative (the variables change in opposite directions). Cramer's V and other measures presented in this chapter assess the overall size of (nondirectional) relationship and are not appropriate measures of directional relationship.

PROBLEMS AND QUESTIONS

Section 7.2

The next three questions use this data: Nine children (75% of the total) served by a child welfare program are reunited with their families and three (25%) are not.

1. What are the odds of being reunited?
2. What are the odds of not being reunited?
3. What is the odds ratio? (This is a trick question; what makes it one?)
4. Six professors at a human services education program (50% of the total) indicate a preference for behavioral theory and six indicate a preference for psychosocial theory. What are the odds that a professor favors behavioral theory?
5. The highest possible value that odds can attain is _____ _____.
6. The lowest possible value that odds can attain is _____.

The next several questions pertain to this data. 20 (25%) of 80 clients classified as having "low skills" versus 50 (62.5%) of 80 classified as having "high skills" obtain employment within six months of beginning to receive welfare assistance.

7. Among those with low skills, what are the odds of obtaining employment?
8. Among those with high skills, what are the odds of obtaining employment?
9. What is the odds ratio calculated so that those with high skills compose the first group? (Consider obtaining employment to be the event of interest.)
10. How many times greater are the odds that clients with high skills will find work than are those odds for clients with low skills?
11. In your own words, interpret the just-calculated odds ratio using the word *likely*.
12. What is the odds ratio calculated so that those with low skills compose the first category? (Consider obtaining employment to be the event of interest.)
13. In your own words, interpret the just-calculated odds ratio using the word *likely*.

14. What mathematical relationship do the two just-calculated odds ratios (5.0 and 0.2) have?
15. 15 of 25 students in a social work class versus 10 of 30 students in a business class support legislation to provide increased medical services to those who are poor. What is the odds ratio? (Consider social work students to be the first group. Consider supporting the legislation as the event of interest.)
16. Under Benefits Plan A, 30% of clients are eligible for a given benefit. Under Benefits Plan B, 60% of clients are eligible. What is the odds ratio? (Consider being eligible to be the event of interest. Consider Plan A to be the first designated group.)
17. Using the same facts as in the prior question but with Plan B considered to be the first designated group, what is the odds ratio?

Section 7.3

18. For each of the following odds ratios, find the odds ratio that would have resulted if the other group had been designated as the first group. (Stated differently, find the reciprocal of each number.)
    a. 4
    b. 0.25
    c. 8
    d. 0.125
19. Which odds ratio conveys the stronger strength of association between variables, 0.5 or 2.0?
20. (T or F) Odds ratios that are reciprocals convey the same size of association.
21. A research study reports an odds ratio of −1.75. What should you conclude?
22. (T or F) Odds ratios are always used to predict the odds of some positive (beneficial) event rather than those of a negative event.
23. (T or F) The odds ratio may be used appropriately whenever both compared percentages are between about 1% and 99%.

Section 7.4

24. Characterize the approximate size/strength of association conveyed by each of the following odds ratios.
    a. 12
    b. 0.20

c. 5

d. 0.70

e. 0.08

f. 2.5

25. (T or F) When one or both percentages in a contingency table are very close to 50%, Table 7.2 provides appropriate descriptors of size of association for the ratio of percentages.

26. In which of the following situations may the descriptors for the odds ratio be applied appropriately?

    a. 8% in Group A experience event versus 4% in Group B

    b. 80% in Group A experience event versus 40% in Group B

    c. 80% in Group A experience event versus 4% in Group B

    d. They may be appropriately applied in all of the above

Section 7.5

27. (T or F) When a contingency table is larger than 2 × 2, the relationship between the variables can be described by a single difference in percentages.

28. (T or F) What the text terms the "average difference in percentages" for a table larger than 2 × 2 is an informal rather than formal statistical procedure.

29. When one combines two or more categories of a variable in a contingency table into one category, the initial categories are said to have been _____.

30. (T or F) When the frequency in a given category is extremely low (say 1 or 2 or 3), this ar-gues *against* combining (collapsing) that category with another category.

31. (T or F) The highest possible value that Cramer's V can attain is 1.0.

32. (T or F) When both variables in a contingency table are dichotomous, phi provides an alternative to the odds ratio for measuring size of association.

Section 7.6

33. If, as one variable increases or decreases, the other also increases or decreases, the relationship between those variables has _____.

In responding to the next several questions, consider (contingency) Table 7PQ.1.

34. What is the level of measurement for both variables?

35. Are the variables associated or independent?

36. Given the level of measurement, is it possible for these variables to have a directional association?

37. Is the association directional or nondirectional?

38. Presume that the categories are coded as indicated in the table [i.e., with 1s, 2s, and 3s so that (a) "against" is a low score and "support" is high and (b) "conservative" is low and "liberal" is high]. With the variables coded this way, is the direction of association positive or negative?

39. (T or F) Cramer's V is the preferred measure of the size of directional association between categorical variables.

40. (T or F) A nominal-level variable with three or more categories can be involved in a directional relationship.

TABLE 7PQ.1	POSITION ON LEGISLATION BY POLITICAL SELF-CHARACTERIZATION		
	POLITICAL SELF-CHARACTERIZATION		
Position on Legislation Q	**Conservative (1) (%)**	**Moderate (2) (%)**	**Liberal (3) (%)**
Against (1)	70	30	10
Neutral (2)	20	40	20
Support (3)	10	30	70

🖥 COMPUTER EXERCISES

For general instructions on computer exercises, see the note in Chapter 2.

1. Calculate and interpret the odds ratio for the impact of adoption (IMPACTD) being evaluated as "very positive" for children adopted into their prior foster home (the designated "first" group) and into a nonfoster home (FOSTER). [In SPSS, *Analyze > Descriptive Statistics > Crosstabs,* click back any unwanted variables, click over FOSTER to "Column(s)" and IMPACTD to "Row(s)," *Cells,* click the box next to "Column(s)" if it is not already checked, *Statistics,* click box next to "Risk," *Continue, OK.*]

   Check your answers: For the FOSTER/IMPACTD odds ratio example, in the "Risk Estimate" table the odds ratio is given in the first row of results and is 1.365. This ratio conveys a weak relationship between type of placement and adoption impact.

   Note: When computing an odds ratio using SPSS, you should verify that the reported odds ratio rather than its reciprocal is the one that you want. In this example, the desired odds ratio must be greater than 1.00, because the percentage of "very positive" impacts (the event) is higher in foster parent adoptions (the designated first group) than in nonfoster adoptions. (In calculating an odds ratio, SPSS regards the designated first group to be the group with the lower numeric code—in this example, nonfoster adoptions are the first group because they are coded as 0 and foster adoptions are coded as 1. Similarly, it regards the designated event to be the event with the lower numeric code—in this example, not being evaluated "very positive" is that event because it is coded as 0 and "very positive" is coded as 1. Hence, in this example SPSS actually calculates the odds ratio that a nonfoster adoption will have an impact other than "very positive." Because both the group and the event are the "opposite" of our interests as stated in the question, the reported odds ratio is correct; if only one of these two had been oppo-

site, SPSS would have calculated a reciprocal. The reciprocal of 1.365 is 0.733.)

2. Calculate the odds ratio that a boy (designated group) rather than a girl will have a handicap (designated event). Also calculate the ratio of percentages. The relevant variables are GENDER and HANDICAP. [In SPSS, *Analyze > Descriptive Statistics > Crosstabs,* click back the variables from the prior question, click HANDICAP over to "Rows" and GENDER over to "Columns" (the "Risk" box in the "Statistics" options should still be checked from the prior question), *OK.*]

   Check your answer: The odds ratio reported by SPSS is 0.813. This represents the odds that a boy (lowest coded and thus designated the "first" group in SPSS) will not have a handicap (not having a handicap is the designated event in SPSS). To obtain the desired odds ratio (boy = designated group, "has handicap" = designated event), we need to take a reciprocal: $1/0.813 = 1.23$. The ratio of percentages (sometimes termed the "risk ratio" or "rate ratio") can be calculated from cell percentages: $21.9\%/18.6\% = 1.18$. The numbers generated in the Risk Estimate table for the "cohorts" are basically ratios of percentages. These numbers can be difficult to interpret. In calculating these ratios, SPSS regards the row variable as the independent variable and the column variable as the dependent variable, which is opposite to the text's recommendation. In the current example, the ratio 0.908 for cohort "male" is obtained as follows: $51.0\%/56.2\% = 0.908$. It may be interpreted as follows: Those without handicaps are 0.908 times as likely to be males as those with handicaps. This interpretation, though correct, is counterintuitive and difficult to understand. (In addition, the text does not recommend the ratio of percentages in a situation where percentages exceed 30%, as here.) If you want ratios of percentages as calculated by SPSS to make sense: (1) make the independent variable the row variable, (2) request row percentages, and (3) give the first (designated) category of the independent variable the lower numeric code. (Recommendation: Don't worry about this and simply calculate these by hand using the cell percentages.)

3. Measure the size of association between FAMETH (family ethnicity) and ONEORTWO (family structure at time of adoption) using Cramer's V. [In SPSS, *Analyze > Descriptive Statistics > Crosstabs*, click back variables from prior exercise, click over FAMETH to "Column(s)" and ONEORTWO to "Row(s)," *Statistics*, click box next to "Phi and Cramer's V," (if necessary, click box next to "Risk" to uncheck it), *Continue, OK.*]

Check your answer: In the Symmetric Measures table, Cramer's V computes to .311, conveying an association of moderate size.

4. Calculate and interpret the odds ratio that an adoption involving a girl (designated the first category) versus one involving a boy will be evaluated "very positive." This example involves the variables GENDER and IMPACTD.

Check your answers: The odds ratio, given in the first row of the Risk Estimate table, is 0.974. Note that a slightly lower percentage (46.4%) of girls' adoptions than boys' adoptions (47.0%) are evaluated very positively. Hence, SPSS has calculated the appropriate odds ratio. The association between GENDER and IMPACTD is extremely weak. From a pragmatic perspective, these variables are unassociated.

5. What is the odds ratio that a child with a handicap (designated group) versus one without a handicap will be placed in a foster adoptive home (designated event)? Relevant variables are HANDICAP and FOSTER.

Check your answer: The odds of being placed in a foster home are 1.773 times greater for those with handicaps (as compared to those without).

6. (Here is an example where you can practice the "Recode" skills that you used in the computer exercise in Appendix C. See the exercise section entitled "Data Transformations" to refresh your memory.) Recode IMPACT (impact of child's adoption on family) into a new dichotomous variable such that "very positive" and "positive" are combined to form one category and "mixed," "negative," and "very negative" are combined to form another. Be sure to use the Recode "Into Different Variables" procedure rather than "Into Same Variables" so that you do not risk permanently altering the value of IMPACT. Give the variable a name and provide variable and value labels. Consider any nonpositive impact to be the event of interest. Calculate and interpret the odds ratio that a single-parent family rather than a two-parent family will experience a nonpositive impact. (The family structure variable is ONEORTWO.)

Check your answer: The odds ratio computes to 0.684. The risk of a nonpositive impact is lower for single-parent adoptions than for two-parent adoptions. The size of association is small. (Depending on values assigned during the recode process, you may have needed to calculate a reciprocal: $1/1.461 = 0.684$.) If prompted to save the data file, you may respond "No" as the newly created variable is not used in subsequent exercises.

NOTES

1. An advantage of the odds ratio is that its value is unaffected by whether one uses odds for the independent or the dependent variable. Still, all of this chapter's examples use the independent variable, dividing odds for one of its categories by the odds for its other category. For instance, dividing the odds of support for Democrats by those for Republicans resulted in an odds ratio of 2.00. One could instead use the dependent variable, dividing the odds of one of its categories by those of the other. For instance, for the example of the child welfare vote, the odds that a supporter will be Democratic are $30/15 = 2.00$, and the odds that a nonsupporter will be Democratic are $20/20 = 1.00$. To derive the odds ratio:

$$\frac{30}{15} \div \frac{20}{20} = \frac{30}{15} \times \frac{20}{20} = \frac{600}{300} = 2.00$$

Thus the odds of being Democratic (rather than Republican) are two times greater for legislators who support the bill than for legislators who do not. The just-completed calculation demonstrates that the odds ratio is unaffected by whether one uses odds for row or column variables to calculate it, a distinct advantage for a measure of association. In contrast, as noted in Chapter 6, the value of the difference in percentages can be affected by the use of row percentages rather than column percentages (or vice versa), an important disadvantage. But to keep interpretation straightforward, one should follow the chapter's examples and use odds for the independent variable in all calculations.

2. The denominators for the two odds used to compute this odds ratio (50 and 70) were derived by subtraction. For instance, if 50% in Program A drop out, it may be deduced that 50% did not experience this event (i.e., did not drop out): 100% − 50% = 50%. Similarly, if 30% in B drop out, then 70% did not: 100% − 30% = 70%.

3. Some researchers might object to the use of *likely* in connection with the odds ratio. They would contend that this word should only be used in connection with probabilities. (Probability is discussed in Chapter 14, Section 14.3.) So long as one uses *likely* in a broad and general way rather than precisely to convey probability, it may be used in connection with odds ratios. All would agree that *likely* may be used in connection with the ratio of percentages.

4. For the average difference in percentages to make sense, each *D%* that composes it should be calculated by subtracting the smaller percentage from the larger. Also, one should follow the recommendation in Chapter 6, Section 6.4, to use those percentages that sum to 100 within categories of the independent variable.

5. The strength of association indicated by a given Cramer's *V* is often modestly stronger than would be suggested by the descriptors in Table 8.1. For instance, via the descriptors, a Cramer's *V* of .30 is a "moderate" association. The actual size of association conveyed by such a Cramer's *V* is perhaps better described as between moderate and strong.

6. A near synonym for directional relationship is *monotonic relationship*. See Toothaker and Miller (1996, p. 615).

CORRELATION AND REGRESSION

8.1 CHAPTER OVERVIEW

To address relationships between interval/ratio-level variables, we begin with the basic concepts underlying *correlation* and a formula for *Pearson's r*, the key correlational measure. Next, we look at selected features of *r*, descriptors of size of association for *r*, and the *coefficient of determination*, r^2. We examine the distinction between *curvilinear* and *linear* association and situations in which to be cautious about interpreting *r*. In the discussion of *regression* we cover the *regression equation*, the *regression line*, and the distinction between regression and correlation. Finally, we look at correlational measures for nominal- and ordinal-level data.

8.2 INTRODUCTION TO CORRELATION

The prior chapter addressed association between nominal-level variables. Our focus shifts now to association of variables that are at the interval/ratio level, which means we are looking at correlation. In a general sense, **correlation** is a synonym for relationship; two variables are correlated if certain values of one tend to "go with" certain values of the other. As an example, if students who study for many hours tend to get high grades and those who study for few hours tend to get low grades, then hours studied and grades are correlated. In a narrow sense, **correlation** refers to relationship as measured by a particular set of correlational measures.

The workhorse correlational measure and this chapter's primary focus is the Pearson correlation coefficient. Symbolized by *r,* the **Pearson correlation coefficient** (or **Pearson's *r***) measures the degree of linear association between two variables that are each at the interval/ratio level of measurement or almost so. A **linear** association is one that can be described by a straight line. Section 8.9 provides further discussion of linear association.

Near its conclusion, this chapter briefly overviews two correlational measures for variables not at the interval/ratio level. But the overwhelming application of correlation is the assessment of relationship between interval/ratio-level variables using Pearson's *r*.

8.3 THE BASICS OF CORRELATION

8.3.1 *Positive and Negative Correlation*

The basic ideas of correlation are similar to those introduced for positive and negative relationship in Chapter 7. If as the values of one variable increase, so also do those of another, these variables are **positively correlated.** This definition uses the word *increase*. An alternate definition that identifies the same pattern from a different perspective is this: If as the values of one variable decrease, so also do those of another, these variables are positively correlated. Whether we focus on increase or decrease, the key point is that values change in the *same* direction. When two variables are **negatively correlated,** the values of one variable increase as those of the other decrease. Or, to identify the same pattern differently, the values of one variable decrease as those of the other increase. The key point is that values change in *opposite* directions.

To add a bit more terminology, when two variables are positively correlated, there is a **positive correlation** between them. When two variables are negatively correlated, there is a **negative correlation** (an *inverse correlation*).

I began writing this chapter in an Olympic year, so examples from track and field are often used. Presume that height jumped in the high jump and distance jumped in the long jump are positively correlated. If this is the case, then those who jump high in the high jump will tend to jump far in the long jump and those who jump "low" in the high jump will tend to jump "short" in the long jump. Not all high high jumpers will be long long jumpers (and not all low high jumpers will be short long jumpers), but this will be the prevailing pattern. When variables are positively correlated, high scores on a first variable tend to go with high scores on the second, and similarly, low scores on the first tend to go with low scores on the second. Stated differently, similar scores tend to go together—highs with highs and lows with lows.

Suppose that height jumped in the long jump and time in the 50-meter run are negatively correlated. If this is the case, then those who jump high in the high jump will tend to have low times (i.e., fast times) in the 50 and those who jump low will tend to have high times (i.e., slow times). When variables are negatively correlated, high scores on a first variable tend to go with low scores on the second, and similarly, low scores on the first tend to go with high scores on the second. Stated differently, dissimilar scores tend to go together—highs with lows and lows with highs.

In our example, height in the high jump and time in the 50-meter run are negatively correlated. Yet those who are *good* long jumpers tend to be *good* sprinters, that is, they tend to run faster. Doesn't this convey that the correlation is positive? No. The direction of the correlation—that is, whether it is positive or negative—is determined not by whether "good" on one variable goes with "good" on another but instead with reference to the values of the variables as they are measured. As height jumped goes up, sprint times tend to go down. Hence the correlation is negative.

8.3.2   *Scatterplots*

Scatterplots display correlations visually. Figure 8.1 presents a scatterplot of the correlation between distance jumped in the long jump and height jumped in the high jump. (The data are hypothetical.) Each marker (small square) in Figure 8.1 represents a case. Height in the high jump is conveyed by a marker's position relative to the vertical axis (Y axis), and distance in the long jump is obtained by its position relative to the horizontal axis (X axis). To learn the height in the high jump that a given marker represents, trace horizontally from that marker to the vertical axis. The point of intersection indicates that height. To learn the distance in the long jump that a marker represents, trace straight down to the horizontal axis. The point of intersection indicates that distance. For instance, the highest marker in Figure 8.1 (it is located in the upper right corner) represents an individual who high-jumped about 6.3 feet and long-jumped slightly more than 20 feet. The pattern made by the markers slants upward from the lower left corner to the upper right corner. The upward slope of this pattern conveys the basic message of positive correlation: As scores on one variable increase, so do those on the other. When

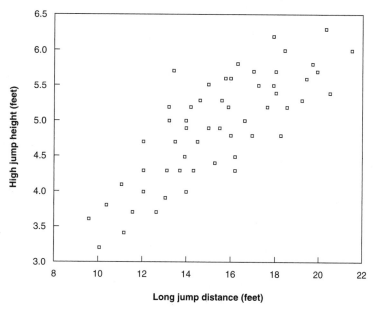

FIGURE **8.1**

A SCATTERPLOT SHOWING POSITIVE CORRELATION

Scores in the high jump and long jump tend to increase or decrease together.

a scatterplot's markers slant upward from lower left to upper right, the displayed variables are positively correlated.

The scatterplot in Figure 8.1 also demonstrates that when variables are positively correlated, high scores on one variable tend to go with high scores on the other, and similarly, low scores tend to go with low scores. For instance, the markers near the upper right corner are for individuals who had high scores on both variables. Similarly, markers near the lower left corner are for those who were low on both.

Figure 8.2 presents a scatterplot that displays the correlation of height in the high jump with time in the 50-meter run. (The data are hypothetical.) The pattern of the markers slants downward from the upper left corner to the lower right corner. As time in the 50-meter run increases, height jumped tends to decrease. Such a downward-sloping pattern from upper left to lower right always conveys a negative correlation. Figure 8.2 also conveys that when a correlation is negative, dissimilar values tend to go together. For instance, markers near the upper left corner convey individuals who had high scores in the high jump but low scores (times) in the 50-meter run. Those in the lower right convey low scores in the high jump and high scores (times) in the 50-meter run.

In the just-presented track and field examples, it is not easy to classify one variable as independent and the other as dependent. When variables can be clas-

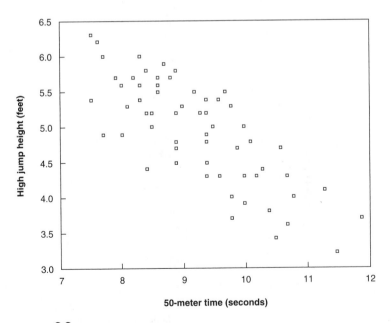

FIGURE 8.2

A SCATTERPLOT SHOWING NEGATIVE CORRELATION

High jump measures tend to decrease as 50-meter run times increase.

sified, the independent variable should be plotted on the horizontal axis (X axis) and the dependent variable should be plotted on the vertical axis (Y axis).

8.3.3 Describing Correlations

Saying that high jump height is positively correlated with long jump distance is the same as saying that long jump distance is positively correlated with high jump height. By shifting the order in which variables are mentioned and how direction is described, the same correlation can be described in four different ways. For instance, each of the following describes the positive correlation between high jump height and long jump distance as displayed in Figure 8.1:

1. As height jumped in the high jump increases, distance jumped in the long jump increases.
2. As height jumped in the high jump decreases, distance jumped in the long jump decreases.
3. As distance jumped in the long jump increases, height jumped in the high jump increases.
4. As distance jumped in the long jump decreases, height jumped in the high jump decreases.

In this example, the two variables cannot be classified easily as independent and dependent. But when one variable is independent and the other dependent, first state the change in the independent variable and second that in the dependent variable. Thus, presuming distance in the long jump to be the independent variable, descriptions 3 and 4 are preferred.

8.4 A FORMULA FOR THE CORRELATION COEFFICIENT

8.4.1 Calculating the Formula

One formula for Pearson's r is:

$$r = \frac{\Sigma(z_x z_y)}{N - 1} \tag{8.1}$$

where r is the correlation coefficient, z_x is the z score on variable X, z_y is the z score on variable Y, and N is the sample size. X and Y are used frequently in formulas. When variables can be classified as independent and dependent, X symbolizes the independent variable and Y symbolizes the dependent variable.

The steps for using formula 8.1 are as follows:

1. Convert scores on both variables to z scores.
2. For each case, multiply the z score on X by that on Y.

3. Sum the products of the z scores.
4. Divide by $N - 1$.

For instance, Table 8.1 shows hypothetical data for the performance of seven people in the high jump and 50-meter run. Step 1, the conversion of scores to z scores, is carried out using formula 5.1 from Chapter 5, Section 5.9. Table 8.2 shows the results.

Step 2 calls for multiplying the z scores. The rightmost column in Table 8.2 presents the results. In Step 3, the products of the z scores are summed, as in the right column of Table 8.2. Finally, in Step 4, the sum from Step 3, -3.862, is divided by $N - 1$ to yield r:

$$r = -3.862/(7 - 1) = -3.862/6 = -.64$$

Hence, the correlation of height jumped in the long jump and time in the 50-meter run is $-.64$.

Formula 8.1 and the foregoing example are presented to help you understand correlation.[1] The correlation coefficient is readily calculated by most spreadsheet software (such as Excel) and statistical programs.

TABLE 8.1   RAW SCORES FOR SEVEN CONTESTANTS

Case	High Jump Height (inches)	50-Meter Run Time (seconds)
Ann	39	9.5
Bill	56	9.2
Jorge	43	8.5
Sally	66	8.7
Gus	56	8.2
Catie	70	7.6
Aaron	53	8.8

TABLE 8.2   STANDARDIZED (z) SCORES FOR THE SEVEN CONTESTANTS

Case	z Score in High Jump	z Score in 50-Meter Run	z Score in Jump × z Score in Run
Ann	−1.404	1.362	−1.912
Bill	.115	.885	0.102
Jorge	−1.047	−.227	0.238
Sally	1.008	.091	0.092
Gus	.115	−.704	−0.081
Catie	1.366	−1.666	−2.263
Aaron	−.153	.250	−0.038
			Sum = −3.862

8.4.2   Understanding the Formula

Think about the high jump/long jump example again. In this example, similar scores tend to go together. Thus, those who score high on the high jump tend to score high on the long jump and those who score low on the high jump tend to score low on the long jump. Recall from Chapter 5 that z scores above the mean have positive values and those below the mean have negative values. Given that similar scores tend to go together, those who score above the mean on the high jump tend to do the same on the long jump. As such, they tend to have positive z scores on both variables. This being the case, the product of their z scores tends to be positive (a positive times a positive equals a positive). Those who score below the mean on the high jump tend to do the same on the long jump. As such, they tend to have negative z scores on both variables. This being the case, the product of their z scores also tends to be positive (a negative times a negative equals a positive). Thus, when similar values "go together" (highs with highs and lows with lows), products of the z scores tend to be positive, so a positive value of r (a positive correlation) results.

When high values tend to be paired with low values (and lows with highs), the products of the z scores are more often negative (a positive times a negative equals a negative), so a negative value of r (a negative correlation) results. This was the case in the just-completed calculation example.

8.5   INTERPRETING r

r may vary from -1.00 to $+1.00$. An r greater than 0.00 conveys a positive correlation, and an r less than 0.00 conveys a negative one. The closer the absolute value of r to 1.00, the larger (and stronger) the correlation. Correlations of -1.00 and 1.00 are **perfect correlations.** When a correlation is perfect, scores on either variable can be predicted *exactly* from scores on the other. Figure 8.3 presents perfect positive and negative correlations. In a perfect correlation, the scatterplot's markers form a straight line. In a perfect positive correlation, markers slant upward from lower left to upper right. In a perfect negative correlation, they slant downward from upper left to lower right. Perfect correlations are almost never encountered in real data. A perfect positive correlation for two variables requires that for each case in the sample, the z score on the first variable must precisely equal the z score on the second.

The "opposite" of perfect correlation is a correlation of 0.00. When the correlation between two variables is 0.00, there is no linear (straight-line) relationship between these variables. The statements about correlations of 0.00 in the next paragraph apply to *most* situations that one encounters. Specifically, they are accurate except when the relationship between variables is *curvilinear.* Curvilinear relationship is somewhat uncommon and is discussed later in the chapter (Section 8.9). The following discussion conveys the general and common meaning of a correlation of 0.00.

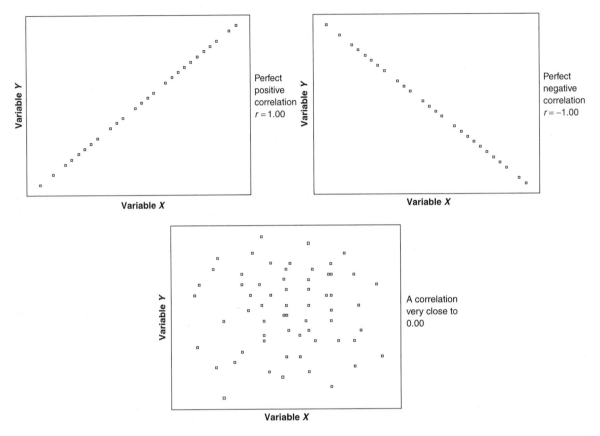

FIGURE **8.3**

PERFECT POSITIVE AND NEGATIVE CORRELATION AND ALMOST NO CORRELATION

With the just-mentioned exception, an r of 0.00 conveys that two variables are unassociated. When r equals 0.00: (1) change (an increase or a decrease) on one variable shows no relationship to change on the second, (2) knowing the value of one variable does not help one to predict that of the other, and (3) the pattern of markers on the scatterplot has neither an upward nor a downward slant but instead takes on a random pattern similar to the "scatter" of buckshot from a shotgun. For example, we might guess that the correlation between grades on a statistics test among human services students and distance jumped in the long jump would be close to 0.00. Those with low, medium, and high grades on the test would be equally likely to have short, medium, or long jumps. Another example of a correlation that we might expect to be close to 0.00 would be that between how much one likes brussels sprouts (measured on a scale from 1 to 100) and one's political orientation (measured on a scale from 1, extremely conservative, to 100, extremely liberal). The bottom scatterplot in Figure 8.3 presents a correlation very close to zero.

TABLE 8.3	DESCRIPTORS OF ASSOCIATION FOR PEARSON'S *r*	
Correlation	**Size of Association**	**Strength of Association**
About .10 (or −.10)	Small	Weak
About .30 (or −.30)	Medium	Moderate
About .50 (or −.50)	Large	Strong
About .70 (or −.70)	Very large	Very strong

A key advantage of the correlation coefficient is ease of interpretation. −1.00 and +1.00 convey the strongest possible linear relationship and 0.00 conveys the absence of such relationship. Note that size of association is conveyed by the *absolute* value of *r*. For instance, a correlation of −.70 indicates a larger (stronger) relationship than does one of .50.

Table 8.3 presents qualitative descriptors for size of relationship for *r*. These descriptors convey relationships of the same size as in similar tables in this book (see Tables 6.4 and 7.2). Size of association is interpreted in the context of social science research rather than mathematically.

Figure 8.4 presents scatterplots for the positive values of *r* that correspond with the qualitative descriptors. As *r* departs from 0.00 and gets closer to 1.00, the shape formed by the markers in the scatterplots comes to resemble less a fat, wide oval and more a skinny, narrow one. The narrower the oval, or stated differently, the more the markers line up in a straight-line (linear) pattern, the stronger the association and the higher the value of *r*. With some practice, you will be able to examine a scatterplot and make a good estimate of the value of *r*. And conversely, you will be able to note the value of *r* and picture the approximate shape of the scatterplot. Figure 8.5 presents scatterplots for the negative values of *r* that correspond to the descriptors in Table 8.3.

For your information, the scatterplot in Figure 8.1 (long jump and high jump) conveys a correlation of .80, and that in Figure 8.2 (50-meter run and high jump) conveys one of −.78. Thus both of these scatterplots display very strong associations, associations that are stronger than the great majority of associations encountered in research. (Of course, these variables are not typical social science variables, and the data are hypothetical.)

8.6   INTERPRETATIONS INVOLVING *r* AND *z* SCORES

8.6.1   *Making Predictions with z Scores*

Regression refers to a group of statistical procedures that are used to predict scores on one variable from those on one or more others (Toothaker and Miller, 1996, p. 199). Pearson's *r* may be used to make predictions involving *z* scores. The

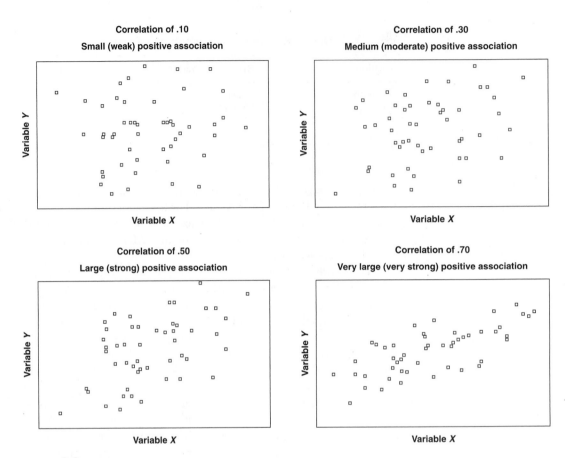

FIGURE 8.4

POSITIVE CORRELATIONS CORRESPONDING TO QUALITATIVE DESCRIPTORS

equation for predicting the z score of a given case on one variable from its z score on a second is termed the **standardized regression equation** (*bivariate standardized regression equation*):

$$\hat{z}_y = r_{xy} z_x \tag{8.2}$$

where $\hat{z}_y$ is the predicted z score on variable Y (the dependent variable). (The caret symbol, ^, is sometimes called a "hat" and designates a predicted score.) In formula 8.2, z_x is the z score on variable X (the independent variable) and r_{xy} is the correlation between X and Y. Formula 8.2 is a *standardized* equation because scores are expressed as standard scores rather than as raw scores. (Standard score is a synonym for z score.) Regression and prediction are covered in greater depth in the regression section of this chapter (Section 8.12).

Equation 8.2 conveys that the best prediction of a case's z score on Y is obtained by multiplying its z score on X by the correlation between these variables.

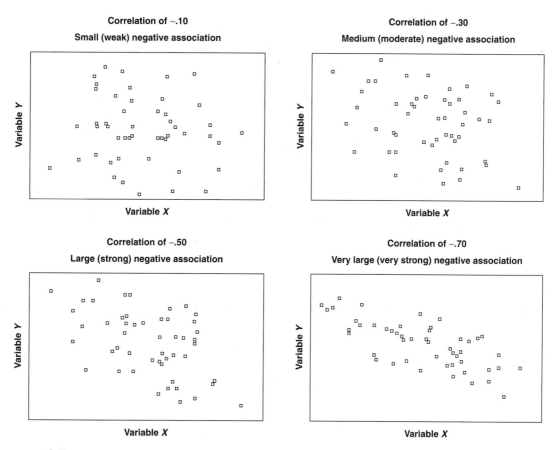

FIGURE **8.5**

NEGATIVE CORRELATIONS CORRESPONDING TO QUALITATIVE DESCRIPTORS

Suppose that Ann's z score on a measure of self-esteem is 0.90 and that the correlation of this measure with a measure of stress is $-.60$. What is the best prediction of Ann's z score on the stress measure?

$$\hat{z}_{stress} = (-.60)(0.90) = -0.54$$

Ann's score on the stress measure is predicted to be slightly more than one-half of a standard deviation below the mean.

8.6.2   *Predicted Change in Standard Deviation Units*

The correlation coefficient conveys the predicted change in standard deviation units for one variable as the other increases by one standard deviation. For instance, an r of .80 between height jumped in the high jump and distance jumped in the long jump conveys that as height jumped in the high jump increases by one standard deviation, predicted distance jumped in the long jump increases by eight-tenths of a standard deviation. This interpretation works both ways: An r of .80 also conveys that as long jump distance increases by one standard deviation, predicted high jump height increases by 0.80 standard deviations. For another example, the correlation between high jump height and time in the 50-meter run, as presented in Figure 8.2, is $-.78$. This conveys that as high jump height increases by one standard deviation, predicted time in the run decreases by 0.78 standard deviations.

As presented in Chapter 5 (Section 5.9), when expressed as z scores, all variables have the same degree of variability. (The standard deviation is 1.00 for all such variables.) Thus r conveys the predicted change in one variable as the other increases by one "equivalent" unit. For instance, the just-presented r of $-.78$ conveys that as high jump height increases by 1.00 unit (relative to its variability), long jump distance decreases by 0.78 unit (relative to its variability).

8.7   CHANGES IN MEASUREMENT AND r

The value of r is not affected by the unit of measurement. For instance, had we measured high jump height in meters rather than in feet, the value of r would not have changed. Similarly, r is not affected by multiplying or dividing one or both variables by a constant. For instance, 1 foot equals 0.3048 meter. To express height in meters, we could multiply each high jump score by 0.3048. This would not affect the correlation between high jump height and any other variable. Similarly, adding or subtracting a constant to one or both variables does not affect the value of r. Suppose we found that the height of the high jump bar was actually one-half inch higher than we had thought, so that we had measured all jumps as one-half inch too low. We could make our measurements accurate by adding this amount to each person's score. Doing so would not affect the correlation of high jump height with any other variable. In sum, the just-provided examples demonstrate that neither multiplying nor dividing by a constant affects the value of r, nor does adding or subtracting a constant. This makes intuitive sense, given that such changes do not affect standardized (z) scores, which are key ingredients in the formula for r.

8.8   THE COEFFICIENT OF DETERMINATION: r^2

Whereas Table 8.3 interprets size or strength of association directly via r, some researchers prefer to do so via r^2 (obtained by squaring r); r^2 is termed the **coefficient of determination.** When one variable is dependent and the other independent, r^2 represents the proportion of variance in the dependent variable that is explained by the independent variable. (See Chapter 4, Section 4.9, to refresh your memory of the variance.) When variables cannot be characterized as independent or dependent, r^2 represents the proportion of variance in each variable that is shared with the other. For instance, when $r = .5$, $r^2 = .5 \times .5 = .25$. In this example, 25% (or the proportion .25) of the variance in one variable is explained by (or shared with) the other.[2]

Figure 8.6 displays visually the meaning of the coefficient of determination. Each circle represents the variance of a standardized variable, that is, of a variable for which all scores are expressed as z scores. The variance of a standardized variable is 1.00. Thus the area of each circle is also 1.00. The overlap of the circles represents explained or shared variance. In Figure 8.6, $r = .50$ and thus r^2 (the shared/explained variance) equals .25 ($.50 \times .50 = .25$). This being the case, 25% of the area of each circle overlaps with that of the other. In Figure 8.6, 75% of the area of each circle does not overlap. This represents the variance of each variable that is unique (unshared). The coefficient of determination may vary from 0 to 1.00. The higher its value, the stronger the association between the variables.

The coefficient of determination is a popular tool. However, it invites misinterpretation. The basic problem is simple: r^2 "sounds" too small. For instance, a correlation of .5 explains "only" 25% of the variance. Hearing this, many conclude that the relationship between the involved variables is also small. Yet it does not follow logically that a mathematically small number conveys a relationship that is small in the context of social science research. A correlation of .50 is considered to represent a large association because correlations larger than this are at least reasonably uncommon in social science research.

Some researchers use r to assess size/strength of association. Others use r^2. Except in the case of perfect correlation, the absolute value of r is always greater than that of r^2. This is so because squaring a number whose absolute value is

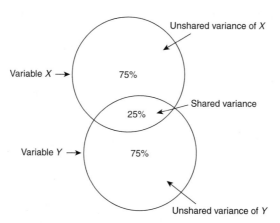

FIGURE **8.6**

GRAPHICAL DISPLAY OF SHARED VARIANCE

less than 1.00 always results in a smaller absolute value (e.g., $.3 \times .3 = .09$, $-.7 \times -.7 = .49$). It is nonsensical (and wrong) to conclude that a relationship is weaker when expressed via one measure (r^2) rather than another (r); either way, it is the same relationship.

In sum, don't be misled by the fact that r^2 sounds small. Between the two measures, r is the more straightforward tool. In particular, the close link between the value of r and the pattern of markers in the scatterplot is helpful. As stated earlier, with practice one can picture the pattern that a given r conveys. One can also learn to picture the degree to which variables change together. This gets to the core of the concept of correlation and gives intuitive meaning to r.

8.9   CURVILINEAR RELATIONSHIP

As stated earlier, there is an exception to the statement that a correlation of 0.00 indicates the absence of relationship between variables. Pearson's r measures the degree of *linear* relationship between variables, that is, the degree to which the relationship (the markers in the scatterplot) assumes a *straight-line* pattern. Note, for instance, that in both Figures 8.1 and 8.2, the markers arrange themselves in straight-line patterns, and thus the depicted relationships are linear. Indeed, one could picture a straight line that would "slice" each pattern of markers in half. In Figure 8.1 (positive correlation) such a line would slant from the lower left to the upper right. In Figure 8.2 (negative correlation), it would slant from upper left to lower right.

In human services research, most relationships found between variables at the interval/ratio level are linear or approximately so. Occasionally, however, relationships are **curvilinear.** In a curvilinear relationship, measurements take on a pattern that is best described by a curve (very occasionally, that curve may have more than one bend) rather than by a straight line. When a relationship is curvilinear, the scatterplot's markers form a curve.

Another sports example can demonstrate a **curvilinear relationship.** Suppose that baseball coaches vary in how hard they pressure children to perform. Some coaches put on a great deal of pressure, others a moderate amount, and others hardly any. If we find a good way to measure the amount of pressure and examine its relationship to the number of games won, we might find a curvilinear relationship. Those coaches who use hardly any pressure may win few games because their players are, presumably, unmotivated (though perhaps happy). Those who use extreme pressure may also win only a few games because their players become too tense to play their best. A medium amount of pressure may provide a winning recipe; coaches who use moderate pressure motivate kids without stressing them out, so they win many games.

Figure 8.7 depicts the (quite strong) relationship between the two variables in this scenario. Number of games won changes in predictable fashion as a function of amount of pressure. The relationship is clearly curvilinear rather than linear. The correlation coefficient (r) is not an appropriate measure of curvilinear relationship and should not be used in such a case. Doing so underestimates size of

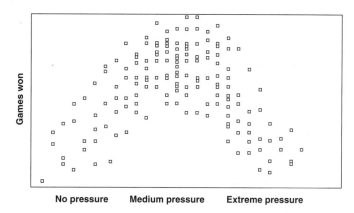

Games won

No pressure   Medium pressure   Extreme pressure

FIGURE **8.7**

CURVILINEAR RELATIONSHIP BETWEEN PRESSURE BY COACH
AND GAMES WON

association. For instance, the Pearson's r between amount of pressure and games won in Figure 8.7 computes to $-.02$, that is, essentially to 0.00. Clearly, this value of r has the potential to mislead. A researcher who did not have access to a scatterplot and neglected to consider the possibility of curvilinear relationship could easily (and mistakenly) conclude that degree of pressure and games won were unassociated. When Pearson's r is close to or equal to 0.00, the correct conclusion is that there is no *linear* relationship.

If a curvilinear relationship is suspected, one should construct a scatterplot and investigate this possibility. The measure called eta squared (η^2), presented in Chapter 9 (Section 9.6.2), is sometimes used to assess nonlinear associations.[3]

8.10 DIRECTIONAL RELATIONSHIP VERSUS LINEAR RELATIONSHIP

The concept of directional relationship was introduced in Chapter 7. It was pointed out that two ordinal-level variables may have a directional relationship, that is, as one increases so does the other (or perhaps the second decreases as the first increases). As numerous examples in this chapter have demonstrated, relationships between variables at the interval/ratio level may also have direction. Indeed, all linear (straight-line) relationships have direction.

However, formally speaking, ordinal-level variables may not be involved in linear relationships. In a linear relationship, one may draw a conclusion pertaining to the amount of change in one variable as the other increases by a given amount. For instance, as high jump height increased by one standard deviation, predicted long jump distance increased by 0.80 standard deviations. One can't draw such a conclusion when an ordinal-level variable is involved. This ties in to basic issues of measurement. With ordinal-level variables, one cannot measure differences between categories. (For instance, one cannot know whether the interval between "excellent" and "good" represents the same difference as does that between "good" and "fair"; see discussion in Chapter 1, Section 1.6.) In sum, relationships involving ordinal-level variables may have direction but may not be linear.

8.11   CAUTIONS IN INTERPRETING *r*

Some cautions in interpreting *r* should be noted. The conditions to watch out for involve cases of very differently shaped distributions, reduced variability, and outlying cases, as detailed next.

8.11.1   *Shape of Distribution*

When the variables differ greatly in their shape of distribution, *r* may have a maximum possible absolute value of less than 1.00. For instance, if one variable has a normal distribution and the other a strongly skewed distribution (either positive or negative), the maximum positive correlation must be less than 1.00. Such a situation would call for caution in applying the qualitative descriptors because the actual strength of association may be somewhat higher than the descriptors suggest.

8.11.2   *Reduced Variability*

Reduced variability can markedly reduce the absolute value of *r*. For instance, suppose you are teaching a group of new mothers, all highly motivated, to learn about child development. You are also studying the correlation between motivation level and amount learned as measured by a test of knowledge about children. Given that *all* the mothers are highly motivated, motivation varies hardly at all. When a variable varies hardly at all, it is exceedingly difficult to study its relationship to other variables. (In effect the "variable" becomes a constant; see Chapter 4, Section 4.11.) In a situation like this, the correlation between motivation level and test score would likely be very close to 0.00. But in a class where motivation varied considerably, it is likely that one would find a reasonably strong relationship between motivation and amount learned.

In sum, when variability is greatly reduced, *r* is not an effective measure; it underestimates the size of association that would otherwise be found.

8.11.3   *Cases That Are Exceptions to the Prevailing Pattern*

A third caution involves cases that are exceptions to the prevailing pattern in the scatterplot. Such cases can greatly affect *r*'s value. For instance, the correlation depicted in Figure 8.8 conveys a correlation of −.54, a large negative correlation. Note the marker in the upper right corner. This case is clearly an exception to the overall pattern. The influence of this case on *r* can be determined by recalculating *r* with the case excluded. Doing so results in an *r* of −.79, a much larger negative correlation.

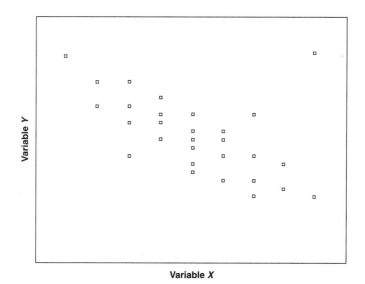

FIGURE 8.8

SCATTERPLOT DEMONSTRATING HOW AN EXCEPTION TO THE PATTERN AFFECTS r

When a single case exerts an inordinate influence on r, some researchers may drop this case, as in our example. Others are more hesitant to do so. One practical solution is to report correlations both with and without the offending case(s) and let readers decide which value of r they find more valid.

8.12   REGRESSION

8.12.1   *Regression Equation and Regression Line*

As mentioned earlier, r represents the expected change in standard deviation units in one variable as another increases by one standard deviation. Thus we can use r to make predictions involving z scores. Sometimes we want a prediction not in terms of standardized units (z scores) but in the original units in which the variables were measured (that is, in raw scores). Regression is the appropriate statistical tool for these purposes.

An example from the special-needs adoption study can illustrate the technique of regression. A key dependent variable is score on the parent-child relationship scale, which, as suggested by its name, probed the closeness and quality of the relationship between parent and child. The scale consists of five items: how well parent and child "got along," communication, trust, respect, and closeness of relationship. All items represented parent reports. Each had a four-point response scale with 4 representing the most positive response and 1 the least positive. Responses to each item were summed, and the sum was divided by the number of items (five) to yield a scale score. The highest possible scale score (resulting from responding 4 to each item) was 4.00 and the lowest possible score (responding 1 to each item) was 1.00.

A second variable in the study was score on a 118-item checklist of child behavior problems (Achenbach, 1991). This was also completed by the parent. For each behavior problem, responses were coded: Not true = 0, Sometimes true = 1, and Often true = 2. The highest possible score on this measure was 236 (118 × 2 = 236) and the lowest was 0.00 (zero). The correlation between score on behavior problems and score on parent-child relationship computed to −.604 (N = 710; only children ages 4 and older were included in this analysis), indicating a strong negative association. Thus, the greater the level of behavioral problems, the less the closeness between parent and child.

Regression focuses on prediction. We might pose the question: "If Sally earns a score of 25 on the behavior problems checklist, what is our best prediction of her family's score on the parent-child relationship scale?" Such a question is addressed by the **regression equation,** which also has the long name of *bivariate unstandardized regression equation.* The regression equation allows researchers to predict the value of a dependent variable, symbolized by Y, based on that of an independent variable, symbolized by X. The predicted values of Y are displayed using the **regression line.** The regression line for the current example is shown in Figure 8.9. Prior to studying the regression equation, let's estimate the parent-child relationship score in Sally's family using the regression line in Figure 8.9. To do so: (1) trace straight up from the value 25 on the X axis (Sally's behavior score) to intersect the regression line, and then from the point of intersection (2) trace left to intersect the Y axis. The Y axis is intersected at about 3.5. This is an estimate, using the method of tracing, of the parent-child relationship score predicted by the regression equation.

The formula for the regression equation is:

$$\hat{Y} = A + BX \tag{8.3}$$

where $\hat{Y}$ is the predicted value of Y (the dependent variable), X is the value of X (the independent variable), A is the constant, and B is the regression coefficient. For formulas for A and B, see Toothaker and Miller (1996, p. 207) or many other statistics books.

The **constant** (or *intercept*), **A,** indicates the predicted value of Y when X equals 0.00. It also indicates the point at which the regression line intersects the Y (vertical) axis. (The just-provided interpretation presumes that the Y axis intersects the X axis where X equals 0.00. On some graphs, this is not the case.) The **regression coefficient, B,** conveys the **slope** of the regression line, that is, the line's change relative to the Y axis as X increases by 1.00. Stated differently, B conveys the predicted change in Y (the change in $\hat{Y}$) as X increases by 1.00.

The regression coefficient, B, and the correlation coefficient, r, can be contrasted. The correlation coefficient, r, is a **standardized coefficient** and thus conveys predicted change with X and Y expressed as z scores (standard scores). As stated earlier, when Y is the dependent variable, r conveys the predicted change in Y in standard deviation units as the value of X increases by one standard

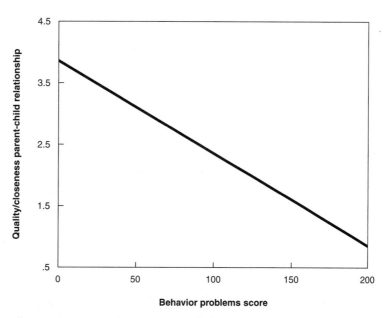

FIGURE **8.9**

REGRESSION LINE

The slope of the line shows a strong negative association between behavior problems and parent-child relationship.

---

deviation. The regression coefficient, B, is an **unstandardized coefficient.** It conveys predicted change with X and Y expressed in their original, unstandardized units of measurement (as raw scores). As stated in the previous paragraph, B indicates the predicted change in Y as X increases by 1.00.

Let's use the names "Relationship Score" for the variable parent-child relationship scale score and "Behavior Score" for the variable behavior problems. Then the regression equation for predicting Relationship Score from Behavior Score for our example is:

Predicted Relationship Score = 3.882 + (−.015 × Behavior Score)

In this equation $A = 3.882$ and $B = -.015$. Given that A equals 3.882, the regression line intersects the Y axis at 3.882. As mentioned earlier, the regression line for this equation is displayed in Figure 8.9. You might want to verify that it does indeed intersect the Y axis at about 3.882. This means that the predicted score on the closeness scale for a family whose child's behavior problems score is 0 is 3.882. B equals −.015. As B is negative, it conveys that the predicted relationship score *decreases* as behavior problems increase. More specifically, B equal to −.015 indicates that as score on the behavior problems scale increases by 1.00, the predicted relationship score decreases by .015. You might want to study the regression line in Figure 8.9 and convince yourself that its slope (i.e., the change in Y as X increases by 1.00) is indeed −.015.[4]

In the prior paragraph, A and B were used to describe the association between behavior score and relationship score. The regression equation may also be used to predict individual scores. For instance, it may be used to predict the relationship score in Sally's family. Recall that Sally's behavior score was 25.0. The best prediction of the parent-child relationship score in Sally's family is:

$$\text{Predicted Relationship Score} = 3.882 + (-.015)(25.0)$$
$$= 3.882 + (-.375$$
$$= 3.882 - .375$$
$$= 3.507$$

This prediction agrees well with the earlier estimate of 3.5 made by tracing values in the regression line graph in Figure 8.9. The just-completed math involved multiplying the regression coefficient, B ($-.015$), by Sally's behavior score (25.0) and then adding the constant, A (3.882).

The regression line is sometimes called the **least-squares line.** If you do the following: (1) for each case, subtract the predicted value for Y (that is, $\hat{Y}$) from the actual value of Y; (2) for each case, square this difference; and (3) add together all the "squared differences," the result is the **sum of squares.** The regression line is the single line that minimizes the sum of squares, that is, makes its value as small as possible. Still another name for the regression line is the **best-fit line.** Among all possible straight lines, it does the best job (judged on the criterion of minimizing the sum of squares) of predicting Y based on X.

The line of "best fit" is indeed a fitting label. Figure 8.10 presents both the regression line and scatterplot for the current example. The regression line in this figure seems to slice the pattern of markers in half. Among all straight lines it does the best job of capturing the pattern of relationship depicted by the markers.

The just-presented regression line was developed from the unstandardized regression equation. One may also develop a regression line based on the standardized equation, that is, with scores expressed as z scores. Such a line conveys the values predicted by the standardized equation $\hat{z}_y = r_{xy}z_x$ (formula 8.2). Figure 8.11 presents a line based on the standardized equation for the high jump and long jump data in Figure 8.1. It also presents the scatterplot for the standardized scores. As you know, r conveys the predicted change in standard deviations for one variable as the other increases by one standard deviation. In the current example r equals .80. Thus, as long jump distance increases by one (1.00) standard deviation, predicted height in the high jump increases by 0.80 standard deviations. The regression line makes this interpretation clearer. When scores are expressed as z scores, the slope of the regression line equals r. Hence, in Figure 8.11, its slope is 0.80.

It may be helpful to verify that the regression line in Figure 8.11 does indeed show the values predicted by the standardized regression equation. For instance, when the z score on long jump is -2.00, the equation predicts a high jump z score of $(.80)$ $(-2.00) = -1.60$. To verify this on the graph, trace up from -2.00 on the X axis to intersect the regression line and then trace horizontally to the left to intersect the Y axis. The Y axis is indeed intersected at about -1.60. Notice that where the z score on long jump is 0.00 (a score at the mean), the predicted z score on high jump is 0.00: $(.80)(0.00) = 0.00$ (also at the mean).

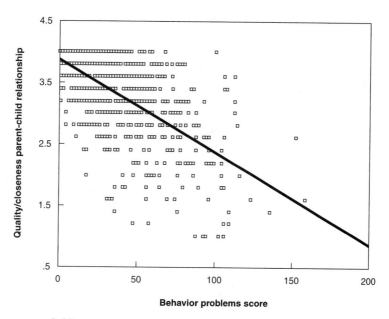

FIGURE 8.10

A Regression Line with Its Scatterplot

The regression line obtained from the regression equation fits with the scatterplot graphed from the same data on behavior problems and parent-child relationship.

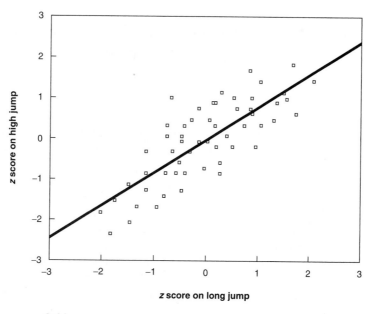

FIGURE 8.11

Regression Line and Scatterplot for Example of High Jump and Long Jump

8.12.2   *Regression Versus Correlation*

The two variables in the current example, closeness of parent-child relationship and behavior problems, were not easily observed, tangible, physical quantities. When variables are tangible and are measured in familiar units, (unstandardized) regression coefficients are particularly easy to interpret and understand. For instance, suppose that a study finds that the regression coefficient (B) for number of prenatal visits as a predictor of infant birthweight, measured in ounces, equals 1.5. This indicates that as number of visits increases by 1 (i.e., for each additional visit), birthweight, on average, increases by 1.5 ounces. When variables are tangible and familiar, regression coefficients have direct, real-world meaning.

In general, regression is the more effective tool for communicating about relationship when variables are tangible, and correlation is more effective when they are subjective and abstract. For instance, in the example of behavior problems and parent-child relationship, the regression coefficient, $-.015$, had no straightforward, intuitive meaning. It took on meaning only when one understood how behavior problems and parent-child relationship closeness were scaled, or measured. In this example, the correlation coefficient ($r = -.604$) did the more straightforward job of conveying relationship.

r and B have complementary roles. The correlation coefficient, r, a standardized coefficient, conveys size of association. The regression coefficient, B, an unstandardized coefficient, conveys relationship in terms of the original units of measure.[5]

8.13   CORRELATION FOR NOMINAL- AND ORDINAL-LEVEL VARIABLES

For a dichotomous variable, we may conceptualize (albeit arbitrarily) one value as high and the other as low. For instance, we could conceptualize "yes" as high and "no" as low. Or (again arbitrarily) we could conceptualize "female" as high and "male" as low. The situation for a dichotomous variable contrasts with that for a nominal-level variable with three or more categories. For such a variable, one may not order categories, even arbitrarily. For instance, one can't put green, brown, and blue eyes in order.

As categories of a dichotomous variable can be conceptualized as low and high, one may compute a correlation between two such variables. This correlation, the correlation between two dichotomous variables, is measured by **phi** (r_{phi}). The formula for phi is basically a shortcut formula for Pearson's r that may be used when both variables are dichotomous. In essence, phi *is* the (Pearson's) r between two dichotomous variables. Its possible values range from -1.00 to 1.00. The descriptors for r in Table 8.3 provide a rough approximation of the size/strength of association indicated by phi.[6] Phi is a viable alternative to the odds ratio for measuring association between dichotomous variables. (For more discussion and a formula, see Glass and Hopkins, 1996, p. 132.)

The correlation between two rank orderings is measured by **Spearman's r** (r_{ranks}). When there are no tied ranks, Spearman's r and Pearson's r have identical values. The formula for Spearman's r is basically a shortcut formula for Pearson's r that may be used when both variables are rank orderings. In essence, Spearman's r is the (Pearson's) r between two rank orderings. The descriptors in Table 8.3 may be used to interpret the size of association indicated by r_{ranks}. (For more discussion and a formula, see Glass and Hopkins, 1996, p. 130.)

As you know, Pearson's r formally requires measurement at the interval/ratio level. Occasionally, researchers bend the rules and use r to describe associations involving one or more variables at the ordinal level. For instance, an important ordinal-level variable in the special-needs adoption study is parent perception of the impact of adoption on the family. It is coded as follows: 5 = very positive, 4 = mostly positive, 3 = mixed, 2 = mostly negative, and 1 = very negative. The correlation of this measure with score on a behavior problems checklist was $-.45$ ($N = 691$; Achenbach, 1991; only children ages 4 and older included in analysis). As the values of both variables can be ordered, this correlation does indeed "make sense." It conveys that the greater the number of problem behaviors, the less positive the impact of the adoption on the family. Clearly, this correlation furthers understanding of the relationship between the two variables.

Though many recommend against using r in situations such as this, those who favor bending the rules have a good argument. If the categories assigned to the values are straightforward, the resulting r will likely convey useful information about the relationship. When calculating r in such a situation, be aware that assignment of a different set of codes would likely result in a somewhat different value.[7]

8.14   CHAPTER SUMMARY

The key measure of association between interval/ratio-level variables is Pearson's r. If one variable increases along with the other, these variables are positively correlated. If one increases as the other decreases, they are negatively correlated. Correlation is presented visually via the scatterplot.

A formula (8.1) for Pearson's r is $r = (\sum(z_x z_y))/(N-1)$. r may vary from -1.00 to 1.00. The greater its absolute value, the larger the size of association. Correlations of -1.00 and of 1.00 are perfect correlations. An r of 0.00 indicates the absence of linear association. Using the Table 8.3 descriptors, a correlation of about .10 (or $-.10$) represents a small (weak) association whereas one of about .50 (or $-.50$) represents a strong one. r conveys the predicted change in standard deviations for one variable as the other increases by one standard deviation. The standardized regression equation (formula 8.2) is $\hat{z}_y = r_{xy} z_x$.

The coefficient of determination, r^2, represents the proportion of variance in one variable that is shared with another. Strength of association often sounds weak when measured using r^2 instead of r.

Pearson's r measures the degree of linear (straight-line) association. When the pattern of association follows a curve, the association is curvilinear. Pearson's r

should not be used in such a case. Relationships between ordinal-level variables may have direction but may not be linear.

When the shape of distribution differs greatly for two variables, the maximum absolute value that r can obtain is typically less than 1.00. Reduced variability also decreases the absolute value of r. Exceptions to the prevailing pattern can greatly influence r's value.

The (unstandardized) regression equation is $\hat{Y} = A + BX$ (formula 8.3). The constant, A, conveys the predicted value of Y where X equals 0.00. The regression coefficient, B, conveys the regression line's slope, that is, the predicted change in Y as X increases by 1.00.

The correlation coefficient, r, is a standardized coefficient. The regression coefficient, B, is an unstandardized coefficient. The regression line minimizes the sum of squares between predicted and actual values of Y. For the standardized regression equation, the regression line's slope equals r. In general, regression is preferred when both variables are tangible, and correlation is preferred when one or both are nontangible.

Phi (r_{phi}) measures correlation between dichotomous variables. Spearman's r (r_{ranks}) does so for rank orderings.

PROBLEMS AND QUESTIONS

Section 8.2

1. A _____ relationship is one that can be described by a straight line.
2. (T or F) The *predominant* use of correlational measures is to assess association between variables at the nominal and ordinal levels of measurement.
3. The workhorse correlational measure is known as the _____ correlation coefficient, which is symbolized by _____.

Section 8.3

4. If as the values of one variable decrease, so also do those of the other, these variables are _____ correlated.
5. If people who work more hours tend to express less enjoyment with life (as measured on some scale) than do those who work fewer hours, then hours worked and enjoyment are _____ correlated.
6. If the markers in a scatterplot slope downward from the upper left to the lower right, the variables displayed in the scatterplot are _____ correlated.

7. (T or F) Saying that variable X is correlated with variable Y is the same as saying that variable Y is correlated with variable X.

Section 8.4

8. In your own words, describe how to calculate r using z scores.
9. If positive z scores on variable X tend to be paired with negative z scores on variable Y, and negative z scores on X with positive scores on Y, then X and Y are _____ correlated.
10. At Athletic U. students take two tests on shooting free throws. On the first test the mean number of shots made for a group of five students is 5.2 with a standard deviation of 1.789. On the second test, these students make an average of 5.8 baskets ($s = 1.304$). The first two columns of Table 8PQ.1 present the number of baskets made by each student on the two tests. Create a similar table and calculate the following:
    a. z scores for each student on Test 1
    b. z scores for each student on Test 2
    c. The product of z scores for each student
    d. The sum of the product of z scores
    e. The correlation of baskets made on Test 1 with baskets made on Test 2

TABLE 8PQ.1			GRID FOR CALCULATION OF STANDARDIZED SCORES		
Student	**Free Throw Test 1**	**Free Throw Test 2**	**z Score on Test 1**	**z Score on Test 2**	**Product of z Scores**
Alex	5	5			
Julio	7	6			
LaKeesha	4	7			
Sandra	7	7			
Rainbow	3	4			
				Sum =	

Section 8.5

11. The value of r may vary from _____ to _____ .

12. Correlations of 1.00 and -1.00 are sometimes termed _____ correlations.

13. In a perfect correlation the dots in the scatterplot form a _____ _____ .

14. Describe in your own words the pattern of markers in a scatterplot when $r = 0.00$. (Assume the absence of curvilinear relationship.)

15. (T or F) The greater the value of r, the larger the association.

16. (T or F) The greater the absolute value of r, the larger/stronger the association.

17. (T or F) The larger the absolute value of r, the less the dots of a scatterplot tend to line up in a straight line.

18. For each of the following pairs, indicate the value of r that conveys the stronger relationship.
   a. .33 or .66
   b. $-.33$ or .66
   c. $-.7$ or $-.2$
   d. $-.92$ or .29

19. Using the descriptors in Table 8.3, use your own words to indicate the approximate strength of relationship conveyed by each of the following correlations. (Assume the absence of curvilinear association.)
   a. $r = .47$
   b. $r = -.32$
   c. $r = .82$
   d. $r = -.11$

20. Interpret the strength of association conveyed by a correlation of 1.24. (Trick question?)

Section 8.6

21. The equation for predicting a case's z score on one variable from its z score on another is termed the (bivariate) _____ regression equation.

22. Describe the standardized regression equation (formula 8.2) in your own words.

23. The correlation between two variables is $-.70$ and their relationship is linear. As one variable increases by one standard deviation, the other tends to _____ by _____ standard deviations.

24. Using the provided information and the standardized regression equation, predict a case's z score on variable Y. (Assume a linear association.)
   a. $r_{xy} = .5; z_x = .24$
   b. $r_{xy} = -.5; z_x = .24$
   c. $r_{xy} = .8; z_x = 2.50$

Section 8.7

25. The correlation between X and Y is $-.30$. The constant 2 is subtracted from all scores on X. The correlation between X and Y following this subtraction is _____ .

26. (T or F) Multiplying scores on variable X by a constant changes the value of the correlation of variable X with variable Y.

Section 8.8

27. Calculate r^2 in each of the following situations:
   a. $r = -.4$
   b. $r = .10$
   c. $r = .70$
   d. $r = -.5$

28. When r is squared to obtain r^2, this coefficient is termed the coefficient of _____ .

29. When one variable is dependent and the other is independent, r^2 conveys the proportion of _____ in the _____ variable that is _____ by the _____ variable.

30. $r^2 = .25$. What is the percentage of explained variance?

31. (T or F) An r^2 of .25 conveys a weak association between variables.

Section 8.9

32. (T or F) The Pearson correlation coefficient is *not* an appropriate tool for measuring the degree of curvilinear association between variables.
33. (T or F) A correlation of 0.00 between two variables *always* conveys the absence of relationship.

Section 8.10

34. (T or F) All directional relationships are linear relationships.
35. (T or F) All linear relationships are directional relationships.
36. (T or F) Strictly speaking, it is not possible for an ordinal-level variable to be involved in a linear relationship.

Section 8.11

37. (T or F) Even when the shape of distribution differs greatly for two variables, one may be confident that the maximum possible absolute value of r is 1.00.
38. Reduced variability typically _____ the absolute value of r.
39. Only clients with the highest level of motivation are selected to participate in a program. In this group the correlation of level of motivation and client rating of effectiveness is .10. What is your best estimate of the correlation that would have been observed if clients with more varied levels of motivation had participated?
    a. .10
    b. Greater than .10
    c. Less than .10

Section 8.12

40. In the regression equation (formula 8.3), A is termed the _____ .
41. In the regression equation, B is a(n) _____ coefficient rather than a standardized one. However, r is a(n) _____ coefficient.
42. In your own words, describe how to interpret B.

43. Other names for the regression line are the _____ - _____ line and the _____ - _____ line.
44. The regression line minimizes the _____ _____ _____ .
45. Consider the regression equation, $\hat{Y} = 3 + (2.5)X$, and indicate the value of each of the following.
    a. The constant, A
    b. The regression coefficient, B
    c. The slope of the regression line
    d. The amount by which $\hat{Y}$ (predicted score on Y) increases as X increases by 1.00
    e. $\hat{Y}$ when $X = 4$
    f. $\hat{Y}$ when $X = 0$
    g. $\hat{Y}$ when $X = -4$
    h. Sally's score on X is -4. What is $\hat{Y}$ for Sally?
    i. Eric's score on X is 5 points higher than Diana's. How many points higher is $\hat{Y}$ for Eric than for Diana?
46. In your own words, why is regression often preferred for tangible, familiar variables and correlation for intangible, unfamiliar ones?

Section 8.13

47. (T or F) The maximum absolute value that r_{phi} can attain is 1.00.
48. The correlation between two dichotomous variables is measured by _____ .
49. (T or F) Pearson's r may be used appropriately when one variable is a nominal-level variable with three or more categories.
50. The correlation between two rank orderings is measured by _____ r, which is symbolized by _____ .

🖥 COMPUTER EXERCISES

For general instructions on computer exercises, see the note in Chapter 2.

1. Calculate and assess the correlation (Pearson's r) between BEHAVTOT (score on behavior problems checklist) and RELSCALE (closeness/quality of parent-child relationship). [In SPSS,

Analyze > Correlate > Bivariate, click over BEHAVTOT and RELSCALE, click on box next to "Pearson" if not already marked, OK.]

Check your answers: The correlation between BEHAVTOT and RELSCALE is −.609. This correlation coefficient conveys a strong negative association.

2. Create a scatterplot depicting the association between BEHAVTOT and RELSCALE. [In SPSS, Graphs > Scatter, be sure graphic next to "Simple" is outlined with the thick black line (if not, click it), Define, click RELSCALE over into "Y axis" space and click BEHAVTOT over to "X Axis" space, OK.]

3. Using statistical software, create a best fit line (least-squares line) for the scatterplot of BEHAVTOT and RELSCALE. [In SPSS, be sure that you are in the Viewer (output display) window, move cursor over the just-created scatterplot, click once to select it, and double-click. This takes you to "SPSS Chart Editor." Chart > Options, under "Fit Line" click the box next to "Total," OK. Observe the best-fit line and close the Chart Editor.]

4. Find and interpret the correlation (Pearson's r) of INTERNAL (internalized behavior problems) and EXTERNAL (externalized behavior problems). [In SPSS, Analyze > Correlate > Bivariate, click over INTERNAL and EXTERNAL (you may also need to click to turn off other variables), OK.]

Check your answers: r = .56, a strong positive correlation.

5. Develop an unstandardized regression equation with the dependent variable RELSCALE and the independent variable BEHAVTOT. As BEHAVTOT increases by 1.00, what is the predicted change in RELSCALE? [In SPSS, Analyze > Regression > Linear, click RELSCALE over into space under "Dependent," click BEHAVTOT over into space under "Independent," OK.]

Check your answers: In the Coefficients table under "Unstandardized Coefficients" and under "B," the value of the constant (A) is 3.896 and the value of B for BEHAVTOT (using scientific notation) is −1.52E−.02, which equals −.0152.

Thus, as BEHAVTOT increases by 1.00, the predicted value of RELSCALE decreases by .00152.

6. What is the correlation between INTERNAL (internalized problems) and RELSCALE? Between EXTERNAL (externalized problems) and RELSCALE? (Hint: you may click over all three variables.)

Check your answers: The correlations of INTERNAL and EXTERNAL with RELSCALE are, respectively, −.448 and −.642.

7. What are the values of the constant (A) and unstandardized regression coefficient (B) in the unstandardized regression equation with the independent variable EXTERNAL and the dependent variable RELSCALE? Interpret B.

Check your answers: Constant = 3.84; B = −1.123. As EXTERNAL increases by 1.00 point, the predicted RELSCALE score decreases by 1.123 points.

NOTES

1. A calculation formula for r is:

$$r = \frac{\frac{\sum XY - \{[(\sum X)(\sum Y)]/N\}}{N - 1}}{s_X s_Y}$$

The notation $\sum XY$ instructs one to multiply each case's score on variable X by its score on variable Y and then to sum these products. The notation $[(\sum X)(\sum Y)]/N$ instructs one to (1) sum scores on X, (2) sum scores on Y, (3) multiply these two sums together, and (4) divide by the sample size. The symbols s_X and s_Y stand for the standard deviations of X and Y. See note 6 at the end of Chapter 4 for a hand calculation formula for the standard deviation.

2. This book presents size of association and strength of association as near synonyms. However, definitions vary; many texts define strength of association as the percentage of explained, or shared, variance (e.g., Toothaker and Miller, 1996, p. 175).

3. There is no single best measure of curvilinear association. The discussion in Cohen and Cohen (1983, pp. 253–270) is excellent but advanced given your knowledge at this time.

4. The following logic should help convince you that the slope is about $-.015$. The regression line intersects the Y axis at 3.882. For simplicity, round this to 3.9. This represents the predicted relationship score when behavior score equals 0.00. Locate the point on the X axis where behavior score equals 100. Trace up to intersect the regression line and then trace horizontally to the Y axis. The Y axis is intersected at about 2.4. Thus, as behavior scores increase from 0 to 100, predicted relationship score decreases from (about) 3.9 to 2.4. This represents a decrease of 1.5: $3.9 - 2.4 = 1.5$. Dividing by 100 estimates the decrease as behavior score increases by 1 point: $1.5/100 = .015$. As we said, a decrease is represented, so $-.015$ is the approximate slope of the regression line and thus the approximate value of B.

5. The standardized coefficient, r, and the unstandardized coefficient B have a straightforward mathematical relationship. If we know the value of B, we may derive r using the equation $r = B(s_X/s_Y)$. If we know the value of r, we may derive B using the equation $B = r(s_Y/s_X)$. In these equations, s_X is the standard deviation of X, and s_Y is that of Y. In our example of behavior score and relationship score, the standard deviation of behavior score (the independent variable, X) is 26.249 and that of parent-child relationship score (the dependent variable, Y) is 0.653. In this example, $r = -.015(26.249/0.653) = -.603$. This result differs from $-.604$ only due to rounding error. Solving for B: $B = -.604(0.653/26.249) = -.015$. (See Toothaker and Miller, 1996, p. 207 for formulas for r and B.)

6. The maximum possible absolute value of phi is less than 1.00 in some situations. This means the actual size of association is often somewhat stronger than suggested by the descriptors in Table 8.3, so they should be applied with some caution. Phi was first presented in Chapter 7 (Section 7.5.3). As stated there, phi may be used to measure association between a dichotomous variable and a nominal-level variable with more than two categories. When used in this way, it should not be conceptualized as Pearson's r. Its most common use by far is to assess association between two dichotomous variables.

7. The correlation between a dichotomous variable and a variable at the interval/ratio level of measurement is termed the *point-biserial correlation* (r_{pb}). See Glass and Hopkins (1996, pp. 133–134).

MORE MEASURES OF SIZE OF ASSOCIATION

9.1 CHAPTER OVERVIEW

Now we are ready to examine the *standardized difference between means* (*SDM*), the preferred measure of size of association when one variable is dichotomous and the other is interval/ratio. Topics pertaining to the *SDM* include formulas, graphical depiction, qualitative descriptors of size of association, cautions in interpretation, and situations with more than two groups. We also discuss an alternative to the *SDM*, *eta squared* (η^2). The latter part of the chapter concentrates on measures of size of directional relationship between ordinal-level variables. Key measures include *Kendall's tau$_b$* (τ_b), *Kendall's tau$_c$* (τ_c), *gamma* (γ), and *Somer's d*.

9.2 INTRODUCTION TO THE STANDARDIZED DIFFERENCE BETWEEN MEANS

As presented in Chapter 3, the mean is the workhorse measure of central tendency. Assessment of relationship when one variable is interval/ratio or almost so and the other is nominal involves comparison of means. When means are precisely equal, variables are unassociated. When means differ, they are associated. Suppose that the mean score on the XYZ self-esteem scale is 45 points in Group A and 45 points in Group B. As these means are equal, group membership (the nominal-level variable) and self-esteem (the almost interval/ratio-level variable) are unassociated. Now suppose instead that the mean self-esteem score is 45 points in Group A and 40 points in Group B. In this example, means differ and therefore the variables are associated.

Sticking with this second example, the next question that might be asked is "How large is the association?" or perhaps "How much of a difference in self-esteem is represented by this difference of 5 points?" Note that self-esteem is abstract and intangible. (It is hard to "reach out and touch" self-esteem.) When the dependent variable is familiar and tangible, one can often answer questions pertaining to size based on experience and common sense. For instance, if members of one weight loss group lose an average of 50 pounds more than those in another, one's reaction might be: "That is a lot of weight."

But how does one make sense of a difference of 5 points in self-esteem? Particularly when the dependent variable is intangible, the best way to assess size of association between a nominal variable and an interval/ratio one is via the standardized difference between means. Symbolized by **SDM, the standardized difference between means** expresses differences in means in terms of the standard deviation observed in the groups. Its formula is:

$$SDM = \frac{\overline{X}_1 - \overline{X}_2}{s_{\text{wg}}} \tag{9.1}$$

where SDM is the standardized difference between means, $\overline{X}_1$ is the mean of Group 1, $\overline{X}_2$ is the mean of Group 2, and s_{wg} is the standard deviation within groups. In formula 9.1, the standard deviations in the two groups are presumed to be equal. Using symbols, $s_1 = s_2$ where s_1 is the standard deviation in Group 1 and s_2 is that in Group 2. Formula 9.1 presumes that the s_{wg} equals these standard deviations. That is, $s_{\text{wg}} = s_1 = s_2$.

Staying with our example, presume that the standard deviation of self-esteem within each group is 10. As such, the standard deviation within groups, s_{wg}, equals 10. The standardized difference between means then is:

$$SDM = \frac{45 - 40}{10} = \frac{5}{10} = 0.50$$

On average, the self-esteem of those in Group A is one-half of a standard deviation higher than the self-esteem of those in Group B. Table 9.1 presents qualitative descriptors for the SDM. According to Table 9.1, the SDM in our example, 0.50, represents a "medium" size of association. Stated differently, the strength of association is moderate. The descriptors in Table 9.1 for the SDM convey associations of the same strength/size as do the corresponding descriptors in tables for the difference in percentages (Table 6.4), the odds ratio (Table 7.2), and the correlation coefficient (Table 8.3).

Although the standardized difference between means is particularly helpful when the dependent variable is intangible, it is also the preferred measure for tan-

TABLE 9.1	DESCRIPTORS OF ASSOCIATION FOR THE **SDM**		
Difference	**Size of Association**	**Strength of Association**
About 0.20 (or −0.20)	Small	Weak
About 0.50 (or −0.50)	Medium	Moderate
About 0.80 (or −0.80)	Large	Strong
About 1.30 (or −1.30) or greater	Very large	Very strong

gible variables. For instance, suppose that a pregnant women's health program implements two interventions designed to help teen mothers give birth to healthy babies. A specific program goal is to reduce the number of low birthweight babies. The following results are observed: (1) the mean birthweight of babies whose mothers who receive Intervention 1 is 5 pounds, 5 ounces (85 ounces), (2) that of babies whose mothers who receive Intervention 2 is 5 pounds, 10 ounces (90 ounces), and (3) the standard deviation in each group is 20 ounces. In this example, the *SDM* computes to:

$$SDM = \frac{85 - 90}{20} = \frac{-5}{20} = -0.25$$

Thus mothers who received Intervention 1 had babies that were, on average, about one-quarter of a standard deviation lighter than for those who received Intervention 2. Referring to Table 9.1, this difference would be characterized as small.

9.3 GRAPHICAL DEPICTION AND INTERPRETATION OF THE *SDM*

Graphical display of the *SDM* can further understanding. Figure 9.1 presents *SDM*s of 0.2, 0.5., 0.8, and 1.3 standard deviations. These correspond respectively to the descriptors small, medium, large, and very large in Table 9.1. The four parts of Figure 9.1 each present two distributions, one for each of the two groups being compared. In terms of formula 9.1, think of one distribution as displaying scores in Group 1 and the other as doing so for Group 2. Each figure assumes that the distributions have (1) normal shapes and (2) equal standard deviations.

The figure in the upper left of Figure 9.1 presents an *SDM* of 0.2, which Table 9.1 classifies as a small difference (small association). Note the extensive overlap between the two distributions in this figure. In contrast, the figure in the lower right of Figure 9.1 presents an *SDM* of 1.3 standard deviations, which Table 9.1 classifies as a very large difference (very large association). Note that the two distributions in this figure are much more distinct than those in the upper left figure. Stated differently, there is much less overlap between the distributions.

The upper right part of Figure 9.1 presents an *SDM* of 0.5, which Table 9.1 calls a medium difference (medium association). In this chapter's first example, those in Group A scored 0.5 standard deviations higher on the XYZ self-esteem scale than did those in Group B. This figure represents that size of association. Think of the left distribution in this figure as representing Group B (the group with the lower mean score in self-esteem) and the right distribution as representing Group A (the group with the higher mean). One can see considerable overlap between these distributions. In other words, a reasonably large percentage of persons in Group B have higher self-esteem than do a reasonably large percentage of persons in Group A. The degree of overlap in this figure is intermediate between that in the two previously described figures. The final part of Figure 9.1 (lower left) conveys a difference of 0.8 standard deviations (an *SDM* of 0.8). This is characterized by Table 9.1 as a large difference (large association).

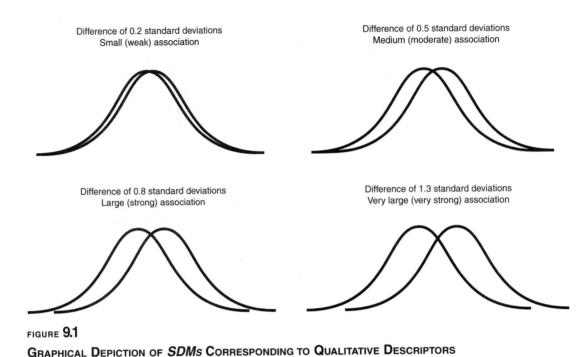

Difference of 0.2 standard deviations
Small (weak) association

Difference of 0.5 standard deviations
Medium (moderate) association

Difference of 0.8 standard deviations
Large (strong) association

Difference of 1.3 standard deviations
Very large (very strong) association

FIGURE 9.1

GRAPHICAL DEPICTION OF *SDMs* CORRESPONDING TO QUALITATIVE DESCRIPTORS

Comparison of the four parts of Figure 9.1 allows us to conclude that the larger the standardized difference between means:

1. The less overlap between the distributions and
2. The more distinct the distributions

Our knowledge of the normal distribution permits further conclusions about the degree of overlap connected with various standard differences in means. Figure 9.2 presents an *SDM* of 1.0. The mean of the group with the higher mean (the group depicted to the right) is one (1.00) standard deviation above that of the group with the lower mean (the group to the left). Just as did Figure 9.1, Figure 9.2 presumes equal standard deviations and normal distributions. In Figure 9.2, a vertical line extends down from the highest point of the curve that describes the group with the higher mean. For a normal distribution, this point represents the mode, the median, and the mean (see Chapter 5). Given that the difference in means between groups is one standard deviation, this line intersects the lower distribution one standard deviation above its mean. Recall from Chapter 5 that in a normal distribution (1) 50% of cases are below the mean and (2) 34% of cases are located between the mean and one standard deviation above the mean. Thus a total of 84% of cases (50% + 34% = 84%) in the group with the lower mean are located to the left of the vertical line. Stated differently, 84% of cases in the lower group have values below the mean in the higher group.

Assessment of the percentage of cases in the lower group with values below the mean of the higher group helps provide an intuitive feel for size of association. For instance, when size of association is small according to Table 9.1 (*SDM* = 0.2),

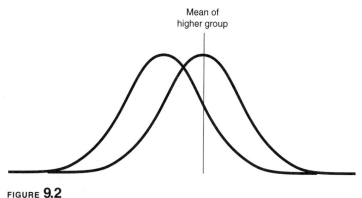

FIGURE **9.2**

A STANDARDIZED DIFFERENCE BETWEEN MEANS OF 1.00

about 60% of cases in the lower group are below the mean of the higher. For the other values in Table 9.1 this percentage is as follows: medium association (SDM = 0.5), about 70%; large association (SDM = 0.8), about 80%; and very large association (SDM = 1.3), about 90%. (All percentages presume normal distributions and equal standard deviations.)

All the just-stated percentages indicate the percentage of cases in the lower group that are below the mean of the higher. The choice of direction was arbitrary. We could equally well have chosen to convey the percentage of cases in the higher group that were above the mean of the lower group. For instance, when an association is very large, approximately 90% of cases in the higher group are above the mean of the lower.

The just-presented graphics and percentages demonstrate that the qualitative descriptors presented in this text characterize size of association within the context of relationships typically observed in social science rather than in a strict mathematical sense. As discussed in Chapter 6, Section 6.7, the pattern in social science is to find associations that are not, mathematically speaking, particularly large. For instance, even when the SDM equals 1.3 (a very large association), one can identify a subgroup of 10% (100% − 90% = 10%) of persons in the group with the lower mean with scores that exceed the mean of the higher group.

9.4 BEGINNING TO WORK WITH REAL-WORLD DATA

So far, discussion of the SDM has invoked two assumptions, normality and equal standard deviations, that will be lacking in most actual data analysis situations. How should one proceed when these assumptions are not met?

When distributions are markedly nonnormal in shape, neither the graphics in Figure 9.1 nor the just-presented percentages will apply precisely. However, when they are reasonably close to normal, these graphics and percentages apply reasonably well. Furthermore, even with markedly nonnormal distributions, the SDM is still a preferred measure for assessing differences between means.

On the other hand, marked differences between the standard deviations in the groups recommend caution. These standard deviations provide the basis for "standardizing" the SDM. When they differ substantially, there is no uniform standard for calculation. Consider the following data:

GROUP	MEAN SCORE OF XYZ SCALE	STANDARD DEVIATION
Group 1	45	10
Group 2	40	20

Using the standard deviation of Group 1 to compute the *SDM*:

$$SDM = \frac{45 - 40}{10} = \frac{5}{10} = 0.5$$

Using the standard deviation of Group 2:

$$SDM = \frac{45 - 40}{20} = \frac{5}{20} = 0.25$$

These two sets of results differ substantially and suggest quite different interpretations of size of association. This example demonstrates that the *SDM* should not be used when standard deviations within the groups differ greatly. As a pragmatic guideline, do not use the *SDM* when the standard deviation in the group with the larger standard deviation is more than about one-third (33%) larger than that in the group with the smaller standard deviation. To determine the percentage by which the larger standard deviation exceeds the smaller: (1) subtract the smaller standard deviation from the larger; (2) divide by the smaller; and (3) multiply by 100. In the current example:

$$\frac{20 - 10}{10} = \frac{10}{10} = 1 \times 100 = 100\%$$

In this example, then, the standard deviation in the larger group is 100% larger than that in the smaller, so the *SDM* is not recommended. This guideline is flexible. If the larger standard deviation exceeds the smaller by an amount modestly larger than the guideline, go ahead and calculate the *SDM*, recognizing that it should be interpreted with some caution. Guidelines for calculating the *SDM* in real-world situations follow.

9.5 CALCULATING THE *SDM* WITH REAL-WORLD DATA

As stated earlier, in real-world research standard deviations within the groups typically differ at least to some degree. Yet formula 9.1 for the *SDM* assumes them to be equal. Thus a method is needed for determining the s_{wg}, the denominator in formula 9.1, when the standard deviations do indeed differ. This section provides procedures for estimating the s_{wg}. Consider the following data pertaining to the XYZ Self-Esteem Scale:

GROUP[1]	MEAN SCORE ON XYZ SCALE	STANDARD DEVIATION
Group 1 ($n_1 = 25$)	45	15
Group 2 ($n_2 = 25$)	40	20

Prior to calculating the *SDM*, one should check whether the sample standard deviations are sufficiently similar to recommend its use:

$$\frac{20 - 15}{15} = \frac{5}{15} = 0.33 \times 100 = 33\%$$

In this example, the larger standard deviation exceeds the smaller by precisely the limit recommended by the guideline, so the *SDM* is an appropriate measure.

Given equal sample sizes, an excellent estimate of the s_{wg} is obtained by taking the average of the two groups' standard deviations:

$$s_{wg} \approx \frac{s_1 + s_2}{2} \tag{9.2}$$

In this formula, the symbol $\approx$ conveys "approximately equal to," s_1 is the standard deviation in Group 1, and s_2 is that in Group 2. In the current example:

$$s_{wg} \approx \frac{15 + 20}{2} = \frac{35}{2} = 17.50$$

Inserting the estimated s_{wg} into the formula for the *SDM*:

$$SDM \approx \frac{45 - 40}{17.5} = \frac{5}{17.5} = 0.286$$

Hence, the mean score in Group 1 is about 0.29 standard deviation units higher than is the mean in Group 2. Assuming that sample sizes are equal and that the 33% guideline is not exceeded, the estimate of the *SDM* calculated with the s_{wg} estimated via formula 9.2 is accurate to within 1%. This level of accuracy is more than enough for getting a good feel for size of association. When precision is required, see the formula in the accompanying endnote.[2]

The preceding calculation presumed equal sample sizes. When group sizes are unequal, a good estimate of the s_{wg} is given by:

$$s_{wg} \approx \frac{n_1 s_1 + n_2 s_2}{n_1 + n_2} \tag{9.3}$$

where n_1 is the sample size in Group 1, n_2 is that in Group 2, s_1 is the standard deviation in Group 1, and s_2 is that in Group 2. For a calculation example, we will continue to use the same data on self-esteem but with different sample sizes:

GROUP	MEAN SCORE OF XYZ SCALE	STANDARD DEVIATION
Group 1 ($n_1 = 30$)	45	15
Group 2 ($n_2 = 20$)	40	20

Using formula 9.3, the standard deviation within groups is estimated to be:

$$s_{\text{wg}} \approx \frac{20(20) + 30(15)}{20 + 30} = \frac{400 + 450}{50} = \frac{850}{50} = 17.0$$

Note that formula 9.3 gives more weight to the group with the larger sample size than to that with the smaller. Thus the estimate of 17.0 is closer to the standard deviation in the larger group ($n_1 = 30$, $s_1 = 15$) than to that in the smaller group ($n_2 = 20$, $s_2 = 20$). Inserting 17.0 into formula 9.1, the estimated standardized difference between means is:

$$SDM \approx \frac{45 - 40}{17.0} = \frac{5}{17.0} = 0.294$$

When the SDM is calculated using formula 9.3 to estimate the s_{wg}, it provides a highly accurate estimate. (Presuming that the 33% guideline is met, it is accurate to within about 3%.) When precision is needed, such as for a formal report, see the formula in the accompanying endnote.[3]

Many social science measures, notably Cohen's d and "effect size," are similar (or in some cases identical) to the standardized difference between means as presented here (see Rosenthal, 1994, pp. 231–244 for these measures).[4] The term *standardized difference between means* (SDM) is (to my knowledge) used only in this text. Most statistical programs do not calculate the SDM. Your best tactic for determining it will be to have the program generate output with means and standard deviations and then to use these for calculation.

9.6 MEASURING SIZE OF ASSOCIATION FOR MORE THAN TWO GROUPS

9.6.1 Calculating an Average Standardized Difference Between Means

The SDM specifically assesses the difference between two groups; it has no easy extension to situations involving three or more groups. Rather than defining a formal extension, I will instead suggest a commonsense approach. One can get a good working estimate of size of association by calculating an "average" standard difference between means. For instance, with three groups—A, B, and C—one would calculate the SDM for the three possible comparisons—A and B, A and C, and B and C—and then compute the average of these comparisons. For four groups one would take the average of A and B, A and C, A and D, B and C, B and D, and C and D. Having carried out calculations, one could use the descriptors in Table 9.1 to interpret the overall size of association. It should be emphasized that such an "average standardized difference between means" is an informal tool rather than a formal measure.[5]

9.6.2 Eta Squared (η^2) and Other Measures

When one variable is dichotomous and the other is at the interval/ratio level, the SDM can become your workhorse tool for assessing size of association. **Eta squared,** also known as the **correlation ratio** and symbolized by η^2, is also an excellent measure of the size of association. (Eta is pronounced "eight-ah.") It has two advantages over the *SDM*. First, it is preferred over the *SDM* when there are two groups and the standard deviation of the larger group exceeds that of the smaller by more than one-third. Second, it may be used with multiple groups, that is, with more than two groups.

Eta squared measures the proportion (percentage) of variance in an interval/ratio-level variable that is explained by a categorical variable. For instance, an η^2 of .40 conveys that 40% of the variance in the interval/ratio variable is explained by the categorical variable. Eta squared may vary from 0.00 (no association) to 1.00 (perfect association). The main problem encountered in interpreting eta squared is that the proportion of explained variance often sounds small. Stated differently, the commonsense (intuited) interpretation of size of association based on η^2 underestimates the actual size of association. For instance, an η^2 of .25 sounds small but nevertheless indicates a reasonably strong association between variables. (This is the same problem encountered in interpreting r^2, as discussed in Chapter 8, Section 8.8.)

The square root of eta squared equals **eta** and is symbolized by η. For instance, when η^2 equals .25, η equals $\sqrt{.25} = .50$. An advantage of η over η^2 is that the descriptors for the Pearson correlation coefficient (see Table 8.3) do a reasonably good job of conveying its size of association.[6] Other measures of size of association for three or more groups include *f*, as presented in Cohen (1988, pp. 273–288) and Aron and Aron (1997, pp. 215–217), and omega squared (ω^2), as presented in Toothaker and Miller (1996, pp. 424, 473). See Glass and Hopkins (1996, pp. 180–182) for further discussion of eta squared.

9.7   MEASURES OF DIRECTIONAL RELATIONSHIP FOR CATEGORICAL VARIABLES

9.7.1   *When to Use These Measures*

Chapter 7 concluded by stating that in Chapter 9 we would introduce several measures that assess the size/strength of directional relationship between ordinal-level categorical variables. Four such measures—Kendall's tau$_b$ (τ_b), Kendall's tau$_c$ (τ_c), gamma (γ), and Somer's *d*—are summarized in this section.

Table 9.2 presents four examples involving relationships between ordinal-level categorical variables. These examples provide guidance in assessing whether relationships have direction, and thus whether to choose a directional or nondirectional measure of size of association. When a relationship has direction, one of the four measures introduced here will generally do the best job of assessing size of association. For simplicity, these measures are termed *directional measures*. When two ordinal-level variables are related (their percentages differ) but there is no directional pattern to this relationship, one of the measures presented in Chapter 7 (Section 7.5.3) for multicategory variables should be used. Among these measures, Cramer's *V* is typically the best choice. For simplicity, these variables are termed *nondirectional measures*. The variables in Table 9.2 are (1) client level

TABLE 9.2	EXAMPLES: ASSOCIATION BETWEEN ORDINAL-LEVEL VARIABLES			
	PROGRESS ON MOST IMPORTANT PROBLEM			
Motivation for Services	**Great Deal (%)**	**Some (%)**	**None (%)**	**Got Worse (%)**
Example 1				
Very	60	25	10	5
Somewhat	45	25	20	10
A little	35	25	25	15
Not at all	30	20	30	20
Example 2				
Very	40	30	20	10
Somewhat	60	25	10	5
A little	40	30	20	10
Not at all	25	30	25	20
Example 3				
Very	60	25	10	5
Somewhat	60	25	10	5
A little	40	30	20	10
Not at all	25	30	25	20
Example 4				
Very	40	30	20	10
Somewhat	25	25	40	10
A little	50	20	15	15
Not at all	25	55	10	10

of motivation for services and (2) client rating of progress on his or her most important problem. A counseling clinic or mental health center might gather such data.

The relationship in Example 1 is clearly a directional one. As level of motivation increases, so does progress made on the client's most important problem. The directional measures introduced here are designed for assessing such associations. In Example 2, the association between level of motivation and rating of progress has a "curved" quality not unlike that described for curvilinear association between interval/ratio variables in Chapter 8. Thus reports of progress become more positive as motivation level increases up to the level of "somewhat" motivated, at which point the direction of relationship reverses. For instance, observe that as motivation level increases from "somewhat" to "very" motivated, client reports on progress become less positive. When a relationship reverses its direction, the directional measures do not assess size of association effectively and a nondirectional measure (for instance, Cramer's V) would be preferred.

Choice of measure can be difficult in some situations. For instance, in Example 3, client ratings become more positive as level of motivation increases from "not at all" to "a little" to "somewhat." At this point, however, the relationship levels off. Thus, those who are "very" motivated report no greater progress than those who are only "somewhat" motivated. The relationship in this example could be characterized as "leveling" but not as reversing itself. All things considered, the directional measures represent the best choice in this situation. In general, these are preferred whenever some reasonably clear directional pattern is observed. In Example 4, the variables are related (as percentages differ), but there is no suggestion of a directional pattern. Directional measures do not effectively assess size of association in situations such as this and a nondirectional measure should be used.[7]

It is often strategic to calculate both directional and nondirectional measures. The nondirectional measures assess the overall size of association without regard to direction. The directional measures complement this perspective by assessing size of directional association. By using both sets of tools, one can probe for both possible types of relationship (nondirectional and directional), thus covering all the bases.

The measures introduced here are designed for measuring directional association when the number of categories (values) is not overwhelmingly large. When both ordinal variables have more than about 10 categories, Spearman's r (r_{ranks}) (see Chapter 8, Section 8.13) provides a good measure of size of association. In essence, computer programs for r_{ranks} convert values (categories) into ranks and then compute the correlation of these ranks.

9.7.2 *Four Measures of Directional Relationship*

Four key measures of directional association between ordinal-level variables—**Kendall's tau$_b$** (τ_b), **Kendall's tau$_c$** (τ_c), **gamma (γ)** and **Somer's *d***—all may vary from a minimum of −1.00 to a maximum of 1.00. When these measures compute to negative values, the direction of relationship is negative. Such values convey that as one variable increases, the other decreases. Positive values indicate a positive relationship, meaning that as one variable increases, so does the other. Given that the values of these measures vary from −1.00 to 1.00, the qualitative descriptors in Table 8.3 for interpreting size of association for Pearson's r can provide some basic guidance in interpretation.[8]

Each of the ordinal measures has some advantages and some weaknesses, so it is difficult to choose a single best measure. This difficulty is a weakness of all the measures. No single measure has moved to the forefront to become a workhorse tool.

Among the measures, tau$_b$ has generated the most enthusiasm from one authority, Blalock (1979, pp. 439–446). Thus, if one wanted to choose one "best" measure, this would be a good choice. One disadvantage of tau$_b$ is that it can obtain values of 1.00 or −1.00 only in a square table (same number of rows and columns; Norusis, 1997, p. 353). Tau$_c$ can obtain these values in any size table and is thus a good choice when the number of rows and columns differs. Somer's d differs from the other statistics in that it computes to a different value depending on which variable in the contingency table is designated as the dependent variable. When one variable in the table is clearly independent and the other is clearly dependent, Somer's d is a good choice. Gamma has the disadvantage that it may obtain its maximum value of 1.00 or −1.00 in situations in which most would not regard the relationship as perfect (that is, as large as it could possibly be). A second disadvantage is that it may compute to be artificially high when the number of categories is limited. In general, all these measures provide a more accurate gauge of size of association when the number of categories is high (say, five, six, or seven) rather than quite low (say, two, three, or four).

All four measures are readily calculated via statistical software packages. Norusis (1999, pp. 360–365) presents an excellent overview of these and related measures.

Table 9.2 presented hypothetical data pertaining to the association between client motivation for services and client progress on the most important problem. For purposes of computer analysis, codes were assigned as follows: motivation, very = 4, somewhat = 3, a little = 2, not at all = 1; progress, great deal = 4, some = 3, none = 2, got worse = 1. The values of the four ordinal measures for the data presented in Example 1 in Table 9.2 are tau_b (τ_b) = .234, tau_c (τ_c) = .226, gamma (γ) = .319, and Somer's d = .226. (This is the value of Somer's d when motivation is treated as the independent variable.) Each measure has a positive value, conveying that client motivation and progress are positively associated. As motivation (presumably the independent variable) increases, so does progress (presumably the dependent variable). Using the descriptors developed for the correlation coefficient, the association between motivation and progress might best be characterized as medium in size or almost so.

Chapter 8 (Section 8.13) discussed whether measures developed for interval/ratio-level variables (particularly Pearson's r) may be used appropriately with ordinal-level variables. When one's primary goal is to learn about and understand data, these measures can be employed. For instance, Pearson's r for the data in Example 1 in Table 9.2 computes to .278, a value similar to those for the four ordinal measures. Indeed, typically the value for r (when applied to ordinal-level variables in a contingency table) is similar to those of the just-presented measures. But when one's primary goal is to conduct an accurate statistical significance test (covered in later chapters), greater caution is needed.

9.8   CHAPTER SUMMARY

When one variable is dichotomous and the other is at the interval/ratio level of measurement or almost so, the standardized difference between means (SDM) is the preferred measure of size of association. Its formula (9.1) is $SDM = (\overline{X}_1 - \overline{X}_2)/s_{wg}$. An SDM of 0.2 represents a small association whereas one of 0.8 represents a large association (see Table 9.1). Assuming normality and equal standard deviations, when an association is characterized as large (SDM = 0.8) about 80% of cases in the "lower" group have values that are below the mean of the "higher" group. The SDM should not be used when the standard deviations of the groups differ markedly, say when the larger standard deviation is more than about one-third larger than the smaller one.

The chapter provides formulas (9.2 and 9.3) for estimating the standard deviation within groups for equal and unequal sample sizes. When the groups' standard deviations are within the one-third guideline, these estimates are highly accurate.

Eta squared, the correlation ratio (η^2), measures the proportion of variance of an interval/ratio-level variable that is explained by a categorical variable. It may be used with more than two groups, a distinct advantage. The square root of η^2 is eta (η). Size of association for η may be interpreted using the guidelines in Table 8.3 for the correlation coefficient.

Four key measures of directional association between ordinal-level categorical variables are Kendall's tau$_b$ (τ_b), Kendall's tau$_c$ (τ_c), gamma (γ), and Somer's d. The range of possible values for all of these is from -1.00 to 1.00. No one of these measures is clearly preferable to the others. Tau$_b$ is an excellent choice when both variables have the same number of categories. Tau$_c$ is a good choice when this is not the case. Somer's d is a good choice when the variables can be classified as independent and dependent.

In general, the directional measures of association presented in this chapter are preferred when relationships have direction, and the nondirectional measures (particularly Cramer's V) presented in Chapter 7 are preferred when this is not the case. It is often strategic to calculate both sets of measures.

PROBLEMS AND QUESTIONS

Section 9.2

1. In your own words, how is the standardized difference between means calculated?
2. Compute the *SDM* for each of the following results.
   a. $\overline{X}_1 = 20$, $\overline{X}_2 = 40$, $s_{wg} = 10$
   b. $\overline{X}_1 = 40$, $\overline{X}_2 = 20$, $s_{wg} = 10$
   c. $\overline{X}_1 = 20$, $\overline{X}_2 = 40$, $s_{wg} = 20$
   d. $\overline{X}_1 = 20$, $\overline{X}_2 = 50$, $s_{wg} = 10$
3. Using the qualitative descriptors in Table 9.1, characterize the size/strength of association conveyed by each of the following.
   a. $SDM = -0.80$
   b. $SDM = 0.80$
   c. $SDM = 2.00$
   d. $SDM = 0.30$
   e. $SDM = -0.53$
4. (T or F) The larger the absolute value of *SDM*, the larger the relationship.

Section 9.3

5. (T or F) In a graphical depiction of the *SDM* such as in Figure 9.1, the greater the overlap between the two distributions, the larger the *SDM*.

6. When an association is characterized as very large ($SDM = 1.3$), about what percentage of cases in the group with the lower mean are below the mean of the group with the higher mean?

Section 9.4

7. (T or F) The *SDM* is an effective and appropriate tool even when the standard deviations of the two groups differ quite markedly.
8. Is the *SDM* an effective measure of size of association in the following situation? Group 1, $\overline{X} = 10$, $s = 8$; Group 2, $\overline{X} = 15$, $s = 18$

Section 9.5

9. For each of the following situations: (1) assume that sample sizes are equal, and (2) use formula 9.2 to estimate the s_{wg}.
   a. $s_1 = 10.00$, $s_2 = 10.00$
   b. $s_1 = 10.00$, $s_2 = 12.00$
   c. $s_1 = 8.0$, $s_2 = 6.0$
10. Consider situation b in the prior question. If the mean in Group 1 is 12 and that in Group 2 is 20, what is the estimated *SDM*? (Assume equal sample sizes.)
11. Using formula 9.3 to estimate the s_{wg}, estimate the *SDM* for the following situation:
    Group 1: $\overline{X} = 22$, $s = 8$, $n = 21$
    Group 2: $\overline{X} = 16$, $s = 10$, $n = 36$

Section 9.6

12. (T or F) The *SDM* is conveniently and formally extended to situations involving three or more groups.

13. Eta squared (the correlation ratio) conveys the proportion of explained _____ .

14. Eta squared, η^2, may range from a minimum possible value of _____ to a maximum possible value of _____ .

15. Using the descriptors for *r* presented in Table 8.3, indicate the approximate strength of association conveyed by η^2 in each of the following. (Note that the value provided is for η^2, not η.)
    a. $\eta^2 = .25$
    b. $\eta^2 = .09$
    c. $\eta^2 = .15$
    d. $\eta^2 = .01$
    e. $\eta^2 = -.5$ (trick question?)

16. (T or F) A disadvantage of η^2 is that its value often sounds small.

Section 9.7

17. Kendall's tau$_b$, Kendall's tau$_c$, gamma, and Somer's *d* all measure . . .
    a. The overall size of association in a contingency table rather than the size of directional association
    b. The size of directional association in a contingency table
    c. Predominantly, the size of association between variables at the nominal level of measurement

18. The four measures mentioned in the prior question may range from a minimum possible value of _____ to a maximum possible value of _____ .

19. (T or F) Cramer's *V* is a preferred measure of the size of directional association.

20. Use the qualitative descriptors for *r* in Table 8.3 to indicate the approximate strength/size of association conveyed by each of the following. Also indicate the direction of association.
    a. Kendall's tau$_b$ = .68
    b. gamma = −.12
    c. Somer's *d* = −.28

 COMPUTER EXERCISES

For general instructions on computer exercises, see the note in Chapter 2.

1. Estimate the standardized difference between means (*SDM*) for the dichotomous independent variable MINORCHI (child's ethnicity: minority or white) and the dependent variable BEHAVTOT (score on behavior problem checklist). Comment on the size of association. [In SPSS, *Analyze > Compare Means > Means,* click BEHAVTOT to "Dependent List" space, click MINORCH to "Independent List" space, *Options* to verify that "Mean," "Number of Cases," and "Standard Deviation" are in "Cell Statistics" space (if not, click these over), *Continue, OK.*]

    Check your answers: No popular computer programs that I am aware of easily calculate the *SDM*. In the MINORCHI/BEHAVTOT example, the estimated s_{wg} is:

    $$s_{wg} = \frac{(26.04)(552) + (26.07)(202)}{552 + 202} = 26.05$$

    and the estimated *SDM* equals $(38.24 - 32.55)/26.05 = 0.22$. The association is small in size.

2. Estimate and interpret the *SDM* for the independent variable ONEORTWO (one-parent versus two-parent family structure) and the dependent variable RELSCALE (closeness/quality of parent-child relationship). [In SPSS, *Analyze > Compare Means > Means* (if necessary, click back variables from prior exercise), click RELSCALE to "Dependent List" space, click ONEORTWO to "Independent List" space, *Options* to verify that "Mean," "Number of Cases," and "Standard Deviation" are in "Cell Statistics" space (if not, click these over), *Continue, OK.*]

    Check your answers:

    $$s_{wg} = \frac{(633)(0.653) + (114)(0.609)}{633 + 114} = 0.646$$

    The estimated *SDM* equals $(3.460 - 3.317)/0.646 = 0.22$, a fairly small difference or association.

3. Calculate Kendall's tau$_b$, Kendall's tau$_c$, gamma, and Somer's d for the independent variable FEELCLOS (closeness of parent-child relationship) and IMPACT (impact of adoption on family). [In SPSS, *Analyze > Descriptive Statistics > Crosstabs*, click back any unwanted variables, click IMPACT to space below "Rows," click FEELCLOS to space below "Columns," *Cells*, click box next to "Column" if not already checked, *Continue, Statistics*, click the boxes next to the four desired statistics (which are in the "Ordinal" area; also, you may want to "uncheck" all other statistics that may be checked), *Continue, OK.*]

Check your answers: In the Directional Measures table, Somer's $d = -.572$ with IMPACT as the dependent variable. In the Symmetric Measures table, Kendall's tau$_b$ = $-.524$, Kendall's tau$_c$ = $-.421$, and gamma = $-.751$.

Note: Each of these measures conveys a strong negative association between FEELCLOS and IMPACT. Why is this association negative rather than positive? Click the icon in the toolbar with a question mark to bring up the "Variables" dialog box. Scroll and highlight FEELCLOS and then IMPACT. Observe that the most positive response on FEELCLOS ("yes, very much so") has the lowest numeric code (1) and that the most positive response on IMPACT has the highest code (5). Thus these two variables are coded in opposite directions. These codings generate the negative association. To reduce confusion, one would do well to recode FEELCLOS so that high codes convey high degrees of closeness and low codes convey low degrees. (To do this, one would recode 1s to 4s, 2s to 3s, 3s to 2s, and 4s to 1s.) With FEELCLOS recoded in this way, the association between FEELCLOS and IMPACT would become positive.

4. Calculate Kendall's tau$_b$, Kendall's tau$_c$, gamma, and Somer's d for the variables EDUCMOM (adoptive mother's education level) and IMPACT (impact of adoption on family). Consider EDUCMOM to be the independent variable. Also compute Pearson's r (it can be found in same dialog box as other requested measures). Finally, interpret these measures.

Check your answers: In the Directional Measures table, Somer's $d = -.108$ with IMPACT as the dependent variable. In the Symmetric Measures table: Kendall's tau$_b$ = $-.117$, Kendall's tau$_c$ = $-.104$, gamma = $-.164$, and $r = -.154$. There is a weak negative association between the mother's education level and the adoption's impact; the lower the education level, the more positive the impact.

NOTES

1. Note that the small n is used rather than the capital N. This is because the number of cases in a group is designated rather than the total number of cases in the study.

2. Given equal sample sizes, when precision is required the s_{wg} is calculated as follows: $s_{wg} = \sqrt{(s_1^2 + s_2^2)/2}$ where s_1^2 is the variance in Group 1 and s_2^2 is that in Group 2. This, in turn, is used as the denominator in formula 9.1.

3. When precision is required and sample sizes are unequal, the SDM should be calculated using the following formula for the s_{wg}:

$$s_{wg} = \sqrt{\frac{(n_1 - 1)s_1^2 + (n_2 - 1)s_2^2}{n_1 + n_2 - 2}}$$

where n_1 is the sample size in Group 1, n_2 is that in Group 2, and s_1^2 and s_2^2 are variances in these groups.

4. In experimental designs, an "effect size" is often computed by subtracting the mean of the control group from that of the experimental and then dividing by the standard deviation of the control group (the group that does not receive the experimental intervention). As such, effect size differs from the SDM as presented here, because the SDM divides by an estimate of standard deviation in both groups (which are presumed to be equal). See Rubin and Babbie (1997, pp. 514–518) or Rosenthal (1994, pp. 231–245).

5. As emphasized in the text, the average SDM is an informal tool. With this in mind, here are some recommendations regarding calculation. First, the SDM formula (9.1) can calculate either a positive or a negative value. In calculating an average SDM, one should compute each SDM that composes it so that its value is a positive (subtract the smaller mean from the larger). Otherwise the average SDM can compute to a value close to 0.00 even when means differ greatly. Second, rather than

estimating a different denominator (s_{wg}) for each comparison, find the average standard deviation within all groups and use this average in all comparisons. (If group sizes are unequal, weight each standard deviation by sample size, using the same logic as in formula 9.3.) With more groups it becomes more likely that the largest s will exceed the smallest s by more than one-third, but the guideline on when to avoid using *SDM* in such cases can be relaxed somewhat in calculating an average *SDM*.

6. The size of association conveyed by a given eta when one variable is nominal and the other is interval/ratio is modestly larger than would be suggested by the descriptors for the correlation coefficient in Table 8.3. The statistic f as presented in Cohen (1988, pp. 273–288) pro-

vides perhaps the most preferred measure of size of association when there are three or more groups.

7. As presented in Chapter 8, Section 8.13, the values of a dichotomous variable can be conceptualized as high and low. Stated differently, they can be ordered. When cases in one category of a dichotomous variable tend to score higher on an ordinal-level variable than do those in the other, that relationship can be conceptualized as having direction. As such, it can often be assessed most effectively by a directional measure.

8. When the number of categories is limited, the actual size of association conveyed by tau_b, tau_c, and Somer's d is often somewhat greater than would be suggested by the descriptors in Table 8.3.

CAUSAL AND NONCAUSAL RELATIONSHIPS

Part Four shifts the focus away from relationship per se to whether a given relationship is causal, that is, whether one variable in a relationship actually affects (causes) another. For instance, suppose that researchers found a positive correlation between the number of hours of violent television shows watched by children and the number of "aggressive" behaviors during recess at school. Based on that information alone, the conclusion should not be drawn that watching violent television causes aggressive behavior. Perhaps kids who watch violent television (relative to those who don't) are (1) more likely to witness actual violence in the home, (2) more likely to experience corporal (physical) punishment, and (3) more likely to be exposed to violence in their neighborhood setting. Any (or some combination) of such factors (rather than the effects of violent television) may be the reason for the association between watching violent television and aggressive behavior. Factors such as these are confounding variables. Chapter 10 presents selected causal models that may explain relationships and stresses the importance of random assignment. Chapter 11 demonstrates how researchers control for confounding variables as they try to determine whether relationships may be causal.

THE ASSESSMENT OF CAUSALITY

10.1   CHAPTER OVERVIEW

We begin Chapter 10 with a general discussion of *causality* and the complications introduced by *confounding variables*. We consider the advantages of *experiments* for drawing causal conclusions and, correspondingly, the disadvantages of *surveys*. In closing, we look at a variety of *causal models* including the *antecedent variable* and *intervening variable* models and distinguish between *direct effects* and *indirect effects*.

10.2   INTRODUCTION TO CAUSALITY

Social research often investigates relationships between variables. For instance, several studies have demonstrated a relationship between children's watching of violence on television and their own aggressive behavior (Lazar, 1994; Comstock and Strasburger, 1990). Sometimes the identification of a relationship is the primary study objective, the end product. Other studies are more ambitious. They seek to determine whether one variable in a relationship *causes* the other. For the issue of television and aggressive behavior, a focus on causality would address the question: "Does watching violence on television *cause* children to behave aggressively?" The issue of **causality** *(causal attribution)* boils down to whether one can determine "what causes what."

This chapter presents a framework for establishing when relationships are likely to be causal, when this is unlikely, and when one simply cannot know. Research design—in particular, differences between experimental and survey designs—is integral to the assessment of causality.

Before we proceed, let's make two basic assumptions. Chapter 6, Section 6.4, clarified that even extremely weak (trivial) relationships are technically considered to be relationships. It makes little sense to probe whether a relationship of trivial size is a causal one. As such, we will presume that all associations presented in this chapter are at least "small" as defined by the qualitative descriptors presented in prior chapters (see Tables 6.4, 7.2, 8.3, and 9.1). Chapter 1, Section 1.13, pointed out that relationships in study samples are sometimes observed simply due to chance (luck of the draw). When an association may well be due to chance, it makes little sense to consider other possible causes. Thus we will presume that all relationships presented in this chapter are sufficiently solid that chance alone is an unlikely explanation. Chapters 14 to 16 focus in depth on the role of chance in relationships.

10.3 WHAT DOES "CAUSE" MEAN IN SOCIAL SCIENCE?

In social science, **cause** is a synonym for "to affect" ("to have an effect") or "to influence." Other words or phrases with nearly identical meanings include "results in," "leads to," "explains," and "increases/decreases the likelihood of." If one variable causes another, it exerts an influence on it. This influence need not be large (though it may be). So, if studying for a test helps even a small amount, we may say that studying *causes* improved test performance. Furthermore, the variable doing the causing (the independent variable) need not be the only one exerting influence. Indeed, in many situations, multiple independent variables affect a dependent variable. For instance, if three variables—studying, having taken a prior course in a similar area, and taking a practice test—all contribute to better test performance, then we may say that each causes improved test performance. When one variable affects another, there is a **causal relationship (causal association)** between them.

Occasionally, it is intuitively obvious that a relationship is not causal. In New York City, researchers have documented a positive association between ice cream consumption and burglaries of residences. On days when New Yorkers eat lots of ice cream, the burglary rate tends to be high. And on days when people refrain from ice cream consumption, these rates are much lower. Does eating ice cream cause burglary? Or is it the reverse; does burglary lead to ice cream eating? The answer to both questions is no. A third variable is responsible for (is the explanation for, the cause of) the association between crime and ice cream consumption. That variable is temperature. On hot days people eat a lot of ice cream. Also on hot days, people are often out of their homes (perhaps on vacation or at the beach). This increases opportunities for burglary. Hence, the association between ice cream consumption and burglary is not causal but instead is due to temperature.

Another example: I passed out a questionnaire to a recent class and found an association between preferring classical as contrasted to rock music and the reporting of aches and pains upon waking in the morning. That is, those who preferred classical music tended to report more aches and pains than did those who preferred rock. Given this association, I concluded that listening to classical music causes aches and pains and recommended that classical fans switch to rock.

Students in this class were of diverse ages. A student informed me that I had failed to consider the possible effects of age. She suggested that older students ("thirty-somethings" and older) were more likely to prefer classical music than were younger students (in their teens and twenties) and also that older students were more likely to experience aches and pains than were younger students. The association between listening to classical music and aching bones was not causal but was instead due to a third variable, age.

10.4   CONFOUNDING VARIABLES

On balance, social scientists are hesitant to conclude that associations are causal. This hesitation stems in part from science's general preference for the conservative and cautious. But the possible presence of confounding variables is the primary cause. As first presented in Chapter 1 (Section 1.7), **confounding variables** are variables that affect the pattern of association between two other variables. Most often, their effect is on size of association, though they may also affect direction of association, or the presence or absence of association. In some situations, the confounding variable may be the sole explanation for (cause of) the association. In the burglary/ice cream example, temperature is a confounding variable. If one could somehow hold the temperature constant, the association between ice cream consumption and burglary would presumably disappear. In the classical music/aching bones example, age is a confounding variable. Among persons of the *same* age, it is doubtful that there is a nontrivial association between preferred music and aches and pains.

Returning to the example of the association between children's watching of violent television and aggressive behavior (Lazar, 1994; Comstock and Strasburger, 1990): Could this association reflect the effects of confounding variables? Perhaps, for instance, children in homes with high levels of violence (partner abuse, severe and frequent corporal punishment, child abuse, tolerance of sibling-on-sibling physical aggression, etc.) tend to watch more violent television than do those without such violence in their homes. Perhaps a general climate of violence, not violent shows on television, is the primary cause of the children's aggressive behavior.

A dictionary defines *confound* as "to fail to discern differences between . . . mix up" or "to increase the confusion of." Confounding variables make it difficult to "unscramble" (determine) the causes of relationships. Several other terms have nearly identical meanings. The term **third variable** conveys that an initially observed relationship between two variables (such as amount of aches and pains and type of music) may be due to or influenced by a third (such as age). Other similar terms include *lurking variable* (here the idea is that an initially observed relationship is due to an unsuspected variable that is "lurking" in the background), *extraneous variable, control variable,* and *nuisance variable.* Social scientists are constantly alert to the possibility that confounding variables may be the explanation for (the cause of) an association between two other variables.

It may be helpful to look at an example from the human services field that demonstrates an initially observed relationship that is due to a confounding variable. Suppose that the mean number of behavior problems per child (as indicated by an instrument filled out by a caretaker) for 100 children in family foster care is 12.0 ($s = 10.0$), whereas that for 100 children in group homes is 18.0 ($s = 10.0$). Does this association, a reasonably large one according to Table 9.1 [$SDM = (12 - 18)/10 = -0.60$)], allow one to conclude that foster family care *causes* a reduction (relative to group home care) in behavior problems?

Table 10.1 introduces the child's age at placement into the analysis. It reveals that (1) younger children were placed more often in foster family care (80 of 100, 80%), whereas older children were placed more often in group homes (80 of 100, 80%); and (2) overall, younger children had fewer behavior problems than did older children: for younger children, $\overline{X} = 10$; for older children, $\overline{X} = 20$ (see the table's rightmost column for this data). Most importantly, Table 10.1 reveals that (1) among younger children, mean behavior scores are equal for those in family foster and group homes ($\overline{X} = 10$; see the "Age 10 or younger" row), and (2) among older children, mean scores are also equal ($\overline{X} = 20$; see the "Age 11 or older" row). Hence, among children of similar ages, type of placement and behavior problems are unassociated.

In this example, the initially observed relationship between type of placement and behavior problems is due to the confounding variable age. The initial relationship is observed because younger children (who most often had few behavior problems) were typically placed in foster family homes and older children (who most often had a higher number of such problems) were typically placed in group homes. In such a situation, one would not want to conclude that group home placement causes behavior problems. Thus Table 10.1 illustrates how a confounding variable (age) can bring about a relationship between two other variables.

TABLE 10.1   AGE ADDED TO PLACEMENT/BEHAVIOR ANALYSIS

	FOSTER FAMILY PLACEMENT		GROUP HOME PLACEMENT		TOTALS	
	$\overline{X}$	n	$\overline{X}$	n	$\overline{X}$	n
Age 10 or younger	10	80	10	20	10	100
Age 11 or older	20	20	20	80	20	100
Totals	12	100	18	100	15	200

Note: $\overline{X}$ = mean number of behavior problems per child; n = number of children in the group. It may be helpful to see how $\overline{X}$ was calculated in the Totals row and Totals column. Consider the Foster Family Placement column for $\overline{X}$. The mean score for 80 youths ages 10 or younger was 10 and that for 20 youths ages 11 or older was 20. The sum of the behavior problems of all youth in this column then is 80(10) + 20(20) = 800 + 400 = 1200. Given the total of 100 youths in this column, the mean score is 1200 ÷ 100 = 12.

10.5   EXPERIMENTAL AND SURVEY DESIGNS

As summarized in Chapter 1, Section 1.8, the two basic quantitative research designs are the survey and the experiment. In **experiments** *(experimental designs)*, researchers *manipulate* the environment. In particular they administer an intervention. As mentioned first in Chapter 1, the **intervention** (also called the **treatment** or the *treatment stimulus*) is what is done to the participant. For instance, one could administer a desensitization regimen to reduce an irrational fear. In addition to administering an intervention, in most experiments the researchers *control* the environment. For instance, they determine factors such as who receives what intervention, when, where, for how long, and how intensely. In sum, experiments are characterized by manipulation and control. In **surveys** *(survey designs)*, the researchers do not manipulate or control the environment. They simply take measurements.

Experiments are preferred for drawing conclusions about causality. The controlled, structured experimental environment allows the researcher to logically rule out the effects of confounding variables and thus to conclude that changes in the dependent variable are indeed caused by the independent variable of key interest (the intervention or treatment). In contrast, in surveys, researchers frequently observe relationships but cannot logically rule out confounding variables as their cause. In a nutshell, the real social world is a complicated place with multiple ongoing events that are potential confounding factors. It is often difficult to pinpoint what caused what.

Experiments, then, are defined by manipulation and control. In general, the greater that control, the greater the confidence the researchers may have that confounding factors are not involved. Broadly speaking, the categories of experimental designs are true experiments, quasi-experiments, and pre-experiments.

Among these three, true experiments are the most preferred for drawing causal conclusions. All true experiments have two or more groups, each of which receives a different intervention. **True experiments** are distinguished and defined by a single characteristic, that being random assignment. As mentioned in Chapter 1 (Section 1.13), **random assignment (randomization)** is the use of methods of chance to assign study participants to groups. Methods of random assignment include flipping coins, drawing names from a hat, using a table of random numbers from a book, and using random numbers generated by a computer.

Although many quasi-experimental designs have two or more groups, none randomly assign participants to groups. *Quasi* means "having some resemblance, usually by possession of certain attributes." **Quasi-experiments** thus have some of the characteristics of true experiments but not all. Quasi-experiments are decidedly better than survey designs for drawing conclusions about causality but decidedly worse than true experiments. The key characteristic that all quasi-experimental designs lack is random assignment.

Whereas all true experiments and many quasi-experiments have two or more groups, only a single group participates in the **pre-experiment.** With respect to drawing causal inferences, these designs are hardly an improvement over surveys.[1] See Rubin and Babbie (1997, pp. 274–309) or many other texts on research methods for further discussion of experimental designs.

10.6 THE ROLE OF RANDOM ASSIGNMENT IN ASSESSING CAUSALITY

The pivotal role of random assignment in making it possible to infer causality can be demonstrated by a study that does not use it. Suppose a statistics instructor receives a new software program that teaches statistics via computer. To test its effectiveness, she designs an experiment in which half the class members use the software during their weekly help sessions (this is the experimental group) and half complete their help sessions as usual with the graduate teaching assistant (the control group). The study's method of assigning students to groups could be termed "student choice." Each student participates in the group of his or her choice. At the semester's end, students take their final exam, scores on which are the dependent variable. Data analysis reveals that the mean score on the final is substantially higher in the software group than in the teaching assistant group. Can one be confident that this relationship is causal, that is, that participation in the software group *caused* the better performance on the final exam? One can be confident only when confounding variables can be logically ruled out.

I can think of at least one such variable that is not ruled out. My hunch is that those with strong math skills were more likely to choose the software group and those with comparatively weaker skills were more likely to opt for the teaching assistant group. I propose that these differing skill levels as the study began—*not* differential effectiveness of the two interventions—provide the primary explanation for (cause of) the results on the final.

What did lead to the better performance of the software group? Due to the lack of random assignment, we cannot logically unravel whether the intervention (the comparative superiority of the software package to the teaching assistant) or possible differences in math skills explain the better test performance of the experimental group. Or perhaps some other confounding variable provides the explanation. Perhaps those who chose the computer software group were, on average, more motivated than those who chose the teaching assistant. Or perhaps those in the teaching assistant group tended to have higher levels of math anxiety.

This example should give you some feel for the quagmire one can encounter in attempting to draw conclusions about causality in designs without random assignment. The literal definition of *quagmire* is a "soft miry land that shakes or yields under the foot." This serves as a good metaphor for the experience of those who attempt to draw causal conclusions in survey and related designs. They can find no firm foundation for such conclusions. Each time they think they have put together a solid line of reasoning that explains a relationship, the land yields underfoot as some new possible confounding variable arises.

As you may have reasoned, random assignment to groups would greatly improve the instructor's ability to draw a causal conclusion in this study. Let's presume that she lets us design the study. Suppose that we put all students' names in a hat, shake it vigorously, and then (with eyes closed) pick out names and assign them randomly to the two groups. Suppose that the study is carried out again and that the same result is observed, that is, better performance in the software group.

When students chose their own groups, we identified several possible confounding variables (differing levels of math skills, differing levels of math anxiety, differing levels of motivation). Can we identify any confounding variables now, given the random assignment?

Let's consider the just-mentioned variables. Is there any reason to think that students in the software group had stronger math skills as the study began? No. All that differentiates the software and teaching assistant groups is the luck of the draw. Clearly, there is no reason to think that one set of names picked randomly from a hat should have better math skills than another. Thus initial level of math skills is not a plausible confounding variable. How about motivation? Clearly, the same logic applies. The luck of the draw won't create groups that differ systematically with respect to motivation. The same logic rules out differing levels of anxiety as a potential explanation for the study results.

Pragmatically speaking, random assignment *eliminates all* confounding variables. When people have been randomly assigned to groups, no logically coherent line of reasoning can be developed that identifies any confounding variables on which groups would be expected to differ in some *systematic* way. At the risk of oversimplifying, given random assignment, researchers may indeed draw causal conclusions. When they see a difference in outcomes between groups, they need not worry that this difference is due to confounding variables but may instead be confident that it reflects the effects of the intervention. They are no longer in a quagmire but on solid ground.

Although random assignment eliminates all *systematic* factors that might affect study results, it does not create precisely identical groups (see Chapter 1, Section 1.13). From a technical perspective, it does not eliminate potential confounding factors but instead *randomly* distributes—that is, "scatters" by luck— these between groups. Random assignment eliminates *systematic* bias, but it cannot totally eliminate differences due to the *random* distribution of factors. Just by chance, students randomly assigned to the software group could have had, on average, better math skills than did those assigned to the teaching assistant. Perhaps this, not the superiority of the software approach, explains their better performance on the final.

You have had only the briefest introduction to inferential statistics, in Chapter 1, Section 1.13. A key purpose of inferential statistics is to see whether chance is a possible explanation for study results. The appropriate statistical test could assess this likelihood. The role of chance is discussed in Chapters 14 to 16. In this chapter we are presuming that relationships are solid enough so that they are not due to chance alone.

Having said that pragmatically speaking, random assignment eliminates potential confounding variables, but that technically it only randomly distributes them, a summary is in order. The pragmatic message is the key one. Pragmatically speaking, random assignment does indeed eliminate the effects of confounding variables. It builds highly similar groups and by so doing enables researchers to draw causal conclusions. When there is no random assignment, the ground is much softer, and researchers are extremely hesitant to draw such conclusions.

Let's divert for a moment away from statistics and into the domain of research. The software/teaching assistant example has overlooked many of the complexities of real-world research. What do we know about this study? Thanks to the random assignment, we know that (1) confounding variables are not responsible for the association between participation in the software group and better performance on the final; therefore, (2) this association in all likelihood is causal, that is, software instruction *causes* better test performance than does teaching assistant instruction.

On the other hand, what don't we know? We know that *some* aspect of the intervention led to a difference in test performance, but we don't know what this aspect is. Perhaps software instruction is, simply put, superior to teaching assistant instruction. However, other possibilities loom. Perhaps the teaching assistant had chronic laryngitis, or broke up with his partner and was emotionally distraught, or was simply a poor instructor. Perhaps the final exam focused more closely on material that was covered by the computer than on that covered by the teaching assistant. Perhaps the summary problems at the conclusion of the software package's lessons were particularly helpful and other parts of the intervention were much less so.[2]

In addition to not knowing what particular aspect(s) of the intervention affected performance, we don't know much about whether the same results would be obtained if, for instance, the study was repeated with a different teaching assistant or at a different university. The discussion of generalizability in Chapter 23, Section 23.2, covers issues such as this. Your research courses cover real-world complexities in much greater detail than does this book. In sum, random assignment is not a magic pill. Even with random assignment, careful, clear thinking is needed in interpreting study results.

10.7 CAUSAL MODELS

10.7.1 Introduction and the Direct Causal Relationship Model

Recognizing that causal attribution (deciding what causes what) is problematic in survey and other nonrandomized designs, researchers have some tools that they use toward this end. This section uses causal models to demonstrate how researchers think about and investigate issues of causality.

A **causal model** (also called a *path diagram*) is a diagram that presents the effects of some variables on others. A straight arrow from one variable to another indicates that the first variable (an independent variable) causes, or affects, the second (a dependent variable). The absence of an arrow between two variables indicates that neither variable directly affects the other. Finally, some diagrams have curved arrows, which indicate that variables are associated but that the reasons for the relationship are unclear. We consider curved arrows in greater depth later.[3] All arrows in this chapter convey positive rather than negative effects or relationships (as one variable changes, the other changes in the same direction). This is to simplify discussion. In real-world research, one sees both positive and negative effects.

The chapter, including several of the models in this section, makes frequent use of the television violence example. Note that the variables are labeled in a "shorthand." For instance, what could be labeled "children's watching of violent television in the home versus not watching violent television" (Figure 10.1) is shortened to "watches violent television." Similarly, "aggressive behavior versus the absence of such behavior" in children is shortened to "behaves aggressively."

The causal model in Figure 10.1 presents perhaps the simplest possible reason why two variables are related: One variable does indeed cause the other. In other words, the relationship depicted in Figure 10.1 is a causal relationship. The direction of causality in this model is depicted by the arrow from "watches violent television" to "behaves aggressively." This arrow goes *directly* from "violent television" to "behaves aggressively" (rather than indirectly through some third variable). This being the case, "violent television" exerts a **direct effect** on "aggressive behavior." As the effect is direct, the relationship between these variables can be characterized as a **direct causal relationship.** The model in Figure 10.1 can, therefore, be described as a **direct causal relationship model.** (The contrast of direct effects and direct causal relationships to indirect effects and indirect causal relationships will be demonstrated shortly.)

10.7.2 Antecedent Variable Model

Other causal models depict different possible explanations for the association between violent television and aggressive behavior. Many of these involve confounding (third) variables. For instance, in the model in Figure 10.2, the confounding variable "violence in the home" causes both "watches violent television" and "behaves aggressively." The absence of an arrow pointing from "watches violent television" to "behaves aggressively" indicates that, according to this model, watching violent television does not cause (exert an influence on) aggressive behavior. When a confounding variable causes each of two other variables, it will generate a relationship between these two. (It will do so even if neither of these two variables exerts a direct effect on the other.) Thus, in this model the association between watching violent television and aggressive behavior is "caused" by (due to) the confounding variable "violence in the home." The situation depicted in the causal model in Figure 10.2—a third variable affecting two other variables and thus bringing about a relationship between these two—is at the crux of the reluctance of social scientists to conclude that associations are causal.

When a variable exerts a direct effect on each of two other variables and by so doing generates a relationship between these variables or affects the size or direction of their association, that variable is an **antecedent variable** (*antecedent*

FIGURE 10.1

A DIRECT CAUSAL RELATIONSHIP MODEL

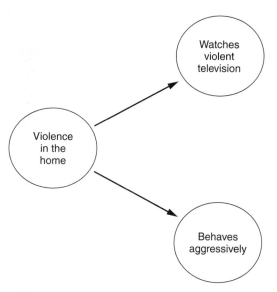

FIGURE 10.2

AN ANTECEDENT VARIABLE MODEL

confounding variable). Hence the model in Figure 10.2 is termed an **antecedent variable model.** The term *antecedent* refers to the fact that the third variable precedes each of the other two in time. In Figure 10.2 "violence in the home" is an antecedent variable.

Let's look at another example of a relationship possibly due to the effects of an antecedent confounding variable. Suppose that clients with chronic and severe mental health problems are discharged from a psychiatric hospital to one of two programs: (1) a halfway house or (2) community residence (they find their own residence and receive extensive casework support). Suppose further that a research study indicates that those discharged to the community residence program experience lower hospital readmission rates than do those discharged to the halfway house. Is the community program more effective, that is, does it *cause* the lower readmission rate? This may indeed be the case. On the other hand, this example contains no information regarding how the decision was made to discharge to one program or other. In most similar situations, staff members discharge to the program that they believe will best meet the client's needs. Let's presume, then, that this assignment was nonrandom. Given the absence of random assignment, an antecedent variable may be involved. For instance, perhaps those with the most serious problems were more often discharged to the halfway house and those with less serious issues were more often discharged to the community program. A difference in severity of client problems, not in program effectiveness, may provide the best explanation of study results. This model is presented in Figure 10.3.

Let's consider one final model of an antecedent variable. Suppose that a researcher observes an association between marijuana use and poor grades.

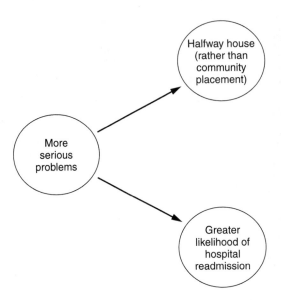

FIGURE **10.3**

AN ANTECEDENT VARIABLE MODEL FROM THE FIELD OF MENTAL HEALTH

Figure 10.4 presents "low motivation" as an antecedent confounding variable that causes both "uses marijuana" and "poor grades." If the model in Figure 10.4 is correct, then marijuana use does not lead to (cause) poor grades.

10.7.3 Intervening Variable Model and Indirect Effects

Figure 10.5 presents a different causal model involving marijuana use, motivation, and grades. In this model, marijuana use causes low motivation and low motivation, in turn, causes poor grades. In this model, motivation is an intervening variable. An **intervening variable** is one that mediates or "passes along" the effect of a first variable (in Figure 10.5, "uses marijuana") to a second ("low grades").

According to this model, does marijuana use cause low grades? One is tempted to say no, because no arrow points *directly* from marijuana use to poor grades. Yet there is an *indirect* causal link between these two. In Figure 10.5, smoking marijuana does indeed affect grades; it does so by decreasing motivation, which in turn leads to lower grades. In this example, marijuana use has an **indirect effect** on grades, one that is passed along by the intervening variable, level of motivation. An indirect effect can be contrasted with a direct effect, which is conveyed by an arrow that leads directly from one variable to another. As already mentioned, in the model in Figure 10.1, violent television exerts a direct effect on aggressive behavior.

Indirect effects may pass through several different intervening variables. To find pairs of variables that are connected via indirect effects, one traces along the

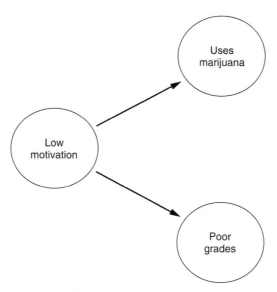

FIGURE **10.4**

AN ANTECEDENT VARIABLE MODEL OF MARIJUANA USE AND GRADES

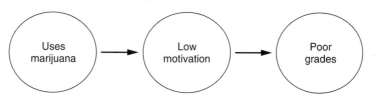

FIGURE **10.5**

AN INTERVENING VARIABLE MODEL OF MARIJUANA USE AND GRADES

arrows, being sure to go only in the direction that they point.[4] For instance, one could envision a complex model in which "watching violent television" leads to "aggressive behavior at school" which leads to "trouble at school" which leads to "labeling as a 'bad' kid" which leads to "increased risk of suspension." Technically, the relationship between a pair of variables connected by indirect effects is a causal relationship, because one variable does indeed affect (even if indirectly) the other. But it clarifies matters to refer to such relationships as **indirect causal relationships.**

Whether a confounding variable is viewed as antecedent or as intervening has important implications for the assessment of causality and, in the real world, for the formulation of policy. For instance, if level of motivation is an antecedent variable as in Figure 10.4, then marijuana use does not cause poor grades. This suggests one set of policy initiatives. If, on the other hand, level of motivation is viewed as an intervening variable as in Figure 10.5, then marijuana use does (indirectly) cause poor grades. This suggests different policy initiatives.

How does one determine whether a confounding variable is antecedent or intervening? How does one "unravel" the causal pattern? This can be exceedingly difficult. Often, one's data provide only limited help. In our example, the same pattern of associations between marijuana use, motivation, and grades could equally well suggest the model in Figure 10.4 (the antecedent variable model) or that in Figure 10.5 (the intervening variable model). Sometimes common sense recommends one model over the other. For instance, it is obvious that an event at Time 2 (later in time) cannot be an antecedent variable to an event at Time 1 (earlier in time). Yet, even with careful, thoughtful interpretation of data, determining the "correct" causal model can be problematic. Often one simply does not know.

Statistical and computer packages are becoming increasingly sophisticated in developing models that "fit" one's data. But (at least as this is written) developing the model that explains the links and connections between one's variables is still largely the province of the researcher. The computer cranks out the numbers (correlations, etc.). The researcher takes the lead in interpreting how those numbers fit together to help explain the social world.[5]

The models presented so far have been straightforward, more so than in most real-world research applications. Let's consider a model in which a variable affects another variable both directly and indirectly. In Figure 10.6, "violence in the home" has a direct effect on "behaves aggressively," as indicated by the arrow that directly connects these variables, and also an indirect effect, as indicated by the path through the intervening variable "watches violent television." The model in

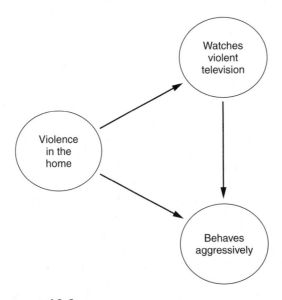

FIGURE **10.6**

A COMBINED MODEL: A VARIABLE WITH BOTH DIRECT AND INDIRECT EFFECTS

Figure 10.6 could be characterized as a combination of the direct causal relationship model and the intervening variable model. Often some combination of the simplified models in this chapter provides the best explanation for a relationship.

10.7.4 *General Confounding Variable Model*

Sometimes two variables are associated but it is difficult or impossible to determine all the causal effects that account for that association. Rather than attempt to do so, it is easier to simply indicate that they are associated. This is done with a curved arrow. For instance, in the model in Figure 10.7, the curved arrow indicates that "violence in the home" and "watches violent television" (children's watching of violent television) are associated. The model does not attempt to indicate the reasons for this association. Some possibilities include (1) watching violent television leads to violence in the home, (2) violence in the home encourages watching violent television, and (3) an antecedent third variable leads to both violence in the home and watching violent television, and thereby generates a relationship between them. In the model in Figure 10.7, violence in the home has a direct causal effect on aggressive behavior. From this model, one cannot determine whether violent television exerts an indirect effect on aggressive behavior, because the reason for the association between violent television and parental violence is not clarified. For instance, if the second explanation above is correct—that violence in the home leads to the watching of violent television—then there is no indirect effect.

In the model in Figure 10.7, violence in the home is indeed a confounding variable affecting the association between television watching and child behavior. As stated earlier, in such a model it is not clear whether the confounding variable is antecedent or intervening or due to some different pattern. We designate this as a **general confounding variable model.**

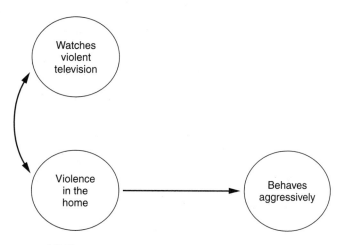

FIGURE **10.7**

A GENERAL CONFOUNDING VARIABLE MODEL

Figure 10.8 presents what to me is an intuitively satisfying causal model. In this model, violent television and parental violence are associated and each exerts a direct effect on child behavior. This model, in essence, is a combination of the direct effects model (see Figure 10.1) and the general confounding variable model (see Figure 10.7).

10.7.5   *Direction of Effect and Other Models*

With the exception of the direct causal relationship model (Figure 10.1), all the models presented have introduced a confounding variable. Not all problems in assessing causality come from confounding variables. It is possible to mistake the **direction of the causal effect.** In this discussion, *direction* is used differently than in Chapters 7, 8, and 9. Here, direction refers not to whether an association is positive or negative but instead to which variable affects which. Suppose that one observed a negative association between level of visiting of family members and degree of depression of nursing home residents. (The greater the visiting, the lower the level of depression.) Figure 10.9 presents two causal models that may account for this association. In Model A, the direction of the causal effect is from "visiting" to "depression." In Model B, the direction is reversed. Interpreting Model B, one would reason that lower levels of depression increase the amount of visiting. (Or, one could say, higher levels of depression reduce the amount of visiting.) In Figure 10.9, it is difficult to know which model provides the better explanation. Each has merit. In Figure 10.9, the direction of the causal effect is unclear.

My research on special-needs adoption (Rosenthal and Groze, 1992) posed an interesting dilemma relating to the direction of an effect. This research revealed a negative association between the adoptive family's participation in family counseling services and the parents' assessment of the overall impact of the child's adoption on the family. Only 28% of responding parents in families that received such

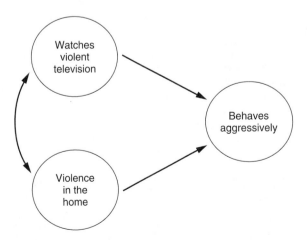

FIGURE **10.8**

COMBINATION OF DIRECT EFFECT AND GENERAL CONFOUNDING VARIABLE MODELS

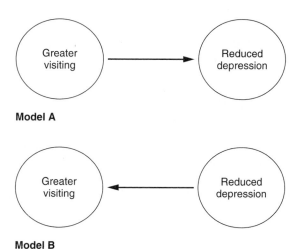

Model A

Model B

FIGURE **10.9**

Two Possible Models When Direction of Causal Effect Is Unclear

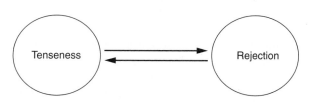

FIGURE **10.10**

A Feedback Model

services indicated that the impact of adoption on their family was "very positive." In contrast, among families that did not receive these services, this percentage was markedly higher, 53%. Do these data suggest that family counseling has a negative impact? Although one can't be sure, the direction of causal influence is more likely in the opposite direction. Presumably, family problems caused families to seek out family counseling services.

In many situations in social science, the direction of a causal effect can be difficult to determine. Sometimes *each* variable affects the other. Such a situation is presented in Figure 10.10. This model conveys that one's tenseness when meeting prospective friends could cause rejection. In turn, this rejection leads to increased tenseness, which causes rejection, and so on. In essence, a feedback loop between the two variables is created. One may envision a feedback loop involving three or more variables. For instance, poor self-esteem leads to substance abuse which leads to poor grades which leads to poor self-esteem which leads to substance abuse, which leads to poor grades and so on. When two or more variables affect each other, they constitute a **feedback model** (also called a *reciprocal model* or *nonrecursive model*). A feedback model could well be applied to Figure 10.9. Perhaps greater visiting reduces depression *and* reduced depression leads to greater visiting (which leads to reduced depression, etc.).

10.8   CHAPTER SUMMARY

The fact of association between two variables is not sufficient for concluding that an association is causal, that is, that one variable causes the other. In social science, *to cause* means "to influence, to affect." Often multiple independent variables affect (cause) a dependent variable.

Confounding variables affect the pattern of association between two other variables. Most often, their effect is on size of association, though they may also affect direction of association, or the presence or absence of association. In some situations, the relationship between two variables may be due entirely to the effects of a confounding variable.

In experiments, researchers manipulate and control the environment. In general, the greater the control, the greater the degree to which causal conclusions can be drawn. The true experiment is characterized by random assignment, the use of methods of chance to assign cases to a group. Pragmatically, random assignment eliminates effects of confounding variables. When random assignment is used, differences in outcome between groups are due to the intervention rather than to a confounding variable. A quasi-experiment has some of the features of a true experiment but lacks randomization. A pre-experiment has little if any advantage over a survey with respect to drawing causal conclusions.

In surveys, the researcher simply takes measurements. Primarily due to confounding variables, it is exceedingly difficult to infer causality using survey results.

A causal model is a diagram that depicts causation. A straight arrow connecting two variables conveys that the first variable (the independent one) exerts a direct effect on (causes) the second (the dependent one). The direct causal relationship model (Figure 10.1) asserts that an independent variable does indeed directly cause a dependent variable.

Several models are based on confounding variables. The antecedent variable model (Figure 10.2) asserts that an antecedent confounding variable affects two other variables and, by so doing, generates a relationship between them. In this model, there is no causal relationship (either direct or indirect) between the two variables in the initial relationship. In an intervening variable model (Figure 10.5), an intervening variable passes along the effect of a first variable to a second. In this model, there is a causal relationship between the initial variables, but it is indirect. Another causal model based on confounding variables is the general confounding variable model (see Figure 10.7).

The direction of a causal effect may be the opposite of what is assumed (see Figure 10.9). Sometimes two or more variables in a relationship influence each other, which can be diagrammed in a feedback model (Figure 10.10).

Problems and Questions

Section 10.2

1. What are some terms with meanings highly similar to or synonymous with "to cause"?

Section 10.3

2. (T or F) All relationships are causal relationships.
3. (T or F) For the relationship between X and Y to be considered causal, X must be the *only* cause of Y or Y must be the *only* cause of X.

Section 10.4

4. Confounding variables may potentially affect...
   a. (T or F) Size of association
   b. (T or F) Direction of association
   c. (T or F) Presence or absence of association
5. What are some other terms with meanings highly similar to or synonymous with confounding variable?

Section 10.5

6. In an experimental design, the researcher _____ and _____ the environment.
7. (T or F) Experimental designs are the preferred design type for drawing causal conclusions.
8. The key distinguishing characteristic that defines the true experiment is _____ _____.
9. _____ -experiments have some but not all of the features of true experiments.
10. Does each of the following designs use random assignment to groups? (Respond with yes or no.)
    a. A staffing committee assigns youths, based on their needs, to Program A or Program B.
    b. A professor picks names out of a hat to decide which of two curricula students will be assigned to.
    c. Participants choose which of three smoking prevention programs they will participate in.
    d. An elder care program uses a computer program that randomly picks which worker will be assigned to incoming clients.

Section 10.6

11. (T or F) Random assignment always results in groups with *precisely identical* characteristics.
12. (T or F) Random assignment eliminates systematic/nonrandom factors that might result in differences between groups.
13. (T or F) Random assignment randomly distributes potentially confounding variables between/among groups.

Section 10.7

14. A(n) _____ _____ is a diagram that presents visually the effects of variables on other variables.
15. In your own words, what does a straight arrow convey?
16. In your own words, what does a curved arrow convey?
17. In a direct causal relationship model, one variable in the initial relationship exerts a(n) _____ effect on the other.
18. In Figure 10.2, "violence in the home" is termed a(n) _____ variable.
19. (T or F) In Figure 10.2, which is an antecedent variable model, "watches violent television" exerts a direct effect on "behaves aggressively."
20. (T or F) In Figure 10.2, "watches violent television" exerts an indirect effect on "behaves aggressively."
21. Examine Table 10.1. Conceptualize age as an antecedent variable that affects both type of placement and behavior problems. Draw this causal model.

Questions 22–29 refer to the following causal model:

$$\text{(A)} \longrightarrow \text{(B)} \longrightarrow \text{(C)}$$

22. The just-presented model is termed a(n) _____ variable model.
23. (T or F) Variable A is termed an intervening variable.
24. (T or F) Variable B is termed an intervening variable.

25. (T or F) One may conclude that variable *A* has no causal effect of any kind on variable *C*.
26. (T or F) Variable *B* exerts a direct effect on variable *A*.
27. (T or F) Variable *A* has an indirect effect on variable *C*.
28. (T or F) Assuming that this model is correct, one may conclude that changes in *A* do not lead to changes in *C*.
29. (T or F) Variables *A* and *C* have an indirect causal relationship.

Questions 30–35 pertain to the following causal model:

30. The text calls this model a(n) _____ _____ _____ model.
31. (T or F) Variable *A* exerts a direct effect on variable *C*.
32. (T or F) Variables *A* and *B* are related.
33. Does variable *A* exert a direct effect on *B*?
34. Is there an indirect causal relationship between *A* and *C*?
35. Give several different possible explanations for the association between *A* and *B*.
36. A study reveals that levels of depression among those in psychotherapy are higher than in the public at large. Researcher A concludes that therapy causes depression. Without introducing a confounding variable, provide an alternative interpretation for study results and draw a causal model of this interpretation.
37. Tension leads to poor golf shots leads to poor scores leads to tension leads to poor shots leads to poor scores. . . . Give the name for the model that describes this situation and draw the model.
38. In each of the following situations, the researcher jumps to a conclusion that may not be true. For each case: (1) suggest an alternative explanation for the described relationship and (2) draw a causal model of your explanation. (As you consider the situations, note that none

involves random assignment to groups. Recognize also that in each case there is more than one alternative explanation.)
a. At a given high school, a researcher finds that youths who are assigned a mentor have lower graduation rates than do youths who are not. The researcher concludes that the mentor program leads to lower graduation rates.
b. A researcher discovers that children who play chess score higher on achievement tests. The researcher concludes that playing chess causes improved performance on such tests.
c. Lower recidivism rates are observed for mental health clients served in an intensive community support program than for those served in a transition house program. Researchers conclude that the community support program is the more effective of the two programs.
d. Children from the child welfare system who are placed in adoptive homes by Program A experience lower disruption rates than do those placed by Program B. Researchers conclude that Program A offers more effective services.

NOTES

1. Only a single group participates in pre-experiments. Pre-experimental designs should not be confused with single-subject designs, in which data typically are gathered on multiple occasions both prior to and following intervention. In pre-experiments, data are gathered at most once prior to intervention (a pretest) and once following intervention (a posttest). See Rubin and Babbie (1997, pp. 309–339) for more on single-subject designs.

2. The factors mentioned in this paragraph would be considered components of the intervention rather than factors external to it, so they would not be considered confounding variables. In contrast, factors such as initial level of math ability and level of anxiety are not components of the intervention; they are external to it. Hence these are potential confounding variables.

3. Some causal models are exceedingly complex, with many variables displayed in a relatively small physical space. In these models, arrows that would otherwise be straight must bend so that they do not bump into unintended variables on their way to the intended variable. Such arrows almost always have the same meaning as do straight arrows in the models presented in this chapter.

4. You might note, for instance, that in Figure 10.2, the antecedent variable model, one cannot trace an indirect path from violent television to aggressive behavior. One is tempted to trace from aggressive behavior to violence in the home, but such a path is not allowed as it goes in the opposite direction of the arrow.

5. As statistical and computer applications become increasingly sophisticated, computers are taking on an ever bigger role. In many ways, they are beginning to develop and refine theory, that is, to determine "what causes what."

CHAPTER 11

CONTROLLING FOR CONFOUNDING VARIABLES

11.1 CHAPTER OVERVIEW

Now that we know to look for a potential confounding variable, we learn how to *control* for one. Different patterns may emerge when this is done, and we consider how to interpret these. *Spurious relationships* and *interaction effects* are two of the possible revelations. We also discuss how to control for two variables and the need for caution in drawing conclusions about causality.

11.2 CONTROLLING FOR A VARIABLE

11.2.1 Basic Concepts

Although survey and other designs without random assignment present many obstacles to researchers who seek to identify causal relationships, several strategies are available to deal with these obstacles. The most common is **controlling for a variable** (*controlling for a confounding variable*). A synonymous term is **holding a variable constant.**

An example from the special-needs adoption study (Rosenthal and Groze, 1992) can illustrate the logic of controlling for a confounding variable. Recall from Chapter 2, Section 2.6, that family ethnicity as a variable took on three values: (1) minority, inracial: minority (nonwhite) parents who adopt a child of the same race as at least one parent; (2) white, inracial: white parents who adopt a white child; and (3) transracial: white parents who adopt a minority child (transracial adoption). Because the transracial group is small ($n = 61$) and for simplicity, we will drop it from this analysis. Also for simplicity, we can simply designate the first two groups as "minority families" and "white families," respectively.

In this study, distinctly positive outcomes were observed for minority families. For instance, 58% of respondents in minority families (126 of 219) reported that the adoption's impact on the family was "very positive." In contrast, only 41% of respondents in white families indicated this (190 of 465).

Given the association between minority ethnicity and positive impact on the family, I asked myself whether the association was causal. Did some characteristic of minority families or communities—greater experience in raising children outside of the nuclear family, greater tolerance for problems (in school, behavior, adjustment) that the children might experience, reduced stigmatization of adoption, more realistic expectations for children, stronger social support systems—cause the better outcomes? Or might a third, confounding variable be responsible? In other words, did differential experiences of minority and white children prior to adoption result in the more positive outcomes observed in minority families?

How does one hunt for a confounding variable? Basically, one must find a variable that is associated with *both* variables involved in the initial association.[1] When such a (confounding) variable can be identified, it influences, at least to some degree, the pattern of the initial association. That is, it affects the size of, the direction of, or the presence/absence of that association. As it is reasonably rare for a confounding variable to actually reverse the direction of an initial association, our primary foci are on size of association and presence/absence of association.

A perusal of various relationships in the adoption study revealed that the variable "age at entry into the adoptive home" was associated with both family ethnicity and impact. As such, it met the basic criteria for a confounding variable and was presumably affecting the size of association between family ethnicity and impact. Age at entry was associated with perceived impact of adoption on the family: the younger the child's age, the more positive the reported impact. Thus, among children who entered their homes prior to their sixth birthday, 54% (237 of 435) of responses were "very positive." Among those who entered their homes after their sixth birthday, this percentage was only 37% (127 of 342). Age at entry into the home was also associated with family ethnicity. In white families, 48% (225 of 467) of children entered the family home subsequent to their sixth birthday; in minority families, this was the case for only 34% (78 of 227) of children.

Having identified a potential confounding variable, age at entry, the next step is to *control* for its influence. When researchers **control** for (**hold constant**) a confounding variable, they essentially change that variable into a constant. For instance, let's try breaking age at entry down into five age groups and then assessing the association of family ethnicity to the percentage of "very positive" responses regarding family impact *within* each age group. Table 11.1 presents these results.

Within each age group presented in Table 11.1, age at entry into the adoptive home varies hardly at all, so it is effectively a constant. This is so because, within each age group, all children entered the home at very nearly the same age. Consequently, within each group, it is logically impossible for age at entry to substantially influence the association of family ethnicity and the impact of adoption. Viewed differently, something that does not vary cannot influence something else. Whatever association is present between the two initial variables within the groups cannot be due to age at entry into the home, which has been transformed into a near constant.

In sum, by controlling for a confounding variable, we eliminate its influence on the initial relationship. We can then assess that relationship in the absence of this influence.

TABLE 11.1	ADOPTION IMPACT BY ETHNICITY, CONTROLLING FOR AGE			
	FAMILIES REPORTING "VERY POSITIVE" IMPACT			
Child's Age at Entry into Adoptive Home	**MINORITY FAMILIES**		**WHITE FAMILIES**	
	%	f	%	f
Birth to 2 years	63	83	60	113
3 to 5 years	55	60	39	128
6 to 8 years	62	50	36	119
9 to 11 years	35	20	26	73
12 years and older	50	4	34	24

11.2.2   Different Patterns

Controlling for a potential confounding variable can result in several different patterns of results. The most common are the following:

1. *Association persists:* Within each group, the association between the initial variables persists at a size nearly the same as (or only modestly weaker than) that prior to control.
2. *Association weakens:* Within each group, the association between the initial variables persists but at a size of association considerably smaller than that prior to control.
3. *Association disappears:* Within each group, the association disappears, that is, one no longer sees an association between the initial two variables (or that association becomes very small).
4. *Association varies by group:* Among the groups, size of association differs markedly; the association may be much larger in some groups than in others, or the direction (positive versus negative) may differ.

The results in Table 11.1 seem to conform best to the first pattern. On balance, the size of the relationships in the groups tends to be only modestly smaller than in the initial relationship. The difference in percentages ($D\%$) in the initial relationship was 17%: 58% − 41% = 17%. In Table 11.1, the average difference in percentages within the subgroups computes to 14%. [To compute this: (1) subtract the percentage of white families from the percentage of minority families for each of the five age groups, (2) sum these differences, and (3) divide by 5.][2]

Given that the size of association in the groups (an average $D\%$ of 14%) is indeed less than that in the initial association (17%), the pattern of results illustrates to some degree the second pattern, a weakening of the association following control. The degree of decrease was modest rather than considerable, however, so most would concur that the results better fit the first pattern.

Note also that the difference in percentages ($D\%$) varies some from group to group. With real-world data, this is the norm. In particular, notice that the difference in percentages between minority and white families is quite large for children who entered the home between the ages of 6 and 8 (62% − 36% = 26%) and quite small for children in the youngest group (63% − 60% = 3%). The variability in the $D\%$ between the different subgroups illustrates the fourth pattern of results, because size of association differs from group to group. Yet, as just mentioned, real data do indeed vary. Most would not regard the degree of variability as large enough to conclude that the results best represent the fourth pattern. In Section 11.5 on interaction effects, we see results that do demonstrate this fourth pattern.

The just-described patterns give an overview of the kinds of results that may be observed when potential confounding variables are controlled for. It would be impossible to provide precise guidelines regarding when results convey one pattern rather than another. As the current examples illustrate, often they convey aspects of more than one. We examine the first three patterns in more detail in the following sections, and the fourth in Section 11.5.

11.2.3 Initial Relationship Persists at About the Same Size

If an initial relationship persists at the same size (or weakens only modestly) when a potential confounding variable is controlled for, one may conclude that the third variable is *not* an important cause of that relationship. How could it be, when the relationship persists at nearly the same size even in the absence of influence from that variable? In such a situation, one holds open the possibility that the initial relationship may be a causal one. In the current example, we would hold open the possibility that some characteristic of minority families and communities does indeed lead to better adoption outcomes. At least in survey research, one may not conclude that the initial relationship is causal, because other confounding variables that have not been controlled for may be involved. For instance, in the current example, possible differences in histories of child abuse and neglect have not been controlled for.

In our example, age at entry was the potential confounding variable but exerted only a minor influence on the association between family ethnicity and family impact. As such, it was almost not a confounding variable at all.

11.2.4 Initial Relationship Weakens but Persists

The second pattern, in which the size of association weakens markedly in the groups but nevertheless an association persists, is encountered frequently in research. Table 11.2 presents hypothetical adoption data that illustrate this pattern. In interpreting Table 11.2, presume that the $D\%$ in the initial relationship continues to be 17%. In Table 11.2, the average difference in the percentage of very positive responses in the five age groups computes to 8.0%. Hence, controlling for age at entry markedly reduces size of association, from a $D\%$ of 17% to an average difference of 8%. Even so, within each age group, family ethnicity (minority versus white) and the impact of adoption continue to be associated. When an initial relationship weakens markedly but nevertheless persists after a confounding variable is controlled for, one may conclude that (1) the confounding variable is not the *sole*

TABLE 11.2 WEAKENED ASSOCIATION WITH CONTROLLED-FOR VARIABLE				
	FAMILIES REPORTING "VERY POSITIVE" IMPACT			
	MINORITY FAMILIES		WHITE FAMILIES	
Child's Age at Entry into Adoptive Home	%	f	%	f
Birth to 2 years	64	83	60	113
3 to 5 year	51	60	42	128
6 to 8 years	57	50	44	119
9 to 11 years	35	20	30	73
12 years and older	46	4	35	24

Note: Data are hypothetical.

cause of the initial relationship (because the relationship persists in the absence of influence from it) and (2) the confounding variable is *partially* the cause of the initial relationship (because the relationship is smaller when the third variable is controlled for than when it is not). The greater the decrease in size from the initial relationship to the relationship(s) in the groups, the greater the presumed influence of the confounding variable.

Consider again the part of an initial relationship that persists following control. For the hypothetical adoption example (Table 11.2), think about the average *D%* of 8%. As just stated, the controlled-for variable cannot be an explanation for that part of the relationship that persists when it is controlled for. At least with respect to this part of the relationship, one may hold open the possibility that the initial relationship is a direct causal one.

11.2.5   *Initial Relationship Disappears*

The third pattern, an important one, is for an initial relationship to disappear when a third variable is controlled for. Such a situation is presented in Table 11.3. The hypothetical data presented in this table pertain to the marijuana use/low motivation/poor grades example used in Figures 10.4 and 10.5 in Chapter 10. As you read Table 11.3, presume that the researcher has found a way to measure motivation level and has controlled for it by dividing the sample into four groups based on level of motivation. Within each group, motivation varies hardly at all; it is very nearly a constant. Let's presume that in the full sample (prior to controlling for motivation), the mean grade point average (GPA) of those who used marijuana was 2.5 and the mean GPA of those who did not was 3.0. Table 11.3 presents mean GPAs for users and nonusers within the four groups defined by level of motivation. Stated differently, it presents mean GPAs controlling for level of motivation. Within each group, mean GPAs of marijuana users and nonusers are very nearly equal. For instance, in the moderate motivation group, these GPAs are, respectively, 2.45 and 2.43. Within each level of motivation—that is, when motivation is controlled for—the association between marijuana use and GPA has very nearly disappeared.

TABLE 11.3	MARIJUANA USE BY **GPA**, CONTROLLING FOR **MOTIVATION LEVEL**	
	MEAN GRADE POINT AVERAGE	
Level of Motivation	**Use Marijuana**	**Do Not Use Marijuana**
Low	2.07	2.09
Moderate	2.45	2.43
High	2.78	2.81
Very high	3.32	3.30

Note: Data are hypothetical.

If a relationship disappears when a confounding variable is controlled for, one concludes that there is no *direct* causal relationship between the variables involved in the initial relationship. Although real-world situations are more complex than textbook examples, the disappearance of a relationship when a confounding variable is controlled for basically indicates that the relationship is explained by one of the three following causal models: the antecedent variable model (see Figure 10.2), the intervening variable model (see Figure 10.5), or the general confounding variable model (see Figure 10.7). The common point in all of these is the absence of an arrow that *directly* connects the two variables involved in the initial relationship. The absence of such an arrow signals the absence of a direct effect between these variables.

As discussed in Chapter 10, identification of the correct causal model can be difficult. Often one is unsure of which model is correct. If one decides in favor of an antecedent variable model, the disappearance of the initial relationship indicates that there is no causal relationship (direct or indirect) between the variables. If one endorses an intervening variable model, it follows that there is (1) no direct causal relationship between the initial variables but that there is (2) an *indirect* causal relationship through the controlled-for (intervening) variable. Still another possibility is the general confounding variable model, presented in Figure 11.1.

By endorsing a general confounding variable model, one may conclude that there is no direct causal relationship between the initial variables. Recall from Chapter 10 that a curved arrow conveys that two variables are associated but does not explain the reason(s) for that association. For instance, the model in Figure 11.1 does not clarify whether (1) marijuana use causes low motivation, (2) low motivation causes marijuana use, (3) marijuana use causes low motivation and low motivation causes marijuana use (i.e., a feedback model; see Figure 10.10), or (4) some third variable causes both marijuana use and low motivation. Because a general confounding variable model does not clarify the reason(s) for the association conveyed by the curved arrow, one does not know whether the initial variables, "uses marijuana" and "poor grades," are linked via an indirect causal relationship. Regarding Figure 11.1, only if "uses marijuana" has a direct effect on "low motivation" is there such a linkage.

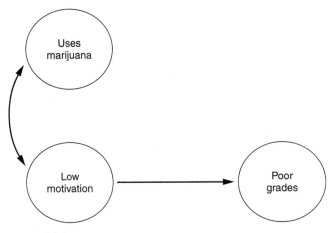

FIGURE **11.1**

A GENERAL CONFOUNDING VARIABLE MODEL PREDICTING GRADES

In sum, from the marijuana use/motivation level/GPA data presented in Table 11.3, one could draw one of the following conclusions:

- Assuming an antecedent variable model (see Figure 10.4), marijuana use does not cause low grades (either directly or indirectly).
- Assuming an intervening variable model (see Figure 10.5), marijuana use (1) does not have a direct causal effect on grades and (2) does have an indirect effect that is mediated by level of motivation.
- Assuming a general confounding variable model (see Figure 11.1), marijuana use (1) does not have a direct effect on grades and (2) no firm conclusion can be reached regarding whether it has an indirect effect.

This example again demonstrates the complexities of drawing causal conclusions. When one has doubt about which model is correct—and this is often—the only solid conclusion to be drawn when a relationship disappears is that there is no direct effect. There is no requirement that one must choose a model. Sometimes the best strategy is to simply hold open the possibility that any of the models, or some combination of them, may be correct.

11.2.6   Spurious Relationships

Now is a good time to introduce a term: A **spurious** relationship is one that disappears when an antecedent variable is controlled for. The dictionary defines spurious as "of falsified or erroneously attributed origin." In essence, a spurious relationship is one that at first glance appears to be causal but with closer attention—that is, with control for an antecedent variable—turns out to be caused by the antecedent variable.[3] Thus, if one assumes an antecedent variable model (see Figure 10.4), the results in Table 11.3 convey that the association between marijuana use and low grades is spurious.

11.3 HOW LARGE AN EFFECT IS A CONFOUNDING VARIABLE LIKELY TO HAVE?

Experienced researchers can predict fairly well the degree to which a confounding variable affects a relationship. Basically, to exert substantial influence the confounding variable must have a *strong* (or reasonably strong) association to *both* variables.[4] In general, the stronger these associations, the greater the influence of the confounding variable.

Consider, for instance, the initial example concerning the influence of the confounding variable age at entry into the home (younger than 6 years versus 6 or older) on the association between family ethnicity (minority versus white) and perceived impact of adoption on the family ("very positive" versus all other responses). In minority families, 48% of children were placed prior to their sixth birthday, as compared to 34% in white families, a difference of 14%: $D\% = 48\% - 34\% = 14\%$. According to the qualitative descriptors for the difference in percentages in Table 6.4, the size of this relationship could best be characterized as medium. Similarly, 54% of respondents in minority families versus 37% in white families evaluated the impact of adoption as "very positive," a difference of 17% ($D\% = 54\% - 37\% = 17\%$), again indicating an association of medium size. In sum, the confounding variable age at entry into home has a relationship of approximately medium size with both variables in the initial relationship.

Even though age at entry has a relationship of medium size with both variables in the initial relationship, it exerts only a modest influence on the size of that relationship. We draw this conclusion because, within the five subgroups of children of similar age, the size of relationship between family ethnicity and impact of adoption on the family is almost as large as in the original group of children of all ages (see Table 11.1). That is, when age is controlled for, the size of relationship shows only a small decrease. In sum, when the strength of association of the confounding variable to each variable in the initial relationship is only moderate (or weaker), that variable typically exerts a relatively small influence on the initial relationship.[5] As stated previously, to have a substantial influence these associations generally must be quite strong.

11.4 CONTROLLING FOR TWO VARIABLES

All the examples so far have controlled for only a single variable. One may control for two or more confounding variables in the same table. Suppose that you analyze data from a university survey concerning graduates' salaries 10 years after graduation. You note that the mean salary for the 100 surveyed women is $40,000 and that for the 100 surveyed men is $50,000. You ask yourself whether this difference suggests discrimination based on gender. You reason that if factors other than gender fully explain the salary differential, then gender discrimination is not a factor. In essence, you want to see whether the relationship between gender and income disappears when controlling for several variables.

Your task then is to identify potential confounding variables and control for them. The graduate's major field comes to mind. You note that 80% of women graduated with majors in the social sciences or humanities whereas 80% of men graduated with majors in the natural sciences. You also note a substantial difference in mean salaries for these fields. The mean salary of social sciences/humanities majors was $38,800 whereas that for natural science majors was $51,200. Major field, then, is associated with both gender and salary, that is, with each of the variables in the initial relationship. It should be controlled for.

Table 11.4 presents the results. These being hypothetical (not real-world) data, the results are quite tidy. You might observe first that men in the natural sciences earn, on average, $10,000 more than do men in the social sciences/humanities ($52,000 versus $42,000) and furthermore that this same differential is present for women ($48,000 versus $38,000). These are not the comparisons of central interest but are presented (1) to help you to interpret the table and (2) to point out the association between major field and salary. The key comparisons compare men's and women's salaries within majors. Within the natural sciences major group, the mean salary of men exceeds that of women by $4000 ($52,000 versus $48,000). Among social sciences/humanities majors, a $4000 gender differential is also found; the mean salary for men is $42,000 whereas that for women is $38,000.

Controlling for major field has reduced the difference between male and female salaries from $10,000 to $4000. Thus, major field was at least partly responsible for the salary differential. Are other confounding variables also influencing the association of gender and income? Presume that the survey probed whether the graduate had taken time off from work to care for a child or other family member. Presume further that taking time off from work does indeed evidence associations to both salary and gender. As such, it is a confounding variable that should be controlled for. Table 11.5 presents results controlling for both major field and taking time off. This table presents four subgroups within which we can assess the male/female salary differential. These are (1) natural sciences majors who took time off, (2) social sciences/humanities majors who took time off, (3) natural science majors who did not take time off, and (4) social sciences majors who did not take time off. Within each of these subgroups, the mean salary of men is $3200 higher than that of women. Thus, controlling for taking time off reduces the salary

TABLE 11.4   GRADUATES' SALARY BY GENDER, CONTROLLING FOR MAJOR

NATURAL SCIENCES MAJORS				SOCIAL SCIENCES/ HUMANITIES MAJORS			
MALES		FEMALES		MALES		FEMALES	
Mean	*n*	Mean	*n*	Mean	*n*	Mean	*n*
$52,000	80	$48,000	20	$42,000	20	$38,000	80

Note: Data are hypothetical.

TABLE 11.5	SALARY BY GENDER, CONTROLLING FOR MAJOR AND TIME OFF						
	NATURAL SCIENCES MAJORS				**SOCIAL SCIENCES/ HUMANITIES MAJORS**		
	MALE		**FEMALE**		**MALE**		**FEMALE**	
Time Off	**Mean**	*n*	**Mean**	*n*	**Mean**	*n*	**Mean**	*n*
Taken	$50,200	8	$47,000	10	$40,200	2	$37,000	40
Not taken	$52,200	72	$49,000	10	$42,200	18	$39,000	40

Note: Data are hypothetical.

differential by an additional $800 (from $4000 to $3200). Just as did major field, it provides a partial explanation for this differential.

A difference still remains after having controlled for two variables. Can we identify additional variables that should be controlled for? Presume that (1) managers earn more on average than do line staff and (2) a higher percentage of men than women are in management. As type of position (management versus staff) is associated with both gender and salary, it should be controlled. We could attempt to create a table controlling for three variables: major field, taking time off, and type of position. Such a table would result in eight different subgroups. (For each of the four groups listed in Table 11.5 there would be two groups, one for managers and the other for line staff.) Clearly, our table is becoming complex. Furthermore, a table with eight subgroups is the simplest table that can control for three variables. Each of the variables in this table had only two categories: $2 \times 2 \times 2 = $ eight subgroups. If each variable had, say, three categories, there would have been 27 subgroups: $3 \times 3 \times 3 = 27$.

Pragmatically speaking, it is usually not practical to control for more than two variables in a single table. Sometimes researchers construct multiple tables to accommodate this issue. For instance, to deal with the management/staff issues, we could construct two separate tables, each structured just like Table 11.5. One table would be for managers, the other for line staff. Having done so, we would continue to follow the logic of comparing male and female salaries within the subgroups.

This text began with univariate statistics (means, standard deviations, etc.), then moved to bivariate statistics (association between two variables). The prior chapter and this one present situations involving three or more variables and thus involve **multivariate** data analysis. But using tables to control for confounding variables provides only the briefest introduction to the capabilities of multivariate analysis. A wide array of multivariate procedures are available for different situations, for instance, for variables at different levels of measurement. Many of these have the capability to control for many different variables. For instance, in multiple regression analysis, the researcher can hold six or seven variables (or more) constant in order to assess relationships. Chapter 22, Section 22.11, introduces and gives an overview of the technique of multiple regression. (See Glass and Hopkins, 1996, or many other texts for discussion of various multivariate procedures.)

As the salary differential example demonstrates, control via the use of tables has limitations. Even so, using tables to control for variables is a straightforward, "workhorse" tool of social scientists, one that you are encouraged to use.

The real limitation in controlling for confounding variables does not lie with choice of methodology (tables versus complex multivariate statistical applications). The fundamental limitation is that, in a nonrandomized study, one can never control for *all* possible confounding variables. In the absence of random assignment, one can basically *never* have a high degree of confidence that an association is causal. For instance, in the salary differential example, we controlled for major field and taking time off and were prepared to control for type of position (management versus staff). Can we identify other potential confounding variables? Perhaps differing percentages of women and men earn graduate degrees. Presumably earning a graduate degree leads to a higher salary. If earning a graduate degree is indeed associated with both gender and salary, it should be controlled for. Perhaps men are more motivated in career by financial rewards and women by other factors. If so, we should find a way to measure and control for this. Clearly, there is no logical end to the list of potential confounding variables. This is the fundamental reason why, even when one has controlled for several key variables, it is difficult to draw causal conclusions in survey and other nonrandomized designs.

11.5   INTERACTION EFFECTS

11.5.1   *Definition and Major Points*

To this point, we have covered three of the four major patterns that may emerge when a confounding variable is controlled for. Thus we have demonstrated that controlling for a potential confounding variable may (1) not affect the size of an initial relationship (or weaken it only marginally), (2) weaken that relationship considerably, or (3) cause that relationship to disappear. The fourth pattern of results is for size of association to differ markedly between subgroups. Such a result is an example of an interaction effect. When there is an **interaction effect (interaction),** the pattern of relationship between two variables differs according to the value of a third variable. This differing pattern of relationship may be reflected by (1) markedly different size of relationship between subgroups, (2) differing direction of association in different subgroups, and/or (3) the presence of association in some subgroup(s) and the lack or near-lack thereof in others.

Let me relay an example that one of my statistics teachers used to help me understand interaction. She presented results from a study that examined the association of gender of lead characters in children's stories with children's interest in those stories. An initial finding was that, on average, children tended to show higher interest when lead characters were boys than when lead characters were girls. When the researcher controlled for gender of reader, an interesting interaction emerged. For female readers, gender of character was not predictive of interest. Girls were equally interested in stories involving female and male lead characters. For boys, the situation was different. They evidenced much greater interest in stories with lead male characters than in those with female characters. Thus the pattern of association between gender of lead character and interest in the story differed for girls and boys. When the pattern of association differs according to the value of a third variable, one has an interaction.

Let's look at an example from the special-needs adoption study (Rosenthal and Groze, 1992). In Table 11.6, the dependent variable is closeness of relationship between parent and child. The higher the score, the closer the relationship (the highest possible score is 4.00). Table 11.6 presents the association between age of child and closeness of relationship controlling for family ethnicity, which was defined near the beginning of this chapter.

Observe that for white, inracial families and even more so for transracial families, as age of child increases, closeness of relationship decreases. Such a pattern would be predicted by the "prevailing wisdom"; one expects greater closeness between parents and children when children are younger than when they are in adolescence. The pattern in minority, inracial homes is distinctly different from that in the other two groups. In minority, inracial families, child's age is essentially unassociated with closeness of association, as indicated by mean scores on closeness that are virtually identical for the three age groups. Thus the pattern of association between age of child and level of closeness differs by ethnicity. This being the case, there is an interaction.

There are almost always two different ways to describe an interaction. The just-presented discussion describes the association between age and closeness of relationship, controlling for family ethnicity. Table 11.6 is titled according to this perspective. Yet Table 11.6 may also be viewed as presenting the association between family ethnicity and closeness of relationship, controlling for age of child. To summarize results from this perspective: (1) for children from birth to 5 years of age the three family ethnicity groups report reasonably similar levels of closeness; (2) for children ages 6 to 11, the trend is toward greater closeness in the minority, inracial group (as evidenced by the higher mean score in this group); and (3) for children ages 12 to 18, this trend becomes even stronger (the difference in means between the minority, inracial group and the other groups becomes larger). From this new perspective, there is an interaction because the pattern of relationship between family ethnicity and closeness to child varies according to the

TABLE 11.6   CLOSENESS SCORE BY AGE, CONTROLLING FOR ETHNICITY

Child's Age at Time of Survey	MINORITY, INRACIAL FAMILIES		WHITE, INRACIAL FAMILIES		TRANSRACIAL FAMILIES	
	Mean	f	Mean	f	Mean	f
Birth to 5 years	3.52	13	3.66	60	3.80	9
6 to 11 years	3.61	112	3.35	207	3.39	23
12 to 18 years	3.46	101	3.02	184	2.96	26

Note: The scores are for parent-child closeness, using a scale where 4.00 indicates the closest relationships.

child's age. Stated differently, the same pattern of association of ethnicity to closeness is not observed for all three age groups.

11.5.2   Interaction Versus Relationship

I described the above interaction in two different ways for learning purposes only. When you describe interactions, don't go to such trouble. Instead, pick the description that makes the most sense—to you, to your audience, according to common sense—and use it. (In the next several paragraphs, I will use the second description above.)

The concepts of interaction and relationship are sometimes confused. Let's determine a distinction by using two sets of "rigged" (hypothetical) results for the closeness/ethnicity/age analysis. In each new set of results, there is no interaction effect. Observe Result A in Table 11.7. In Result A, for all three age groups, family ethnicity and closeness of relationship are unassociated (technically, their association is trivial, because group means differ by so little). In Result B in Table 11.8, for all three age groups, family ethnicity and closeness of relationship are associated. Within each age group, greater closeness is observed in the minority, inracial group than in the other two. Furthermore, the size of association, indicated by the size of the difference between the means, is very nearly equal in each group.

Result A and Result B differed. In B, family ethnicity and closeness were associated. In A, they were not (technically, their association was of trivial size). Whether two variables are associated is *not,* per se, pertinent to the assessment of whether there is an interaction. What both sets of results have in common is that the *pattern* of association between family ethnicity and closeness is *the same* in all three age groups. Stated differently, the pattern of association *does not* vary according to child's age. This is the key point. When the pattern of association does not vary for the different categories of the controlled-for variable, there is no interaction.

Both sets of results contrast with the actual study results as presented in Table 11.6. In the real results, the pattern of association between ethnicity and closeness varies according to age group. As such, there is an interaction. In Results A and B, the pattern of association does not vary by age group. Thus no interaction effect occurs for either of these sets of results.[6]

TABLE 11.7   RESULT A: SAME LACK OF ASSOCIATION IN EACH AGE GROUP

Child's Age at Time of Survey	MINORITY, INRACIAL FAMILIES		WHITE, INRACIAL FAMILIES		TRANSRACIAL FAMILIES	
	Mean	f	Mean	f	Mean	f
Birth to 5 years	3.63	13	3.66	60	3.62	9
6 to 11 years	3.48	112	3.49	207	3.45	23
12 to 18 years	3.31	101	3.30	184	3.33	26

Note: Data are hypothetical.

TABLE 11.8	RESULT B: SAME SIZE OF ASSOCIATION IN EACH AGE GROUP					
Child's Age at Time of Survey	**MINORITY, INRACIAL FAMILIES**		**WHITE, INRACIAL FAMILIES**		**TRANSRACIAL FAMILIES**	
	Mean	**f**	**Mean**	**f**	**Mean**	**f**
Birth to 5 years	3.81	13	3.51	60	3.42	9
6 to 11 years	3.68	112	3.38	207	3.39	23
12 to 18 years	3.57	101	3.20	184	3.23	26

Note: Data are hypothetical.

11.5.3   *Exploring Data*

This chapter has primarily emphasized control for variables as a tool for assessing whether relationships are causal. The key idea to carry with you from this discussion is not that most relationships are not causal but instead that assessing causality is often an uncertain and difficult undertaking. In addition to their role in the assessment of causality, the methods presented in this chapter are equally important as tools for learning about one's data. By exploring data carefully and by examining associations under varied conditions, one can often identify unexpected relationships and interactions. It is somewhat uncommon for researchers to find interactions. They are usually excited to do so, and readers are often intrigued by them.[7,8]

11.6   CHAPTER SUMMARY

To determine the influence of a potential confounding variable, one controls for that variable, that is, holds it constant. Potential confounding variables are associated with *both* variables in the initial relationship.

A straightforward way to control for a confounding variable is to create groups composed of cases with the same (or highly similar) values on that variable. Within groups, the controlled-for variable becomes, effectively, a constant. Several different patterns may emerge. If the size of association in the groups differs hardly at all from that in the initial association, one concludes that the controlled-for variable is not an important cause of the relationship. When the association persists in the groups but at a reduced size, one concludes that the effects of the confounding variable provide a partial but not a full explanation for the initial relationship.

When an initial relationship disappears, one concludes that there is no direct causal relationship between the initial variables. The precise conclusion reached for this pattern of results depends on the causal model: For the antecedent variable model, one concludes that there is no causal effect (direct or indirect); for the intervening variable model, that there is no direct effect but that there is an indirect effect from the controlled-for variable; and for the general confounding variable model, that there is no direct effect and that no firm conclusion can be reached regarding an indirect effect. A spurious relationship is one that disappears when an antecedent confounding variable is controlled for.

To exert substantial influence, a confounding variable must (generally speaking) have reasonably strong associations with *both* variables in the initial relationship. The stronger these associations, the greater the influence. One may control for two or more variables.

An interaction occurs when the pattern of relationship between two variables differs according to the value of a third variable. Key "patterns" of interaction are (1) markedly different size of relationship in different groups, (2) differing direction of association in different groups, and/or (3) the presence of association in some group(s) and the lack thereof in others.

PROBLEMS AND QUESTIONS

Section 11.2

1. A phrase synonymous with controlling for a (confounding) variable is holding a variable _____.

2. (T or F) Most confounding variables that substantially influence the size of an initial association are associated with only one of the variables in that initial association.

3. When a confounding variable is controlled for (as, for instance, age is in Table 11.1), that confounding variable ceases to be a variable and becomes essentially a(n) _____.

4. (T or F) Consider the associations of X and Y within categories of the controlled-for confounding variable Z. Within categories of Z, Z has little (if any) effect on the size of the association between X and Y.

5. In various situations, controlling for a confounding variable may result in . . .
   a. Only a marginal change in size of association
   b. A marked reduction in size of association
   c. The disappearance of the association
   d. All of the above

6. X and Y are strongly associated. The variable Z is controlled for. Within categories of Z, X and Y are unassociated (or the association is extremely weak). In this example, the associa-

tion between X and Y _____ when Z was controlled for.

7. In Table 10.1, when age is controlled for, the relationship between type of placement (family foster or group home) and number of behavioral problems . . .
   a. Is just as strong within the age subgroups as in the initial relationship
   b. Is somewhat weaker within the age subgroups than in the initial relationship
   c. Disappears

8. (T or F) If an initial relationship persists at about the same size when a potential confounding variable Z is controlled for, one may conclude that Z is not an important cause of (explanation for) that relationship.

Questions 9–11 pertain to the following causal model:

9. This model is a(n) _____ variable model.

10. If this model is correct, when A is controlled for the relationship between B and C will _____.

11. Given that this is an antecedent variable model and that the relationship between the two ini-

tial variables (B and C) disappears when a confounding variable (A) is controlled for, the relationship between B and C is termed a(n) _____ relationship.

12. If this model is correct . . .
    a. B exerts no direct effect on C
    b. B exerts no indirect effect on C
    c. B exerts no effect whatsoever (direct or indirect) on C
    d. The relationship between B and C is due to A
    e. All of the above

Questions 13–15 pertain to the following causal model:

13. The model is a(n) _____ variable model.
14. If this model is correct, when one controls for B the relationship between A and C will _____.
15. In this model . . .
    a. A has no effect whatsoever on C
    b. A has a direct effect on C
    c. A has an indirect effect on C
    d. All of the above
16. An initial relationship between X and Y disappears when Z is controlled for. Presume that it is plausible that either an antecedent variable model or an intervening variable model is correct. Which of the following conclusions is correct?
    a. There is no direct effect of X on Y or of Y on X.

    b. Neither X nor Y has any effect (direct or otherwise) on the other.
    c. X exerts a direct effect on Y or Y does so on X.
    d. X exerts an indirect effect on Y or Y does so on X.

Section 11.3

17. (T or F) Even when a confounding variable has a relationship of small to medium size with both variables involved in an initial relationship, it typically exerts a substantial influence on the size of the initial relationship.
18. (T or F) Generally speaking, to exert substantial influence on the size of a relationship, a confounding variable should have a reasonably strong association with both variables involved in that relationship.

Section 11.4

19. (T or F) In survey designs, it is exceedingly difficult (if not impossible) to control for all potentially confounding variables.

Section 11.5

20. For each of the four studies in Table 11PQ.1, indicate whether there is an interaction effect (yes or no), and if there is an interaction effect, describe it in your own words.

TABLE 11PQ.1 **HOSPITAL READMISSION BY GENDER AND TREATMENT TYPE**

Study Number	MEN READMITTED (%)		WOMEN READMITTED (%)	
	Community Treatment	Traditional Treatment	Community Treatment	Traditional Treatment
1	15	25	22	32
2	15	25	25	15
3	33	44	33	44
4	20	20	20	40

Note: Data are hypothetical.

COMPUTER EXERCISES

For general instructions on computer exercises, see the note in Chapter 2.

1. Examine the association of FAMETH3 (family ethnicity) to IMPACT (impact of adoption), controlling for AGEHOM3 (child's age at entry into home coded in three categories). [In SPSS, *Analyze > Compare Means > Means,* click IMPACT to "Dependent List," click AGEHOM3 to "Independent List," click "Next" next to "Layer 1 of 1," click FAMETH over to "Independent List," *OK.*]

   To interpret the SPSS results, in the "Report" table, first assess the results presented in the bottom quarter of the table (titled TOTAL), which are the results prior to controlling for AGEHOM3. To assess associations controlling for AGEHOM3, look at the top three-quarters of the table. The results do not show a definitive pattern. By and large, the relationship between FAMETH and IMPACT holds at nearly the initial strength when AGEHOM3 is controlled for. Some interaction is suggested, because the difference in mean IMPACT between inracial families and other families differs somewhat by age. This difference is, generally speaking, much smaller in the "birth to 3 years" group than in the other age groups. (In the "birth to 3 years" group, IMPACT is actually most positive in the transracial group.)

2. Assess the association between MINORCH (child's ethnicity) and IMPACTD (dichotomous variable measuring impact) without and then with control for AGEHOM3 (child's age at ethnicity). [In SPSS, *Analyze > Descriptive Statistics > Crosstabs,* click IMPACTD to space under "Rows" and MINORCH to space under "Columns," *Cells,* click box next to "Column," *Continue, OK.* Examine the results. *Analyze > Descriptive Statistics > Crosstabs* brings back the Crosstabs dialog box. Click AGEHOM3 over into space below "Layer 1 of 1," *OK.*]

   Check your answers: Initial (bivariate) contingency table reveals that when child's ethnicity is other than white, respondents are more likely to respond "very positive" (55% versus 44%). When controlling for AGEHOM3, an interaction appears to emerge. When age is 3 or under, responses do not vary according to MINORCH (62% in each group responded "very positive"). For older children, responses are more positive when the child is of minority ethnicity.

3. Assess again the association between MINORCH and IMPACTD (you generated the necessary table in exercise 2). Next, assess this association controlling for ONEORTWO (one-parent versus two-parent adoption). (Hint: ONEORTWO will be the "Layer 1 of 1" variable.)

   Check your answers: Results suggest a weak interaction effect. Among two-parent families, impact is more positive in families with minority children (51.9% versus 42.3% respond "very positive"). Among single-parent families, impact is very slightly more positive in families with white children (60.0% versus 57.4% respond "very positive").

NOTES

1. In some situations a variable related very strongly to one variable in an initial relationship and not at all to the other could influence the size of that relationship. Typically, that influence is small. A third variable can be involved in an interaction (interactions are discussed in Section 11.5) even when it is not related to both variables in the initial relationship.

2. Summing the differences in percentages and then dividing by the number of subgroups is similar to the procedures involved in calculating the average difference in percentages as described in Chapter 7, Section 7.5.1. Both the average difference in percentages and the procedures described here are informal tools for approximating the overall degree of relationship in a table. In carrying out the procedures described here, one should always subtract the same percentage. In the current example, the percentage for white families (presuming that

this is the second designated category) is always sub-tracted from that for minority families (presuming that this is the first). This rule applies even if the difference computes to a negative number. The math for the cur-rent calculation is:

$$D\% = [(63 - 60) + (55 - 39) + (62 - 36)$$
$$+ (35 - 26) + (50 - 34)] \div 5$$
$$= (3 + 16 + 26 + 9 + 16) \div 5$$
$$= 70 \div 5 = 14.0$$

3. Many social scientists (e.g., Cohen and Cohen, 1983, p. 93) also use the term *spurious* when the general confounding variable model is assumed and the initial re-lationship disappears. The term should not be used with the intervening variable model, as an indirect causal ef-fect is still present with this model.

4. There are some exceptions to this guideline. In par-ticular, a confounding variable having an *extremely* strong association to one variable could exert substantial influence even if it had only a small association to the other variable.

5. We might also want to determine how much influ-ence age of adoption has on the association of family eth-nicity and impact of adoption. Recall that the difference in percentages was 17% in the initial relationship and that the average difference in percentages was 14% within the subgroups. We can subtract 14% from 17% (17% − 14% = 3%) and conclude that of the initial *D%* of 17%, the direct effects of age of adoption explain a dif-ference of 3%. We can also conclude that the remaining difference of 14% is not caused by the direct effects of age of adoption.

6. We have defined *interaction* as the situation in which the pattern of association between two variables differs according to a third variable. This statement is both correct and consistent with this chapter's focus on controlling for confounding variables. Technically, how-ever, interaction occurs between two *independent* vari-ables. So, for instance, in Table 11.6 the interaction is be-tween family ethnicity and age of child. To be more pre-cise, one would say, "There is an interaction between family ethnicity and age of child in the prediction of closeness of relationship." Technically, it is incorrect to say that there is an interaction between either (1) family ethnicity and closeness of relationship or (2) age of child and closeness of relationship. Formally, the interaction is between the independent variables.

7. The pattern of association of a third variable to the variables in an initial relationship can be used to identify third variables that substantially influence the size of that relationship; basically, only third variables with strong re-lationships to both variables in the initial relationship ex-ert substantial influence. On the other hand, the pattern of association to the initial variables does not convey which third variables may be involved in interactions. For instance, presume that a third variable is indeed in-volved in an interaction. Suppose further that one exam-ines the association of this variable to each of the vari-ables in the initial relationship. It is possible for this variable to be unassociated with both variables. In sum, the pattern of association to the initial variables cannot be used to "hunt down" potential interactions.

8. An interaction effect occurs when the pattern of as-sociation varies according to the value of a third variable. Chapters 14 and 15 discuss how relationships sometimes occur simply due to chance (see also Chapter 1, Section 1.13). In the same way, the pattern of association for dif-ferent values of a third variable can also vary simply by chance. The appropriate statistical significance test can discern whether chance alone is a likely or an unlikely ex-planation for variability in the pattern of association. When chance is an unlikely explanation, the interaction is presumed to be due to real factors and is statistically significant. This text does not cover how to test whether an interaction is significant (see Glass and Hopkins, 1996, pp. 482–535; Toothaker and Miller, 1996, pp. 467–506; or discussion of two-way, or factorial, analysis of variance in many texts).

INFERENTIAL STATISTICS: BEGINNING APPLICATIONS

Part Five presents the basics of inferential statistics, that is, of how researchers draw conclusions about whole populations based on data from samples. Chapter 12 discusses different types of samples and demonstrates how characteristics of random samples are used to estimate characteristics of populations. Chapter 13 presents confidence intervals (similar to the "margins of error" often mentioned in newscasts in connection with political polls).

Chapter 14 introduces statistical significance tests. Researchers use significance tests to decide whether a difference in a sample may simply be due to chance or reflects a real difference. For instance, suppose that one places 1000 names in a hat and, at random, draws 10 names to be in Group A and 10 in Group B. Those in A receive Relaxation Treatment A and those in B receive Relaxation Treatment B. Following these treatments, those in Group A, on average, have higher relaxation scores than do those in B. On the basis of such small samples, one cannot be confident that Treatment A is actually more effective than B. The observed difference may be due to the "luck of the draw," that is, to chance. Perhaps, for instance, those assigned to Group A were more relaxed to begin with.

Chapter 15 presents a first statistical significance test and introduces the hypothesis testing model for carrying out such tests. Chapter 16 introduces the concept of statistical power and discusses what statistical significance does and does not mean.

AN INTRODUCTION TO INFERENTIAL STATISTICS

12.1 CHAPTER OVERVIEW

We first distinguish the features of inferential statistics from those of descriptive statistics, which we have already studied. To know whether inferential statistics can be used in a study, we look for three key characteristics of *random samples* and for whether *independence of observations* applies. We consider how nonrandom sampling can lead to *bias*, and conversely, how random sampling leads to *representativeness*. We also get a new definition for a *statistic* of a sample as distinguished from a *parameter* of a whole population. We examine the characteristics of an *estimator* and the two types of estimates, *point estimates* and *interval estimates*. *Sampling error* and *sampling distributions* are introduced and defined. The *central limit theorem* allows us to develop the *sampling distribution of the mean*.

12.2 DESCRIPTIVE VERSUS INFERENTIAL STATISTICS

Descriptive statistical procedures describe the study sample. Chapters 3 to 9 cover a variety of univariate and bivariate procedures that may be used for this purpose.

The purpose for which a procedure is used, rather than the procedure per se, determines whether we are engaged in descriptive or inferential statistics. If we use the mean of a randomly selected study sample to estimate the mean of the population from which it was selected, we are not describing our study sample. Instead we are drawing conclusions about the population. This being the case, we are not engaged in descriptive statistics, which by definition confines itself to study sample description. Instead, we have entered the domain of inferential statistics. **Inferential statistical procedures** are tools for drawing conclusions about populations based on observations from samples randomly selected from those populations. (To simplify discussion, when it is readily apparent that the population being referred to is the "population from which the sample was selected," this text often states simply "population.")

12.3   CHARACTERISTICS OF RANDOM SAMPLES

For a sample to be a random sample, it should be selected by a *formal* method of chance. Consider the population of students at a school of social work or human services. Appropriate formal methods of chance for selecting students include (1) putting the names of *all* students in a hat, shaking well, and drawing names, (2) using a table of random numbers (you will probably encounter these in your research class), and (3) programming a calculator or computer software package to pick the sample. Another way to select a sample would be to stand at the school's front door and have those who walk through fill out a questionnaire. Selection by such a methodology also involves an element of chance. For instance, perhaps some students just happen to have classes scheduled when the sample is being taken and so are included. Perhaps someone gets a flat tire and so, by "bad" luck, is not included. A sample taken this way—even though chance plays an informal role—is not a random sample.[1]

A second basic characteristic of a random sample is that each case has an *equal* chance of being selected. To ensure this, one typically develops a list of *all* cases in the population and selects randomly from this list.[2]

A third characteristic of a random sample, **independence of selection,** states that the selection of each case is independent of the selection of each other case. The following is an example of a sampling methodology that violates the assumption of independence of selection:

> Suppose that you want to observe the television viewing habits of children at an elementary school. Let's say that the principal provides you with a list of all families at the school. You cut up the list, put the family names in a hat, and draw out, say, 25 families for your study. As some families have more than one child enrolled, your study sample numbers more than 25 children. Let's say that it numbers 35. You go to the homes and record the viewing habits of each child.

Your sample of 35 children does not meet the independence of selection assumption. If one child in a family was selected, so was each other enrolled child in that family. Looked at from the opposite perspective, if one child from a family was not selected, neither were any others.

Given that this sample does not meet the independence of selection assumption, it is not, strictly speaking, a random sample.[3] A better sampling method would have been to (1) obtain a list of all children rather than of all families and (2) select children randomly from this list. The resulting sample would then meet the assumption of independence of selection.

Don't confuse random sampling with random assignment as discussed in Chapters 1 (Section 1.13) and 10 (Section 10.6). Random sampling is a method for selecting cases for one's study. When sampling is random, the inferential procedures presented in this and subsequent chapters may be used to generalize sample results to the population from which the sample was selected. Random assignment (randomization) refers to the use of random methods to assign cases to groups *within* an experimental study. Random assignment bears on the issue of causality. When assignment is random, one can be much more confident that a difference between groups is due to the treatment intervention rather than to a confounding variable.

12.4   RANDOM SAMPLING AND REPRESENTATIVENESS

Why is random sampling so important in research and statistics? One may reason from conditions in a sample to those in a population only when that sample possesses the quality of **representativeness.** When a sample is **representative** of a population, the characteristics of the sample are similar to those of the population. For instance, if the television viewing habits of the 35 children in your study sample are similar to those of the population of children at the elementary school, then that sample is representative of that population with respect to television viewing. Representativeness does not have a precise mathematical definition but instead conveys the general notion of similarity.

Only by pure luck is a sample (random or nonrandom) ever *perfectly* representative. Stated differently, only by luck are the characteristics of the sample *exactly* like those of the population. Even with a random sample, the luck of the draw enters in. Thus characteristics of a sample almost always differ at least somewhat from those of the population. The great advantage of a random sample over a nonrandom one is that luck is the *only* factor that causes differences between sample and population. Stated differently, in a random sample only *random* factors affect representativeness. One need not be concerned about *systematic* bias.

As presented in Chapter 1 (Section 1.11), a sample is **biased** if its characteristics differ systematically from those of the population about which one seeks to make inferences. Random samples have no systematic bias. In contrast, when samples are nonrandom, there is often good reason to suspect bias.

For instance, suppose that a social work professor who studies the career aspirations of students uses data gathered in the three classes that she teaches to draw conclusions about career aspirations of the full population of students at the school. Suppose further that she teaches courses primarily related to child welfare. It is likely, then, that many of the students who take her classes (particularly if these are electives) will have career aspirations in child welfare work. We have good reason to suspect that, taken as a group, her sample has greater interest in child welfare careers than does the full population of social work students at the school. Stated differently, we suspect that the career aspirations of the study sample, relative to those of the population, are systematically biased in the direction of greater interest in child welfare. If 70% of the professor's students indicated interest in a career in child welfare, we would not want to conclude that a similar percentage in the population shared that interest. Recognizing the likely direction of bias in the sample, our best guess would be that the percentage of students in the population interested in a child welfare career would be lower than the 70% in the sample.

The probable bias in the just-described sample is reasonably straightforward. To give an even more straightforward example, suppose that a study of student opinions about the degree of support for public welfare programs is being conducted and that a researcher administers a questionnaire in this area to a sample of social work students. Almost certainly, social work students as a group are more supportive of public welfare programs than are university students as a whole. Thus, relative to the population of students at the university, the social work sample will likely be biased in the direction of greater support.

When a sampling method is nonrandom, one is never sure that bias is present. Perhaps my conjectures about bias in the previous examples were wrong. For instance, perhaps social work students are not more supportive of public welfare programs than other students. Although one is never sure that bias is present in a nonrandom sample, the more important point is that one is never sure that it is not. As a general rule, science prefers to err on the cautious side. Since bias cannot be ruled out in nonrandom samples, they are generally regarded as being nonrepresentative.

One never knows *for sure* that a random sample is representative. (As stated earlier, the luck of the draw causes sample characteristics to differ from those of the population.) But the tools of inferential statistics enable the researcher to estimate how similar or different the characteristics of a random sample are likely to be from those of the population. When random samples are very small, the luck of the draw is large. For instance, suppose that 50% of people in the United States (the population) support the Democratic presidential candidate and 50% support the Republican candidate. Suppose further that we draw a random sample of five people. Because the sample is so small, just by luck all five (100%) might support, say, the Democratic candidate. Such a sample is not representative because the sample percentage differs so markedly from that in the population. As sample size increases, however, the luck of the draw decreases and random samples become increasingly representative. Thus, with the exception of very small samples, random samples are generally regarded as being representative. As such, they may be used to draw conclusions about the populations from which they have been selected.

Before we conclude our discussion of random sampling, one more point should be made: Inferential statistical procedures may not be used to draw conclusions about a population different from the one from which the study sample was randomly selected. This does not say that a study of, say, career aspirations of social work students at a given school would not inform us about those of students at a neighboring school. Indeed, most research studies do yield results with some degree of applicability beyond the population from which the study sample was selected. For instance, if the school at which the study was conducted and the neighboring school share many common characteristics—similar student body, similar course offerings, similar size, similar backgrounds of faculty, and so on—good reasons exist for thinking that career aspirations may indeed be similar among students in these two settings. However, drawing conclusions about populations different from that used to select the study sample is not within the realm of inferential statistics. Inferential statistics is a set of mathematics-based tools for drawing conclusions about the population from which a sample has been randomly selected.

The logic for assessing the applicability of study findings to different populations or settings is not based in mathematical reasoning and is not the province of inferential statistics. Concepts and tools for this purpose are presented in Chapter 23, Section 23.2, which discusses generalizability.

12.5 INDEPENDENCE OF OBSERVATIONS

As already stated, to use inferential statistical procedures, one needs a random sample. We have discussed three characteristics of random samples: (1) cases are selected via a formal method of chance, (2) cases have an equal chance of selection, and (3) the selection of each case is independent from that of each other case. To qualify for inferential statistics, the study sample should also possess a fourth characteristic. This fourth characteristic is termed *independence of observations* or simply *independence.* As a rough working definition, two cases are independent— that is, they meet the **independence of observations (independence)** assumption—when they do not share some common factor or event that makes their scores similar. That common factor is ordinarily (1) extraneous to the purpose of the research study and (2) not taken into account by the research design (for instance, not controlled for). When the independence assumption is not met, cases (observations) are said to be **dependent** and one's data have a problem termed **dependency.**[4] A key reason for dependency is that the actions of one study participant influence those of another.

Independence and dependence are conveyed better by example than by definition. Consider two studies of two different interventions designed to enhance assertiveness. In the first study, presume that the intervention is administered via a CD-ROM on a computer. Each participant carries out the intervention (a packaged module designed to enhance assertiveness) at home in privacy. Presume that the intervention in the second study is an assertiveness group. In group format, clients practice assertiveness skills, encouraging and reinforcing one another as they progress through the program. In both studies, presume that the study sample has been randomly selected from a large population.

The study of the CD-ROM intervention clearly meets the independence assumption. In particular, given that participants do not come into contact with one another, the actions of one cannot influence those of another.

The independence assumption is tricky to assess in the group intervention study. For instance, perhaps good progress for one participant "rubs off" on others. Or perhaps the opposite is true—a group member with a destructive personality hinders others' progress. Or perhaps subgroups (cliques) have formed. If so, those within the given subgroups will likely influence the progress of others in their group. Any of these group dynamics could lead to similar scores among subgroups of participants and, by so doing, introduce dependency. If these dynamics, or any others, introduce dependency, inferential statistical procedures should not, formally, be used.

In real-world human services research, the independence assumption presents a dilemma. Many human services studies bring participants together for interaction. Applied strictly, the independence assumption could invalidate numerous studies. There is no easy resolution. Often there is no way to know whether the independence assumption has been met. Furthermore, if it has not been met, and therefore dependency has been introduced, it can be difficult to know whether the degree of dependency is large enough to cause problems in one's analysis.

Again, there is no easy resolution. In human services research, the most common approach to independence issues is to assume that cases are independent unless there is convincing evidence to the contrary. In the just-described group intervention example, for instance, the researcher might well reason that it cannot easily be established that the independence assumption has not been met and, therefore, carry out the called-for inferential procedure.

Let's consider a clear violation of the independence assumption. Suppose that one student copies another's answers on a test that is used as an outcome measure in a study. Clearly, these two observations (test scores) are not independent. In such a situation, most researchers would exclude the copied score from the study sample.

So, except when clearly violated, the pragmatic decision is to assume that the independence assumption has been met. To recap, one may use inferential statistical procedures if the study sample is a random one and meets the independence of observations assumption.

12.6   STATISTICS AND PARAMETERS

Chapter 1 provided a general definition of *statistic:* a numerical summary of data. *Statistic* also has a specific meaning that differentiates it from *parameter.* **Statistics** are numerical characteristics of samples. **Parameters** are numerical characteristics of populations (Toothaker and Miller, 1996, p. 16). For instance, the mean of a sample is a statistic whereas that of a population is a parameter. Much of inferential statistics involves the use of sample statistics to estimate population parameters. For instance, the mean of a random sample estimates the mean in the population from which it was selected. Similarly, the standard deviation and variance in a random sample estimate their corresponding population parameters. When a sample statistic is used to estimate a population parameter, that statistic is termed an **estimator (inferential statistic).** (Or one may simply continue to use the term *statistic.*)

For the most part, sample statistics are symbolized by letters from the Roman alphabet (the same letters used in English), and population parameters are symbolized by Greek letters. Some key statistics and their corresponding parameters are presented in Table 12.1.

TABLE 12.1   **SELECTED INFERENTIAL STATISTICS AND POPULATION PARAMETERS**

Statistic or Parameter	Symbol for Sample Statistic	Symbol for Population Parameter	Spelling of Greek Letter	Pronunciation of Greek Letter
Mean	$\overline{X}$	μ	mu	mew
Standard deviation	s	σ	sigma	sigma
Variance	s^2	σ^2	sigma	sigma
Proportion	p	π	pi	pie

Note: The symbol for the proportion in the population, π, is the same as that for the circumference of a circle. The symbol for the proportion in a sample, p, is the same as that for probability, which is introduced in Chapter 14, Section 14.3.

The formula for the z score of a sample was presented in Chapter 5, Section 5.9. As symbols for the mean and standard deviation in a population have been introduced, the formula for the z score in a population may be presented:

$$z = \frac{X - \mu}{\sigma} \tag{12.1}$$

where X is the score of an individual case; the Greek symbols are listed in Table 12.1.

12.7 CHARACTERISTICS OF ESTIMATORS

Good estimators are both efficient and unbiased (Glass and Hopkins, 1996, pp. 242–247).[5] An **efficient** estimator requires a minimum of cases to generate a good estimate. Efficiency is basically a matter of relative efficiency. For instance, the mean is a more efficient estimator of central tendency than is the median. Given equal sample sizes, the sample mean, on average, provides more precise estimates of the population mean than does the sample median of the population median. The other estimators in Table 12.1 are also efficient estimators.

An **unbiased** estimator tends to neither overestimate nor underestimate a parameter. The mean and proportion of a sample are both unbiased estimators of their corresponding population parameters. You may recall that Chapter 4 provided two formulas for both the variance and the standard deviation. When calculated with $N - 1$ in the denominator (formula 4.7), the variance of a random sample is an unbiased estimator of the population variance. This is the key reason why this formula is preferred. When calculated with N in the denominator (formula 4.6), the variance of a sample provides a slightly biased estimate of the population variance.

Given that the use of $N - 1$ in the denominator makes the sample variance an unbiased estimator, common sense suggests that it would do the same for the standard deviation. In this situation, common sense leads us astray. The use of

$N - 1$ in the denominator of the standard deviation (formula 4.5) greatly reduces the amount of bias in the standard deviation but does not entirely eliminate it. Even with this adjustment, the standard deviation of a random sample, s, tends to underestimate that in a population, σ, by an extremely small amount. As such, s is a biased estimator. The degree of bias is so small that, for practical purposes, we may disregard it.

The mean $(\overline{X})$, the variance (s^2), and proportion (p) are efficient and unbiased and thus are the preferred estimators of their respective population parameters. Indeed these statistics provide the *best possible* estimates of their respective parameters. The standard deviation (s) is efficient and its degree of bias is exceedingly small. The standard deviation in a sample, then, is the preferred estimator of that in the population. One may use these sample statistics to estimate the respective population parameters only when the study sample is a random one.

At this point, an example of how to use the just-discussed estimators is in order. Suppose that you work in child welfare services in a large state and have access to a large computerized data file with a variety of information pertaining to all children listed as victims on abuse and neglect reports. You draw a random sample of 100 reports from this large population of reports. The mean age of children in your sample is 8.5 years with a variance of 24.01 years and a standard deviation of 4.9 years. The mean, the variance, and the standard deviation are all the preferred estimators of their respective population parameters. As such, you would estimate that (1) the population mean, μ, equals 8.5 years; (2) the population variance, σ^2, equals 24.01 years; and (3) the population standard deviation, σ, equals 4.9 years.

Suppose also that 40% of reports in your sample involve abuse (physical or sexual) and 60% involve neglect. (As you know, proportions and percentages present the same information in different ways. Hence all of the points already made about proportions apply to percentages.) The percentage in a random sample is, therefore, an unbiased estimate of that in the population from which it has been selected. Thus 40% (abuse reports) and 60% (neglect reports) are the best estimates of the population percentages. Expressed as proportions, the best estimates are that π (the population proportion) equals .40 for abuse reports and .60 for neglect reports.

In examples above, each statistic estimates a single value. For instance, the sample mean estimates the population mean. When a statistic estimates a specific value, that estimate is a **point estimate.** Thus 40% is a point estimate of the percentage of abuse cases in the population. A disadvantage of a point estimate is that one does not know how close that estimate is likely to be to the population parameter. We know that 40% is the best estimate of the population percentage that we can make using our sample data. But how good an estimate is this? Is it likely to be accurate to within 5%, 10%, or perhaps 20% of the population percentage? We would like to be able to answer such questions.

In addition to point estimates, researchers make interval estimates. Rather than stating a specific value as does a point estimate, an **interval estimate** specifies a range within which the population value (parameter) is likely to be located. Thus, rather than making an estimate of 40%, for instance, as would a point estimate, an interval estimate states a likely range, for instance, "between 35 and 45%." The advantage of the interval estimate is that by specifying a range of likely values, it does convey a sense of how "good" one's estimate is. In general, as sample size increases, one is able to specify an increasingly smaller (narrower) range of likely values. In other words, as sample size goes up, one's estimate becomes more accurate.

12.8 SAMPLING ERROR AND SAMPLING DISTRIBUTIONS

Sample statistics only *estimate* population parameters. For instance, due to the luck of the draw, the mean in your random sample of 100 child abuse and neglect cases almost certainly differs by some amount from that in the population. Indeed, only by pure luck would the mean in your sample *exactly* equal that in the population. The difference between a sample statistic and a population parameter is known as **sampling error:**

$$\text{Sample error} = \text{sample statistic} - \text{population parameter} \qquad (12.2)$$

The mean in your sample was 8.5 years. If that in the population was 9.0 years, then sampling error would equal $8.5 - 9.0 = -0.5$ year. The just-described situation is unrealistic because the population parameter was known. In real-world research, only a sample of cases are selected from the population and the population parameter is unknown. As such, the just-provided formula for sampling error cannot be carried out and the exact amount of sampling error cannot be determined. Even if the exact amount of sampling error remains unknown, the tools of inferential statistics allow researchers to estimate it. Stated differently, researchers can estimate how close the sample statistic is likely to be to the population parameter.

The key tool for estimating the likely degree of similarity between the sample statistic and the population parameter is the sampling distribution. A **sampling distribution** is the theoretical distribution of a statistic that results from selecting an infinite number of random samples of the same size from a given population (all samples are selected from the same population).[6] The cases of a sampling distribution are the statistics from each sample. For instance, suppose that one (1) selects an infinite number of random samples of fixed size from a population, (2) calculates the mean of each sample, and (3) records these means. By so doing, one would build a frequency distribution composed of sample means. In a nutshell, a sampling distribution is a frequency distribution that is composed of statistics. The just-described sampling distribution, composed of sample means, is particularly important in statistics.

A **sampling distribution of the mean,** also known as the **sampling distribution of $\overline{X}$,** is a frequency distribution composed of the means of an infinite number of random samples of the same size, all selected from the same population. An important statistical theory, the **central limit theorem,** states three key points about the sampling distribution of $\overline{X}$:

1. Its mean equals the mean in the population from which samples were randomly selected.
2. Its standard deviation equals the standard deviation in the population from which the samples were randomly selected divided by the square root of the sample size.
3. As sample size increases, its shape approaches normality (approaches that of a normal distribution).

The third point is especially important. In particular, notice that no mention is made of the shape of the distribution in the population from which samples were selected. Thus, even when the shape of this distribution is *nonnormal*, the shape of the sampling distribution of $\overline{X}$ approaches normality. We may carry the third point one step farther and state that for almost all distributions that one encounters in social science research—normal, skewed, flat, bimodal, and other shapes—the shape of the sampling distribution of $\overline{X}$ will be normal or nearly so whenever sample size is 100 or greater.[7] The standard deviation of the sampling distribution of $\overline{X}$ is termed the **standard error of the mean** and is symbolized by $\sigma_{\overline{X}}$ According to point 2, its formula is:

$$\sigma_{\overline{X}} = \frac{\sigma}{\sqrt{N}} \tag{12.3}$$

where $\sigma_{\overline{X}}$ is the standard error of the mean, σ is the standard deviation in the population, and N is the size of the randomly selected samples.

The example on child abuse reports can be used to "build" a sampling distribution of $\overline{X}$. Presume that the mean age of children in the full population of all child abuse reports is 9.0 years with a standard deviation of 5.0 years. Note that these population parameters differ somewhat from the statistics of the random sample presented earlier ($\overline{X} = 8.5$, $s = 4.9$). This is to be expected. Due to sampling error, sample statistics and population parameters almost always differ. Figure 12.1 presents the frequency distribution of children's ages in the population. This distribution is distinctly nonnormal. (The vertical axis in Figure 12.1 does not list the actual number of children of each age, but the bars' heights do convey the relative numbers. It is presumed that this population is an extremely large one, with perhaps 100,000 or so cases.)

Suppose we select an infinite number of random samples of size 100 from this population and plot the mean of each. What will this sampling distribution of $\overline{X}$ look like? More specifically, what will be its mean, standard deviation, and shape? The central limit theorem addresses these questions about the sampling distribution of $\overline{X}$:

1. Point 1 in the previous list tells us that its mean equals the mean in the population from which the samples were selected. The mean, therefore, equals 9.0 years.
2. Point 2 states that its standard deviation (that is, the standard error of the mean, $\sigma_{\overline{X}}$ equals the standard deviation in the population from which samples were selected divided by the sample size:

$$\sigma_{\overline{X}} = 5.0/\sqrt{100} = 5.0/10 = 0.50 \text{ year}$$

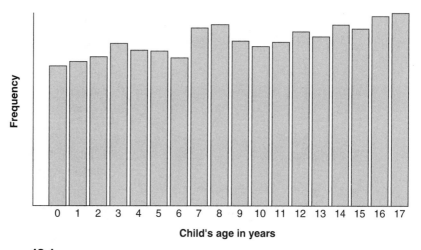

FIGURE **12.1**

DISTRIBUTION OF CHILDREN'S AGES IN THE POPULATION

3. Point 3 and the subsequent discussion tell us that, given that sample size is 100, its shape is extremely close to normal. (This is so even though the population distribution is nonnormal.)

As the shape of the sampling distribution of $\overline{X}$ is very close to normal, the characteristics of the normal curve can be used to describe it. In a normal distribution, about 68% of cases are within one standard deviation of the mean and about 95% of cases are within two standard deviations. Given that the mean of the distribution is 9.0 years and its standard deviation is 0.50 year, about 68% of the sample means in the distribution are located between 8.50 and 9.50 years (9.0 ± 0.50) and about 95% of these means are located between 8.00 and 10.00 years [9.0 ± (2 × 0.50)]. Figure 12.2 presents this sampling distribution of $\overline{X}$. In sum, using the central limit theorem and when $N \geq 100$, one can describe the sampling distribution of $\overline{X}$ for virtually all situations that are encountered in social science research.

12.9 SAMPLE SIZE AND THE SAMPLING DISTRIBUTION OF $\overline{X}$

A fundamental concept in inferential statistics is that as sample size increases, sampling error tends to decrease. Stated differently, as sample size increases, sample statistics become increasingly similar to population parameters.

This concept can be applied to the sampling distribution of $\overline{X}$. Thus the standard deviation of the sampling distribution of $\overline{X}$ (the standard error of the mean, $\sigma_{\overline{X}}$), $\sigma_{\overline{X}} = \sigma/\sqrt{N}$, conveys the amount of "spread" of sample means around the population mean. When $\sigma_{\overline{X}}$ is large, sample means are greatly

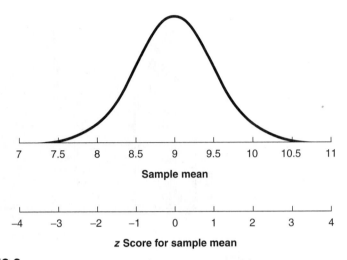

7   7.5   8   8.5   9   9.5   10   10.5   11

Sample mean

−4   −3   −2   −1   0   1   2   3   4

***z* Score for sample mean**

FIGURE **12.2**

SAMPLING DISTRIBUTION OF THE MEAN FOR CHILDREN'S AGES

The top label for the horizontal axis presents the sample means via raw scores and the bottom axis does so via *z* scores.

dispersed. When it is small, sample means tend to cluster close to the population mean. As study of the formula reveals, the standard error of the mean varies as a function of sample size. As N increases, $\sigma_{\bar{X}}$ decreases.

The child abuse example can be used to demonstrate the link between sample size and sampling error. Recall that the mean age in the population of reports was 9.0 years with a standard deviation of 5.0 years. We have already built one sampling distribution of $\bar{X}$ based on sample size of 100 (see Figure 12.2). Let's build two more, one based on a sample size of 400 and one on 1600. The characteristics of the three distributions are presented in Table 12.2. In Table 12.2, as sample size increases, the standard error of the mean decreases.

Figure 12.3 presents visual comparisons of the three sampling distributions. As sample size increases, the sample means cluster closer and closer to the population mean. This demonstrates that as sample size increases, sample means become increasingly similar to the population mean. It also illustrates the general point that as sample size increases, sample statistics provide increasingly accurate estimates of population parameters.

TABLE 12.2   CHANGE IN SAMPLING DISTRIBUTION OF $\bar{X}$ WITH LARGER SAMPLES

Sample Size	Mean	Standard Error of the Mean ($\sigma_{\bar{X}}$)	Shape
100	9.0	$5/\sqrt{100} = 5/10 = 0.50$	Very close to normal
400	9.0	$5/\sqrt{400} = 5/20 = 0.25$	Very close to normal
1600	9.0	$5/\sqrt{1600} = 5/40 = 0.125$	Very close to normal

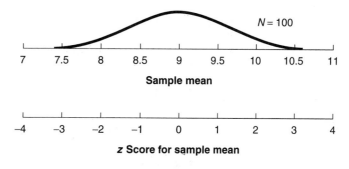

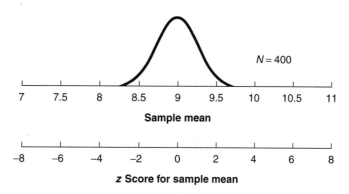

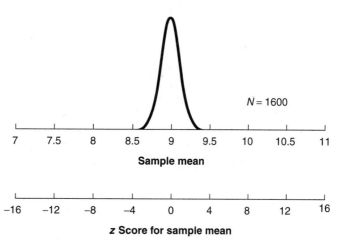

FIGURE **12.3**

SAMPLING DISTRIBUTIONS OF $\overline{X}$ BASED ON THREE DIFFERENT SAMPLE SIZES

In real-world research, researchers do not select an infinite number of random samples. Instead they select one sample and use the central limit theorem, along with methods presented in Chapter 13, to build the sampling distribution. They never know *exactly* how close their study sample mean is to the population mean. (Stated differently, they never know which case their study mean represents in the sampling distribution.) Yet, via the sampling distribution, they can estimate the expected closeness. When sample size is large, one can typically make a very close estimate, because sample means are more tightly clustered. Chapter 13 demonstrates how researchers use sampling distributions to make interval estimates about the likely range within which population parameters are located.

12.10   Chapter Summary

Descriptive statistical procedures describe the study sample. Inferential statistical procedures are used to draw conclusions about populations based on observations from study samples randomly selected from those populations.

Inferential procedures may only be used with random samples. For a sample to be a random sample, (1) cases must be selected via a formal method of chance, (2) each case must have an equal chance of being selected, and (3) the selection of each case must be independent of that of each other case.

When a sample is representative, its characteristics are similar to those of the population. A sample is biased if its characteristics differ *systematically* from population characteristics.

When samples are nonrandom, one typically suspects bias, and thus these samples are regarded as nonrepresentative. In a random sample, only *random* factors (luck of the draw) affect representativeness. With the exception of very small samples, random samples are regarded as representative. Thus they may be used to draw inferences about the populations from which they were selected.

Two cases in a sample meet the independence of observations assumption when they do not share some common factor that makes their scores similar. When this assumption is not met, cases are dependent. Pragmatically, one should assume independence unless there is convincing evidence to the contrary.

Statistics are numerical characteristics of samples. Parameters are numerical characteristics of populations. When a statistic is used to estimate a parameter, it is termed an estimator. Sample statistics are symbolized by Roman letters. Population parameters are symbolized by Greek letters.

Good estimators are efficient and unbiased. An efficient estimator requires a minimum of cases to generate a good estimate. An unbiased estimator tends to neither overestimate nor underestimate a parameter. The sample mean ($\overline{X}$), sample variance (s^2), and sample proportion (p) are efficient and unbiased. The sample standard deviation, s, is efficient and has extremely little bias.

Point estimates state a specific value. Interval estimates state a range of likely values. Sampling error is the difference between the sample statistic and the population parameter. As sample size increases, sampling error tends to decrease.

A sampling distribution is the theoretical distribution of a statistic that results from selecting an infinite number of random samples of the same size from a given population. The cases of a sampling distribution are the statistics from each sample.

The central limit theorem states three key points about the sampling distribution of $\overline{X}$: (1) its mean equals the mean in the population; (2) its standard deviation equals the standard deviation in the population divided by the square root of the sample size; and (3) as sample size increases, its shape approaches normality. The standard deviation of the sampling distribution of $\overline{X}$ is termed the standard error of the mean: $\sigma_{\overline{X}} = \sigma/\sqrt{N}$ (formula 12.3). As sample size increases, the standard error of the mean decreases.

PROBLEMS AND QUESTIONS

Section 12.2

1. Inferential statistical procedures are tools for drawing conclusions about _____ based on _____ that are _____ selected from these _____.

Section 12.3

2. For a sample to be a random sample, it must be selected via a(n) _____ method of _____.

3. For each of the following, indicate whether a formal method of chance is used in selecting the sample. (Respond yes or no.)
   a. People who enter a mall at a given time are asked to respond to a questionnaire.
   b. Students volunteer to participate in a professor's research study.
   c. Names are randomly picked from a hat for participation in a professor's research study.
   d. A computer program randomly selects numbers that determine who will receive a questionnaire.

4. (T or F) A basic characteristic of a random sample (as presented in this text) is that each case has an equal chance of being selected.

5. In your own words, what does the independence of selection criterion state?

6. For each situation, indicate whether the independence of selection criterion is met.
   a. Names of students are randomly selected from a hat.

b. Households are randomly selected in a survey. All adults in each household are interviewed. (Consider a case to be an adult rather than a household.)
   c. Researchers conducting a study on children randomly select families to be in their study. When a family is selected, all children in that family are studied. (Consider a case to be a child rather than a family.)

Section 12.4

7. Define *representativeness* in your own words.

8. (T or F) Representativeness has a precise mathematical definition.

9. (T or F) In a random sample, systematic bias affects representativeness.

10. In a nonrandom sample . . .
    a. There is always systematic bias.
    b. There is often reason to suspect bias.
    c. Assuming adequate sample size, representativeness is ensured.

11. A student surveys student members of the Young Republicans Club regarding their degree of support for public welfare programs. Do you think that the sample results are representative for the population of students at the university? If you think bias is present, state its likely nature, or direction. Respond in your own words.

12. Very small random samples . . .
    a. Are representative
    b. Have both systematic and random error
    c. May not be representative due to the luck of the draw

Section 12.5

13. Explain, in your own words, the concept of independence of observations.

14. When the independence of observations assumption is not met, cases are said to be _____ and one's data have a problem termed _____.

15. Provide an example from the field of mental health in which the independence assumption may have been be violated.

16. From the field of education, provide a clear example of violation of the independence assumption.

Section 12.6

17. The characteristics of samples are termed _____ and those of populations are termed _____.

18. When a sample statistic is used to estimate a population parameter, that statistic is termed a(n) _____ or a(n) _____ _____.

19. Statistics are symbolized by letters from _____ the alphabet and parameters by letters from the _____ alphabet.

Section 12.7

20. Two qualities of a good estimator are _____ and _____.

21. An efficient estimator requires a(n) _____ of cases to generate a good estimate.

22. The quality of unbiasedness conveys that an estimator tends to neither _____ nor _____ the parameter.

23. Indicate the symbols for both the sample statistic and the population parameter for the following:
    a. Mean
    b. Standard deviation
    c. Variance
    d. Proportion

24. Assuming random sampling, indicate whether each of the following sample statistics is a biased or unbiased estimate of its counterpart in the population.
    a. $\overline{X}$
    b. s

c. s^2
d. p

25. The mean of a randomly selected sample is 10 and its standard deviation is 6. Estimate the mean and standard deviation of the population from which the sample was selected.

26. In a given sample, $\overline{X} = 10$ and $s = 6$. What are your best estimates of μ and σ?

27. Sample A, randomly selected from Population A, has a mean of 10 and a standard deviation of 6. Estimate the mean and standard deviation of population B.

28. In a randomly selected sample, 28% of adults indicate that they agree with a given statement. What is your best estimate of the proportion of adults who agree with that statement in the population from which the sample was selected?

29. In a given randomly selected sample, $p = .25$. What is your best estimate of π?

30. When a statistic estimates a specific value, that estimate is termed a(n) _____ _____.

31. A(n) _____ _____ specifies a range within which a population parameter is likely to be located.

Section 12.8

32. The difference between a sample statistic and a population parameter is termed _____ _____.

33. The mean of a sample is 20 and the mean of the population from which it was randomly selected is 18. What is the sampling error?

34. In your own words, define sampling distribution.

35. The cases of a sampling distribution are the _____ from each sample.

36. In your own words, describe the sampling distribution of $\overline{X}$.

37. In your own words, what three points does the central limit theorem state regarding the sampling distribution of $\overline{X}$?

38. The standard deviation of the sampling distribution of $\overline{X}$ is termed the _____ _____ of the _____ and is symbolized by _____.

39. Almost without exception, whenever N is ≥ 100, one may assume that the shape of the sampling distribution of $\overline{X}$ is close to _____.

40. For each example in Table 12PQ.1 indicate the following regarding the sampling distribution of the mean: its mean, its standard deviation ($\sigma_{\overline{X}}$, the standard error of the mean), and its shape.

41. For Example 1 in the prior question, indicate the approximate percentage of means (cases) in the sampling distribution of $\overline{X}$ that are located in the following ranges.
    a. $\mu \pm 1$ standard deviation (24 to 26)
    b. $\mu \pm 2$ standard deviations (23 to 27)
    c. $\mu \pm 3$ standard deviations (22 to 28)

Section 12.9

42. As sample size increases, the size of $\sigma_{\overline{X}}$ _____.

43. (T or F) Other things being equal, as sample size increases, the researcher can make an increasingly accurate estimate of the population mean.

44. (T or F) In real-world research, researchers select an infinite number of samples (or at least an exceedingly large number) so that they can construct the sampling distribution of $\overline{X}$.

 COMPUTER EXERCISES

For general instructions on computer exercises, see the note in Chapter 2.

1. Treating the sample as a random sample from an extremely large population, what is the esti-

mated population mean for FCOH (score on family closeness/cohesion scale)? [In SPSS, *Analyze > Descriptive Statistics > Descriptives,* click over FCOH, *Options,* verify that box next to "Mean" is checked (if not, click it), *Continue, OK.*]

Check your answer: The sample mean, 40.26, provides the best estimate of the population mean. The estimated population mean for FCOH, thus, is 40.26.

2. Treating the sample as a random sample from an extremely large population, what is the estimated proportion of the population that evaluates the impact of adoption on their family as "very positive"? Use IMPACTD (0 = other than "very positive," 1 = "very positive"). [In SPSS, *Analyze > Descriptive Statistics > Frequencies,* click over IMPACTD (you may want to click back any other variables), *OK.*]

Check your answer: The percentage of respondents responding "very positive" as indicated in the Valid Percent column is 46.8%. (Recall that valid percents are calculated with missing cases excluded, that is, using only valid cases.) The percentage 46.8% corresponds to the proportion .468. This is the proportion of the sample who responded "very positive" and thus represents the best estimate of that in the population.

3. What is the estimated population mean for AGECHIY (child's age at time of survey)?

Check your answer: Estimated population mean for AGECHIY is 10.83 years.

TABLE 12PQ **EXAMPLES RELATED TO THE SAMPLING DISTRIBUTION OF $\overline{X}$**

Example	Mean of Populaton (μ)	Standard Deviation of Population (σ)	Shape of Population from Which Samples Were Randomly Selected	Sample Size (N)
1	25	10	Negative skew	100
2	25	10	Negative skew	400
3	25	10	Negative skew	16
4	25	25	Flat	100
5	40	16	Leptokurtic	256

NOTES

1. There are many methods of random sampling. Simple random sampling, systematic sampling, stratified sampling, and cluster (or area) sampling are among the best known. The simplest and most common is simple random sampling. For instance, putting names in a hat and then selecting names at random generates a simple random sample. This text often uses the term *random sampling* when, strictly speaking, *simple random sampling* should have been used. When methods of random sampling other than simple random sampling are used, the inferential procedures presented in this text may not yield accurate results. Fortunately, many random samples are indeed simple random samples, so the presented procedures work well in most situations. One other point: By some definitions, to generate a simple random sample, one should sample with *replacement;* that is, after selecting a case, one should replace that case for possible selection a second time. The practical implications of whether one samples with or without replacement are, typically, negligible (Kish, 1965, pp. 36–45).

2. Strictly speaking, the statement that "each case has an equal chance of being selected" applies to many but not all random sampling methods. It does indeed hold true in simple random sampling. (See endnote 1 for a comment on simple random samples.)

3. Strictly speaking, we should say that such a sample is not a *simple* random sample. It could still meet the definition of random sample via a more complex sampling method. (See endnote 1.)

4. As emphasized, the definition is a rough one. Formally, cases are also dependent if some common factor causes scores to be dissimilar rather than similar. Another term for independence of observations is *statistical independence.* Some statistical techniques are appropriate with dependent observations. In essence, such techniques adjust for dependency and, by so doing, remove it.

5. A third quality is consistency. A *consistent* estimator becomes increasingly precise as sample size increases (Glass and Hopkins, 1996, pp. 242–247).

6. Typically the population is assumed to be infinitely large. As such, one may, theoretically, select an infinite number of samples.

7. For many populations, the shape of the sampling distribution of $\overline{X}$ will be nearly normal for sample sizes much smaller than 100. Basically, the more skewed the shape of the population, the larger the sample size that is required for normality. Except where the population is extremely skewed, a sample size of about 30 is sufficient. For the present discussion, the key point is that normality can be assumed for almost all populations whenever $N \geq 100$.

Confidence Intervals for Means and Proportions

13.1 Chapter Overview

In this chapter we undertake the construction of *confidence intervals*. After examining the logic that underlies their formation, we work with 95% and 99% *confidence intervals* for means. Next, we do the same for proportions. In closing, we discuss three general issues pertaining to the interpretation of confidence intervals.

13.2 Confidence Intervals for Means

13.2.1 Definition

When researchers use inferential statistics to determine the likely range within which a parameter is located, that estimate is an interval estimate. A synonym and more common term for interval estimate is *confidence interval*. Thus a **confidence interval** is the probable range within which a population parameter is located. The most common confidence interval in the social sciences is the 95% confidence interval. The **95% confidence interval** (.95 *confidence interval*) is the interval within which one is 95% confident that the population parameter is located. Learning how to construct this interval is a key goal of this chapter.

13.2.2 Underlying Theory

Suppose that we select an infinite number of samples of fixed size from a given population and calculate and plot the mean of each. The result is a sampling distribution of $\overline{X}$. Presume also that sample size is 100 or larger. According to the central limit theorem, this sampling distribution of $\overline{X}$ has (1) a mean equal to the population mean, that is, to the mean of the population from which samples have been randomly selected; (2) a standard deviation equal to the population standard deviation divided by the square root of the sample size ($\sigma_{\overline{x}} = \sigma/\sqrt{N}$); and (3) given that $N \geq 100$, a nearly normal shape. As you know, the "cases" of this sampling distribution are sample means.

Suppose that we randomly select a sample mean from this sampling distribution of $\overline{X}$ and draw a line that extends two standard deviations ($2 \times \sigma_{\overline{x}}$) in both directions from that mean. Would the range of values spanned by that line include the mean of the sampling distribution? We cannot know for sure.

However, we do know that about 95% of cases in a normal distribution are located within two standard deviations of the mean. From the central limit theorem and because $N \geq 100$, we know that the sampling distribution has a nearly normal shape. Putting these two facts together, we know that about 95% of sample means are located within two standard deviations of the sampling distribution's mean. This being the case, we may conclude that for 95% of sample means, a line extended two standard deviations in both directions from the sample mean includes the sampling distribution mean. It is simply a shift in perspective to the conclusion that we may have 95% confidence (be 95% confident) that a line extended two standard deviations in both directions from any randomly selected sample mean does so. (If lines extended from 95% of sample means include the distribution mean, one may be 95% confident that this is so for any given one.)

According to the central limit theorem, the mean of the sampling distribution of $\overline{X}$ equals the population mean. Thus we may be 95% confident that a line extended two standard deviations in both directions from any given sample mean includes the population mean. Our study sample mean is simply one randomly selected mean in the sampling distribution. Hence, we may be 95% confident that a line extended two standard deviations in both directions from it includes the population mean. Shifting perspective just a bit and stating the same point in a longer way: We may be 95% confident that a line extended two standard deviations in both directions from the mean of our study sample includes the mean of the population from which that sample was selected.

The just-presented discussion is the nuts and bolts of the logic behind the formation of 95% confidence intervals for means. By extending a line two standard deviations in both directions from our study sample mean, we establish a range within which we are 95% confident that the population mean is located. The logic underlying confidence intervals presumes that the study sample has been selected randomly from the population. If it has not been, we may not form confidence intervals. (Note that in this text, the term *population* typically refers to the population from which one's study sample has been randomly selected.)

To demonstrate confidence intervals, we will continue to make use of the child maltreatment data from Chapter 12. As presented there, in the full population of maltreatment reports (the complete file at the state computerized data registry), the mean age of children equals 9.0 years with a standard deviation of 5.0 years. The central limit theorem describes the sampling distribution of $\overline{X}$ for this population. When $N = 100$, the sampling distribution of $\overline{X}$ has a mean of 9.0 years, a standard deviation (standard error of the mean) of 0.50 year ($\sigma_{\overline{x}} = 5/\sqrt{100} = 0.50$), and a shape close to normal. This sampling distribution is presented in Figure 12.2 in the prior chapter.

As just demonstrated, we may be 95% confident that a line extended two standard deviations from a study sample mean includes the population mean. For the child maltreatment example, the standard deviation of the sampling distribution $(\sigma_{\bar{X}})$ is 0.50 year. Thus two standard deviations represents one year ($0.50 \times 2 = 1.00$). This being the case, we may be 95% confident that a line extended one year in both directions from a given mean includes the population mean of 9.0 years.

Figure 13.1 presents lines extending one year (two standard deviations) in both directions from five means, each of which may be thought of as a study sample mean. In Figure 13.1, the lines extended from study sample means A, B, and C include the mean of the sampling distribution and, therefore, the population mean. For instance, the line for A extends from approximately 7.7 years to 9.7 years, a range that includes the population mean of 9.0 years. On the other hand, the lines for means D and E do not include the mean of the sampling distribution and, therefore, do not include the population mean.

The lines presented in Figure 13.1 are, in essence, 95% confidence intervals. For 95% of sample means in the sampling distribution of $\bar{X}$, lines extended two standard deviations in both directions include the population mean. Stated differently, 95% of 95% confidence intervals include this mean. The lines extending from means A, B, and C are examples of such confidence intervals. For 5% of means, lines extended two standard deviations in both directions do not include the population mean. Stated differently, 5% of 95% confidence intervals do not include this mean. The lines extending from means D and E are examples of this 5%. In real-world research one doesn't know for sure whether a 95% confidence interval extended from the study sample mean includes the population mean. One can, however, be 95% confident that it does so, or, viewed differently, 5% "confident" that it does not.

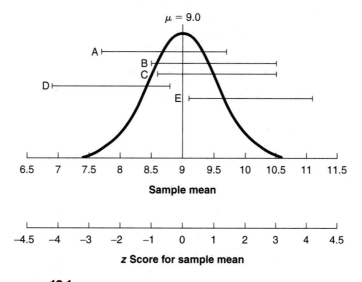

FIGURE **13.1**

FIVE **95% CONFIDENCE INTERVALS**

13.2.3   Real-World Application

In real-world research, researchers don't select an infinite number of random samples to build a sampling distribution. Instead, they draw only a single sample (the study sample) and use the central limit theorem in conjunction with the principles presented next to build the sampling distribution.

Point 2 of the central limit theorem states that the standard deviation of the sampling distribution is equal to the standard deviation in the population divided by the sample size. Yet, from a single random sample one cannot know the standard deviation in the population. The only way to know this precisely would be to "sample" *all* cases. Of course, if one did so, there would be no need for a confidence interval, for if all cases were sampled, the population mean would be known precisely.

There is a straightforward way out of this dilemma. As stated in Chapter 12, the standard deviation in a random sample is an excellent estimator of the standard deviation in the population. For almost all situations in social science research, whenever sample size (N) is 100 or greater, the standard deviation s in a random sample (such as the study sample) is a highly accurate estimator of that in the population, σ. Whenever $N \geq 100$, the degree of accuracy is so great that s and σ are almost without exception very nearly equal, symbolized as $s \approx \sigma$. As stated several times, the standard deviation of the sampling distribution of $\overline{X}$ equals the population standard deviation divided by the square root of the sample size: $\sigma_{\overline{X}} = \sigma/\sqrt{N}$. Whenever $N \geq 100$, a highly accurate estimate of $\sigma_{\overline{X}}$ can be obtained by dividing s by $\sqrt{N}$. The formula is:

$$s_{\overline{X}} = \frac{s}{\sqrt{N}} \tag{13.1}$$

where $s_{\overline{X}}$ is the estimate of the standard error of the mean. Given that $N \geq 100$, $s_{\overline{X}}$ and $\sigma_{\overline{X}}$ are almost without exception very nearly equal: $s_{\overline{X}} \approx \sigma_{\overline{X}}$.

One final point: This discussion has emphasized that about 95% of cases of the normal distribution are within two standard deviations of the mean. More precisely, 95% of cases in a normal distribution are within 1.96 standard deviations of the mean (see Table A.1 in Appendix A). For greater accuracy, 1.96 rather than 2.00 is used in formulas.

13.2.4   Formulas and Computation

The following formulas for confidence intervals of the mean may be used whenever sample size is 100 or greater. As such, they will be designated as *large sample formulas*. (Chapter 17 presents formulas for smaller sample sizes.) The **95% confidence interval of the mean** is the interval within which one is 95% confident that the population mean is located. The first large sample formula is:

$$95\%\,CI \text{ of } \mu = \overline{X} \pm 1.96\left(\frac{s}{\sqrt{N}}\right) \tag{13.2}$$

where 95%CI of μ is the 95% confidence interval of the mean, $\overline{X}$ is the mean of the randomly selected study sample, s is its standard deviation, and N is the sample size. An alternative formula is:

$$95\%CI \text{ of } \mu = \overline{X} \pm 1.96(s_{\overline{X}}) \tag{13.3}$$

where $s_{\overline{X}}$ is the estimate of the standard error of the mean. As $s_{\overline{X}} = s/\sqrt{N}$, formulas 13.2 and 13.3 are equivalent.

Continuing with the child maltreatment example, we can now compute a confidence interval. In the prior chapter, we supposed that you had selected a random sample of 100 cases from the large statewide database of child maltreatment cases. The mean age of victims in your study sample was 8.5 years with a standard deviation of 4.9 years. To calculate the 95% confidence interval for the population mean:

1. Divide s by $\sqrt{N}$:

$$s_{\overline{X}} = \frac{4.9}{\sqrt{100}} = 0.49$$

2. Multiply by 1.96:

$$0.49 \times 1.96 = 0.96$$

3. Add and subtract from $\overline{X}$:

$$95\%CI \text{ of } \mu = 8.5 \pm 0.96 = 7.54 \text{ to } 9.46$$

As stated earlier, although we never know for sure whether a particular 95% confidence interval captures the mean, we do know that 95% of 95% confidence intervals do so, so we have 95% confidence for any given one. Thus we can be 95% confident that the mean age in the population is located in the range from 7.54 years and 9.46 years. Sometimes researchers use the term *captures:* We are 95% confident that the interval from 7.54 to 9.46 captures (includes) the population mean.

As sample size increases, the characteristics of samples increasingly resemble those of populations. As you would suspect, as sample size increases, the width of the 95% confidence interval decreases. For instance, let's compute a 95% confidence interval keeping all things the same except that we now assume a sample size of 400. In other words, $\overline{X} = 8.5, s = 4.9, N = 400$. To compute the confidence interval:

1. Divide s by $\sqrt{N}$:

$$s_{\overline{X}} = \frac{4.9}{\sqrt{400}} = \frac{4.9}{20} = 0.245$$

2. Multiply by 1.96:

$$0.245 \times 1.96 = 0.48$$

3. Add and subtract from $\overline{X}$:

$$95\%CI \text{ of } \mu = 8.50 \pm 0.48 = 8.02 \text{ to } 8.98$$

The increased sample size results in a narrower 95% confidence interval, that is, in a more precise range within which one has 95% confidence that the population mean is located.

As stated earlier, the mean age for the full population of maltreatment reports was 9.0 years. If we continue to presume this to be the case, then this particular confidence interval does not capture the population mean. (It just misses.) Hence this particular 95%CI is one of the 5% of such intervals that do not capture the mean. (Of course, in real-world research one has no way to know whether a particular interval does or does not capture the mean.)

Sometimes 95% confidence is not enough. For instance, suppose that a state legislator comes across your report on child maltreatment and phones you about it. We will presume that your report states that the 95% confidence interval for the mean age extends from 7.54 years to 9.46 years. (This was the confidence interval when sample size equaled 100.) You explain to the legislator that this indicates that one can be 95% confident that the mean age for the full population of children is in the range from 7.54 years to 9.46 years. She tells you that 95% confidence is not sufficient and that, given the importance of the legislative changes in child welfare that she will be proposing, 100% confidence is required. You explain to her that, short of studying the full population, there is no way of being *100%* confident about the mean age. It was mentioned earlier that your sample was drawn from a large computerized database. You suggest to her that she contact the chief data analyst at the child welfare agency so that she may gain access to this database. She responds: "There is no time. The hearing is in two hours." Perhaps, she suggests, if we could be 99% confident rather than just 95% confident, that would satisfy the legislators who will be voting. You say that you can calculate such an interval and that you will call her back in five minutes.

A **99% confidence interval** is the interval within which one is 99% confident that the population parameter is located. It is constructed via the same logic as is a 95% interval. In a normal distribution, 99% of cases are located within 2.58 standard deviations of the population mean (see Table A.1 in Appendix A). Hence (given that $N \geq 100$), if we extend a line 2.58 standard deviations in both directions from the mean of a randomly selected sample, we can be 99% confident that this line includes the population mean. In the long run, 99% of 99% confidence intervals capture the mean.

The **99% confidence interval of the mean** is the interval within which one is 99% confident that the population mean is located. The "large sample formula" assumes a sample size of least 100:

$$99\%CI \text{ of } \mu = \overline{X} \pm 2.58\left(\frac{s}{\sqrt{N}}\right) \tag{13.4}$$

An alternative formula is:

$$99\%CI \text{ of } \mu = \overline{X} \pm 2.58(s_{\overline{X}}) \tag{13.5}$$

Assume that the child maltreatment data remain the same: $\overline{X} = 8.5$, $s = 4.9$, $N = 100$. The 99% confidence interval is:

$$8.5 \pm 2.58\left(\frac{4.9}{\sqrt{100}}\right) = 8.5 \pm 2.58\left(\frac{4.9}{10}\right) = 8.5 \pm 1.26 = 7.24 \text{ to } 9.76$$

Having finished your calculation, you phone the legislator back and inform her that you are 99% confident that the mean age of children is in the interval that ranges from 7.24 years to 9.76 years. Unfortunately, the legislator is again frustrated and responds: "I wanted to be more confident about the children's mean age, but you have given me a wider range than before. How can this be?" Given the same sample size, and other things being equal, 99% confidence intervals are always *wider* than are 95% confidence intervals. This should make intuitive sense: To be more confident that the interval contains the population parameter, one must specify a wider range.

Although our state legislator had hoped otherwise, 99% confidence intervals aren't "better" than 95% confidence intervals. And, by the same token, 95% intervals aren't "better" than 99% intervals. In deciding which interval to use, researchers have a trade-off. They may either specify a more precise (narrower) interval (the 95%*CI*) but have less confidence that it captures the mean (95% versus 99%), or they may specify a less precise (wider) interval (the 99%*CI*) but have greater confidence (99% versus 95%) that it does so.

To truly improve one's estimate, one can't simply use a different confidence interval. Instead, one must select a larger sample, which reduces the likely sampling error. Sticking with the current example ($\overline{X} = 8.5$, $s = 4.9$), increasing the sample size to 400 results in the following 99% confidence interval:

$$8.5 \pm 2.58\left(\frac{4.9}{\sqrt{400}}\right) = 8.5 \pm 2.58\left(\frac{4.9}{20}\right) = 8.5 \pm 0.63 = 7.87 \text{ to } 9.13$$

Notice that the increase in sample size reduces the width of the confidence interval. Hence, when sample size was 100, the 99%*CI* for the same mean and standard deviation extended from 7.24 years to 9.76 years. Both of the just-mentioned intervals do include the population mean.

In sum, confidence intervals for population means can be calculated in straightforward fashion. The confidence interval for the mean is a common procedure, one that you will use often and that is available on many statistical software packages. We now move on to confidence intervals for proportions.

13.3 CONFIDENCE INTERVALS FOR PROPORTIONS

The construction of confidence intervals for proportions (percentages) draws on the same statistical theory that underlies the construction of those for means. We will continue to make use of the random sample of 100 maltreatment reports. Our interest shifts now to type of maltreatment, abuse or neglect. In your sample, 40% of reports were for abuse and 60% were for neglect. In real-world research, one doesn't know the characteristics of the population. For teaching purposes, let's presume that 43% (.43) of maltreatment reports in the full database (that is, in the full population) pertain to abuse and 57% (.57) pertain to neglect. (A commonsense understanding of sampling error will tell you that the statistics in your sample, 40% and 60%, probably differ somewhat from their corresponding population parameters.)

Confidence intervals for proportions are formed most often for dichotomous variables. Given that it has only two values, the shape of the distribution of a dichotomous variable can never assume the smooth continuous shape of a normal curve. Figure 13.2 presents the distribution of abuse and neglect reports in the population (the full maltreatment database). This distribution clearly has a non-normal shape. If we select an infinite number of random samples of the same size from this distribution and, for each, calculate and plot the proportion of abuse cases, we would have a **sampling distribution of the proportion** (a **sampling distribution of p**). Via the central limit theorem we know the following about the sampling distribution of p:

1. Its mean equals the proportion in the population. This proportion is symbolized by π (pi).
2. Its standard deviation equals $\sqrt{\pi(1 - \pi)/N}$.
3. As sample size increases, its shape approaches normality.

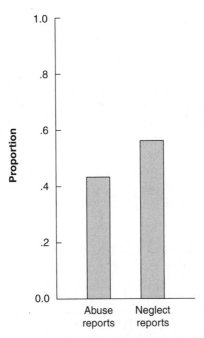

FIGURE **13.2**

DISTRIBUTION IN THE POPULATION:
PROPORTION OF ABUSE AND NEGLECT REPORTS

The standard deviation of the sampling distribution of p is termed the **standard error of the proportion** and is symbolized by σ_p. Step 2 in the preceding list provides a formula:

$$\sigma_p = \sqrt{\frac{\pi(1 - \pi)}{N}} \tag{13.6}$$

where N is the size of the randomly selected sample and π is the population proportion.

Recall that the sampling distribution of $\overline{X}$ has a nearly normal shape whenever sample size is 100 or greater. The sampling distribution of p has a nearly normal shape whenever the guidelines in Table 13.1 are met. When the population proportion (π) is close to .50, the sampling distribution of p is nearly normal even for very small samples. In contrast, when it is close to 0.00 or close to 1.00, very large samples are needed.[1]

To see how the guidelines work, let's apply them to the current example. Presume that our interest is in the proportion of abuse reports rather than neglect reports. The proportion of abuse reports in the population is .43, that is, $\pi = .43$. When $\pi = .43$, the needed sample size to ensure an approximately normal sampling distribution is 13, according to Table 13.1. As our study sample size ($N = 100$) is greater than 13, the shape of the sampling distribution of the proportion will indeed be approximately normal.[2]

On the basis of the central limit theorem and given that the sample size guideline is met, we may draw the following conclusions regarding the sampling distribution of p for abuse reports:

1. Its mean equals the proportion in the population (π), which is .43.

2. Its standard deviation, the standard error of the proportion, equals:

$$\sigma_p = \sqrt{\frac{(.43)\,(.57)}{100}} = \sqrt{\frac{.245}{100}} = \sqrt{.00245} = .0495$$

3. Its shape is close to normal.

Proportion (π or p)[a]	Needed Sample Size
.50	10
.40 to .49 and .51 to .60	13
.30 to .39 and .61 to .70	20
.20 to .29 and .71 to .80	60
.10 to .19 and .81 to .90	180
.05 to .09 and .95 to .99	440
.02 to .04 and .96 to .98	1200
.01 or .99	2400
<.01	25 ÷ proportion
>.99	25 ÷ (1 − proportion)

TABLE 13.1 SAMPLE SIZE FOR NEARLY NORMAL SAMPLING DISTRIBUTION OF p

Note: Adapted from Samuels and Lu, 1992, pp. 228–231.
[a]Some applications of this table make use of π. Other applications make use of p.

Figure 13.3 presents this sampling distribution of p. Given that its shape is nearly normal, about 95% of sample proportions are within 1.96 standard deviations of the population proportion (multiply 1.96 by the standard deviation: $1.96 \times .0495 = .097$). Hence, if we were to extend a line of length .097 in both directions from each sample proportion, 95% of these lines would capture the population proportion. Such being the case, we can be 95% confident that such a line extended from any single randomly selected proportion does so. Using the same logic, we may be 95% confident that such a line extended from a study sample proportion includes the proportion of the population from which the study sample was randomly sampled.

In constructing the sampling distribution depicted in Figure 13.3, the population proportion, π, was used to compute the standard error of the proportion, σ_p. In real-world research, one does not know π. Recall from Chapter 12 (Section 12.7) that the proportion in the sample, p, is the preferred estimate of that in the population, π. Hence p may be substituted into formula 13.6 to yield an estimate of the standard error of the proportion, σ_p This formula is:

$$s_p = \sqrt{\frac{p(1 - p)}{N}} \tag{13.7}$$

where s_p is the estimate of the standard error of the proportion, p is the sample proportion, and N is the sample size.

This estimate is sufficiently accurate for forming confidence intervals whenever the sample size guidelines in Table 13.1 are met. (When these are met, $\sigma_p \approx s_p$.) Hence, when these guidelines are met, σ_p may be used in formulas for confidence

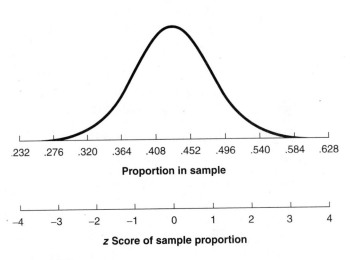

FIGURE **13.3**

SAMPLING DISTRIBUTION OF THE PROPORTION OF ABUSE REPORTS

intervals. When they are not, the formulas in this chapter should not be used.[3] The **95% confidence interval of the proportion** is the interval within which one is 95% confident that the population proportion is located. One formula is:

$$95\%CI \text{ of } \pi = p \pm 1.96\sqrt{\frac{p(1-p)}{N}} \tag{13.8}$$

where $95\%CI$ of π is the 95% confidence interval of the proportion, p is the study sample proportion, and N is the sample size. An alternative formula is:

$$95\%CI \text{ of } \pi = p \pm 1.96(s_p) \tag{13.9}$$

where s_p is the estimate of the standard error of the proportion.

We may now compute a confidence interval for the child abuse example. A first step is to confirm that sample size is adequate. In our earlier use of Table 13.1, we used π as a reference for the guidelines. In actual research situations, π is unknown, so one uses p. In the study sample, 40% of cases were abuse cases, so $p = .40$. When $p = .40$, the needed sample size is 13. The study sample size is 100 ($N = 100$). As 100 is greater than 13, the sample size guideline is met and the confidence interval may be computed.

1. Calculate s_p, the estimate of the standard error of the proportion:

$$s_p = \sqrt{\frac{.40(1-.40)}{100}} = \sqrt{\frac{.4(.6)}{100}} = \sqrt{\frac{.24}{100}} = \sqrt{.0024} = .049$$

2. Multiply by 1.96:

   $1.96 \times .049 = .096$

3. Add and subtract from p (the sample proportion):

   $95\%CI$ of $\pi = .40 \pm .096 = .304$ to $.496$

The $95\%CI$ of π spans the interval from .304 to .496. This being so, one can be 95% confident that the population proportion of abuse reports is somewhere in the range from .304 to .496. Expressed in percentages, one can be 95% confident that somewhere between 30.4% and 49.6% of reports are abuse reports.[4]

Perhaps you are also interested in constructing a 99% confidence interval for the proportion of abuse reports. A **99% confidence interval of the proportion** is the interval within which one is 99% confident that the population proportion is located. The formulas are:

$$99\%CI \text{ of } \pi = p \pm 2.58\sqrt{\frac{p(1-p)}{N}} \tag{13.10}$$

$$99\%CI \text{ of } \pi = p \pm 2.58(s_p) \tag{13.11}$$

where $99\%CI$ of π is the 99% confidence interval of the proportion.

The estimate of the standard error of the proportion, s_p, was calculated earlier. To find the $99\%CI$, insert s_p into formula 13.11.

$$99\%\,CI \text{ of } \pi = .40 \pm 2.58(.049) = .40 \pm .126 = .274 \text{ to } .526$$

As always (given identical data), the 99% interval (.274 to .526) is wider than the 95% interval (.304 to .496).

13.4   THREE MORE POINTS

In closing, three more points should be made. First, the chapter's formulas formally assume that samples have been randomly selected from populations that are infinite in size. In the real world, there are no such populations. For instance, in 1999 the population of the United States was about 270 million. From a pragmatic perspective the formulas work well whenever the sample represents 10% or less of the population. When the sample represents more than 10% of the population, they result in intervals that are too wide and thus are not recommended.[5]

Second, although counterintuitive, it is almost always the case that the width of a confidence interval (for both means and proportions) is affected hardly at all by the size of the population from which it is randomly selected. For instance, a random sample of 100 persons from a small town of 1000 will result in a confidence interval of approximately the same width as will a random sample of similar size drawn from the *entire* United States population. The size of the *sample*—not that of the population from which the sample is selected—is the primary determinant of the width of the confidence interval.

This does not say that it is just as easy to draw a random sample of persons from a very large population (the United States) as from a small one (the town of 1000). Also, "identical" confidence intervals from different-sized populations represent different numbers of people. For instance, a confidence interval extending from 50% to 60% (a range of 10%) in the United States represents approximately 27 million people (10% of 270 million). In the small town of 1000, such a confidence interval represents 100 people (10% of 1000).

The third point concerns nonresponse. So far, this chapter has assumed that all randomly selected cases do indeed become part of the study sample. In survey research, however, typically a given percentage does not respond. For instance, a response rate of 70% is excellent for a mailed questionnaire (Rubin and Babbie, 1997, p. 352). One problem with nonresponse is that sample size decreases, so confidence intervals get wider. Yet the greater problem concerns representativeness and possible bias. Typically, people choose not to respond for particular reasons. For instance, those who were dissatisfied with agency services may be less likely to respond to a services satisfaction questionnaire than those who were satisfied. The major issue raised by nonresponse is that one has no way to know whether the opinions of nonresponders are similar to or different from those of responders. (Obviously, one cannot know the opinion of someone who does not respond.)

Suppose that one selects a large random sample but gets substantial nonresponse. One can be confident that the opinions of the *responding* sample will be representative of those in the population who *would also have returned the questionnaire* had it been sent to them. Obviously, this is not the population of interest. When there is substantial nonresponse, opinions in the responding sample may well be biased relative to those in the full population.

There is no easy way to deal with nonresponse. In general, one should be alert to possible bias whenever nonresponse is substantial (say, about 15% or higher).

13.5 CHAPTER SUMMARY

A synonym for interval estimate is confidence interval, the likely range within which a population parameter is located. The 95% confidence interval is the interval within which one is 95% confident that the population parameter is located.

From logic based on the central limit theorem, one may have 95% confidence that a line extended about two standard deviations from a study sample mean captures the mean of the population from which that sample was randomly selected. Such a line conveys a 95% confidence interval.

One never knows for sure whether a particular 95% confidence interval captures the mean. Given that 95% of 95% confidence intervals do so, one may have 95% confidence for any given one.

Whenever sample size is 100 or greater, the standard error of the mean can be estimated accurately by $s_{\overline{X}} = s/\sqrt{N}$ (formula 13.1). One formula (13.3) for the 95% confidence interval for the mean is $95\%CI$ of $\mu = \overline{X} \pm 1.96(s_{\overline{X}})$.

A 99% confidence interval is the interval within which one is 99% confident that the population parameter is located. Ninety-nine percent of 99% confidence intervals include the population parameter.

Given equal sample sizes, and other things being equal, 99% confidence intervals are wider than 95% confidence intervals. One has greater confidence (99%) that a 99%CI includes the mean than that a 95%CI does so (95%). As sample size increases (other things being equal), the width of a confidence interval decreases.

Via the central limit theorem, one knows the following about the sampling distribution of the proportion: (1) its mean equals π, (2) its standard deviation equals $\sqrt{\pi(1 - \pi)/N}$, and (3) as N increases, its shape approaches normality. The standard error of the proportion, σ_p, is estimated by formula 13.7: $s_p = \sqrt{p(1 - p)/N}$.

The formulas for confidence intervals for proportions yield sufficiently accurate results whenever the sample size guidelines in Table 13.1 are met. One formula for the 95%CI of π is $95\%CI$ of $\pi = p \pm 1.96(s_p)$ (formula 13.9).

The chapter makes three closing points. First, its formulas work well only when the sample represents about 10% or less of the population. Second, the width of the confidence interval is typically affected hardly at all by the size of the population from which the sample is selected. Third, nonresponse can bias study results.

PROBLEMS AND QUESTIONS

Section 13.2

1. What term is essentially a synonym for interval estimate?
2. Define confidence interval in your own words.
3. The _____ _____ _____ is the interval within which the researcher is 95% _____ that the population parameter is located.

Questions 4–9 pertain to the sampling distribution of $\overline{X}$.

4. (T or F) Given sample size of 100 or more, a line extended two standard deviations (two standard errors, that is, $\sigma_{\overline{X}} \times 2$) in both directions from a randomly selected sample mean always includes the population mean (μ).
5. (T or F) Given sample size of 100 or more, about 95% of sample means are located within two standard deviations $\sigma_{\overline{X}} \times 2$) of the population mean (μ).
6. (T or F) Given sample size of 100 or more, a line extended two standard deviations in both directions ($\sigma_{\overline{X}} \times 2$) from the study sample mean always includes the mean of the population from which that sample was randomly selected.
7. (T or F) Given sample size of 100 or more, a line extended two standard deviations($\sigma_{\overline{X}} \times 2$) in both directions from the study sample mean always includes the mean of the population from which that sample was randomly selected.
8. (T or F) Given sample size of 100 or more, one can be 95% confident that a line extended two standard deviations ($\sigma_{\overline{X}} \times 2$) in both directions from the study sample mean includes the mean of the population from which that sample was randomly selected.
9. The line described in the prior question comes very close to describing the _____ _____ _____ of the _____.
10. Given sample size of 100 or more, _____ provides a highly accurate estimate of σ.
11. What is the formula for $s_{\overline{X}}$, the estimate of $\sigma_{\overline{X}}$?

12. In your own words, describe how to calculate a 95% confidence interval.
13. In a normal distribution, 95% of cases are located within (exactly) _____ standard deviations of the mean.
14. Using formula 13.2 or 13.3, calculate 95% confidence intervals of μ for the examples in Table 13PQ.1.

TABLE 13PQ.1	EXAMPLES FOR COMPUTING CONFIDENCE INTERVALS OF μ		
Example	$\overline{X}$	N	s
1	50	100	10
2	50	100	20
3	50	400	20
4	50	1600	20
5	50	9	6

15. As sample size increases (other things being equal), the width of the 95% confidence interval of μ _____.
16. In the long run, what percentage of 95% confidence intervals do indeed include the unknown population parameter?
17. A(n) _____ _____ _____ is the interval within which one can be 99% _____ that the unknown population parameter is located.
18. Calculate 99% confidence intervals for Examples 2, 3, and 4 in Table 13PQ.1.
19. Given that all other influencing factors are equal, a 95% confidence interval is _____ than a 99% confidence interval.
20. Given that all other influencing factors are equal, a 99% confidence interval is _____ than a 95% confidence interval.
21. In the long run, what percentage of 99% confidence intervals do indeed include the unknown population parameter?

Section 13.3

22. What three points does the central limit theorem state about the sampling distribution of p?
23. Explain in your own words how to calculate the standard error of the proportion, σ_p (see formula 13.6).

24. For the following population proportions (π's), indicate the needed sample size so that the sampling distribution of the proportion will have an approximately normal shape. Use Table 13.1 for reference.
    a. .83
    b. .04
    c. .43
    d. .25
    e. .91

25. Calculate the standard error of the proportion, σ_p, in the following situations.
    a. $N = 50, \pi = .40$
    b. $N = 50, \pi = .60$
    c. $N = 100, \pi = .60$

26. In real-world confidence interval problems, the population proportion, π, is unknown and is estimated by _____ (symbol), the _____ proportion.

27. The symbol for the estimate of σ_p is _____.

28. Estimate the standard error of the proportion in the following situations. (Note: The situations are the same as in problem 25 except that the sample proportion rather than the population proportion is provided.)
    a. $N = 50, p = .40$
    b. $N = 50, p = .60$
    c. $N = 100, p = .60$

29. For the three situations in problem 28, indicate whether sample size is sufficient for the formation of confidence intervals.

30. Calculate the 95% confidence intervals of π for the situations in problem 28.

31. Calculate the 99%CI of π for the situations in problem 28.

Section 13.4

32. (T or F) The formulas presented in this chapter work very well even when the sample represents up to about 50% of the population.

33. (T or F) In most situations, the width of the confidence interval for both means and proportions is affected hardly at all by the size of the population from which the sample is selected.

34. (T or F) The greatest problem caused by nonresponse ordinarily does not relate to issues of bias or representativeness but rather to the increased width of the confidence interval.

 COMPUTER EXERCISES

For general instructions on computer exercises, see the note in Chapter 2.

1. Treating the sample as a random sample from an extremely large population, what are the mean, standard deviation, estimated standard error of the mean, and 95% confidence interval of the mean for BEHAVTOT (behavior problem checklist score)? [In SPSS, *Analyze > Descriptive Statistics > Descriptives*, click over BEHAVTOT, *Options*. Make sure the boxes next to "Mean," "Std. deviation," and "S.E. mean" are checked. (Click any that are not checked.) If any unwanted statistics are checked, click these to unmark them. *Continue, OK.*]

   Check your answers: Regarding BEHAVTOT: $\overline{X} = 36.65$, $s = 26.12$, $s_{\overline{X}} = 0.95$, and thus 95%CI of $\mu = 36.65 \pm 1.96(0.95) = 34.79$ to 38.51. Note that one could use the t distribution and the one-sample t test procedure (to be presented in Chapter 17) to carry out this problem. [The SPSS menu commands for this are *Analyze > Compare Means > One-Sample T Test.*]

2. Treating the sample as a random sample from a much larger population and making use of the variable GENDER (coded as 0 = boy, 1 = girl), what are (1) the estimated standard error of the proportion of girls in the population, and (2) the 95% confidence interval of the proportion of girls? [In SPSS, *Analyze > Descriptive Statistics > Frequencies* (if necessary, click back any unwanted variables), click over GENDER, *Statistics*, click/mark box next to "S.E. mean" (unmark any unwanted statistics), *Continue, OK.*]

Check your answers: In the frequency distribution table for GENDER, the "Valid Percent" column indicates that the percentage of girls is 47.9; hence this proportion is .479. The estimated standard error of the proportion is .0177. This proportion, which may be in scientific notation form, is listed under "Std. Error Mean" in the Statistics table. When a variable is coded with 0s and 1s as is GENDER, the standard error of the proportion and the standard error of the mean are one and the same. The 95% confidence interval for the proportion is:

$$.479 \pm 1.96(.0177) = .444 \text{ to } .514$$

3. Regarding family income, what are the mean, the standard deviation, the estimated standard error of the mean, and the 95% confidence interval of the mean? [In SPSS, the appropriate variable is INCOMEK, family income coded in thousands of dollars ($1000s).]

Check your answers: As income is coded in $1000s, you need to multiply the SPSS results by 1000 to get correct answers. For family income: mean = $35,650, standard deviation = $22,250, and estimated standard error of the mean = $870. The 95%CI is:

$$\$35,650 \pm 1.96 (\$870) = \$33,995 \text{ to } \$37,355$$

NOTES

1. Samuels and Lu (1992, pp. 228–231) developed three rules that differ in terms of how close an approximation to a normal distribution is desired. Table 13.1 presents the most relaxed rule, the one with the least strict approximation standards. For the next, "middle" standard, sample sizes required for the 10 categories in Table 13.1 (listed from top to bottom) are:

10, 13, 47, 125, 400, 960, 2650, 5400,
56 ÷ proportion, 56 ÷ (1 − proportion)

For their strictest standard, these are (from top to bottom):

26, 40, 170, 500, 1570, 3760, 10,400, 21,400,
221 ÷ proportion, 221 ÷ (1 − proportion)

Confidence intervals based on the relaxed standards (those in Table 13.1) may be thought of as being "very nearly" accurate. Where greater precision is required, one should use one of the two just-presented standards. For still greater precision, see note 3.

2. For a dichotomous variable, the necessary sample size according to Table 13.1 is always the same for each of the two categories. For instance, had we chosen the neglect category ($\pi = .57$), the needed sample size would also have been 13.

3. See Glass and Hopkins (1996, pp. 325–330) for the Ghosh method, which provides more precise confidence intervals than those presented here, particularly when sample size is small. When sample size is very small, confidence intervals formed via the binomial distribution (Toothaker and Miller, 1996, pp. 257–260) will also be more accurate than those presented here.

4. To calculate a 95% confidence interval for the proportion of neglect cases, one could insert this proportion (.60) into formula 13.8 or 13.9 and carry out the computations. Alternatively, one could subtract each of the limits for the interval for abuse reports from 1.00: 1.00 − .304 = .696; 1.00 − .496 = .504. Hence the 95% interval for neglect reports is from .504 to .696.

5. This note demonstrates how to use a correction factor to adjust this chapter's formulas when the sample represents more than 10% of the population. The margin of error is the amount that is added and subtracted from the sample result. For instance, in formula 13.9, the margin of error equals $1.96(s_p)$. The proportion of a population that is included in a random sample is termed the sampling ratio. The correction factor is derived by (1) subtracting the sampling ratio from 1.00 and (2) taking the square root. For instance, if the sampling fraction is .20, the correction factor calculations are (1) 1.00 − .20 = .80 and (2) $\sqrt{.80} = .894$. The correction factor is used to adjust the margin of error. To do so, multiply the margin of error by the factor. For instance, the 95% confidence interval for abuse reports calculated earlier spanned the interval from .304 to .496. In this situation, the margin of error was .096. Assuming a sampling ratio of .20 and, therefore, a correction factor of .894, the adjusted margin of error is .894 × .096 = .086. The confidence interval therefore becomes .40 ± .086 = .314 to .486.

THE LOGIC OF STATISTICAL SIGNIFICANCE TESTS

14.1 CHAPTER OVERVIEW

Before you begin to use *statistical significance tests*, this chapter provides you with a solid introduction to the concepts behind them, including the basics of *probability*. We discuss *hypothesis pairs*, the *null hypothesis* and *research hypothesis*, and *directional* versus *nondirectional* hypotheses. In-depth discussion focuses on the logic of statistical significance tests including the role of chance, when to *accept* or *reject* the null, and *statistical significance levels*.

14.2 INTRODUCTION TO SIGNIFICANCE TESTING

Chapter 1 (Section 1.13) identified two major functions of inferential statistical procedures (Toothaker, 1986, p. 18). The first, estimation, is carried out via point estimates and interval estimates (confidence intervals). The second is decision making, the primary tool for which is the statistical significance test. As presented in Chapter 1, Section 1.13, a **statistical significance test (hypothesis test)** is an inferential statistical procedure conducted to determine how likely it is that a study result is due to chance, or luck.

14.3 PROBABILITY

14.3.1 *Definition and Formula*

Prior to discussion of significance testing, an introduction to probability is in order. The **probability** that an event with a given characteristic will occur equals the number of events with that characteristic divided by the total number of events:

$$\text{Probability of event with given characteristic} = \frac{\text{Number of events with characteristic}}{\text{Total number of events}} \quad (14.1)$$

For instance, suppose that ten therapists attend a staff meeting regarding a given case. Suppose further that four of these favor intervention via group therapy and that six favor intervention via individual therapy. You are the supervisor. You put the names of the ten therapists in a hat, shake the hat, and randomly pick one name.

What is the probability that the therapist whose name is picked favors a group therapy intervention? The number of events (therapists) with the characteristic of interest (favor group intervention) is four. The total number of events is ten. The probability of randomly selecting a therapist who favors the group intervention is $4/10 = .4$.

To give another example: What is the probability of flipping an unbiased coin and having it turn up heads? The number of events with the characteristic is one (one side of the coin is heads). The number of possible events is two (the coin has two sides). Hence the probability that the coin will turn up heads is $1/2 = .5$.

Note that probabilities are expressed as proportions. For instance, in our examples, the probabilities were, respectively, .4 and .5. Probabilities, in essence, are proportions. Thus a second formula for probability is:

$$\text{Probability of event with given characteristic} = \text{Proportion of events with characteristic} \tag{14.2}$$

For instance, in the first example the proportion of therapists who favored group intervention was .4: $4/10 = .4$. This was also the probability of selecting such a therapist.

Probability may range from 0.00 to 1.00. It is 0.00 when there is no chance of the event and 1.00 when there is absolute certainty. For instance, if no therapists favored group intervention, the probability of randomly selecting such a therapist would be $0/10 = 0.00$. If all ten favored group intervention, this probability would be $10/10 = 1.00$. Probability is symbolized by p. Thus, if the probability of an event is .30, $p = .30$. Note that the symbol for probability is the same as that for proportion.

14.3.2   *Probability and the Normal Distribution*

As the next series of chapters demonstrates, many statistical significance tests are based on the normal distribution, so let's work through a few probability problems based on this distribution.

What is the probability of randomly selecting from a normal distribution a case that is located within one standard deviation of the mean? As has by now been burned into your brain, 68% of cases in a normal distribution are within one standard deviation of the mean. Therefore, the proportion of such cases is .68. Hence the probability of randomly selecting a case located within one standard deviation of the mean is .68, that is, $p = .68$.

A second problem: What is the probability of randomly selecting from a normal distribution a case located two or more standard deviations below the mean, that is, with a z score of -2.00 or lower? As Table A.1 (in Appendix A) indicates, the proportion of cases in this area of the normal curve is .0228. Hence $p = .0228$.

14.4   NULL AND RESEARCH HYPOTHESES

In hypothesis (significance) testing, the researcher decides which of two hypotheses, the null hypothesis or the research hypothesis, best describes a population condition. To keep things simple, this chapter expresses these hypotheses via words rather than mathematical symbols. Just as for confidence intervals, we assume that samples have been randomly selected from wider populations. When such is not the case, statistical significance tests are not valid procedures (an exception is presented in Chapter 16, Section 16.8). As you read, keep in mind the concept of sampling error. Due to sampling error (chance, luck of the draw, random variation, etc.), study sample results typically differ at least somewhat from population conditions.

The **null hypothesis** (the **null**) states that a given condition is true in the population. For instance, a null could state, "In the population from which the study sample was randomly selected, the mean score on the XYZ self-esteem test is 100 points." The **research hypothesis (alternative hypothesis)** states a logically opposite condition. In our example, for instance, the research hypothesis would state, "In the population from which the study sample was randomly selected, the mean score on the XYZ self-esteem test is not 100 points." Null and research hypotheses go together as a **hypothesis pair.** For instance, the just-stated hypotheses may be presented together as a hypothesis pair:

> *Null hypothesis:* In the population from which the study sample was randomly selected, the mean score on the XYZ self-esteem test is 100 points.
> *Research hypothesis:* In the population from which the study sample was randomly selected, the mean score on the XYZ self-esteem test is not 100 points.

The research hypothesis *always* negates the null. If one hypothesis is true, the other must be false. Thus, if the null is true, the research hypothesis is false. If the research hypothesis is true, the null is false.

A hypothesis pair pertains to the *population* from which the study sample was randomly selected, but researchers carry out statistical procedures using *sample* data. As such, they never know for certain which hypothesis statement is true and which is false. The only way to know this definitively would be to "sample" the entire population. Yet, if they did so, there would be no need for a significance test (for they would have complete knowledge of the population and thus know definitively which hypothesis was correct). Given that the hypothesis pair always pertains to the population that was randomly sampled, one may state the pair without specific mention of this. For instance, our hypothesis pair may be shortened to:

> *Null hypothesis:* The mean score on the XYZ self-esteem test is 100 points.
> *Research hypothesis:* The mean score on the XYZ self-esteem test is not 100 points.

When the population from which one has randomly sampled is not mentioned explicitly, it is understood that the hypothesis pair pertains to it.

14.5   A COMMON PATTERN FOR HYPOTHESIS PAIRS

In actual human services research, null hypotheses typically state that two variables are unassociated. The form of the statement varies according to the level of measurement of the involved variables:

When both variables are at the nominal level of measurement, null hypotheses typically state that percentages (proportions) are equal.

When one variable is at the nominal level and the other is at the interval/ratio level or almost at this level, null hypotheses typically state that means are equal.

When both variables are at the interval/ratio level or almost at this level, null hypotheses typically state that their correlation (as measured by Pearson's r) equals 0.00.

Although these three statements differ, each conveys the same underlying idea: In the population from which one has randomly sampled, two variables are unassociated.

The research hypothesis is, in essence, a statement that the null is false. As the null typically states that variables are not associated, the research hypothesis typically states that they are:

When both variables are at the nominal level, research hypotheses typically state that percentages (proportions) are not equal.

When one variable is nominal and the other is at the interval/ratio level or almost at this level, research hypotheses typically state that means are not equal.

When both variables are at the interval/ratio level or almost at this level, research hypotheses typically state that their correlation (as measured by Pearson's r) does not equal 0.00.

The following null and research hypothesis pair is typical in a situation with one variable at the nominal level (gender) and the other at the interval/ratio level or almost so (self-esteem as measured on a multi-item scale is almost at the interval/ratio level):

Null: Mean self-esteem scores of women and men are equal.
Research: Mean self-esteem scores of women and men are not equal.

The next hypothesis pair is typical of those involving two nominal-level variables:

Null: The percentage of clients who become pregnant in prevention Program A is equal to the percentage of clients who become pregnant in Program B.
Research: The percentage of clients who become pregnant in prevention Program A is not equal to the percentage of clients who become pregnant in Program B.

A typical pair when both variables are at the interval/ratio level:

Null: The correlation (Pearson's r) between number of visits of family members and level of depression of nursing home patients equals 0.00.
Research: The correlation (Pearson's r) between number of visits and level of depression of nursing home patients does not equal 0.00.

Note the common pattern across these examples. In each, the null states that variables are not associated and the research states that they are. Note that no statement was made about a typical hypothesis pair for variables at the ordinal level of measurement. Significance tests involving ordinal-level variables are carried out somewhat less commonly than those for variables at other levels. Largely because of this, this text deemphasizes tests for ordinal variables. Assuming that one's interest is in directional relationship (see Chapter 7, Section 7.6), the hypothesis pair for two ordinal-level variables often states, in essence:

Null: There is no directional relationship.
Research: There is a directional relationship.

Null and research hypothesis pairs do not *always* focus on the presence or absence of association. Sometimes, for instance, the null states that a population parameter equals some value and the research hypothesis states that it does not. The example pertaining to the XYZ self-esteem scale (this chapter's first example) illustrated this pattern.

14.6 Directional and Nondirectional Hypothesis Pairs

14.6.1 *Definitions and Examples*

There are two types of hypothesis pairs: nondirectional pairs and directional pairs.[1] As its name suggests, a **nondirectional hypothesis** does not state a direction. In a nondirectional hypothesis pair, the null states the logical condition "equal" and the research states the condition "not equal." All of the hypothesis pairs presented so far have been nondirectional. In each instance, the null hypothesis stated "equal" and the research hypothesis stated "not equal."

Directional hypotheses do state a direction. They make use of the logical operators "less than" and "greater than." To be specific, the null hypothesis in a directional pair states either of two logical conditions: "less than or equal to" or "greater than or equal to." The research hypothesis states either "less than" or "greater than." As with all hypothesis pairs, the research hypothesis negates the null. Hence the direction stated in the research hypothesis is always opposite to that stated in the null. When the null states "less than or equal to," the research hypothesis states "greater than." When the null states "greater than or equal to," the research hypothesis states "less than." The just-presented examples can be restated as directional hypothesis pairs. For instance, the example involving the XYZ self-esteem test can be restated as:

Null: The mean self-esteem score is less than or equal to 100 points.
Research: The mean self-esteem score is greater than 100 points.

This hypothesis pair may also be stated using the opposite directions (guidance regarding which direction is preferred is presented shortly):

Null: The mean self-esteem score is greater than or equal to 100 points.
Research: The mean self-esteem score is less than 100 points.

The other examples may also be restated as directional hypothesis pairs:

Null: The percentage of teens who become pregnant in Program A is greater than or equal to the percentage who become pregnant in Program B.
Research: The percentage of teens who become pregnant in Program A is less than the percentage who become pregnant in Program B.

Null: The correlation (Pearson's r) between family visiting and level of depression of nursing home clients is greater than or equal to 0.00.
Research: The correlation (Pearson's r) between family visiting and level of depression of nursing home clients is less than 0.00.

To save space, the last two directional hypothesis pairs are not repeated in opposite directions.

14.6.2 Guidelines for Usage

Although the decision regarding whether to use a directional or nondirectional hypothesis pair rests with the researcher, guidelines for decision making are clear. Directional hypotheses are used when prior research, theory, logic, or common sense provides a *compelling* reason for expecting that the study result will be in a particular direction. For instance, a considerable body of research (Lazar, 1994; Comstock and Strasburger, 1990) indicates that viewing violent television leads to increased violent behavior. A researcher conducting a study in this area would *strongly* expect to find that the greater the amount of violent television viewed, the greater the amount of violent behavior. Given the strong expectation for results to be in a given direction, a directional hypothesis pair would be preferred.

In a directional hypothesis pair, the research hypothesis always states the direction that is consistent with expectations and the null always states the direction that runs counter to expectations. For instance, in the just-presented example the pair would be:

Null: The correlation (r) between the amount of violent television watched and the amount of violent behavior is less than or equal to 0.00.
Research: The correlation (r) between the amount of violent television watched and the amount of violent behavior is greater than 0.00.

Nondirectional hypotheses are used when theory, research, logic, or common sense do not provide a *compelling* reason for expecting that a result will be in a given direction. For instance, for the earlier example pertaining to self-esteem of women and men, presume that a group of researchers sees no compelling reasons to think that self-esteem is higher for either gender. Hence they would prefer a nondirectional pair for a study in this area. Similarly, presuming that Program A and Program B are both relatively new and untested programs of pregnancy prevention, one would most likely use a nondirectional hypothesis pair to compare their effectiveness. On the other hand, given compelling reasons for favoring one program over the other, one would likely choose a directional hypothesis.

As stated earlier, the choice of a directional or nondirectional hypothesis pair rests ultimately with the researcher. If you are in doubt regarding which type of pair to use, a nondirectional one is recommended. These are much more common in actual research. At a guess, more than 95% of the hypotheses in research journals related to human services are nondirectional. Use directional hypotheses only when you are almost certain regarding direction. Human services research is a fairly new endeavor. In most research studies, prior theory and research are not sufficiently compelling to justify directional hypotheses. Other reasons for preferring nondirectional hypotheses are discussed in the next chapter.[2]

14.7 SAMPLING ERROR AND THE NULL HYPOTHESIS

Remember once again that due to sampling error, sample statistics and population parameters almost always differ. Suppose that researchers studying self-esteem select a random sample of students from the population of students at a university and formulate a nondirectional hypothesis pair. To remind you that hypothesis statements always apply to populations, the following hypothesis pair specifically states this:

> *Null:* In the population from which the study sample was randomly selected, mean self-esteem scores of women and men are equal.
> *Research:* In the population from which the study sample was randomly selected, mean self-esteem scores of women and men are unequal.

Presume that, in the study sample, the mean self-esteem score is higher for men than for women. What is the cause of this association? There are two possible explanations:

1. *The null hypothesis is true* (mean self-esteem scores of women and men are equal in the population). The association in the sample is due solely to sampling error (the fact that sample statistics and population parameters differ due to chance).
2. *The research hypothesis is true* (mean self-esteem scores of women and men differ in the population). The association in the sample is not due solely to sampling error. The fundamental reason for the association in the sample is that the variables are indeed associated in the population.

Short of sampling the entire population, one cannot determine definitively which hypothesis is true. However, via significance tests, researchers can determine whether the null or the research hypothesis provides the better explanation for the study result.

One uses different significance tests in different situations. For instance, a particular test examines differences in means, another those in percentages, another correlations, and so on. Though there is a test for almost any situation that one can imagine, each conveys the same basic message: Statistical significance tests convey the probability of obtaining one's study sample result given that the null is true in the population from which one's sample was randomly selected.

Every significance test tests the null hypothesis. The assumption is made that the null is true. This assumed to be the case, the test calculates the probability of obtaining the study sample result. When this probability is low (just how low will be discussed shortly), one reasons that it is unlikely that the null is true. When it is not sufficiently low, one reasons that the null may be true.

An example from the realm of coin flips can demonstrate the logic of hypothesis testing. Suppose you notice that a particular coin is bent. Curious about whether this affects how it lands, you develop a nondirectional hypothesis pair:

Null: The coin comes up heads 50% of the time.
Research: The coin does not come up heads 50% of the time.

Your hypothesis pair pertains to the full *population* of coin flips, that is, to the results that would be obtained if you flipped the coin an infinite number of times. You don't have time to flip the coin indefinitely, so let's suppose that you flip it 100 times. Suppose that it comes up heads 94 times and tails 6 times. Intuitively, you know that, given a true null (an unbiased coin), the chances of obtaining this result are tiny. You can't rule out the possibility that the null is true with 100% certainty. There is always the chance, even if infinitesimally small, that the null is true and the discrepancy between the study sample result (94% heads) and the population condition stated in the null (50% heads) is due solely to sampling error (luck). In other words, you cannot *prove* that the null is false.

Yet, as the likelihood of obtaining such a result given a true null is exceedingly small, you may conclude that it is *likely* that the null is false. Viewed from a different perspective, you may conclude that it is unlikely that sampling error (chance, luck, etc.) is the sole cause of the study sample result. Clearly, the obtained results are inconsistent with a true null.

When sampling error alone is an unlikely explanation for the study sample result, one **rejects the null hypothesis** and **accepts the research hypothesis.** Such is indeed the case in the current situation. Hence you would reject the null hypothesis that the population percentage of heads is 50% and accept the research hypothesis. You would conclude that the percentage in the population is not 50%.

Now let's put a different spin on the results of your coin toss study. Suppose that the coin comes up heads 55 times and tails 45 times. In this situation, study sample results (55%) differ from the condition stated in the null (50%). Yet you know intuitively that this difference may simply reflect sampling error (luck). Stated differently, you know intuitively that, given a true null, this particular result would not be unlikely. Though it does not *prove* that the null is true, it provides no strong reason for thinking otherwise. This study sample result is consistent with a true null hypothesis. (From a slightly different perspective, the result is not sufficiently inconsistent with the null for one to conclude that the null is likely false.)

When sampling error alone is a plausible (not unlikely) explanation for the study sample result, one **accepts the null hypothesis** and **rejects the research hypothesis.** In the just-described situation, sampling error (chance) is indeed a plausible explanation for the study result. Hence you would accept the null hypothesis that the population percentage is 50% and reject the research hypothesis that this percentage is other than 50%.

Statistical significance tests test the *null* hypothesis. The researcher's initial decision concerns the null. As you know, the research hypothesis negates the null. The decision on the research hypothesis follows logically from that on the null. When the null is accepted, the research hypothesis is always rejected. When the null is rejected, the research hypothesis is always accepted. An alternative term for *accepts the null* is *fails to reject the null*. Section 14.10 explains in depth why *fails to reject* is, perhaps, the better of the two. For now, we use both terms.

14.8 STATISTICAL SIGNIFICANCE LEVELS

Though different significance tests have different formulas, all result in a probability, symbolized by p. This probability has two important interpretations. The first has already been mentioned: The probability resulting from a significance test conveys the probability of obtaining the study sample result given a true null. Though this first interpretation relates most directly to the formal hypothesis testing model, which is developed in the next chapter, the second is perhaps more important and is the basic nuts-and-bolts meaning of significance testing that you will carry beyond this class. The second interpretation is this: The probability resulting from a significance test conveys the probability that the study sample result is due to chance alone (sampling error alone). For instance, if the probability given by the test is .26, that is, $p = .26$, this conveys that (1) the probability of obtaining the sample result given a true null is .26 and (2) the probability that the sample result is due to chance alone is .26. These two probabilities are one and the same. (They are different sides of the same coin.) For instance, given a true null in the population, it follows logically that chance alone is the explanation for the difference between the condition stated in the null and the sample result. Reversing this logic: If chance alone explains the difference between the condition stated in the null and the sample result, it follows logically that the null is true. The two probabilities are always equal.

In communicating about the probability resulting from a significance test, one may simply say "the probability of obtaining the study sample result." This is understood to have the same meaning as "the probability of obtaining the study sample result given a true null" and "the probability that the study sample result is due to chance alone." Hence, given the probability presented in the prior paragraph, we could simply say: The probability of obtaining the study sample result is .26.

Before we proceed, it should be mentioned that the probabilities resulting from statistical tests accurately convey the probability of the study sample result only when the appropriate test for a given situation is carried out. If one carries out an inappropriate test, the test's probability may be inaccurate. This problem is discussed in depth in Chapter 15, Section 15.3. All discussion in the current chapter presumes that an appropriate test has been conducted.

The null is rejected when the probability of obtaining the study sample result, as conveyed by the significance test, is sufficiently low. How low does this probability need to be? By convention, social science has adopted two major **statistical significance levels,** the .05 statistical significance and the .01 statistical significance level:

- At the **.05 statistical significance level,** researchers accept (fail to reject) the null hypothesis (and therefore reject the research hypothesis) when the probability of obtaining the study sample result, as indicated by the significance test, is greater than .05. They reject the null hypothesis (and therefore accept the research hypothesis) when this probability is less than or equal to .05.
- At the **.01 statistical significance level,** researchers accept (fail to reject) the null hypothesis (and therefore reject the research hypothesis) when the probability of obtaining the study sample result, as indicated by the significance test, is greater than .01. They reject the null hypothesis (and therefore accept the research hypothesis) when this probability is less than or equal to .01.

For ease of communication, *statistical significance level* may be shortened to *significance level* or simply *level*. The probability connected with the chosen significance level is termed **alpha** (α, a letter from the Greek alphabet). Thus, when the .05 level is selected, $\alpha = .05$. When the .01 level is selected, $\alpha = .01$. Sometimes the phrase to *set alpha* is used. For instance, when we select the .05 significance level, we "set α to .05."

The researcher customarily chooses the significance level prior to conducting the statistical test. The .05 level is used most frequently. Occasionally, researchers choose significance levels different from .05 and .01. When the .10 significance level is used, the null is rejected if the probability resulting from the significance test is less than or equal to .10. When the .001 level is used, the null is rejected if this probability is less than or equal to .001.

When the probability resulting from the test is less than or equal to the probability associated with the chosen statistical significance level ($\leq \alpha$), that result is **statistically significant.** When this probability is greater, it is not. So, suppose that a researcher selects the .05 significance level and conducts the appropriate significance test, which yields a probability of .02 ($p = .02$). As .02 is less than .05, this result is statistically significant. To be more specific, it is *statistically significant at the .05 level.* In this situation, the researcher would reject the null hypothesis and therefore accept the research hypothesis. Suppose that a researcher chooses the .05 level, conducts the appropriate test, and obtains a probability of .17 ($p = .17$). As .17 is greater than .05, this result is not statistically significant at the .05 level. The researcher would accept the null hypothesis and therefore reject the research hypothesis.

When a result is statistically significant, it has achieved **statistical significance.** Statistical significance and acceptance of the research hypothesis go hand in hand. When a result is statistically significant, one rejects the null and accepts the research hypothesis. When a result is not statistically significant one accepts (fails to reject) the null and rejects the research hypothesis.

Rejection of the null at the .01 significance level is a more convincing rejection than is rejection at the .05 level. When one rejects at the .01 level, the probability that the study sample result is due to chance alone is less than or equal to .01 (one in a hundred). When one rejects at the .05 significance level, this probability is less than or equal to .05 (five in a hundred).

One may attach degrees of confidence to the decision to reject the null. A rejection at the .01 level means one is 99% confident that the null is indeed false. A rejection at the .05 level means one can be 95% confident that this is the case.

14.9 ROLE OF NULL AND RESEARCH HYPOTHESES IN SCIENTIFIC INQUIRY

Peruse the null hypotheses that have been presented so far in this chapter. They are, for lack of a better word, boring. Time and time again, the null is a humdrum statement: All is the same, everything is equal, there is no difference, nothing is related (yawn). Indeed, the dictionary definition of null is "amounting to nothing." Perhaps you are wondering "What is the purpose of the null?"

Science has a deeply rooted preference for the simplest, most straightforward explanation. Consider the study of relationships between variables, a central focus of scientific inquiry. Researchers frequently face the task of explaining why two variables are associated in their study sample. The null hypothesis provides the simplest, most straightforward explanation. It asserts that (1) the variables are unassociated in the population from which the study sample was randomly selected, and that (2) the only reason for the association in the study sample is sampling error (chance, luck of the draw). Science prefers such a "simplest possible" explanation. So long as the sample result is consistent with the null, there is no reason to reject it.

The research hypothesis offers a more complex explanation. It asserts that an association is observed in the sample not solely because of chance but also, and more fundamentally, because an association truly exists in the population. Science will accept this more complex explanation only when a simpler one (i.e., the null) does not suffice.

In sum, significance testing examines whether the simplest possible explanation—sampling error—is a plausible explanation for the association observed in the study sample. When it is, the canons of science do not permit one to consider a more complex explanation. For instance, if the higher self-esteem for male students than for female students in a study sample may be due simply to sampling error (the luck of the draw of random samples), it makes little sense to seriously consider other explanations. On the other hand, if one can rule out sampling error as a plausible cause (it can never be ruled out with 100% certainty), then the traditions of science give permission to think about *real* (and more interesting) explanations.

Real explanations are explanations other than sampling error (chance). Perhaps men are more assertive in advocating for their rights and this enhances self-esteem. Perhaps contradictory messages about academic success undermine self-esteem in women. It makes good sense to consider real differences only when one can be confident that an association is not simply due to luck. When researchers accept the research hypothesis, they are, in essence, concluding that some real difference—something more than sampling error—explains their study sample result. Acceptance of the null, on the other hand, conveys that the result may be due simply to chance.

Just as the name *null* conveys well the meaning of this hypothesis, *research hypothesis* is also a well-chosen term. In research in the human services, the research hypothesis typically carries the message that the researcher hopes will be borne out by the study. For instance, one might seek to demonstrate that a newly developed pregnancy prevention intervention is more effective than an existing one, or to identify factors associated with enhanced functioning of clients in nursing homes.

The research hypothesis often expresses the new ideas that can improve human services practice. As scientists, human services researchers strive to be objective. As humans, they often root for the research hypothesis.

14.10   ACCEPTING VERSUS FAILING TO REJECT

When the probability of obtaining the study sample result is greater than the statistical significance level (greater than α), one accepts the null hypothesis. The term *accepts* is potentially misleading. It is important to see that by accepting the null one does *not* conclude that it is likely that the null is true.

Consider evidence in a murder trial. Suppose that a blood test establishes that the blood at the murder scene matches—is consistent in many ways with and shows no inconsistencies with—the blood of the defendant. By itself, such evidence does not necessarily establish that the blood at the scene is likely that of the defendant. Establishing that the blood is consistent with the defendant's blood does not establish that it is not also consistent with that of others.

In the same way, establishing that the "evidence" in the research study is consistent with the null does not demonstrate that this evidence is not consistent with other hypotheses. Consider our example involving the bent coin. In this example, the null hypothesis stated: "The coin comes up heads 50% of the time." In our second study, it came up heads 55 times in 100 flips (55%). We accepted the null, reasoning that the difference between 50% and 55% could well reflect luck (sampling error). Yet this study sample result was also consistent with many other hypotheses that we did not test. For instance, had we hypothesized that the coin came up heads 60% of the time, we would not have been surprised by the result (55%). The sample result, then, is also consistent with this hypothesis.

Thus acceptance of the null does not indicate that the sample result is inconsistent with the research hypothesis (or with any other hypothesis). Acceptance simply indicates that the result is consistent with the null. (Or, to be more precise, it is not so inconsistent as to lead to rejection.) As already stated, the null provides the simplest explanation of results. From the perspective of science, the simplest explanation is best. So, acceptance of the null conveys that results are consistent with the simplest, and therefore the best, explanation.

As stated earlier, a better term than *accept the null* is **fail to reject the null.** In accepting the null, one doesn't conclude that it is likely that the null is true. Instead, one concludes that the study sample result does not provide sufficient reason for concluding otherwise. As both *accepts the null* and *fails to reject* are in common use, this text continues to use both. However, it emphasizes *fail to reject*. This term best conveys the meaning of the decision to "accept" the null.

When one fails to reject (accepts) the null, the decision to reject the research hypothesis follows automatically. (These decisions are, in essence, one and the same.) Rejection of the research hypothesis does not imply either that the research hypothesis is false or that it is likely that it is false. It simply conveys that study findings were not sufficient to reject a simpler hypothesis, the null. In a sense, by failing to reject the null, one makes no decision at all on the research hypothesis. As the simpler explanation (the null) suffices, one gives no consideration to the more complex one (the research).

One more analogy from the field of law can increase understanding. In rendering a verdict in a criminal trial, a jury is not asked to find the defendant guilty or innocent but rather guilty or not guilty. A finding of not guilty does not indicate that a defendant *is* innocent or even that it is likely that the defendant is innocent. Instead it conveys that innocence is plausible at some level greater than a reasonable doubt. In the same vein, when one accepts the null, this does not establish that the null *is* true or that it is likely that it is true. Instead it conveys that it is plausible that the null is true (that results do not convey sufficient grounds for concluding otherwise). When one fails to reject (accepts) the null, one has at least a reasonable doubt that it is true.

On the other hand, continuing with the legal analogy, when one rejects the null, one judges it to be false beyond a reasonable doubt. The researcher can be confident, though not certain, that it is indeed false (and confident, though not certain, that the research hypothesis is true).

To sum up:

> When chance alone (sampling error alone) provides a plausible explanation for the study sample result, one fails to reject (accepts) the null and rejects the research hypothesis. Such a result is not statistically significant.

> When chance alone (sampling error alone) does not provide a plausible explanation for the study sample result, one rejects the null and accepts the research hypothesis. Such a result is statistically significant.

14.11   CHAPTER SUMMARY

A general formula (14.1) for probability is:

$$\text{Probability of event with given characteristic} = \frac{\text{Number of events with characteristic}}{\text{Total number of events}}$$

Probability (p) may range from 0.00 to 1.00. It is 0.00 when there is no chance of an event and 1.00 when there is absolute certainty.

Hypothesis statements pertain to the population from which one has randomly selected the study sample. The null hypothesis states that a given condition is true. The research hypothesis states a logically opposite condition. Typically, null hypotheses state that variables are not associated and research hypotheses state that they are. Null and research hypotheses go together as a hypothesis pair.

A nondirectional hypothesis does not state a direction. A directional hypothesis does do so. Directional pairs are used when there are compelling reasons for expecting results in a given direction. Nondirectional pairs are used when this is not the case and are much more common.

Two possible explanations for an association in one's study sample are (1) the null is true, and thus the association is due solely to sampling error, or (2) the research hypothesis is true, and thus the association is not due solely to sampling error (real factors are also involved).

Significance tests convey (1) the probability of obtaining one's study sample result given a true null and (2) the probability that the study sample result is due to chance alone. These two probabilities are one and the same.

Every significance test tests the null. When the probability of obtaining the study result given a true null is sufficiently low, one rejects the null and accepts the research hypothesis. When it is not, one fails to reject (accepts) the null and rejects the research hypothesis.

The two major statistical significance levels are the .05 level and the .01 level. At the .05 level, one accepts the null (and therefore rejects the research hypothesis) when the probability resulting from the significance test is greater than .05. One rejects the null (and therefore accepts the research hypothesis) when this probability is less than or equal to .05. The probability connected with the significance level is termed *alpha* (α).

When a result is statistically significant, chance alone is not a plausible explanation. When it is not, chance alone is a plausible explanation. When a result is statistically significant, one rejects the null and accepts the research hypothesis. When it is not, one accepts (fails to reject) the null and rejects the research hypothesis.

The null offers the simplest explanation. Science will accept a more complex one (the research hypothesis) only when the null does not suffice. Acceptance of the research hypothesis conveys that some *real* difference—something more than sampling error—explains the result.

In accepting the null, one doesn't conclude that it is likely that the null is true but instead that the study result does not provide sufficient grounds for concluding otherwise. A better term than *accepts* is *fails to reject*.

PROBLEMS AND QUESTIONS

Section 14.2

1. A term synonymous with statistical significance test is _____ _____.

Section 14.3

2. From memory, state the general formula for probability.
3. Probability may range from a minimum of _____ to a maximum of _____.
4. A wilderness experience program can serve 16 youths. 40 youths want to participate. Names will be drawn randomly from a hat. For any given youth, what is the probability of being selected to participate?
5. What symbol does this text use for probability? For proportion?
6. Given a normal distribution, what is the probability of each of the following?
   a. Randomly selecting a case at the mean or higher
   b. Randomly selecting a case located within one standard deviation of the mean
   c. Randomly selecting a case with a z score of 1.00 or higher

Section 14.4

7. The _____ hypothesis states that a given condition is true in the population. The _____ hypothesis, also called the _____ hypothesis, states a condition logically _____ to that stated in the null.
8. A null and its corresponding research hypothesis, taken together, are termed a(n) _____ _____.
9. (T or F) The statements made by a hypothesis pair pertain to the study sample rather than to the population from which that sample was selected.

Section 14.5

10. (T or F) Null hypotheses typically state that variables are associated.

11. When both variables are at the nominal level, null hypotheses typically state that _____ are equal.
12. When one variable is at the interval/ratio level and the other is at the nominal level, null hypotheses typically state that _____ are equal.
13. When both variables are at the interval/ratio level, the null typically states that the _____ between these variables is _____.
14. The research hypothesis, in essence, states that the null is _____.
15. (T or F) *All* hypothesis pairs concern the presence or absence of association.

Section 14.6

16. In a nondirectional hypothesis pair, the null states the logical condition _____ and the research/alternative hypothesis states the condition _____ _____.
17. _____ hypotheses state a direction and make use of the logical operators _____ _____ and _____ _____.
18. Indicate whether the following research hypotheses are part of a directional or a nondirectional hypothesis pair.
   a. A higher percentage of women than men choose careers in the human services.
   b. Women and men are not equally likely to choose careers in the human services.
   c. The mean levels of self-esteem of men and women differ.
   d. The mean level of self-esteem is higher for men than for women.
19. State a nondirectional hypothesis pair.
20. State a directional hypothesis pair.
21. State the just-stated directional hypothesis pair with the direction reversed.
22. (T or F) On balance, directional (rather than nondirectional) hypothesis pairs are used when theory, research, logic, or common sense suggests a compelling reason to expect that a study result will be in a particular direction.
23. (T or F) In a directional hypothesis pair, the _____ hypothesis states the direction that is consistent with expectations and the _____ hypothesis states the opposite direction.

24. (T or F) Ultimately, the choice to use a directional or a nondirectional hypothesis pair rests with the researcher.

25. (T or F) In actual research, directional hypothesis pairs are more commonly used than are nondirectional pairs.

Section 14.7

26. When the null is true, the association in the study sample is due solely to _____ _____.

27. When the research hypothesis is true, the fundamental reason that an association is observed in the sample is that there is indeed a(n) _____ in the population.

28. (T or F) Statistical significance tests allow researchers to determine definitively—that is, with 100% confidence—which hypothesis is true.

29. (T or F) Significance tests indicate the probability of obtaining study results given a true null.

30. When sampling error alone is an unlikely explanation for the study sample result, one _____ the _____ hypothesis and accepts the _____ hypothesis.

31. When sampling error alone is a plausible explanation for the study sample result, one accepts the _____ hypothesis and _____ the _____ hypothesis.

32. Statistical significance tests test the _____ hypothesis.

33. When the null is accepted, the research hypothesis is always _____. When the null is rejected, the research hypothesis is always _____.

Section 14.8

34. The threshold for decision making is termed the _____ _____ _____.

35. The probability associated with the selected statistical significance level is termed _____ and is symbolized by _____.

36. What does alpha equal when the .05 significance level is used? When the .01 level is used?

37. At the .05 statistical significance level, the researcher accepts (fails to reject) the null when the probability given by the significance test is greater than _____ and rejects the null when this probability is _____ _____ or _____ _____ _____.

In responding to the remaining questions, presume that the statistical significance test that is carried out is indeed an appropriate one.

38. The probability given by a statistical significance test conveys which of the following?
   a. Given a true null, the probability of obtaining the study sample result
   b. The probability that the study sample result is due to chance alone
   c. The probability of obtaining the study sample result
   d. All of the above

39. At the .01 statistical significance level, the researcher accepts (fails to reject) the null when the probability given by the significance test is greater than _____ and rejects the null when this probability is _____ _____ or _____ _____ _____.

40. (T or F) The significance level is customarily chosen subsequent to carrying out the statistical test.

41. When the probability given by the statistical test is less than or equal to the probability associated with the statistical significance level (less than or equal to α), the result is said to be _____ _____.

42. A researcher selects the .05 significance level. The significance test indicates the probability of obtaining the study sample result due to chance alone is .12. This result is statistically significant. (T or F)

43. The probability resulting from a significance test is .03. Is this result statistically significant at the .05 level? (Yes or No)

44. The probability of obtaining a given result as indicated by a significance test is .03. Is this result statistically significant at the .01 level? (Yes or No)

45. When researchers reject the null at the .05 statistical significance level, they can be _____ % confident that the null is false. When they reject at the .01 level, they may be _____ % confident that this is the case.

46. Statistical significance tests indicate the probability that the study sample result is due to _____ _____ alone. Another name for sampling error is _____ . Significance tests also indicate the probability of obtaining the study sample result given that the _____ hypothesis is _____ .

47. (T or F) When a study sample result is statistically significant, chance alone is a likely explanation for that result.

48. (T or F) When a study sample result is statistically significant at the .01 level, the probability that the result is due to chance alone is less than or equal to .01.

49. A researcher uses the .05 significance level. The probability yielded by the statistical significance test is .48. Respond to each of the following:
    a. (T or F) This result is statistically significant at the .05 significance level.
    b. (T or F) One would accept (fail to reject) the null.
    c. (T or F) One would reject the null.
    d. (T or F) One would accept the research hypothesis.
    e. (T or F) One would reject the research hypothesis.
    f. (T or F) The probability that the study result is due to chance alone is .48.
    g. (T or F) The probability of obtaining the study result given a true null is .48.
    h. (T or F) The probability of obtaining the study result is .48.
    i. (T or F) Chance alone is a plausible explanation for the study result.
    j. (T or F) One can be confident that the null is false.

50. A researcher uses the .01 level. The probability yielded by the statistical significance test is .002. Respond to each of the following:
    a. (T or F) This result is statistically significant at the .01 significance level.
    b. (T or F) One would accept (fail to reject) the null.
    c. (T or F) One would reject the null.
    d. (T or F) One would accept the research hypothesis.

e. (T or F) One would reject the research hypothesis.
f. (T or F) The probability that the study result is due to chance alone is .002.
g. (T or F) The probability of obtaining the study result given a true null is .002.
h. (T or F) The probability of obtaining the study result is .002.
i. (T or F) Chance alone is a plausible explanation for the study result.
j. (T or F) One can be confident that the null is false.

Section 14.9

51. The _____ hypothesis offers the simplest, most straightforward explanation of the study sample result.

52. (T or F) The research hypothesis offers a more complex explanation than does the null.

53. (T or F) Science prefers complex explanations to simple ones.

54. (T or F) The "human side" of the researcher tends to root for the alternative (research) hypothesis rather than for the null.

Section 14.10

55. A better term than *accept the null* is _____ to _____ the _____ .

56. A researcher fails to reject (accepts) the null in a study. Which of the following conclusions are therefore valid (correct), and which are not?
    a. It is likely that the null is true.
    b. The study sample result is consistent with (not inconsistent with) the null.
    c. The null is the only hypothesis that is consistent with study results.
    d. The null provides a plausible explanation for the study result.
    e. It is likely that the research hypothesis is false.

NOTES

1. The use of the term *direction* in connection with hypothesis testing has considerable similarity to its use in describing types of relationship (positive or negative), as

introduced in Chapter 7 (Section 7.6). The use of direction in connection with hypotheses should not be confused with the direction of a causal effect, which was discussed in Chapter 10, Section 10.7.

2. As mentioned earlier, hypothesis statements most often focus on whether two variables are related. In this context, it was stated that null hypotheses state that variables are unassociated. Formally, this statement is not accurate when the hypothesis pair is directional. The null in a directional hypothesis pair actually states that one of two conditions is true: (1) the variables are unassociated (the "equal to" condition) or (2) the variables are associated in the direction that runs counter to expectations (the "greater than" or the "less than" condition). Consider, however, that when researchers are uncertain regarding direction, they select a nondirectional hypothesis pair. The selection of a directional pair conveys that there is no pragmatic chance that the direction of association is in the direction stated in the null. As such, even a directional null is basically a statement that two variables are unassociated.

THE LARGE SAMPLE TEST OF THE MEAN AND NEW CONCEPTS

15.1 CHAPTER OVERVIEW

To get some practice with significance testing and an introduction to many statistical concepts, we use the *large sample test of* $\overline{X}$ to work on an example of research findings. The four-step *hypothesis testing model* provides our structure. We consider *assumptions* of statistical tests and get the specific assumptions for the large sample test. We examine the role of sampling distributions in significance testing and find out how to more explicitly interpret test results than in the prior chapter. *Two-tailed* and *one-tailed* tests and *rejection regions* are introduced. *Test statistic* is defined, as is the *sampling distribution of a test statistic*. The probabilistic nature of hypothesis testing is emphasized in a discussion of *type I* and *type II errors*.

15.2 A MODEL FOR HYPOTHESIS TESTING

Four basic steps make up the **hypothesis testing model,** which is the model for carrying out statistical significance tests and making decisions regarding one's hypothesis pair (Glass and Hopkins, 1996, p. 258). These steps are:

1. State the hypothesis pair. These are the null and the research hypotheses; the pair may be directional or nondirectional.
2. Choose a statistical significance level. That is, set a value for alpha (α); usually the .05 level or the .01 level is selected.
3. Carry out the appropriate statistical significance test. The appropriate test is determined by levels of measurement and other factors we discuss later.
4. Make a decision regarding the hypothesis pair:
    - If the probability resulting from the significance test is greater than the probability associated with the significance level (greater than alpha), accept (fail to reject) the null hypothesis and reject the research hypothesis.

- If the probability resulting from the significance test is less than or equal to that associated with the chosen significance level (less than or equal to alpha), reject the null hypothesis and accept the research hypothesis.

As presented in the prior chapter (Section 14.8) (and presuming that an appropriate test has been carried out), the probability resulting from the statistical test conveys (1) given a true null, the probability of obtaining the study sample result, (2) the probability that the study sample result is due to chance alone, and (stated more simply) (3) the probability of obtaining the study sample result.

The steps in the model will be introduced gradually over the course of the chapter. To demonstrate the model, we need a specific statistical significance test.

The **large sample test of the mean,** also known as the **large sample test of $\overline{X}$,** examines whether the mean of a sample differs to a statistically significant degree from a hypothesized value. It may be used when sample size is 100 or greater. The presentation of this test demonstrates concepts that underlie all significance tests. Quite often, we detour from the large sample test of $\overline{X}$ to illustrate these concepts. For instance, let's first consider the assumptions of a test.

15.3   ASSUMPTIONS OF STATISTICAL SIGNIFICANCE TESTS

15.3.1   Definition and Assumptions of the Large Sample Test of $\overline{X}$

Statistical significance tests are based on **assumptions,** conditions that must be met for the test to yield a precisely accurate probability. Significance tests convey the probability that a study result is due to chance. Whenever a test assumption is not met, the probability given by the test differs (at least to some degree) from the actual probability that the result is due to chance. Stated differently, when an assumption is not met, the test has some degree of inaccuracy. The assumptions of the large sample test of $\overline{X}$ are (1) normality (that the sample has been selected from a population that is normally distributed), and (2) that the standard deviation (σ) in the population from which the study sample was randomly selected is known.

A statistical test may be either robust or nonrobust to an assumption. When a test is **robust,** an assumption may be violated with only a minor effect on accuracy. For instance, the large sample test of $\overline{X}$ is robust to the normality assumption. When this test is carried out in the absence of normality, the probability that it yields does indeed differ from the actual probability that the result is due to chance. However, presuming that $N \geq 100$, the degree of inaccuracy is extremely small. For all practical purposes, then, the test's probability is highly accurate. As such (and stated for a second time), the large sample test is robust to the normality assumption. When a test is nonrobust to an assumption, violation of the assumption can greatly affect accuracy.

The second assumption, that the population standard deviation (σ) is known, can never really be met. The only way to know the value of σ would be to "sample" the entire population. If this was done, one would have no reason to carry out the test, because the entire population having been sampled, the value of the population mean (μ) would be known.[1]

As Chapter 13 (Section 13.2) emphasized, whenever sample size is 100 or greater, the standard deviation of the study sample, s, provides an excellent estimate of σ. Just as s is used to estimate σ in forming confidence intervals, it may also be used in the large sample test of $\overline{X}$. As long as sample size is 100 or greater, the use of s rather than σ has a negligible impact on accuracy. Hence, given that sample size is 100, the large sample test of $\overline{X}$ is robust to the assumption that σ is known. It should not be used when sample size is smaller than 100.[2] The level of measurement of the dependent variable should be interval/ratio or almost so.

15.3.2 Assumptions Common to All Tests

As we begin to study specific tests, recall from Chapter 12 that random sampling is an implicit assumption of all inferential statistical procedures. The three key characteristics of a random sample are that (1) selection of cases takes place via a formal method of chance, (2) all cases have an equal chance of selection, and (3) the selection of each case is independent from that of each other case. A second assumption for all statistical tests is the independence of observations assumption, a rough definition for which is that cases do not share some common factor that makes their scores similar (see discussion in Chapter 12, Section 12.5). Because random sampling and independence of observations are assumed for *all* inferential procedures, no specific mention of these will be made as the assumptions of each statistical test are presented.[3]

15.4 THE FIRST TWO STEPS OF THE HYPOTHESIS TESTING MODEL

Now for a working example of the large sample test of $\overline{X}$. Presume that you are interested in improving the parenting skills of parents of elementary school-age children and that you develop an intervention with this purpose in mind.

From the population of all parents of elementary school children in your city, you randomly select 100 parents (each from a different family) to take part in your program. All agree to do so. Following the program, you administer a scale that measures parenting skills. Let's say that the scale is scored so that higher scores indicate better parenting skills and lower scores indicate worse skills. Presume also that in a previous large-scale research project, this scale was administered to a very large, representative sample of parents of elementary school children from across the United States. Finally, presume that the mean scale score in this large sample was 100 points.

Let's say that the mean scale score of the 100 parents in your study sample is 105 points with a standard deviation of 20 points. Your interest is in comparing parenting skills of those in your sample to those in the large representative sample. The mean score in your sample is five points higher. Is this difference due only to sampling error, or can you be confident that sampling error alone is not the explanation and that the difference reflects the effects of *real* rather than chance factors?

Up to now, we have avoided the use of statistical symbols in the discussion of hypothesis testing. We now begin to use symbols. Often, both statistical symbols and words are used. Let's carry out the first two steps of the hypothesis testing model for our example.

1. State the hypothesis pair.

We will specify a nondirectional hypothesis pair (directional pairs will be demonstrated later). In a nondirectional pair for the large sample test of $\overline{X}$ the null states that the mean of the population from which the study sample was randomly selected equals some value. The research hypothesis states that it does not equal this value. For our example:

(Null) H_0: $\mu = 100$ points
(Research) H_1: $\mu \neq 100$ points

This hypothesis pair uses statistical symbols. It is customary to designate the null hypothesis as $\boldsymbol{H_0}$ (hypothesis-zero) and the research hypothesis as $\boldsymbol{H_1}$ (hypothesis-one). Recall that μ is the statistical symbol for the population mean. Expressing the same hypotheses in words:

Null: The mean in the population from which the study sample was randomly selected equals 100 points.
Research: The mean in the population from which the study sample was randomly selected does not equal 100 points.

The decision to use a nondirectional pair rather than a directional one reflects a conservative approach on our part. It acknowledges that the mean in the population from which the study sample was selected could potentially be either greater than or less than 100. In essence, the null asserts that if you could administer the parenting intervention to the full population of elementary school parents in your city, their mean score on the parenting skills measure would equal 100 points.

2. Choose a significance level.

We will use the .05 statistical significance level, that is, we will set alpha to .05 ($\alpha = .05$).

15.5   STATISTICAL TESTS AND SAMPLING DISTRIBUTIONS

The basic job of all statistical significance tests is to determine the probability of obtaining the study sample result under the assumption that the null hypothesis is true. Significance tests use sampling distributions to carry out this task. Different tests use different distributions. The large sample test of $\overline{X}$ is based on the sampling distribution of $\overline{X}$, which was introduced in Chapter 12 (Section 12.9). Recall that a sampling distribution of $\overline{X}$ is the distribution that would result if one picked an infinite number of random samples of a given size from a population and, for each sample, recorded its mean.

What would the sampling distribution of $\overline{X}$ look like for our example if the null was indeed true? In other words, what would the sampling distribution of $\overline{X}$ look like if an infinite number of random samples of size 100 were selected from a population with a mean of 100? The central limit theorem and related points presented in Chapter 13 (Section 13.2) provide the answer. Recall from Chapter 13 that when sample size is 100 or greater, (1) the standard deviation in a random sample, s, provides a highly accurate estimate of that in the population, σ, and (2) the shape of the sampling distribution will be very close to normal for almost any distribution that one might encounter in social science research. Thus, according to the central limit theorem, the sampling distribution of $\overline{X}$ for our example will have the following characteristics:

1. Its mean will equal that in the population (μ). Hence (given a true null) its mean will be 100 points.
2. Its standard deviation (the standard error of the mean, $\sigma_{\overline{X}}$) will equal the standard deviation in the population, divided by the square root of the sample size: $\sigma_{\overline{X}} = \sigma/\sqrt{N}$. Given that $N \geq 100$, $\sigma_{\overline{X}}$ will be approximately equal to the standard deviation in the sample divided by the square root of the sample size: $\sigma_{\overline{X}} \approx s/\sqrt{N}$, $\sigma_{\overline{X}} \approx s_{\overline{X}}$). The standard deviation of the study sample is 20. Thus $\sigma_{\overline{X}} \approx 20/\sqrt{100} = 20/10 = 2.0$ points. Expressed in words, the standard deviation of the sampling distribution of $\overline{X}$ will be approximately 2.0 points.
3. Given that sample size is 100, its shape will be very close to normal.

Figure 15.1 presents a distribution with the three just-described characteristics: a mean of 100, a standard deviation of 2.0, and a normal shape. Given a true null ($\mu = 100$), this distribution very closely approximates the sampling distribution of $\overline{X}$. It cannot describe this distribution exactly because (1) σ is estimated rather than known and (2) the shape of the sampling distribution of $\overline{X}$ is very close to but not necessarily *precisely* normal. Pragmatically, the approximation is so good that we will indeed refer to this distribution as the sampling distribution of $\overline{X}$.

Note that Figure 15.1 and all subsequent figures in this chapter have two X axes. They display sample means in their original measurements (as raw scores) on the top X axis and as z scores on the bottom axis. Expressed as z scores, the mean of the distribution in Figure 15.1 is 0.00, its standard deviation is 1.00, and its shape is normal. For now, most discussion focuses on the raw scores as presented in the top axis.[4]

We may use our knowledge of the normal distribution to draw a variety of conclusions about the sampling distribution of $\overline{X}$ as presented in Figure 15.1. Many of these provide different perspectives on the same information.

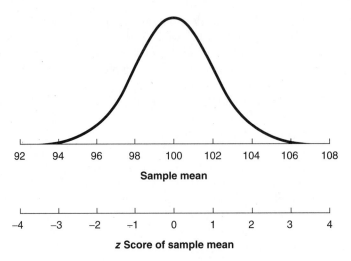

FIGURE **15.1**

SAMPLING DISTRIBUTION OF $\overline{X}$ FOR PARENTING SKILLS SCORE

Given a true null, the sampling distribution of $\overline{X}$ has a mean of 100, a
standard deviation extremely close to 2.0, and a shape extremely close
to normal.

In a normal distribution, 95% of cases are located within 1.96 standard deviations of the mean. Multiplying the highly accurate estimate of the standard deviation of the sampling distribution, 2.00, by 1.96 informs us that 95% of sample
means are located within 3.92 points ($2.0 \times 1.96 = 3.92$) of the population mean
($\mu = 100$, as stated in the null). Thus 95% of sample means are located between
96.08 ($100 - 3.92 = 96.08$) and 103.92 ($100 + 3.92 = 103.92$).[5]

Likewise, 5% of sample means differ from the value stated in the null by
3.92 or more points, that is, they are either ≤ 96.08 or ≥ 103.92. Given that the
normal curve is symmetrical, 2.5% of means are ≤ 96.08 ($5\%/2 = 2.5\%$) and
2.5% are ≥ 103.92. Figure 15.2 presents the sampling distribution with its upper and lower 2.5% tails designated.

The just-presented conclusions pertained to percentages. We may also determine probabilities. For instance, what is the probability of randomly selecting a
mean that is either ≤ 96.08 or ≥ 103.92? As 5% of cases have such means, this
probability is .05: $5\%/100\% = .05$.

To ask another question: What is the probability of randomly selecting a sample mean that is greater than or equal to the study sample mean, that is, of selecting a mean ≥ 105? To determine this probability, we need to compute a z score for
the study sample mean and then refer to the normal distribution table, Table A.1
in Appendix A. This z score is computed as follows: $z = (105 - 100)/2 = 2.50$. (The
study sample mean is $2\frac{1}{2}$ standard deviations above the sampling distribution's
mean.) Table A.1 indicates that the proportion of cases in a normal distribution with
z scores greater than or equal to 2.50 is .0062. Thus the probability of randomly selecting a mean that is greater than or equal to the study sample mean is .0062.

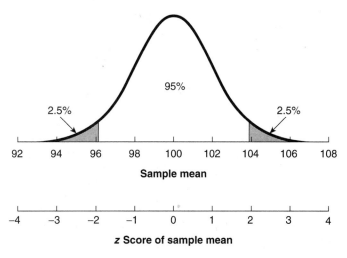

FIGURE **15.2**

**PARENTING SKILLS SCORE: SAMPLING DISTRIBUTION OF $\overline{X}$
WITH 2.5% TAILS**

A related but different question is: What is the probability of randomly selecting a mean that differs from the value stated in the null ($\mu = 100$) by as much as or more than the study sample mean does, in other words, of selecting a mean that differs by five or more points in *either* direction? Stated differently, what is the probability of randomly selecting a mean that is either ≤ 95 or ≥ 105? As the normal curve is symmetrical, the proportion of means ≤ 95 is the same as that of means ≥ 105. Hence the probability of randomly selecting a mean ≤ 95 is .0062. The probability of randomly selecting a mean either ≤ 95 or ≥ 105 is .0062 + .0062 = .0124. Thus the probability of randomly selecting a mean that differs from the mean stated in the null by as much as or more than the mean of the study sample is .0124.

One's study sample mean is viewed as a single (randomly selected) mean in the sampling distribution. Recognizing this, we reach the following conclusions:

- Given a true null, the probability of obtaining a mean as extreme as or more extreme than the study sample mean is .0124.
- The probability that sampling error alone (chance alone) could lead to a mean as extreme as or more extreme than the study sample mean is .0124.

In the preceding statements, a given result is "more extreme" than another if it differs more from the condition stated in the null than does the other. (For instance, in the current example a sample mean of 107 differs from the mean stated in the null, $\mu = 100$, by more than does one of 105, and thus it is more extreme.) Figure 15.3 presents probabilities that pertain to the study sample mean.

The discussion in this section has, in effect, carried out the large sample test of $\overline{X}$ informally. Prior to doing so formally, you need more information on (1) how to interpret significance tests and (2) the role of nondirectional versus directional hypothesis pairs, as discussed in the next two sections.

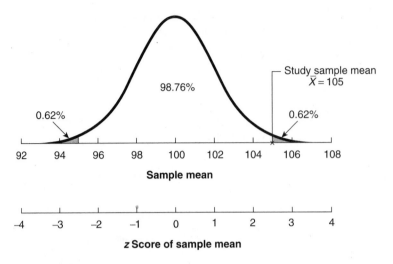

FIGURE 15.3

PROPORTION OF MEANS MORE EXTREME THAN THE STUDY SAMPLE MEAN

The shaded areas in the sampling distribution are more extreme than our sample mean of 105, whether they are in the same or the opposite direction.

15.6 EXPLICIT INTERPRETATIONS OF THE RESULTS OF STATISTICAL SIGNIFICANCE TESTS

Chapter 14 emphasized that the probabilities given by significance tests convey (1) given a true null, the probability of obtaining the study sample result, and (2) the probability that the study sample result is due to chance alone (sampling error alone). We may now make these interpretations more explicit. The probabilities resulting from statistical significance tests convey both of the following:

1. Given a true null, the probability of obtaining a result as extreme as or more extreme than the study sample result
2. The probability that chance alone could lead to a result as extreme as or more extreme than the study sample result

The two just-stated probabilities are, in essence, one and the same and are always equal. These new interpretations provide two equivalent guidelines for when to accept or reject the null:

The null is accepted when, given a true null, the probability of obtaining a result as extreme as or more extreme than the study sample result is greater than the probability associated with the significance level ($>\alpha$). It is rejected when, given a true null, this probability is less than or equal to the probability associated with the significance level ($\leq\alpha$).

The null is accepted when the probability of obtaining a result as extreme as or more extreme than the study sample result due to chance alone is greater than the probability associated with the significance level ($>\alpha$). It is rejected when this probability is less than or equal to the probability associated with the significance level ($\leq\alpha$).

We may also add two more interpretations of the probabilities yielded by significance tests, though they won't be emphasized to the same degree. Significance tests convey:

1. The proportion of cases in the sampling distribution that are as extreme as or more extreme than the study sample result
2. Given a true null, the probability of randomly selecting from the sampling distribution a sample result that is as extreme as or more extreme than the study sample result

All of the interpretations just presented presume that an appropriate test has been carried out. When a test's assumptions are violated and the test is not robust to these assumptions, the probability yielded by the test can differ markedly from the just-mentioned probabilities.

15.7   THE IMPLICATIONS OF A DIRECTIONAL VERSUS A NONDIRECTIONAL HYPOTHESIS

In the current example, the hypothesis pair is nondirectional. Assume for the moment that the research hypothesis is true, that is, that the actual (unknown) mean of the population from which the study sample was selected does not equal 100. As the research hypothesis does not state a direction, the actual population mean may be either greater than 100 or less than 100. The statistical test needs to take both of these possibilities into account.

The decision to accept or reject the null is based on the location of the study sample mean in the sampling distribution. When the hypothesis pair is nondirectional, sample means near the center of the distribution are viewed as consistent with the null. Given a true null, these represent expected and likely results. As one moves away from the center toward the tails, results become increasingly less likely and less consistent with a true null. Means in the extreme tails are viewed as inconsistent with the null because, given a true null, the probability of randomly selecting such an extreme mean is extremely low. Such means can be thought of as unexpected and unlikely given a true null. Though one can never prove that the null is false, a study sample mean so extreme conveys that this is likely the case.

With a nondirectional hypothesis, study sample results in both the lower and upper tails of the sampling distribution of $\overline{X}$ may lead to rejection of the null. When results in *both* tails of a sampling distribution may result in rejection of the null, the statistical test is a **two-tailed test.**

When the hypothesis is directional, only study sample results in the tail of the sampling distribution that is in the direction stated in the research hypothesis are viewed as inconsistent with the null and only such results may lead to its rejection. When results in only one tail of the sampling distribution may lead to rejection of the null, the statistical test is a **one-tailed test.** Whenever one specifies a directional hypothesis, the statistical test is one-tailed. Stated differently, directional hypotheses and one-tailed tests go together.

In most situations (including that for the large sample test of $\overline{X}$), nondirectional hypotheses and two-tailed tests go together. That is, when one specifies a nondirectional hypothesis, one uses a two-tailed test. (An exception is discussed later in the text and need not concern us now.)

The areas of the sampling distribution that result in rejection of the null are termed **rejection regions** (Toothaker, 1986, p. 316) or **critical regions.** Two-tailed tests have two rejection regions, one in each tail. The proportion of cases located in the rejection regions (for two regions, the combined proportion from each region) is equal to the probability associated with the chosen significance level, that is, to alpha (α). For instance, when the .05 level is used, and thus $\alpha = .05$, this proportion is .05. When there are two regions, an equal percentage is located in each. Thus, for a two-tailed test when $\alpha = .05$, 2.5% of cases are in the rejection region in the upper tail and 2.5% are in the region in the lower tail.

Given a true null, the probability that the study sample result will be located in a rejection region is equal to the proportion of cases in these regions. As just stated, when the .05 level is used (and thus $\alpha = .05$), this proportion is .05. Hence, when $\alpha = .05$ (given a true null), the probability that the sample result will be in a rejection region is .05.

Sample results in the rejection region(s) are viewed in the same way as those in the tails. Thus, among different possible results (given a true null), such results are the least likely and the most unexpected. When a result is in a rejection region, one rejects the null.

15.8   CARRYING OUT THE STATISTICAL TEST VIA THE SAMPLING DISTRIBUTION

Because our example states a nondirectional hypothesis, a two-tailed statistical significance test is required. Thus there will be two rejection regions, one in each tail. As we have chosen the .05 statistical significance level (set α to .05), each region consists of the 2.5% of cases in its respective tail of the sampling distribution of $\overline{X}$. Earlier in the chapter, we determined for our working example on parenting skills that 2.5% of means in the sampling distribution of $\overline{X}$ had values of 103.92 or greater and that 2.5% had values of 96.08 or less. These values define the rejection regions. The sampling distribution and its two rejection regions are depicted in Figure 15.4.

The null should be rejected only if the probability of obtaining a result as extreme as or more extreme than the study result is less than or equal to the probability associated with the selected significance level. As we selected the .05 level ($\alpha = .05$), this probability must be less than or equal to .05.

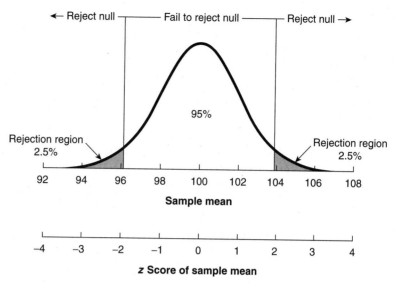

FIGURE 15.4

REJECTION REGIONS FOR A TWO-TAILED TEST WHEN $\alpha = .05$

The curve is the sampling distribution of $\overline{X}$ for parenting skills score.

All means in the rejection regions meet this criteria. Consider first the means that define the regions, 103.92 and 96.08. Five percent of sample means are as extreme as or more extreme than these. Hence the probability of obtaining (via random sampling) a mean as extreme as or more extreme than the defining means is .05. As the defining means are the least extreme means in the rejection regions, this probability is less than .05 for all other means. In sum, all means in the rejection region (the defining ones and all others) meet the criteria and result in rejection of the null. For each mean not in a rejection region, the probability of randomly sampling a mean that is as or more extreme is greater than .05. Therefore, means not in the rejection region lead to acceptance of the null.

Figure 15.5 presents the study sample mean ($\overline{X} = 105$) and the rejection regions. The study mean is located in a rejection region. As such, it meets the rejection criteria and our decision is to reject the null.

The decision regarding the research hypothesis follows automatically from that on the null. As the null is rejected, the research hypothesis is accepted. We conclude that the mean of the population from which your study sample was selected does not equal 100.

The values associated with the rejection region(s) convey a range of results that lead to rejection. Sometimes one's interest is specifically in the probability connected with the study sample. As determined earlier, in our example (given a true null), the probability of obtaining a mean as extreme as or more extreme than the study sample mean is .0124 (see Figure 15.3).

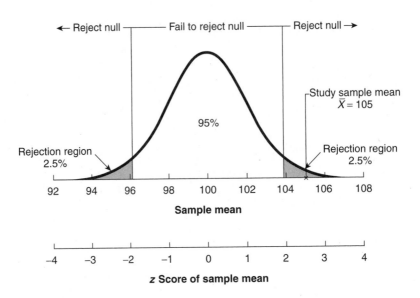

FIGURE **15.5**

STUDY SAMPLE MEAN AND REJECTION REGIONS WHEN $\alpha = .05$

Note the location of the study sample mean within one of the rejection regions for a two-tailed test. The curve is the sampling distribution of $\overline{X}$.

15.9   COMMUNICATING ABOUT RESULTS

Chapter 14 introduced two reasonably straightforward interpretations of the probabilities resulting from significance tests: (1) given a true null, the probability of obtaining the study sample result, and (2) the probability that the study sample result is due to chance alone. The current chapter made these interpretations more explicit, adding to them the phrase "as extreme as or more extreme than the study sample result." These more explicit interpretations communicate more precisely what the probability given by the test conveys. In particular, they draw attention to the key role of the sampling distribution in the logic of hypothesis testing. However, these more explicit interpretations are cumbersome and wordy. In the everyday language of statistics, the shorter interpretations from Chapter 14 are used more often than are the longer ones developed in this chapter. It is understood that the shorter interpretations have the same meaning as their longer counterparts. For instance, saying "the probability that the study sample mean is due to chance alone is .0124" is a shorthand and more convenient way to say "the probability that chance alone could result in a mean as extreme as or more extreme than the study sample mean is .0124."

As pointed out in Chapter 14, one may shorten interpretation still further and state simply "the probability of obtaining the study sample mean is .0124." Though this statement mentions neither "chance alone" nor "given a true null," it is a shorthand way of saying both that "the probability that the study sample mean is due to chance alone is .0124" and that "given a true null, the probability of obtaining the study sample mean is .0124." (Recall from Section 14.8 in Chapter 14 that these two probabilities are one and the same.)

In sum, there are several different ways to communicate about the results of significance testing. Among these different ways, the shortened version using "chance alone" (i.e., the probability that the study sample result is due to chance alone) is used most often and comes closest to capturing the everyday meaning of significance test results. Rather than using a single way to interpret the probabilities resulting from significance tests, this text interprets these probabilities in different ways as it covers different tests.

One of the most effective ways to communicate the probability resulting from a significance test is to use the symbol for probability. For instance, in the current example, $p = .0124$. One final note on communicating about significance test results: The phrase *chance alone* is sometimes shortened simply to *chance*. Hence, one may say "the probability that the study result is due to chance is .0124."

15.10   FINISHING THE EXAMPLE
USING THE FORMULA

In the prior section, we carried out the statistical significance test conceptually by referring to the sampling distribution of $\overline{X}$. As stated earlier, all statistical tests are based on sampling distributions. By understanding the logic underlying the sampling distribution, one understands how the test does its job. Yet one need not understand the inner workings of an automobile engine to drive a car. In the same vein, one need not understand the sampling distribution to carry out a statistical significance test. Formulas are provided for this purpose. One formula is:

$$z \approx \frac{\overline{X} - \mu}{\left(\dfrac{s}{\sqrt{N}}\right)} \tag{15.1}$$

where $\approx$ is the "approximately equal to" sign, z is a highly accurate estimate of the z score of the study sample mean with respect to the sampling distribution of $\overline{X}$, $\overline{X}$ is the study sample mean, μ is the value of the population mean stated in the null, s is the standard deviation in the sample, and N is the sample size. A second and equivalent formula is:

$$z \approx \frac{X - \mu}{s_{\overline{X}}} \tag{15.2}$$

where $s_{\overline{X}}$ is the estimate of the standard error of the mean. As you recall from formula 13.1, $s_{\overline{X}} = s/\sqrt{N}$.[6] In both just-presented formulas, the standard deviation of the sampling distribution of $\overline{X}(\sigma_{\overline{X}})$ is estimated rather than known. As such, both compute highly accurate estimates of z scores rather than exact z scores. This is why the approximately equal sign ($\approx$) is used. As mentioned before, when $N \geq$

100, the degree of inaccuracy introduced by estimating $\sigma_{\bar{X}}$ is negligible. We now return to step 3 of the hypothesis testing model.

3. Carry out the test.

First we need to calculate the estimate of the standard error of the mean:

$$s_{\bar{X}} = \frac{20}{\sqrt{100}} = \frac{20}{10} = 2.00$$

Next we calculate z via formula 15.2:

$$z \approx \frac{105 - 100}{2.00} = 2.50$$

The result obtained from calculation of a statistical significance test formula—in the current example, z—is the **test statistic (obtained statistic).** Given that the large sample test formula calculates a value for z, we refer to our result as the "obtained z."

Continuing to use the hypothesis model to finish the example, we execute step 4:

4. Make a decision regarding the hypothesis pair.

All statistical tests have **decision rules,** that is, specific criteria by which the decision to accept or reject the null is made. Rules for decision making for the large sample test of $\bar{X}$ vary according to whether a one-tailed or a two-tailed test is used and according to the chosen significance level. For a two-tailed large sample test of $\bar{X}$ using the .05 significance level, the decision rule is:

Fail to reject (accept) the null whenever the absolute value of the obtained z is less than 1.96. Reject the null whenever the absolute value of the obtained z is greater than or equal to 1.96.

Given that the absolute value of our obtained z, 2.50, is greater than 1.96, we reject the null hypothesis and therefore accept the research hypothesis. Recall from Chapter 14 (Section 14.8) that rejection of the null and statistical significance go hand in hand. Hence the difference between the mean in your study sample ($\bar{X} = 105$) and that in the large national population ($\mu = 100$) is a statistically significant one. To be more explicit, this difference is statistically significant at the .05 level via a two-tailed significance test (nondirectional hypothesis). The probability that this difference is due to chance alone (sampling error alone) is $\leq .05$. Interpreted from a different perspective, given a true null, the probability of obtaining the study sample result is $\leq .05$.

15.11   THE SAMPLING DISTRIBUTION OF A TEST STATISTIC

So far we have concentrated on the sampling distribution of a *sample* statistic, that being the mean. Just as sample statistics have sampling distributions, so also do *test* statistics. Basically, the **sampling distribution of a test statistic** is the distribution that would result if one (1) selected an infinite number of random samples of a given size; (2) for each sample, calculated the test statistic; and (3) recorded that statistic for each sample. Stated differently, this sampling distribution is the distribution of the test statistic that would be obtained by replicating the study an infinite number of times. The sampling distribution of a test statistic given a true null is key to determining the probability of the study result.

When both of the assumptions of the large sample test of $\overline{X}$ are met, and given a true null, the sampling distribution of the test statistic z has a precisely normal shape, a mean of 0.00, and a standard deviation of 1.00. In the real world these assumptions cannot be met: σ is estimated and no population is exactly normal. As such, in most real-world research, even when the null is true, the sampling distribution of the test statistic z does not have these *precise* characteristics. However, when $N \geq 100$ and given a true null, it almost always comes *extremely* close to having these. When Figures 15.1 to 15.8 are interpreted via the numbers in their bottom axis (the z scores), they present normal distributions with means of 0.00 and standard deviations of 1.00. These distributions very closely approximate the sampling distribution of the test statistic z when the null is true. Stated differently, they very closely approximate the distribution of test results that would be obtained from repeating the study an infinite number of times under the assumption of a true null.

In essence, either formula (15.1 or 15.2) for the large sample test converts the study sample mean into a z score within the sampling distribution of $\overline{X}$. As this sampling distribution has a nearly normal shape, one simply refers to the normal distribution table (Table A.1 in Appendix A) to determine the probability of a result. Notice that the values of z in the decision rules derive from the normal distribution. For instance, in a normal distribution, 5% of cases differ from the mean by 1.96 standard deviations or more. Thus 1.96 is used in the decision rule for a two-tailed test when $\alpha = .05$.

The values of a test statistic that determine whether one accepts or rejects the null are termed the **critical values** (*critical value* for a one-tailed test). In this example, the critical values of z are -1.96 and 1.96.

15.12 A MORE RELAXED INTERPRETATION OF STUDY RESULTS

The hypothesis testing model allows one to make decisions about the null and research hypotheses. Yet the assessment of data does not end with these decisions. Let's step back from the model to get a more commonsense perspective on results.

In the parenting skills example we made the decision, using the hypothesis testing model, to accept the research hypothesis. The research hypothesis does not state a direction, but instead simply states that the mean of the population from which the study sample was selected does not equal 100. Strictly speaking, this is the only conclusion that we may draw via the model; we may not conclude that the population mean is greater than 100. Sometimes one needs to "step outside" of the model to fully interpret a study result.

Although the model does not address this point explicitly, when one rejects the null in a nondirectional hypothesis pair, the actual (unknown) population condition most likely differs from the value stated in the null in the same direction as does the sample result. For instance, given that our sample mean ($\overline{X} = 105$) is greater than the value stated in the null ($\mu = 100$), the actual population mean is also likely to be greater. To pave the way for further interpretation, we need to break from the model and conclude that it is likely that the population mean is greater than 100.

Such a stepping outside of the model opens the way for a pragmatic, commonsense interpretation. When the null is rejected, this informs the researcher that chance alone is not a likely explanation for the study sample result. Thus the researcher seeks to determine what *real*, nonchance factors might be responsible. When a sample result is in a given direction, it makes no sense to think critically about factors that might have caused it to be in the *other* direction. Hence, in our example, rejection of the null opens the way to consider why the parenting skills of those in your sample are *more* effective than those of people in the national sample. In sum, when a result is statistically significant with a nondirectional hypothesis pair, one's primary focus in interpreting that result should be on factors that may explain why it differs from the null in the direction that it does.

15.13   STATISTICAL SIGNIFICANCE AND CAUSALITY

By rejecting the null, we have concluded that chance alone is not a likely explanation for the higher mean in your sample. Stated differently, we have decided that something *real* provides that explanation. This brings up the question of just *what* real factor(s) were at work. Here are some possibilities:

- Your intervention did indeed enhance parenting skills.
- The parenting skills in your city were high prior to your intervention (this, not your intervention, explains the higher score).
- Because they liked you and sensed how much you wanted to help them, the parents in your sample "fudged" their responses in a positive direction.
- The simple fact of getting some extra attention rather than the scientific components of your treatment program led to increased parenting skills.
- Any or all of the above, or perhaps something else.

As Chapters 10 and 11 demonstrated, the assessment of causality is a cautious and complex undertaking. The fact of statistical significance does not allow one to conclude what *particular* real thing explains the study sample result. It simply lets one rule out sampling error as a likely or plausible cause. When sampling error can be ruled out, critical thinking about the issues of causality as raised in Chapters 10 and 11 is in order.

On the other hand, when chance cannot be ruled out, it makes little sense to consider such issues. Why think seriously about the cause of a relationship when that relationship may simply be due to the luck of the draw?

15.14   EFFECT OF CHOICE OF SIGNIFICANCE LEVEL ON OUTCOME OF SIGNIFICANCE TESTS

Having stepped outside of the hypothesis testing model, we now return to it. Sometimes one selects the .01 statistical significance level rather than the .05 level. The decision-making rule for a two-tailed large sample test of $\overline{X}$ using the .01 significance level is as follows:

Fail to reject (accept) the null whenever the absolute value of the obtained z is less than 2.58. Reject the null whenever the absolute value of the obtained z is greater than or equal to 2.58.

As already calculated, our obtained z is 2.50. As the absolute value of 2.50 is less than 2.58, our decision, using the .01 significance level (that is, with α set to .01), is to fail to reject the null. Our study result is not statistically significant at the .01 level. Use of the .01 level results in a different decision than did the .05 level.

In a normal distribution, 1% of cases are located more than 2.58 standard deviations from the mean, 0.5% in each tail. For a two-tailed test when $\alpha = .01$, the most extreme 0.5% of cases in the upper tail composes one rejection area and the same percentage in the lower tail composes the other. As the estimated standard deviation of the sampling distribution of $\overline{X}$ is 2.0, 99% of means are located between 94.84 and 105.16 ($2.00 \times 2.58 = 5.16$; $100 \pm 5.16 = 94.84$ to 105.16). This represents the range within which the null is accepted. Means less than or equal to 94.84 or greater than or equal to 105.16 lead to its rejection. These areas define the rejection regions.

Figure 15.6 presents the rejection regions and the study sample mean. The sample mean is not located in a rejection region—it just misses. The probability that the study result is due to chance alone exceeds .01, so we fail to reject (accept) the null and reject the research hypothesis. Hence, for a two-tailed test at the .01 level, the difference between the mean of your study sample and that of the large national sample is not a statistically significant one.

The different decisions reached using the two significance levels demonstrate that, other things being equal, it is more difficult to reject the null when the .01 level is used than when the .05 level is used. This is because rejection at the .01 level requires a larger difference from the condition stated in the null than does that at the .05 level. This can be seen by comparing Figures 15.5 and 15.6. At the .05 level, a difference of 3.92 points from the population mean of 100 is sufficient for rejection. At the .01 level, this difference increases to 5.16 points. Choice of the .01 level reduces the likelihood of accepting the research hypothesis.

As mentioned in Chapter 14, Section 14.9, the research hypothesis typically carries with it the key idea that the researcher seeks to affirm. Why would

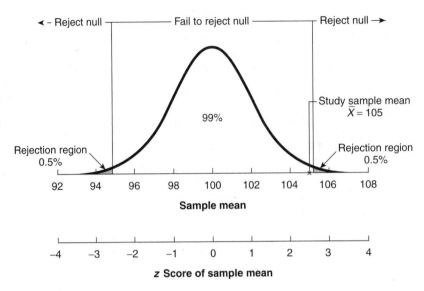

FIGURE **15.6**

STUDY SAMPLE MEAN AND REJECTION REGIONS WHEN $\alpha = .01$

The same study sample mean as in Figure 15.5 is outside the rejection regions for a two-tailed test when the significance level changes to .01.

one choose the .01 level when this lessens the likelihood of accepting the "favored" hypothesis?

15.15   TYPE I AND TYPE II ERRORS

As mentioned earlier, researchers never know for sure whether their decision regarding the null is correct. The choice of significance level, .01 or .05, bears directly on the likelihood of type I error. When a **type I error** is made, one rejects a null that is in reality true. Stated differently, one accepts a false research hypothesis.

Suppose that a research team conducts 100 statistical significance tests, in each case using the .05 significance level. Suppose also that in each case (unknown to the researchers), the null hypothesis is true. How often will they mistakenly reject this true null, that is, how often will they make a type I error? When the .05 level is chosen, 5% of sample results are located in the rejection region(s) of the sampling distribution. Hence (given a true null), the probability of obtaining a result that will lead to rejection is .05. Viewed differently, in the long run (given a true null), 5% of study sample results (.05) lead to rejection of the null at the .05 level. Thus our best guess is that, given 100 tests, our researchers will mistakenly reject the null about five times (5% of 100 tests is five). Stated differently, we expect that they will make about five type I errors.

The probability of a type I error is equal to the probability associated with the significance level, that is, to α. When $\alpha = .05$, this probability is .05; when $\alpha = .01$, it is .01. Choosing the .01 level rather than the .05 level reduces the risk of type I error by a factor of five (.05/.01 = 5 times). If the just-described experiment (100 tests, null true in each case) was repeated using the .01 level, our best guess would be that the researchers would mistakenly reject the null only once (100 × .01 = 1 time).

The cause of type I error is simply sampling error. The researchers have had the bad luck of drawing an atypical result in a tail of the sampling distribution. Of course, having drawn only a single sample result (and not having access to the full population), they have no way to know that they have done so. All that they can know is that, given a true null, the probability of a type I error—that is, the probability that the study result is due to sampling error alone—is .05 (1 in 20) if they have chosen the .05 level and .01 (1 in 100) if they have chosen the .01 level.

Rejections of the null at the .01 level are more convincing than are those at the .05 level, because the probability that the study result is due to sampling error is lower. Researchers typically choose to use the .01 level when the negative consequences of mistakenly rejecting the null are great.

For instance, suppose that in a clinical trial, a new drug designed to reduce hallucinations among clients with schizophrenia does so more effectively than a traditional drug and that the difference in effectiveness is statistically significant at the .05 level. Suppose also that the new drug is suspected of slightly increasing the risk of kidney problems. Given that the difference in effectiveness is significant at the .05 level, the likelihood that this difference is due to sampling error alone (chance alone) is .05 (1 in 20). Considering the possible side effects, a 1 in 20 likelihood may be too great. In a situation like this, one would want to virtually rule out the possibility that the study result simply reflected sampling error. In such a situation, one might well set α to .01 and by so doing reduce the risk that the difference simply reflects chance to 1 in 100. (Of course, if the risk of kidney problems was high enough, even a 1 in 100 chance might not justify a decision to use the drug.)

Although setting alpha to .01 (rather than to .05) reduces the risk of type I error, it increases the risk of type II error. A **type II error** occurs when one fails to reject (accepts) a null that is in actuality false. Stated differently, type II error is the error of rejecting a true research hypothesis. Choice of the .01 level (rather than the .05 level) increases the probability of a type II error, because the areas of the sampling distribution that result in acceptance of the research hypothesis (i.e., the rejection regions) are smaller. (To see this, compare Figures 15.5 and 15.6.) Choosing the .01 level (rather than the .05 level) makes it more difficult to accept the research hypothesis. The probability of a type II error is termed **beta** (pronounced "bait-ah"), symbolized by the Greek letter β. (This text does not present a method for calculating beta.)

The probabilities of a type I versus a type II error are in tension. Choice of the .01 level (rather than the .05 level) reduces the risk of type I error but increases that of type II error. Choice of the .05 level reduces the risk of type II error but increases that of type I error. The trick is to find the right balance between one type of error and the other.

As already mentioned, the .05 level is used most frequently, mainly due to tradition. By tradition, social science is typically willing to accept a 5% risk of reject-

TABLE 15.1	DECISION MAKING AND THE NULL AND RESEARCH HYPOTHESES	
	TRUE STATE OF AFFAIRS IN THE POPULATION	
Decision	**Null Is True**	**Null Is False**
Fail to reject (accept) the null	Correct decision	Incorrect decision; type II error
Reject the null	Incorrect decision; type I error	Correct decision

ing a true null. Occasionally, researchers use the .10 level, which increases the risk of type I error to 10%. The .001 level, used occasionally, reduces the risk of type I error to 1 in 1000 (to .001).

Decision making in hypothesis testing is probabilistic. One can never *prove* with *100%* certainty which hypothesis is correct. Table 15.1 summarizes the possible relationships between the true state of affairs in the population (unknown to the researcher) and the decisions made in hypothesis testing.

As Table 15.1 demonstrates, four scenarios are possible: (1) the null is true and the correct decision (fail to reject) is made, (2) the null is true and the incorrect decision (reject) is made, (3) the null is false and the correct decision (reject) is made, and (4) the null is false and the incorrect decision (fail to reject) is made. The researchers, of course, know the decision they have made but never know for certain that this decision is correct.[7]

15.16   TWO-TAILED VERSUS ONE-TAILED TESTS

When the hypothesis pair is directional, the significance test is one-tailed. A one-tailed test has only one rejection region, its location differing according to the direction stated in the research hypothesis. When the research hypothesis states "greater than," the rejection region is in the upper (positive) tail. When it states "less than," the rejection region is in the lower (negative) tail. As with a two-tailed test, the proportion of cases in the rejection region equals the probability associated with the chosen significance level (equals α). When the .05 level is used, this proportion is .05. When the .01 level is used, it is .01.

The parenting skills example can be repeated using a directional hypothesis pair and therefore a one-tailed test. Using the four-step hypothesis testing model, we start with step 1:

1. State the hypothesis pair.

H_0: $\mu \leq 100$ H_1: $\mu > 100$

Stated in words:

Null: The mean in the population from which the study sample was randomly selected is less than or equal to 100 points.

Research: The mean in the population from which the study sample was randomly selected is greater than 100 points.

The decision to state a directional hypothesis pair conveys that prior research, theory, common sense, or logic indicate convincingly that the expected direction is as stated in the research hypothesis. Certainly, a solid rationale for a directional hypothesis can be generated in this example. Your intervention is designed to improve parenting skills. As such, the commonsense expectation is for better parenting skills in your study sample (which has received the intervention) than in the large, representative sample (which has not). Note that the expected direction of results is stated in the research hypothesis rather than in the null.

2. Choose the significance level.

We will use the .05 significance level (set α to .05).

3. Carry out the test.

The same formula is used, resulting in same test statistic regardless of whether a one-tailed or a two-tailed test is used. The value of the obtained z was calculated earlier in the chapter. It is 2.50.

4. Make a decision.

For a one-tailed large sample test when $\alpha = .05$ and the research hypothesis specifies "greater than," the decision rule is to:

Fail to reject (accept) the null if the obtained z is less than 1.645. Reject the null if z is 1.645 or greater.

In our example, the obtained z equals 2.50: $(105 - 100)/2 = 2.50$. As 2.50 is greater than 1.645, we reject the null and therefore accept the research hypothesis. Hence, from the perspective of a one-tailed test at the .05 level ($\alpha = .05$), the study result is a statistically significant one.

In making our decision, we simply followed the steps of the hypothesis testing model. It will be helpful to see how the sampling distribution of $\overline{X}$ and its rejection region relate to this decision. These are presented in Figure 15.7. As the research hypothesis states "greater than" and $\alpha = .05$, the rejection region is the upper 5% tail of the sampling distribution. In a normal distribution, 5% of cases are located 1.645 or more standard deviations above the mean. Hence any sample mean located 1.645 or more standard deviations above the mean of the sampling distribution results in rejection of the null. In our example, the mean of the sampling distribution of $\overline{X}$ is 100 and its standard deviation is 2.00. A mean of 103.29 is 1.645 standard deviations above the mean: $100 + (1.645 \times 2.00) = 103.29$. Therefore all means greater than or equal to 103.29 result in rejection. As our mean is 105, the null is rejected.

As Figure 15.7 demonstrates, only sample means located in the upper tail of the distribution result in rejection. Compare Figure 15.7 with Figure 15.5, which presents the areas of acceptance and rejection for our example for a two-tailed test. In both figures, $\alpha = .05$. For both figures, direct your attention to the rejection regions in the *upper* tails. Notice that this region is larger for the one-tailed

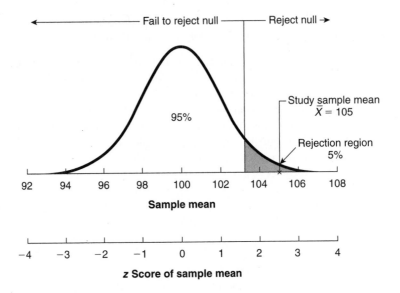

FIGURE **15.7**

STUDY SAMPLE MEAN AND REJECTION REGION FOR ONE-TAILED TEST, α = .05

When the research hypothesis states a direction (here, it states "greater than"), the significant results are in one tail only. The curve is the sampling distribution of $\overline{X}$ for parenting skills score.

test (it represents 5% of the area of the distribution) than for the two-tailed test (2.5%). Notice also that with a one-tailed test, study sample results closer to the value stated in the null result in rejection. For instance, in the current example, means greater than or equal to 103.29 result in rejection. For a two-tailed test, this value is 103.92.

This comparison of Figures 15.5 and 15.7 demonstrates an important point: Presuming that the population parameter does indeed differ in the expected direction, use of a one-tailed test (rather than a two-tailed one) increases the likelihood of rejecting the null. Simply put, it is easier to reject the null with a one-tailed test. When one's expectation of direction is solid, a one-tailed test is often the best choice. (It is not unlike having your cake and eating it too.)

Often a researcher's interest is in the probability of obtaining the particular study sample result. When a test is two-tailed, one considers cases that are as or more extreme in both directions. For the study sample mean ($\overline{X}$ = 105), this proportion is .0124, so p = .0124. For a one-tailed test, one considers only cases that are as or more extreme in the direction stated in the research hypothesis. Stated differently, (1) when the research hypothesis states less than, one considers only cases less than or equal to the study sample result, and (2) when it states greater than, one considers only cases greater than or equal to the study sample result. In the current example, the research hypothesis states "greater than." The proportion of means greater than or equal to the study sample mean is .0062, so p = .0062.

In this example, use of a one-tailed test (rather than a two-tailed one) cuts the probability of the study result in half. This is always the case when the study result is in the expected direction. Via a one-tailed test, then, our study result is viewed as an even less likely result than was the case via a two-tailed test.[8]

With a one-tailed test, sample results in the tail that is in the direction opposite to that stated in the research hypothesis do not result in rejection of the null no matter how far out in the tail they may be. Via the hypothesis testing model, such results are viewed as consistent with the null hypothesis.

Suppose, for instance, that the mean of your sample had been not 105 but 90. This result is not in the rejection region of the sampling distribution for a one-tailed test when $\alpha = .05$ (see Figure 15.7). Thus you would fail to reject (would accept) the null and conclude that the population mean was less than or equal to 100. When the sample mean is 90, the z obtained via the significance test formula is -5.00: $(90 - 100)/2.00 = -5.00$. In a normal distribution, the proportion of cases that are five or more standard deviations from the mean is less than .000001 (less than 0.0001%). Had a two-tailed test been used, you would have rejected the null (resoundingly).

Failure to reject the null in such a situation points out the potential for one-tailed tests to yield misleading results. Let's step outside the formal hypothesis testing model and interpret these findings from a broader, commonsense perspective. The basic meaning of failing to reject (accepting) the null is that sample results are consistent with the notion of "sameness" (no difference, equality, etc.). In the current example, study results provide compelling evidence that those who received your intervention have *less* effective parenting skills than do those in the large national sample. Failing to reject the null in this situation—although it is the correct decision according to the hypothesis testing model—runs contrary to the basic "there is no difference" notion that this decision conveys.

In a paradoxical situation such as this, the formal hypothesis testing model conveys a misleading message. Most researchers would probably (1) acknowledge that a directional hypothesis was used when it should not have been and (2) repeat the statistical analysis using a nondirectional hypothesis pair and therefore a two-tailed test. Such a test would reject the null. We have previously noted that nondirectional hypotheses and thus two-tailed tests are preferred in the absence of a compelling reason to expect a result in one direction. The difficulty in interpreting one-tailed tests when results are in the unexpected direction is an important reason for this preference.

15.17 MORE DECISION RULES FOR THE ONE-TAILED, LARGE SAMPLE TEST OF $\overline{X}$

The decision rule has already been given for a one-tailed, large sample test of $\overline{X}$ when the research hypothesis states "greater than" and $\alpha = .05$. When direction is the same but $\alpha = .01$ (i.e., the .01 statistical significance level is used), the decision-making rule is as follows:

Fail to reject (accept) the null if the obtained z is less than 2.33. Reject the null if the obtained z is 2.33 or greater.

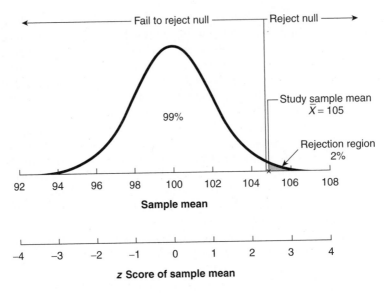

FIGURE **15.8**

STUDY SAMPLE MEAN AND REJECTION REGION FOR A ONE-TAILED TEST, α = .01

The research hypothesis states that μ will be *greater than* 100 for your population, and the .01 significance level is chosen.

In a normal distribution, 1% of cases are located 2.33 or more standard deviations above the mean (see Table A.1 in Appendix A). Returning to our study sample mean of 105, our obtained z of 2.50 is greater than 2.33. As such, our decision is to reject the null. Note that when α was set to .01 but our test was two-tailed, our decision was to accept the null (see Figure 15.6). This again demonstrates that the choice of a directional hypothesis, and therefore a one-tailed test, increases the likelihood of rejecting the null. Figure 15.8 shows the rejection region for a one-tailed test when α = .01 and the research hypothesis states "greater than." It is the upper 1% of the sampling distribution. As Figure 15.8 shows, the null is rejected for all sample means 2.33 or more standard deviations above the mean. Given that the estimated standard deviation of the sampling distribution of $\overline{X}$ is 2.00, it is rejected for all sample means greater than or equal to 104.66: $100 + 2.33(2.00) = 104.66$.

The decision rule for a one-tailed test when the research hypothesis states "less than" and α = .05 is:

Fail to reject (accept) the null if the obtained z is greater than −1.645. Reject the null if the obtained z is less than or equal to −1.645.[9]

In the situation just described, the most extreme 5% of cases in the sampling distribution's lower tail is the rejection region. In our example, all means less than or equal to 96.71 result in rejection of the null: $100 − 1.645(2.00) = 96.71$.

The decision rule for a one-tailed test when the research hypothesis states "less than" and α =.01 is:

Fail to reject (accept) the null if the obtained z is greater than -2.33. Reject the null if the obtained z is less than or equal to -2.33.

In this situation, the most extreme 1% of cases in the lower tail is the rejection region. In our example, all means less than or equal to 95.34 result in rejection: $100 - 2.33(2.00) = 95.34$.

15.18 CHAPTER SUMMARY

The hypothesis testing model's steps are: (1) state the hypothesis pair, (2) choose a statistical significance level (set alpha), (3) carry out the test, and (4) make a decision.

Assumptions are conditions that must be met for a test to yield precisely accurate probabilities. When a test is robust to an assumption, that assumption may be violated with only a minor effect on accuracy. The large sample test of $\overline{X}$ assumes normality and that σ is known. It is robust to the normality assumption. When $N \geq 100$, s may substitute for σ with minimal loss of accuracy. The nondirectional null for the large sample test states that the mean of the population from which the study sample was randomly selected equals some given value.

The null is designated as H_0 and the research hypothesis as H_1. The probabilities yielded by significance tests convey (1) given a true null, the probability of obtaining a result as extreme as or more extreme than the study sample result, and (2) the probability that chance alone could lead to a result as extreme as or more extreme than the study sample result. All tests make use of sampling distributions.

When the hypothesis pair is nondirectional, the significance test is almost always two-tailed. When it is directional, it is one-tailed. The areas of the sampling distribution that result in rejection of the null are termed rejection regions. Two-tailed tests have two such regions, one in each tail. One-tailed tests have a single rejection area located in the tail corresponding to the direction stated in the research hypothesis. The proportion of cases in the rejection region(s) is equal to the probability associated with the chosen significance level, that is, to alpha (α). The null is rejected when the probability of a study result as indicated by the significance test is less than or equal to α. One formula (15.2) for the large sample test of $\overline{X}$ is $z = (\overline{X} - \mu)/s_{\overline{X}}$.

All statistical tests have decision rules, that is, criteria by which one decides whether to accept or reject the null. The result obtained from carrying out a test's formula is termed the test statistic.

The sampling distribution of a test statistic is the distribution that would result if one selected an infinite number of random samples of a given size and for each sample calculated and recorded the test statistic. When $N \geq 100$ and given a true null, the sampling distribution of the test statistic z very closely resembles a normal distribution of z scores.

The values that determine whether one accepts or rejects the null are termed critical values. It is more difficult to reject at the .01 level than at the .05 level.

One never knows for certain whether the decision made on the hypotheses is correct. A type I error rejects a true null hypothesis. Its probability equals α. A type II error fails to reject (accepts) a false null. Its probability equals beta (β). Choice of the .01 level (rather than the .05 level) reduces the risk of type I error but increases that of type II error. Choice of the .05 level (rather than the .01 level) reduces the risk of type II error but increases that of type I error.

Presuming that the population parameter does indeed differ in the expected direction, it is easier to reject the null with a one-tailed test than with a two-tailed test. Statistical significance rules out sampling error as a likely or plausible cause but does not allow one to conclude what particular real factor is involved.

PROBLEMS AND QUESTIONS

Section 15.2

1. State the four steps of the hypothesis testing model.

Section 15.3

2. In your own words, what is a test assumption?
3. When violation of an assumption results in only a minor loss of accuracy, a statistical test is _____ to that assumption.
4. What are the two assumptions of the large sample test of $\overline{X}$?
5. Given sample size of 100 or more, the large sample test of $\overline{X}$ is _____ both to the normality assumption and to the assumption that σ is known.
6. As _____ _____ and _____ of _____ are assumed for all inferential procedures, this text makes no specific mention of these for the different tests that are presented.

Section 15.4

7. The symbols for the null and research (alternative) hypotheses are, respectively, _____ and _____.

Section 15.5

8. A null hypothesis states that the mean for a given population is 10.0 points. In a random sample of 100 cases, $s = 5.0$. Given that the null is true, provide the following for the sampling distribution of $\overline{X}$: mean, standard deviation, shape.

9. For the just-presented sampling distribution of $\overline{X}$, what is the probability of randomly selecting a sample with a mean in the following areas?
   a. Greater than or equal to 10
   b. Greater than 10.5
   c. Less than 9.5
   d. Either greater than 10.5 or less than 9.5
10. Continuing to think about the same data, presume that the mean of the researcher's sample is 10.5. In your view, is this sample result consistent with the null that $\mu = 10$? Why?
11. Answer the same questions as in problem 10 except presume that the sample mean equals 11.5.

Section 15.6

12. The probabilities resulting from statistical tests convey, given a true null, the _____ of obtaining a result as _____ as or more _____ than the study sample result.
13. The probability indicated by a given statistical test is .17. Presuming that it is the appropriate test and that assumptions are met, what percentage of cases in the sampling distribution are as extreme as or more extreme than the study sample result?

Section 15.7

14. (T or F) With a nondirectional null, one uses a(n) _____-tailed large sample test of $\overline{X}$.
15. (T or F) With a two-tailed test, only results in the upper tail result in rejection of the null.
16. When the hypothesis pair is _____, only results in the tail that is located in the direction

stated in the _____ hypothesis may result in rejection of the null.

17. The area(s) of the sampling distribution that result in rejection of the null are termed the _____ region(s).

18. When $\alpha = .05$, what proportion of cases are located in a rejection region of the sampling distribution? When $\alpha = .01$?

19. As a general rule, nondirectional hypotheses and _____-tailed statistical tests go together.

20. Given a true null, the probability of obtaining a study sample result in a rejection region is equal to _____.

21. When the study sample result is located in a rejection region, one should _____ the null and _____ the research hypothesis.

22. When the study sample result is not located in a rejection region, one should _____ to _____ (that is, _____) the null, and _____ the research hypothesis.

Sections 15.8 and 15.10

23. $H_0: \mu = 25.00$, $H_1: \mu \neq 25$; $\overline{X} = 23.4$, $s = 12.0$, $N = 144$. Based on the just-provided information, respond to the following:

   a. Is the hypothesis pair directional or nondirectional?

   b. Given a true null, what are the mean, standard deviation, and shape of the sampling distribution of $\overline{X}$?

   c. What is the z score of the study sample mean in the sampling distribution of $\overline{X}$?

   d. Given a true null, what is the probability of obtaining a mean as low as or lower than the study sample mean?

   e. Given a true null, what is the probability of obtaining a sample that differs in *either* direction from the condition stated in the null by as much as does the study sample mean or by even more than this?

   f. Is the appropriate statistical test one-tailed or two-tailed?

   g. From the perspective of a two-tailed test, what is the probability of obtaining the study sample result or an even more extreme result, given a true null?

   h. Given that $\alpha = .05$, is the probability resulting from the statistical test greater than or less than α?

   i. Given that $\alpha = .05$, what proportion of cases are located in the rejection area in each of the tails of the sampling distribution?

   j. Is the study sample mean located in a rejection area?

   k. The appropriate decisions are to _____ the null and to _____ the research hypothesis.

   l. What is the probability that the study sample result is due to chance alone? (Consider both tails of the sampling distribution.)

24. For a two-tailed large sample test of $\overline{X}$ when $\alpha = .05$, what is the decision rule?

Section 15.11

25. The result that is obtained from calculation of a test formula is termed the _____ _____.

26. (T or F) Test statistics have sampling distributions.

27. Presuming that sample size is ≥ 100 and given a true null, indicate the mean, standard deviation, and shape of the sampling distribution of the test statistic z as calculated via formula 15.1 or 15.2.

28. The values of a test statistic that define the boundaries of the rejection regions are termed the _____ values.

Sections 15.12 and 15.13

29. When a result is statistically significant, one may conclude that something other than _____ _____ is the likely explanation for the study sample result.

30. (T or F) Even when chance is a plausible explanation for the study result, the text advises one to seriously consider what *real* factors are the likely cause of that result.

Section 15.14

31. (T or F) Choice of significance level never has an effect on the decision regarding the null.

32. (T or F) Other things being equal, it is more difficult to reject at the .01 level than at the .05 level.

33. H_0: $\mu = 50.00$, H_1: $\mu \neq 50$; $\overline{X} = 61.0$, $s = 50$, $N = 100$. Respond to the following:
   a. The appropriate statistical test is _____ -tailed.
   b. The obtained z is _____.
   c. Given that the .05 level is selected ($\alpha = .05$), what decision is reached regarding the null?
   d. Had the .01 level been selected ($\alpha = .01$), what decision would have been reached regarding the null?
   e. (T or F) From the perspective of a two-tailed test, the probability of obtaining the study sample result or an even more extreme result is greater than .01.

34. Given the same significance level (α) and other things being equal, if one considers *only* the half of the sampling distribution of $\overline{X}$ that is in the direction stated in the research hypothesis (the upper half when "greater than" is stated; the lower half when "less than" is stated), then ...
   a. (T or F) The rejection region is larger for a one-tailed test than for a two-tailed test.
   b. (T or F) The value that defines the rejection region is closer to the value stated in the null for a one-tailed test than for a two-tailed test.

Section 15.15

35. When a(n) _____ _____ error is made the researcher rejects a null that is in reality true. Stated differently, the researcher accepts a(n) _____ research hypothesis.
36. When the null is true, the probability of a type I error equals _____.
37. In reality (and unknown to the researcher) a given null is true. The researcher conducts 1000 statistical tests with α set to .01. What is the best estimate of the number of type I errors that will occur?
38. (T or F) Rejections at the .05 level are more convincing than are those at the .01 level.
39. (T or F) Setting α to .01 (rather than to .05) reduces the risk of type I error.
40. When a type II error is made, one accepts a(n) _____ that is in reality _____.

41. The probability of a type II error is termed _____ and is symbolized by _____.
42. (T or F) In any given situation, the higher the risk of type I error the lower the risk of type II error.
43. (T or F) In hypothesis testing, one can never prove with 100% certainty which hypothesis is correct.

Sections 15.16 and 15.17

44. (T or F) When the null hypothesis states "greater than," the rejection region is in the upper (positive) tail.
45. What is the decision-making rule for a one-tailed large sample test of $\overline{X}$ when the research hypothesis states "greater than" and $\alpha = .05$?
46. What proportion of cases in a normal distribution have z scores greater than 1.645?
47. H_0: $\mu \leq 50.0$, H_1: $\mu > 50.0$; $\overline{X} = 58.5$, $s = 50.0$, $N = 100$. Respond to the following:
   a. Is the hypothesis pair directional or non-directional?
   b. Is the appropriate test one-tailed or two-tailed?
   c. Is the study result in the expected direction?
   d. Calculate z.
   e. What proportion of cases in the sampling distribution of $\overline{X}$ have means greater than or equal to the study sample mean?
   f. From the perspective of a one-tailed test and given a true null, what is the probability of obtaining the study sample result or an even more extreme result?
   g. Presume that α is set to .05. What decision should be made regarding the null? Regarding the research hypothesis?
   h. Had the .01 significance level been selected instead, what would the just-mentioned decisions have been? (The test is still one-tailed.)
   i. Presume that the hypothesis pair is nondirectional (H_0: $\mu = 50.00$, H_1: $\mu \neq 50$) and that $\alpha = .05$. What would the just-mentioned decisions have been?
48. H_0: $\mu \leq 50.0$, H_1: $\mu > 50.0$; $\overline{X} = 35.0$, $s = 50.0$, $N = 100$. Respond to the following:

a. Calculate the test statistic z.

b. Given that $H_0 = 50$, about what proportion of samples in the sampling distribution of $\overline{X}$ have a mean less than or equal to the mean of the study sample?

c. About what proportion of cases in the sampling distribution of $\overline{X}$ differ in either direction from the value stated in the null (50) by as much as or more than does the study sample mean?

d. Is a one-tailed or a two-tailed test indicated?

e. What tail (upper or lower) is the rejection region located in?

f. Is the study sample result in the expected direction or in the unexpected direction?

g. Given that $\alpha = .05$ (and note the one-tailed test): via the hypothesis testing model, what decision is reached regarding the null?

h. In your own words, why is the decision to fail to reject the null in this situation a misleading one?

 ## COMPUTER EXERCISE

For general instructions on computer exercises, see the note in Chapter 2.

1. The mean FACES cohesion score (FCOH) in a large representative sample was 39.8. (Results were given to only one decimal place, so consider this mean to be 39.80.) Using data supplied by the SPSS Descriptives procedure, carry out a large sample test of $\overline{X}$ to test the null that the mean cohesion score equals this value. Use the .05 significance level and a two-tailed test. [In SPSS, *Analyze > Descriptive Statistics > Descriptives*, click over FCOH, *Options*, if they are not already checked click the boxes next to "Mean" and "Std. Error" to highlight them (and click any checked boxes for statistics that you do not want so as to uncheck them), *Continue, OK.*]

Check your answers: The mean FCOH score is 40.26 and the estimated standard error of

the mean is 0.20. Thus $z \approx (40.26 - 39.80)/0.20 \approx 2.30$. The decision rule for a two-tailed large sample test of $\overline{X}$ at the .05 level calls for rejection when the absolute value of the obtained z is ≥ 1.96, so the null is rejected. (An easier way to carry out a highly similar test is to use the one-sample t test as presented in Chapter 17. In SPSS: *Analyze > Compare Means > One-Sample T Test.*)

NOTES

1. Most statistics texts recommend that the large sample test of $\overline{X}$ should be used only when sigma (σ) is known. As one hardly ever has such knowledge, examples of the large sample test are often artificial. See Toothaker and Miller (1996, pp. 314–318) or almost any introductory text for an example of how the large sample test of $\overline{X}$ is implemented in those occasional instances when σ is known. As Chapter 17 demonstrates, in actual research situations, the one-sample t test is almost always preferred to the large sample test.

2. The large sample test of $\overline{X}$ typically yields quite accurate results with samples as small as about 20. The primary reason for not using it with samples smaller than 100 is that another statistical test, the one-sample t test presented in Chapter 17, is preferred in these circumstances.

3. In some random sampling procedures, the chance of selection for each case is not equal but is known. So long as the chance of selection is known, skilled statisticians can adjust for any bias introduced by unequal probabilities of selection. (See note 2 in Chapter 12.)

4. The general formula for z score in a population (formula 12.1) is $z = (X - \mu)/\sigma$. This formula involves division by the standard deviation of the population, σ. In contrast, the z score of a sample mean in the sampling distribution of $\overline{X}$ in our example is calculated by dividing by an (extremely accurate) *estimate* of the standard deviation, $s/\sqrt{N}$, rather than by the precise standard deviation, $\sigma/\sqrt{N}$. As such, the z scores presented in Figure 15.1 (and subsequent figures) should be viewed as extremely accurate estimates of z scores rather than as precise z scores. When $N \geq 100$, the degree of inaccuracy introduced by this estimation has little pragmatic impact.

5. Because the standard deviation of the sampling distribution is estimated (with very high accuracy) rather

than known, the range within which 95% of cases are located is very close to but not exactly equal to 96.08 to 103.92. Given that $N \geq 100$, the degree of inaccuracy is extremely small.

6. The general formula for the z score in a population is $z = (X - \mu)/\sigma$. The standard deviation of the sampling distribution of $\overline{X}$ is $\sigma_{\overline{x}} = \sigma/\sqrt{N}$. Hence the following formulas would precisely calculate a z score with respect to the sampling distribution of $\overline{X}$: $z = (\overline{X} - \mu)/(\sigma/\sqrt{N})$ and $z = (\overline{X} - \mu)/\sigma_{\overline{x}}$. As already mentioned, in almost all real-world research situations, σ is unknown, so these formulas cannot be calculated.

7. Given a true null, the probability of making the correct decision (accept the null) equals $1 - \alpha$. Thus, when $\alpha = .05$, this probability is .95 $(1 - .05 = .95)$. Given a false null, the probability of a correct decision equals $1 - \beta$ (β is the probability of accepting a false

null). Further discussion of these issues is found in Chapter 16.

8. Very occasionally for a one-tailed test, the study result is in the direction opposite to that stated in the research hypothesis. In this situation, (1) when the research hypothesis states "greater than," the probability of the study result, p, equals the proportion of cases with greater or equal values, and (2) when it states "less than," p equals the proportion with lesser or equal values. For instance, suppose that in the current example (in which the research hypothesis states "greater than") the study sample mean had been 98.0. The proportion of means in the sampling distribution greater than or equal to 98.0 is .8413. Hence the probability of this result is .8413 $(p = .8413)$.

9. Do not misinterpret the meaning of "less than -1.645." For instance, -1.50 is *greater* than -1.645; -3.00 is *less* than -1.645.

CHAPTER 16

STATISTICAL POWER AND SELECTED TOPICS

16.1 CHAPTER OVERVIEW

The more *statistical power* that a significance test can give us, the more likely we are to find an association if one does exist. We discuss statistical power in depth, in particular focusing on how sample size affects power. Next, we consider five other factors that influence power and guidelines for approximating power. We also discuss three topics related to significance: (1) the use of statistical tests when one's study sample has not been randomly selected, (2) guidelines for communicating about associations and significance, and (3) common misinterpretations of statistical significance.

16.2 STATISTICAL POWER

As presented in Chapter 15, the error of failing to reject a false null is termed a type II error and its probability equals beta (β). Closely related to beta is the concept of power. The **power (statistical power)** of a statistical test is the probability that it will reject a false null. Stated differently, power is the probability that the test will accept a true research hypothesis.

Power and beta are opposites. Given a false null, beta is the probability of making an incorrect decision (failing to reject the null) and power is the probability of making a correct one (rejecting it). Power and beta sum to 1.00, logically enough. Given a false null, only two events are possible, a correct decision (reject) or an incorrect one (fail to reject). These being the only events, their probabilities must sum to 1.00. For instance, when power equals .7, beta equals .3: .7 + .3 = 1.00. Given that beta (β) and power sum to 1.00:

$$\text{Power} = 1 - \beta \qquad (16.1)$$

$$\beta = 1 - \text{Power} \qquad (16.2)$$

These two equations reveal that (given a false null), the greater the power, the lower the probability of a type II error.

In most situations, researchers seek to learn something new. Typically, that something is conveyed by the research hypothesis. What researchers want, then, is to conduct a significance test that has a good chance of rejecting the null if it is false. Stated differently, they want their test to have good power. Power is a good thing. Given a true research hypothesis, the higher the power, the higher the probability of a correct decision, and thus the greater the likelihood that study results will reveal the "something new" that the researchers seek to find.

16.3   SAMPLE SIZE AND POWER

Though many factors influence power, sample size is the most important by far. When sample size is low, power is typically low. Conversely, when it is large, power is typically high. Before we use numerical examples, let's discuss further the influence of sample size.

When the null is true (which is unknown to the researcher), sampling error alone can cause the study sample result to differ from the condition stated in the null. When the research hypothesis is true (again, unknown), both sampling error and real factors can cause this difference. The statistical test seeks to determine whether the study result reflects only sampling error or whether real factors are also involved.

Though we never know the precise amount of sampling error, we do know that as sample size increases, sampling error tends to decrease. When sample size is small, a great deal of sampling error is likely to be present. Small sample size makes the job of the statistical test difficult. When sample size is small, the potential amount of sampling error can be so large that the test cannot do a good job of determining whether real factors are also involved. In this situation, the large effects of sampling error can overwhelm and obscure those of real factors.

An analogy can convey the problem. Suppose that you are driving across Oklahoma—the heart of "tornado alley"—straining to hear a faint radio signal. Unfortunately, the static in the background is so strong that you cannot be sure of what the announcer is saying. You think he is saying that a tornado (something quite real) has been spotted in the ominous clouds that you see ahead. As in your attempt to hear the radio signal's message, researchers tune in to the message of their study sample result. If this message is obscured by "static" and "background noise," that is, by sampling error, they may never discern the true situation. They may mistakenly conclude that the null hypothesis is true (no tornado) when in reality the research hypothesis is true (find shelter). In sum, when sample size is small, the real effect that one hopes to find can easily become "lost" in the sampling error. In such a situation, the probability of an incorrect decision (type II error) is high and power is low.

16.4   SOME EXAMPLES OF HOW SAMPLE SIZE AFFECTS POWER

Let's examine the influence of sample size by using the parenting skills example presented in the prior chapter. In this example, the nondirectional hypothesis pair was as follows:

Null: The population mean is 100 points.
Research: The population mean is not 100 points.

As the pair is nondirectional, we will use a two-tailed large sample test. We will set alpha (α) to .05 (use the .05 level). For learning purposes, we will carry out the study three times, each time with a different sample size: 100, 400, and 1600. Presume that in each study the standard deviation of the sample is 20 points. Given sample size of at least 100, the standard deviation in the sample (s) provides an excellent estimate of that in the population (σ). For all three studies, presume that the study sample mean is 97 points.

Figure 16.1 presents (assuming a true null) the sampling distribution of the mean for the three studies.[1] As demonstrated in Chapters 12 and 13, as sample size increases, the standard deviation of the sampling distribution decreases. Stated differently, as sample size increases, sample means cluster closer to 100. For each sample size, Figure 16.1 presents the rejection regions (the areas that result in rejection of the null). As sample size increases, sample means closer to the value stated in the null ($\mu = 100$) lead to its rejection. For instance, when sample size equals 100, the null is rejected when means differ by about four points or more. When it is 400, this difference is about two points. When it is 1600, it is about one point.

Figure 16.1 also presents the location of the study sample mean ($\overline{X} = 97$) with respect to each sampling distribution. When sample size is 100, the study sample mean is not located in a rejection region, so we fail to reject the null. For both of the larger samples, it is in a rejection region, so we reject the null.

Figure 16.1 illustrates a basic effect of sample size: Other things being equal, as sample size increases, increasingly smaller differences result in rejection. Given that a null hypothesis is indeed false, as sample size increases, it becomes increasingly easier to reject that null.

Having carried out the large sample test of $\overline{X}$ informally via the sampling distribution of $\overline{X}$, let's now do so via its formula (formula 15.1). When sample size is 100:

$$z \approx \frac{97 - 100}{\left(\dfrac{20}{\sqrt{100}}\right)} = \frac{97 - 100}{\left(\dfrac{20}{10}\right)} = \frac{-3}{2} = -1.50$$

When it is 400:

$$z \approx \frac{97 - 100}{\left(\dfrac{20}{\sqrt{400}}\right)} = \frac{97 - 100}{\left(\dfrac{20}{20}\right)} = \frac{-3}{1} = -3.00$$

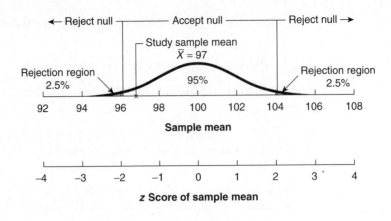

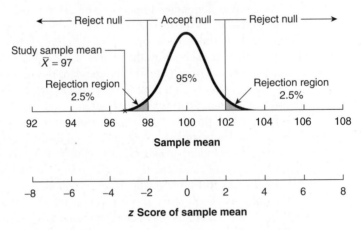

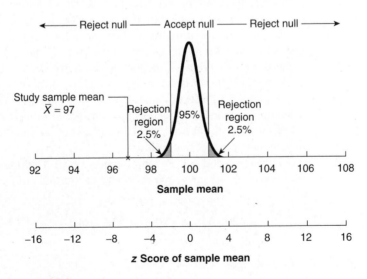

FIGURE **16.1**

INCREASED POWER WITH LARGER SAMPLE SIZES

The three curves represent the sampling distribution of $\overline{X}$ for three different sample sizes: $N = 100$ (top), 400 (middle), 1600 (bottom). All three rejection regions are for a two-tailed test, $\alpha = .05$.

When it is 1600:

$$z \approx \frac{97 - 100}{\left(\dfrac{20}{\sqrt{1600}}\right)} = \frac{97 - 100}{\left(\dfrac{20}{40}\right)} = \frac{-3}{.5} = -6.00$$

The decision-making rule for a two-tailed large sample test when $\alpha = .05$ is to reject the null if the absolute value of the obtained z is greater than or equal to 1.96. Hence the null is rejected when sample size is 400 and 1600 but is accepted when it is 100. (Thus, as must be the case, results obtained via the formula confirm those obtained earlier via the sampling distribution.)

As sample size increases (other things being equal), so does power. In our example, power—the opportunity to reject a false null—increased as sample size increased from 100 to 400 to 1600. Yet, for each of these sample sizes, power was at least adequate. Even when sample size equaled 100, a difference of only about four points was sufficient for rejection. In each situation, then, given a false null, we had a fairly good opportunity for reaching the correct decision.

When sample size is very small, very large differences are typically required to reject the null. The size of the required difference can be so large that the statistical test does not have a realistic opportunity to do so. To make this point, we need to ignore the recommendation in the prior chapter (Section 15.3) that the large sample test of $\overline{X}$ should be carried out only when sample size is 100 or greater. Let's conduct a large sample test with a sample size of nine. We keep all other facts the same: same hypothesis pair, same standard deviation in the population (20 points), two-tailed test, $\alpha = .05$, and, finally, $\overline{X} = 97$.

Figure 16.2 presents the sampling distribution of $\overline{X}$. As you interpret Figure 16.2, block from your mind that we have violated a condition for carrying out the test. For the sake of discussion, presume that Figure 16.2 accurately portrays the sampling distribution, so that test results are also accurate.[2] The mean of the sampling distribution in Figure 16.2 is 100. Its standard deviation equals $20/\sqrt{9} = 20/3 = 6.67$. Notice that a very large difference from the condition stated in the null ($\mu = 100$) is needed for it to be rejected. For instance, the study sample mean of 97 is nowhere near either rejection region. Even a mean of, for instance, 112 is not sufficient for rejection. Indeed, a sample mean either greater than or equal to 113.07 or less than or equal to 86.93 is required to reject the null: $100 \pm (1.96 \times 6.67) = 86.93$ to 113.07.

In Figure 16.2 power is low. As the wide span of the sampling distribution conveys, when sample size is small, sampling error alone can be responsible for extremely large differences. In such a situation, the effect (if any) of real factors can be buried somewhere beneath the presumed large effects of sampling error. In such a situation, the statistical test cannot effectively unscramble real differences from sampling error.

In sum, when sample size is small, statistical power is almost always low and the risk of type II error is, therefore, almost always high. In such circumstances, the researcher typically does not have a fair and realistic opportunity to reject the null. Low power, primarily due to inadequate sample size, is a fairly common problem in human services research.

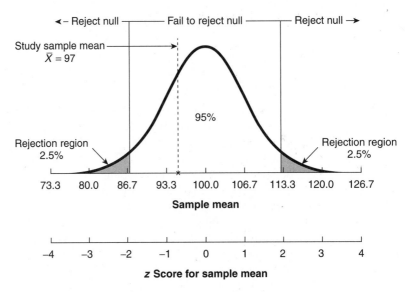

FIGURE 16.2

EFFECT ON POWER OF VERY SMALL SAMPLE SIZE

Rejection regions are far from the mean of the sampling distribution of $\overline{X}$ when $N = 9$. Except for sample size and the scale of the art, all other facts are as for the three curves in Figure 16.1 (including two-tailed test, $\alpha = .05$).

Let's look at a hypothetical example to illustrate the effects of small sample size. For instance, suppose that the human services agency where you work designs an experiment to test the effectiveness of a program to prevent out-of-home placement of children. Ten families are randomly assigned to the new family preservation unit and ten to traditional, ongoing services. One year later, you discover that only 3 of 10 children (30%) in the new program but 7 of 10 (70%) in the traditional program required out-of-home placement. Enthusiastic about the apparent success of the new program, you conduct the appropriate statistical test for determining whether the difference in percentages between the programs, 40% (70% − 30% = 40%) is statistically significant. (This test is the chi-square test of independence, presented in Chapter 20.) The test indicates that the probability that this difference is due to chance is .13. As this probability ($p = .13$) is greater than that associated with your chosen significance level (presume that you had chosen the .05 level), you fail to reject the null.

The problem here is low statistical power. The small sample size makes it exceedingly difficult to reject the null. This example illustrates why *fail to reject the null* better expresses your decision than does *accept the null*. In accepting the null you do not conclude that it is likely that the null is true but only that it provides a plausible explanation. In this example, the statistical test doesn't have sufficient power to examine effectively whether sampling error or a real difference is at work. In a situation like this, the logic of science favors the simplest explanation (sampling error) and so the null is "accepted."

Though discouraged by the results of the initial statistical test, your agency continues the experiment for a second year. At the end of the second year, only 6 of 20 children (30%) in the new program in contrast to 14 of 20 (70%) of children in the traditional program require placement. In this example, the difference in percentages ($D\% = 70\% - 30\% = 40\%$) continues to be the same but sample size has increased. (Presume that you continue to use the .05 level.) This time, the statistical test results indicate that $p = .009$ (that the probability of the study sample result is .009). As .009 is less than .05, this result is statistically significant at the .05 level, so the null is rejected.[3] This demonstrates that, as sample size increases, so does one's opportunity to reject the null.

When sample size is small, even large associations (large differences) are often not statistically significant. Conversely, when sample size is very large, even small associations are often significant. For instance, the research on special-needs adoption found a negative correlation of −.10 between the parent's report of the adopted child's enjoyment of school and the family's income (Rosenthal and Groze, 1992). Thus, the higher the family income, the lower the child's reported enjoyment of school. Although this correlation indicated only a weak association, it was statistically significant at the .01 level using a two-tailed test of Pearson's r. (This test tests the null that the population correlation is 0.00. It is presented in Chapter 22, Section 22.2.) How could such a weak correlation be statistically significant?

A statistically significant difference is one that is not likely to be due solely to sampling error. When sample size is very large, there is very little sampling error. Because sampling error is minimal, one can be confident that the sample result is very similar to the actual population condition. In the current example, the study sample size was indeed quite large ($N = 599$). As such, there was little sampling error. This made the significance test's job an easy one. Even though the difference between the sample statistic ($-.10$) and the hypothesized population parameter (0.00) was small, the statistical significance test could discern that this difference was unlikely to be due to sampling error (the effects of sampling error were minimal due to the large sample size).

One more example can reinforce your understanding of how large sample size enhances power. One of my statistics teachers informed my class that in a given academic achievement test for high school students, female students outscored males by an extremely small margin. As I recall, the mean score of female students was about one-fortieth of a standard deviation higher ($SDM = .025$), an amount eight times smaller than this text's categorization of a small association or difference ($SDM = .20$; see Table 9.1). This difference was statistically significant (at, I believe, the .01 level). How could such a tiny difference be statistically significant? My professor went on to say that the test had been given to tens of thousands of students across the prior decade and that results had been aggregated to form one huge study sample of more than 100,000. Due to the huge sample size, sampling error was reduced to almost nothing. As such, even the tiniest difference could be discriminated from sampling error and thus was sufficient for rejecting the null.

The statistical power in the just-described study was exceedingly high, close to 1.00. In practical terms, a difference of one-fortieth of a standard deviation has no real-world import.

In sum, with large samples one typically has an excellent opportunity to reject the null. Even small differences are usually sufficient to do so. In other words, with large sample size, one ordinarily has excellent statistical power.

A common mistake that students make is to merge size of association and statistical significance together into one concept. These two concepts are separate and distinct and it is important to grasp this. Size of association refers to the degree to which two variables vary together. Statistical significance (or lack thereof) pertains to the probability that a relationship or difference is due to chance. Don't make the mistake of assuming that because an association is statistically significant it must, necessarily, be a large association. The just-presented academic test example demonstrates that this is not always the case. Similarly, don't make the mistake of assuming that because an association is large, it necessarily is statistically significant. The example on placement prevention demonstrates the fallacy of this assumption. In sum, when a relationship is statistically significant, simply say to yourself, "It is not likely to be due to chance."

16.5   OTHER FACTORS THAT INFLUENCE POWER

16.5.1   Overview

Power is the ability of a statistical test to detect a false null. Sample size is the single factor that most influences power. Other factors include (1) the choice of significance level, (2) whether one's hypothesis pair is directional or nondirectional, (3) the anticipated size of association or difference, (4) the amount of variability, and (5) the particular statistical test that is used.

16.5.2   Significance Level

The probability of a type II error, beta, is lower when the .05 level is used than when the .01 level is used, because the rejection areas of the sampling distribution are larger. Hence the choice of the .05 level rather than the .01 level (other things being equal) increases power. To see this, compare Figures 15.5 and 15.6. The choice of the .10 level increases power still more.

16.5.3   Directional Hypotheses and One-Tailed Tests

When theory, research, common sense, or logic indicates that the population parameter differs in a particular direction from the value stated in the null, power is increased by use of a directional hypothesis pair, which calls for a one-tailed test. With a one-tailed test (presuming that results are in the expected direction), results closer to the value stated in the null lead to rejection. To see this point, compare Figures 15.5 and 15.7, focusing on the upper halves of the sampling distributions. When the one-tailed test is used, a difference of 3.29 points (a score of 103.29 or greater) results in rejection. When the test is two-tailed, this difference is 3.92 points (103.92 or greater). In sum, when the population parameter is indeed in the expected direction, a directional hypothesis (one-tailed test) increases the likelihood of rejecting the null, that is, it increases power.[4]

16.5.4   Expected Size of Association or Difference

Power is enhanced when one expects a large association or difference rather than a smaller one. For instance, suppose that you compare student anxiety levels about one month into the semester (a time when things are sailing along smoothly for most) with those toward the end (as exams come up and papers are due). Your expectation would be for anxiety to be a *great deal* higher near the semester's end.

As you know, the null typically states "no difference." Hence your expectation is for the study sample result (large difference) to differ greatly from the condition stated in the null (no difference). Given that the expected difference from the condition stated in the null is large, even a substantial amount of sampling error may not be sufficient to obscure it. The expectation of a larger difference thus increases the opportunity to reject the null. Stated differently, it enhances power.

When one expects a very large association or difference, small or moderate sample size is generally sufficient for good power. On the other hand, the expectation of a small difference reduces power. When one expects a small association or difference, very large sample size is generally required for good power.

16.5.5   Variability

Variability has an interesting relationship to statistical power. On the one hand, one can have so much variability that power is reduced. This occurs when excessive variability is caused by variables that are extraneous to the relationship of interest. Suppose, for instance, that one studies which of two therapy approaches is more effective at reducing depression among clients using outpatient mental health services. In addition to type of approach, many other factors influence depression. These might include age, gender, relationship with partner, living situation, stress, success at work, economic well-being, support systems, family connections, social skills, amount of exercise, diet, medication, sleep habits, health, exposure to toxic substances, religiosity, exposure to discrimination, degree of repressed anger, and events of the particular day. Saying that all these factors influence depression is the same as saying that they all cause variability in depression. The greater the variability introduced by variables extraneous to the variable of interest, the more difficult it becomes to detect the influence of that variable. In sum, the greater the variability due to extraneous factors, the lower the statistical power.[5]

More common and more serious than the problem of excessive variability is that of inadequate variability. When variability is very low, power is almost always quite limited. Let's use an example from the field of pregnancy prevention. Suppose that 100 unmarried teens are randomly assigned to Program A and 100 to Program B. Now let's propose two different hypothetical sets of results for the total sample, that is, for all 200 participants. Result 1: among all participants, 8 become pregnant within the study's follow-up time and 192 do not. Result 2: 80 become pregnant and 120 do not.

Which set of results is preferred? Given that the goal of both programs is pregnancy prevention, the preferred outcome is Result 1. But from the perspective of statistical power, Result 2 is preferred. The "problem" with Result 1 is that it is next to impossible to determine which Program, A or B, is more effective. Even if results favor one program—presume that six participants (6%) in A but only two (2%) in B became pregnant—the number of pregnancies is too low for meaningful comparison. Viewed differently, there is insufficient variability (in each program, almost all did not become pregnant) to conduct a meaningful statistical significance test. The power of the test will be so low that there is almost no possibility of rejecting the null.

Using the chi-square test of independence (covered in Chapter 20), the probability that the just-described difference (6% in one group versus 2% in the other) is due to sampling error alone is .149.[6] Hence we fail to reject (accept) the null. We conclude that the two programs are equally effective in terms of pregnancy prevention.

Let's supply some numbers and percentages for Result 2. Let's say that 50 participants (50%) became pregnant in A in comparison to only 30 (30%) in B. Each group, then, has a considerable variability in outcomes. Stated differently, in each group a sizable percentage of participants become pregnant and a sizable percentage do not. The situation is the opposite of that in Result 1 when almost all participants experienced the same outcome (not becoming pregnant). This greater amount of variability in Result 2 makes the job of the statistical test easier. It increases statistical power. The probability that the just-mentioned difference (50% versus 30%) is due to chance alone is .004 (computed via the chi-square test of independence). Hence the null that the two programs are equally effective in preventing pregnancy would be rejected at the .01 level. (This presumes that the .01 level was selected.)

The just-presented example demonstrates how low variability in the dependent variable (Result 1) can reduce power and, conversely, how high variability (Result 2) can enhance it. These same points apply to the independent variable as well. For instance, suppose that you are interested in the association between the independent variable of minority or majority status (minority ethnicity versus white) and employment status (obtained a human services job versus did not) among recent graduates of your educational program. Presume that the graduating class consists of 93 (93%) white students but only 7 (7%) minority students. Due to the limited variability of minority/majority status, a statistical test of its association to employment status will have very low power. Only an extremely large difference between the percentages of white and minority students who obtain employment will lead to rejection of the null. More equal numbers of minority and majority students—that is, greater variability in minority/majority status—would increase power.

In sum, although excessive variability introduced by extraneous factors reduces statistical power, the more central point is that one usually wants reasonably high variability in both the independent and dependent variables. When the variability of either is very low, power is reduced.

16.5.6   Choice of Statistical Significance Test

Some statistical tests have greater power than do others. In general, the higher the level of measurement required by the test, the greater its power. For instance (other things being equal), statistical tests that require interval-level measurement most often have greater power than do those that require ordinal-level measurement. The practical implication is that one should strive for the highest possible level of measurement. By so doing, one can use a more powerful test, and increase the likelihood of rejecting the null. Chapter 22 (Section 22.4) discusses the distinction between parametric and nonparametric tests. As a general rule, parametric tests have somewhat greater power than do nonparametric ones.

16.6   How Much Power Is Enough?

By tradition, scientists have reached a rough consensus that power of about .80 or above may be regarded as good. Thus power below about .80 is viewed as less than adequate, or as poor. When power is .80, the statistical significance test has an 80% chance of rejecting a false null. In this situation, beta (the probability of failing to reject a false null) is .20. This is the probability of a type II error. Just as .80 is the traditionally accepted standard for power, the .05 statistical significance level is the "traditional" significance level. At the .05 level, the risk of a type I error—rejecting a true null—is .05. The traditions of science thus accept a risk of type II error that is four times higher than that for type I error (.20/.05 = 4 times). This reflects the conservative bias of science in favor of the null. The error of rejecting a true null is regarded as a more costly mistake than is that of failing to accept (rejecting) a true research hypothesis.

Note the use of *fail to accept* in regard to the research hypothesis. When statistical power is low, this phrase better describes the researcher's decision than does *reject*. It captures the reality that, with inadequate statistical power, one does not have a realistic opportunity to accept the research hypothesis.

16.7   How Large Should Sample Size Be?

A frequently asked question is, "How large should my sample be?" When statistical significance testing will be conducted, this question translates to "How large should my sample be to have good statistical power?" As power is influenced by many factors besides sample size, this question is exceedingly difficult to answer. The complete and best answer is provided in Cohen's classic *Statistical Power Analysis for the Behavioral Sciences* (1988). It estimates power at various sample sizes, also taking into account the other factors that have been discussed here. Several software programs are available for estimating power.

Keeping in mind that it is an oversimplification, you can use Table 16.1 as a rough guide that relates sample size and power. As you interpret Table 16.1,

TABLE 16.1	A ROUGH GUIDE: SAMPLE SIZE AND STATISTICAL POWER	
Study Sample Size	Rough Estimate of Likely Statistical Power	Comments
Less than 50	Poor/low	Only very large associations or differences are likely to result in rejection of the null
51 to 200	Fair/moderate	Good opportunity for rejecting null for large associations or differences but less opportunity in other situations
201 to 500	Good/fairly high	Good opportunity for rejecting the null in most situations; power may not be sufficient to reject the null for small associations or differences
501 to 2000	Excellent/ very high	Excellent opportunity to reject null in most situations; good opportunity to do so even when associations or differences are small
2001 or more	Exceptional/ extremely high	Excellent opportunity to reject null even when associations or differences are small; even trivial (extremely small) differences may result in rejection

consider factors besides sample size that affect power. For instance, when variability is very low, power is likely to be less than Table 16.1 suggests. When you expect a very large difference, power will likely be greater. Similarly, the use of a directional hypothesis (and thus a one-tailed test) may well increase power. In Table 16.1, "Study Sample Size" refers to the total number of people in one's study sample rather than to the number in a specific group. When the numbers in each group differ greatly—say when 90% are in one group versus 10% in another—power will ordinarily be less than is suggested by Table 16.1.

16.8   "IMAGINARY" AND REAL POPULATIONS

A basic premise of our discussion of inferential statistical procedures has been that these are valid only when the study sample has been randomly selected from a wider population. The reality of social science research is that inferential statistical procedures are often used when this is not the case. This is true both for confidence intervals and statistical significance tests but applies more to significance tests, so let's focus on those.

Our working example for the large sample test of $\overline{X}$ (in Chapter 15) proposed that you administered a parenting skills intervention to a random sample of parents selected from a large population of elementary school parents in a given town. As such, this example was in accord with the premise that the study sample should be randomly selected from a larger population. Suppose we restructure the sampling methodology for this study and state that the 100 parents who participated were selected in some other manner. Let's say, for instance, that they represent the entire population of parents who responded to an announcement about your program in the local paper. Hence those in your study sample don't represent any wider group. When the sample is not randomly selected from any larger population, what purpose, if any, is served by conducting a significance test? Indeed, should statistical tests even be conducted?

Researchers disagree on the answer to these questions and we can't resolve that disagreement here. A fairly substantial minority of researchers take the strict stance that significance testing should only be conducted when the study sample is a random sample from a larger population.[7] A majority believe that significance tests serve a useful purpose even when there is no larger population.

The most important application of statistical significance tests is to determine whether an association (or difference) in one's study sample is due simply to chance or instead reflects real differences. The majority of researchers hold this question to be both relevant and meaningful even when the study sample has not been selected randomly. For instance, suppose that you are a mental health professional at a center that serves those with serious mental illness. Perhaps you notice that clients served by Unit A, which has a vigorous community outreach program, seem less likely to require psychiatric hospitalization than do those served by Unit B. You compare unit logs of clients served in the past year and your hunch is borne out. You find that only 20 of 100 clients in Unit A versus 50 of 100 in Unit B required hospitalization. Presume that these 200 clients were not selected from any wider population, but instead represent the full population of clients served by these units in the year. Outcomes for Unit A seem superior but you don't want to conclude that this is the case if the difference may be due just to chance. To find this out, you need to conduct a significance test. (The appropriate test is the chi-square test of independence, presented in Chapter 20.)

A minority of researchers would take the position that you should not conduct a significance test. They would do so because (1) there is no wider population to which statistical inferences can be made and (2) the concept of sampling error makes no sense when everyone in the population is included in the study.

The majority would recommend that you should go ahead and conduct a significance test. Yet significance tests assume random sampling from a wider population. Thus, in recommending a significance test, they are also recommending that you assume random sampling (even though there has been no such sampling). Their logic follows roughly this sequence:

1. It is important to determine whether chance alone is a plausible cause of the association.
2. To determine this, I must conduct a significance test.
3. Significance tests assume random sampling from a wider population.
4. I will assume random sampling so that a test can be carried out to resolve the role of chance.

In sum, their recommendation would be to assume random sampling from a wider population even though there is no such real population. This population then is hypothetical, abstract, or assumed, or, one could even say, *imaginary*.

When the population is assumed rather than real, conclusions pertaining to it don't have practical, real-world importance. In our example, the probability indicated by the statistical test (a chi-square test of independence) computes to less than .001. Assuming that we had selected the .01 significance level, we would reject the null. Thus we would conclude that it is unlikely that the null hypothesis (equal percentages in the two units) is true in the population from which the study sample was selected. Yet, given that this population is imaginary, this conclusion has dubious meaning. Stated differently, it makes no practical difference whether the null is likely or unlikely to be true among a group of imaginary people. Our study sample results can't be generalized statistically to any *real* population beyond the study sample.

Unlike the imaginary study population, the study sample consists of *real* people. Conclusions pertaining to it do have real-world meaning. In particular, the low probability associated with the statistical test ($p < .001$) conveys that the study sample results are not likely to be due to chance alone. Even if we can't generalize statistically to a larger population, we can be confident that something real (something more than chance) made a difference *for the study sample*.

The statistically significant finding invites us to consider what real factors explain the study results. For instance, no mention was made of random assignment to units. As such, a confounding variable may be at work. Perhaps those in Unit A had, on average, less severe illnesses than did those in Unit B. Perhaps this rather than the superiority of the community-outreach approach explains the lower hospitalization rate in Unit A. Whatever the cause, one needs to be confident that chance has been ruled out as a plausible cause before theorizing about real explanations. In sum, it makes good common sense to rule out chance even when there has been no random sampling. The practical message is that you should indeed go ahead and conduct statistical significance tests even when the population is imaginary.

16.9   COMMUNICATING ABOUT ASSOCIATION AND SIGNIFICANCE

In communicating about an association, a good practice is to always state whether that association is statistically significant. Suppose that you write "Variables A and B are associated" but make no mention of significance. Some readers will reason (1) if the association was not statistically significant, the author would not have indicated that the variables were associated, and therefore (2) the association is statistically significant. Others will wonder whether the association is significant. Still others will assume that the association is not significant because no mention of this was made. The way to avoid such confusion is to make direct mention of significance or the lack thereof.[8]

Some researchers counsel that when an association in a sample is not statistically significant, one may simply say: "A and B are unassociated." I find such language misleading as it fails to convey that, in the study sample, the variables are indeed associated. The best approach, again, is to clarify the issue of significance. Thus one might state "Variables A and B were associated in the sample but this association was not statistically significant" or perhaps "The association between A and B was not significant."

One problem with continually stating whether or not an association is statistically significant is simply that "statistically significant" is such a mouthful. Notice that in the previous couple of paragraphs, I sometimes resorted to stating "significant" rather than "statistically significant." This is an acceptable practice. The danger in so doing is that some readers will attach the dictionary meaning of *significance* to your association and assume that the association is important.

The quickest way to communicate statistical significance or the lack thereof is via the probability symbol, p. As mentioned earlier, p indicates the probability resulting from the statistical test. When an association is statistically significant at the .01 level, one may state "A and B were associated, $p < .01$." When an association is not statistically significant at the .05 level, one may state "The association was not significant, $p > .05$." Via the p symbol, one conveys whether the association is significant *and* the significance level. This is preferable to simply stating that the association is or is not significant. With the advent of computers, the precise probability of a study result is often available. Hence one may write "A and B were associated, $p = .023$."

In reporting significance, the hypothesis testing model differs from common practice in one way. In the model, one chooses a significance level prior to carrying out the test. Furthermore, one does not change to another level after having carried out the test (some regard such a change as cheating). For instance, in our second family preservation experiment in Section 16.4, we chose the .05 level. The probability of the study result was .009. Even though .009 is less than .01, we did not switch to the .01 level but instead reported the result as significant at the .05 level. In actual research, things are more relaxed, and it is customary to report significance at the lowest significance level that has been achieved. For instance, in an actual research situation, one would report the study result ($p = .009$) as significant at the .01 level.

16.10 WHAT STATISTICAL SIGNIFICANCE IS AND IS NOT

Statistical significance is recognized as the most important concept in statistics and data interpretation and is clearly the cornerstone around which social science research is organized. A key problem, however, is that statistical significance is too often viewed as the *only* important concept. Because such extreme attention is focused on statistical significance, its meaning becomes blurred with other important but less recognized aspects of data analysis. Thus, when an association is statistically significant, some students (and sometimes researchers) make the mistake of assuming that this association is also necessarily (1) large (strong), (2) causal, (3) generalizable to many settings, and (4) important. Statistical significance has one primary meaning—that chance alone is not the likely explanation for an association or difference. Interpret it in this way and you will not go wrong. Don't make the mistake of blurring its meaning with these other distinct and important concepts.

TABLE 16.2	VALID CONCLUSIONS FROM STATISTICAL SIGNIFICANCE TESTS
If study result is not statistically significant:	**If study result is statistically significant:**
Fail to reject (accept) the null hypothesis; reject the research hypothesis.	Reject the null hypothesis; accept the research hypothesis.
Study sample result is consistent with the null hypothesis. (It is somewhat more accurate to say that the result is not inconsistent with the null.)	Study sample result is consistent with the research hypothesis.
Probability resulting from the statistical significance test is greater than the probability associated with the statistical significance level (greater than alpha, α).	Probability resulting from the statistical significance test is less than or equal to the probability associated with the statistical significance level (less than or equal to alpha, α).
Probability of obtaining the study sample result is greater than the probability associated with the significance level ($>\alpha$).	Probability of obtaining the study sample result is less than or equal to the probability associated with the significance level ($\leq\alpha$).
Given a true null, the probability of obtaining the study sample result is greater than the probability associated with the significance level ($>\alpha$).	Given a true null, the probability of obtaining the study sample result is less than or equal to the probability associated with the significance level ($\leq\alpha$).
Given a true null, the probability of obtaining a result as extreme as or more extreme than the study sample result is greater than the probability associated with the significance level ($>\alpha$).	Given a true null, the probability of obtaining a result as extreme as or more extreme than the study sample result is less than or equal to the probability associated with the significance level ($\leq\alpha$).
Probability that the study sample result is due to chance alone (sampling error alone) is greater than the probability associated with the significance level ($>\alpha$).	Probability that the study sample result is due to chance alone (sampling error alone) is less than or equal to the probability associated with the significance level ($\leq\alpha$).
Probability that chance alone (sampling error alone) could lead to a result as extreme as or more extreme than the study sample result is greater than the probability associated with the significance level ($>\alpha$).	Probability that chance alone (sampling error alone) could lead to a result as extreme as or more extreme than the study sample result is less than or equal to the probability associated with the significance level ($\leq\alpha$).
The proportion of cases in the sampling distribution that are as extreme as or more extreme than the study sample result is greater than the probability associated with the significance level ($>\alpha$).	The proportion of cases in the sampling distribution that are as extreme as or more extreme than the study sample result is less than or equal to the probability associated with the statistical significance level ($\leq\alpha$).
Plausible (not unlikely) that the difference between the condition stated in the null and the study sample result is due to chance alone (sampling error alone).	Unlikely that the difference between the condition stated in the null and the study sample result is due to chance alone (sampling error alone).
One should not conclude that the difference between the condition stated in the null and the study sample result is due to something real (it may well be due to chance alone).	Likely that the difference between the condition stated in the null and the study sample result is due to something real (it's unlikely to be due to chance alone).
It is plausible (not unlikely) that the null hypothesis is true. (One may not conclude that it is likely that the null is true.)	It is likely that the research hypothesis is true. It is likely that the null hypothesis is false.

TABLE 16.2 CONTINUED	
If study result is not statistically significant:	**If study result is statistically significant:**
Insufficient grounds for concluding that the null hypothesis is false and that the research hypothesis is true.	Confident (though not 100% sure) that the research hypothesis is true. Confident that the null hypothesis is false.
If the .05 statistical significance level was used ($\alpha = .05$), one is less than 95% confident that the null hypothesis is false (and that the research hypothesis is true). At the .01 level ($\alpha = .01$), one is less than 99% confident.	If the .05 statistical significance level was used ($\alpha = .05$), one is 95% confident that the null hypothesis is false (and that the research hypothesis is true). At the .01 level ($\alpha = .01$), one is 99% confident.
Do not say that results *prove* that the null hypothesis is true.	Do not say that results *prove* that the research hypothesis is true.
(If the hypothesis pair pertains to an association) study results do not provide sufficient grounds for concluding that variables are associated in the population from which the study sample was randomly selected. Association in the study sample may be due to chance alone.	(If the hypothesis pair pertains to an association) it is likely that the variables are associated in the population from which the study sample was randomly selected. Unlikely that the association in the study sample is due to chance alone.

Chapter 23 (Section 23.4) presents an integrated model for data interpretation that brings together the five just-mentioned concepts—statistical significance, size of association, causality, generalizability, and importance. In contrast to the first three concepts, generalizability and importance have not been discussed in depth so far in this text. Chapter 23 provides this discussion (see Sections 23.2 and 23.3).

Having just cautioned you on what statistical significance is not, now seems an opportune time to summarize what it is. Valid conclusions pertaining to statistical significance or the lack thereof are summarized in Table 16.2. The right column lists valid conclusions that may be drawn when results are statistically significant. All are basically different ways of saying the same thing. The left column lists conclusions that may be drawn when results are not statistically significant. These are also different ways of saying the same thing. Underlying the conclusions in Table 16.2 is the assumption that an appropriate significance test has been carried out. When this is not the case, some of the conclusions do not hold.

This chapter and the prior two have presented the theory, logic, and meaning of significance testing. In Chapters 17 to 22 the focus shifts to key statistical significance tests that are used commonly in human services research.

16.11   CHAPTER SUMMARY

A statistical test's power is the probability that it will reject a false null. Power and beta (β) sum to 1.00, and power $= 1 - \beta$ (formula 16.1).

The most important factor influencing power is sample size. As sample size increases (other things being equal), so does power. When sample size is very small, the size of the difference required to reject the null can be so large that the test does not have a realistic opportunity to do so. In this situation, the probability of an incorrect decision (a type II error) is most often high and power is low. As sample size increases, increasingly smaller relationships and differences result in rejection of the null. When sample size is very large, the probability of a type II error is most often low and power is high.

When sample size is small, even large associations (large differences) in a sample are often not statistically significant. Conversely, when it is very large, even small associations (small differences) are often significant.

Besides sample size, five factors influencing power are (1) the significance level (alpha), (2) whether the hypothesis pair is directional or nondirectional, (3) the anticipated size of association, (4) the amount of variability, and (5) the particular test that is used. Choice of the .05 level (rather than the .01 level) increases power. Presuming that the population parameter is in the expected direction, a directional hypothesis (and therefore a one-tailed test) increases power. The larger the expected size of association or difference, the greater the power. When the variability of either the independent or dependent variable is very low, power is reduced. On the other hand, excessive variability due to extraneous variables also reduces power. As a general rule, the higher the level of measurement required by the statistical test, the greater its power.

By tradition, scientists regard power of about .80 or above as good. When power is .80, the significance test has an 80% chance of rejecting a false null.

Most researchers recommend statistical significance testing even when the study sample has not been selected randomly from any wider population. Though conclusions pertaining to the population have dubious meaning, those pertaining to the study sample make real-world sense. In particular, the role of chance can be assessed. To avoid confusion, one should always state whether an observed association is statistically significant.

Mistakenly, many regard statistical significance as the *only* important concept in data interpretation. The key meaning of statistical significance—that chance alone is an unlikely explanation—often becomes blurred with other concepts.

Problems and Questions

Section 16.2

1. Power is the _____ that a statistical test will reject a(n) _____ _____ hypothesis, or stated differently, that it will accept a(n) _____ _____ hypothesis.

2. Power and β (beta) sum to _____ .

3. When the probability of a type II error (β) equals .30, power equals _____ .

4. The greater the power, the lower the probability of a(n) _____ _____ error.

5. (T or F) Good/high statistical power is preferable to poor/low power.

Section 16.3

6. The most important factor influencing power is _____ _____ .

7. When sample size is small, power is usually _____ and when it is large, power is usually _____ .

Section 16.4

8. Other things being equal, as sample size increases, the amount of difference from the condition stated in the null that is necessary for rejection of the null _____ .

9. H_0: $\mu = 100$, $s = 40$, $\alpha = .05$ (two-tailed test). For each of the following sample sizes, indicate (1) $s_{\bar{X}}$ (estimated standard error of the mean) and (2) the approximate difference from the condition stated in the null that is necessary for rejection via the large sample test of $\bar{X}$.
   a. 100
   b. 400
   c. 1600

10. (T or F) When sample size is very small, even large associations in one's study sample may not be statistically significant.

11. (T or F) When sample size is very large, even small associations in one's study sample may be statistically significant.

12. (T or F) Statistically significant associations are always large associations.

Section 16.5

13. (T or F) Other things being equal, use of the .05 statistical significance level rather than the .01 level increases power.

14. (T or F) Presuming that the population parameter does indeed differ in the expected direction and other things being equal, use of a one-tailed test rather than a two-tailed test increases power.

15. (T or F) Other things being equal, the greater the anticipated association or difference, the less the statistical power.

16. (T or F) Other things being equal, the greater the variability in the dependent variable that is due to extraneous factors, the greater the power.

17. In Study A, 4% of youth offenders in the study commit an offense subsequent to treatment (recidivate), and 96% do not. In Study B, these percentages are, respectively, 27% and 73%.

Presume that sample size is 200 in both studies and that both studies have two treatment groups with 100 in each group. In which study is the statistical test of the association of type of treatment to recidivism likely to have greater power?

18. (T or F) Very restricted (low) variability in either the independent or dependent variable can lead to reduced (low) statistical power.

19. (T or F) In general, the lower the level of measurement, the greater the statistical power.

Section 16.6

20. Science has reached a rough consensus that power of about _____ or higher may be regarded as good.

21. When power is .80, a statistical test has a(n) _____ % chance to reject a false null.

Section 16.7

22. Using Table 16.1, the rough guide to assessing power, indicate the approximate power ("very high," "poor," etc.) expected with studies with the following sample sizes.
   a. 25
   b. 100
   c. 5000
   d. 700

Section 16.8

23. (T or F) All researchers recommend that statistical significance testing should never be carried out when the study sample has not been randomly selected.

24. (T or F) According to this text, statistical conclusions pertaining to the study sample (in particular regarding the role of chance) have real-world meaning even when the study sample has not been randomly selected.

Section 16.9

25. (T or F) The text recommends that one should state whether associations in the study sample are statistically significant.

26. In significance testing, what does p convey?

27. Presume that $\alpha = .05$ and that $p = .03$. Does this p convey a statistically significant result?

28. When $\alpha = .01$, does $p = .03$ convey a statistically significant result?

Section 16.10

29. Statistically significant associations are always . . .
    a. (T or F) Large
    b. (T or F) Causal
    c. (T or F) Widely generalizable
    d. (T or F) Important
30. Which from the following list does not go with the others? Statistically significant, fail to reject the null, probability of result $< \alpha$, variables likely associated in population, unlikely to be due to chance.
31. (T or F) When a result is statistically significant, this proves that the null is false.

NOTES

1. As the standard deviation of the sampling distribution of $\overline{X}$ is estimated (very accurately by $S/\sqrt{N}$) rather than known, the distributions in Figure 16.1 closely approximate but do not present precisely the sampling distribution of $\overline{X}$.

2. A better test (the one-sample t test, see Chapter 17, Sections 17.6 and 17.7) is available when sample size is less than 100. The large sample test of $\overline{X}$ would indeed yield accurate results with a sample size of nine if (1) the population from which the sample was selected was normally distributed and (2) the population standard deviation (σ) was known. Given these conditions, the sampling distribution in Figure 16.2 would also be accurate. The current discussion seeks to demonstrate how very small sample size affects power. Obviously, this is difficult when the only test presented so far requires a sample size of 100. In sum, in the interest of learning, one should assume that sampling distribution as presented in Figure 16.2 is accurate.

3. Formally, one should not change the selected significance level. For instance, although $p = .009$, which is less than .01, the result is reported as significant at the .05 level (not the .01 level) because the .05 level was selected. See the discussion at the end of Section 16.9.

4. When one has no knowledge or expectation regarding the direction of results, the use of a one-tailed versus a two-tailed test has no effect on power. (In this situation, one would always use a two-tailed test.)

5. Multivariate statistical procedures can take into account variability introduced by extraneous variables and thus increase power (see Chapter 22, Section 22.11).

6. Fisher's exact test (see Chapter 20, note 1) would also be appropriate in this situation. Via this test, $p = .279$.

7. A considerably larger minority believe that significance tests should only be conducted when (1) the study sample is a random sample, or (2) subjects have been randomly assigned to groups, or (3) both points 1 and 2 are true.

8. In some research studies, researchers are interested only in describing sample results. The key issues addressed by significance testing—whether associations are due to chance, and so on—simply are not related to the study's goals. As such, no significance tests are conducted. When this is the case, this should be clarified so that the kinds of confusion described in the text do not result.

SELECTED SIGNIFICANCE TESTS AND A DATA INTERPRETATION MODEL

Chapters 17 to 22 present a variety of statistical significance tests designed for different situations. For instance, some tests examine whether sample means differ to a statistically significant degree. Others do so for percentages. For most tests, the text presents the underlying logic, cautions regarding use, the formula, a computational example, and an example using statistical software. Key tests covered include the independent samples t test, the dependent samples t test, the chi-square test of independence, a statistical significance test for correlation, and analysis of variance.

Finally, Chapter 23 integrates material from throughout the text and presents a model for data interpretation.

The *t* Distribution and One-Sample Procedures for Means

17.1 Chapter Overview

When sample size is small, inferential statistical procedures should not be based on the normal distribution, and we now consider the reasons in greater depth. For many smaller samples we can use the *t distribution* because it changes along with *degrees of freedom*, which are related to sample size for the tests in this chapter. Inferential procedures using the *t* distribution include confidence intervals as well as statistical significance tests. This chapter presents one such significance test, the *one-sample t test*. We also discuss whether tests involving means may be used with ordinal-level data.

17.2 The Normal Distribution and Small Samples

As presented in Chapter 15, one formula (15.2) for the large sample test of $\overline{X}$ is:

$$z \approx \frac{\overline{X} - \mu}{s_{\overline{X}}}$$

In this formula, $s_{\overline{X}}$ is an estimate of the standard deviation of the sampling distribution of $\overline{X}(\sigma_{\overline{X}})$. Recall from Chapter 15 (Section 15.11) that the sampling distribution of a test statistic is the distribution that would be obtained if one (1) took an infinite number of random samples and each time (2) calculated the formula for the statistic in question and recorded the result. Whenever sample size is 100 or greater and the null is true, the sampling distribution of the test statistic z comes very close to being a normal distribution with a mean of 0.00 and a standard deviation of 1.00. (Stated differently, it comes very close to being a distribution of normally distributed z scores.) This being the case, one may refer to the table of areas of the normal distribution (Table A.1 in Appendix A) to learn probabilities and use the decision rules presented in Chapter 15. Whenever $N \geq 100$, $s_{\overline{X}}$ provides a highly accurate estimate of $\sigma_{\overline{X}}$ ($s_{\overline{X}} \approx \sigma_{\overline{X}}$). However, when $N < 100$ this is no longer so. Partly because of this, when $N < 100$, the sampling distribution of the test statistic z as presented in formula 15.2 does not come extremely close to being a distribution of normally distributed z scores. Even when the shape of the population from which samples are selected is normal (and given a true null), it differs in at least two key ways. First, its standard deviation is larger than 1.00. Second, its shape is leptokurtic. As presented in Chapter 5, Section 5.6, leptokurtic distributions are more peaked than normal distributions and—more importantly for the current discussion—have thicker and more elongated tails. In addition, when the sample is selected from a skewed population, the sampling distribution of the test statistic z can also have a skewed shape.

Due to the just-mentioned differences, when $N < 100$ one may not (1) determine the probability of obtaining the study sample mean by reference to a table of the normal distribution (Table A.1) or (2) use the decision rules presented for the large sample test. For similar reasons, when $N < 100$, the formulas for confidence intervals for means in Chapter 13 (all of which are based on the normal distribution) do not yield accurate confidence intervals. In sum, when N is less than 100 and, therefore, $s_{\overline{X}}$ does not accurately estimate $\sigma_{\overline{X}}$, inferential statistical procedures involving means should not be based on the normal distribution.[1]

A general definition of a z score is a score minus the mean, divided by the standard deviation. The z that formula 15.2 calculates comes close to meeting this definition but does not quite do so. In particular, formula 15.2 does not divide by the standard deviation of the sampling distribution of $\overline{X}$($\sigma_{\overline{X}} = \sigma/\sqrt{N}$) but instead by an *estimate* of this ($s_{\overline{X}} = s/\sqrt{N}$). As stated above, so long as $N \geq 100$, $s_{\overline{X}}$ and $\sigma_{\overline{X}}$ are almost exactly equal, so the z that formula 15.2 calculates very nearly equals the z that would have been obtained by dividing by $\sigma_{\overline{X}}$. From a pragmatic perspective, we may regard it as a z and therefore may use the procedures mentioned in the preceding paragraph (decision rules, the normal distribution table, etc.). However, strictly speaking, formula 15.2 does not calculate a z score.

When one takes a score, subtracts the mean, and divides not by the standard deviation but by an *estimate* of the standard deviation, the result of that calculation is not a z score but a ***t* score,** also called a ***t*.** Given a true null, the sampling distribution that would result from selecting an infinite number of samples and each time carrying out the just-described calculation is not described best by a normal distribution but by a ***t* distribution.** Thus (if certain assumptions we discuss later are met and if the null is true) the sampling distribution of $(\overline{X} - \mu)s_{\overline{X}}$ (the right side of formula 15.2) follows a t distribution.

Strictly speaking, formula 15.2 is a formula for t rather than z. Though the one-sample t test is presented later in the chapter, its formulas are presented now. One formula rewrites formula 15.2 as a formula for t:

$$t = \frac{\overline{X} - \mu}{s_{\overline{X}}} \tag{17.1}$$

The other, mathematically equivalent to 17.1, rewrites formula 15.1:

$$t = \frac{\overline{X} - \mu}{s/\sqrt{N}} \tag{17.2}$$

In these formulas, t is the test statistic for the one-sample t test. When $N <$ 100, inferential procedures involving means (both confidence intervals and hypothesis tests) should be based on the t distribution. Before examining the t distribution, let's get an introduction to degrees of freedom.

17.3   DEGREES OF FREEDOM

Almost all statistical procedures that are presented from this point forward require calculation of the number of degrees of freedom. **Degrees of freedom (df)** are the number of independent values that remain after mathematical restrictions have been applied. For instance, suppose that you have 25 cases in a sample and compute the sample mean, $\overline{X}$. Suppose further that you inform a colleague of (1) the value of $\overline{X}$ and (2) the values of 24 of the 25 cases. With this information, the colleague could figure out the value of the 25th case. As this situation is described, the 25th case is not "free" to vary; instead, its value can be determined from the values of the other 24 cases and the mean.

Now presume that you wish to calculate the standard deviation of this sample, that is, s. (The formula for s is $s = \sqrt{\Sigma(X - \overline{X})^2/(N - 1)}$, formula 4.5.) Because $\overline{X}$ appears in the formula for s, only 24 cases (24 X's) have an opportunity to vary independently. Once the values of 24 cases and $\overline{X}$ have been plugged into the formula, the value of the 25th case is known. In this example, s, which in turn estimates the population standard deviation (σ), is based on $N - 1$, or 24, degrees of freedom. Even though the sample has 25 cases, for purposes of calculating s, it has only 24 independent values. Stated differently, the sample has 24 degrees of freedom.

You may have wondered why the formula for s uses $N - 1$ rather than N in the denominator. $N - 1$ represents the degrees of freedom. In any given sample, there are only $N - 1$ opportunities for values to vary independently around the mean.

Degrees of freedom is ultimately an abstract, mathematical concept that is difficult to define with words. As one text states: "Do not expect a flash of insight that will give this concept rich, intuitive meaning" (Hopkins and Glass, 1978, p. 193). Fortunately, one does not need a "rich" understanding to use degrees of freedom. This text supplies straightforward methods for calculating degrees of freedom for all statistical procedures when this information is needed.

17.4   CHARACTERISTICS OF THE t DISTRIBUTION

17.4.1   A Family of t Distributions

Unlike the normal distribution, the t distribution is not a single distribution but is instead a family of distributions whose characteristics (shape, etc.) change according to the number of degrees of freedom. Stated differently, there is a different

t distribution for each different degree of freedom. A **family** of distributions is basically a group of distributions that are derived by common procedures or formulas. Like the normal distribution, the t distribution is a theoretical distribution rather than an empirical one.

This chapter presents two procedures based on the t distribution, confidence intervals for means and the one-sample t test. The formulas for both involve calculation of the standard deviation in the study sample (s). As just demonstrated, calculations of s have $N - 1$ degrees of freedom. Thus both procedures are based on t distributions with $N - 1$ degrees of freedom. (Chapter 18 demonstrates how the t distribution is used in two additional procedures, the independent samples t test and the dependent samples t test. The degrees of freedom for these procedures are presented in that chapter.)

How do the t distribution's characteristics change as degrees of freedom change? For the procedures presented now, this question may also be stated as: How do the t distribution's characteristics change as sample size changes? In answering these questions, primary attention is directed to the t distribution's shape.

When sample size is small (say 5 or so) and thus degrees of freedom are low (when $N = 5$, $df = 4$), the shape of the t distribution differs considerably from that of the normal distribution. Specifically, it is leptokurtic (peaked) with much thicker and much more stretched-out tails. As sample size increases, the shape of the t distribution becomes less leptokurtic and increasingly comes to resemble that of the normal distribution. When sample size is about 20 ($df = 19$), the t distribution's shape is quite similar to that of the normal distribution. When it is 100 ($df = 99$) or greater, the shapes of the t and normal distribution are almost indistinguishable. When sample size is infinity (a real-world impossibility) these distributions are identical. Figure 17.1 presents t distributions with three different degrees of freedom.[2]

By now, you are familiar with the kinds of statements that can be made about percentages of cases and the normal distribution. For instance, 95% of cases in a normal distribution are located within 1.96 standard deviations of the mean. Similarly, 99% of cases in a normal distribution are within 2.58 standard deviations of the mean. Rephrasing in terms of z scores, 95% of cases are located between a z

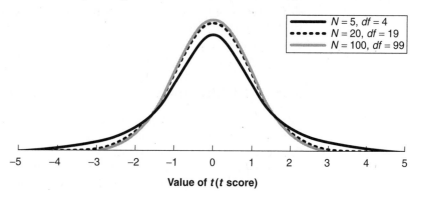

FIGURE **17.1**

t DISTRIBUTION FOR THREE DIFFERENT SAMPLE SIZES

score of -1.96 and a z score of $+1.96$, and 99% of cases are located between a z score of -2.58 and a z score of 2.58.

For the t distribution, the value of t within which given percentages of cases are located varies according to the degrees of freedom, that is (for the procedures in this chapter), according to the sample size. When sample size is 5 ($df = 4$), 95% of cases are located between a t score of -2.78 and a t score of 2.78. When sample size is 20 ($df = 19$), 95% of cases are located between t scores of -2.09 and 2.09. When sample size is 100 ($df = 99$), 95% of cases are located between t scores of -1.98 and 1.98. When our interest is in the values of t within which 99% of cases are located, these are $N = 5$ ($df = 4$), -4.60 to 4.60; $N = 20$ ($df = 19$), -2.86 to 2.86; and $N = 100$ ($df = 99$), -2.63 to 2.63.

Note that when sample size is 5 ($df = 4$), the positive and negative values of t within which 95% and 99% of cases are located are much larger than are the corresponding values of z for the normal distribution (95%, 2.78 versus 1.96; 99%, 4.60 versus 2.58). This is so because a t distribution with four degrees of freedom has a strongly leptokurtic shape; in particular, it has extremely thick and elongated tails. On the other hand, when N is 100, the positive and negative values of t within which 95% and 99% of cases are located differ hardly at all from the corresponding values of z for the normal distribution (95%, 1.98 versus 1.96; 99%, 2.63 versus 2.58). This is so because the shape of a t distribution with 99 degrees of freedom is almost indistinguishable from that of a normal distribution. Figure 17.2 presents visually the values of t within which 95% of cases are located for the three t distributions that have been discussed.

The t distribution's changing shape plays a role in its delivery of accurate results. When $N < 100$, $s_{\bar{X}}$ estimates $\sigma_{\bar{X}}$ with more than inconsequential error. In general, the smaller the sample size, the greater the error. By changing its shape, the t distribution takes the likely amount of error in estimating $\sigma_{\bar{X}}$ into account. When sample size is small, the t distribution assumes thick, elongated tails, in effect spreading out the sampling distribution so that, for instance, confidence intervals become appropriately wider. With larger samples, the likely amount of error is small. As such, the t distribution alters its shape only slightly from that of the normal distribution to adjust for this error. Because the t distribution adjusts its shape according to the likely amount of error, statistical procedures based on it yield accurate results. (This assumes that procedures are used appropriately and that assumptions are met.)

17.4.2   t Distribution and the Normality Assumption

Before closing our discussion of the t distribution's characteristics, we need to consider a final point. The sampling distribution of the test statistic t as presented in formulas 17.1 and 17.2 can be *precisely* described by a t distribution only when the study sample is randomly selected from a normally distributed population. However, even when this population is nonnormal, as sample size increases, the sampling distribution of the test statistic t very quickly assumes a shape that closely approximates that of a t distribution. The key criterion that determines how quickly a t distribution is approximated is the degree of skewness. When only a modest skew

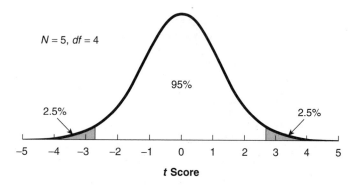

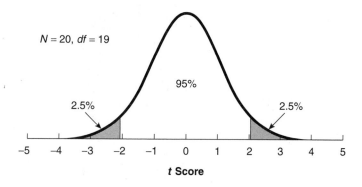

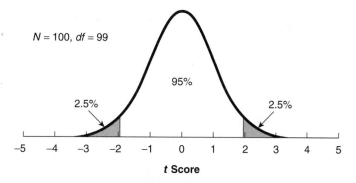

FIGURE **17.2**

LOCATION OF 95% OF CASES FOR THREE *t* DISTRIBUTIONS

occurs in the population from which the study sample is selected (and given a true null), the sampling distribution of *t* closely approximates a *t* distribution even for extremely small samples (say, when $N \geq 8$). As skewness increases, so does the required sample size. However, even for strongly skewed populations (and given a true null), this sampling distribution approximates a *t* distribution for quite small samples (say, when $N \geq 30$). Table 17.1 lists the degree of skewness in the population and the required sample size. The basic message of Table 17.1 is that the

	SKEWNESS AND SAMPLE SIZE
TABLE 17.1	TO APPROXIMATE A *t* DISTRIBUTION

Skewness in Population[a]	Sample Size Required
Normal	2[b]
Modest skew	About 8
Moderate skew	About 15
Strong skew	About 30
Extreme skew	About 60[c]

[a]Refers to the shape of distribution of the population from which the study sample was randomly selected.
[b]Two is the minimum sample size required to compute the test statistic *t*. Whenever the population has a precisely normal distribution, and given a true null, the test statistic *t* precisely follows a *t* distribution. (This is so for all sample sizes.)
[c]If a distribution was skewed to an "extremely" extreme degree (more so than depicted in the most skewed figures in Figures 5.4 and 5.6), a sample size larger than 60 could be required.

required sample size is small even when skewness is quite marked. As you peruse Table 17.1, you may want to refer to Figures 5.4 and 5.6 for the shape of distribution conveyed by modest, moderate, strong, and extreme skew.

17.5 CONFIDENCE INTERVALS FOR MEANS FOR SMALL SAMPLES

Whenever sample size is less than 100, the *t* distribution rather than the normal distribution should be used to form confidence intervals for means. The *t* distribution may also be used when sample size is 100 or greater, though in this circumstance the resulting confidence intervals differ hardly at all from those obtained via formulas based on the normal distribution (formulas 13.2 to 13.5). One confidence interval formula based on the *t* distribution is:

$$CI \text{ of } \mu = \overline{X} \pm t(s/\sqrt{N}) \tag{17.3}$$

An alternative formula is:

$$CI \text{ of } \mu = \overline{X} \pm t(s_{\overline{X}}) \tag{17.4}$$

As you know, $s_{\overline{X}}$ is the estimate of the standard error of the mean and equals $s/\sqrt{N}$. Table A.2 in Appendix A presents critical values of *t* and values of *t* to use in forming confidence intervals. In formulas 17.3 and 17.4, *t* represents the value of *t* in Table A.2 that corresponds to the desired confidence interval with the appropriate degrees of freedom.

Formulas 17.3 and 17.4 yield highly accurate confidence intervals whenever the sample size guidelines in Table 17.1 are met. As stated above, degrees of freedom equal $N - 1$.

For a computational example, suppose that you select a random sample of 25 children in foster care and determine that they have experienced a mean of 4.35

placements with a standard deviation of 1.2 placements. That is, $N = 25$, $\overline{X} = 4.35$, and $s = 1.2$. Presume that the shape of the population distribution has only a moderate degree of positive skew and that you want to determine a 95% confidence interval. Prior to making calculations, you should check that the sample size guidelines in Table 17.1 are met. When the population has a moderate skew, the sample size of 25 exceeds the guideline of 15. As such, you may proceed with calculations:

1. Estimate $s_{\overline{X}}$:

$$\frac{1.2}{\sqrt{25}} = \frac{1.2}{5} = 0.24$$

2. Compute the degrees of freedom $(N - 1)$: $25 - 1 = 24$.
3. Locate the appropriate value of t in Table A.2.

The leftmost column in Table A.2 indicates degrees of freedom. Trace down this column to find the row with 24. Trace across the row until you intersect the column labeled at the top "Values of t for 95%CI." The t at this intersection is 2.064. This t indicates the number of standard deviations within which 95% of cases are located in a t distribution with 24 degrees of freedom.

4. Multiply the t from Table A.2 by $s_{\overline{X}}$: $2.064\,(0.24) = .495$.
5. Add and subtract the results of step 4 from $\overline{X}$ to determine the confidence interval:

$$95\%\ CI\ of\ \mu = 4.35 \pm .495 = 3.855\ to\ 4.845$$

Hence you can be 95% confident that the population mean, μ, is located in the range from 3.855 placements to 4.845 placements. Sometimes Table A.2 does not list the precise number of degrees of freedom. When this is so, one uses the next smaller listed number. For instance, when N is 70, $df = 70 - 1 = 69$. Table A.2 has no row corresponding to 69 degrees of freedom. It does, however, list values of t for 60 degrees of freedom, so these would be used. For a 99% confidence interval rather than a 95% one, one traces down the column labeled "Values of t for 99%CI."

It might be interesting to compare the results of our just-computed confidence interval with the interval that would have resulted had we used one of the large sample formulas presented in Chapter 13. Formula 13.2 is $95\%CI = \overline{X} \pm 1.96(s/\sqrt{N})$. Via this formula: $95\%CI\ of\ \mu = 4.35 \pm 1.96\,(1.2/\sqrt{25}) = 3.88\ to\ 4.82$. The confidence interval computed via the t distribution is slightly wider than that computed via the large sample formula. As you know, the large sample formula is based on the normal distribution. The confidence interval based on the t distribution must be slightly wider if it is to accommodate the thicker tails of this distribution. In a normal distribution, 95% of cases are within 1.96 standard errors $[(1.96 \times \sigma_{\overline{X}}) \approx (1.96 \times s_{\overline{X}})]$ of the mean; hence this value is used in formula 13.2. In a t distribution with 24 degrees of freedom, 95% of cases are within 2.064 estimated standard errors $(2.064 \times s_{\overline{X}})$; hence this value is used.

Confidence intervals based on the normal distribution essentially assume that one can make a "perfect" estimate of the standard deviation in the population from which the sample was selected, and thus a perfect estimate of the standard deviation of the sampling distribution (that is, of $\sigma_{\overline{X}}$). In contrast, confidence intervals based on the t distribution adjust for the likely error in these estimates and thus are wider. Ultimately, confidence intervals based on the t distribution are more accurate than those based on the normal distribution. Whenever N is 100 or greater, the degree of increased accuracy is so small that one may use a formula based on either distribution.

17.6   Introduction to the One-Sample t Test

17.6.1   Background

Just as does the large sample test of $\overline{X}$, the **one-sample t test** examines whether the mean of a sample differs significantly from a hypothesized value. When $N < 100$, the large sample test can be inaccurate, so the one-sample t test should be used. When $N > 100$, the one-sample t test and the large sample test yield highly similar results, those of the one-sample t test being slightly more accurate. The one-sample t test sees more than occasional use and is preferred to the large sample test of $\overline{X}$ even when sample size exceeds 100. The large sample test of $\overline{X}$ is rarely used in actual research. Its primary use is in teaching students the logic of significance testing.

17.6.2   Assumptions and Levels of Measurement

A formal assumption of the one-sample t test is that the population from which the sample is selected is normally distributed. However, the test is highly robust to this assumption and yields highly accurate probabilities if the sample size guidelines for the t distribution presented in Table 17.1 are met. (Recall that when a test is robust to an assumption, that assumption may be violated with only a minimal effect on accuracy.)

Notice that the assumption regarding shape of distribution pertains to the *population* distribution. In real-world research situations, one never knows for certain what this shape is, because the study sample comprises only *some* of the cases in the population. How does one resolve the dilemma that this test assumption requires information that one does not have? Basically, one presumes that the shape of the population distribution is reasonably similar to that in the sample. Thus, if the shape of the sample distribution is reasonably close to normal, one assumes that this is so in the population. Similarly, if the study sample is markedly skewed, presumably this is also the case in the population. As common sense suggests, the larger the sample, the better the inference that can be made about the shape of the population distribution. Hence, with small samples, one should recognize that inferences about the population distribution should be made cautiously. From a pragmatic perspective, one needs a sample size of at least 15 in order to make a reasonably good inference about the likely shape of the population distribution.[3]

The one-sample *t* test and other tests of means can yield inaccurate results when there are extreme outliers. With larger samples (say 50 or larger), outliers usually are not a major concern, because the other observations reduce their influence. With small samples, they are more problematic. For instance, the one-sample *t* test would not be recommended with the following data:

6, 7, 7, 8, 8, 8, 8, 9, 9, 9, 9, 10, 10, 32

In this situation the value 32 would pull the mean markedly in a positive direction, which could lead to an incorrect decision regarding the null. Even with small samples the one-sample *t* test may be used with values that are "somewhat" extreme but not enough so to be classified as outliers. For instance, it could be used with the following data:

6, 7, 7, 8, 8, 8, 8, 9, 9, 9, 9, 10, 10, 15

The *t* test presumes measurement at the interval/ratio level or almost so.

17.6.3 *Hypotheses*

The hypothesis pairs for the one-sample *t* test are the same as those for the large sample test of $\overline{X}$. The nondirectional hypothesis pair may be stated as follows:

Null: The mean of the population from which the study sample was randomly selected equals some value.
Research: The mean of the population from which the study sample was randomly selected is not equal to the value stated in the null.

Stated in mathematical symbols:

$$H_0: \ \mu = A \qquad H_1: \ \mu \neq A$$

where μ symbolizes the mean of the population from which the study sample was selected and A is a given value.

One way to state the directional hypothesis pair is:

Null: The mean of the population from which the study sample was randomly selected is less than or equal to some value.
Research: The mean of the population from which the study sample was randomly selected is greater than the value stated in the null.

In mathematical symbols:

$$H_0: \ \mu \leq A \qquad H_1: \ \mu > A$$

When the hypothesized difference is in the opposite direction, this pair states:

Null: The mean of the population from which the study sample was randomly selected is greater than or equal to some value.
Research: The mean of the population from which the study sample was randomly selected is less than the value stated in the null.

In mathematical symbols:

$$H_0: \; \mu \geq A \qquad H_1: \; \mu < A$$

17.6.4   Distribution and Degrees of Freedom

The one-sample test is based on the t distribution. As presented earlier in this chapter, a t distribution's characteristics vary according to degrees of freedom. For the one-sample t test, degrees of freedom equal $N - 1$. When the normal distribution is used in statistical significance testing, the critical value(s) for the test statistic do not vary according to sample size. For instance, for a two-tailed test at the .05 level, the critical values for z for the large sample test are 1.96 and -1.96, regardless of sample size. (Recall that critical values are the values that define the values of the test statistic that result in rejection of the null.)

As the shape of the t distribution varies according to its degrees of freedom, so do the critical values. Table A.2 in Appendix A presents the critical values of t for various degrees of freedom. These values are listed for the .01 and .05 significance levels for both one-tailed and two-tailed tests. To locate the critical t: (1) trace down the leftmost column to locate the appropriate degrees of freedom and (2) trace across the row to find the appropriate type of test (one-tailed versus two-tailed) and significance level ($\alpha = .05$ or $\alpha = .01$). If the precise degrees of freedom are not listed, use the closest lower number.

Take a moment to study the critical values of t in Table A.2. Notice that as degrees of freedom increase, these values decrease and become closer to those for the large sample test of $\overline{X}$. Such a pattern is expected because, as degrees of freedom increase, the shape of the t distribution increasingly comes to resemble that of the normal distribution. The formulas for the one-sample t test (formulas 17.1 and 17.2) were provided earlier (Section 17.2).

When the hypothesis pair is nondirectional, the one-sample test is two-tailed. When it is directional, it is one-tailed with the rejection region located in the direction stated in the research hypothesis.

17.6.5   Decision Rules

For the one-sample t test with a nondirectional hypothesis pair, and therefore a two-tailed test, the decision rules are as follows:

Fail to reject (accept) the null if the absolute value of the obtained t is less than the value of t in Table A.2.

Reject the null if the absolute value of the obtained t is greater than or equal to the value of t in Table A.2.

For directional hypothesis pairs, the test is one-tailed. When the research hypothesis states "greater than":

Fail to reject (accept) the null if the obtained t is less than the value of t in Table A.2.

Reject the null if the obtained t is greater than or equal to the value of t in Table A.2.

When the research hypothesis states "less than":

Fail to reject (accept) the null if the obtained t is greater than the negative[4] of the t in Table A.2.

Reject the null if the obtained t is less than or equal to the negative of the t in Table A.2.

17.7 Carrying Out the One-Sample t Test

17.7.1 A Working Example

Suppose that all mental health centers in a large state administer an instrument that measures social functioning skills to all clients admitted during a given month and that the mean for these clients is 50.00 points. Suppose that you work in a mental health center in a small neighboring state and are interested in comparing the level of functioning of clients at your center with those in the large state. You have sufficient resources to administer the instrument to 25 clients, so you select a random sample and do so. The mean score of these 25 clients is 45.00 points with a standard deviation of 15 points. Stating your results via statistical symbols: $N = 25$, $\overline{X} = 45.00$, $s = 15.00$. Presume that the distribution of scores in the study sample has a moderate positive skew.

You seek to determine whether your study sample mean differs significantly from 50.00, the mean of the client population in the neighboring state. The one-sample t test is the appropriate tool.

A first step is to check that the sample size guidelines in Table 17.1 are met. The study sample size of 25 is sufficient for one to infer that the sample and population have similar shapes. (The population referred to is that from which the sample was selected.) Given that the sample has a moderate positive skew, you may conclude that the population also has such a skew. According to Table 17.1, when skew is moderate, a sample size of about 15 is sufficient for the one-sample t test to yield accurate results. As $N = 25$, sample size is sufficient and you may proceed. Following the hypothesis testing model as presented in Chapter 15, Section 15.2:

1. State the hypothesis pair:

   H_0: $\mu = 50.00$ H_1: $\mu \neq 50.00$

You have chosen a nondirectional hypothesis pair, presumably because no prior theory or research suggested a strong reason for believing that social functioning at your mental health center was either greater than or less than that in the neighboring state.

2. Choose a significance level.

Presume that you choose the .05 level, that is, that you set alpha (α) to .05.

3. Carry out the test.

The first task is to compute $s_{\bar{X}}$:

$$s_{\bar{X}} = \frac{15.00}{\sqrt{25}} = \frac{15.00}{5} = 3.00$$

Next, insert the appropriate values into formula 17.1 and carry out the computations:

$$t = \frac{45.00 - 50.00}{3.00} = \frac{5.00}{3.00} = -1.67$$

4. Make decision regarding the hypothesis pair.

Prior to making a decision, you need to determine the degrees of freedom:

$$df = N - 1 = 25 - 1 = 24$$

As the hypothesis pair is nondirectional, the test is two-tailed. To locate the critical value of t in Table A.2: (1) trace down the degrees of freedom column to 24 and (2) trace across to the column for a two-tailed test when $\alpha = .05$. The value of t in Table A.2 is 2.064. The absolute value of the obtained t ($|-1.67| = 1.67$) is less than the t in Table A.2. Under the decision-making rule for a nondirectional pair (two-tailed test), we fail to reject (accept) the null. We conclude that the difference between your study sample mean ($\bar{X} = 45$) and that in the larger state ($\mu = 50$) may simply be due to chance (sampling error).

17.7.2 Carrying Out the Test via the Sampling Distribution

Although one may carry out the one-sample t test without viewing the sampling distribution, the sampling distribution furthers understanding. Figure 17.3 presents an approximation of the sampling distribution of $\bar{X}$ that is based on the t distribution. This is the expected distribution of results given a true null. Figure 17.3 also shows the rejection regions and the study sample mean, $\bar{X} = 45.00$. For a two-tailed, one-sample t test when $df = 24$ and $\alpha = .05$, the rejection regions include all sample means with t scores ≥ 2.064 or ≤ -2.064. The study sample mean was not located in either rejection region; hence the correct decision was to accept the null.

In this example, the probability of obtaining a sample mean as extreme as or more extreme than the study sample mean exceeds .05. Stated differently, the probability that the study result is due to chance alone (sampling error alone) exceeds .05. Your data do not provide sufficiently convincing evidence for concluding that the mean level of social functioning of the population of clients at your clinic differs from that of the population of clients in the neighboring state.

17.7.3 The Example with a Directional Hypothesis Pair

Let's work through this example once more, this time assuming that you had compelling reasons for believing that clients at your clinic functioned, on average, at a lower level than those in the neighboring state. Given such an expectation, you

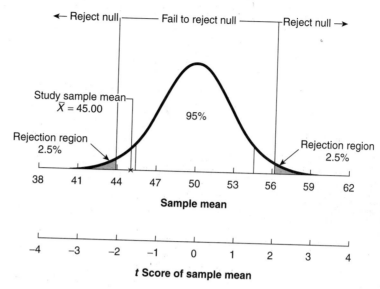

FIGURE 17.3

SAMPLING DISTRIBUTION OF $\overline{X}$ BASED ON THE *t* DISTRIBUTION

The study sample mean and rejection regions are indicated for the one-sample *t* test. The test is two-tailed, *df* = 24, α = .05.

would be justified in stating a directional hypothesis pair. The research hypothesis conveys the direction of your expectations:

$$H_0: \mu \geq 50.00 \qquad H_1: \mu < 50.00$$

Presume that α continues to be .05. Given that the hypothesis pair is directional, the test is one-tailed. For a one-tailed *t* test with *df* = 24 and α = .05, the value of *t* in Table A.2 is 1.711. Given that the research hypothesis states "less than or equal to," the decision-making rule calls for rejection when the obtained *t* is less than (more negative than) −1.711. In this example, the obtained *t* (already calculated to be −1.67) just misses achieving significance. Even via the one-tailed test, the probability that your results are due to sampling error exceeds .05, so your decision is still to accept the null. Figure 17.4 presents an approximation of the sampling distribution of $\overline{X}$, the rejection region, and the study sample mean.

17.8 ORDINAL-LEVEL MEASUREMENT AND TESTS INVOLVING MEANS

All tests involving means formally require measurement at the interval/ratio level. Almost all researchers concur that these tests may be used with data that "almost" meet the interval/ratio standard (multi-item attitudinal scales and the like). The

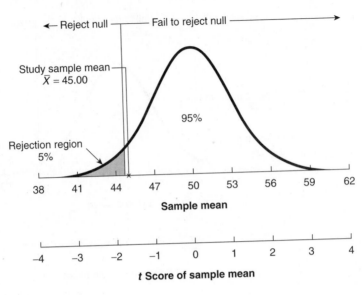

FIGURE **17.4**

REJECTION REGION FOR A ONE-TAILED TEST

Information is the same as for the sampling distribution in Figure 17.3 ($\overline{X}$ = 45.00, *df* = 24, α = 05) except that the research hypothesis states "less than."

more difficult question is whether they may be used with categorical ordinal-level variables (those with response categories like "always, often, sometimes, never" or "strongly agree, agree, disagree, strongly disagree," etc.). Many contend that such use can yield inaccurate probabilities and instead recommend tests designed for categorical ordinal-level variables. (These tests are presented in Chapter 22.)

Others contend that if a test can provide useful information, one should carry it out. They argue that tests for ordinal-level variables tend to be cumbersome, little used, and poorly understood and that tests of means (1) are straightforward, (2) are in common use, (3) are well understood, (4) have greater statistical power, and (5) almost always yield reasonably accurate results.

Should tests of means be used with ordinal-level variables? To a related question, Hubert Blalock (1979, p. 441), author of a definitive statistics text, responded: "There is no simple answer to this kind of question, although mounting evidence suggests that, practically speaking, it will *usually* make little difference with respect to one's conclusions." He suggests that one carry out both sets of tests and compare results.

A pragmatic approach is this: If testing for differences in means directly addresses the core of a research question and you believe that the values (1, 2, 3, 4, 5, etc.) assigned to the categories are straightforward, then go ahead and test. In such a situation, regard the test's probability as approximate rather than exact and recognize that a test designed for ordinal-level data would likely yield similar but not identical results.

17.9   CHAPTER SUMMARY

When $N < 100$, inferential procedures involving means should be based on the t distribution. The t distribution is a family of distributions whose shape changes according to degrees of freedom (sample size minus 1 for the procedures in this chapter). When sample size is very small (say 10 or less), the t distribution has a distinctly more peaked shape than does the normal distribution. In particular, its tails are much thicker and are elongated. As sample size increases, its shape increasingly resembles that of the normal distribution. When $N \geq 100$, the shapes of the t and normal distributions are almost identical. For the t distribution, the positive and negative value of t between which 95% (and 99%) of cases are located varies by degrees of freedom.

The sampling distribution of the test statistic t for the one-sample t test precisely follows a t distribution only when the population from which the study sample is selected is normally distributed. However, as sample size increases, this sampling distribution very quickly takes on the shape of the t distribution. Even for a strongly skewed population, a sample size of about 30 is sufficient.

Degrees of freedom (df) are the number of independent values that remain after mathematical restrictions have been applied. For confidence intervals for means and the one-sample t test, the appropriate t distribution has $N - 1$ degrees of freedom.

Whenever sample size is less than 100, confidence intervals for means should be based on the t distribution. These intervals are highly accurate whenever the sample size guidelines in Table 17.1 are met. A formula (17.3) is CI of $\mu = \overline{X} \pm t(s_{\overline{X}})$. Whenever N is 100 or greater, confidence intervals calculated via the t distribution and via the normal distribution are almost identical.

Just as does the large sample test of $\overline{X}$, the one-sample t test examines whether a sample mean differs significantly from a hypothesized value. It is highly robust to the normality assumption and yields accurate results whenever the sample size guidelines in Table 17.1 are met. (The researcher uses the shape of the sample distribution to infer the probable shape of the population distribution.) A formula (17.1) is $t = (\overline{X} - \mu)/s_{\overline{X}}$. The test may be one-tailed (directional hypothesis pair) or two-tailed (nondirectional pair). Critical values vary according to degrees of freedom.

PROBLEMS AND QUESTIONS

Section 17.2

1. (T or F) Given a true null, one may correctly presume that the sampling distribution of the test statistic z [as calculated via formula 15.2, $z \approx (\overline{X} - \mu)/s_{\overline{X}}$ comes extremely close to being a normally distributed distribution of z scores even when $N < 100$.

2. When $N < 100$, the standard deviation of the sampling distribution of the test statistic z (formula 15.2) is _____ than 1.00, and the shape of this distribution is _____ with _____, _____ tails.

3. (T or F) When $N < 100$, one may correctly assume that $s_{\overline{X}} \approx s_{\overline{X}}$.

4. (T or F) When $N < 100$, inferential statistical procedures involving means should *not* be based on the normal distribution.

5. When one subtracts the mean from a score and divides by an *estimate* of the standard deviation, the resulting score is termed a _____ score.

6. (T or F) When $N \geq 100$ ($df \geq 99$), the characteristics of a normal distribution and those of a t distribution are *precisely* identical.

7. (T or F) Whenever $N \geq 100$ ($df \geq 99$), the characteristics of a normal distribution and those of a t distribution are extremely similar.

Section 17.3

8. Define degrees of freedom in your own words.

9. When one calculates the standard deviation of a sample, how many degrees of freedom are there?

10. Suppose that $N = 50$. One calculates s via formula 4.5 (with $N - 1$ in the denominator). What are the degrees of freedom?

Section 17.4

11. A _____ of distributions is a group derived via common procedures or formulas.

12. The following questions pertain to the shape of the t distribution. All are true/false questions.
    a. It is an empirical distribution.
    b. Its shape stays the same as sample size and degrees of freedom change.
    c. Its shape changes as sample size and degrees of freedom change.
    d. As sample size and df increase, its shape becomes increasingly similar to that of a normal distribution.
    e. Whenever $N \geq 10$ ($df \geq 99$), its shape will be indistinguishable from that of a normal distribution.
    f. Whenever $N \geq 100$ ($df \geq 99$), its shape will be extremely close to normal.
    g. As sample size and df increase, the value of t within which 95% of cases are located decreases.

13. The following questions pertain to the sampling distribution of the test statistic t given a true null. In all questions, the term *population* refers to the population from which the study sample was randomly selected.

a. In your own words, how is this distribution derived?

b. (T or F) This distribution *precisely* follows a t distribution even when the population has a nonnormal distribution.

c. (T or F) Even for nonnormal populations, as sample size (and therefore the number of degrees of freedom) increases, it fairly quickly assumes a shape that closely approximates a t distribution.

d. (T or F) As the degree of skew in the population increases, the sample size necessary to approximate a t distribution increases.

e. When the degree of skewness in the population is moderate, about how large a sample is required for this distribution to approximate a t distribution? When the degree of skewness is strong?

Section 17.5

14. Whenever $N < 100$, the _____ distribution rather than the _____ distribution should be used to form confidence intervals for means.

15. Determine degrees of freedom (df), the estimate of the standard error of the mean ($s_{\bar{X}}$), and the 95% confidence interval of the mean (95%CI of μ) for each of the following. In each situation, *skew* refers to the degree of skew in the population from which the study sample was randomly selected. (As you work on each problem, be alert to the issue of whether sample size is large enough for the sampling distribution of the test statistic t to approximate a t distribution.)
    a. $N = 49$, $\bar{X} = 40.0$, $s = 21.0$, skew is strong
    b. $N = 25$, $\bar{X} = 60.0$, $s = 30.0$, skew is moderate
    c. $N = 9$, $\bar{X} = 40.0$, $s = 21.0$, skew is extreme

16. Calculate 99%CI of μ for part b in problem 15.

Section 17.6

17. The one-sample t test assumes that the population from which the study sample is randomly selected is _____ distributed. It is _____ to this assumption.

18. (T or F) The one-sample t test may be used appropriately when study sample size is very

small (N of about 10) and there are extreme outliers.

19. (T or F) The hypothesis pairs for the one-sample t test are the same as those for the large sample test of $\bar{X}$.

20. (T or F) The one-sample t test is primarily designed for use with ordinal-level data.

Section 17.7

21. Consider the following. H_0: $\mu = 80.0$ and H_1: $\mu \neq 80.0$. $N = 36$, $\bar{X} = 89.0$, $s = 18.0$, shape of distribution of study sample: moderate positive skew, $\alpha = .05$.
    a. State the research hypothesis in words.
    b. What test should be used to test the null?
    c. Is sample size large enough for carrying out the test? [That is, is it large enough so that (given a true null) the sampling distribution of the test statistic t will approximate a t distribution?]
    d. Is the hypothesis pair directional or nondirectional?
    e. Is the appropriate statistical test one-tailed or two-tailed?
    f. How many degrees of freedom are there?
    g. What is/are the critical value(s) of t?
    h. What is $s_{\bar{X}}$?
    i. What is the obtained t?
    j. What is the decision regarding the null? The research hypothesis?
    k. Is it likely that the null is true?
    l. (T or F) One can be at least 95% confident that the null is false and that the research hypothesis is true.
    m. If one were to draw the sampling distribution of the test statistic t, given a true null, would the study sample result be located in a rejection region?
    n. Stepping outside of the hypothesis testing model, is it more likely that μ (the population mean) is greater than the value stated in the null or that it is less than this value?

22. H_0: $\mu \geq 60.0$, H_1: $\mu < 60.0$. $N = 64$, $\bar{X} = 57.0$, $s = 16.0$, shape of distribution of study sample: moderate positive skew, $\alpha = .05$. For these data, respond to questions a through m from problem 21.

Section 17.8

23. (T or F) All researchers concur that the one-sample t test should never, under any circumstances, be used with ordinal-level data.

 # Computer Exercises

For general instructions on computer exercises, see the note in Chapter 2.

1. Assuming the study sample to be a random one from a larger population, what is the 95% confidence interval of μ for FCOH (family closeness/cohesion score)? [In SPSS, *Analyze > Compare Means > One Sample T Test*, click over FCOH, set test value to 0 if it isn't already, *Options*, type **95** in the space next to "Confidence Interval" if not already done, *Continue, OK.*]

   Check your answers: In the One-Sample Test box, the 95%CI of μ for FCOH extends from 39.88 to 40.65. (Note: When using SPSS's One-Sample T Test to find a confidence interval, you must have the test value set at 0. If it is not, the interval will be inaccurate.)

2. Carry out a one-sample t test to test the nondirectional null that the mean in the adoption sample is 39.8. (This is the mean for the very large sample on which norms for the cohesion score are based.) [In SPSS, follow the same instructions as in exercise 1 except enter 39.80 for Test Value.] Use the .05 level, and note that the test is two-tailed.

   Check your answers: The One-Sample Test box indicates that the test is statistically significant at the .05 level ($p = .019$). (It is unfortunate that the mean score for the normative sample was only given to one decimal place—39.8—as this makes the test less accurate than would have been ideal.) The "Mean Difference" equals the sample mean minus the test value: 40.26 − 39.80 = 0.46. The "95% Confidence Interval of the Difference" is a confidence interval for the value of the mean difference in the study population.

3. Birthweights in ounces of a random sample of babies of mothers who participated in prenatal education classes are (16 ounces = 1 pound):

96, 115, 83, 92, 133, 109, 112, 108, 121, 79, 114, 109

Calculate the 95% confidence interval of $\overline{X}$. (Presume that the degree of skew in the population is modest, so that sample size is adequate for an accurate confidence interval.) [In SPSS, enter these data in a new data set (*File > New > Data*) and perform the calculation. (You need not save any changes to the adoption data set or the data set created for this question.)]

Check your answer: 95%*CI* of μ = 95.94 to 115.89.

NOTES

1. Given a true null, when $N < 100$, the sampling distribution of the test statistic t comes reasonably close to being a normal distribution of z scores whenever both of the following conditions are met: (1) N is not small (is greater than about 30) and (2) the shape of the distribution from which the study sample was selected is not skewed to an extreme degree. When either of these conditions is not met, it does not come close to being such a distribution.

2. In examining the distributions in Figure 17.1, one is tempted to say that when $N = 5$ the t distribution is "flatter" than is the case when, for instance, $N = 100$. After all, at the point when $t = 0$ (this is the mean, median, and mode for all three presented t distributions), the curve for the $N = 5$ distribution is lower than is that for the $N = 100$ distribution. Even though the $N = 5$ curve is lower at this point, it is nonetheless somewhat more pointed (peaked) in its shape. Pragmatically, the key difference in shape between the normal distribution and the family of t distributions is the thicker and more elongated tails in the t distribution.

3. With very small samples, researchers often use substantive knowledge to supplement study sample data. For instance, if numerous large-scale studies of a given variable all indicate that this variable is nearly normally distributed, researchers studying this variable with a very small sample (say $N = 5$) would likely presume a nearly normal distribution in their study population.

4. For instance, the negative of 5 is -5. The negative of 3.27 is -3.27.

Independent Samples t Test and Dependent Samples t Test

18.1 Chapter Overview

In this chapter you learn to use two common tests based on the *sampling distribution of the difference between means*. The first test is the *independent samples t test* with its two distinct formulas, the *unequal variances formula* and the *equal variances formula*. The second test, used when the observations form *dependent pairs*, is the *dependent samples t test*. In this test, increased correlation between scores increases the power of the test. The dependent samples t test also has two formulas, including the straightforward *difference score formula*.

18.2 The Sampling Distribution of the Difference Between Means

18.2.1 *Brief Overview of the Independent Samples* t *Test*

The one-sample t test, discussed in the last chapter, determines the probability of obtaining a given sample mean under the null hypothesis that the mean in the population from which that sample was randomly selected equals some stated value. The **independent samples t test** compares means in two samples, each selected randomly from a different population. It determines the probability of obtaining these sample means under the null hypothesis that means are equal in these populations. It is one of the two or three most commonly used statistical tests.

18.2.2 *A New Sampling Distribution*

Statistical significance tests are based on sampling distributions. For instance, the one-sample t test is based on the sampling distribution of $\overline{X}$. The independent samples t test is based on the sampling distribution of the difference between means.

A **sampling distribution of the difference between means,** also known as the **sampling distribution of $\overline{X}_1 - \overline{X}_2$,** is the hypothetical distribution that would result if one (1) selected a random sample of a given size from a population and computed its mean ($\bar{X}_1$), (2) selected a random sample of a given size (it need not be of the same size as that in the first sample) from a second population and computed its mean ($\bar{X}_2$), (3) subtracted the mean of the second sample from that of the first ($\bar{X}_1 - \bar{X}_2$), (4) recorded this difference in a frequency distribution, and (5) repeated steps 1 to 4 an infinite number of times. (In repeating the steps, all samples selected from the first population should be of the same size and all samples selected from the second population should be of the same size.)

The central limit theorem conveys the following about the sampling distribution of $\bar{X}_1 - \bar{X}_2$:

1. Its mean equals the difference between the means in the populations from which the samples have been selected, that is, $\mu_1 - \mu_2$, where μ_1 is the mean in the first population and μ_2 is that in the second.
2. Its standard deviation, symbolized by $\sigma_{\bar{X}_1 - \bar{X}_2}$ and known as the **standard error of the difference between means,** is:

$$\sigma_{\bar{X}_1 - \bar{X}_2} = \sqrt{\frac{\sigma_1^2}{N_1} + \frac{\sigma_2^2}{N_2}} \qquad (18.1)$$

where σ_1^2 is the variance (σ^2) in the first population, σ_2^2 is that in the second, and N_1 and N_2 are the respective sample sizes. (Recall that the variance is the square of the standard deviation.)
3. Its shape approaches normality as sample size increases.

According to Point 1, when samples are selected from populations with equal means ($\mu_1 = \mu_2$), the mean of the sampling distribution of $\bar{X}_1 - \bar{X}_2$ is $\mu_1 - \mu_2 = 0.00$. Using Point 2, one may easily calculate the standard deviation of this sampling distribution.

Point 3 conveys that the shape of the sampling distribution of $\bar{X}_1 - \bar{X}_2$ approaches normality even when the shape of the distribution in one or both populations is nonnormal. Table 17.1 in the previous chapter presents sample size guidelines for the one-sample t test. The sampling distribution of $\bar{X}_1 - \bar{X}_2$ will have an approximately normal shape whenever both samples meet these guidelines. For instance, if the first sample is selected from a population with a strong skew, its sample size should be at least 30. If the second is selected from a population with a moderate skew, its sample size should be at least 15 (see Table 17.1).[1]

Suppose that one has two populations with the following characteristics:

Population 1: $\mu_1 = 25.00$, $\sigma_1 = 10.00$
Population 2: $\mu_2 = 25.00$, $\sigma_2 = 8.00$

Presume that one develops a sampling distribution of $\bar{X}_1 - \bar{X}_2$ by picking an infinite number of samples of size 20 ($N_1 = 20$) from Population 1 and size 16 ($N_2 = 16$) from Population 2, each time subtracting the mean of the second sample ($\bar{X}_2$) from that of the first ($\bar{X}_1$). Presume that both populations are moderately skewed. What are the characteristics of this sampling distribution?

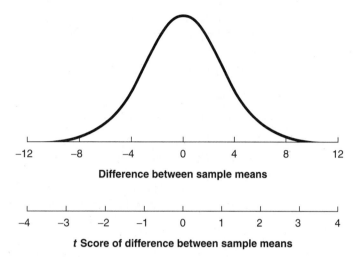

FIGURE **18.1**

SAMPLING DISTRIBUTION OF THE DIFFERENCE BETWEEN MEANS

Its mean equals $\mu_1 - \mu_2$: $25.00 - 25.00 = 0.00$. Via formula 18.1, its standard deviation equals:

$$\sigma_{\bar{X}_1 - \bar{X}_2} = \sqrt{\frac{10^2}{20} + \frac{8^2}{16}} = \sqrt{\frac{100}{20} + \frac{64}{16}} = \sqrt{5 + 4} = \sqrt{9} = 3.00$$

As both sets of samples meet the size guidelines in Table 17.1, the shape of the sampling distribution is approximately normal. Figure 18.1 presents this sampling distribution of $\bar{X}_1 - \bar{X}_2$.

18.3 THE INDEPENDENT SAMPLES *t* TEST: INTRODUCTION AND THEORY

18.3.1 *Hypotheses*

The independent samples *t* test tests the null hypothesis that the means of two populations are equal. The hypothesis pair may be directional or nondirectional. Recall from Chapter 1 (Section 1.13) that the term *group* indicates cases that have the same value on a study's key independent variable. For instance, in a study focused on gender, women would compose one group and men the other. As used in the hypothesis pairs that follow, *group* and *sample* are synonyms.

The nondirectional hypothesis pair is:

Null: The mean of the population from which Sample 1 (Group 1) was selected equals the mean of the population from which Sample 2 (Group 2) was selected.

Research: The mean of the population from which Sample 1 (Group 1) was selected is not equal to that of the population from which Sample 2 (Group 2) was selected.

Stated in mathematical symbols, this pair is:

$$H_0: \quad \mu_1 = \mu_2 \qquad H_1: \quad \mu_1 \neq \mu_2$$

One way to express the directional pair is:

Null: The mean of the population from which Sample 1 (Group 1) was selected is less than or equal to that of the population from which Sample 2 (Group 2) was selected.

Research: The mean of the population from which Sample 1 (Group 1) was selected is greater than that of the population from which Sample 2 (Group 2) was selected.

In mathematical symbols:

$$H_0: \quad \mu_1 \leq \mu_2 \qquad H_1: \quad \mu_1 > \mu_2$$

If the hypothesized difference is in the opposite direction, the directional pair is:

$$H_0: \quad \mu_1 \geq \mu_2 \qquad H_1: \quad \mu_1 < \mu_2$$

When the pair is nondirectional, the independent samples t test is two-tailed. When the pair is directional, it is one-tailed.

18.3.2   Basic Assumptions

The independent samples t test (1) requires measurement at the interval/ratio level or almost so, (2) assumes that both populations are normally distributed but is highly robust to violations of this assumption, and (3) yields accurate probabilities whenever each sample meets the sample size guidelines presented in Table 17.1.[2] It should not be used when one (or both) of the samples is very small and has extreme outliers. An additional assumption, the equality of variances assumption, applies in some situations. This assumption is discussed in the next section.

18.3.3   Two Formulas and the Equality of Variances Assumption

In real-world research, one does not know the standard deviation of the sampling distribution of the difference between means, $\sigma_{\overline{X}_1 - \overline{X}_2}$, and thus must estimate it. This estimate is symbolized by $s_{\overline{X}_1 - \overline{X}_2}$. A general formula for the independent samples t test is:

$$t = \frac{\overline{X}_1 - \overline{X}_2}{s_{\overline{X}_1 - \overline{X}_2}} \tag{18.2}$$

where t is the test statistic, $\overline{X}_1$ is the mean of the first sample (group), $\overline{X}_2$ is that of the second, and $s_{\overline{X}_1 - \overline{X}_2}$ is the estimate of the standard error of the difference between means.

The independent samples t test has two other formulas, each appropriate in a different situation. Unlike formulas that have been presented for some other procedures, these two formulas are not mathematically equivalent. Thus—with an important exception—they yield different values of t. The exception involves the situation in which sample sizes are equal, that is, when n_1 (sample size in the first group) equals n_2 (that in the second). When $n_1 = n_2$, the two formulas yield identical values of t. Though the formulas yield identical values of t with equal sample sizes, degrees of freedom differ. Thus, even with equal sample sizes, one needs to know when to use each. The two formulas differ in terms of how they estimate the standard error of the difference between means, that is, $\sigma_{\overline{X}_1 - \overline{X}_2}$.

In the first formula, $\sigma_{\overline{X}_1 - \overline{X}_2}$ is estimated by:

$$s_{\overline{X}_1 - \overline{X}_2} = \sqrt{\frac{s_1^2}{n_1} + \frac{s_2^2}{n_2}} \tag{18.3}$$

where $s_{\overline{X}_1 - \overline{X}_2}$ is the estimate of the standard error of the difference between means, s_1^2 is the variance of the sample randomly selected from the first population, s_2^2 is that of the sample randomly selected from the second population, n_1 is the number in the first sample (group), and n_2 is the number in the second. Recall from Chapter 2 (Section 2.2) that n (not capitalized) signifies the number in a group rather than in the full study sample. The first formula for the independent samples t test, known as the **unequal variances formula,** is:[3]

$$t = \frac{\overline{X}_1 - \overline{X}_2}{\sqrt{\frac{s_1^2}{n_1} + \frac{s_2^2}{n_2}}} \tag{18.4}$$

In the second formula, the method for estimating $\sigma_{\overline{X}_1 - \overline{X}_2}$ is more complex:

$$s_{\overline{X}_1 - \overline{X}_2} = \sqrt{\left(\frac{(n_1 - 1)s_1^2 + (n_2 - 1)s_2^2}{n_1 + n_2 - 2}\right)\left(\frac{1}{n_1} + \frac{1}{n_2}\right)} \tag{18.5}$$

The second formula for t, known as the **equal variances formula,** is:

$$t = \frac{\overline{X}_1 - \overline{X}_2}{\sqrt{\left(\frac{(n_1 - 1)s_1^2 + (n_2 - 1)s_2^2}{n_1 + n_2 - 2}\right)\left(\frac{1}{n_1} + \frac{1}{n_2}\right)}} \tag{18.6}$$

As already mentioned, each formula is appropriate in a different situation. The unequal variances formula is used when the variance of the population from which the first sample was selected and that from which the second was selected are unequal ($\sigma_1^2 \neq \sigma_2^2$). When these population variances are equal ($\sigma_1^2 = \sigma_2^2$), that is, when the **equality of variances** assumption (*homogeneity of variances assumption*) is met, the equal variances formula yields more accurate probabilities, so it is used.[4]

In real-world research, researchers cannot know definitively whether or not population variances are equal, so they can never be sure of which to use. This decision is typically made via an **equality of variances test** (*homogeneity of variances test*). This test's null hypothesis states that population variances are equal ($\sigma_1^2 = \sigma_2^2$), and its research hypothesis states that they are not ($\sigma_1^2 \neq \sigma_2^2$). When the test rejects the null, one should use the unequal variances formula. When it fails to reject (accepts) the null, one should, in most cases, use the equal variances (an exception will be noted shortly). Typically, the .05 statistical significance level is selected for the test. Equality of variances tests are usually carried out via statistical software programs as part of the t test procedures and hence are not covered in depth here (see Glass and Hopkins, 1996, pp. 430–437).

As just stated, there is an exception to the rule that the equal variances formula should be used whenever the equality of variances test fails to reject the null hypothesis of equal population variances. The equality of variances test has limited power when sample size is small, say when $n_1 + n_2$ is less than about 50. When this is the case, it may well fail to reject the null ($\sigma_1^2 = \sigma_2^2$) even when population variances differ quite markedly. This is a type II error, one of failing to reject a false null.

The equal variances formula is robust to the equality of variances assumption when sample sizes are equal ($n_1 = n_2$). Stated differently, with equal sample sizes, the independent samples t test yields highly accurate probabilities even if the equal variances formula is mistakenly used when population variances differ ($\sigma_1^2 \neq \sigma_2^2$). However, when sample sizes differ, violation of the equal variances assumption can lead to inaccurate probabilities.[5] As discussed above, when sample size is small, the equality of variances test may fail to reject the null even when population variances differ considerably. My recommendation is to always use the unequal variances formula when all of the three following conditions are present: (1) sample size is small ($n_1 + n_2 < 50$), (2) sample sizes are unequal, (3) sample variances differ more than modestly (when the larger variance is 50% or more larger than the smaller). Stated differently, when all three conditions are present, one should use the unequal variances formula even when the equality of variances test fails to reject the null. In all other situations—that is, whenever not all three conditions are present—one should use the unequal variances formula when the equality of variances test rejects the null and the equal variances formula when it fails to do so.

18.3.4 Distribution, Degrees of Freedom, and Decision Rules

Regardless of which formula is used, the sampling distribution of the test statistic t for the independent samples t test is described best by a t distribution.[6] As mentioned earlier, degrees of freedom differ for the two formulas. For the unequal variances formula, degrees of freedom are given by a rather complex formula (Moore and McCabe, 1993, p. 538):

$$df = \frac{\left(\dfrac{s_1^2}{n_1} + \dfrac{s_2^2}{n_2}\right)^2}{\dfrac{1}{n_1 - 1}\left(\dfrac{s_1^2}{n_1}\right)^2 + \dfrac{1}{n_2 - 1}\left(\dfrac{s_2^2}{n_2}\right)^2} \tag{18.7}$$

Sometimes formula 18.7 does not yield a whole number for degrees of freedom. One need not be concerned about this. When the equal variances formula is used, the formula for degrees of freedom is more straightforward: $df = n_1 + n_2 - 2$. Decision rules are precisely the same as those for the one-sample *t* test presented in Chapter 17 (see Section 17.6.5).

18.4 CARRYING OUT THE INDEPENDENT SAMPLES *t* TEST

18.4.1 A Note on Calculations

As mentioned earlier, the two formulas yield identical values of *t* when sample sizes are equal ($n_1 = n_2$). As comparison of the formulas reveals, the unequal variances formula (18.4) is more straightforward than is the equal variances formula (18.6). In the interest of simplicity, all calculation problems at the end of the chapter have equal sample sizes to allow use of the simpler unequal variances formula. In contrast to *t*, computation of degrees of freedom is simpler when equal variances can be assumed. (In this case: $df = n_1 + n_2 - 2$.) Whenever the unequal variances formula is used, requiring the more complex degrees of freedom formula (18.7), the number of degrees of freedom is simply provided in all problems. (There is no reason to carry out this tedious calculation when most statistical software readily provides degrees of freedom.)

18.4.2 A Calculation Example

Suppose that you teach 32 parents to monitor (count) the number of times per day that they nag their elementary school-age children. Suppose further that you randomly assign 16 parents to Group 1, which receives Method 1 of parenting skills training, and 16 parents to Group 2, which receives Method 2. Following intervention, parents monitor (count) their nagging behaviors for a week with the following results:

Group (Sample) 1: $n = 16$, $\overline{X} = 22.00$ behaviors, $s = 6.00$ behaviors

Group (Sample) 2: $n = 16$, $\overline{X} = 28.00$ behaviors, $s = 11.00$ behaviors

Presume that in each group, the shape of the distribution of nagging behaviors has a moderate positive skew.

Prior to carrying out the *t* test we should verify that sample size is adequate according to Table 17.1. Given that the degree of skew in both samples is moderate, we presume a similar degree of skew in the populations from which they were selected. When skew is moderate, Table 17.1 recommends minimum sample sizes of 15 or so. Hence the sample size is adequate in both groups ($n = 16$).

Next, we need to determine which formula to use. A quick glance at the results reveals that the standard deviation in Group 1 ($s = 6.00$) is considerably smaller than that in Group 2 ($s = 11.00$). This suggests that population variances differ and that the equality of variances assumption is not met. An equality of variances test (not presented) did indeed result in rejection of the null of equal variances ($p < .05$), so the unequal variances formula for t will be used. We may now apply the hypothesis testing model.

1. State the hypothesis pair.

   We state a nondirectional pair:

   Null: The mean number of nagging behaviors in the population from which Group 1 was randomly selected is equal to that in the population from which Group 2 was randomly selected.

   Research: The mean number of nagging behaviors in the populations from which Groups 1 and 2 were randomly selected are not equal.

   In symbols, this pair is:

   H_0: $\mu_1 = \mu_2$ H_1: $\mu_1 \neq \mu_2$

2. Choose a statistical significance level (that is, set α).

We select the .05 level. As the hypothesis pair is nondirectional, the statistical test is two-tailed.

3. Carry out the statistical significance test.

The first step is to calculate the denominator, $s_{\overline{X}_1 - \overline{X}_2}$, the estimate of the standard deviation of the sampling distribution of $\overline{X}_1 - \overline{X}_2$. Using formula 18.3:

$$s_{\overline{X}_1 - \overline{X}_2} = \sqrt{\frac{36}{16} + \frac{121}{16}} = \sqrt{\frac{157}{16}} = \sqrt{9.81} = 3.13$$

Note that the sample variances, 36 and 121, were obtained by squaring the sample standard deviations ($6^2 = 36$, $11^2 = 121$). The next step is to plug $s_{\overline{X}_1 - \overline{X}_2}$ into formula 18.2:

$$t = \frac{22.00 - 28.00}{3.13} = \frac{-6.00}{3.13} = -1.92$$

4. Make a decision.

As already mentioned, decision rules are the same as those for the one-sample t test. For a two-tailed test, the decision rule calls for rejection of the null if the absolute value of the obtained t is greater than the absolute value of the t in Table A.2 in Appendix A. To use Table A.2, one must calculate degrees of freedom using formula 18.7, the appropriate formula when variances are unequal. Via formula 18.7, there are 23.20 degrees of freedom. Just as for the one-sample t test, when the exact number of degrees of freedom is not listed, one uses the closest lower number listed, which is 23. For a two-tailed test with 23 degrees of freedom, the critical value of t at the .05 level ($\alpha = .05$) is 2.069. As the absolute value of the obtained t, 1.92, is less than 2.069, we fail to reject (accept) the null, and thus reject the research hypothesis. From the perspective of a two-tailed test at the .05 level, the difference between the sample means is not statistically significant.

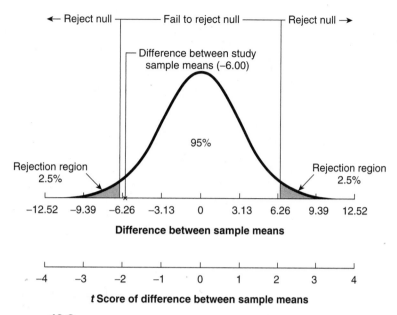

FIGURE **18.2**

t TEST RESULTS

The difference between study sample means is not within either rejection region
for a two-tailed test, $\alpha = .05$.

Given a true null, the probability of obtaining the difference obtained in the study
or an even larger difference exceeds .05. In sum, study results do not provide
sufficient grounds for concluding that population means differ.

Figure 18.2 presents the results visually. Interpreted via the top X axis (the
raw scores), the distribution presented in Figure 18.2 very closely approximates
the sampling distribution of $\bar{X}_1 - \bar{X}_2$, given a true null.[7] Interpreted via the
bottom axis (the *t* scores), the distribution in Figure 18.2 (1) is a *t* distribution with
23.20 degrees of freedom and (2) closely approximates the sampling distribution
of the test statistic *t*, given a true null. In a *t* distribution with 23.20 degrees of
freedom, 95% of cases have values between about -2.069 and 2.069. These values (the critical values) define the rejection regions. The obtained *t* in the study
sample, -1.92, is not located in a rejection area; hence the decision to fail to reject the null. The obtained *t* in this example is nearly sufficient for rejecting the
null. Had there been convincing evidence prior to the study to suggest that
Method 1 (the intervention for Group 1) would be more effective at reducing nagging, we might instead have formulated a directional hypothesis pair:

$$H_0: \quad \mu_1 \geq \mu_2 \qquad H_1: \quad \mu_1 < \mu_2$$

When the research hypothesis states "less than," one rejects the null when the
obtained *t* is less than the negative of the *t* in Table A.2 for a one-tailed test. For

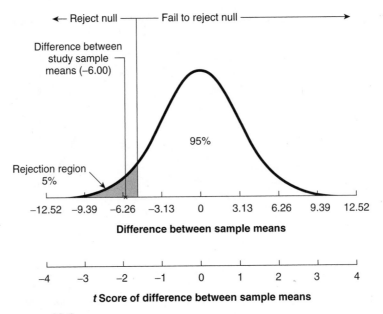

FIGURE **18.3**

REJECTION REGION FOR A ONE-TAILED TEST

The research hypothesis states "less than"; otherwise the information is the same as for the sampling distribution in Figure 18.2 (the difference between study sample means is −6.00, α = .05).

23 degrees of freedom, the t in Table A.2 for a one-tailed test when α = .05 is 1.714. The negative of this t is −1.714. The obtained t, −1.92, is indeed less than −1.714, so the null is rejected. Hence, from the perspective of a directional hypothesis, we conclude that the mean level of nagging is indeed lower for Method 1 than for Method 2. Figure 18.3 presents these results.

Presume for the moment that we have indeed rejected the null, that is, presume that we had formulated a directional hypothesis and obtained the results presented in Figure 18.3. Given these assumptions, some comments regarding the drawing of causal conclusions may be useful here. Because the null is rejected, we may conclude that chance alone (sampling error alone, the luck of the randomization, etc.) is an unlikely explanation for the difference between group means. Therefore some *real* factor (or factors) is presumably at work. In the current example, parents were randomly assigned to groups. As discussed in earlier chapters, random assignment eliminates confounding variables (see Chapter 1, Section 1.13, and Chapter 10, Section 10.6). Thus we may conclude that the real factor causing the difference between means is not a confounding variable on which the two groups differ. Instead, because of the random assignment, we may deduce that the likely causal agent is indeed the treatment intervention. The current results indicate that Method 1 may indeed *cause* a greater reduction in nagging behavior than does Method 2. Stated differently, Method 1 appears to be the more effective intervention. Had results been statistically significant but the assignment to groups nonrandom, we could have concluded that results were unlikely to be due to chance alone but could not have ruled out confounding variables.

18.4.3   Independent Samples t Test on the Computer

The best way to carry out an independent samples *t* test is via computer. A key independent variable in the special-needs adoption study is family structure, that is, whether the child was adopted into a single-parent or a two-parent family (Rosenthal and Groze, 1992). An important dependent variable is the adoptive parent's perception of the impact of the child's adoption on the family. Possible responses and assigned codes are 5, "very positive"; 4, "mostly positive"; 3, "mixed; positives and negatives about equal"; 2, "mostly negative"; and 1, "very negative." Though this variable is at the ordinal level of measurement, an independent samples *t* test was, nonetheless, performed (see Chapter 17, Section 17.8). The test examines mean family impact scores in single-parent and two-parent adoptions. Let's assume a nondirectional hypothesis pair (so we use a two-tailed test) and set α to .05. Table 18.1 presents *t* test results as generated by the SPSS for Windows program. Some help in interpreting the SPSS output is in order. First, note that the

TABLE 18.1   SPSS FOR WINDOWS INDEPENDENT SAMPLES *t* TEST RESULTS

Group Statistics

	FAMSTR Family	N	Mean	Std. Deviation	Std. Error Mean
IMPACT Impact of Adoption on Family	one parent	155	4.2903	.9186	.0738
	two parent	623	4.1284	.9452	.0379

Independent Samples Test

		Levene's Test for Equality of Variances		t-test for Equality of Means						
									95% Confidence Interval of the Mean	
		F	Sig.	t	df	Sig. (2-tailed)	Mean Difference	Std. Error Difference	Lower	Upper
IMPACT Impact of Adoption on Family	Equal variances assumed	.002	.961	1.919	776	.055	.1619	.0844	−.0037	.3275
	Equal variances not assumed			1.952	241.680	.052	.1619	.0829	−.0014	.3253

means for both groups are greater than 4, which corresponds to a response of "mostly positive." Thus, in both single- and two-parent families, the overall impact of adoption on the family is distinctly positive. Observe that the mean score is modestly higher for one-parent families than for two-parent families. Subtracting the second group mean, 4.1284, from the first, 4.2903, yields what the program labels as the "Mean Difference," which is .1619. The column labeled "Std. Error Mean" presents the estimated standard error of the mean ($s_{\bar{X}}$, the estimated standard deviation of the sampling distribution of $\bar{X}$) for both one-parent and two-parent families. (Recall that this is estimated by dividing the standard deviation in the sample by the square root of the sample size. You might want to verify for yourself that $.9186/\sqrt{155} = .0738$, and similarly, that $.945/\sqrt{623} = .0379$.)

Note that the standard deviations in the two groups, .9186 and .9452, are very similar. Given such similarity, one would expect that the equality of variances test would fail to reject (accept) the null of equal population variances. SPSS tests this assumption via Levene's test, which yields a probability of .961. Presuming that the .05 significance level has been selected for this test, .961 is greater than .05, so the null of equal population variances is indeed accepted. As such, the equal variances formula should be used. Referring to the "Equal variances assumed" row, the obtained t is 1.919 with 776 degrees of freedom. (Degrees of freedom equal $n_1 + n_2 - 2 = 155 + 623 - 2 = 776$.) Given a true null, the probability of the study result is .055 (see the column labeled "Sig. (2-tailed)." As this probability exceeds (just barely) the chosen significance level, .05, we fail to reject the null of equal means in the two populations. Study results do not provide sufficient grounds for concluding that parents in single-parent families assess the impact of their child's adoption on their family more positively than do those in two-parent families.

18.5   THE INDEPENDENCE ASSUMPTION

As applied to t tests involving differences in means, the independence of observations assumption (see Chapter 12, Section 12.5) conveys that observations in the two samples must *not* be linked as pairs. For instance, in our example on nagging, all of the observations in Group 1 were independent from those in Group 2. There was no logical "pairing" across the samples. Similarly, in the just-presented example for special-needs adoption, all of the observations in the first sample (the single-parent families) were independent from those in the second sample (two-parent families). In such a situation, one has independent samples and the independent samples t test is the appropriate test.

Consider a different situation. Suppose that a group of parents participate in your parenting skills class and that you obtain nagging scores both prior to your intervention, a **pretest,** and following it, a **posttest.** Observations in your pretest sample are not independent from those in the posttest sample but instead are logically linked. Suppose that one of the parents is named Cindy. Cindy's pretest score is not independent from her posttest score. Instead, her pretest and posttest scores form a logically linked pair. These two observations are said to be dependent. Stated differently, they form a **dependent pair** (*matched pair*).

Dependent observations most commonly occur when two measurements are taken for each study participant. This was the case in the just-provided example. Some other situations include "naturally occurring pairs" (Toothaker, 1986, p. 406)—brothers and sisters, spouses, partners, twins, roommates, and so on—as well as studies when subjects have been "matched." For instance, in some research designs, researchers identify pairs of people with similar characteristics on key variables and then assign one member of each matched pair to one intervention and the other to a second.

When all the observations in two samples form dependent pairs, the samples are said to be **paired samples** (or **dependent samples**). Other terms with nearly identical meanings are *correlated samples, related samples,* and *matched samples.*

The independent samples *t* test should be conducted only when the two samples are independent, that is, when there are no logically linked pairs across samples.[8] When all observations form dependent pairs, that is, when one has paired samples, the dependent *t* test is the appropriate statistical tool.

18.6   The Dependent Samples *t* Test

18.6.1   A First Formula, Basics, and Implications for Statistical Power

The **dependent samples *t* test** is used when observations in each sample form pairs, that is, with paired (dependent) samples. Some alternative names for the dependent samples *t* test include *t test for pairs, t test for matched samples, t test for correlated samples,* and *t test for related samples.*

With paired samples, the observations within each pair are dependent rather than independent. However, each *pair* of observations is independent from each other pair. Stated differently, though the independence of observations assumption does not hold for individual observations, it does hold with respect to the different pairs. As for the independent samples *t* test, there are two formulas for the dependent samples *t* test. We briefly consider the first formula and then focus on the second. Unlike the situation for the independent samples *t* test, the two formulas for the dependent samples *t* test are mathematically equivalent. Though they appear quite different, they yield identical results. For both formulas, (1) degrees of freedom equal $N - 1$, where N is the number of *pairs,* (2) decision rules are the same as for the independent samples test, and (3) the hypothesis pair may be either directional (one-tailed test) or nondirectional (two-tailed test). For the first formula, the hypothesis pairs are identical to those for the independent samples test. (For the second, as will be demonstrated later, one conceptualizes these pairs differently.) The first formula is:

$$t = \frac{\bar{X}_1 - \bar{X}_2}{\sqrt{\dfrac{s_1^2}{N} + \dfrac{s_2^2}{N} - 2r_{12}(s_1/\sqrt{N})(s_2/\sqrt{N})}} \tag{18.8}$$

where t is the test statistic, $\bar{X}_1$ and $\bar{X}_2$ are the sample means, s_1^2 is the variance of the first sample, s_2^2 is the variance of the second sample, r_{12} is the correlation between scores in the two samples, s_1 is the standard deviation of Sample 1, s_2 is the standard deviation of Sample 2, and N is the number of pairs.

The key difference between this formula (18.8) and the unequal variances formula for the independent samples t test (formula 18.4) is the additional term on the right side of the denominator. Study of formula 18.8 reveals that as the positive correlation between scores (r_{12}) increases, the denominator becomes smaller. As the denominator becomes smaller, the same difference in means results in a larger absolute value of t. This, in turn, increases the likelihood of rejecting the null or, stated differently, increases statistical power. When the correlation between scores is very strong, power can be increased greatly.

This increase in power can be demonstrated by reworking the example for nagging scores. Suppose that you (1) randomly select 16 parents, (2) administer a pretest on nagging, (3) carry out your intervention (the parenting class), and (4) administer a posttest. Presume a nondirectional hypothesis (and thus a two-tailed test) and selection of the .05 level. Presume the following results:

Pretest (Sample 1): $n = 16$, $\bar{X} = 22.00$ behaviors, $s = 6.00$ behaviors

Posttest (Sample 2): $n = 16$, $\bar{X} = 28.00$ behaviors, $s = 11.00$ behaviors

These data are identical to those presented earlier to demonstrate the independent samples t test. (Means, sample sizes, and standard deviations are all unchanged.) Presume first that the correlation between pretest and posttest scores is 0.00 ($r_{12} = 0.00$). Via formula 18.8, the obtained t is -1.92:[9]

$$t = \frac{22.00 - 28.00}{\sqrt{\dfrac{36}{16} + \dfrac{121}{16} - 2(0.00)(6/\sqrt{16})(11/\sqrt{16})}} = \frac{-6.00}{\sqrt{\dfrac{157}{16}}} = \frac{-6.00}{\sqrt{9.81}}$$

$$= \frac{-6.00}{3.13} = -1.92$$

For 16 pairs, and therefore 15 degrees of freedom ($16 - 1 = 15$), the critical t in Table A.2 is 2.131. As the absolute value of the obtained t is less than 2.131, we fail to reject the null.

Let's carry out the test again, this time assuming a strong positive correlation, $r_{12} = .70$, between pretest and posttest scores:

$$t = \frac{22.00 - 28.00}{\sqrt{\dfrac{36}{16} + \dfrac{121}{16} - 2(0.70)(6/\sqrt{16})(11/\sqrt{16})}}$$

$$= \frac{-6.00}{\sqrt{9.81 - 2(0.70)(1.50)(2.75)}}$$

$$= \frac{-6.00}{\sqrt{3.85}}$$

$$= -3.05$$

The obtained t is -3.05. Its absolute value, 3.05, exceeds the critical t in Table A.2 (2.131), so the null is rejected. The comparison between the two examples illustrates the substantial increase in power that typically results when scores are strongly correlated. In general, the greater the positive correlation, the greater the increase in power. When scores are strongly correlated (which is typical when pretest and posttest scores are compared), the dependent samples t test has much greater power than one would estimate from simply examining the number of pairs. In such a situation, Table 16.1, which relates power to sample size, likely underestimates power.

18.6.2   A Better Calculation Formula

The prior formula was presented to (1) show the link between the independent and dependent samples tests and (2) demonstrate that a strong correlation between scores increases power. For calculation, and for simplicity in general, the difference score formula is preferred.

A case's **difference score** is calculated by subtracting its score on Sample 2 from that on Sample 1. Suppose that Sally scores 42 on a depression measure on a pretest (Sample 1) and scores 37 on a posttest (Sample 2). Her difference score is $42 - 37 = 5$. If Juan scores 28 on the pretest and 31 on the posttest, his difference score is $28 - 31 = -3$. One version of the **difference score formula** for the dependent samples t test is:

$$t = \frac{\overline{X}_{dif}}{s_{dif}/\sqrt{N}} \tag{18.9}$$

where $\overline{X}_{dif}$ is the mean of the difference scores, s_{dif} is the standard deviation of these scores, and N is the number of pairs. A second version of this same formula is:

$$t = \frac{\overline{X}_{dif}}{s_{\overline{X}dif}} \tag{18.10}$$

where $s_{\overline{X}dif}$ estimates the standard deviation of the sampling distribution of $\overline{X}$ for the difference scores and equals $s_{dif}/\sqrt{N}$.

When one uses the first-presented dependent samples t test formula (18.8), hypothesis pairs for the dependent and independent samples tests are one and the same. The difference score formulas point out an alternative way to express the hypothesis pair. For these formulas, the nondirectional hypothesis pair can be stated as:

Null: In the population from which the sample was randomly selected, the mean of the difference scores equals 0.00.
Research: In the population from which the sample was randomly selected, the mean of the difference scores does not equal 0.00.

In symbols, the nondirectional pair is:

$$H_0: \quad \mu_{\text{dif}} = 0 \qquad H_1: \quad \mu_{\text{dif}} \neq 0$$

where μ_{dif} represents the population mean of the difference scores.
  Via symbols, the directional pairs are:

$$H_0: \quad \mu_{\text{dif}} \geq 0 \qquad H_1: \quad \mu_{\text{dif}} < 0 \qquad \text{and} \qquad H_0: \quad \mu_{\text{dif}} \leq 0 \qquad H_1: \quad \mu_{\text{dif}} > 0$$

Using the difference score formula (18.9 and 18.10), the dependent samples t test is essentially a one-sample t test (see Chapter 17, Sections 17.2 and 17.6) where the dependent variable is the difference score and the mean of that variable is hypothesized to be 0.00. Problems at the end of this chapter use the difference score formula rather than the first-presented formula (18.8) for the dependent samples t test.

18.6.3 *Applying the Hypothesis Testing Model via the Difference Score Formula*

The special-needs adoption study questionnaire was readministered to adoptive parents about four years after the initial administration (Rosenthal and Groze, 1994). A scale assessing closeness of relationship between parent and child was completed at both administrations. The highest possible scale score was 4.0 and the lowest possible score was 1.0. The higher the score, the greater the closeness between parent and child. A total of 281 parents completed the instrument at both administrations. The mean score was lower at the second administration. A dependent samples t test was conducted to see if this decrease was statistically significant. Study results were:

First administration: $N = 281$, $\overline{X} = 3.40$, $s = 0.612$

Second administration: $N = 281$, $\overline{X} = 3.11$, $s = 0.769$

The standard deviation of difference scores (s_{dif}) equaled 0.545.
  Before we carry out the hypothesis testing model, a key point should be made: The mean difference score (the mean of the difference scores) is always equal to the difference between the sample means. For instance, for the just-presented data, the difference between the samples means is $3.40 - 3.11 = 0.29$. As such, we know that the mean difference score also equals 0.29. Proceeding now with the model:

1. State the hypothesis pair.

The nondirectional hypothesis pair is:

Null: The mean difference score on the parent-child closeness scale in the population from which the sample was randomly selected equals 0.00.

Research: The mean difference score on the parent-child closeness scale in the population from which the sample was randomly selected does not equal 0.00.

2. Choose a significance level (set α).

The .01 level is selected (α is set to .01).

3. Carry out the test.

$$t = \frac{0.29}{0.545/\sqrt{281}} = \frac{0.29}{0.545/16.76} = \frac{0.29}{0.0325} = 8.92$$

4. Make a decision.

Degrees of freedom equal $N - 1$: $281 - 1 = 280$. When the exact number of degrees of freedom is not listed in Table A.2, one uses the closest lower number. This is 200. As the hypothesis pair is nondirectional, the test is two-tailed. For a two-tailed test at the .01 significance level, the *t* in Table A.2 is 2.601. The absolute value of the obtained *t*, 8.92, exceeds 2.601. Hence the null is rejected and the research hypothesis is accepted.

The significance test informs us that the reduced closeness in parent-child closeness is unlikely to be due to chance alone. The elimination of chance as a plausible explanation invites us to theorize about what real factors are involved. The second administration took place about four years after the first. At the time of the second administration, a much greater percentage of children in the study were in adolescence. Presumably, the reduced parent-child closeness is at least partly due to this.

18.6.4   Assumptions

Before we close our discussion of the dependent samples *t* test, its assumptions should be stated. The dependent samples *t* test assumes that difference scores are normally distributed in the population from which the sample was randomly selected (Toothaker, 1986, p. 413). The best way to infer the shape of the distribution of difference scores in the population is to examine their shape in the sample. The sample size guidelines in Table 17.1 may be applied with sample size considered to be the number of pairs. (When guidelines are not met, probabilities may be inaccurate.) The level of measurement should be interval/ratio or almost so.

18.7   CHAPTER SUMMARY

Based on the sampling distribution of the difference between means, the independent samples *t* test examines whether a difference between the means of two independent samples is statistically significant. The sampling distribution of $\overline{X}_1 - \overline{X}_2$ has three key characteristics: (1) Its mean equals the difference in means in the populations from which the samples were selected ($\mu_1 - \mu_2$). (2) Its standard deviation, the standard error of the difference between means ($\sigma_{\overline{X}_1 - \overline{X}_2}$), equals $\sqrt{\sigma_1^2/N_1 + \sigma_2^2/N_2}$. (3) Its shape approaches normality as sample size increases.

In real-world research, $\sigma_{\bar{X}_1-\bar{X}_2}$ is estimated by $s_{\bar{X}_1-\bar{X}_2}$. As $\sigma_{\bar{X}_1-\bar{X}_2}$ is estimated rather than known, the shape of the sampling distribution of $\bar{X}_1 - \bar{X}_2$ is described best by a t distribution.

The two formulas for the independent samples t test differ in how they calculate $s_{\bar{X}_1-\bar{X}_2}$. The unequal variances formula (18.4) is used when population variances differ, $\sigma_1^2 \neq \sigma_2^2$. The equal variances formula (18.6) is used when these are equal, $\sigma_1^2 = \sigma_2^2$. Except when sample sizes are equal, these formulas yield different values of t. For both, the nondirectional null states that population means are equal: $H_0: \mu_1 = \mu_2$.

The unequal variances formula (18.4) is relatively straightforward, $t = (\bar{X}_1 - \bar{X}_2)/\sqrt{s_1^2/n_1 + s_2^2/n_2}$, although calculation of its degrees of freedom is laborious (formula 18.7). The equal variances formula (18.6) is more complex, although its degrees of freedom are straightforward: $df = n_1 + n_2 - 2$.

One conducts an equality of variances test to see which formula should be used. This test's null is $\sigma_1^2 = \sigma_2^2$. When the test rejects the null, one uses the unequal variances formula. When it fails to do so, the equal variances formula is preferred except when all three of the following are present: (1) sample size is small ($n_1 + n_2 < 50$), (2) sample sizes are unequal, (3) sample variances differ more than modestly.

For the independence of observations assumption to apply, cases may not be linked as pairs. When cases are not linked, one has independent samples and uses the independent samples t test. When cases form pairs, one has dependent (paired) samples and uses the dependent samples t test.

The two formulas for the dependent samples t test yield identical results and have identical degrees of freedom: $N - 1$, where N is the number of pairs. As the first formula (18.8) demonstrates, the greater the positive correlation between scores, the greater the statistical power.

The second formula, the difference score formula (18.9 and 18.10), is more straightforward. To determine a case's difference score, subtract its score on Sample 2 from that on Sample 1. One difference score formula (18.9) is $t = \bar{X}_{\text{dif}}/(s_{\text{dif}}/\sqrt{N})$. When the difference score formula is used, the nondirectional null states that the mean difference score equals 0.00.

Both t tests require measurement at the interval/ratio level or almost so. Both assume normality but are highly robust to this assumption. For both, the hypothesis pair may be either nondirectional (two-tailed test) or directional (one-tailed).

PROBLEMS AND QUESTIONS

Section 18.2

1. The independent samples t test is based on the sampling distribution of the _____ between _____.

2. In your own words, describe how a sampling distribution of the difference between means is formed.

3. What is the symbol for the standard error of the difference between means?

4. $\mu_1 = 50$, $\sigma_1 = 20$, $n_1 = 100$; $\mu_2 = 60$, $\sigma_2 = 18$, $n_2 = 81$. Both population distributions have

only a modest degree of skew. Given these data, provide the following information about the sampling distribution of $\overline{X}_1 - \overline{X}_2$:
a. Its mean, $\mu_1 - \mu_2$
b. Its standard error, $\sigma_{\overline{X}_1 - \overline{X}_2}$
c. Its shape

Section 18.3

5. (T or F) The hypothesis pair for the independent samples *t* test may be either directional or nondirectional.
6. Express the nondirectional null hypothesis for the independent samples *t* test in symbols.
7. The independent samples *t* test assumes that the populations from which samples are randomly selected are _____ distributed. It is _____ to violations of this assumption.
8. (T or F) The two formulas for the independent samples *t* test (the unequal variances formula and the equal variances formula) always yield identical results.
9. (T or F) When n_1 equals n_2, the equal variances formula and the unequal variances formula yield identical values of *t*.
10. The equal variances formula is used when population variances are _____ . The unequal variances formula is used when they are _____ .
11. (T or F) In real-world research, the researcher knows definitively whether σ_1^2 equals σ_2^2.
12. What is the name of the test used to decide whether variances are equal?
13. What is the null for the equality of variances test?
14. When the null for the equality of variances test is rejected, one uses the _____ variances formula.

15. (T or F) When the equality of variances test fails to reject the null of equal population variances, one *always* uses the equal variances formula.
16. In your own words, when the equality of variances test fails to reject the null, when should one use the unequal variances formula?
17. (T or F) Even though the equal and unequal variance formulas yield different results with unequal *n*'s, degrees of freedom are always the same for each.
18. (T or F) Whenever sample sizes are equal, degrees of freedom are the same for the two formulas.

Section 18.4

19. At a mental health center, 50 clients who have problems pertaining to depression are identified. All agree to participate in a randomized experiment. Half (Group 1) are randomly assigned to a cognitive-behavioral intervention and half (Group 2) to a psychosocial-based intervention. Following treatment, a depression scale is administered. (The higher the scale score, the greater the depression.) Results are shown in Table 18PQ.1.
    a. What statistical test should be used to assess whether the difference in means is statistically significant?
    b. What is the nondirectional null?
    c. Considering the degree of skew, are sample sizes adequate for carrying out an independent samples *t* test?
    d. Are the 50 clients a random or a nonrandom sample? (This is a trick question.)
    e. In essence, one's hypothesis pair pertains

| TABLE 18PQ.1 | COMPARISON OF DEPRESSION IN TWO TREATED GROUPS | | | |

Intervention	$\overline{X}$	*s*	*n*	Shape of Sample Distribution
Cognitive-behavioral	48.0	10	25	Moderate positive skew
Psychosocial	59.0	12	25	Moderate positive skew

Note: Data are hypothetical.

to the extremely large population from which the study sample or samples were randomly selected. In this study, is this extremely large population real (composed of real people) or imaginary (abstract, hypothetical, theoretical)?

f.   (T or F) Even though the just-described population is imaginary and thus the study samples are not truly random samples, many researchers would indeed say that a statistical test may be conducted.

g.   Even though the sampling process was not random, the process of assignment to groups was random. Comment on how this affects the degree to which causal conclusions can be drawn.

h.   Just as a rough estimate, what is the standardized difference between means (SDM)?

i.   Presume that the equality of variances test results in acceptance of the null (p > .05). Which formula for the independent samples t test should be used?

j.   Via formula 18.3, what is the estimate of the standard error of the difference between means, $s_{\bar{X}_1 - \bar{X}_2}$?

k.   Via formula 18.4, what is the value of t?

l.   Should degrees of freedom be those that apply to the equal variances formula or to the unequal variances formula?

m.   What is the formula for degrees of freedom? How many degrees of freedom are there?

n.   Given that α = .05 and that the test is two-tailed, what are the critical values of t?

o.   What values of t result in rejection?

p.   What is your decision regarding the null? The research hypothesis?

q.   Is it likely or unlikely that the study result is due to chance alone (sampling error alone)?

r.   (T or F) One can be 95% confident that the null is false.

s.   (T or F) One may conclude that it is likely that the null is false in the extremely large population(s) from which the study samples were assumed to be randomly selected. (To some degree, this is a trick question.)

t.   The answer to the previous question is

True. Does this conclusion have real-world meaning? Explain.

u.   (T or F) One may be 95% confident that the study sample result is due to something real (something other than sampling error).

v.   The answer to the prior question is True. Does this conclusion have real-world meaning?

w.   (T or F) The something real that caused the study result is quite likely a confounding variable.

20. Consider the following data:

Group 1: n = 30, $\bar{X}$ = 40.00 behaviors, s = 8.00 behaviors
Group 2: n = 30, $\bar{X}$ = 45.00 behaviors, s = 20.00 behaviors

Presume that both samples have only a modest degree of skew, that the research hypothesis is $\mu_1 < \mu_2$, that the .05 significance level is selected (α = .05), and that the null of equal variances was rejected in the equality of variances test. Respond to the following.

a.   Are sample results in the expected direction?

b.   What is the null?

c.   Given the degree of skew, are sample sizes sufficient so that results will be reasonably accurate?

d.   Which formula for the t test should be used?

e.   Via formula 18.3, what is $s_{\bar{X}_1 - \bar{X}_2}$?

f.   What is t?

g.   Via formula 18.7, df = 38.05. What is the critical value of t and what values of t lead to rejection of the null?

h.   What is your decision regarding the null? the research?

i.   Is it plausible that the difference in means is due simply to sampling error/chance?

j.   (T or F) One may be 95% confident that the null is false.

21. Consider the following data:

Group 1: n = 10, $\bar{X}$ = 20.00, s = 10.00
Group 2: n = 25, $\bar{X}$ = 15.00, s = 15.00

Presume that the degree of skew is modest in both samples. Presume that the null hypothesis of equal population variances is accepted via an equality of variances test.

a. What is s_1^2? What is s_2^2?

b. How can it be that the null of equal population variances is accepted even though the sample variances differ considerably?

c. Should the equal or unequal variances formula be used? Why?

22. Consider the following data:

Group 1: $n = 36$, $\overline{X} = 20.00$, $s = 16.00$
Group 2: $n = 36$, $\overline{X} = 15.00$, $s = 15.00$

Calculate *df*, $s_{\overline{X}_1 - \overline{X}_2}$, and *t*, and state your decision regarding the null. Presume that the hypothesis pair is nondirectional, that $\alpha = .01$, and that the equality of variances test fails to reject the null of equal population variances.

Section 18.5

23. Observations taken prior to intervention are termed a _____ . Those taken subsequent to intervention are termed a _____ .

24. Two observations that are paired ("linked") form a _____ pair.

25. When all observations in two samples form matched/dependent pairs, these samples are termed _____ samples.

26. Each of the following items lists two samples. Indicate whether these samples are dependent (paired) or independent.

a. Brothers; sisters of these brothers.

b. Those who receive Intervention X; others who receive Intervention Y.

c. Clients take pretest; same clients take posttest.

d. A group of clients receive an intervention. Each member of the group is "matched" with someone of similar age, sex, gender, and problem type who did not receive the intervention.

e. Women in a human relations class; the men in that class.

Section 18.6

27. Other things being equal, as the positive correlation between the scores of dependent pairs increases, the denominator of the dependent samples *t* test (formula 18.8) becomes

_____ and the absolute value of *t*, therefore, becomes _____ .

28. Other factors being equal, as the positive correlation increases, the size of the difference between means that is necessary to reject the null _____ .

29. When the correlation between pretest and posttest scores is strong (and positive), power is often much _____ than would be expected given the number of pairs.

30. How are degrees of freedom calculated for the dependent samples *t* test?

31. (T or F) The calculation formulas for the dependent samples *t* test (formula 18.8 versus the difference score formulas, 18.9 and 18.10) yield identical results and have the same number of degrees of freedom.

32. Sally's score in Sample 1 is 25. Her score in Sample 2 is 30. What is Sally's difference score?

33. Fred's scores are 22.5 in Sample 1 and 20.3 in Sample 2. What is Fred's difference score?

34. In terms of difference scores, how is the null hypothesis for the dependent samples *t* test expressed?

35. (T or F) The mean of the difference scores equals the difference between the sample means.

36. Consider the following data:

Pretest (Sample 1): $n = 36$, $\overline{X} = 20.00$, $s = 16.00$
Posttest (Sample 2): $n = 36$, $\overline{X} = 15.00$, $s = 15.00$

The standard deviation of difference scores (s_{dif}) equals 12.00. The distribution of difference scores has a moderate negative skew. Presume that the hypothesis pair is nondirectional and that $\alpha = .05$. For these data, answer the following questions.

a. What is the appropriate statistical test for testing the significance of the difference in means?

b. Given the amount of skew, is sample size (the number of pairs) sufficient?

c. What is the difference between means $(\overline{X}_1 - \overline{X}_2)$?

d. What is the mean of the difference scores?
e. What is the number of pairs?
f. What is the standard error of the mean of the difference scores, $s_{\bar{X}\text{dif}}$?
g. What is the obtained t?
h. How many degrees of freedom are there?
i. Is the appropriate test one-tailed or two-tailed?
j. What are the critical values of t?
k. What is your decision regarding the null hypothesis? Regarding the research hypothesis?
l. Is it likely that the observed difference in means is due simply to chance/sampling error?
m. Can you be at least 95% confident that the null is false?

37. The dependent samples t test is based on the assumption that difference scores are _____ distributed. It is _____ to this assumption.

 ## COMPUTER EXERCISES

For general instructions on computer exercises, see the note in Chapter 2.

1. Carry out an independent samples t test to determine whether the mean score on RELSCALE (closeness/quality of parent-child relationship) differs significantly by FOSTER (adoption by prior foster parents versus "new" parents). [In SPSS, *Analyze > Compare Means > Independent Samples T Test*, click RELSCALE over into the space beneath "Test Variable(s)," click FOSTER over into the "Grouping Variable" space, *Define Groups:* type **0** into space next to "Group 1" and **1** into space next to Group 2 (0 conveys adoptions that are not by foster parent and 1 those that are), *Continue, OK.*] Carry out a two-tailed test at the .05 level.

Check your answers: In the Independent Samples Test table, Levene's test for equality of variances is significant ($p < .05$). Thus the null of equal population variances is rejected and the "Equal variances not assumed" test is preferred.

The two-tailed probability of this test, listed in the "Sig. (2-tailed)" column, is highly significant, $p = .000$. The null of equal mean scores in foster and nonfoster adoptions is rejected.

2. Carry out an independent samples t test to determine whether the mean score on RELSCALE (closeness/quality of parent-child relationship) differs significantly by GENDER (gender of adoptive child). [In SPSS, *Analyze > Compare Means > Independent Samples T Test*, click back FOSTER, click GENDER over to "Grouping Variable" space, *Define Groups:* type **0** into space next to "Group 1" and **1** into space next to Group 2 (0 conveys boys, 1 conveys girls), *Continue, OK.*] Carry out a one-tailed test where the research hypothesis states that girls have greater closeness and $\alpha = .05$.

Check your answers: In the Independent Samples Test table, Levene's test for equality of variances is significant ($p < .05$). Thus the null of equal population variances is rejected and the "Equal variances not assumed" test is preferred. Results are in the expected direction (though just barely so), so we may divide the two-tailed probability by 2 to obtain the one-tailed probability: $.637/2 = .3185$. As $p > .05$, the null is accepted.

3. Carry out a two-tailed dependent samples t test with α set to .01 to determine whether there is a statistically significant difference between score on INTERNAL ("withdrawn" kinds of behavioral problems) and that on EXTERNAL ("acting out"/aggressive problems). [In SPSS, *Analyze > Compare Means > Paired-Samples T Test*, highlight (select) both INTERNAL and EXTERNAL and click them over, *OK.*]

Check your answers: In the Paired Samples Statistics table, the mean for EXTERNAL is .4486 and that for INTERNAL is .2588. In the Paired Samples Test table, the mean score on EXTERNAL minus that on INTERNAL is $.4486 - .2588 = .1897$. This difference is highly significant, $p = .000$ (two-tailed test).

4. Determine whether the mean IMPACT (impact of adoption on family) scores differ significantly at the .05 level (two-tailed test) for children with and without handicaps (HANDICAP; 0 = no handicap, 1 = handicap).

Check your answer: Because the null of equal population variances is accepted, $p = .561$, the equal variances formula should be used. In the independent samples t test (equal variances formula), the mean scores do not differ significantly: $t (778) = 0.171$, $p = .865$.

NOTES

1. Table 17.1 provides basic working guidelines. A close approximation to normality is often reached more rapidly than these guidelines suggest.

2. As you know, the researcher infers the shape of the population distribution from that of the sample (see discussion in Chapter 17, Section 17.6). With very small samples, the shape of the population distribution may differ markedly from that of the sample, so some caution should be used in applying the sample size guidelines in Table 17.1. However, if one uses a nondirectional hypothesis pair and thus conducts a two-tailed test, highly accurate results will typically be obtained when sample size comes even reasonably close to meeting the guidelines. On the other hand, with a directional hypothesis and therefore a one-tailed test, the guidelines should be followed more strictly. In such a situation, one should conduct the independent samples t test only with reasonable confidence that the guidelines are met.

3. When a t test is carried out via the unequal variances formula, it is often referred to as Welch's t test or as an AWS (for Aspin-Welch-Satterthwaite) procedure (Toothaker and Miller, 1996, p. 422).

4. In the equal variances formula, the left side of the denominator estimates the population variance:

$$\left(\frac{(n_1 - 1)s_1^2 + (n_2 - 1)s_2^2}{n_1 + n_2 - 2} \right)$$

Because this formula is used when variances are equal ($\sigma_1^2 = \sigma_2^2$), only one population variance must be estimated. The equal variances formula pools together data from both samples to estimate of the population variance, so it is sometimes termed the *pooled variance formula*. (The left side of the denominator is often termed the *pooled variance estimate*.) In contrast, the unequal variances formula estimates two different variances, σ_1^2 and σ_2^2. It is sometimes termed the *separate variances formula*.

5. As a general rule, the probabilities yielded by the two formulas differ markedly only when *both* of the following conditions are true: (1) the sample standard deviations differ markedly (the larger standard deviation is 50% or more larger than that of the smaller) and (2) sample sizes differ markedly (the larger sample is at least 50% larger than the smaller). In general, the larger the difference between the sample standard deviations and the larger the difference in sample sizes, the greater the difference in the probabilities indicated by the formulas.

6. When the unequal variances formula is used, the sampling distribution of the test statistic t cannot be precisely described by a t distribution (Moore and McCabe, 1993, p. 532), but the approximation is close enough so that the t distribution may be used with limited loss of accuracy.

7. Because the population variances, σ_1^2 and σ_2^2, are estimated rather than known, Figures 18.2 and 18.3 can only approximate the sampling distribution of $\bar{X} - \bar{X}_2$. Interpreted by the top axis, the distribution in Figure 18.2 is the distribution that would result if one took the following steps: (1) selected a random sample of size 16 from a normally distributed population where $\sigma = 6.0$, (2) selected a random sample of similar size from a second normally distributed population with a mean equal to that of the first where $\sigma = 11.0$, (3) subtracted the second mean from that of the first, (4) recorded that difference, and (5) repeated steps 1 through 4 an infinite number of times.

8. When only a small percentage of cases (say 10% or less) are dependent (linked), the researcher may either (1) randomly select one member from each pair to be excluded from the study and then conduct an independent samples t test or (2) carry out the test, recognizing that the probability yielded by the test is not likely to be precisely accurate.

9. The obtained t, -1.92, is identical to that obtained earlier via the independent samples t test. When r_{12} equals 0.00, the denominator's right side term drops out, so the dependent samples t test formula (18.8) becomes essentially identical to the unequal variances formula for the independent samples test (formula 18.5). (Although formula 18.5 uses n_1 and n_2 and formula 18.8 uses N, given equal sample sizes, $n_1 = n_2 = N$, where n_1 is the number of cases in Group 1, n_2 is that in Group 2, and N is the number of pairs.)

SINGLE SAMPLE TESTS OF PROPORTIONS

19.1 CHAPTER OVERVIEW

Considering the many variables measured at the nominal level—male or female, intervention programs A, B, or C—we need a way to test for significant differences for these variables. Such tests are based on differences between proportions, which convey variability between nominal categories. We begin with the *one-sample test of a proportion*. Next we use a new distribution, the *chi-square distribution*, and a statistical test based on it, the *one-variable chi-square test*. Discussion of this test introduces *expected* and *observed proportions*, and *expected* and *observed frequencies*. We work with both hand and computer calculations.

19.2 ONE-SAMPLE TEST OF A PROPORTION

19.2.1 Introduction and When to Use It

The **one-sample test of a proportion,** also known as the **one-sample test of p,** examines whether a sample proportion, p, differs significantly from some stated value. For instance, suppose that an instrument that assesses child behavior problems is administered to a random sample of 25,000 children from across the United States and that 10% (.10) of children obtain scores that are sufficiently high to indicate the presence of serious behavior problems. Suppose further that you are a school social worker at an elementary school in an economically depressed area. Major layoffs have recently occurred at the area's key employer. Teachers at your school tell you that increased numbers of children are presenting with behavior problems. You administer the behavior problems instrument to the 200 children at your school and determine that, as defined by the instrument, 17% have serious problems. Can you conclude that the percentage (proportion) of serious behavior problems in your school differs significantly from 10%, the percentage in the large sample? To answer this question, you need to determine the probability that a sample of size 200 in which p (the sample proportion) equals .17 would be randomly selected from a population in which π (pi, the population proportion) equals .10.

Like confidence intervals for proportions, the one-sample test of p is based on the sampling distribution of the proportion (the sampling distribution of p). The standard deviation of this distribution, which is the standard error of the proportion, σ_p, equals $\sqrt{\pi(1-\pi)/N}$, according to formula 13.6. Its shape is quite close to normal whenever the sample size guidelines presented in Table 13.1 are met.

19.2.2 Basics

The one-sample test of p yields highly accurate results whenever the sample size guidelines in Table 13.1 are met. In evaluating the guidelines, one uses the value of π stated in the null rather the proportion (p) obtained in the sample.[1] The nondirectional hypothesis pair (two-tailed test) states:

> *Null:* The proportion in the population from which the study sample was randomly selected equals a given value.

> *Research:* The proportion in the population from which the study sample was randomly selected does not equal this given value.

In mathematical symbols this pair is:

$$H_0: \quad \pi = A \qquad H_1: \quad \pi \neq A$$

where π is the proportion in the population from which the study sample was randomly selected and A is some given value. In symbols, the directional hypothesis pairs (one-tailed test) are:

$$H_0: \quad \pi \leq A \qquad H_1: \quad \pi > A \qquad \text{and} \qquad H_0: \quad \pi \geq A \qquad H_1: \quad \pi < A$$

One formula for the one-sample test of p is:

$$z = \frac{p - \pi}{\sqrt{\pi(1-\pi)/N}} \tag{19.1}$$

where p is the proportion in the study sample, π is the proportion stated in the null, and N is the sample size. A second (mathematically equivalent) formula is:

$$z = \frac{p - \pi}{\sigma_p} \tag{19.2}$$

where σ_p is the standard error of the proportion given a true null and equals $\sqrt{\pi(1-\pi)/N}$.

The decision rules for the one-sample test of p are the same as those for the large sample test of $\overline{X}$ (see Chapter 15, Sections 15.10, 15.11, 15.14, 15.16, and 15.17). To expedite discussion, the decision rule for a nondirectional hypothesis pair using the .05 significance level is repeated here:

> When the absolute value of the obtained z is less than or equal to 1.96, fail to reject (accept) the null.

When the absolute value of the obtained z is greater than 1.96, reject the null.

19.2.3 Carrying Out the Behavior Problems Example

We may now proceed with the behavior problems example. A first step is to check that the sample size guidelines for proportions in Table 13.1 have been met. As previously stated, the hypothesized proportion (π) rather than the study sample proportion (p) is used for this purpose. When π equals .10, the minimum required sample size according to Table 13.1 is 180. The study sample size, $N = 200$, exceeds this, so the test may be carried out.

1. State the hypothesis pair.

The combination of a solid explanation for the apparent increase in behavior problems (the stress generated by the plant closing) and preliminary data (the teachers' reports of increased problems) argues in favor of a directional hypothesis pair. However, choice of the type of pair rests ultimately with the researcher. Given that nondirectional pairs are far more common in research and given this text's preference for these pairs (see the last four paragraphs of Section 15.16 in Chapter 15), the pair will be nondirectional:

Null: The proportion of children with serious behavior problems in the population from which the study sample was randomly selected equals .10.

Research: The proportion of children with serious behavior problems in the population from which the study sample was randomly selected does not equal .10.

In symbols, these hypotheses are:

$$H_0: \quad \pi = .10 \qquad H_1: \quad \pi \neq .10$$

2. Choose the significance level (set alpha, α).

We will set α equal to .05 (use the .05 significance level).

3. Carry out the test.

The first step is to determine the standard error of the proportion:

$$\sigma_p = \sqrt{\frac{.10(1-.10)}{200}} = \sqrt{\frac{.10(.90)}{200}} = \sqrt{\frac{.09}{200}} = \sqrt{.00045} = .021$$

Next, σ_p is inserted into formula 19.2:

$$z = \frac{.17 - .10}{.021} = \frac{.07}{.021} = 3.30$$

4. Make a decision.

The decision rule for a two-tailed test when $\alpha = .05$ calls for rejection of the null when the absolute value of the obtained z is 1.96 or greater. As the absolute of the

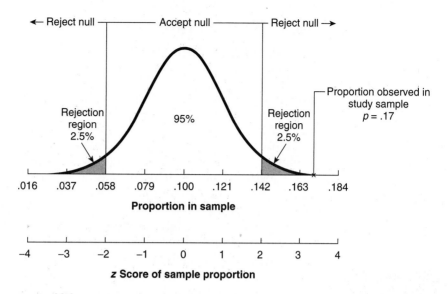

19.1

STATISTICAL SIGNIFICANCE OF SAMPLE PROPORTION WITH BEHAVIOR PROBLEMS

The sampling distribution of the proportion is based on data from a national sample and has a mean of .10. In comparison, one school has a proportion of .17 children with serious behavior problems. The rejection regions are for a one-sample test of the proportion with a two-tailed test and $\alpha = .05$. (Data are hypothetical.)

obtained z, 3.30, exceeds 1.96, the null is rejected. At the .05 level (two-tailed test), study results do indeed achieve statistical significance. Results of the significance test indicate that the elevated level of behavior problems in your school is unlikely to be due solely to chance. As such, you may conclude that real factors (perhaps the layoffs at the plant) are likely also involved. Figure 19.1 presents results visually.

Note that even though the study sample for this example was not actually selected from any larger population—all students in the school were tested—a statistical significance test was nonetheless carried out. As presented in Chapter 16, Section 16.8, most researchers agree that tests may be carried out in the absence of random sampling. In such situations, conclusions about the study sample do make real-world sense. For instance, in this study, we concluded that chance alone was an unlikely explanation for the increased behavior problems in this sample. However, a conclusion about a population would not make real-world sense. For instance, in the current example the test results allow us to conclude that the null ($\pi = .10$) is probably not true in the population from which the sample was randomly selected. No such population actually exists. (It is abstract, or imaginary.) As such, this conclusion, though correct, has no real-world meaning.

19.3 INTRODUCTION TO THE ONE-VARIABLE CHI-SQUARE TEST

The one-sample test examines whether a single proportion differs significantly from a hypothesized proportion. The **one-variable chi-square test** (*goodness-of-fit chi-square test*) examines whether the overall distribution of proportions for a categorical variable differs significantly from a set of hypothesized proportions. Chi (pronounced "ki" as in "kite") is symbolized by the Greek letter χ, so the test is also designated as the **one-variable χ^2 test.** Like the one-sample test of p, it is not a workhorse but is used more than occasionally.

An example can clarify how the one-variable χ^2 test is used. Suppose that you are a social work student and that your school of social work offers three concentrations for students to choose from in the second year of their master's program: (1) a direct practice concentration, (2) a community practice concentration, and (3) a combined concentration integrating direct and community practice. You wonder whether students are (1) more likely to choose some concentration(s) than others or (2) equally likely to choose each concentration, and you decide to study this topic. If students are equally likely to choose each, then in the large population of students from which the study sample will be selected,[2] one-third will choose each concentration. Stated as proportions, the proportion selecting each concentration will be .33: 1.00/3 = .33. This is the null hypothesis.

Suppose that among 90 students, the actual distribution of proportions is as follows: direct practice, $p = .50$ (45 students, 45/90 = .50); community practice, $p = .22$ (20 students, 20/90 = .22); and combined practice, $p = .28$ (25 students, 25/90 = .28.) Given a true null, what is the probability of obtaining such proportions? Do these differ sufficiently from those stated in the null so that we may conclude that they are unlikely to be due to chance? The one-variable χ^2 test addresses questions such as these.

19.4 THE CHI-SQUARE DISTRIBUTION

Recall that the sampling distribution of a test statistic is the distribution that would be obtained if one selected an infinite number of random samples and for each sample calculated and recorded the test statistic. Given a true null and given that sample size guidelines to be presented later are met, the sampling distribution of the test statistic χ^2 closely follows (that is, comes extremely close to being) a chi-square (χ^2) distribution. Rather than covering the statistical theory underlying the **chi-square (χ^2) distribution,** this text simply defines it as the key distribution for significance tests involving differences between proportions. We examine two statistical tests for which the test statistic is χ^2, the one-variable χ^2 test presented here and the χ^2 test of independence presented in the next chapter.

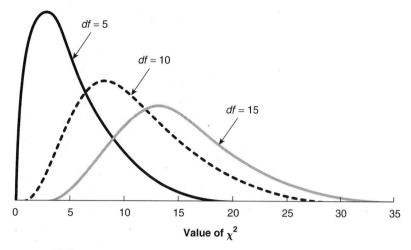

FIGURE 19.2

THREE CHI-SQUARE DISTRIBUTIONS

Like the t distribution, the χ^2 distribution is a family of distributions that take on different characteristics according to degrees of freedom. A unique χ^2 distribution corresponds to each degree of freedom. For the one-variable χ^2 test, degrees of freedom equal the number of categories minus 1. If J symbolizes the number of categories, then $df = J - 1$. In the concentration choice example, there are three concentrations, so $df = 3 - 1 = 2$.[3] Hence, given a true null and adequate sample size, the distribution of test statistic χ^2 for this example will closely follow a χ^2 distribution with two degrees of freedom.

Let's examine some selected characteristics of the χ^2 distribution. Most importantly, the mean of a χ^2 distribution equals its degrees of freedom. For instance, the mean of a χ^2 distribution with five degrees of freedom is 5.[4] Second, all χ^2 distributions are positively skewed. The degree of skew decreases as the degrees of freedom increase. Figure 19.2 presents χ^2 distributions for three selected degrees of freedom. (For the theory that underlies the χ^2 distribution, see Glass and Hopkins, 1996, pp. 422–428, or many other texts.)

As already stated, given a true null and adequate sample size, the sampling distribution of the test statistic χ^2 for the one-variable χ^2 test closely follows a χ^2 distribution with $J - 1$ degrees of freedom. This being the case (given a true null and adequate sample size), one expects the obtained χ^2 to be reasonably close to (not to differ greatly from) the mean of the χ^2 distribution that it follows. (The obtained χ^2 would differ greatly from this distribution's mean only if, by the luck of the draw, it was located in a tail of the distribution.) A χ^2 distribution's mean equals its degrees of freedom. Hence, with five degrees of freedom, one expects the obtained χ^2 to be reasonably close to 5. In the concentration choice example, degrees of freedom equal two, so you would expect (given a true null and adequate sample size) the obtained χ^2 to be reasonably close to this.

On the other hand, when the null is false, one expects the obtained χ^2 to be larger than the number of degrees of freedom, often considerably so. For instance, given a false null, you would expect the obtained χ^2 for the concentration choice example to be larger than 2.

In sum, values of χ^2 not greatly different from the number of degrees of freedom ($J - 1$ for the one-variable χ^2 test) are consistent with a true null. Values of χ^2 considerably greater than this indicate that the null may well be false. The exact value of χ^2 necessary for rejection (the critical value) varies according to the degrees of freedom. Table A.3 in Appendix A presents critical values for χ^2 distributions with differing degrees of freedom. (Use of this table is demonstrated later in the chapter.) All statistical tests based on the χ^2 distribution are one-tailed tests. They have only one rejection region, which is always in the distribution's upper tail.

Values of χ^2 less than the degrees of freedom are consistent with the null hypothesis. In effect, such values indicate that the amount of sampling error in one's study sample is less than the expected or typical amount, given a true null.

19.5   EXPECTED AND OBSERVED PROPORTIONS AND FREQUENCIES

Before we discuss the one-variable χ^2 test in detail, an introduction to expected proportions, expected frequencies, observed proportions, and observed frequencies is in order. These terms are used for both the one-variable χ^2 test and for the χ^2 test of independence presented in the next chapter. This chapter defines the terms as they apply to the one-variable χ^2 test.

A category's **expected proportion** (or if percentages are used, its *expected percentage*) conveys the predicted proportion of responses for that category, given a true null. Expected proportion equals the proportion stated in the null; they are basically one and the same. For instance, in the example of choice of concentration, the null states that the proportion in each category (concentration) is .33 ($\pi = .33$). That is, the expected proportion for each category is .33. A category's **expected frequency** is the predicted frequency of responses for that category, given a true null. To compute expected frequency, one multiplies the proportion stated in the null (the expected proportion) by the sample size (N). For instance, the expected frequency for each category in the concentration choice example is .33(90) = 30. A category's **observed proportion** is the actual proportion of responses in that category (*observed percentage* is the actual percentage). For instance, the observed proportion choosing direct practice is 45/90 = .50. Finally, a category's **observed frequency** is the actual frequency of responses in that category. For instance, the observed frequency of direct practice students is 45.

19.6 CARRYING OUT THE
ONE-VARIABLE CHI-SQUARE TEST

19.6.1 Background, Sample Size, and Decision Rules

The one-variable χ^2 test is used most often with nominal-level variables. It may be used with ordinal-level variables but is less than optimal in this situation. With one exception, it yields sufficiently accurate probabilities whenever the *average* expected frequency equals at least four.[5] The exception involves situations with only two categories. In this case, use the sample size guidelines in Table 13.1. In assessing these guidelines, one uses the hypothesized proportions (π) rather than the sample proportions (p). An example of how to use these is presented later in the chapter. When sample size guidelines are met (and given a true null), the test statistic χ^2 for the one-variable χ^2 test closely follows a χ^2 distribution with $J - 1$ degrees of freedom, where J is the number of categories. (See Glass and Hopkins, 1996, p. 335 for greater information on sample size guidelines.)

All hypothesis pairs for the one-variable χ^2 test are nondirectional. The general form of the hypothesis pair is as follows:

Null: Each proportion in the population from which the study sample was randomly selected equals some given value.
Research: At least one proportion in the population from which the study sample was randomly selected differs from the value stated for it in the null.

The proportions stated in the null must sum to 1.00. (Proportions in our last example sum to 0.99 rather than to 1.00 due to rounding error.)

Rejection of the null conveys that at least one proportion differs significantly from the value stated for it in the null. Rejection does not allow one to conclude which specific proportion differs or whether more than one does so. One may think of the one-variable χ^2 test as testing the full distribution of proportions. When the null is rejected, one concludes that the distribution in the population from which the study sample was selected is not identical to that described in the null.

One formula for the one-variable χ^2 test is:

$$\chi^2 = N\left(\sum \frac{(p_o - p_e)^2}{p_e} \right) \tag{19.3}$$

where N is the sample size, Σ is the summation sign, p_o is the observed proportion for a category, and p_e is the expected proportion for a category. Study of formula 19.3 reveals that the greater the difference between observed and expected proportions, the greater the obtained χ^2, and thus the greater the likelihood of rejecting the null. (Another formula, easier for hand calculation, is presented shortly.)

Decision rules for the one-variable χ^2 test are to:

Fail to reject (accept) the null if the obtained χ^2 is less than the critical value listed in Table A.3 in Appendix A.

Reject the null if the obtained χ^2 is greater than or equal to the critical value listed in Table A.3.

Chapter 15 (Section 15.7) stated the following guideline: Use a one-tailed test with a directional hypothesis pair and a two-tailed test with a nondirectional pair. It also stated that there is an exception to this guideline. The guideline applies only to statistical tests for which the hypothesis pair may be either directional or nondirectional. For some tests, the hypothesis pair is always nondirectional; a directional pair is not allowed. Contrary to the guideline, tests that permit only a nondirectional hypothesis are always *one*-tailed. The one-variable χ^2 test is such a test; its hypothesis pair is always nondirectional, so it is always one-tailed.

In sum, the one-variable χ^2 test can examine whether study sample proportions (observed proportions) differ from hypothesized proportions (expected proportions) to a statistically significant degree but cannot examine the direction of these differences.[6] The test's rejection region is always in the upper tail.

19.6.2 *Applying the Hypothesis Testing Model*

We may now apply the hypothesis testing model to the data for student choice of concentration. As already stated, for accurate results, the average expected frequency should be at least four. To calculate the average expected frequency, one divides the sample size by the number of categories. Sample size is 90 and the number of categories is three: 90/3 = 30. The average expected frequency of 30 exceeds four. Hence the test will yield accurate results and we may proceed.

1. State the hypothesis pair.

   Null: In the population from which the study sample was randomly selected, the proportion is .33 for each concentration.

   Research: In the population from which the study sample was randomly selected, the proportion is not .33 for each concentration.

2. Select the significance level (set α).

The .05 significance level will be used (α = .05).

3. Carry out the test.

Formula 19.3 demonstrates that the one-variable χ^2 test examines whether observed proportions (those in the study sample) differ from expected proportions (those hypothesized for the population) to a degree that is greater than would be expected by chance. However, an easier (and mathematically equivalent) formula for hand calculation is:

$$\chi^2 = \sum \frac{(f_o - f_e)^2}{f_e} \tag{19.4}$$

where f_o is the observed frequency in a category and f_e is the expected frequency.

Recall that expected frequency is derived by multiplying the proportion stated in the null (the expected proportion) by the sample size. As calculated earlier, the

TABLE 19.1	CALCULATION OF χ^2 FOR CHOICE OF CONCENTRATION				
Category	f_o	f_e	$f_o - f_e$	$(f_o - f_e)^2$	$(f_o - f_e)^2/f_e$
Direct	45	30	15	225	7.50
Community	20	30	−10	100	3.33
Combined	25	30	−05	25	0.83
				Sum = χ^2 =	11.86

expected frequency for each category is .33(90) = 30. Formula 19.4 directs one to do the following for each category: (1) subtract the expected frequency from the observed frequency, (2) square this difference, and (3) divide by the expected frequency. For step 4, the summation sign (Σ) directs one to sum the results from step 3. These steps are best carried out with a grid like the one in Table 19.1.

  4. Make a decision.

Degrees of freedom equal the number of categories minus 1: $df = 3 - 1 = 2$. Consulting Table A.3 in Appendix A, at the .05 significance level, the critical value for a χ^2 statistic with two degrees of freedom is 5.99. As the obtained χ^2, 11.86, exceeds this, the null is rejected. We conclude that at least one proportion in the population from which the study sample was selected differs from the value stated for it in the null. Or, viewing it differently, we conclude that the overall distribution of proportions in this population differs from that stated in the null.

  Figure 19.3 presents the study results and demonstrates that the probability that our study result is due to chance alone is less than .05. Hence we make the decision to reject.

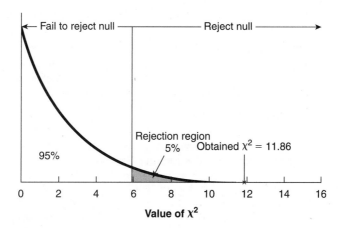

FIGURE 19.3

ONE-VARIABLE CHI-SQUARE TEST INDICATING SIGNIFICANCE OF RESULT

The χ^2 distribution for $df = 2$ puts the obtained χ^2 test statistic well within the rejection region at the .05 significance level.

19.6.3   A Computer-Assisted Example

Most software packages readily compute the one-variable χ^2 test, so let's conduct a test using the SPSS for Windows program. So far this chapter has presented data as proportions rather than as percentages. For a change of pace, we use percentages for this example.

In the 1980s, I analyzed injuries sustained from child abuse and/or neglect for the Colorado Department of Social Services. From the period of 1977 to 1985, children in Colorado sustained 1474 serious injuries (Rosenthal, 1988). These injuries included brain damage, skull fracture, broken bones, dislocations, internal injuries, serious burns, and serious cuts and bruises. Boys sustained 826 of these injuries (56.04%) and girls sustained 648 (43.96%). According to the 1980 Census (General Population Characteristics, Table 20), there were 924,365 people aged 0 (birth) to 19 in Colorado in 1980. Of these, 472,669 were boys (51.13%) and 451,696 were girls (48.87%). If risk for serious injury was equal for boys and girls, one would expect that 51.13% of such injuries would be sustained by boys and 48.87% by girls. These are the expected percentages. Multiplying by sample size (N) provides expected frequencies: for boys $1474 \times .5113 = 753.66$; for girls $1474 \times .4887 = 720.34$. The hypothesis pair may be stated as:

Null: 48.87% of children who sustain serious injuries due to child abuse/neglect are girls and 51.13% are boys.

Research: At least one percentage differs from what is stated in the null.

With only two categories, as is the case here, the sample size guidelines in Table 13.1 should be met. As mentioned earlier, one uses hypothesized proportions rather than observed ones. It is also the case that one need check only one of the two proportions against the guidelines. (Whenever the guidelines are met by one proportion, they will, necessarily, be met by the other.) The hypothesized proportion for the category "girls" is 48.87%. For this percentage, the minimum recommended sample size is 13. The study sample size, $N = 1474$, greatly exceeds this, so we may proceed with the test.

Results from the SPSS for Windows software package are presented in Table 19.2. Note that the SPSS program labels its output with terms slightly

TABLE 19.2   ONE-VARIABLE χ^2 TEST: SERIOUS CHILD ABUSE INJURY BY GENDER

GENDER gender of child				Test Statistics	
	Observed N	Expected N	Residual		
female victims	648	720.3	−72.3	Chi-Square[a]	14.210
male victims	826	753.7	72.3	df	1
Total	1474			Sig.	.0002

[a] 0 cells (.0%) have expected frequencies less than 5. The minimum expected cell frequency is 720.3

Note: The tables are edited output from SPSS for Windows.

different from those used so far in our discussion. What we have termed *observed frequency* is listed under "Observed N." Similarly, *expected frequency* is listed under "Expected N." The "Residual" represents the difference between "Observed N" and "Expected N." The obtained χ^2 is 14.21 with one degree of freedom. Degrees of freedom are listed in the "df" row in the Test Statistics table. With two categories, degrees of freedom are $2 - 1 = 1$. Computer programs provide exact probabilities. As presented in the "Sig." row, given a true null, the probability of obtaining a result as extreme as or more extreme than the study result is .0002. (Only two in every 10,000 randomly selected samples yield results this extreme.) As .0002 is less than .01, the null is rejected. Because the hypothesis pair was nondirectional, our formal conclusion via the hypothesis testing model is simply that the percentages in the study population differ from those stated in the null. Reasoning in a more relaxed manner (see Chapter 15, Section 15.12), we may conclude that the percentage of boys who sustain serious injury exceeds their Colorado population percentage and that the percentage of girls who do so falls below theirs.

The just-presented example of the one-variable χ^2 test is more representative of typical applications than was the earlier one on choice of concentration, because the proportions stated in the null represent those in a real comparison population (the population of children in Colorado). In the choice of concentration example, these proportions represented an abstract population. (That population could be described as the population in which the same proportions prefer each concentration.) Within the constraint that hypothesized proportions should add up to 1.00, researchers ultimately may specify any proportions they choose. The chosen proportions should make good theoretical sense and good common sense.

The abuse injury example demonstrates that hypothesized percentages need not be equal. Rather than 50% and 50%, these were 51.13% and 48.87%.[7]

19.7 CHAPTER SUMMARY

The nondirectional null for the one-sample test of p states that the proportion in the population from which the study sample was randomly selected equals some given value. The hypothesis pair may be directional (one-tailed test) or nondirectional (two-tailed). Decision rules are the same as those for the large sample test of $\overline{X}$. One formula (19.2) is $z = (p - \pi)/\sigma_p$. The one-sample test of p yields accurate probabilities whenever the size guidelines in Table 13.1 are met. One uses the proportion stated in the null (π) to assess these guidelines.

Based on the chi-square (χ^2) distribution, the one-variable chi-square (χ^2) test examines whether the proportions observed for a categorical variable differ significantly from proportions stated in the null. The χ^2 distribution is a family of distributions that take on different characteristics according to degrees of freedom. The mean of a χ^2 distribution equals its degrees of freedom.

Given a true null and adequate sample size, one expects the obtained χ^2 for the one-variable χ^2 test to be reasonably close to $J - 1$ (where J is the number of categories). When the null is false, one expects the obtained χ^2 to be larger, often considerably so. Statistical tests based on the χ^2 distribution are one-tailed, with the rejection region located in the upper tail.

Expected proportion is the predicted proportion, given a true null. For the one-variable χ^2 test, this equals the proportion stated in the null. Expected frequency is the predicted frequency, given a true null. The observed proportion is the actual proportion of responses. Finally, the observed frequency is the actual frequency of responses.

Except when there are two categories, the one-variable χ^2 test yields accurate results whenever the average expected frequency is four or greater. When there are two categories, one consults the size guidelines in Table 13.1. The hypothesis pair is always nondirectional.

The null states that each proportion in the population from which the study sample was randomly selected equals some given value. Rejection of the null indicates that the proportion for at least one category differs from the value stated for it in the null. The preferred calculation formula (19.4) is $\chi^2 = \Sigma[(f_o - f_e)^2/f_e]$.

PROBLEMS AND QUESTIONS

Section 19.2

1. (T or F) The decision rules for the one-sample test of p are the same as those for the large sample test of $\overline{X}$.

2. For the one-sample test of p, is the test statistic a t statistic or a z statistic?

3. In a very large representative sample, the proportion of public welfare participants who secure jobs within three months that pay more than minimum wage is .15. Among 250 clients who participate in a demonstration program, this proportion is .25.

   a. What test should be used to examine whether the proportion in the demonstration program differs significantly from that in the large sample?

   b. State the nondirectional hypothesis pair for the test.

   c. In examining whether sample size is adequate (using Table 13.1) should p (.25) or π (.15) be used?

   d. Is sample size adequate?

   e. Calculate σ_p, the standard error of the proportion.

   f. Calculate z (carry out the test).

g. Given that $\alpha = .05$, what is your decision regarding the null? The research?

h. Given a true null, is the probability of obtaining the sample result or an even more extreme result greater than .05 or less than .05?

i. Is the probability that chance alone explains the difference between the sample proportion ($p = .25$) and the hypothesized proportion ($\pi = .15$) greater than or less than .05?

4. A community mental health program sets a goal that 80% of its clients will not be readmitted to a psychiatric hospital. The actual percentage for their first 100 clients is 90%. You wish to determine whether the actual percentage differs from the targeted percentage to a statistically significant degree.

   a. State the nondirectional hypothesis pair for the test.

   b. In examining whether sample size is adequate (using Table 13.1), should p (.90) or π (.80) be used?

   c. Is sample size adequate?

   d. Calculate σ_p.

   e. Calculate z (carry out the test).

   f. Given that you select the .05 level, what is your decision regarding the null? The research?

   g. Is the probability that the study sample result is due only to chance/sampling error greater than or less than .05?

h. Is the difference between the actual percentage (90%) and the targeted percentage (80%) a statistically significant one?
i. Can you be confident that the null is false?

Section 19.4

5. Like the t distribution, the χ^2 distribution is a _____ of distributions that takes on different characteristics according to the _____ of _____.
6. What is the mean of a χ^2 distribution with six degrees of freedom?
7. All χ^2 distributions are _____ skewed. The degree of skewness _____ as degrees of freedom increase.
8. When the value of the obtained χ^2 is considerably greater than the degrees of freedom, this indicates that the null may well be _____.
9. All statistical tests based on the χ^2 distribution are _____ -tailed. The rejection region is always located in the _____ tail.

Section 19.5

10. The expected proportion equals the proportion stated in the _____. When one multiplies the expected proportion by the total number of responses (sample size), they derive the _____ _____.
11. The actual proportion of responses is termed the _____ _____. The actual frequency is termed the _____ _____.

Section 19.6

12. With one exception, the one-variable χ^2 test typically yields accurate results when the _____ expected frequency is _____ or greater.
13. (T or F) The one-variable χ^2 test examines the *direction* in which observed proportions differ from expected proportions.
14. (T or F) The one-variable χ^2 test examines whether observed proportions differ from expected proportions to a degree that is greater than would be expected by chance alone.
15. A new county social services agency is located in a county in which 35% of residents are Hispanic, 25% are Asian American, 20% are Native American, 10% are African American, and 10% are white. Of the first 50 clients served, 24% are Hispanic, 20% are Asian American, 14% are Native American, 16% are African American, and 24% are white. You wish to examine whether the actual percentages served in the different groups differ to a statistically significant degree from the groups' percentages in the county.
   a. What is the appropriate statistical significance test for this purpose?
   b. What is the average expected frequency?
   c. Is the average expected frequency sufficient for carrying out the test?
   d. State the null.
   e. What are the expected proportions?
   f. What are the expected frequencies?
   g. What are the observed proportions?
   h. What are the observed frequencies?
   i. Using formula 19.4 for the calculation, what is χ^2?
   j. How many degrees of freedom are there?
   k. Presume that the .01 significance level was selected (i.e., $\alpha = .01$). What is the critical value of χ^2?
   l. What is your decision regarding the null? Regarding the research hypothesis?
   m. Do the percentages served differ to a statistically significant degree from the percentages in the county?
   n. Are these study results likely to be due to chance alone?
16. An agency has four programs, A, B, C, and D. The director hypothesizes that one-quarter of clients can best be served by each program. Among the first 80 clients served, 26 are evaluated as best served by A, 16 as best served by B, 23 as best served by C, and 15 by D. Your task is to determine whether actual (observed) percentages differ from the hypothesized (expected) percentages to a statistically significant degree.
   a. Is sample size sufficient for a one-variable χ^2 test?
   b. What are the expected frequencies?
   c. What is the value of χ^2?
   d. How many degrees of freedom are there?

e. What is the critical value of χ^2 given that $\alpha = .05$?

f. Should you accept or reject the null?

g. Is the probability that study sample results are due to chance alone greater than .05 or less than this?

h. Does the result indicate that it is likely that the null is true?

i. Is the result consistent with the null?

17. Answer the same questions presented in the prior problem but with the change that observed frequencies are A, 28; B, 14; C, 25; D, 13.

COMPUTER EXERCISES

For general instructions on computer exercises, see the note in Chapter 2.

1. Using a one-sample test of p, test the null that the proportion of scores in the clinical range for BEHCLIN (0 = not clinical, 1 = clinical) is .10, the approximate proportion in a representative sample. The test should be two-tailed, with α set to .01. [In SPSS, *Analyze > Nonparametric Tests > Binomial,* click BEHCLIN to "Test Variable List," type **.10** in space by "Test Proportion," *OK.*

    Check your answers: In the Binomial Test table, the one-tailed probability of the result is .000. Though the table is labeled Binomial Test, a one-sample test of p as presented in the chapter has actually been carried out. With *Binomial* selected, SPSS conducts a binomial test when sample size is small and the one-sample test of p when it is not. (See note 1 at the end of this chapter for a comment on the binomial test.) For most statistical tests (assuming that the result is in the expected direction), one simply doubles the one-tailed probability to obtain a two-tailed one. For technical reasons (a sampling distribution that is both asymmetric and discrete rather than symmetric and continuous), this is not recommended for the binomial test. However, as just stated, it is the case that a one-sample test of p has been carried out. Hence one may double the one-tailed probability (.000) to obtain the two-tailed one (still .000).

As $p < .01$, the null that $\pi = .10$ is rejected. Note the "Based on Z approximation" message below the Binomial Test table. When this message appears, a one-sample test of p has been conducted, and thus the one-tailed probability may be doubled to obtain a two-tailed one.

2. In the large representative sample on which norms for the FACES Cohesion scale were based, families were classified into four types based on their level of cohesion: (1) disengaged (16.3%), (2) separated (33.8%), (3) connected (36.3%), and (4) enmeshed (13.6%). Using a one-variable chi-square test, test the null hypothesis that the percentages in the hypothetical population from which the adoption sample was randomly selected (presume the sample to have been selected in this fashion) match those in the nonrepresentative sample. [In SPSS, *Analyze > Nonparametric Tests > Chi-Square,* click over FCOH4, click button next to "Values," type **16.3** in space next to "Values," *Add,* and repeat for **33.8**, **36.3**, and **13.6** (note that these sum to 100), *OK.*]

    Check your answers: According to the Test Statistics table, the one-variable chi-square test for FCOH4 does not achieve significance with 3 degrees of freedom. $\chi^2 = 4.61$, $p > .05$. We fail to reject the null.

3. Test the null hypothesis that the proportion of children with handicaps (HANDICAP: 0 = no handicap, 1 = handicap) is .25 (two-tailed test, $p = .01$).

    Check your answers: A less than optimal aspect of the SPSS Binomial procedure is that it can be difficult to figure out the group for which the test proportion is tested. For instance, presuming that you entered .25 in the test proportion space, it may be that the SPSS program has tested the probability that the proportion of children *without* handicaps is .25 (instead of that the proportion *with* handicaps is .25.) So check this in the Binomial Test table. If the incorrect group has been tested (the group tested is the first group listed in the table), one option is to enter the proportion equal to $1 - p$ in the test proportion box. Testing this proportion for the incorrect group results in the same probability as testing the desired proportion for the correct group. Thus, for our example, you may well need to enter the proportion .75 (1 − .25 = .75) and rerun the test.[8] The "Based on Z approximation" message appears, indicating that a one-sample test of p has been conducted. Hence the one-tailed probability given by SPSS (.002) may be doubled to obtain the two-tailed probability. As $p = .004$, the null is rejected.

NOTES

1. When the sample size guidelines for the one-sample test of p are not met, the binomial test may be used. The null and research hypotheses for the binomial test are the same as those for the one-sample test of p with the exception that the pair is almost always directional. See Toothaker and Miller (1996, pp. 256–260) for more on the binomial test and the binomial distribution.

2. As in the prior example, the existence of a wider (larger) population from which the study sample is selected is assumed so that a statistical test may be carried out.

3. Recall that degrees of freedom equal the number of independent pieces of information after mathematical restrictions have been applied. Suppose that (as in our example) a variable has three categories and that we know the frequency in the first two categories and the total number of cases. By subtraction, we can determine the frequency in the third category. In this context, the third category is not free to vary (take on any frequency) but is instead constrained. Thus degrees of freedom are not three but instead $3 − 1 = 2$.

4. The mode of a χ^2 distribution (the high point of the curve) equals the number of degrees of freedom minus 2.

5. When the number of categories is large (say, about eight or more), an average expected frequency of three is sufficient. When one or more expected frequencies are very small (say, less than 0.5), the probabilities given by the test can be somewhat inaccurate. Such very small expected frequencies cause greater concern when the number of categories is small (say, about five or fewer) than when this is large. For further information on sample guidelines see Roscoe and Byars (1971) or Koehler and Larantz (1980).

6. Basically, in some situations the concept of direction does not apply. For instance, one may use a single procedure to test whether a single parameter is greater than or less than some value (or than a second parameter) but cannot do so when three or more are involved. When the one-variable χ^2 test is used in situations involving three or more proportions, the concept of direction does not apply, so the hypothesis pair is always nondirectional. When there are only two proportions, the concept of direction may be applied; see note 7.

7. The abuse injury example of the one-variable χ^2 test had two categories, girls and boys. With two categories, one may conduct either a one-sample test of p or a one-variable χ^2 test. For instance, we could have computed a one-sample test of p to test whether the proportion of boys differed significantly from 51.13 (their proportion in the population) or, alternatively, a one-sample test of whether the proportion of girls differed significantly from 48.87. With two categories, the probability (p) resulting from a two-tailed (nondirectional) one-sample test of p equals that resulting from a one-variable χ^2 test. Even though they appear very different, these two tests are mathematically equivalent. The advantage of the one-sample test of p is that one may specify either a directional or a nondirectional hypothesis, and thus either a one-tailed or a two-tailed test. When a one-variable χ^2 test has two categories, a one-tailed probability for the one-sample test of p may also be obtained by dividing the probability yielded by the χ^2 test by two. (This presumes that results are in the expected direction.)

8. The SPSS binomial procedure (as best as I can determine) tests the proportion for the group that corresponds to the value of the first case in the data set. For instance, for the variable HANDICAP, the value of the first case is 0 (no handicap), hence the proportion is tested for the no handicap group. The "cut point" option (see Binomial Test dialog box) is perhaps a better way to designate groups.

The Chi-Square Test of Independence

20.1 Chapter Overview

It's time to learn to use the *chi-square* (χ^2) *test of independence,* perhaps the most common statistical test of significance. We discuss the test's sampling distribution, the hypothesis pair, definitions of expected and observed frequencies and of expected and observed proportions, and a computational formula. But it's important to remember, as an example at the end of the chapter emphasizes, that the χ^2 test of independence is not a measure of size of association.

20.2 Introduction to the Chi-Square Test of Independence

The second test based on the chi-square distribution, the **chi-square test of independence (χ^2 test of independence),** assesses the probability that an association between two categorical variables is due to chance. Among all statistical tests, it may be the most used and best known. It is often referred to simply as the *chi-square* (χ^2) *test.*

To demonstrate the χ^2 test, we will use an example first presented in Chapter 7 (Section 7.5). This example, taken from the special-needs adoption study (Rosenthal and Groze, 1992), examined the association between the presence (versus the absence) of serious behavior problems and family ethnicity. Family ethnicity defines three groups of adopting families: (1) minority, inracial: that is, minority (nonwhite) parents who adopt a child of the same race as at least one parent; (2) white, inracial: white parents who adopt a white child; and (3) transracial: white parents who adopt a minority child (transracial adoption). Table 20.1, a contingency table, displays the association between these variables. (See Section 6.4.1 in Chapter 6 if you need to refresh your mind regarding how to interpret a contingency table.)

TABLE 20.1	FAMILY ETHNICITY BY SERIOUSNESS OF BEHAVIOR PROBLEMS			
	Minority, Inracial	White, Inracial	Transracial	
Child has serious behavior problems	59	194	20	273
	29%	47%	37%	40.7%
Child does not have serious behavior problems	142	222	34	398
	71%	53%	63%	59.3%
	201	416	54	671

In Table 20.1, the percentage of children with serious behavior problems differs by family ethnicity. Thus, 29% of minority, inracial families, 47% of white, inracial families, and 37% of transracial families reported such problems. Percentages differ, so the variables are associated. This association in the study sample does not permit one to conclude that there is also an association in the population from which the sample was randomly selected. Perhaps the variables are unassociated in this population and the association in the sample reflects sampling error (chance).

20.3   SELECTED CHARACTERISTICS OF THE χ^2 TEST

20.3.1   Sample Size Requirements

The χ^2 test of independence yields highly accurate probabilities whenever the average expected frequency for the cells of the contingency table is at least six (6.00). For the 2×2 contingency table only, an additional condition should be met: The minimum expected frequency in each cell should be at least one (1.00).[1] When the minimum expected frequency for all cells in a table is three (3.00) or greater, χ^2 probabilities are accurate even when the average frequency is less than six.

20.3.2   Hypothesis Pair

The null for the χ^2 test may be presented in two basic ways. First, and most basically, it states that two variables are unassociated (independent) in the population from which the study sample was randomly selected:

> *Null:* In the population from which the study sample was randomly selected, the two variables are unassociated (independent).

> *Research:* In the population from which the study sample was randomly selected, the two variables are associated.

Recall from Chapter 6 that variables in a contingency table are unassociated when (1) column percentages are equal or (2) row percentages are equal. Recall also that whenever one set of percentages is equal, so is the other (see Chapter 6, Section 6.4). Thus the null may also be stated with reference to the percentages in the contingency table:

> *Null:* In the population from which the study sample was randomly selected, column percentages are equal.

> *Research:* In the population from which the study sample was randomly selected, column percentages differ.

If one chooses to focus on row percentages, the hypotheses are:

> *Null:* In the population from which the study sample was randomly selected, row percentages are equal.

> *Research:* In the population from which the study sample was randomly selected, row percentages differ.

Or the hypothesis pair may be stated simply as:

> *Null:* In the population from which the study sample was randomly selected, percentages are equal.

> *Research:* In the population from which the study sample was randomly selected, percentages differ.

The hypothesis pair is always nondirectional. For instance, a research hypothesis statement would not state that a higher percentage of behavior problems would be observed in one category of family ethnicity than in another. Expression of the hypothesis pair in mathematical symbols is cumbersome and not particularly helpful, so we won't use them.

20.3.3 *Distribution and Degrees of Freedom*

Assuming a true null and that sample size requirements are met, the sampling distribution of the test statistic χ^2 for the test of independence closely follows a chi-square (χ^2) distribution. Just as for the one-variable test, when the null is true, one expects the obtained χ^2 to be reasonably close to (not to differ greatly from) the number of degrees of freedom. Values of χ^2 considerably larger than the degrees of freedom may indicate that the null is false. For the chi-square test of independence, the formula for degrees of freedom is:

$$df = (R - 1)(C - 1) \tag{20.1}$$

where R is the number of rows in the contingency table and C is the number of columns. In our example, the contingency table (Table 20.1) has two rows and three columns. The calculation,[2] then, is $df = (2 - 1)(3 - 1) = (1)(2) = 2$.

As is the case for the one-variable χ^2 test, the χ^2 test of independence is always a one-tailed test. The rejection region is always located in the upper tail of the distribution.

20.4   FORMULAS AND DECISION RULES

20.4.1   Formulas

The χ^2 test of independence assesses whether observed proportions differ from expected proportions to a degree that is greater than would be expected due to sampling error (chance) alone. A cell's observed proportion is simply the proportion for that cell. For instance, in Table 20.1, the observed column proportion of children with serious behavior problems in minority, inracial families is .29 (29%). A cell's expected proportion is the expected proportion given a true null. The formula for a cell's expected column proportion is:

$$p_e = \text{(row margin total)}/N \tag{20.2}$$

where row margin total is the number of cases in the row in which the cell is located and N is the number of cases in the table. The formula for a cell's expected row proportion is:

$$p_e = \text{(column margin total)}/N \tag{20.3}$$

where column margin total is the number of cases in the column in which the cell is located and N is the number of cases in the table.

All cells in a given row always have the same expected column proportion. For Table 20.1, the expected column proportion for each cell in the first row is $(273/671) = .407$. For each cell in the second row, this proportion is $(398/671) = .593$. Similarly, all cells in a given column have the same expected row proportion. Researchers sometimes refer to observed and expected percentages rather than proportions. For instance, the expected cell percentage for each cell in the first row in Table 20.1 is 40.7%.

Although the χ^2 test is best conceptualized as examining differences between expected and observed proportions, the easiest hand-calculation formula involves expected and observed frequencies. This formula (19.4) is the same as that preferred for the one-variable test. For convenience, it is repeated here:

$$\chi^2 = \sum \frac{(f_o - f_e)^2}{f_e} \tag{19.4}$$

For the χ^2 test of independence, expected frequency refers to the predicted frequency for a cell of the contingency table, given a true null. A cell's expected frequency is given by:

$$f_e = \frac{\text{(row margin total)} \times \text{(column margin total)}}{N} \tag{20.4}$$

The easiest way to compute expected frequencies is to (1) create a contingency table with row and column totals and N but with the cells left empty, and (2) for each cell, carry out formula 20.4. Table 20.2 presents such a table with calculations. Note that expected frequencies need not equal whole numbers.

TABLE 20.2   **EXPECTED FREQUENCY OF SEVERE BEHAVIOR PROBLEMS**

	Minority, Inracial	White, Inracial	Transracial	
Child has serious behavior problems	$\frac{(273)(201)}{671} = 81.78$	$\frac{(273)(416)}{671} = 169.25$	$\frac{(54)(273)}{671} = 21.97$	273 (40.7%)
Child does not have serious behavior problems	$\frac{(398)(201)}{671} = 119.22$	$\frac{(398)(416)}{671} = 246.75$	$\frac{(398)(54)}{671} = 32.03$	398 (59.3%)
	201	416	54	671

Note: Cells show calculations for expected frequency.

TABLE 20.3   **EXPECTED BEHAVIOR PROBLEMS BY FAMILY ETHNICITY**

	Minority, Inracial	White, Inracial	Transracial	
Child has serious behavior problems	81.78 40.7%	169.25 40.7%	21.97 40.7%	273 40.7%
Child does not have serious behavior problems	119.22 59.3%	246.75 59.3%	32.03 59.3%	398 59.3%
	201	416	54	671

Note: Top number in each cell is expected frequency; bottom number is expected column percentage.

For instance, in minority, inracial families the expected frequency of children with serious behavior problems is 81.78.

Table 20.3 presents a contingency table composed of expected frequencies and expected percentages. These are the precise frequencies and percentages that would be expected given a true null, that is, in the absence of any sampling error. As mentioned earlier, two variables are unassociated when row or column percentages are identical. In Table 20.3, column percentages are indeed identical for each of the three family ethnicity groups. Hence, in Table 20.3, behavior problems and family ethnicity are unassociated or, one may say, independent. All contingency tables composed of expected frequencies and expected percentages present a condition of independence. The χ^2 test examines whether actual study results differ sufficiently from the condition of independence for one to conclude that these results are not due to chance alone.[3] (In actual research, one would not create a table composed of expected frequencies and percentages. Table 20.3 was created for learning purposes.)

20.4.2 *Decision Rules*

Decision rules are precisely the same as for the one-variable χ^2 test. One fails to reject (accepts) the null if the obtained χ^2 is less than the critical value in Table A.3 in Appendix A. One rejects the null if the obtained χ^2 is greater than or equal to the critical value.

20.5 CARRYING OUT THE χ^2 TEST

20.5.1 *Applying the Hypothesis Testing Model*

We will continue with the example involving family ethnicity and serious behavior problems. For the χ^2 test to yield an accurate probability, the average expected frequency should be six or greater. To find the average expected frequency, one divides N (the total number of cases) by the number of cells. Table 20.1 has six cells. The average expected frequency, therefore, is 671/6 = 111.8. This greatly exceeds six. As an alternative to verifying that the average expected cell frequency was greater than six, we could have verified that the minimum expected frequency was greater than three. Expected frequencies were calculated in Table 20.2. The minimum expected frequency is 21.97 (upper right corner). As this is greater than three, sample size is adequate. With the sample size requirement met, we may proceed with the χ^2 test:

1. State the hypothesis pair.

   Null: In the population from which the study sample was randomly selected, family ethnicity and the presence (versus absence) of a serious behavioral problem are unassociated.

   Research: In the population from which the study sample was randomly selected, family ethnicity and the presence (versus absence) of a serious behavioral problem are associated.

   One may also choose to state the hypothesis pair via percentages:

   Null: In the population from which the study sample was randomly selected, the percentage of children with serious behavior problems is equal in each of the three family ethnicity groups.

   Research: In the population from which the study sample was randomly selected, the percentage of children with serious behavior problems is not equal in all three family ethnicity groups.[4]

2. State the significance level (set α).

The .01 statistical significance level is selected. (With a large sample size like this, use of the .01 level rather than the .05 level reduces the likelihood that an extremely weak association will achieve statistical significance.)

3. Carry out the test.

Expected frequencies have already been calculated, so we may proceed with the χ^2 formula (19.4). For each cell in the contingency table, the formula directs one to (1)

TABLE 20.4   CALCULATION OF χ^2 FOR FAMILY ETHNICITY AND BEHAVIOR

Cell	f_o	f_e	$f_o - f_e$	$(f_o - f_e)^2$	$(f_o - f_e)^2/f_e$
Upper left	59	81.78	−22.78	518.93	6.35
Upper middle	194	169.25	24.75	612.56	3.62
Upper right	20	21.97	−1.97	3.88	0.18
Lower left	142	119.22	22.78	518.93	4.35
Lower middle	222	246.75	−24.75	612.56	2.47
Lower right	34	32.03	1.97	3.88	0.12
				Sum = χ^2 =	17.09

subtract the expected frequency from the observed frequency, (2) square this difference, and (3) divide by the expected frequency. Finally (step 4), the summation sign directs one to sum the results for step 3. Calculations are best carried out via a grid like the one in Table 20.4.

4. Make a decision on the null.

We need to calculate the degrees of freedom first. The contingency table has two rows and three columns, so $df = (3 - 1)(2 - 1) = (2)(1) = 2$. Referring to Table A.3 in Appendix A, the critical value for a χ^2 distribution with two degrees of freedom at the .01 level ($\alpha = .01$) is 9.21. As the obtained χ^2, 17.09, exceeds the critical value, the null is rejected. The differences between expected and obtained percentages are unlikely to be due to chance alone. We accept the research hypothesis and conclude that family ethnicity and likelihood of serious behavior problems are indeed associated in the study population. Figure 20.1 presents these results.

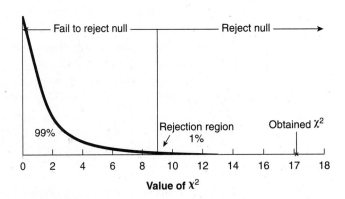

FIGURE 20.1

RESULTS FOR FAMILY ETHNICITY/BEHAVIOR EXAMPLE

The obtained χ^2 of 17.09 is in the rejection region, so the null is rejected. The χ^2 distribution is for two degrees of freedom, and $\alpha = .01$

20.5.2 *Comments on the Example*

A formal conclusion from the χ^2 test pertains to the full contingency table rather than to specific categories. For instance, on the basis of the just-computed statistically significant χ^2, one may not conclude that the percentage of children with serious behavior problems in minority, inracial families differs to a statistically significant degree from that in white, inracial families. Such a conclusion disregards that the transracial group was also included in the calculation of χ^2.[5]

Less formally, however, researchers typically examine the pattern of results for the different categories as they seek to understand and make sense of the data. In this example, the low percentage of children with serious problems in minority, inracial families (29%) clearly stands out and directs attention to this point.

As you know by now, the fact of statistical significance rules out chance (random variation, sampling error, luck of the draw) as a likely explanation, but it does not speak to what particular real factors are involved. In the present example, for instance, at least two possible explanations come to mind: (1) The minority, inracial parents have excellent parenting skills and these skills lead to comparatively lower levels of behavior problems in their children. (2) The children who entered minority, inracial homes tended to have less traumatic preadoption experiences than did those in other homes and this (not better parenting skills) explains why these children have fewer problems. This example demonstrates that the fact of association alone (even statistically significant association) does not allow one to infer causality.

20.6 A COMPUTER-ASSISTED EXAMPLE

The χ^2 test of independence is included in all statistical packages. Table 20.5 is a contingency table produced by the SPSS for Windows package. (It presents the same information as did Table 20.1.) The variable SERIBEH, short for serious behavior problems, is the row variable, and FAMETH, short for family ethnicity, is the column variable. The table was created and the χ^2 test was carried out via the "Crosstabs" procedure. The SPSS program computes three chi-square tests. The χ^2 formula provided in this chapter is for the Pearson χ^2 in SPSS, so let's direct our attention to it. The probability associated with the obtained χ^2 is .00019. Given a true null, results as extreme as those presented in the contingency table are expected only 19 times in every 100,000 samples. In this situation we can be extremely confident that (1) the null is false and (2) our result is not due to chance alone.[6,7]

Now is a convenient time to provide the format for presenting χ^2 results in journal articles or when space is limited. The current results would be reported as:

$$\chi^2 (2, N = 671) = 17.095, p < .01$$

or as:

$$\chi^2 (2, N = 671) = 17.095, p = .00019$$

The first number inside the parentheses conveys the degrees of freedom.

TABLE 20.5   SERIOUS BEHAVIOR PROBLEMS BY FAMILY ETHNICITY

Chi-Square Tests

SPSS Output	Value	df	Asymp. Sig. (2-sided)
Pearson	17.095[a]	2	.00019
Chi-Square Likelihood Ratio	17.456	2	.00016
Linear-by-Linear Association	8.041	1	.00457
N of Valid Cases	671		

[a] 0 cells (.0%) have expected count less than 5. The minimum expected count is 21.97.

SERIBEH serious behavior problems?
FAMETH Family Ethnicity Crosstabulation

SPSS Output		FAMETH Family Ethnicity			Total
		Minority, Inracial	White, Inracial	Transracial	
SERIBEH serious behavior problems?	has problems	59	194	20	273
		29.4%	46.6%	37.0%	40.7%
	does not have problems	142	222	34	398
		70.6%	53.4%	63.0%	59.3%
Total		201	416	54	671
		100.0%	100.0%	100.0%	100.0%

Note: SPSS for windows output.

20.7 ORDINAL VARIABLES AND THE CHI-SQUARE TEST OF INDEPENDENCE

When both variables in the contingency table are ordinal, the relationship between them may well be a directional one. Although one may test whether such relationships achieve significance by using a χ^2 test of independence, it is not preferred for this situation. The χ^2 test can examine the degree to which observed and expected percentages differ, but it cannot assess whether such differences take on a directional pattern. It may well miss (fail to detect) a directional pattern and consequently fail to reject the null. As an example, consider Table 20.6, a contingency table of (1) motivation for services by (2) progress on most important problem (this table is adapted from Table 9.2 in Chapter 9). A directional

TABLE 20.6   PROGRESS BY MOTIVATION FOR SERVICES

Motivation for Services	PROGRESS ON MOST IMPORTANT PROBLEM					
	Great Deal	Some	None	Got Worse		
Very	12	5	2	1	20	
	60%	25%	10%	5%	25%	
Somewhat	9	5	4	2	20	
	45%	25%	20%	10%	25%	
A little	7	5	5	3	20	
	35%	25%	25%	15%	25%	
Not very	5	5	6	4	20	
	25%	25%	30%	20%	25%	
	33	20	17	10	80	
	41%	25%	21%	13%	100%	

pattern is evident: As level of motivation increases, so does reported progress on the most important problem. Even though this pattern is clear and sample size is adequate ($N = 80$), the χ^2 test does not reach significance. χ^2 computes to 7.30, which with nine degrees of freedom [$df = (4 - 1)(4 - 1) = 9$] is not significant at the .05 level. As just discussed, these results may be stated as χ^2 (9, $N = 80$) = 7.30, $p > .05$.

Chapter 22 (Section 22.6) discusses several significance tests that are particularly designed for examining directional associations between ordinal-level categorical variables like those in Table 20.6. The preferred tests include those for tau_b (τ_b), tau_c (τ_c), gamma (γ), and Somer's d.[8]

20.8   THE χ^2 STATISTIC IS NOT A MEASURE OF SIZE OF ASSOCIATION

Suppose that two delinquency prevention experiments are conducted and that these are identical except for sample size. Presume that in the first experiment, 20 youths are randomly assigned to Method A and 20 to Method B, and in the second experiment, 200 are so assigned to each method. Presume also that outcomes are identical in terms of the percentage of success (no delinquent act committed during follow-up period) and failure (one or more delinquent acts committed). Let's say that in both experiments 80% of youth in Method A and 60% in Method B experience successful outcomes. Both studies then show the same size of association ($D\% = 80\% - 60\% = 20\%$) between method and outcome. The task of the χ^2 test is to determine whether the association between method and outcome is statistically significant. Table 20.7 presents contingency tables for the two experiments. (The row labels "Success" and "Failure" apply to both tables.)

TABLE 20.7 EFFECT OF SAMPLE SIZE ON CHI-SQUARE TEST OF INDEPENDENCE

	FIRST EXPERIMENT			SECOND EXPERIMENT	
Outcome	Method A	Method B		Method A	Method B
Success	16	12		160	120
	80%	60%		80%	60%
Failure	4	8		40	80
	20%	40%		20%	40%
Total Frequency	20	20		200	200

Although the size of association in the two experiments is identical, obtained χ^2's differ. In the first, smaller experiment, χ^2 equals 1.90. With one degree of freedom, this χ^2 is not statistically significant ($p = .17$), so one fails to reject the null. However, the obtained χ^2 in the second, larger experiment equals 19.0, which is significant ($p = .0001$) and leads to rejection of the null.[9]

The differing values of χ^2 despite the same size of association demonstrate that the χ^2 test is *not* a measure of size of association. It *is* a test of statistical significance. As such, its function is to determine the probability that study results are due to chance. The probabilities resulting from statistical tests are highly dependent on sample size. Other things being equal, the greater the sample size, the greater the likelihood of rejecting the null. That is, to repeat a point from Chapter 16, the greater the sample size, the greater the power.[10]

20.9   CHAPTER SUMMARY

Based on the χ^2 distribution, the χ^2 test of independence assesses the probability that an association between two categorical variables is due to chance. With the exception of 2×2 tables, it yields accurate probabilities whenever the average expected frequency is at least six or greater. In a 2×2 table, an additional requirement is a minimum expected frequency of one (1.00) in each cell.

The null hypothesis (always nondirectional) may be stated in two ways: (1) in the population from which the study sample was randomly selected, percentages are equal, or (2) in this population, variables are unassociated (independent). Via formula 20.1: $df = (R - 1)(C - 1)$.

The preferred hand-calculation formula is the same as that for the one-variable χ^2 test (formula 19.4). A cell's expected column proportion is given by formula 20.2: $p_e = $ (row margin total)/N. All cells in a given row have identical expected column proportions. To compute a cell's expected frequency: (1) multiply its row margin total by its column margin total and (2) divide by N (formula 20.4).

The χ^2 test of independence examines whether observed proportions differ from expected proportions to a greater degree than expected from chance alone. The hypothesis pair is always nondirectional. It is a one-tailed test. One rejects the null if the obtained χ^2 is greater than or equal to the critical χ^2 in Table A.3. One's formal conclusion pertains to the full contingency table rather than to specific categories (pairs) of variables.

The χ^2 test is not preferred for testing directional associations. It is not a measure of size of association.

PROBLEMS AND QUESTIONS

Section 20.3

1. With the exception of a 2×2 table, the χ^2 test of independence yields accurate probabilities whenever the _____ expected frequency is at least _____. Also, probabilities are accurate whenever the _____ expected frequency is at least _____.

2. (T or F) In most situations, the χ^2 test of independence assesses not just the degree to which percentages differ from expectations but also the direction of these differences.

3. Most basically, the nondirectional null for the χ^2 test of independence asserts that two categorical variables are _____.

4. Is the hypothesis pair for the χ^2 test of independence directional or nondirectional?

5. Calculate degrees of freedom for χ^2 tests based on contingency tables of the following sizes:
   a. 3×4
   b. 5×2
   c. 6×4
   d. 2×2

6. 100 students attend a graduate school of counseling psychology. 50 attend a workshop on human sexuality. Of the 50 students who attend the workshop, 40 agree with the statement "Sexual orientation is *not* predominantly a matter of choice." Of the 50 who do not attend, 32 agree. Your task is to conduct a χ^2 test of independence to examine whether workshop attendance (or lack thereof) and opinion (agree versus any other response) on the statement have a statistically significant association.
   a. State the nondirectional null in terms of association or the lack thereof.
   b. State the nondirectional null via percentages. Do so by stating the percentages in the two attendance categories (attend and do not attend) who agree with the statement.

c. What are the expected frequencies?

d. Is sample size sufficient for conducting the χ^2 test? (Note that two dichotomous variables are involved.)

e. Although they are not used in the computation of χ^2, what are the observed proportions? (State these so that they sum to 100 within categories of "attend.")

f. Are the variables associated or independent in the sample?

g. Although they are not used in computation, what are the expected percentages (or proportions)? (State these so that they sum to 100 within categories of "attend.")

h. Are the expected percentages identical to the observed percentages?

i. What is the value of the test statistic χ^2?

j. How many degrees of freedom are there?

k. Presuming that the .05 statistical significance level was selected, what is the critical value of χ^2?

l. Express results succinctly, as they might appear in a journal article, for instance.

m. What is your decision regarding the null? The research hypothesis?

n. (T or F) One may be 95% (or more) confident that the association in the study sample is not due simply to chance.

o. Presume for the moment that different results had been obtained and the null had been rejected rather than accepted (with those attending more likely to agree). Such being the case, should you conclude with confidence that attending the workshop *caused* greater agreement?

7. Presume the same situation as in the prior question except that all numbers are doubled. Hence, of 100 students who take the workshop, 80 agree with the statement. Of 100 students who do not take the workshop, 64 agree. (Hint: See note 9 at the end of this chapter.)

a. What is the obtained χ^2?
b. Is the obtained χ^2 statistically significant?
c. What is your decision regarding the null? The research hypothesis?
d. May one be 95% confident that the association in the study sample is not due simply to chance?
e. May one appropriately conclude that workshop attendance *causes* greater agreement?

8. Table 20PQ.1 presents hypothetical data on the possible association between choice of concentration by social work graduate students and their employment status in the field of social work five years after graduation. Regarding these data …
a. Calculate the percentage employed in social work for each of the four concentration areas.
b. What is the expected (column) proportion for each cell in the "employed in social work" row? In the "not employed in social work" row?
c. In the sample, are the variables associated?
d. Just from eyeballing the table, how would you characterize the size/strength of association?
e. What is the value of χ^2?
f. How many degrees of freedom are there?
g. Given that α is set to .05, what is the critical value of χ^2?
h. What is your decision regarding the null? The research hypothesis?
i. Is the obtained χ^2 statistically significant at the .05 level?
j. Express results succinctly, as they might appear in a journal article.

k. Is it plausible that the association in the sample simply reflects sampling error?

Section 20.7

9. (T or F) The χ^2 test of independence is particularly sensitive to and adept at discerning directional relationship between categorical or-dinal-level variables.

Section 20.8

10. (T or F) The χ^2 test of independence is a measure of size/strength of association.
11. All other things being equal (observed proportions, size of association, etc.), as sample size increases, the value of the obtained χ^2 _____.

 COMPUTER EXERCISES

For general instructions on computer exercises, see the note in Chapter 2.

1. Via the chi-square test of independence, examine whether the association between FOSTER (adoption by prior foster parents: yes/no) and IMPACTD (adoption's impact evaluated as very positive: yes/no) is a statistically significant one. [In SPSS, *Analyze > Descriptive Statistics > Crosstabs*, click IMPACTD over to space beneath "Row(s)," click FOSTER over to space beneath "Columns," *Statistics*, click box next to "Chi-square," *Continue* (then, if you want column percentages, *Cells*, click box next to "Col-

TABLE 20.QP.1	EMPLOYMENT STATUS 5 YEARS AFTER GRADUATION				
	CONCENTRATION				
Employed in Social Work	**Children and Family**	**Mental Health**	**Health**	**Community Practice**	**Total**
Yes	40	34	30	46	150
No	10	16	10	14	50
Total	50	50	40	60	200

umn," *Continue*), *OK.*] Use the .01 level of significance.

> Check your answers: Regarding FOSTER and IMPACTD, we fail to reject the null at the .01 level: $\chi^2 (1, N = 772) = 4.560, p = .033$ in the Chi-Square Tests table.

2. Examine whether the association between FAMETH (family ethnicity) and HANDICAP (does child have handicap?) is significant via the chi-square test of independence. [In SPSS, *Analyze > Descriptive Statistics > Crosstabs* (if necessary, click back variables from prior problem), click HANDICAP over to space beneath "Row(s)", click FAMETH over to space beneath "Columns," *Statistics*, click box next to "Chi-square" if it is not already checked, *Continue* (if you want Column percentages, *Cells*, click box next to "Column" if it is not already checked), *Continue, OK.*] Use the .01 level.

> Check your answers: Regarding FAMETH and HANDICAP, the null is rejected at the .01 level: $\chi^2 (2, N = 760) = 17.44, p = .000$ in the Chi-Square Tests table.

3. Test the (nondirectional) null that the proportion of children with handicaps is equal in one- and two-parent families. This involves the variables HANDICAP (independent variable) and ONEORTWO (dependent). Use the .01 level.

> Check your answers: Via the Pearson Chi-Square test: $\chi^2 (1, N = 773) = 5.11, p = .024$. Hence proportions do not differ significantly at the .01 level, and we fail to reject the null.

NOTES

1. For the 2×2 table, the minimum expected frequency should be at least 1.00. For other tables, results can be inaccurate when a substantial percentage of cells (say, 33% or more as a rough guideline) have expected frequencies less than 1.00. Guidelines for minimum and average frequencies may be relaxed modestly when the .05 level rather than the .01 level is used. (Stated differently, at the .05 level, highly accurate results are typically observed whenever frequencies come close to meeting the guidelines.) When guidelines are not met for a 2×2 table, Fisher's exact test is generally preferred to the χ^2 test. Fisher's test uses essentially the same hypothesis pairs as does the χ^2 test. Whenever the frequency guidelines are met (or at the .05 level, when they are nearly met), the χ^2 test is preferred to Fisher's test because the probability yielded by Fisher's test is typically higher than the actual probability that the result is due to chance (Norusis, 1997, p. 305). For more on Fisher's test, see Blalock (1979, pp. 292–297). For a 2×2 table, many statistical packages compute χ^2 with the Yates correction. Glass and Hopkins (1996, p. 335) recommend not using this correction. For more on required expected frequencies, see Roscoe and Byars (1971), Camilli and Hopkins (1978), and Camilli and Hopkins (1979). See also note 7 in this chapter.

2. Consider a 2×2 contingency table in which one knows (1) the row margin totals, (2) the column margin totals, and (3) the frequency of the upper left cell. Subtracting the cell frequency of the upper left cell from the margin total for the upper row provides the frequency for the upper right cell. Subtracting the upper left cell frequency from the left column margin total provides the frequency for the lower left cell. The only remaining frequency is for the lower right cell. This may be calculated either by (1) subtracting the frequency for the upper right cell from the right column margin total or (2) subtracting the frequency for the lower left cell from the lower row margin total. Thus, knowing the frequency of only one cell and the margin totals, one may calculate frequencies for the others. Given that the marginal totals are known (which by definition is always the case), only one cell frequency is independent in a 2×2 contingency table. As such, there is only one degree of freedom. The degrees of freedom formula for such a table computes as follows: $(2 - 1)(2 - 1) = (1)(1) = 1$. You may use analogous logic to fill out contingency tables of various sizes and, by so doing, get a feel for the logic of the degrees of freedom formula.

3. I have characterized the χ^2 test of independence as testing whether observed proportions differ sufficiently from expected proportions for one to conclude that chance is not a likely explanation. One may also view this test as testing whether observed frequencies differ sufficiently from expected frequencies for this conclusion to be reached. Or one may view the test more broadly as testing whether observed results (expressed as either proportions or frequencies) differ sufficiently from expected results. Expected results are, in essence, the results predicted in the absence of any sampling error.

4. The key idea expressed in the research hypothesis using percentages is that at least one percentage (proportion) differs from one or more of the others. If π_1

represents the hypothesized population proportion with serious behavior problems for Group 1 and π_2 and π_3 do the same for Groups 2 and 3, the null may be expressed as $\pi_1 = \pi_2 = \pi_3$. The research hypothesis cannot be readily expressed in symbols, because there is no symbol to express the idea that at least one percentage differs.

5. To examine associations involving only selected categories, one could construct a 2×2 contingency table composed only of the pertinent categories and carry out the χ^2 test. A problem with doing so is that, particularly for larger tables, many possible pairs of categories can be compared. If one compares many, just by chance one or more pairs are likely to have a significant difference. This problem is magnified when one purposively selects given pairs. The logic of multiple comparisons discussed in Chapter 21, Section 21.7, applies here. Glass and Hopkins (1996, pp. 467–468) present a specific multiple comparison (the Marascuilo method) for comparing pairs in a contingency table, which is greatly preferred over carrying out tests of different pairs.

6. To determine precisely how confident one may be that the null is false (and that the research hypothesis is true), one may (1) subtract the probability given by the test from 1.00 and (2) multiply by 100. For instance, this probability in the current example is .00019: $(1.00 - .00019) \times 100 = 99.981\%$. One may be 99.981% confident that the null is false. As another example, if $p = .08$: $(1.00 - .08) \times 100 = 92\%$ confident.

7. The SPSS Crosstabs output produces three different χ^2 statistics: the Pearson χ^2, the likelihood ratio χ^2, and the linear-by-linear association χ^2. The formula presented in this book is for the Pearson χ^2 and, as such, I recommend it. The likelihood ratio χ^2 test may also be used. With small sample sizes, Pearson's χ^2 test and a likelihood χ^2 test can yield somewhat different probabilities. When frequency guidelines are almost but not fully met, it can be difficult to decide whether the probability yielded by Pearson's χ^2 test is sufficiently accurate for de-

cision making. In such a situation, the probability yielded by the likelihood ratio χ^2 test provides a useful check. When both probabilities yield the same decision regarding the null, one has increased confidence in results. (One should not use either of these χ^2 tests when the frequency guidelines are markedly violated. See note 1.) With large sample sizes, the probabilities yielded by the two just-described tests are very similar (Norusis, 1997, p. 305). For discussion of the linear-by-linear association χ^2 test, see the next note.

8. Whenever the chi-square is selected within the crosstabs procedure, the SPSS for Windows program conducts a special chi-square test of linear-by-linear association. This test, which always has one degree of freedom, may be used to examine whether a directional association in a contingency table is significant. For Table 20.6, this χ^2 computes to 6.90, which with $df = 1$ is significant at the .01 level. This test is a good alternative for assessing directional association in contingency tables. It should not be used with nominal-level variables. Formally it assumes interval-level measurement (i.e., equal spacing between categories), so results should be interpreted with some degree of caution when measurement is at the ordinal level.

9. You might note that, given that observed percentages remain the same, the obtained χ^2 increases in direct proportion to sample size. For instance, the sample size in the second experiment in Table 20.7 is 10 times larger than that in the first experiment, and so is the value of χ^2: 19.0 versus 1.90.

10. For two dichotomous variables, a two-tailed *z test of a difference in proportions* (Glass and Hopkins, 1996, p. 337) and the χ^2 test of independence are essentially identical tests and yield identical probabilities. An advantage of the *z* test is that it may be either one-tailed or two-tailed. To obtain the probability for a one-tailed *z* test, divide that for the χ^2 test in half. (This presumes that results are in the expected direction.)

ANALYSIS OF VARIANCE

21.1   CHAPTER OVERVIEW

We now consider a key statistical test, *analysis of variance (ANOVA)*. We begin with underlying theory including the *mean square within*, the *mean square between*, and the *F distribution*, the sampling distribution on which ANOVA is based. Computation is demonstrated via hand and computer. We discuss *multiple comparison* procedures and close with a discussion of statistical *fishing*.

21.2   INTRODUCTION TO ANOVA

The independent samples t test assesses differences in means between two independent samples. **Analysis of variance,** also known as **ANOVA,** assesses differences in means between two or more independent samples. Though ANOVA may be used when there are only two samples, most researchers prefer the t test in this circumstance. Hence ANOVA is typically used for three or more samples. For two samples, a two-tailed (nondirectional) independent samples t test (equal variances formula only) and ANOVA yield identical probabilities. Although they appear different, these two tests are mathematically equivalent.

So far, this text has used the standard deviation as its almost exclusive measure of variability. As its name suggests, analysis of variance is based on the variance rather than the standard deviation. Recall that s^2 symbolizes the variance of a sample, and σ^2 does so for a population. As presented in Chapter 4 (Section 4.9), the standard deviation is the square root of the variance and the variance is the square of the standard deviation. (To refresh your memory of the variance, see Chapter 4, Section 4.9.)

Before we examine the logic of ANOVA, an additional piece of information is needed. As first presented in Chapter 12, Section 12.8, the central limit theorem informs us that the standard deviation of the sampling distribution of $\overline{X}$ (the standard error of the mean) equals the population standard deviation divided by the square root of the sample size: $\sigma_{\bar{X}} = \sigma/\sqrt{N}$. The central limit theorem also states that the variance of the sampling distribution of $\bar{X}$ equals the population variance divided by the sample size: $\sigma_{\bar{X}}^2 = \sigma^2/N$.

21.3   UNDERLYING THEORY: THE LOGIC OF ANOVA

21.3.1   *Key Assumptions and Null Hypothesis*

ANOVA assumes that the populations from which samples (groups) have been selected (1) are normally distributed and (2) have equal variances. For the discussion that follows, we also assume that sample sizes, n's, are equal. ANOVA's null hypothesis states that all samples were randomly selected from populations with equal means. In statistical symbols:

$$\mu_1 = \mu_2 = \ldots = \mu_J$$

where μ_1 is the population mean for the first sample and μ_2 is that for the second. The subscript J stands for the "last" group. For instance, given five groups, $J = 5$. The ellipsis dots ($\ldots$) convey the unlisted groups. For instance, with five groups, the null is:

$$\mu_1 = \mu_2 = \mu_3 = \mu_4 = \mu_5$$

Even when the null is true, sample means differ (vary) due to sampling error. ANOVA informs the researcher whether the variability in sample means (1) may be due to sampling error alone or (2) is more likely due to both sampling error and *real* differences between the population means.

21.3.2   *Two Estimates of the Population Variance*

ANOVA generates two estimates of σ^2. the population variance. These are the key to understanding ANOVA.

First, the logic underlying the first estimate of σ^2: Recall that ANOVA assumes (1) normal distributions and (2) equal variances. The null asserts that population means are equal. Thus, when the null is true, all of the populations from which samples have been selected share the same mean, the same shape, and the same variance. In essence, when the null is true, all populations have *exactly* the same characteristics. Thus, given a true null, all of the study samples (groups) may be viewed as randomly selected samples from a *single* population. Recall from Chapter 4 (Section 4.9) that s^2 (the variance in a sample) provides an unbiased estimate of σ^2 (the variance in the population from which the sample was randomly selected). If one has, for instance, five samples, one has five different estimates of σ^2. Assuming equal sample sizes, the best estimate of σ^2 is obtained by finding the average variance, s^2, in the samples. This first estimate of the population variance, based on the average variance *within* each group, is termed the **mean square within,** symbolized by MS_W.

Now the logic behind the second estimate of σ^2: As just stated, when the null is true, each sample represents a randomly selected sample from a single population. This being the case, the sample means form a miniature sampling distribution of $\overline{X}$. For instance, with five samples, the sample means form a sampling distribution composed of five means.

Suppose for the moment that you had a full sampling distribution of $\overline{X}$ composed of means from an infinite number of samples and that you knew the variance of this sampling distribution but not that of the population from which samples had been selected. As stated above, the variance of the sampling distribution of $\overline{X}$ is given by $\sigma_{\overline{X}}^2 = \sigma^2/N$. Multiplying both sides by N results in $N\sigma_{\overline{X}}^2 = \sigma^2$. This may also be expressed as $\sigma^2 = N\sigma_{\overline{X}}^2$. Stated in words, the variance in the population equals the variance of the sampling distribution of $\overline{X}$ times the sample size.

The sampling distribution of $\overline{X}$ in ANOVA is a miniature distribution rather than a full one composed of an infinite number of means. As such, one cannot determine the exact population variance, σ^2. but one may estimate it. To estimate σ^2. multiply the variance of the sample means (the variance of the mini–sampling distribution) by the sample size, n. Thus the estimate of σ^2 is $ns_{\overline{X}}^2$, where $s_{\overline{X}}^2$ is the variance of the sample means. (The use of a small n conveys that sample size refers to the size of a single sample/group rather than to the total number of cases in the full study sample.) This second estimate of the population variance, based on the variance *between* the group means, is termed the **mean square between** (MS_B).

When the null is true, one expects the MS_W and the MS_B to have reasonably similar values because the only factor causing them to differ is sampling error. No systematic factor leads one estimate to be larger or smaller than the other.

Suppose instead that the null is false, that is, that one or more pairs of population means differ. Differences *between* population means do not affect the MS_W, as this estimate is generated from the variance *within* each group. On the other hand, differences between population means do affect the means of the samples. When population means differ, this causes the sample means to spread out more than would be expected just from sampling error. The MS_B is based on variance *between* the sample means. When population means differ, this increases the expected spread (variance) of the sample means ($s_{\overline{X}}^2$), and thus the expected value of the MS_B ($ns_{\overline{X}}^2$) In sum, when the null is false, one expects the MS_B to be larger than the MS_W. This is the essential logic of ANOVA.

When the MS_W and the MS_B are similar in size, the variability (differences) between the group means may well be due only to sampling error. When the MS_B is considerably larger than the MS_W, this suggests that some population means do indeed differ.

21.3.3   *The* F *Distribution*

How much larger than the MS_W does the MS_B have to be before the null of equal population means can be rejected? This question is addressed by the **F distribution,** the sampling distribution on which ANOVA is based. An **F ratio** (or simply **F**) is formed by dividing one population variance estimate by another. In the case of ANOVA, one divides the MS_B by the MS_W:

$$F = \frac{MS_B}{MS_W} \tag{21.1}$$

When the null is true, one expects the F ratio to be reasonably close to 1.00 (because the MS_B and the MS_W are expected to be reasonably equal in size). When the null is false, one expects the F ratio to exceed 1.00 (because the MS_B is expected to be larger than the MS_W).

Like the t distribution and the χ^2 distribution, the F distribution is not a single distribution but a family of distributions that takes on different shapes and has different critical values depending on degrees of freedom. Each F distribution has two different degrees of freedom, one corresponding to its numerator and one to its denominator. In ANOVA, degrees of freedom for the MS_B (the numerator) equal the number of groups (designated by J) minus 1: $df = J - 1$. Degrees of freedom for the MS_W (the denominator) equal the total number of cases in the full study sample, N, minus the number of groups: $df = N - J$. Suppose a study has six groups with 10 people in each group: df for the $MS_B = 6 - 1 = 5$; df for the $MS_W = 60 - 6 = 54$.

All F distributions are positively skewed. Most importantly for ANOVA (regardless of degrees of freedom), the mean of each F distribution is very close to 1.00. When the null is true and assumptions are met, the F ratio in ANOVA (the test statistic F) follows an F distribution with degrees of freedom corresponding to those for the MS_B (numerator) and MS_W (denominator). See Glass and Hopkins (1996, p. 430) for greater detail on the F distribution.

21.4   PARTICULARS OF ANOVA

21.4.1   Assumptions and Levels of Measurement

As previously stated, ANOVA assumes that (1) population distributions are normally shaped and (2) population variances are equal. With both equal and unequal sample sizes, ANOVA is highly robust to the normality assumption. For two groups, the sample size guidelines in Table 17.1 apply. For three or more samples/groups, and assuming that no populations are highly skewed, ANOVA yields reasonably accurate results even with very small sample sizes, say, when the smallest sample (group) size is about 10 or greater. (When one is confident that all population distributions are reasonably close to normal in shape, it is safe to use ANOVA with even smaller samples, say when the smallest $n \geq 5$.) When one or more cases is an extreme outlier (e.g., 5, 6, 8, 8, 9, 10, 42) and sample size is small, ANOVA can yield inaccurate probabilities. Given *equal* sample sizes, it is robust to the equal variances assumption.

With unequal sample sizes, ANOVA is not robust to this assumption. The greater the disparity in sample sizes, the less robust it is. Thus, when both sample sizes and sample variances differ substantially, ANOVA results can be inaccurate. The assumption of equal population variances is typically assessed by an equality of variances test similar to that used for the independent samples t test. With unequal n's, the probabilities yielded by ANOVA can be presumed to be accurate only under both of the following conditions: (1) the null of equal variances is accepted and (2) one's equality of variances test has adequate statistical power.[1,2] (One's total sample size, N, should be at least 50 or so for this test to have adequate power.) ANOVA presumes interval/ratio-level measurement or almost so. (See Glass and Hopkins, 1996, pp. 402–405, for greater detail on ANOVA assumptions.)

21.4.2 Hypothesis Pair

The hypothesis pair in ANOVA is always nondirectional:

Null: The means of all populations from which samples have been randomly selected are equal.

Research: All population means are not equal.

In symbols, the null is $H_0 = \mu_1 = \mu_2 = \ldots = \mu_J$. Because no symbol conveys the idea that all means are not equal, the research hypothesis cannot be stated using mathematical symbols.[3] For three or more groups, when rejecting the null, one may conclude that all population means are not equal but may not draw a conclusion regarding which particular pair(s) of means differ.

21.4.3 Distribution and Test Statistic

The test statistic in ANOVA is F (the F ratio), with the formula $F = MS_B/MS_W$. The two numbers for degrees of freedom are found as follows: for MS_B (the numerator), $df = J - 1$; for MS_W (the denominator), $df = N - J$. ANOVA is always a one-tailed test with the rejection region located in the upper tail.

To determine F, one first calculates the MS_W and the MS_B. When sample sizes are equal:

$$MS_W = \frac{s_1^2 + s_2^2 + \ldots + s_J^2}{J} \tag{21.2}$$

where J is the number of groups/samples, s_1^2, s_2^2, and s_J^2 are the sample variances, and . . . stands for samples not mentioned explicitly in the formula. This formula simply computes the average variance within the groups. Whether or not sample sizes are equal, the MS_W equals the sum of squares within, the SS_W, divided by its degrees of freedom. The most common formula for the MS_W is:

$$MS_W = \frac{SS_W}{df \text{ for } MS_W} \tag{21.3}$$

The **sum of squares within** (SS_W) is the sum of squared deviation scores around the sample (group) means. To calculate the SS_W, for *each* sample (1) find its mean, (2) subtract each case's score from that mean to determine a deviation score, (3) square each deviation score, and (4) sum the squared deviation scores. Finally (step 5), sum the results of step 4 across all samples. The formula for the SS_W is:

$$SS_W = \sum (X_1 - \bar{X}_1)^2 + \sum (X_2 - \bar{X}_2)^2 + \ldots + \sum (X_J - \bar{X}_J)^2 \tag{21.4}$$

where X_1 represents each case in Sample 1, $\overline{X}_1$ is the mean of Sample 1, X_2 represents each case in Sample 2, $\overline{X}_2$ is the mean of Sample 2, X_J represents each case in Sample J, $\overline{X}_J$ is the mean of Sample J, and the dots represent samples not listed.

In ANOVA terminology, the mean of *all* scores is the **grand mean,** and it is used to calculate the MS_B. To determine the grand mean, sum the scores for all cases and divide by N (the total number of cases in the study sample). The MS_B equals the **sum of squares between** (SS_B) divided by its degrees of freedom:

$$MS_B = \frac{SS_B}{df \text{ for } MS_B} \tag{21.5}$$

To compute the SS_B: (1) compute the grand mean, (2) subtract the mean of each sample from the grand mean, (3) square each difference in step 2, (4) multiply each squared difference by the number of cases in that sample, and (5) sum the results of step 4. The formula for the SS_B is:

$$SS_B = n_1(\overline{X}_1 - \overline{X}_{grand})^2 + n_2(\overline{X}_2 - \overline{X}_{grand})^2 + \ldots + n_J(\overline{X}_J - \overline{X}_{grand})^2 \tag{21.6}$$

where n_1 is the number of cases in Sample 1, $\overline{X}_1$ is the mean of Sample 1, n_2 is the number of cases in Sample 2, $\overline{X}_2$ is the mean of Sample 2, n_J is the number of cases in Sample J, $\overline{X}_J$ is the mean of Sample J, and $\overline{X}_{grand}$ is the grand mean.

21.4.4   Critical Values and Decision Rules

Table A.4 in Appendix A lists critical values for F. To use Table A.4, find the critical value that corresponds to (1) the degrees of freedom for the MS_B (numerator; listed across the top), (2) degrees of freedom for the MS_W (denominator; listed down the left column,) and (3) the alpha level (significance level). When the exact number of degrees of freedom is not listed for the MS_B (numerator), use the closest larger number. When it is not listed for the MS_W (denominator), use the closest smaller number. The decision rules are:

Fail to reject (accept) the null when the obtained F is less than the critical value of F in Table A.4.

Reject the null when the obtained F is greater than or equal to the critical value of F in Table A.4.

21.5   HAND-CALCULATION EXAMPLE

With the easy accessibility of statistical software, one need not carry out ANOVA calculations by hand. However, a demonstration may help you understand the ANOVA test of significance. Suppose that 12 students, four each in three study groups, answer the following number of questions correctly on a brief quiz:

GROUP 1	GROUP 2	GROUP 3
3, 5, 5, 7	4, 5, 7, 8	6, 7, 7, 8

The null states that population means are equal: $\mu_1 = \mu_2 = \mu_3$. Presume that the .05 significance level is chosen. To carry out the ANOVA calculations:

1. Calculate the grand mean:

   $3 + 5 + 5 + 7 + 4 + 5 + 7 + 8 + 6 + 7 + 7 + 8 = 72,$ $72/12 = 6$

2. Calculate the mean of each group:

   Group 1: $3 + 5 + 5 + 7 = 20,$ $20/4 = 5$
   Group 2: $4 + 5 + 7 + 8 = 24,$ $24/4 = 6$
   Group 3: $6 + 7 + 7 + 8 = 28,$ $28/4 = 7$

3. Calculate the SS_W via formula 21.4:

   Group 1: $(3 - 5)^2 + (5 - 5)^2 + (5 - 5)^2 + (7 - 5)^2 =$
   $$4 + 0 + 0 + 4 = 8$$
   Group 2: $(4 - 6)^2 + (5 - 6)^2 + (7 - 6)^2 + (8 - 6)^2 =$
   $$4 + 1 + 1 + 4 = 10$$
   Group 3: $(6 - 7)^2 + (7 - 7)^2 + (7 - 7)^2 + (8 - 7)^2 =$
   $$1 + 0 + 0 + 1 = 2$$

   Summing the results for the groups: $8 + 10 + 2 = 20$.

4. Calculate the MS_W via formula 21.3, that is, divide the SS_W by the degrees of freedom for the MS_W ($N - J$):

   $20/(12 - 3) = 20/9 = 2.22$

5. Calculate the SS_B via formula 21.6:

   $4(5 - 6)^2 + 4(6 - 6)^2 + 4(7 - 6)^2 = 4(1) + 4(0) + 4(1) = 8$

6. Determine the MS_B via formula 21.5, that is, divide the SS_B by the degrees of freedom for the MS_B ($J - 1$):

   $8/(3 - 1) = 8/2 = 4.00$

7. Divide the MS_B by the MS_W to form the F ratio:

   $F = 4.00/2.22 = 1.80$

Consulting Table A.4 for degrees of freedom 2 (numerator) and 9 (denominator) when $\alpha = .05$, the critical value of F is 4.26. As the obtained F, 1.80, is less than 4.26, we fail to reject the null and conclude that the differences between the group means may well be due to sampling error. Study results are not statistically significant.

Figure 21.1 presents an F distribution with degrees of freedom 2 (numerator) and 9 (denominator). Given a true null and presuming that ANOVA assumptions are met, the obtained F ratio (test statistic F) is 4.26 or greater in 5% of randomly selected samples. F ratios greater than or equal to 4.26 are located in the rejection region. The test statistic F in our study was not located in the rejection region, so the null was accepted.

In interpreting the just-computed results, two cautions should be noted. First, sample size (n) was only 4. As such, the sample distributions provide little help in assessing whether the population distributions meet assumptions. If one or more population distributions is highly skewed, the test result (probability) may be inaccurate. Second, due to the small sample size, statistical power is very low.

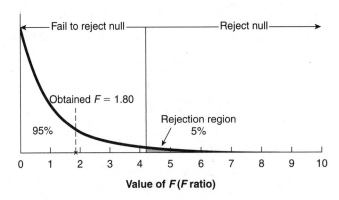

FIGURE **21.1**

F Distribution (*df* = 2,9) and Rejection Region
(α = .05)

The difference in quiz scores between study groups 1, 2, and 3 is
not significant, as shown by the obtained *F* of 1.80 located in the
region where the null is accepted.

21.6   Computer Calculation Example

Examples from previous chapters have used the family ethnicity variable from the
special-needs adoption study (Rosenthal and Groze, 1992). The three family ethnicity groups are as follows: Group 1, minority, inracial (minority parents who adopted
a minority child of the same race as at least one parent); Group 2, white, inracial
(white parents who adopt a white child); and Group 3, transracial (white parents who
adopt a minority child). Parents filled out an instrument indicating the severity of behavioral problems in the home. The higher the score, the greater the severity of
problems. As the behavior problems instrument (Achenbach, 1991) was designed
for children ages four and older, only such cases are included in the analysis.

The current example makes use of the SPSS for Windows statistical package
to assess whether mean behavior problems scores differ significantly among the
three groups. The null states that all three means are equal: H_0: $\mu_1 = \mu_2 = \mu_3$.
We will use the .01 significance level.

Table 21.1 presents the SPSS output. The Descriptives table conveys that the
mean behavior problems score is highest in the white, inracial group, intermediate in the transracial group, and lowest in the minority, inracial group. Observe
that standard deviations in all three groups are very similar.

As would be expected given the similarity of group standard deviations, the
test of equality of population variances (as presented in the Test of Homogeneity
of Variances table) results in acceptance of the null of equal population variances:
H_0: $\sigma_1^2 = \sigma_2^2 = \sigma_3^2$. (The probability for this test's result was .793. Presuming that
the .05 level was chosen, we would have rejected the null if this probability had
been less than or equal to .05.) Because the equality of variances assumption is
met, our ANOVA results should be quite accurate.

TABLE 21.1 **ANOVA Results: Behavior Problems in Family Ethnicity Groups**

Descriptives

			N	Mean	Std. Deviation	Std. Error	95% Confidence Interval for Mean	
							Lower Bound	Upper Bound
CBCTOT behavior problems score	FAMETH family ethnicity	minority, inracial	208	31.13	25.80	1.79	27.60	34.66
		white-inracial	433	40.21	26.23	1.26	37.74	42.69
		transracial	55	36.20	26.07	3.52	29.15	43.25
		Total	696	37.18	26.37	1.00	35.22	39.14

Test of Homogeneity of Variances

	Levene Statistic	df1	df2	Sig.
CBCTOT behavior problems score	.232	2	693	.793

ANOVA

		Sum of Squares	df	Mean Square	F	Sig.
CBCTOT behavior problems score	Between Groups	11648.4	2	5824.2	8.559	.000
	Within Groups	471586.7	693	680.5		
	Total	483235.2	695			

Note: SPSS for Windows output.

The table labeled ANOVA is typically termed an **ANOVA table** (or an *ANOVA summary table*). To understand it better, let's see how some of the numbers in this table were derived. We focus first on the degrees of freedom column, "df." The degrees of freedom listed in the "Between Groups" row (2) is that for the MS_B. This formula is $df = J - 1$, where J is the number of groups. There are three groups, so $df = 3 - 1 = 2$. The degrees of freedom listed in the "Within Groups" row (693) is that for the MS_W. This formula is $df = N - J$. The study sample size (N) is 696 (see the Descriptives table). Hence $df = 696 - 3 = 693$. Each mean square is computed by dividing its corresponding sum of squares by its degrees of freedom:

$$MS_B = (11648.4)/2 = 5824.4 \qquad MS_W = (471586.7)/693 = 680.5$$

Finally, note that the F ratio is computed by dividing the mean square between by the mean square within:

$$F = 5824.2/680.5 = 8.559$$

As listed in the "Sig." column in the ANOVA table, given a true null, the probability of obtaining an F of 8.559 is .000. This probability is less than the selected significance level ($\alpha = .01$), so the null is rejected. We conclude that the differences between the group means are unlikely to be due to chance alone and instead reflect real differences.

In contrast to the prior ANOVA example where sample size was very small ($N = 12$), sample size in this example was very large ($N = 696$). As such, power was excellent. With excellent power, even small associations often achieve significance. One should not make the mistake of assuming that because a result is statistically significant, size of association is necessarily large. In the current example, size of association can best be characterized as small to medium. For instance, the largest difference in means between groups, that between minority families and white, in-racial families is about one-third of a standard deviation: $SDM \approx (40.21 - 31.13)/26.09 = 0.36$ (the denominator is s_{wg}, estimated via formula 9.3). For greater detail regarding ANOVA see Glass and Hopkins (1996), Toothaker and Miller (1996), or many other statistics books.

21.7   MULTIPLE COMPARISON PROCEDURES

Suppose that an analysis of variance with five groups (samples) yields statistically significant results. This informs us that it is unlikely that all population means are equal. The next logical step in the data analysis process is to identify pairs of means that differ to a statistically significant degree. One approach for so doing is to conduct independent samples t tests for each pair. A disadvantage of this approach is that the number of tests needed increases rapidly with the number of groups. The number of t tests necessary to compare all possible pairs of means is $[J(J - 1)]/2$, where J is the number of groups. With five groups, 10 t tests are needed: $[5(5 - 1)]/2 = 10$. As you recall, the probability of a type I error, the error of rejecting a true null, equals the probability associated with the statistical significance level (α). For instance, when the .05 level is used, the probability of a type I error is .05. This probability applies to *each* statistical test, that is, to each comparison between means.

When a series of comparisons is carried out, the probability of a type I error for *at least one* comparison in the series is greater than that for any single comparison. For instance, given five groups and therefore 10 comparisons, and with α set to .05 (and assuming a true null, that is, that all population means are equal), the probability of a type I error on at least one comparison equals approximately .40. There is intuitive logic behind this result. Each comparison has a 5% chance that sampling error will result in rejection. Even though this chance is small for any single comparison, given enough comparisons, sampling error may well prevail at least once.

In sum, when multiple t tests are conducted, the probability of making at least one type I error can greatly exceed the chosen significance level.[4] Multiple comparison procedures were developed to deal with this problem. At the risk of oversimplification, most **multiple comparison** procedures adjust the risk of type I error so that it applies to the whole series of comparisons rather than to each specific one. For instance, given five groups, and therefore 10 possible comparisons, by using an appropriate multiple comparison procedure, one could set the risk of type I error to .05 for the whole series of 10 comparisons. (Given that this risk is .05 for the series, it is less than this for any single comparison.)

Multiple comparison procedures reduce the possibility that a comparison will reach significance due to chance and are clearly preferable to conducting multiple *t* tests. Most statistical packages have easy-to-use multiple comparison procedures. Some of the better-known multiple comparisons are the Bonferroni, SNK, and Tukey procedures.[5] (See Toothaker and Miller, 1996, pp. 483–512, or Glass and Hopkins, 1996, pp. 444–481, for further discussion.)

21.8 FISHING EXPEDITIONS

21.8.1 The Dangers of Fishing

Regarding comparisons between means, the prior section stated: "When a series of comparisons is carried out, the probability of a type I error for *at least one* comparison in the series is greater than that for any single comparison." This same idea may be extended to all statistical tests and to research studies in general.

For instance, suppose that in a given study one has five independent variables and three dependent variables. In such a study, one has 15 different combinations of independent variables with dependent variables. Thus, to examine each combination, one would need to conduct 15 statistical significance tests ($5 \times 3 = 15$). Presume that (unknown to the researcher) the null is true for each combination. Stated differently, presume that in the study population, each independent variable is unassociated with each dependent variable. Suppose that the .05 level is used for each test. What is the probability that at least one of the 15 tests will be significant? This probability computes to about .54.[6] In other words, even though the null is true in each instance, the odds of finding at least one statistically significant association are better than 50/50. This example supports the key concept: When a series of statistical significance tests is carried out, the probability of a type I error for *at least one* test in the series is greater than that for any single test.

The basic message is that if enough tests are conducted, sooner or later one or more will achieve significance. Conducting many, many tests searching for one or more to achieve significance is referred to as a "fishing expedition" or, more simply, as **fishing.** Most researchers discourage fishing. In the worst cases, those who fish simply probe the associations of all possible variables without any guidance from theory and without critical thinking. Sooner or later, inevitably, they "catch a fish," that is, they find a statistically significant association.

The number of tests conducted is only part of the problem. In addition to carrying out a great many tests, researchers sometimes report only those test results that are statistically significant.

When a given study involves only a single significance test and the null is rejected at the .05 level, one can be 95% confident that it is false. When a study involves a reasonably small number of tests and these have been planned for ahead of time, one may have basic confidence in results (but should recognize that the likelihood of a significant finding increases with the number of tests). When a researcher carries out a great many tests with scant attention to the guiding theory on which the study is based—and particularly, if results are reported selectively—one should be skeptical. Here, the likelihood that a particular significant result is due to chance may greatly exceed the significance level. In this situation (given the .05 level), one should have *much less than* 95% confidence that the null is false.

21.8.2 *The Dangers of Not Fishing*

As we have just discussed the dangers of fishing, this is a good time to point out problems associated with the opposite orientation, that is, to *only* investigate associations clearly articulated by prior theory and hypotheses. The problem with such an orientation is akin to putting on blinders, that is, to seeing only what one wants to see. Suppose that we have three variables: Variable A, Variable B, and Variable C. We design a study to assess the association of A and B, which is theorized to be large and highly significant. We consider C to be an unimportant variable; it's included in the study only as an afterthought. Now suppose that study results show (1) no association between A and B and (2) a large, significant (and unexpected) association between A and C. If we adopt the strictest possible stance against fishing, we would not report the association between A and C. (Indeed, with such a stance we would never even discover this association because we would focus our sole attention on the association between A and B.)

Many key scientific discoveries involve discovery of the unexpected, and fishing is a route toward such discovery. With powerful computers that effortlessly crank out numbers and tests, it seems foolish not to exploit the full information in one's data set. The computational ability we have today contrasts markedly with that of statisticians 70 years ago, who computed each correlation and test by hand. On the other hand, excessive fishing without attention to theory and without critical reasoning does little to advance knowledge and calls to mind the phrase "Garbage in: Garbage out." So, the best approach is to find the right balance between (1) the key ideas conveyed by theory and (2) some amount of fishing.

21.9 CHAPTER SUMMARY

Analysis of variance (ANOVA) examines differences in means between two or more independent samples. The null states that all samples (groups) have been randomly selected from populations with equal means. The hypothesis pair is always nondirectional.

ANOVA generates two estimates of the population variance, the mean square within (MS_W), based on variances within groups, and the mean square between (MS_B), based on the variance between group means. When the MS_W and the MS_B have similar values, differences between group means may well be due only to sampling error. When the MS_B is considerably larger than the MS_W, population means may indeed differ and the null may be false. The MS_W is typically calculated by dividing the sum of squares within (SS_W) by the degrees of freedom for the MS_W $(N - J)$. The MS_B is calculated by dividing the sum of squares between (SS_B) by the degrees of freedom for the MS_B $(J - 1)$.

ANOVA is based on the F distribution. To compute F in ANOVA, divide the MS_B by the MS_W: $F = MS_B/MS_W$ (formula 21.1). When the null is true, one expects F to be reasonably close to 1.00. When it is false, one expects F to be greater than 1.00, often considerably so.

ANOVA assumes that populations are normally distributed and have equal population variances. It is robust to the normality assumption. Given equal sample sizes, ANOVA is robust to the equal variances assumption. With unequal sample sizes, it is not.

One fails to reject (accepts) the null when the obtained F is less than the critical value in Table A.4. It is rejected when the obtained F equals or exceeds this value. ANOVA is a one-tailed test.

When a series of pairs of means are compared via independent samples t tests, the probability of a type I error for at least one comparison in the series exceeds that for any given comparison. Most multiple comparison procedures adjust the risk of type I error so that it applies to the whole series of comparisons rather than to each particular pair.

Conducting many, many statistical tests searching for one to achieve significance is termed fishing. When multiple, unplanned tests are conducted and results are reported selectively, one should be skeptical. A balance between planned-for and exploratory analyses is often a good combination.

PROBLEMS AND QUESTIONS

Section 21.2

1. (T or F) With two groups, ANOVA and a two-tailed independent samples t test (equal variances formula) yield identical probabilities.
2. What is the formula for the variance of the sampling distribution of $\overline{X}$?

Section 21.3

3. ANOVA assumes that the populations from which samples have been selected are _____ distributed and have _____ variances.
4. In your own words, what does the null for ANOVA state?
5. State the null in symbols.
6. In ANOVA, one derives two estimates of the population _____.
7. When the null is true, the two estimates of the population _____ are expected to be about _____.

8. The first estimate of the population variance, based on the variance within _____, is termed the _____ _____ _____.
9. Given equal sample sizes, the MS_W equals the _____ variance _____ each group.
10. The second estimate of the population variance, based on the variance _____ group means, is termed the _____ _____ _____.
11. When sample sizes are equal and the null is true, the sample means form, in effect, a miniature _____ _____ of _____.
12. When sample sizes are equal, the mean square between is derived by multiplying the variance of the sample _____ by _____ (symbol).
13. The MS_W is based on the variance _____ groups. The MS_B is based on the variance _____ groups.
14. (T or F) When the null is true, one expects the MS_W and the MS_B to have very different values.
15. Differences between population means cause the sample means to _____ out more than would be expected due to _____ _____ alone.

16. When the null is false, one expects the mean square _____ to be larger than the mean square _____.

17. ANOVA is based on the _____ distribution. By dividing the MS_B by the MS_W, one derives an _____ _____.

18. When the null is true, one expects the F ratio to equal approximately _____. When the null is false, one expects the F ratio to be _____ than 1.00.

19. (T or F) When the obtained F is less than 1.00, one always accepts the null.

20. All F distributions are _____ skewed.

Section 21.4

21. (T or F) ANOVA is robust to the assumption that samples are selected from normally distributed populations.

22. (T or F) Even when sample sizes differ considerably, ANOVA is robust to the equality of variances assumption.

23. (T or F) When sample sizes are equal, ANOVA is robust to the equality of variances assumption.

24. Given three or more groups, is the hypothesis pair in ANOVA directional or nondirectional, or can it be either of these?

25. (T or F) The ANOVA statistical test is always _____-tailed.

26. (T or F) ANOVA focuses on whether a specific pair of means differs rather than on the overall variability of means.

Section 21.5

27. How is the sum of squares within calculated?

28. To calculate the MS_W, one divides the SS_W by the _____ of _____ for the MS_W, that is by _____ (formula for df for MS_W).

29. How is the sum of squares between calculated?

30. To calculate the MS_B, one divides the SS_B by the _____ of _____ for the MS_B, that is, by _____ (formula for df for MS_B).

31. What is the formula for F (F ratio)?

32. Indicate the degrees of freedom first for the MS_B and second for the MS_W for the following situations.
    a. $N = 40, J = 5$

b. $N = 100, J = 3$

c. $N = 28, J = 4$

33. A given study has three groups, each with $n = 10$. The variances of these groups are $s_1^2 = 8.0$, $s_2^2 = 9.0$, $s_3^2 = 7.0$.
    a. What is the average variance within the groups?
    b. If one assumes equal variances in the populations from which samples were selected, what is the best estimate of the population variance?
    c. What is the MS_W?
    d. What is df for the MS_W?

34. Given the provided information, compute F for each situation.
    a. $MS_B = 3.3, MS_W = 2.2$
    b. $MS_B = 7.8, MS_W = 2.6$
    c. $MS_B = 6.0, MS_W = 8.0$
    d. $MS_B = 6.0, MS_W = 1.5$

35. Indicate whether each of the following F ratios would result in acceptance or rejection of the null at (1) the .05 significance level and (2) the .01 level.
    a. $F = 5.83, df = 2$ (MS_B) and 30 (MS_W)
    b. $F = 5.03, df = 2$ (MS_B) and 30 (MS_W)
    c. $F = 1.97, df = 5$ (MS_B) and 50 (MS_W)

Section 21.6

36. A given study has five groups with 21 people in each group.
    a. Fill in the missing information for the ANOVA test in Table 21PQ.1 and respond to the questions that follow.
    b. When $\alpha = .05$, what is the critical value of F?
    c. Does the obtained F indicate a statistically significant difference in group means?
    d. Is the obtained F consistent with (not inconsistent with) the null?

TABLE 21PQ.1   ANOVA TEST

Source	df	Sum of Squares	Mean Squares	F Ratio
Between groups		360.00		
Within groups		4500.00		

e. What is your decision regarding the null?

f. Do the results suggest it is plausible that the difference in group means may be due simply to chance?

TABLE 21PQ.2   ANOVA TEST

Source	df	Sum of Squares	Mean Squares	F Ratio
Between groups	3	300.00		
Within groups	96	960.00		

37. The questions for this problem are based on the incomplete ANOVA table in Table 21PQ.2.
    a. How many groups were in this study?
    b. Assuming equal sample sizes, what was the sample size in each group?
    c. What is the MS_B, the MS_W, and F?
    d. When $\alpha = .01$, what is the critical value of F?
    e. At the .01 level, what is your decision regarding the null?
    f. Is it plausible (i.e., is it not unlikely) that the difference between means is due simply to chance?

Section 21.7

38. Assuming a true null, the probability of a type I error equals _____.

39. Given a true null, when multiple independent samples t tests are conducted, the probability of making at least one type I error is _____ than _____.

40. Assuming a true null, when multiple independent samples t tests are conducted with $\alpha = .05$, the probability that the null will be rejected for at least one test is _____ than _____.

41. What is the name of the set of procedures that addresses the problem of increased probability of type I error when many pairs of means are compared?

Section 21.8

42. (T or F) Assuming a true null, when many different statistical tests are conducted in a study, the probability of rejecting the null on at least one test exceeds that probability for any given single test.

43. (T or F) In general, one should be more skeptical when results of many varied tests are reported than when the result of a single, planned-for test is reported.

44. (T or F) This text advocates that one should *never* go fishing.

45. In your own words, what is the advantage of fishing?

COMPUTER EXERCISES

For general instructions on computer exercises, see the note in Chapter 2.

1. Via analysis of variance, see whether there is a statistically significant association between mean score on RELSCALE (quality/closeness of parent/child relationship) and FAMETH (family ethnicity). [In SPSS, *Analyze > Compare Means > One-Way ANOVA*, click RELSCALE over to space below "Dependent List," click FAMETH over to space below "Factor," *Options*, click boxes next to "Descriptive" and "Homogeneity-of-variance" so that these are checked, *Continue, OK*.] Use the .05 level.

   Check your answers: In the Test of Homogeneity of Variances table, the Levene statistic is highly significant, $p = .000$. Given that sample sizes also differ, the accuracy of the ANOVA results is in some question. Given that (1) the differences in standard deviations are moderate and (2) results in the ANOVA table are highly significant, $F(2,732) = 14.93$, $p = .000$, it is unlikely that the inaccuracy introduced by the unequal variances is serious enough to result in a different decision regarding the null. (See note 1 at the end of the chapter.) Hence the null of equal means is rejected.

2. Via analysis of variance, see whether mean BEHAVTOT (score on behavior checklist) scores differ significantly for the different categories of FCOH4 (FACES cohesion categories). [In SPSS, follow the procedures outlined in the previous

exercise but with BEHAVTOT clicked into the space below "Dependent List" and FCOH4 into that below "Factor."] Use the .05 level.

Check your answers: The Levene test rejects the null of equal population variances, $p = .001$. However, as sample variances do not differ greatly and as the F ratio is highly significant, $p = .000$, we can be reasonably safe in deciding to reject the null. (See note 1 at the end of the chapter.)

3. Via analysis of variance, see whether mean age at entry into the home (AGEHOMEY) differs significantly ($p = .01$) by family ethnicity (FAMETH).

Check your answers: As the homogeneity of variances test is not significant ($p = .080$), the null of equal population variances is accepted. Mean age at entry into the home does differ significantly, $F(2,754) = 11.10$, $p < .01$. (In particular, children in white, inracial homes entered at older ages.)

NOTES

1. As a practical matter, ANOVA's probabilities will be reasonably accurate when both of the following conditions are met: (1) the largest sample standard deviation is no more than 50% larger than the smallest and (2) the largest sample size is no more than 50% larger than the smallest. These guidelines may be relaxed for three or more samples/groups. Glass and Hopkins (1996, pp. 405–406) discuss weaknesses in the Levene test, which is often used to test equal variances, and recommend the Welch and Brown-Forsythe modifications to ANOVA when both variances and sample sizes differ. (These modifications are akin to the procedures used in the unequal variances formula for the independent samples t test; see Chapter 18, Section 18.3.)

2. When both sample sizes and population variances are unequal, the probability resulting from ANOVA will be inaccurate, at least to some degree. When larger samples are selected from populations with greater variability and smaller samples from those with lesser, the actual probability that the result is due to chance is less than the probability resulting from ANOVA. When larger samples are selected from populations with lesser variability and smaller samples from those with greater, the actual probability that the result is due to chance is greater than that resulting from ANOVA (Glass and Hopkins, 1996, pp. 404–405). Sometimes an inaccurate ANOVA probability does not prevent one from making a correct decision on the null. For instance, presume the following: (1) the .05 level is selected, (2) the probability yielded by ANOVA is .04, and (3) larger samples are selected from less variable populations (as indicated by smaller sample standard deviations) and smaller samples are selected from more variable ones (larger sample standard deviations). In such a situation, one can deduce that the actual probability that the result is due to chance is less than that indicated by ANOVA (less than .04). Hence, one may safely reject the null at the .05 level.

3. When there are only two groups, the research hypothesis may be expressed as H_1: $\mu_1 \neq \mu_2$.

4. The approximate probability of at least one error equals $1 - (1 - \alpha)^C$ where C is the number of comparisons. For 10 comparisons, $1 - (1 - .05)^{10} = 1 - (.95)^{10} = 1 - .60 = .40$. This probability is approximate because each comparison is not independent of each other comparison.

5. The term *contrast* is often used to refer to comparisons between the groups involved in an ANOVA. An important type of contrast is a *linear polynomial contrast*. Sometimes groups can be ordered from lowest to highest. For instance, suppose that youths in Group 1 receive one hour per week of tutoring services, those in Group 2 receive two hours, those in Group 3 receive three hours, and those in Group 4 receive four hours. Perhaps the pattern of results suggests an increase in mean grade point average (GPA, the dependent variable) as number of hours increases. A linear polynomial contrast can assess whether a directional pattern of differences between means—in this example, the increase in mean GPA as tutoring hours increases—reaches statistical significance. In SPSS, linear contrasts are accessed via the One-Way ANOVA procedure. See Glass and Hopkins (1996, pp. 462–467) for more on this and related contrasts.

6. In this example, the number of combinations equals the number of independent variables times the number of dependent variables: $5 \times 3 = 15$. The approximate probability equals $1 - (1 - .05)^{15} = 1 - .46 = .54$. Had the .01 level been selected, the approximate probability would have been $1 - (1 - .01)^{15} = 1 - .86 = .14$.

SELECTED STATISTICAL TESTS

22.1 CHAPTER OVERVIEW

The *statistical significance test of Pearson's r* is another of the most-used measures of significance. We study it closely, including its hypothesis pairs and the effects that sample size has on it. Statistical software for the test produces a *correlation matrix*, which we interpret. We turn next to the distinction between *parametric* and *nonparametric* tests and overview a variety of nonparametric tests for ordinal-level data, all available in statistical software. These include the *significance test of Spearman's r*, tests for categorical variables, and tests for independent and dependent samples. We discuss the comparative advantages and disadvantages of parametric versus nonparametric procedures. Finally, we overview *multiple regression analysis*.

22.2 STATISTICAL SIGNIFICANCE TEST OF PEARSON'S *r*

22.2.1 Basic Logic

The Pearson correlation coefficient, *r*, measures the degree of linear association between continuous variables, as discussed in Chapter 8. Even when the correlation in the population from which one's sample has been selected equals 0.00, the obtained *r* almost always differs from this due to sampling error. The **significance test of Pearson's *r*** conveys the probability of obtaining one's study sample correlation given that the population correlation is 0.00. It is one of the two or three most frequently conducted statistical tests.

22.2.2 Assumptions and Levels of Measurement

The significance test of *r* presumes measurement at the interval/ratio level or almost so. Although the test is based on the assumption that both variables are normally distributed in the population from which the sample was selected, it is robust to this assumption and yields reasonably accurate results whenever the degree of skewness is not severe (Toothaker and Miller, 1996, p. 388).[1] When one or more distributions is strongly skewed, the test of Spearman's r (r_{ranks}; Section 22.5) is a good alternative. The combination of very small sample size and outliers can introduce inaccuracy.

22.2.3 Hypothesis Pairs

Both nondirectional and directional hypothesis pairs may be formulated. The nondirectional hypothesis states:[2]

> *Null:* The correlation (Pearson's r) in the population from which the study sample was randomly selected equals 0.00.
> *Research:* The correlation (Pearson's r) in the population from which the study sample was randomly selected does not equal 0.00.

The population correlation is termed rho (pronounced as in "*row* your boat") and is symbolized by the Greek letter ρ. In symbols, the nondirectional pair is:

$$H_0: \quad \rho = 0 \qquad H_1: \quad \rho \neq 0$$

Two sets of directional hypothesis pairs, one for each direction, may be stated:

$$H_0: \quad \rho \leq 0 \qquad H_1: \quad \rho > 0 \qquad \text{and} \qquad H_0: \quad \rho \geq 0 \qquad H_1: \quad \rho < 0$$

22.2.4 Sampling Distribution of r

If one picks an unlimited number of random samples of a given size from a population in which rho (ρ) equals 0.00 and, for each, calculates and plots r, one could build a **sampling distribution of the test statistic r.** Statistical theory tells us that (1) the mean of that distribution equals 0.00; (2) presuming that assumptions are met, its shape is normal; and (3) as sample size increases, its standard deviation decreases. Figure 22.1 presents the sampling distribution of r for three different sample sizes, presuming that assumptions are met. Distribution A is for an unlimited number of samples of size 20. Distribution B is for a sample size of 50 and C is for one of 200. Observe that as sample size increases, values of r cluster more tightly around 0.00. Figure 22.1 also presents rejection regions.

As Figure 22.1 demonstrates, the larger the sample size, the smaller the absolute value of r needed to reject the null. The top and middle figures in Figure 22.1 present rejection regions for a two-tailed test where $\alpha = .05$. When sample size is 20 (Distribution A), values of r less than or equal to $-.468$ or greater than or equal to .468 result in rejection of the null hypothesis that ρ (rho) equals 0. When sample size is 50 (Distribution B), values less than or equal to $-.276$ or greater than or equal to .276 result in rejection. Distribution C presents the rejection area for a one-tailed test where $N = 200$, $\alpha = .05$, and the research hypothesis states the direction "less than." In this figure, the null is rejected whenever r is less than or equal to $-.117$.

Figure 22.1 demonstrates that as sample size increases, it becomes easier to reject the null. (To make the same point in a different way: As sample size increases, so also does statistical power.)

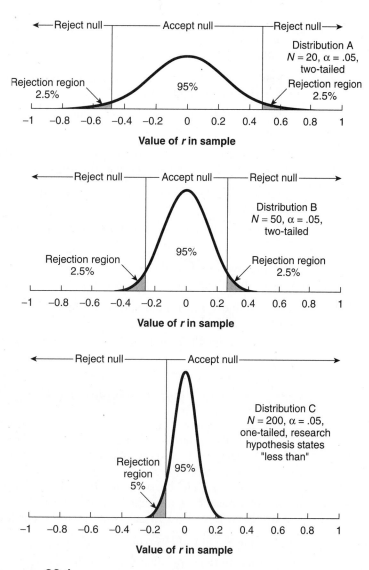

FIGURE 22.1

SAMPLING DISTRIBUTION OF *r* FOR THREE DIFFERENT SAMPLE SIZES

Population correlation (ρ) equals 0.00.

22.2.5   *Carrying Out the Test via a Table*

A straightforward way to assess the significance of r is to consult a table of critical values. We will follow this approach. Table A.5 in Appendix A presents critical values of Pearson's r for (1) .01 and .05 significance levels, (2) one-tailed and two-tailed tests, and (3) varied degrees of freedom. For testing the significance of r, degrees of freedom equal $N - 2$, where N is the number of cases in the study sample.

22.2.6 Decision Rules

When the hypothesis pair is nondirectional, the test of r is two-tailed. In this case:

> Fail to reject (accept) the null when the absolute value of the obtained r is less than the r in Table A.5.

> Reject the null when the absolute value of the obtained r is greater than or equal to the r in Table A.5.

When the hypothesis pair is directional, the test is one-tailed. If the research hypothesis states "greater than," the rejection region is in the upper tail. In this case:

> Fail to reject (accept) the null if the obtained r is less than the r in Table A.5.

> Reject the null if the obtained r is greater than or equal to the r in Table A.5.

When the research hypothesis states "less than," the rejection region is in the lower tail. In this case:

> Fail to reject (accept) the null if the obtained r is greater than the negative of the r in Table A.5.

> Reject the null if the obtained r is less than or equal to the negative of the r in Table A.5.

22.2.7 Carrying Out the Hypothesis Testing Model

In Rosenthal and Groze's (1992) study of outcomes of special-needs adoptions, the correlation between family income and closeness of relationship between parent and child (measured by responses to five questions that were summed together to generate a scale score) was $-.21$ ($N = 635$). Thus, as family income increased, closeness of parent-child relationship tended to decrease. (When r equals $-.21$, the size of association would generally be characterized as being between medium and small; see Table 8.3.) To carry out the hypothesis testing model:

1. State the hypothesis pair.

    Null: In the population from which the sample was randomly selected, the correlation of family income and closeness of parent-child relationship equals 0.00.

    Research: In the population from which the sample was randomly selected, the correlation of family income and closeness of parent-child relationship is not equal to 0.00.

Neither prior theory or research suggests compelling reasons for expecting the correlation to be in one direction rather than the other, so a nondirectional hypothesis pair is formulated.

2. Select a statistical significance level.

The .01 level is selected (α is set to .01). With large samples, researchers typically choose the .01 level rather than the .05 level. With large samples, very weak associations are often sufficient for rejection of the null. Choosing the .01 level increases the size of association required for rejection and, by so doing, reduces the likelihood that an association of trivial size (for instance, $r = .06$) will achieve significance.

3. Carry out the test.

Since we are consulting a table of critical values (Table A.5), there is no test to carry out. As stated above, $r = -.21$.

4. Make a decision.

The test of r has $(N - 2)$ degrees of freedom: $635 - 2 = 633$. Table A.5 does not list this precise number of degrees of freedom. When the exact number is not listed, one uses the next lower listed number. This is 600. For a two-tailed test with 600 degrees of freedom where $\alpha = .01$, the critical value of r in Table A.5 is .105. As the absolute value of the obtained r is greater than the critical value, the null hypothesis that the correlation of family income and closeness is 0.00 is rejected.[3] Given that the .01 level was used, we can be 99% confident that the association between income and closeness is not due to chance alone.

22.3   A CORRELATION MATRIX

Sometimes one wants to examine correlations among several variables. Table 22.1 presents an SPSS-generated **correlation matrix** that presents correlations among five variables in the adoption study (Rosenthal and Groze, 1992). A brief description of these variables is needed to interpret their correlations: The higher the parent-child relationship score, the closer the relationship between parent and child. Behavior problems score is the score on a behavior checklist (Achenbach, 1991; higher scores indicate more problems). Education level is measured on a five-point scale (higher score indicates greater education). Overall impact is also on a five-point scale (higher score indicates more positive impact). Finally, family income is measured in $1000 increments.

A correlation matrix allows one to explore correlations between the various combinations of variables. Each correlation is listed twice. For instance, the correlation between score on the behavior problems scale and that on the parent-child relationship scale is found in both the first row, second column and also in the second row, first column. This correlation, $-.609$, conveys a large negative association between these variables.

The asterisks "flag" statistically significant correlations. All correlations achieve significance at the .05 level. (As you know, with large sample sizes even weak associations often achieve significance.) Of all the correlations, those involving family income may be most interesting. In addition to being negatively associated with the impact of adoption on the family, income is positively associated with behavior problems score and negatively associated with closeness of parent-child relationship.

TABLE 22.1   A CORRELATION MATRIX FROM THE SPECIAL-NEEDS ADOPTION STUDY

Correlations

		behavior problems score	parent-child relationship score	mean educ. level of parents	family income	impact of adoption on family
Pearson Correlation	behavior problems score	1.000	−.609**	.075*	.092*	−.557**
	parent-child relationship score	−.609**	1.000	−.194**	−.213**	.696**
	mean educ. level of parents	.075*	−.194**	1.000	.391**	−.143**
	family income	.092*	−.213**	.391**	1.000	−.170**
	impact of adoption on family	−.557**	.696**	−.143**	−.170**	1.000

** Correlation is significant at the 0.01 level (2-tailed).
* Correlation is significant at the 0.05 level (2-tailed).

Note: The smallest sample size for any correlation in the matrix is 633. The table is SPSS for Windows output.

Note that all the correlations in a straight line from the upper left corner of the matrix to the lower right corner are 1.00. These correlations represent the correlation of each variable with itself. Such correlations are always 1.00.

22.4   PARAMETRIC AND NONPARAMETRIC TESTS

The basic distinction between parametric statistical tests and nonparametric statistical tests is that **parametric tests** assume that the population from which the study sample was randomly selected has some particular distributional shape, whereas **nonparametric tests** make no such assumption. Almost all commonly used parametric tests assume this distribution to be normally distributed. Pragmatically, then, the key distinction is that parametric tests assume normality whereas nonparametric tests do not. We have covered the following parametric tests: the large sample test of $\overline{X}$. the one-sample t test, the independent samples t test, the dependent samples t test, analysis of variance, and the significance test of r. Each assumes normality.

The following can be characterized as nonparametric: the one-sample test of p, the one-variable χ^2 test, and the χ^2 test of independence. None of these assumes normality.

Many consider the distinction between parametric and nonparametric tests to be confusing and not particularly useful (Glass and Hopkins, 1996, p. 212). Consider, for instance, that all the above-mentioned parametric tests presume measurement at the interval/ratio level. In contrast, the above-mentioned nonparametric tests all involve nominal-level data. The next several sections present nonparametric tests designed for ordinal-level data. Each of these is considered to be nonparametric because it does not assume normality. Yet, it should be intuitive that neither a nominal-level nor an ordinal-level variable can be normally distributed. (For instance, neither can ever assume the smooth distributional shape of the normal curve.) In effect, the parametric/nonparametric distinction is unneeded. Pragmatically, tests that require interval/ratio-level measurement are classified as parametric and tests for nominal- and ordinal-level variables are classified as nonparametric.[4]

The next several sections overview about a dozen nonparametric tests for ordinal-level variables. Each sees fairly limited use. Detailed discussion can be found in many texts (see Siegel and Castellan, 1988; Blalock, 1979; Conover, 1980; Toothaker and Miller, 1996).

22.5   STATISTICAL SIGNIFICANCE TEST OF SPEARMAN'S r

The hypothesis pairs for the statistical **significance test of Spearman's r (significance test of r_{ranks})** are the same as those for the test of Pearson's r except that they apply to ranks. For instance, given two variables, X and Y, the nondirectional hypothesis for Spearman's r would state: In the population from which the study sample was randomly sampled, the correlation of rank order on X with rank order on Y is 0.00.

As presented in Chapter 8 (Section 8.13), the formula for Spearman's r is basically a shortcut formula for Pearson's r that may be used for rank orderings. Even though Pearson's r and Spearman's r have identical values (or nearly so when the data include tied scores)[5] for rank-ordered variables, special considerations are required for testing the significance of r_{ranks}. When sample size is greater than or equal to 30, the critical values (those that result in rejection of the null) of Pearson's r and r_{ranks} are nearly identical. Hence, presuming that $N \geq 30$, the easiest way to test r_{ranks} is to consult the table of critical values for r (Table A.5). When $N < 30$, the critical values of r and r_{ranks} differ, so one should carry out a test specifically designed for Spearman's r. This test is best carried out by computer software.

As presented earlier in this chapter, the significance test of Pearson's r assumes that both interval/ratio-level variables are normally distributed in the population from which the study sample was selected. When one or both is very strongly skewed, this test's probabilities may be inaccurate. In such a situation, one may (1) convert scores on both variables into ranks and (2) conduct a test of r_{ranks}. As a test of r_{ranks} does not require normality, its accuracy is unaffected by the skewed distribution of the initial scores. One only occasionally encounters variables that are measured initially via rank orderings. On the other hand, one frequently encounters very strongly skewed interval/ratio-level variables. As such, the most common use of the test of r_{ranks} is with such strongly skewed variables.

A disadvantage of opting to use the test of r_{ranks} is that results must be interpreted in terms of ranks rather than original scores. Also, converting interval-level scores into ranks throws away information; it converts precise measurements into cruder ones. When one or both initial variables are strongly skewed, one must make a judgment. One strategy is to carry out tests of both r on the initial scores and r_{ranks} on the ranks and compare. Results are often highly similar.

22.6   TESTS OF ASSOCIATION BETWEEN TWO ORDINAL-LEVEL CATEGORICAL VARIABLES

Chapter 7 (Section 7.6) introduced the concept of directional association between two ordinal-level variables. In a positive directional association, as one variable increases in value, so also does the other. In a negative directional association, as one variable increases, the other decreases. Four measures of directional association between categorical, ordinal-level variables were presented in Chapter 9: Kendall's tau$_b$ (τ_b), Kendall's tau$_c$ (τ_c), gamma (γ), and Somer's d. Each of these may vary between -1.00 and $+1.00$. For each, the value 0.00 indicates the absence of association. The statistical significance of each may be tested, although the procedures for so doing are beyond our scope. (See Blalock, 1979, pp. 439–443.)

The hypothesis pair for all four tests may be either directional or nondirectional. In each case, the nondirectional null hypothesis is that the measure (tau$_b$, tau$_c$, gamma, or Somer's d) equals 0.00 in the population from which the study sample was randomly selected. The easiest way to carry out these tests is via computer packages.[6] Either a two-tailed test (with a nondirectional hypothesis pair) or a one-tailed test (with a directional pair) may be conducted. The probabilities generated by computer programs usually assume a two-tailed test. For a one-tailed test, one may divide the two-tailed probability in half, assuming that results are in the expected direction.

22.7   TESTS FOR VARIABLES AT THE ORDINAL LEVEL: INDEPENDENT SAMPLES

The **Mann-Whitney U test** examines differences in ranks in two independent samples (groups). For instance, suppose that 10 children with low self-esteem are randomly assigned to a "talking" therapy group and 10 to an "activities" therapy group and that at the conclusion of these groups, the children draw pictures of themselves. Next, suppose that the 20 pictures are shuffled together and that an expert in child development assigns each picture a score from 1 to 100 according to the "degree of positive self-esteem" that is expressed. (On the rating scale, presume that 1 represents the lowest possible esteem and 100 the highest possible esteem.) Because the pictures have been shuffled, the expert does not know which therapy group is associated with the pictures, but the researcher does have this information. Next, ranks can be assigned to the scores. For instance, the picture with the highest ranked score could be given the rank 20, the one with the next highest score that of 19, and so on down to the lowest score, which would be assigned the rank 1.[7,8] The calculations of the Mann-Whitney U test (which are beyond our scope) make use of these ranks rather than the original scores.

One way to state the nondirectional null for the Mann-Whitney U test is this: In the populations from which samples/groups were selected, mean ranks are equal. Hence, in the current example this null would state: Mean rank in self-esteem is equal in the populations from which the two therapy groups were selected. Though the Mann-Whitney test's formula deals with ranks, the hypothesis pair may also be expressed with respect to medians. Hence, an alternative way to state the nondirectional null is: In the populations from which samples/groups were selected, medians are equal. The hypothesis pair may be either nondirectional (use a two-tailed test) or directional (use a one-tailed test). The Mann-Whitney test is best carried out via computer. It should not be used when variances of scores or ranks differ greatly in the two groups.[9]

When sample size is very small and one suspects that population distributions are strongly skewed, the Mann-Whitney U test provides a good alternative to the independent samples t test. (In such a situation, the independent samples t test can yield inaccurate results.)

The Mann-Whitney U test is used with two independent samples and rank-ordered data. The **Kruskal-Wallis test** is an extension of the Mann-Whitney test to situations with two or more independent samples. It bears the same relationship to the Mann-Whitney U test as does analysis of variance to the independent samples t test.

The null for the Kruskal-Wallis test states that mean ranks (or medians) are equal in the different samples. The hypothesis pair is always nondirectional. One may not draw conclusions about whether particular pairs of mean ranks differ or about the direction of differences. The test is not recommended when the variances of ranks differ greatly between groups (see note 9 at the end of the chapter).

Like the Mann-Whitney U test, the **Kolmogorov-Smirnov test** is used with two independent samples and a dependent variable at the ordinal level of measurement. The Mann-Whitney test is preferred when that variable is a rank ordering. Although the Mann-Whitney test may be used when the dependent variable is categorical, the Kolmogorov-Smirnov test is perhaps preferred (Blalock, 1979, p. 266). For instance, the Kolmogorov-Smirnov test would be well suited for assessing whether men and women differ regarding their support for a proposed maternal-child health policy measured on a four-point scale (4 = strongly support, 3 = support, 2 = oppose, 1 = strongly oppose; this is the categorical ordinal-level variable). The null hypothesis for this test is difficult to state in words. Basically, it assesses whether the overall pattern of responses is higher in one group than in the other. Each of the three just-mentioned tests is best carried out via a computer package.

22.8   TESTS FOR VARIABLES AT THE ORDINAL LEVEL: DEPENDENT SAMPLES

Each of the three just-presented tests is used with independent samples. The **sign test** is a handy test when one has two dependent (paired) samples and ordinal-level measurement. Recall from Chapter 18 (Section 18.6.4) that the dependent samples t test can yield inaccurate results if *both* of the following conditions are met: (1) the distribution of population difference scores is strongly skewed (one infers that distribution from the sample distribution) and (2) sample size is very small. In such a situation, the sign test is an excellent alternative.

To illustrate the sign test, suppose that all children in an elementary school use a five-point scale to rate the degree of "toughness" in discipline of (1) their father and (2) their mother. These two ratings are dependent because the same person (the child) makes each. Presume that a rating of 1 conveys the lowest level of strictness and a rating of 5 conveys the highest. Suppose that for each child, we compare the toughness rating for each parent. Three basic outcomes are possible: (1) the father is rated as tougher than the mother, (2) the mother is rated as tougher than the father, or (3) both parents earn the same toughness rating, that is, mother and father are tied on toughness.

The first step in the sign test is to exclude all tied cases. The null hypothesis states that in the population from which the sample of nontied cases was randomly selected, 50% of outcomes are in each direction. For instance, in our toughness example, the nondirectional null would assert that (ties excluded) 50% of children view their father as the tougher disciplinarian and that 50% of children view their mother as tougher. The hypothesis pair may be directional or nondirectional. Either a one-tailed or a two-tailed test may be used. The sign test is best carried out via computer software.

Continuing with the example, presume that a sample of 23 children rated both their mother and father regarding toughness with the following outcomes: 14 rated their father as tougher, 6 rated their mother as tougher, and 3 gave each parent the same rating (tied). Presume that we wish to conduct a two-tailed test using the .05 significance level. The first step is to discard the three ties. Among the 20 remaining cases, 70% (14 of 20) rated their father as tougher and 30% (6 of 20) rated their mother as tougher. The two-tailed probability, as calculated by the SPSS for Windows program, is .115. This probability (the probability that the result may be due to chance) exceeds .05 and thus we fail to reject the null.

Another alternative to the dependent samples t test is the **Wilcoxon signed ranks test** (also known as the *Wilcoxon matched pairs test*). The Wilcoxon test takes into account not only the direction of difference in ratings but also the size of the difference. For instance, suppose that a given child rated her father as 5 (the toughest possible rating) and her mother as 1 (the least tough rating). This represents a difference of 4: $5 - 1 = 4$. Such a pair of ratings represents a larger difference than would, for instance, a rating of 4 for the father and 1 for the mother: $4 - 1 = 3$. By taking into account size of differences, some additional precision is gained.

The hypothesis pair for the Wilcoxon signed ranks test may be stated in terms of medians. For instance, in the current example the nondirectional null could be stated as follows: In the population from which the sample was randomly selected, median toughness ratings for mothers and fathers are equal. The tests may be either two-tailed (with a nondirectional pair) or one-tailed (with a directional pair). The Wilcoxon test should not be used when sample variances differ greatly (see note 9 at the end of the chapter) and should be used cautiously when the number of categories is limited (say, about five or fewer).[10]

The **Friedman test** (also known as the *Friedman two-way analysis of variance*) is used with two or more dependent samples and ordinal-level measurement. As an example, suppose that each student at a school of social work rank orders the level of anxiety that he or she experiences in four classes: research, human behavior, policy, and practice. For instance, if an individual student experiences the greatest anxiety in research, he would assign this class the rank order 1. Perhaps his anxiety is lowest in practice; this class then would be assigned the rank ordering of 4. Each student in the class would complete this process. The Friedman test uses the null hypothesis that the mean ranks (or median ranks) in the different study conditions are equal. For instance, in this example it would test the null that the mean ranks assigned to each of the four classes are equal. Rejection of the null conveys that the difference in mean ranks is greater than would be expected by chance. In the current example, rejection of the null would indicate that students experience differing levels of anxiety in the different classes. (See Siegel, 1956, pp. 166–172, or Toothaker and Miller, 1996, pp. 611–615, for detailed information on this test.)

The hypothesis pair for the Friedman test may also be stated in terms of medians and is always nondirectional. Statistically significant test results apply to all involved groups rather than to particular pairs. The Friedman test should be used cautiously when sample variances differ greatly (see note 9 at the end of the chapter).

22.9   TESTS FOR DICHOTOMOUS VARIABLES: DEPENDENT SAMPLES

A final nonparametric test, **McNemar's test,** tests differences in percentages (proportions) between two dependent samples. The nondirectional null hypothesis states that percentages are equal.

As an example, presume that you have a caseload of 60 clients with severe mental illness. Two paraprofessionals are assigned to help you manage this caseload. Let's say that in the month just before the paraprofessionals begin, 50% (30 of 60) of clients keep their medication appointments, and that in the paraprofessionals' first month of work, 67% (40 of 60) do so. Presuming that the same clients compose your caseload at both occasions, the two samples (the "before" sample and the "after" sample) are dependent. Via McNemar's test, you could examine whether the change in percentages (from 50% to 67%) was statistically significant (or was instead likely to represent chance fluctuation). When one has three or more dependent samples, **Cochran's Q** may be used to test the null that proportions are equal.

22.10   PARAMETRIC TESTS VERSUS NONPARAMETRIC TESTS

The choice of the "right" statistical test can be difficult. The parametric statistical tests presented in this text all assume interval-level measurement and normally distributed populations. Social scientists frequently work with variables that do not meet one or both of these assumptions (or they may not be able to determine whether these assumptions are met). In such situations, they must choose between conducting the parametric test even though assumptions are potentially violated or, instead, conducting a nonparametric test.

Let's consider the advantages of choosing a parametric test. Fortunately, the key parametric tests—significance test of Pearson's r, both t tests, analysis of variance—are quite robust to violations of the normality assumption and typically yield highly accurate probabilities even for distinctly nonnormal distributions. Further, as already mentioned, most researchers are comfortable using these procedures even when data are not strictly at the interval level (for instance, with scores on psychological tests and attitudinal instruments).

The just-mentioned tests are the workhorses of social science. Their greatest advantage is perhaps that most everyone with some statistical training has a basic familiarity with them. Still another advantage is that these tests are logically tied to a variety of well-known multivariate statistical procedures. Thus researchers may conveniently (1) conduct the appropriate (bivariate) parametric test and then (2) move on to a more sophisticated multivariate test that builds on the principles and ideas of the simpler procedure.

In contrast, fewer nonparametric multivariate techniques are well known. Thus, for the most part, the nonparametric procedures for ordinal-level variables that have been discussed here do not logically set the stage for more complex (and often more informing) multivariate analysis.

In general, parametric statistical tests have greater statistical power than do their nonparametric alternatives. Thus, when the null is indeed false, one is generally more likely to obtain a correct result showing statistical significance with a parametric test than with its nonparametric counterpart. The degree of difference in power is usually modest. As a rough guideline, sample sizes often need to be approximately 10% larger to have the same power with nonparametric tests as with their parametric alternatives. Exact percentages vary greatly by test and by specific situation. (See Toothaker and Miller, 1996, pp. 601–602, for greater detail on the power of nonparametric tests.)

Based on the just-mentioned factors, my overall preference is for the parametric tests. Yet, others have different views. The nonparametric tests require neither the normality assumption nor interval-level measurement. When these requirements are violated or not assuredly met, the probabilities given by the appropriate nonparametric test will generally be somewhat more accurate than those of the corresponding parametric tests. When one's ordinal-level data are categorical with a limited number of categories—for instance, a four-point response scale: excellent, good, fair, poor—most researchers would recommend a nonparametric test designed for such data rather than a parametric test. (See related discussion in Chapter 17, Section 17.8.)

Given the ease of statistical testing via computer packages, one alternative is to conduct both the appropriate parametric test and its nonparametric alternative and compare probabilities. Hopefully, these will be reasonably similar. When similar results are yielded by different methods, one gains greater confidence in these. It is good science to use multiple procedures and techniques to cross-check one's findings and, by so doing, gain new information. It is not good or legitimate science to test data via every possible statistical test until one finally finds a test that yields a statistically significant result. This is analogous to visiting many medical doctors to find one who provides the desired advice. (And this is fishing of the worst kind; see Chapter 21, Section 21.8.)[11,12,13]

22.11   MULTIPLE REGRESSION ANALYSIS

This chapter concludes our discussion of statistical procedures, but first let's get a glimpse into the world of multivariate statistical analysis. Multivariate procedures involve three or more variables. The most commonly used such procedure is multiple regression.

In **multiple regression analysis,** several **predictors** (independent variables) are entered into an equation that predicts a dependent variable. Multiple regression produces two sets of coefficients, B's and β's (betas, pronounced "bait-ahs"). B's are unstandardized, meaning they convey change in terms of original units (raw scores). (The B's in multiple regression are the same as those in bivariate regression; see Chapter 8, Section 8.12.1.) β's are standardized, meaning they convey change in terms of standard deviation units. β's in multiple regression have much in common with r, the correlation coefficient (see Section 8.12.1).

The key difference between B and β and their respective bivariate counterparts (B and r, respectively) is that B and β convey change while *controlling for* other variables in the analysis:

- The unstandardized coefficient (B) for a given predictor conveys the predicted change in original units (raw scores) in the dependent variable when the predictor increases by 1.00 original unit, controlling for other predictors in the analysis.
- The standardized coefficient (β) for a given predictor conveys the predicted change in standard deviation units in the dependent variable when the predictor increases by 1.00 standard deviation, controlling for other predictors in the analysis.

Table 22.2 presents a multiple regression analysis involving four of the five variables presented in the correlation matrix in Table 22.1. The dependent variable is score on the parent-child relationship scale; the other three variables are independent variables. Let's focus first on the unstandardized coefficients, the B's. For instance, the B of $-.0154$ for behavior problems score conveys that, controlling for the influence of family income and parental education, as behavior problems score

TABLE 22.2   MULTIPLE REGRESSION PREDICTING PARENT-CHILD RELATIONSHIP SCORE

Coefficients[a]

Model	Unstandardized Coefficients		Standardized Coefficients	t	Sig.
	B	Std. Error	Beta		
1 (Constant)	4.185	.067		62.404	.000
CBCTOT Behavior Problems Score	−.0154	.001	−.600	−19.290	.000
INCOMEK Income in 1000s	−.0037	.001	−.122	−3.591	.000
EDUC Mean parent educ. level	−.0530	.021	−.087	−2.566	.011

[a.] Dependent Variable: RELSCALE Quality/Closeness Parent-Child Relationship

Note: An SPSS-generated multiple regression example.

increases by 1.00, predicted parent-child relationship score decreases by .0154. Because both behavior problems and parent-child relationship are measured on unfamiliar scales, one can't make any intuitive sense of size of association from this coefficient.[14]

On the other hand, β's do begin to convey size of association. The β of −.600 for behavior problems indicates that, controlling for the influence of family income and parental education, as behavior problem score increases by one (1.00) standard deviation, predicted parent-child relationship score decreases by .600 standard deviations. One may use the qualitative descriptors for r to interpret size of association for β (see Table 8.3). Hence, the β for behavior problems conveys a strong negative association between behavior problems and parent-child relationship. Both family income and parental education have weak negative associations (their β's are −.122 and −.087 respectively) to closeness of parent-child relationship.[15]

In bivariate regression, the constant indicates the predicted value of the dependent variable (Y) when the independent variable (X) equals 0.00 (see Section 8.12.1). In multiple regression, it indicates the predicted value of the dependent variable when all predictors (independent variables) equal 0.00. The constant of 4.185 in Table 22.2 conveys that when all three predictors have the value 0.00, the predicted parent-child relationship score is 4.185.

As you interpret Table 22.2, remember that variables not included in the analysis are not controlled for. Also remember that in a survey design, one can never control for all possible confounding variables. One more caution is advised in interpreting multiple regression results. In interpreting any given coefficient, one should think of multiple regression as controlling reasonably well but not perfectly for other variables in the analysis. For further information on multiple regression, see Toothaker and Miller (1996, pp. 220–226), or Glass and Hopkins (1996, pp. 131–140).[16]

22.12   CHAPTER SUMMARY

The statistical significance test of Pearson's r examines whether the r obtained in one's study sample differs significantly from 0.00. Though normality is assumed for both variables, it is reasonably robust to this assumption. A correlation matrix presents the correlations among a group of variables.

Parametric tests assume that the study population has some particular distributional shape (a normal one, almost always) whereas nonparametric tests make no such assumption. Parametric tests are used predominantly with interval/ratio-level variables and nonparametric tests with nominal- and ordinal-level variables.

When both variables are rank-ordered, the preferred test is a significance test of r_{ranks}. When results from a test of Pearson's r may be inaccurate, the test of r_{ranks} is an excellent alternative.

One may test the significance of four measures of directional association between categorical, ordinal-level variables: tau_b, tau_c, gamma, and Somer's d. For each test, the nondirectional null states that the measure equals 0.00 in the study population.

The Mann-Whitney U test examines differences in ranks in two independent samples. The nondirectional null states that mean ranks (or, alternatively, medians) are equal. It is an alternative to the independent samples t test.

The Kruskal-Wallis test extends the Mann-Whitney test to situations with two or more independent samples. The Kolmogorov-Smirnov test is preferred when one has two independent samples and an ordinal-level categorical variable.

The sign test and the Wilcoxon signed ranks test are used with two dependent (paired) samples and ordinal-level measurement. These are alternatives to the dependent samples t test. The Friedman test is used when one has two or more dependent samples and ordinal-level measurement. When samples are dependent and the variable of interest is dichotomous, McNemar's test is the best choice.

Principal advantages of parametric tests over nonparametric ones include (1) greater familiarity, (2) connection to multivariate procedures, and (3) greater statistical power. On the other hand, when any of a parametric test's assumptions are not met, the probabilities given by its nonparametric counterpart may be more accurate.

In multiple regression analysis, multiple predictors predict a dependent variable. Both the unstandardized (B's) and standardized (β's) coefficients convey change for one predictor while controlling for other predictors in the analysis.

PROBLEMS AND QUESTIONS

Section 22.2

1. (T or F) The significance test of Pearson's r assumes that both variables are normally distributed.
2. (T or F) The significance test of Pearson's r is

at least reasonably robust to the normality assumption.
3. State the nondirectional hypothesis pair for Pearson's r in symbols.
4. As sample size increases, the standard deviation of the sampling distribution of r _____.
5. Given a nondirectional hypothesis pair, as sam-

ple size increases, the _____ value of r that is necessary to reject the null _____.

6. A study finds that the greater the degree of health problems experienced by residents in a nursing home, the more frequent the visiting of family members: $r = .32$, $N = 102$.
   a. Is this correlation positive or negative?
   b. State the nondirectional hypothesis pair in symbols.
   c. How many degrees of freedom are there?
   d. When $\alpha = .01$ (and assuming a nondirectional null), what are the critical values of r?
   e. State the specific values of r that result in rejection of the null.
   f. What is your decision regarding the null?
   g. How confident can you be that the null is false?
   h. Is the relationship in the sample likely to be due to chance alone?
   i. Are you inclined to conclude that visiting leads to increased health problems? If not, what is a more likely explanation for the relationship?

7. Consider the information in Table 22PQ.1. For each situation presented in Table 22PQ.1...
   a. State the null in symbols.
   b. Indicate the degrees of freedom.
   c. State the critical value(s).
   d. Indicate your decision on the null.

Section 22.4

8. (T or F) Nonparametric tests assume that the population from which the study sample is randomly selected has some particular shape.

TABLE 22PQ.1

Situation	N	r	Research Hypothesis	α
#1	52	−.26	$r < 0.00$	.01
#2	52	−.26	$r < 0.00$	.05
#3	52	−.26	$r \neq 0.00$	.05
#4	72	−.26	$r \neq 0.00$	.05
#5	72	−.26	$r \neq 0.00$	.01

9. (T or F) All of the parametric tests presented in this text assume that the population from which the study sample is randomly selected has a normal shape.

10. (T or F) Pragmatically speaking, all (or almost all) tests that require interval/ratio-level measurement are parametric tests.

11. (T or F) The independent samples t test is an example of a nonparametric test.

Section 22.5

12. (T or F) Even when one or both distributions are *extremely* skewed, the significance test of Pearson's r is recommended above the test of Spearman's r.

13. In your own words, when is the test of r_{ranks} most often used?

14. Indicate a disadvantage of the test of Spearman's r for which interval/ratio-level scores have been transformed into ranks.

15. (T or F) When $N \geq 30$, critical values of r and r_{ranks} are very similar.

Section 22.6

16. Using symbols, state the nondirectional null for a statistical significance test involving tau_b.

17. In your own words, what does the nondirectional null state for significance tests of tau_b, tau_c, gamma, and Somer's d?

18. (T or F) The hypothesis pair for the four measures mentioned in the prior question may be either directional or nondirectional.

Section 22.7

19. (T or F) The Mann-Whitney U test assumes that samples have been selected from normally distributed populations.

20. (T or F) The Mann-Whitney U test is used with dependent rather than independent samples.

21. State the nondirectional null for the Mann-Whitney U test in two different ways.

22. What test extends the Mann-Whitney test to situations involving two *or more* independent samples?

23. The Kolmogorov-Smirnov test is perhaps preferred to the Mann-Whitney test when the dependent (ordinal-level) variable is a _____ variable rather than a rank ordering.

Section 22.8

24. Is the sign test used with dependent or independent samples?

25. In your own words, what does the nondirectional null hypothesis for the sign test state?

26. What information does the Wilcoxon matched pairs test take into account that the sign test does not?

27. The Friedman test is used with two or more _____ samples and _____ -level measurement.

Section 22.9

28. Does McNemar's test have more similarity to an independent samples *t* test or to a dependent samples *t* test?

29. Is McNemar's test used with dependent (paired) samples or independent samples?

30. (T or F) McNemar's test examines whether proportions in two dependent samples differ to a statistically significant degree.

31. For each of the following, indicate (1) whether samples are independent or paired (dependent) and (2) whether McNemar's test may be used.

    a. 30% of women (first sample) versus 15% of men (second sample) agree with social policy X.

    b. At pretest (first sample), 80% of clients report severe fear of snakes; at posttest (second sample), only 35% do so.

    c. 25% of teenage girls (first sample) versus 40% of their brothers (second sample) indicate that their first choice in music is hard rock.

    d. 45% of Republicans (first sample) versus 85% of Democrats (second sample) support legislation designed to prevent elder abuse.

Section 22.10

32. List several advantages of parametric tests.

33. List a disadvantage of parametric tests.

34. List an advantage of nonparametric tests.

35. List several disadvantages of nonparametric tests.

36. (T or F) The choice between a parametric and a nonparametric test is always a straightforward and easy one.

Section 22.11

37. What does the unstandardized regression coefficient, *B*, convey?

38. What does the standardized regression coefficient, β, convey?

39. (T or F) β conveys change/association in terms of standardized variables (*z* scores) rather than unstandardized ones.

40. (T or F) Multiple regression methods control quite well even for variables/predictors that are not in the regression equation.

 # Computer Exercises

For general instructions on computer exercises, see the note in Chapter 2.

1. Examine whether the correlation between INTERNAL (internalized behavioral problems score) and EXTERNAL (externalized behavioral problem score) is statistically significant at the .01 level in a two-tailed test. [In SPSS, *Analyze > Correlate > Bivariate*, click over the two variables, *OK*.]

   Check your answer: As indicated by the Correlations table, the correlation between INTERNAL and EXTERNAL (*r* = .56) is statistically significant at the .01 level.

2. Generate a correlation matrix for the variables INTERNAL, EXTERNAL, FCOH (family cohesion), RELSCALE (closeness of parent-child relationship), and IMPACT. [In SPSS, *Analyze > Correlate > Bivariate*, click over the needed variables, *OK*.]

3. Carry out a significance test of Spearman's *r* for RELSCALE (closeness of parent-child relationship) and AGEHOMYT (child's age in years at entry into home, "truncated"). [In SPSS, *Analyze > Correlate > Bivariate*, click back any unwanted variables if necessary, click over RELSCALE and AGEHOMYT, click box

next to "Spearman" (and if desired, click the box next to "Pearson" to uncheck this correlation), *OK.*] Use the .01 level and a two-tailed test.

Check your answer; Spearman's *r* computes to −.361, which is significant at the .01 level.

4. Using Kendall's tau$_b$, Kendall's tau$_c$, gamma, and Somer's *d*, examine whether there is a statistically significant (directional) relationship between the independent variable FEELCLOS (closeness of parent-child relationship) and the dependent variable ENJOYSCH (child's enjoyment of school). [In SPSS, *Analyze > Descriptive Statistics > Crosstabs,* click ENJOYSCH to space below "Rows," click FEELCLOS to space below "Columns," *Statistics,* click the boxes next to the four desired statistics (which are in the "Ordinal" area) and uncheck any other procedures that may be checked, *Continue, OK.*] Use the .01 level and a two-tailed test.

Check your answer: For each of the four measures, results are highly significant, *p* = .000.

5. Using the Mann-Whitney *U* test and the Kolmogorov-Smirnov test, examine whether the association between IMPACT (impact of adoption on family) and FOSTER (whether adoptive parents were the child's foster parents) is statistically significant. [In SPSS, *Analyze > Nonparametric Tests > 2 Independent Samples,* click IMPACT over to space under "Test Variable List," click FOSTER to space below "Grouping Variable," *Define Groups,* type **0** into space next to "Group 1" and **1** into space next to "Group 2" (0 and 1 are the values of FOSTER), *Continue,* click boxes next to "Mann-Whitney U" and "Kolmogorov-Smirnov Z" so that both are checked, *OK.*] Use the .05 level and a two-tailed test.

Check your answer: The two-tailed probability for the Mann-Whitney *U* test computes to .001 and that for the Kolmogorov-Smirnov test computes to .009. Hence, the null of no association between the variables is rejected by both tests.

6. Although a dependent samples *t* test would be preferred, carry out the sign test and the Wilcoxon signed ranks test for the variables INTERNAL (mean response on internal behavior problem items) and EXTERNAL (mean response on external behavior problem items). [In SPSS: *Analyze > Nonparametric Tests > 2 Related Samples,* highlight (select) both INTERNAL and EXTERNAL and click over this "pair," click boxes next to "Wilcoxon" and "Sign" so that both are checked, *OK.*] Use the .01 level and a two-tailed test.

Check your answers: Both the Wilcoxon test and the sign test yield highly significant results, *p* = .000 for both tests. One may conclude that EXTERNAL and INTERNAL scores differ to a statistically significant degree.

7. Carry out a multiple regression analysis with the dependent variable IMPACT (impact of adoption on family) and the predictors AGEHOMEY (child's age at entry into home), FOSTER (foster parent adoption), INCOMEK (family income in 1000s of dollars), and BEHAVTOT (behavior problems score). [In SPSS, *Analyze > Regression > Linear,* click IMPACT over to space under "Dependent," click the four predictors over to the space under "Independent(s)," verify that "Method" is "Enter," *OK.*] Use the .05 level and a two-tailed test.

Check your answers: Focusing attention on the Coefficients table, which shows results for each predictor, controlling for other predictors in the table, only FOSTER does not have a statistically significant association to IMPACT. Note that INCOMEK has a negative association (as income increases, the impact of adoption is assessed less positively). Among the different predictors, BEHAVTOT has the strongest association to IMPACT, β = −.524, a strong negative association. All probabilities (shown in the "Sig." column) are for a two-tailed test.

NOTES

1. Another formal assumption of the test of r is that of *bivariate normality,* which means not only that the two variables are normally distributed but also that taken as a pair, they are jointly normally distributed. Description of bivariate normality is beyond our scope. Violation of this assumption typically introduces substantial inaccuracy only when one or more of the variables is very strongly skewed (Toothaker and Miller, 1996, p. 388).

2. For discussion of how to test a null that correlation in the population (rho) equals some value other than 0.00, see discussion of Fisher's z transformation in Glass and Hopkins (1996, pp. 355–356) or many other texts.

3. One may test the significance of r via the formula $t = r/s_r$ with degrees of freedom equal to $N - 2$. In this formula, s_r is the estimate of the standard error of r (the estimate of the standard deviation of the sampling distribution of r). The formula for s_r is given by $s_r = \sqrt{(1 - r^2)/(N - 2)}$. In the current example:

$$s_r = \sqrt{\frac{1 - .21^2}{635 - 2}} = \sqrt{\frac{1 - .044}{633}} = \sqrt{\frac{.956}{633}} = .039$$

Solving for t: $t = .21/.039 = 5.38$ with $635 - 2 = 633$ degrees of freedom. Table A.2 does not list this exact number of degrees of freedom. The closest lower number is 200. When $\alpha = .01$ for a two-tailed test, the critical t is 2.601. The obtained t, 5.38, exceeds this, so the null is rejected.

4. Definitions of nonparametric and parametric differ from text to text. Toothaker and Miller (1996, pp. 578–580) state that the null for a nonparametric test pertains to an entire population distribution whereas that for a parametric one pertains to a specific parameter. Another term for parametric test is *distribution-free test.*

5. How are ranks assigned when scores are tied? Suppose that one obtained the following scores on some measure (scores have been ordered from high to low): 27, 22, 22, 19, 14, 12. Observe that there are two 22s tied for the second highest rank. When scores tie, they should be assigned the mean of the ranks that would otherwise have been assigned. In the current example, if the two 22s had not tied, one score would have been assigned the rank 2 and the other the rank 3. Hence, the rank that should be assigned to each score is $(2 + 3) \div 2 = 2.5$. The ranks that would be assigned to the sample of scores would then be as follows: (1) 27, (2.5) 22, (2.5) 22, (4) 19, (5) 14, (6) 12.

6. The linear-by-linear association χ^2 test may also be used to measure directional association of ordinal-level categorical variables. See note 8 at the end of Chapter 20.

7. Another way to score self-esteem would be to have the expert simply rank order the pictures from highest to lowest.

8. An alternative way to assign ranks would be: highest score 1, next highest 2, . . . , lowest 20. Also, see note 5 on how to deal with tied ranks.

9. For instance, presume that the following ranks are assigned: Group A, 1, 2, 4, 8, 10, 11; Group B, 3, 5, 6, 7, 9. In this example, mean ranks are equal ($\overline{X} = 6$) but the variances differ. Clearly, ranks in Group B are clustered much more closely than those in Group A. In such a situation, the Mann-Whitney test is not recommended.

10. The level of measurement required for the Wilcoxon signed ranks test is interval (Conover, 1971, p. 207) or almost so (Blalock, 1979, p. 270). For instance, given ordinal-level measurement one may not conclude that the difference in toughness conveyed by a rating of 4 for the father and 1 for the mother, $4 - 1 = 3$, is precisely the same as that conveyed by a rating of 5 for the father and 2 for the mother, $5 - 2 = 3$. Yet the Wilcoxon signed ranks test essentially assumes this to be the case. When one's data are clearly ordinal and the number of categories is limited (say four or fewer), the sign test is perhaps preferred to the Wilcoxon signed ranks test.

11. If the probabilities differ substantially, one should either report both probabilities or report the higher probabilities only. When there is a discrepancy, science prefers to err on the conservative side; that is, to accept the null rather than to reject it.

12. Data transformation is often used when test assumptions are violated. In *data transformation,* some common mathematical manipulation is applied to each score. Examples of transformations are (1) adding a constant to each score, (2) multiplying each score by a constant, (3) converting each score to a z score, (4) squaring each score, (5) taking the square root of each score, and (6) taking the log of each score. Recall that when sample size is very small and distributions are highly skewed, the independent samples t test can yield inaccurate results. Presume that scores in one's first study group are 2, 4, 6, 7, 8, 10, 15, 32. These scores are positively skewed and, additionally, 32 is an outlier. We may transform these scores by calculating logs. The resulting logs (ordered from low to high) are 0.69, 1.39, 1.79, 1.95, 2.08, 2.30, 2.71, and 3.47. Observe that, following transformation, the distribution of scores has neither a marked positive

skew nor an outlier. Presume that scores in the second group had the same pattern (positive skew and a positive outlier) and that taking logs removed both of these problems. Having transformed both sets of scores, one could conduct an independent samples t test using the logs. Given that the shapes of the transformed scores are no longer distinctly nonnormal, this t test would yield accurate results. Taking logs is often the best way to transform a variable with a highly positive skew into one that more closely approximates a normal distribution. Data transformations are also used to turn curvilinear relationships into linear ones. Discussion of transformation may be found in Cohen and Cohen (1983, pp. 260–272), Norusis (1997, pp. 432–433, 515–532), and Glass and Hopkins (1996, pp. 89–98).

13. When assumptions have been violated, statistical tests can yield inaccurate probabilities. Presuming that one comes reasonably close to meeting a test assumption (does not violate it blatantly), only a small amount of inaccuracy has likely been introduced. Often one can be confident that the amount of inaccuracy is not sufficient to result in a different decision regarding the null. For instance, when test results indicate that $p = .001$ and α has been set to .05 (and if no assumptions have been blatantly violated), one can be confident that the decision on the null is unaffected, because .001 differs greatly from .05. On the other hand, when test results indicate that $p = .045$ and α has been set to .05, even a small amount of inaccuracy could affect the decision on the null because .045 differs hardly at all from .05.

14. To make intuitive sense of the B's, one would need to know precisely how each variable was scaled. Limitations of space here do not allow such description.

Except for the fact that one has controlled for other variables in the analysis, interpretation of B's in multiple regression follows the same logic as that in bivariate regression. Refer to Chapter 8, Section 8.12.2, if you wish to refresh your memory on this.

15. When a predictor is dichotomous, β sometimes underestimates size of association. When one category of a dichotomous predictor is coded 1 point higher than is the other (for instance: male = 0, female = 1), B conveys the amount by which the predicted score for the higher-coded group exceeds that for the lower. For instance, a B of 2.5 for the variable gender conveys that the predicted score for women is 2.5 points higher than that for men.

16. In other reading about multiple regression, you may encounter several statistics not presented in the text. The *multiple correlation coefficient* (R or *multiple R*) is the correlation between predicted and actual values of the dependent variable (Y). The *squared multiple correlation coefficient* (R^2 or *multiple R^2*) is the square of R and conveys the proportion of variance in Y that is explained by the regression equation. The *adjusted R^2* (*adjusted multiple R^2*) is preferred to R^2 as it provides a better estimate of the variance explained in the population from which the study sample was randomly selected. R^2 tends to overestimate this variance. Closely related to the standardized regression coefficient (β) is the *partial correlation coefficient*, which may be interpreted as the correlation between two variables when one controls for a third variable. (Or, in some instances, more than one variable is controlled for.) See Glass and Hopkins (1996, pp. 168–170) or many other texts for more on partial correlation.

GENERALIZABILITY, IMPORTANCE, AND A DATA INTERPRETATION MODEL

23.1 CHAPTER OVERVIEW

Statistical methods provide a great deal of knowledge about study results, but researchers need to be able to go beyond that to determine how useful the results are. We begin by discussing how to assess *generalizability,* including the importance of *degree of similarity* in this assessment. Next, we consider the concept of *importance,* emphasizing the distinction between importance and statistical significance. Finally, we examine the five-part *balanced model for data interpretation* and apply it to examples of research studies.

23.2 GENERALIZABILITY

23.2.1 *Inferential Statistics and Generalizability*

All research studies are conducted in a particular setting, or to use a fancier word, in a particular context. A dictionary definition of context is "the interrelated conditions in which something exists or occurs." The context of a research study represents the particular characteristics of that study—the time, the place, the study sample (age, gender, ethnicity, etc.), the sampling method, the research design, the specific measures used, the intervention (if any), the people who implement the intervention, those who record the data (i.e., interviewers), the researchers whose study it is.

For purposes of our discussion, the population from which the study sample was selected will not be considered part of the study context. This somewhat arbitrary decision is made because ultimately the study sample participates in the study, not the population from which that sample is selected. To simplify discussion, the population from which the study sample is selected is often referred to as the "study population."

Both researchers and "consumers" (readers) are often interested in whether the same or different study results would be obtained were a given study to be carried out in a different context, that is, in a setting in which one or more of the particulars have changed. For instance, if you read a research report about a highly effective program serving unmarried mothers in a rural, southwestern state, you might wonder whether that program would also be effective with your caseload of unmarried mothers in an urban setting in a northeastern state. Such concerns are addressed by the concept of generalizability. The **generalizability** of a study result may be defined as the expected similarity between the study result and the result that would be obtained if the study was carried out in a different setting or context.

When similar results are expected, one has high generalizability, or, one may say, the results are highly **generalizable.** When quite different results are expected, one has limited (low) generalizability. The degree of generalizability is often difficult to assess. In some situations, one can do little more than make a best guess, or a conjecture. Often study results are highly generalizable to some new settings but not generalizable to others.

Researchers use two sets of tools to assess generalizability. The first set is the inferential statistical procedures that have been presented in the past eleven chapters. Researchers use these to generalize study sample results to the population from which that sample was randomly selected. Confidence intervals for percentages illustrate this process. One takes a random sample from a population, finds the percentage in the sample, and then establishes a confidence interval for the population. Using the logic of inferential statistics, the study's result has been generalized from one context or setting (the study sample) to a different one (the study population).

One's degree of confidence in generalizations made using statistical logic is known precisely. For instance, the researcher may state: "I am 95% percent confident that the true percentage for this population is located between 42 and 49%." Similarly, in hypothesis testing, the researcher who rejects the null at the .01 statistical significance level can be 99% confident that the null is indeed false in the population from which the study sample was randomly selected.

As emphasized many times, as sample size increases, the characteristics of a random sample become increasingly similar to those of the population from which the sample was selected. Thus, given large enough sample size, one can make *accurate* statements about the study population based on the randomly selected study sample. For instance, given large enough sample size, one may specify a narrow confidence interval. To summarize, given large enough sample size, inferential statistical tools allow one to make accurate generalizations with a high and known level of confidence.

If generalization based on statistical logic can be made confidently and with accuracy, what is the downside? The great limitation, of course, is that such generalization may only be made to the population from which the study sample was selected. This poses different problems depending on the sampling methodology.

As Chapter 16 (Section 16.8) pointed out, sometimes a study sample is not a random sample from any wider population. In such situations, there is no real-world population to which one may make statistical generalizations. In other studies, the study sample may be a random one but the population from which it has been selected may be quite limited in its scope. For instance, suppose that a professor randomly selects 50 students from the 250 who attend that school and tests an intervention for reducing anxiety experienced in statistics courses. The professor may (and indeed should) use the logic of inferential statistics to generalize results from the study sample to the full population of students at that school. For instance, a confidence interval could be set for the mean level of anxiety that would be observed if the intervention could have been administered to all students.

However, such statistically based logic may not be used to assess the results that would be obtained if the study was carried out, for instance, in a neighboring school. This is because students in this second school are not part of the population from which the study sample was selected.

In my first statistics class, the professor sternly admonished: "Don't generalize beyond the population from which the study sample has been randomly selected." This admonition injected appropriate caution but at the same time paralyzed my thinking. I wondered, "Does each study have relevance to only one specific population, that being the one from which the sample was randomly selected?" The answer is no.

The primary purpose of *some* studies is indeed to learn about the study population. Large-scale surveys are the best example of such studies. The researcher randomly selects a sample from a large (sometimes national) population and studies the sample to learn about that population. Yet, in other studies, one's intent is to develop knowledge that can be applied beyond the population from which one has sampled. Many experiments come to mind here. For instance, the results of the just-described intervention pertaining to math anxiety hopefully have some relevance beyond the professor's specific school. A better admonishment for students might be: "The *tools of inferential statistics* may not be used to make generalizations beyond the population from which the study sample has been sampled."

Pragmatically, this statement is correct. In the interest of clarity, an exception will be pointed out. Occasionally, random methods are used to select more than just the study sample. For instance, presume that an educational experiment seeks to compare the effect of Curriculum A to that of Curriculum B. Presume that, in addition to the random selection and random assignment of students, (1) participating schools are randomly selected from a wider population of schools and (2) participating teachers are randomly selected from the population of teachers within the selected schools. Because random methods were used to select both schools and teachers, the logic of inferential statistics in this study may indeed be used to generalize results to (1) the population of schools from which the sample of schools was selected and (2) the population of teachers within those schools from which the sample of teachers was selected. Formally speaking, statistical logic may be used to generalize findings to any aspect of a study that has been randomly selected. Hence, a more technically correct admonishment is: "The tools of inferential statistics may not be used to make generalizations concerning any aspect of a study that has not been randomly selected."

Yet social scientists do attempt to generalize study findings beyond the study context and beyond the study population, for instance, to different times, to different settings, and to populations other than the study population. The logic of inferential statistics may not be applied to this endeavor. Another kind of logic is required. This second set of tools is presented in this chapter, but first a hypothetical vignette will demonstrate just how limited the context of a study is, and therefore how limited the reach of statistical inference is:

In January 1999, all 200 elementary students in Superrural, Oklahoma, took part in a study on television violence. For one week, 100 students were randomly assigned to a daily two-hour regimen of violent television consisting of the following (hypothetical) shows (*Shoot 'em Up, Blow 'em Up, Blow 'em Every Which Way*, etc.). Mr. Macho coordinated and facilitated this group. For the same week, the other 100 students were randomly assigned to nonviolent television shows (*Best Friends, Share with Your Neighbor, Best Friends II*, etc.). Ms. Peace was this group's coordinator. Both groups watched 40-inch television sets from 9 A.M. to 11 A.M. At the lunchtime recess, playground observations were made by trained observers using the (hypothetical) Playground Observation Tool (POT). Statistical analysis indicated significantly more aggressive behavior in the violent television group than in the nonviolent television group ($p < .01$). Expressed in standard deviation units, the difference in means on the POT was 0.8 ($SDM = 0.8$).

For the sake of discussion, let's presume a carefully crafted study, accurate measurement, and researchers who had no "axe to grind" that may have biased results. Given the results as just described, we may conclude that the association between violent television and aggressive behavior (1) is unlikely to be due to chance (because it is statistically significant), (2) is a reasonably large association (because a difference of 0.8 standard deviations conveys a large difference in means), (3) is presumably a causal association (because the students were randomly assigned to groups).

Let's pose some questions pertaining to generalizability. Would we observe similar results (in other words, a reasonably similar size of association) if we carried out the study, say, ...

- in 2004 rather than 1999?
- in New York, New York, rather than Superrural, Oklahoma?
- in a junior high school in a neighboring town?
- with a predominantly African American population in the deep South?
- on a 20-inch rather than a 40-inch television?
- with the viewing session in the afternoon rather than the morning and for two weeks rather than one?
- for a different selection of violent and nonviolent television shows?
- with coordinators other than Mr. Macho and Ms. Peace?
- using some instrument other than the POT?

The answers to such questions are beyond the reach of inferential statistical logic. One can't use statistical logic to generalize the study result to any wider real-world population, as no such population exists. One can't use statistical logic to generalize to different times of the day, types of shows, group leaders, and so on because these aspects of the study were not randomly selected.

Some mistakenly assume that because a study result is statistically significant, this same result will be observed in a different context or setting. Sometimes this is the case. For instance, perhaps the same results would be obtained if Mr.

Passive and Ms. Hottemp coordinated the study. Perhaps very similar results would be obtained in New York. (Perhaps not.) The key point is that the logic and tools of inferential statistics do not address such issues. It is easy to forget (or to simply never consider at all) just how *particular* and how *specific* is the context of each study, and, therefore, how limited is the reach of statistical reasoning.

One more example can demonstrate just how easy it is to overinterpret results. Perhaps a mental health center wishes to determine whether Intervention A or Intervention B is more effective in reducing depression. Presume that random assignment is used to assign clients to the two interventions. Presume that A is delivered by three therapists who favor this approach and B by three who favor it. Presume that the reduction in depression is, to a statistically significant degree, greater among those who receive A than those who receive B. Given the random assignment to groups, we may conclude that A *causes* greater reduction than does B. Again, the key point to grasp is that this conclusion is only valid within the particular context and setting of the study (and with respect to the wider population, if any, from which the study sample was randomly selected). For instance, one cannot—at least via statistical logic and tools—conclude that the same results will be observed with a different group of therapists. For that matter, one does not know whether the better results for A are found because (1) A truly is more effective than B or (2) the three therapists who delivered A are more effective (better therapists) than those who delivered B. Generalizing outside of the study context requires caution.

23.2.2 *Generalization via Nonstatistical Logic*

The logic of inferential statistics is used to assess generalizability to the population (if any) from which the sample was randomly selected and to any other aspects of the study that may have been selected randomly. For all other situations, a different logic is needed. This logic is grounded not in statistical concepts and procedures but instead in critical thinking and common sense.

The key tool for assessing generalizability beyond the study context is one's qualitative judgment of the **degree of similarity** between the context of the study and the context to which one seeks to generalize. The greater that similarity, the greater the expected generalizability. The less that similarity, the less the expected generalizability. The fact that similarity is the key tool for assessing generalizability is so grounded in common sense that many texts make no mention of it. By failing to do so, they create the mistaken impression that critical reasoning with careful attention to similarity is unscientific and has no role whatsoever in understanding and interpreting data. My view is the opposite. I see such reasoning as at the heart of scientific inquiry. Campbell's principle of "proximal similarity" makes explicit the importance of similarity: "As scientists we generalize with most confidence to applications most similar to the setting of the original research" (Campbell, 1986, p. 75). (*Proximal* means "situated close to.")

Let's see how similarity guides us in assessing the generalizability of the study results presented in the vignette. The concept of similarity would suggest that we would have greater reason to expect similar findings in, for instance, a neighboring school than in a school in a highly urbanized setting such as New York. In general, the greater the similarity to that neighboring school—size, socioeconomic status, rural versus urban, and so on—the greater the expected generalizability of study findings.

Would the study results generalize to a different selection of television shows? A very clever researcher might have randomly selected a "sample" of violent shows from the population of such shows and done the same for nonviolent shows. Then inferential statistics could have tackled this question and provided some reasonably definitive answers. In the absence of such a random selection process, our best strategy will be to compare the characteristics of the shows used in the study with "typical" violent shows. Perhaps the shows in the study do share many characteristics with most other violent shows. This would nudge our thinking toward the conclusion that the study results could indeed be generalized across many television shows. On the other hand, perhaps the shows selected for the study were a particularly violent group. If typical violent shows tend to be much less violent than those in the study, we would, presumably, be cautious regarding possible generalizability to a broader selection of shows.

The study results, via the POT instrument, indicate that violent television viewed in the school setting appears to lead to aggressive behavior in the school setting (or at least leads to such behavior during the lunchtime recess). May we conclude that violent television at home also affects aggressive behavior in the home/neighborhood setting? In other words, can we generalize the study results to the home setting? There is no easy answer. My inclination is that such a conclusion may stretch study findings too far. The circumstances of home and neighborhood differ in important ways from those of the school. Hence, we might want to recommend caution regarding such generalization. For instance, in writing a journal article on the study, we might caution the reader not to jump to such a conclusion. Perhaps I am being too cautious in this reasoning. Indeed, when one attempts to generalize outside of the study context, it is difficult to know whether one is being too cautious or too bold.

Although similarity is clearly the fundamental consideration, we draw on other sources of information in assessing generalizability. In particular, the variability of the study sample is important. When the study sample represents a large cross section of people from diverse backgrounds, we ordinarily expect greater generalizability than when it represents only a narrow, fairly homogeneous group. This is the case even when the sample has not been randomly selected. Clearly, we also call on our substantive knowledge of the area being studied as we consider generalizability issues. For instance, an expert on violence and television could call on this knowledge in interpreting the results presented in the vignette.

The process of replication is at the heart of establishing generalizability. **Replication** refers to carrying out a study a second (or third, fourth, or fifth, etc.) time. In replicating, one does not carry out the study in the *exact* same way. Indeed, it is logically impossible to do so because, even if nothing else differs, the time (date) of the second study necessarily differs from that of the first. Rather than carrying out the exact same study, researchers strategically vary and change key characteristics of the study. When one sees similar results across different characteristics—times, settings, populations, research methods, and so on—one's confidence in the generalizability of those results increases commensurately. Clearly, the best way to find out whether the vignette result generalizes to the home setting is to replicate the study in this setting.

When results differ sharply as some aspect of the study changes, this suggests that study results don't generalize across that particular aspect. For instance, if a different selection of violent shows yielded a very different result—say, no difference in violent playground behavior between the two study groups—this would suggest that study results do not generalize well across a variety of different television shows.

Given scarce resources, replication is often a luxury. There may be only one article in the empirical literature on the particular intervention that you are planning to use with a client. In such a situation, you won't be able to compare the results of different replications to help determine the likely results of the intervention for your client. Your best assessment tool in this situation will be your informed judgment of the similarity (or difference) between your client's particulars and those of the clients in the research study. The greater that similarity, the greater the expected similarity of results, that is, the greater the expected generalizability.

Generalization to the population from which one has randomly sampled is based on statistical logic. Given large enough sample size, such generalization can be made with confidence and accuracy. Generalization in relationship to any other study characteristic—to different populations, to different measures, to different people delivering the intervention, and so on—is based on nonstatistical logic. Generalizations based on nonstatistical logic should be made with a spirit of caution (the knowledge that one may be wrong). In comparison to statistically based generalization, one makes generalizations based on nonstatistical logic with less confidence and less accuracy. This is why many texts make no mention of this process and some professors admonish "Do not do this."

Generalization outside of the study context requires a leap of faith—and critical thinking skills, common sense, and sometimes practice wisdom—to draw conclusions not merited by the research design per se. Although some admonish against this, there is no pragmatic alternative. All studies are lodged in a specific context. Without permission to generalize beyond that context, results never logically have real-world applicability or relevance. So although one must generalize cautiously, one must nevertheless attempt to do so.

One final comment is in order. It rarely makes sense to state simply "These study results have high generalizability" or "They have low generalizability." Generalizability makes sense only when talking about the specific setting to which one seeks to generalize. Thus a study's results may have high generalizability to Setting A and low generalizability to Setting B.

23.3   IMPORTANCE

As you know, the search for relationships between variables is at the heart of much of social science research. So far this text has introduced four concepts that are key to this endeavor: (1) *statistical significance:* whether the relationship is likely to be due to chance; (2) *size (strength) of relationship:* the degree to which two variables tend to change or vary together; (3) *causality:* whether one variable affects the other; and (4) *generalizability:* the degree to which a similar relationship or study result will be found in a different context or setting. The fifth key concept is importance.

Importance may be defined as the importance (or potential importance) that a relationship or study result has in the real world. Other terms with similar meanings include *practical importance, practical significance,* and *substantive significance* (Rubin and Babbie, 1997, p. 518). In assessing importance, the other four key concepts are considered because they bear on it. That is, associations that are statistically significant, strong, causal, and generalizable *tend to be* more important than those that are not. Even so, importance stands on its own as a distinct and separate issue.

An association that is statistically significant, strong, causal, and highly generalizable can be unimportant. A example might be an intervention that is remarkably effective at improving skills at shooting tiddlywinks. Tiddlywinks is a game for kids that has come to be synonymous with time spent in inconsequential activity. A human services professional's reaction on hearing about such results would likely be: "Who cares? What one scores in tiddlywinks has no relevance to social issues that confront people and society." At least from a human services perspective, study results are unimportant.

It is possible for an association (or study result) to be not statistically significant, yet important. For instance, consider a large-scale randomized true experiment with two treatment groups for at-risk youth. Presume that youth in one group are served in their own homes by community-based programs and that those in the other are served in placement settings (group homes, residential placements, etc.). Let's say that outcomes on a variety of measures—delinquency rates, school performance, behavior problems, self-esteem—are similar in the two groups. Stated differently, let's presume that the association of approach (in-home versus placement) to each outcome measure is both (1) not statistically significant and (2) very weak in strength. Such findings suggest that neither intervention is more effective than the other.

Yet such seemingly unremarkable results could have important implications for service delivery. From a public policy perspective, the in-home approach keeps families intact, and thus is preferred. Presume also that the in-home approach is less expensive. This being the case, study results indicate that a program that is preferable from both policy and economic perspectives yields outcomes that are equivalent to one that is less preferable on both counts. In this context, study results are not so unremarkable after all. These statistically nonsignificant results could well lead to *important* changes, that is, to increased development of in-home services.

Do you see how misleading the term "statistically *significant*" is? In part because of this term, students often confuse "*statistical* significance" with real-world significance, that is, with importance. Many statistically significant results do indeed have real-world significance. But these two concepts are distinct. When a result (or association) is statistically significant, we can be confident that it is not due to chance. (And the other interpretations presented in Table 16.2 apply as well.) Yet it does not follow logically that the result is necessarily important in the real world. It may be or it may not be.

The importance of an association or study result is determined ultimately via qualitative judgment. Though it is difficult to provide guidelines for assessing importance, some comments are in order.

Clearly one considers the particular result and the research design. Associations that are statistically significant, strong in magnitude, presumably causal, and/or highly generalizable stand a greater chance of having practical importance than do those that are not. Importance is not the same thing as newsworthiness. Yet it is simply the nature of social science inquiry that the discovery that something makes a difference is more likely to be important than a discovery that something does not.

The crux of importance is the presumed bearing that study results have for the real world. For instance, when a new intervention reduces depression among mental health patients to a greater degree than does a traditional one, the researcher or practitioner would try to assess whether switching to the new intervention would make an important difference in clients' lives. Would their depression be reduced to a degree that would be meaningful to them and that would help them better carry out tasks of living? Such a question can be difficult to answer and requires assessment from varied perspectives.

In counseling/therapy with individuals, the term *clinical significance* is synonymous with importance. An example demonstrating clinical significance may be helpful. Perhaps a behavior modification intervention reduces the misbehavior of a given child in the school setting by only a modest degree. Yet perhaps this modest reduction is just the amount that is necessary to reduce stress for the teacher to a manageable level. Hence the modest reduction may be an important one.

Expert knowledge in one's substantive area is important in the assessment of importance. For instance, a researcher with expert knowledge in pregnancy prevention can better evaluate study results in this area than can one without such knowledge.

Questions regarding importance are largely nonstatistical. For the most part, statistical experts can agree about statistical questions. For instance, they can agree about the width of a confidence interval. Experts are likely to disagree about importance because there are no set tools for establishing it. Even if the process for assessing importance is difficult to describe and even if experts disagree, this process is nonetheless a vital one. Whenever you assess research results, you will ultimately have to make some judgment about the importance of those results. Considerations of importance are ultimately the same as those of meaning. One cannot avoid asking, "What is the meaning of this result for the real world?"

23.4   A BALANCED MODEL
FOR DATA INTERPRETATION

This section seeks to build a **balanced model for data interpretation** based on five factors: (1) statistical significance, (2) size of association, (3) causality, (4) generalizability, and (5) importance. The term *balanced* reflects my belief that when each factor holds reasonably equal "weight" and is accorded reasonably equal "importance," the interpretation of data is balanced and begins to be comprehensive.

The typical interpretation of data is unbalanced. It is heavily tilted toward the assessment of statistical significance and pays scant, uneven attention to other concepts in the model. Statistical significance is the most misinterpreted concept in data interpretation.

Most misinterpretations of statistical significance follow a common pattern. People attach meanings to statistical significance that are only tangentially connected to it (if at all). These misinterpretations inevitably involve one of the other four factors in the model. Thus, people conclude that statistically significant relationships are necessarily (1) large, (2) causal, (3) generalizable, and/or (4) important. Such reasoning does not follow logically and is incorrect.

Let's examine these illogical conclusions. First, some statistically significant associations represent large associations between variables, but others do not. In particular, recall that when sample size is large, associations of weak or moderate strength often achieve statistical significance (see Chapter 16, Section 16.4). Regarding the second conclusion, recall that much of the assessment of causality hinges on the research design. In survey designs, the problem of confounding variables is persistent. It is not uncommon for statistically significant associations to be caused by confounding variables. Third, with the exception of generalization to the population from which the study sample was selected (and to other randomly selected aspects of the study), statistical significance and generalizability are separate issues. One may have a statistically significant association that has very limited generalizability. Conversely, an association or result that is not statistically significant could have generalizability to a wide variety of settings. As an example, although the results for the study of in-home versus placement treatment for at-risk youth did not achieve statistical significance, perhaps they are widely generalizable to different regions of the United States. Finally, the connection between statistical significance and importance was just discussed. Some statistically significant associations are important. Others are not.

The same mistake is made in the other direction. People conclude that because an association is not statistically significant it also is necessarily (1) small in size, (2) not causal, (3) not generalizable, and (4) unimportant.

These (for the most part) illogical conclusions may also be examined. First, it does not follow that because an association is not statistically significant, it is necessarily small in size. In particular, when sample size is small (and therefore power is typically low), even reasonably strong/large associations may not be statistically significant. The second conclusion above holds reasonably well. When an association is not statistically significant, it may well be due to chance factors. As such, one has no grounds for concluding that it is causal. Third, as we have noted, generalizability is not, per se, connected to statistical significance. A result that is not statistically significant can be highly generalizable to many settings. Finally, as the in-home versus placement services example demonstrated, an association may be both (1) not statistically significant and (2) important.

The key to balanced interpretation is to treat the five concepts as separate and distinct. Interpretation becomes muddled when two or more concepts are scrambled together into one. In particular, do not inappropriately extend the meaning of statistical significance into areas that properly belong with the other concepts. As already stated, a statistically significant association is one that is not likely to be due to chance (sampling error). This is, pragmatically speaking, its core and only meaning.

To summarize, the key parts of the balanced data interpretation model are:

1. *Statistical significance:* whether the relationship is likely to be due to chance
2. *Size (strength) of association:* the degree to which the values of one variable vary, differ, or change according to those of the other
3. *Causality:* whether one variable affects the other
4. *Generalizability:* the degree to which a similar relationship or study result will be found in a different context or setting
5. *Importance:* the real-world implications of study results

The model makes several assumptions. Most basically, it assumes that the study of relationships is a key goal of the study. This holds for most studies. Experimental studies, for instance, focus on the association of the treatment intervention to the outcome variable. Similarly, a key goal of many surveys is the discovery of relationships. The occasional study reports purely univariate statistical data. The model should not be applied to such studies.

The model's third point pertains to causality. Some studies, notably many surveys, have a purely descriptive purpose; they describe results but do not seek to explain them. When a study's purpose is purely descriptive, questions pertaining to causality do not apply. In such a situation, one should simply drop the consideration of causality from the model and instead work with a four-point model (statistical significance, strength of association, generalizability, importance).

In discussing the model, I sometimes interchange the words *study result* and *relationship.* Pragmatically, the study of relationship is at the heart of most human services research. The key results of one's study are often one and the same as the relationships obtained.

23.5 AN EXAMPLE OF THE MODEL

Let's see how the model might be applied in data interpretation. As we have so often, let's use an example from the special-needs adoption study. To summarize the study:

> Rosenthal and Groze (1992) surveyed about 800 families who had adopted children with special needs from public agencies in three Midwestern states: Oklahoma, Kansas, Illinois. Special needs are factors that can delay or prevent timely adoption. Important special needs include older age at adoption, handicaps, developmental disabilities, emotional/behavioral problems, sibling group status, and minority ethnicity. The mean age of children when they entered their adoptive home was 5.52 years. Sixty-two percent of the children were white, 22% were African American, and 16% were from other ethnic backgrounds or were biracial. The study included 382 girls and 415 boys. The initial survey (a mailed questionnaire) was carried out in 1988. The response rate was 60%.

A central purpose of the study was to examine the quality of relationship between parents and children. The study found "close" parent-child relationships in most study families. The correlation between the adoptive parent's income at the time of the survey and the closeness (quality) of the responding parent's relationship to the adoptive child was $-.21$, $p < .01$ ($N = 635$). In other words, as family income increases, the closeness of relationship decreases.

My recommendation is to proceed through the parts of the model in the order in which the model presents them. We begin, therefore, with the assessment of statistical significance. The relationship between family income and closeness is indeed statistically significant ($p < .01$) and therefore unlikely to be due to chance factors. Some real factors are responsible for the association. In interpreting statistical significance, one should consider the power of the statistical test. In this situation, primarily due to the large sample size, statistical power is excellent.

As emphasized above, the other concepts of the model are not necessarily linked to statistical significance. Even so, statistical significance, in a sense, forms a gateway through which the relationship should pass prior to consideration of the other concepts. Having established that the association between income level and closeness is not likely to be due to chance, we may now assess its size. Referring to Table 8.3, a correlation of $-.21$ is about halfway between $-.10$, the guideline for small association, and $-.30$, that for medium association. Though these are general guidelines only, they clearly tell us that the association is not a large and compelling one. As income increases, closeness *tends* to decrease, but this pattern is comparatively weak. With a correlation of $-.21$, many families do not fit the prevailing pattern. Thus some wealthy families have high levels of closeness and some poor families have low levels.

It is important to treat size of association as its own distinct concept. Consider for the moment the implications of improperly extending the meaning of statistical significance to also include size of association. The following chain of illogical reasoning could result: (1) the association is statistically significant; (2) therefore, it is large (this is the key logical error); and (3) therefore, only low-income parents should be recruited for parenting special-needs children. Such a mistaken policy would exclude many middle- and upper-income people who would make fine adoptive parents.

Having established that there is an association and having assessed the size of that association, the next step in the interpretative model is the assessment of causality. As stated earlier, when an association is not statistically significant, one ordinarily would not theorize about issues pertaining to causality. Here, as the association is statistically significant, some real (nonchance) factors are presumably causing it. What might such factors be?

One possibility is that the association is a causal one, in other words, that low-income families and/or their communities possess some characteristics that do indeed facilitate closer relationships with children. At the risk of speculation, we may consider some of these possible characteristics. One such possibility is that low-income families may be more genuinely accepting of the children for "who they are." Perhaps, on the other hand, middle- and upper-income families tend to have goals that are too lofty given the children's background. For instance, they might expect very high achievement in schools. Perhaps lower-income families tend to use straightforward, practical methods of discipline and these methods tend to work better than the intellectualized methods of other families. Perhaps the communities in which low-income families live are more similar to those of the adoptees' family of origin than are the circumstances of other families, and this similarity facilitates integration into the home.

In the previous paragraph I have theorized (or some would say speculated). Perhaps I have gone too far out on a limb, where there is no solid, data-based support for my ideas. Yet the fact of a statistically significant association rules out chance as a likely explanation and thus invites reasoned speculation. The just-presented theories attempted to find characteristics of lower-income adoptive homes or communities that facilitate closeness. But perhaps these families do not possess such characteristics to a greater degree than do middle- and upper-income families. Perhaps the observed association reflects the influence of a confounding variable. The research design is a survey, and as you know, in survey designs confounding variables can be the explanation for (cause of) associations. The basic strategy for identifying potential confounding variables is to think of variables that are associated with both of the variables in the initial association.

Two such variables pop into my mind. (Obviously, I have the advantage of having worked with the data.) The first such variable is the age of the child in the home. As children get older, relationships with parents become less close, as a general rule. Also, as children age, parents tend to move up the ladder at work and increase their salaries. Perhaps, then, lower-income parents tend to be closer to their children because their children tend to be younger. A second possible variable relates to the family ethnicity, which has been discussed elsewhere in this text (see Chapter 2, Section 2.6). Minority respondents tended to have particularly close relationships with their children, somewhat more so than white respondents. In addition, minority families had lower mean incomes. Perhaps some characteristic of minority families explains the negative association between income level and closeness. Indeed, it could be very difficult to unscramble whether lower income or minority family ethnicity (or neither) is a key causative factor.

Given the potential that several confounding variables may be involved, the preferred approach would be some kind of multivariate statistical analysis, presumably a multiple regression analysis, that would include all such variables (see Chapter 22, Section 22.11). Such an analysis could control for their effects, though not perfectly. As Chapters 10 and 11 cautioned, in a survey design, one can never control for all potentially confounding third variables. Hence, regardless of the results of the regression analysis, one would be cautious in drawing causal inferences. As you know, with experimental designs using randomization, one may be much more confident in attributing causality than one can with survey designs.

So far, using the model, we have (1) concluded that the association is not due to chance, (2) concluded that it is fairly small (or medium) in size, and (3) recognized the complexities of drawing causal inferences. Next, we should consider issues of generalizability. Additional information on the sampling design can help in assessing generalizability. In Oklahoma and Kansas, the survey was mailed to all families who adopted children ages four and older under the auspices of the public social service agency during a four-year interval, approximately from 1984 to 1988. In Illinois, the survey was mailed to a random sample of families who were receiving adoptive financial subsidies in 1988. Given that the sampling process was random in Illinois, the study result can be generalized with reasonable confidence to the full population of families who were receiving subsidies in 1988. With the exception of this population, there are no other real populations to which results may be generalized via inferential statistical logic. Other issues of generalizability must be addressed based on the concept of similarity.

As we begin to consider generalizability, let's stop for a moment and note the response rate of 60%. Classes in research deal in depth with bias that can result from nonresponse. For now, suffice it to say that we have no data from 40% (100% − 60% = 40%) of the adoptive families to whom surveys were mailed. Their opinions and characteristics may differ greatly from those of respondents. We have no solid way to know. We hold open the possibility that the study results may not generalize to these families. Perhaps parents in these families tended to have less close relationships with their adoptive children than did those in responding families. This may have influenced their decision not to respond.

A second generalizability consideration pertains to time. The survey was mailed more than ten years prior to the writing of this chapter (1999). Perhaps several more years have elapsed as you are reading this. To the degree that conditions and circumstances in the field of special-needs adoption have changed, you would want to be cautious in presuming that similar results would be observed today.

All three states are Midwestern states. Would the same negative association between income and closeness be observed in other regions of the nation? There are no easy answers here. I would note that many of the circumstances in the backgrounds of special-needs children are similar across the United States. Many, for instance, experience severe abuse and/or neglect, and many are placed outside of their home for extended periods prior to the adoption. These similar experiences nudge one's thinking toward a tentative conclusion that similar results might be observed in different regions.

As the discussion on generalizability indicated, replication is a key tool for establishing the generalizability or lack thereof of study results. Several studies have indeed found (weak) associations between lower socioeconomic status and better adoptive outcomes (Jaffee and Fanshel, 1970; McWhinnie, 1967, cited in Zwimpfer, 1983; Davis and Bouck, 1955; Ripple, 1968). As such, the result in this study does not appear to be a fluke but instead seems to be part of a pattern of results. The fact that similar results have been observed in a variety of studies in different times and different regions bodes well for generalizability.

Generalizability outside of the study context is never an easy process. In, say, 2006, in your private (rather than public) child welfare agency, should you expect to find modestly closer relationships between parents and children in lower-income special-needs adoptive families than in middle- and upper-income families? Perhaps this conclusion stretches the study result too far from its initial context. However, the results from this study and from others with similar results suggest, at a minimum, that lower-income families are an important and positive resource for special-needs children.

As this discussion proceeds, you may be experiencing one of the major frustrations of research. Real-world research, even when well planned, has a habit of leaving more questions unanswered than answered. Clear, definitive conclusions are more the exception than the rule.[1]

The final part of the data interpretation model asks you to consider the importance, that is, the *meaning*, of the study result or association. Does the fact that particularly close parent-child relationships were observed in lower-income families have any real-world significance? Often one must call on substantive knowledge of the content area to address the question. Each year about 18,000 children are adopted under the auspices of public agencies for child welfare (Tatara, 1988). More than half of these have special needs. Hence the study results appear to have relevance for a reasonably large group of children and families. As this book is written, there are critical shortages of adoptive homes for children with special needs. On balance, more families are interested in adopting younger, healthy, and often white babies than in adopting those with special needs. The study results suggest that a variety of families from all walks of life—in particular parents from lower socioeconomic backgrounds and minority parents—can successfully adopt special-needs children. In this author's opinion, the study results do have real-world importance for recommending active recruitment of prospective parents from varied backgrounds.

23.6   COMMENTS ON THE MODEL

As you may have surmised, the data interpretation model moves progressively from quantitative decision making that yields clear conclusions into qualitative decision making that often yields less-than-clear conclusions. Thus issues of statistical significance can be addressed with 100% clarity—an association either is or is not significant at a given level. Assessments of size of association are somewhat more subjective—no absolute standards support such judgments, and what is large in one setting may not be so in another. The assessment of causality involves statistical tools, in particular, controlling for possible confounding variables. Yet, particularly in survey designs, this assessment can become exceedingly complex and ultimately involves at least some measure of qualitative judgment. The process of generalizing often takes one "beyond one's data." Pragmatically speaking, it can boil down to making a carefully reasoned "best guess." Finally, the assessment of importance ultimately requires subjective, qualitative judgment.

Books can provide precise rules for statistical decision making. The same precision cannot be provided for the broader, more qualitative aspects of data interpretation. Most statistics texts spend inordinate time in the clear waters of inferential statistics and almost none in the murky waters of generalizability and importance. By not providing guidance in these areas, these texts inadvertently suggest that they are unimportant. Critical reasoning in these areas is both difficult *and* important. Data interpretation requires careful and precise thinking. Hopefully, this chapter can help you strike a balance between being so careful that your thinking is paralyzed and reasoning recklessly. Careful and cautious critical reasoning—but with a dash of creativity—is what is needed.

23.7   CHAPTER SUMMARY

All research studies are conducted in a particular context. The generalizability of a study result is the expected similarity between the study result and the result that would be obtained if the study were carried out in a different context. Researchers use two different sets of tools to assess generalizability.

The tools of inferential statistics are used to make generalizations to (1) the population (if any) from which the study sample was randomly selected and (2) the population (if any) from which any other aspect of the study was randomly selected. Given large enough sample size, such generalizations can be made with high and known confidence. Statistical logic may not be used to make generalizations beyond the study population or regarding any aspect of the study that has not been randomly sampled.

The logic for generalizing beyond the study context is grounded predominantly in critical thinking and common sense. The key tool is one's qualitative judgment of the degree of similarity between the context of the study and the context to which one seeks to generalize. The greater that similarity, the greater the expected generalizability. Other factors considered include the variability of the sample and substantive knowledge. Replication in varied settings is central to establishing generalizability. Generalizations based on nonstatistical logic should be made cautiously and with the knowledge that one may be wrong.

The *importance* of a relationship or study result refers to the importance that it has in the real world. Although statistical significance bears on importance, importance and statistical significance are distinct concepts. A relationship may be statistically significant and unimportant.

The balanced model for data interpretation includes five factors: (1) statistical significance, (2) size of association, (3) causality, (4) generalizability, and (5) importance. Statistical significance is often accorded too much importance. Many mistakenly conclude that a statistically significant association is also necessarily (1) large, (2) causal, (3) generalizable, and/or (4) important. Each factor in the model is distinct. When each is given reasonably equal consideration, data interpretation is balanced and has the potential to be comprehensive.

PROBLEMS AND QUESTIONS

Section 23.2

1. A near synonym for "particular setting" is _____.

2. Define generalizability.

3. (T or F) The tools of inferential statistics may appropriately be used to generalize to the population from which the study sample was randomly selected.

4. (T or F) The tools of inferential statistics may appropriately be used to make generalizations to populations distinct from that from which the study sample was randomly sampled.

5. (T or F) Given large enough sample size, generalizations that use the tools of inferential statistics can often be made with known and considerable confidence.

6. What is misleading about the statement "Do not generalize beyond the population from which the study sample has been randomly sampled"?

7. The key tool for assessing the degree of generalizability beyond the study context (and beyond the population from which the sample was randomly selected) is degree of _____.

8. (T or F) In general, the greater the similarity between the setting/context to which one seeks to generalize and the setting/context of the research study, the greater the presumed generalizability.

9. Greater generalizability is expected when one's study sample has diverse and varied characteristics than when it is homogeneous and unvaried.

10. (T or F) The typical way to replicate a study is to keep all aspects of the study exactly the same.

11. (T or F) Generally speaking, one has more confidence in generalizations made with inferential statistical logic and applied to the population from which one has randomly sampled than one has in generalizations made with nonstatistical logic and applied to other populations and settings.

Section 23.3

12. (T or F) A study that does not yield statistically significant results cannot be an *important* study.

13. (T or F) Importance and statistical significance have essentially identical meanings.

14. (T or F) Importance and practical significance have very similar meanings.

15. What term from counseling/therapy with individuals has a meaning highly similar to importance?

16. Is it possible for an association to be statistically significant, strong, causal, and *unimportant?*

Section 23.4

17. What are the five factors in the balanced data interpretation model?

18. In typical "unbalanced" data interpretation, which factor is commonly accorded the greatest importance?

19. (T or F) Statistically significant associations are necessarily causal associations.

20. (T or F) The text recommends treating the five factors in the model as highly overlapping (nearly synonymous) rather than as distinct and separate.

21. Give an example of a relationship or study result that is both statistically significant and unimportant.

Integrative Problems

The problems that follow pull together material from throughout the text and guide you through the data interpretation model.

22. Two community mental health centers serve clients with chronic and severe mental health problems in a large urban city in the northeastern United States. Mental health center A uses a model in which mental health workers make frequent visits to clients who live in their own residences. At mental health center B, clients live in halfway houses with social workers on these premises. 30 of 200 clients (15%) at A versus 50 of 200 (25%) at B require psychiatric hospitalization within 12 months of beginning treatment. A chi-square test of independence indicates that this difference in percentages reaches significance in a two-tailed test, $p < .05$.

   The questions that follow for this problem are phrased in a general way so they can also be used for the next five problems. In particular, .05/.01 refers to the significance level specified for the problem. For all problems, assume a nondirectional hypothesis pair.

   a. What is the nondirectional null?

   b. Roughly, what is the statistical power of the statistical test in this situation?

   c. Is the relationship statistically significant at the .05/.01 level? (Respond with respect to the appropriate level, .05 or .01, given the information provided.)

   d. Is the probability that the study sample result is due solely to chance greater than .05/.01 or less than or equal to .05/.01?

   e. Given a true null, is the probability of obtaining the study sample result (or an even more extreme result) greater than .05/.01 or less than or equal to .05/.01?

f. Can you be at least 95%/99% confident that the null is false, or is your level of confidence less than this? (Respond with respect to the appropriate confidence level, 95% or 99%, given the information provided.)

g. What are your decisions regarding the null and research hypotheses?

h. How strong/large is the relationship?

i. Can you conclude that the relationship is causal? Why or why not? If you believe that the relationship may not be causal, indicate what confounding variables or other factors might explain the relationship.

j. Can the results be generalized statistically to any real, nonimaginary population?

k. In what other settings/populations do you think reasonably similar results might be obtained? Stated differently, to what settings/populations do you think results can be generalized using the logic of similarity?

l. Give an example of a setting/population to which you would be hesitant to generalize results.

m. Are the results important for the helping professions? Why or why not?

The questions for the prior problem also apply to each of the following problems.

23. At an exclusive private mental health clinic in southern California, 100 clients with issues related to depression are randomly assigned to one of two treatment approaches, A or B. On the Rainbow Depression Inventory, those in approach A evidence lower depression scores ($\overline{X} = 25.0$, $s = 10.0$, $n = 50$) than do those in B ($\overline{X} = 30.0$, $s = 10.0$, $n = 50$). An independent samples t test indicates that the probability of this result is less than .05.

24. Two large-scale welfare reform innovations are introduced in Oklahoma. The "search" approach emphasizes help with job searching and the "education" approach emphasizes educational/vocational training. 4000 clients are randomly assigned to each approach. 80% of those in "education" versus 78% of those in "search" find jobs within a specified time period. These results achieve significance, $p < .05$.

25. A random sample of 600 eleven-year-old boys is selected from all such boys in a six-state region in the southeastern United States. They are asked to participate in a randomized study pertaining to which of two types of video game controllers provides more effective and realistic action. All boys in the sample agree to participate. 300 are randomly assigned to the "palm-module" controller and 300 to the "joystick-style" controller. Results are as follows on a multi-item scale that measures controller effectiveness (high score conveys greater effectiveness): palm-module group, $\overline{X} = 60.0$, $s = 10.0$; joystick group, $\overline{X} = 40.0$, $s = 10.0$. An independent samples t test indicates a significant difference in means, $p < .01$.

26. A medium-size Midwestern town implements an experiment designed to test the effectiveness of an education program to prevent drug use among teens and preteens. From the total of 1000 age-appropriate youth, 200 are randomly selected to be in the study. All agree to participate. The intervention is quite intensive and involves components such as education, role play, video, and a celebrity advocating against drugs. One year after the program, students fill out a questionnaire that includes the question "Have you used marijuana in the past six months?" Of the 200 youth who received the intervention, 24% (48) respond affirmatively. This percentage is 25% (200 of 800) for the youth who did not receive the intervention. According to a chi-square test of independence, the difference in percentages is not significant, $p > .05$.

27. The juvenile justice agency in a large western state classifies its services into two basic types: (1) home based and (2) placement based. A large-scale follow-up study finds that those youth whose primary service was home based were far less likely to commit offenses subsequent to services than were those whose primary service was placement based. Specifically, only 10% of 1540 youth in home-based services committed offenses as compared to 33% of 750 youth in placement-based services. This difference in percentages is statistically significant, $p < .01$.

Note

1. A comment on the link between causality and generalizability is in order. The primary purpose of some research studies, notably experiments, is to enable researchers to draw solid causal conclusions. When a study has such a purpose but does not succeed in this end (for instance, when confounding variables cannot be ruled out), it typically makes little sense to consider issues pertaining to generalizability. In other words, if one has no confidence regarding "what caused what" within the study context, generalizing outside of it most often serves no useful purpose.

Tables

PROPORTION OF CASES IN SELECTED AREAS OF THE NORMAL DISTRIBUTION

TABLE A.1

z or −z	Cases Between Mean and z or −z	Cases > z or < −z	z or −z	Cases Between Mean and z or −z	Cases > z or < −z
0.00	.000	.500	1.04	.351	.149
0.02	.008	.492	1.06	.355	.145
0.04	.016	.484	1.08	.360	.140
0.06	.024	.476	1.10	.364	.136
0.08	.032	.468	1.12	.369	.131
0.10	.040	.460	1.14	.373	.127
0.12	.048	.452	1.16	.377	.123
0.14	.056	.444	1.18	.381	.119
0.16	.064	.436	1.20	.385	.115
0.18	.071	.429	1.22	.389	.111
0.20	.079	.421	1.24	.393	.107
0.22	.087	.413	1.26	.396	.104
0.24	.095	.405	1.28	.400	.100
0.26	.103	.397	1.30	.403	.097
0.28	.110	.390	1.32	.407	.093
0.30	.118	.382	1.34	.410	.090
0.32	.126	.374	1.36	.413	.087
0.34	.133	.367	1.38	.416	.084
0.36	.141	.359	1.40	.419	.081
0.38	.148	.352	1.42	.422	.078
0.40	.155	.345	1.44	.425	.075
0.42	.163	.337	1.46	.428	.072
0.44	.170	.330	1.48	.431	.069
0.46	.177	.323	1.50	.433	.067
0.48	.184	.316	1.52	.436	.064
0.50	.191	.309	1.54	.438	.062
0.52	.198	.302	1.56	.441	.059
0.54	.205	.295	1.58	.443	.057
0.56	.212	.288	1.60	.445	.055
0.58	.219	.281	1.62	.447	.053
0.60	.226	.274	1.64	.449	.051
0.62	.232	.268	1.645	.4500	.0500
0.64	.239	.261	1.66	.452	.048
0.66	.245	.255	1.68	.454	.046
0.68	.252	.248	1.70	.455	.045
0.70	.258	.242	1.72	.457	.043
0.72	.264	.236	1.74	.459	.041
0.74	.270	.230	1.76	.461	.039
0.76	.276	.224	1.78	.462	.038
0.78	.282	.218	1.80	.464	.036
0.80	.288	.212	1.82	.466	.034
0.82	.294	.206	1.84	.467	.033
0.84	.300	.200	1.86	.469	.031
0.86	.305	.195	1.88	.470	.030
0.88	.311	.189	1.90	.471	.029
0.90	.316	.184	1.92	.473	.027
0.92	.321	.179	1.94	.474	.026
0.94	.326	.174	1.960	.4750	.0250
0.96	.331	.169	1.98	.476	.024
0.98	.336	.164	2.00	.477	.023
1.00	.341	.159	2.02	.478	.022
1.02	.346	.154	2.04	.479	.021

z or −z	Cases Between Mean and z or −z	Cases > z or < −z	z or −z	Cases Between Mean and z or −z	Cases > z or < −z
2.06	.480	.020	2.62	.4956	.0044
2.08	.481	.019	2.64	.4959	.0041
2.10	.482	.018	2.66	.4961	.0039
2.12	.483	.017	2.68	.4963	.0037
2.14	.484	.016	2.70	.4965	.0035
2.16	.485	.015	2.72	.4967	.0033
2.18	.485	.015	2.74	.4969	.0031
2.20	.486	.014	2.76	.4971	.0029
2.22	.487	.013	2.78	.4973	.0027
2.24	.487	.013	2.80	.4974	.0026
2.26	.488	.012	2.82	.4976	.0024
2.28	.489	.011	2.84	.4977	.0023
2.30	.489	.011	2.86	.4979	.0021
2.32	.490	.010	2.88	.4980	.0020
2.326	.4900	.0100	2.90	.4981	.0019
2.34	.490	.010	2.92	.4982	.0018
2.36	.491	.009	2.94	.4984	.0016
2.38	.491	.009	2.96	.4985	.0015
2.40	.492	.008	2.98	.4986	.0014
2.42	.492	.008	3.00	.4987	.0013
2.44	.493	.007	3.10	.4990	.0010
2.46	.493	.007	3.20	.4993	.0007
2.48	.493	.007	3.30	.4995	.0005
2.50	.4938	.0062	3.40	.4997	.0003
2.52	.4941	.0059	3.50	.4998	.0002
2.54	.4945	.0055	4.00	.49997	.00003
2.56	.4948	.0052	1.645	.4500	.0500
2.576	.4950	.0050	1.960	.4750	.0250
2.58	.4951	.0049	2.326	.4900	.0100
2.60	.4953	.0047	2.576	.4950	.0050

6.1				
TABLE A.2	**VALUES OF *t* FOR CONFIDENCE INTERVALS AND CRITICAL VALUES FOR THE *t* DISTRIBUTION**			

	VALUES OF *t* FOR 95% *CI*	**VALUES OF *t* FOR 99% *CI***		
		Critical Values ($|t|$)		
	Two-Tailed Test		**One-Tailed Test**	
df	$\alpha = .05^a$	$\alpha = .01^b$	$\alpha = .05^c$	$\alpha = .01^d$
1	12.706	63.657	6.314	31.821
2	4.303	9.925	2.920	6.965
3	3.182	5.841	2.353	4.541
4	2.776	4.604	2.132	3.747
5	2.571	4.032	2.015	3.365
6	2.447	3.707	1.943	3.143
7	2.365	3.499	1.895	2.998
8	2.306	3.355	1.860	2.896
9	2.262	3.250	1.833	2.821
10	2.228	3.169	1.812	2.764
11	2.201	3.106	1.796	2.718
12	2.179	3.055	1.782	2.681
13	2.160	3.012	1.771	2.650
14	2.145	2.977	1.761	2.624
15	2.131	2.947	1.753	2.602
16	2.120	2.921	1.746	2.583
17	2.110	2.898	1.740	2.567
18	2.101	2.878	1.734	2.552
19	2.093	2.861	1.729	2.539
20	2.086	2.845	1.725	2.528
21	2.080	2.831	1.721	2.518
22	2.074	2.819	1.717	2.508
23	2.069	2.807	1.714	2.500
24	2.064	2.797	1.711	2.492
25	2.060	2.787	1.708	2.485
26	2.056	2.779	1.706	2.479
27	2.052	2.771	1.703	2.473
28	2.048	2.763	1.701	2.467
29	2.045	2.756	1.699	2.462
30	2.042	2.750	1.697	2.457
35	2.030	2.724	1.690	2.438
40	2.021	2.704	1.684	2.423
50	2.009	2.678	1.676	2.403
60	2.000	2.660	1.671	2.390
80	1.990	2.639	1.664	2.374
100	1.984	2.626	1.660	2.364
120	1.980	2.617	1.658	2.358
200	1.972	2.601	1.653	2.345
500	1.965	2.586	1.648	2.334

[a] $\pm t$ = Value of *t* within which 95% of cases are located
[b] $\pm t$ = Value of *t* within which 99% of cases are located
[c] $\pm t$ = Value of *t* above or below which 95% of cases are located
[d] $\pm t$ = Value of *t* above or below which 99% of cases are located

TABLE A.3	CRITICAL VALUES FOR THE CHI-SQUARE DISTRIBUTION

Degrees of Freedom	SIGNIFICANCE LEVEL			
	.10	.05	.01	.001
1	2.71	3.84	6.63	10.83
2	4.61	5.99	9.21	13.82
3	6.25	7.81	11.34	16.27
4	7.78	9.49	13.28	18.47
5	9.24	11.07	15.09	20.52
6	10.64	12.59	16.81	22.46
7	12.02	14.07	18.48	24.32
8	13.36	15.51	20.09	26.12
9	14.68	16.92	21.67	27.88
10	15.99	18.31	23.21	29.59
11	17.28	19.68	24.72	31.26
12	18.55	21.03	26.22	32.91
13	19.81	22.36	27.69	34.53
14	21.06	23.68	29.14	36.12
15	22.31	25.00	30.58	37.70
16	23.54	26.30	32.00	39.25
17	24.77	27.59	33.41	40.79
18	25.99	28.87	34.81	42.31
19	27.20	30.14	36.19	43.82
20	28.41	31.41	37.57	45.31
21	29.62	32.67	38.93	46.80
22	30.81	33.92	40.29	48.27
23	32.01	35.17	41.64	49.73
24	33.20	36.42	42.98	51.18
25	34.38	37.65	44.31	52.62
26	35.56	38.89	45.64	54.05
27	36.74	40.11	46.96	55.48
28	37.92	41.34	48.28	56.89
29	39.09	42.56	49.59	58.30
30	40.26	43.77	50.89	59.70
35	46.06	49.80	57.34	66.62
40	51.81	55.76	63.69	73.40
50	63.17	67.50	76.15	86.66
60	74.40	79.08	88.38	99.61
70	85.53	90.53	100.43	112.32
80	96.58	101.88	112.33	124.84
100	118.50	124.34	135.81	149.45

TABLE A.4   CRITICAL VALUES FOR THE *F* DISTRIBUTION

df for MS_W (Denominator)	α	\multicolumn{10}{c}{df FOR MS_B (NUMERATOR)}

df for MS_W (Denominator)	α	1	2	3	4	5	6	7	8	10	12
1	.05	161.4	199.5	215.7	224.6	230.2	234.0	236.8	238.9	241.9	243.9
	.01	4052	4999	5403	5625	5764	5859	5928	5981	6056	6106
2	.05	18.51	19.00	19.16	19.25	19.30	19.33	19.35	19.37	19.40	19.41
	.01	98.50	99.00	99.17	99.25	99.30	99.33	99.36	99.37	99.40	99.42
3	.05	10.13	9.55	9.28	9.12	9.01	8.94	8.89	8.85	8.79	8.74
	.01	34.12	30.82	29.46	28.71	28.24	27.91	27.67	27.49	27.23	27.05
4	.05	7.71	6.94	6.59	6.39	6.26	6.16	6.09	6.04	5.96	5.91
	.01	21.20	18.00	16.69	15.98	15.52	15.21	14.98	14.80	14.55	14.37
5	.05	6.61	5.79	5.41	5.19	5.05	4.95	4.88	4.82	4.74	4.68
	.01	16.26	13.27	12.06	11.39	10.97	10.67	10.46	10.29	10.05	9.89
6	.05	5.99	5.14	4.76	4.53	4.39	4.28	4.21	4.15	4.06	4.00
	.01	13.75	10.92	9.78	9.15	8.75	8.47	8.26	8.10	7.87	7.72
7	.05	5.59	4.74	4.35	4.12	3.97	3.87	3.79	3.73	3.64	3.57
	.01	12.25	9.55	8.45	7.85	7.46	7.19	6.99	6.84	6.62	6.47
8	.05	5.32	4.46	4.07	3.84	3.69	3.58	3.50	3.44	3.35	3.28
	.01	11.26	8.65	7.59	7.01	6.63	6.37	6.18	6.03	5.81	5.67
9	.05	5.12	4.26	3.86	3.63	3.48	3.37	3.29	3.23	3.14	3.07
	.01	10.56	8.02	6.99	6.42	6.06	5.80	5.61	5.47	5.26	5.11
10	.05	4.96	4.10	3.71	3.48	3.33	3.22	3.14	3.07	2.98	2.91
	.01	10.04	7.56	6.55	5.99	5.64	5.39	5.20	5.06	4.85	4.71
11	.05	4.84	3.98	3.59	3.36	3.20	3.09	3.01	2.95	2.85	2.79
	.01	9.65	7.21	6.22	5.67	5.32	5.07	4.89	4.74	4.54	4.40
12	.05	4.75	3.89	3.49	3.26	3.11	3.00	2.91	2.85	2.75	2.69
	.01	9.33	6.93	5.95	5.41	5.06	4.82	4.64	4.50	4.30	4.16
13	.05	4.67	3.81	3.41	3.18	3.03	2.92	2.83	2.77	2.67	2.60
	.01	9.07	6.70	5.74	5.21	4.86	4.62	4.44	4.30	4.10	3.96
14	.05	4.60	3.74	3.34	3.11	2.96	2.85	2.76	2.70	2.60	2.53
	.01	8.86	6.51	5.56	5.04	4.69	4.46	4.28	4.14	3.94	3.80
15	.05	4.54	3.68	3.29	3.06	2.90	2.79	2.71	2.64	2.54	2.48
	.01	8.68	6.36	5.42	4.89	4.56	4.32	4.14	4.00	3.80	3.67
16	.05	4.49	3.63	3.24	3.01	2.85	2.74	2.66	2.59	2.49	2.42
	.01	8.53	6.23	5.29	4.77	4.44	4.20	4.03	3.89	3.69	3.55
17	.05	4.45	3.59	3.20	2.96	2.81	2.70	2.61	2.55	2.45	2.38
	.01	8.40	6.11	5.18	4.67	4.34	4.10	3.93	3.79	3.59	3.46
18	.05	4.41	3.55	3.16	2.93	2.77	2.66	2.58	2.51	2.41	2.34
	.01	8.29	6.01	5.09	4.58	4.25	4.01	3.84	3.71	3.51	3.37
19	.05	4.38	3.52	3.13	2.90	2.74	2.63	2.54	2.48	2.38	2.31
	.01	8.18	5.93	5.01	4.50	4.17	3.94	3.77	3.63	3.43	3.30
20	.05	4.35	3.49	3.10	2.87	2.71	2.60	2.51	2.45	2.35	2.28
	.01	8.10	5.85	4.94	4.43	4.10	3.87	3.70	3.56	3.37	3.23

df for MS_W (Denominator)	α					df FOR MS_B (NUMERATOR)					
		1	2	3	4	5	6	7	8	10	12
21	.05	4.32	3.47	3.07	2.84	2.68	2.57	2.49	2.42	2.32	2.25
	.01	8.02	5.78	4.87	4.37	4.04	3.81	3.64	3.51	3.31	3.17
22	.05	4.30	3.44	3.05	2.82	2.66	2.55	2.46	2.40	2.30	2.23
	.01	7.95	5.72	4.82	4.31	3.99	3.76	3.59	3.45	3.26	3.12
23	.05	4.28	3.42	3.03	2.80	2.64	2.53	2.44	2.37	2.27	2.20
	.01	7.88	5.66	4.76	4.26	3.94	3.71	3.54	3.41	3.21	3.07
24	.05	4.26	3.40	3.01	2.78	2.62	2.51	2.42	2.36	2.25	2.18
	.01	7.82	5.61	4.72	4.22	3.90	3.67	3.50	3.36	3.17	3.03
25	.05	4.24	3.39	2.99	2.76	2.60	2.49	2.40	2.34	2.24	2.16
	.01	7.77	5.57	4.68	4.18	3.85	3.63	3.46	3.32	3.13	2.99
26	.05	4.23	3.37	2.98	2.74	2.59	2.47	2.39	2.32	2.22	2.15
	.01	7.72	5.53	4.64	4.14	3.82	3.59	3.42	3.29	3.09	2.96
27	.05	4.21	3.35	2.96	2.73	2.57	2.46	2.37	2.31	2.20	2.13
	.01	7.68	5.49	4.60	4.11	3.78	3.56	3.39	3.26	3.06	2.93
28	.05	4.20	3.34	2.95	2.71	2.56	2.45	2.36	2.29	2.19	2.12
	.01	7.64	5.45	4.57	4.07	3.75	3.53	3.36	3.23	3.03	2.90
29	.05	4.18	3.33	2.93	2.70	2.55	2.43	2.35	2.28	2.18	2.10
	.01	7.60	5.42	4.54	4.04	3.73	3.50	3.33	3.20	3.00	2.87
30	.05	4.17	3.32	2.92	2.69	2.53	2.42	2.33	2.27	2.16	2.09
	.01	7.56	5.39	4.51	4.02	3.70	3.47	3.30	3.17	2.98	2.84
32	.05	4.15	3.29	2.90	2.67	2.51	2.40	2.31	2.24	2.14	2.07
	.01	7.50	5.34	4.46	3.97	3.65	3.43	3.26	3.13	2.93	2.80
35	.05	4.12	3.27	2.87	2.64	2.49	2.37	2.29	2.22	2.11	2.04
	.01	7.42	5.27	4.40	3.91	3.59	3.37	3.20	3.07	2.88	2.74
40	.05	4.08	3.23	2.84	2.61	2.45	2.34	2.25	2.18	2.08	2.00
	.01	7.31	5.18	4.31	3.83	3.51	3.29	3.12	2.99	2.80	2.66
45	.05	4.06	3.20	2.81	2.58	2.42	2.31	2.22	2.15	2.05	1.97
	.01	7.23	5.11	4.25	3.77	3.45	3.23	3.07	2.94	2.74	2.61
50	.05	4.03	3.18	2.79	2.56	2.40	2.29	2.20	2.13	2.03	1.95
	.01	7.17	5.06	4.20	3.72	3.41	3.19	3.02	2.89	2.70	2.56
60	.05	4.00	3.15	2.76	2.53	2.37	2.25	2.17	2.10	1.99	1.92
	.01	7.08	4.98	4.13	3.65	3.34	3.12	2.95	2.82	2.63	2.50
75	.05	3.97	3.12	2.73	2.49	2.34	2.22	2.13	2.06	1.96	1.88
	.01	6.99	4.90	4.05	3.58	3.27	3.05	2.89	2.76	2.57	2.43
100	.05	3.94	3.09	2.70	2.46	2.31	2.19	2.10	2.03	1.93	1.85
	.01	6.90	4.82	3.98	3.51	3.21	2.99	2.82	2.69	2.50	2.37
150	.05	3.90	3.06	2.66	2.43	2.27	2.16	2.07	2.00	1.89	1.82
	.01	6.81	4.75	3.91	3.45	3.14	2.92	2.76	2.63	2.44	2.31
250	.05	3.88	3.03	2.64	2.41	2.25	2.13	2.05	1.98	1.87	1.79
	.01	6.74	4.69	3.86	3.40	3.09	2.87	2.71	2.58	2.39	2.26
1000	.05	3.85	3.00	2.61	2.38	2.22	2.11	2.02	1.95	1.84	1.76
	.01	6.66	4.63	3.80	3.34	3.04	2.82	2.66	2.53	2.34	2.20

TABLE A.5   CRITICAL VALUES FOR PEARSON'S *r*

N	df	TWO-TAILED TEST $\alpha = .05$	TWO-TAILED TEST $\alpha = .01$	ONE-TAILED TEST $\alpha = .05$	ONE-TAILED TEST $\alpha = .01$
3	1	.997	1.000	.988	1.000
4	2	.950	.990	.900	.980
5	3	.878	.959	.805	.934
6	4	.811	.917	.729	.882
7	5	.754	.875	.669	.833
8	6	.707	.834	.621	.789
9	7	.666	.798	.582	.750
10	8	.632	.765	.549	.715
11	9	.602	.735	.521	.685
12	10	.576	.708	.497	.658
13	11	.553	.684	.476	.634
14	12	.532	.661	.458	.612
15	13	.514	.641	.441	.592
16	14	.497	.623	.426	.574
17	15	.482	.606	.412	.558
18	16	.468	.590	.400	.543
19	17	.456	.575	.389	.529
20	18	.444	.561	.378	.516
21	19	.433	.549	.369	.503
22	20	.423	.537	.360	.492
23	21	.413	.526	.352	.482
24	22	.404	.515	.344	.472
25	23	.396	.505	.337	.462
26	24	.388	.496	.330	.453
27	25	.381	.487	.323	.445
29	27	.367	.471	.311	.430
32	30	.349	.449	.296	.409
37	35	.325	.418	.275	.381
42	40	.304	.393	.257	.358
47	45	.288	.372	.243	.338
52	50	.273	.354	.231	.322
62	60	.250	.325	.211	.295
72	70	.232	.302	.195	.274
82	80	.217	.283	.183	.257
102	100	.195	.254	.164	.230
142	140	.165	.216	.139	.195
202	200	.138	.181	.116	.164
302	300	.113	.148	.095	.134
402	400	.098	.128	.082	.116
602	600	.080	.105	.067	.095
1002	1000	.062	.081	.052	.073

Review of Basic Math

B.1 BASIC OPERATIONS, TERMS, AND SYMBOLS

When two numbers are added (or, one may say, summed) the result is termed a **sum.** For instance:

$3 + 3 = 6$ The sum is 6.

When one number is subtracted from another, the result is termed a **difference.** For instance:

$5 - 4 = 1$ The difference is 1.

When two numbers are multiplied, the result is termed a **product.** For instance:

$2 \times 4 = 8$ The product is 8.

When one number is divided by another, the result is termed a **quotient.** For instance:

$6 \div 2 = 3$ The quotient is 3.

Sometimes symbols different from these are used. A slash indicates division. For instance: $6/2 = 3$. A horizontal bar also conveys division:

$$\frac{6}{2} = 3$$

In expressions involving division, the number that is divided (that is, the number above the horizontal bar) is termed the **numerator.** The number by which one divides (the number below the horizontal bar) is termed the **denominator.**

When one or both of two numbers are inside parentheses and have no symbol between them, multiply them. For instance:

$(2)(4) = (2) \times (4) = 2 \times 4 = 8$

$2(4) = 2 \times (4) = 2 \times 4 = 8$

B.2   ADDITIONAL SYMBOLS

Here is a list of symbols with which you may or may not be familiar and examples of how they are used:

$<$	less than $(5 < 7)$
$>$	greater than $(7 > 5)$
$\leq$	less than or equal to $(3 \leq 5$ and also $5 \leq 5)$
$\geq$	greater than or equal to $(6 \geq 2$ and also $6 \geq 6)$
$\approx$	approximately equal to $(8.6532 \approx 8.6533)$
$\pm$	add and subtract $(5 \pm 3 = 5 - 3$ and $5 + 3$; these equal 2 and 8)

Another symbol that you may not have encountered is the **summation sign, Σ**. The summation sign instructs one to sum whatever follows. Hence the expression $\Sigma\,(2, 3, 8, 9, 5)$ directs one to sum 2, 3, 8, 9, and 5:

$$\Sigma\,(2, 3, 8, 9, 5) = 2 + 3 + 8 + 9 + 5 = 27$$

B.3   ORDER OF OPERATIONS

An important rule to remember: Always carry out operations inside parentheses first. For instance:

$$(2 + 4)/(2 + 1) = 6/3 = 2$$

When more than one set of parentheses are needed, brackets [ ] and then braces { } are used. Operations in the innermost set, the parentheses, should be carried out first, then those in brackets, then those in braces. For instance:

$$[8 + (3 \times 4)] \div 5 = (8 + 12) \div 5 = 20 \div 5 = 4$$

Assuming that operations within parentheses, brackets, and braces have been carried out, multiplication and/or division should be carried out prior to addition and/or subtraction. For instance:

$$7 + 3(5) = 7 + 15 = 22$$

B.4   POSITIVE AND NEGATIVE NUMBERS AND ABSOLUTE VALUES

You will encounter both **negative numbers** (those with values less than 0) and **positive numbers** (those with values greater than 0). Negative numbers are designated by the negative sign. The **negative sign** (minus sign, $-$) is the same as the subtraction symbol and conveys subtraction from 0 (zero). Hence, -5 conveys the negative number "negative 5," which equals $0 - 5$ (that is, $0 - 5 = -5$). The **pos-**

itive sign (plus sign, +) is the addition symbol and conveys 0 plus a number. For instance, +5 conveys "positive 5," which equals 0 + 5 (that is, 0 + 5 = +5). However, when a number is a positive number, one need not designate this by a sign. Stated differently, whenever there is no sign, a number can be assumed to be positive. For instance, 5 designates +5 (positive 5). (One need not write +5; simply writing 5 is sufficient.)

Some tips regarding addition and subtraction involving negative numbers:

Adding a negative number yields the same result as subtracting a positive number. Thus, to add a negative number, change its sign to positive and subtract. For instance: 4 + (−2) = 4 − 2 = 2. Sometimes the result is a negative number; for instance: 2 + (−4) = 2 − 4 = −2.

Subtracting a negative number yields the same result as adding a positive number. Thus, to subtract a negative number, change its sign to positive and add. For instance, 4 − (−2) = 4 + 2 = 6. Again, the result may be a negative: for instance, −4 − (−2) = −4 + 2 = −2.

To sum a group of numbers, some of which are positive and some of which are negative, follow these steps: (1) sum the positive numbers, (2) change the negative numbers to positives and sum, and (3) subtract the sum in step 2 from the sum in step 1. For instance, to sum the numbers 5, −3, 6, −2, −1:

Step 1: 5 + 6 = 11
Step 2: 3 + 2 + 1 = 6
Step 3: 11 − 6 = 5

Some rules to remember regarding multiplication and division are:

A positive number multiplied by or divided by a positive yields a positive. For instance:

$4 \times 2 = 8$ and $4/2 = 2$

A negative number multiplied by or divided by a negative yields a positive. For instance:

$(-4)(-2) = 8$ and $(-4)/(-2) = 2$

A positive number multiplied or divided by a negative, and also a negative number multiplied or divided by a positive, yields a negative. For instance:

$(4)(-2) = -8$ and $(4)/(-2) = -2$
$(-4)(2) = -8$ and $(-4)/(2) = -2$

The **absolute value** of a number is its value without regarding its sign. Or, stated differently, it is the positive value of the number. For instance, the absolute value of −5 is 5 (positive 5). Similarly, the absolute value of 5 is 5. Absolute value is symbolized by vertical bars on both sides of a number. Hence |−3| conveys the absolute value of minus 3, which is 3.

It may be helpful to clarify the meaning of "less than" (symbolized by $<$) and "greater than" (symbolized by $>$) as these apply in situations involving negative numbers. Obviously, for instance, $5 > 2$ and $2 < 5$. It may be less obvious whether the following expressions are true: $-5 < -2$; $-5 < 2$; and $2 > -5$. All these expressions are indeed true. In considering whether a given number is greater than or less than another, one considers actual values, *not* absolute values. For instance, -5 is not greater than -2 but is less than -2. On the other hand, the absolute value of negative 5 (which is 5) is greater than the absolute value of negative 2 (which is 2). In symbols this last statement is $|-5| > |-2|$.

This text uses the term the **negative of** to convey the negative number that is opposite in sign to a given positive number. For instance, as used in the text, -7 is the negative of 7 and -1.87 is the negative of 1.87. (This is not a formal term in mathematics, but it is helpful for several applications in the text.)

B.5 SQUARES, SQUARE ROOTS, EXPONENTS, AND POWER

The **square** of a number (or, one may say, a number squared) equals that number multiplied by itself. For instance, 6 squared $= 6 \times 6 = 36$. The symbol for a number squared is the superscript 2, that is, ^{2}. Thus, 6 squared is symbolized by 6^2, and the equation is $6^2 = 6 \times 6 = 36$.

The square root of, say, X is the number that when multiplied by itself yields X. For instance, the square root of 36 is 6, because $6 \times 6 = 36$. Another way to define square root is to say that the square root of X is the number that when squared yields X. With this definition, the square root of 36 is 6 because $6^2 = 36$. Square roots are designated by the radical symbol (also known as the square root symbol), $\sqrt{}$. Hence, in symbols, $\sqrt{36} = 6$.[1]

The **power** to which a number is raised conveys the number of times that a number appears in an expression in which it is multiplied by itself. When a number is squared it is raised to the second power, because a number appears twice in an expression in which it is squared. For instance, $6 \times 6 = 6^2$, which equals 6 to the second power. The power to which a number is raised always appears as a superscript (that is, in the same style of notation used for squaring). Hence, 8^3 conveys 8 raised to the third power:

$8^3 = 8 \times 8 \times 8 = 512$. (Note that 8 appears three times in this expression.)

(Do not confuse the power to which a number is raised with statistical power, which is presented in Chapter 16.)

The number (superscript) that conveys the power to which a number is raised is termed an **exponent.** Hence, in the expression 8^3, the exponent is 3.

In reading computer output, you may encounter scientific notation. Scientific notation expresses numbers making use of 10 raised to a given power. The power to which 10 is raised (the exponent of 10) conveys the number of places by which the decimal point must be moved to express the number in conventional format. Here are some examples:

NUMBER IN SCIENTIFIC NOTATION	NUMBER IN STANDARD FORMAT
-8.77×10^2	-877
2.37×10^8	$237{,}000{,}000$
6.32×10^{-4}	0.000632

In the first example, the exponent is 2. Because the exponent is positive, the decimal point is moved two places to the right to express the number conventionally. In the final example, the exponent, -4, is negative. As such, one moves the decimal point four places to the left to express the number conventionally.

B.6   FRACTIONS

Almost all the numbers that we have dealt with so far have been **whole numbers,** that is, numbers that do not involve fractions or decimals. For instance, 3132, 11, and 0 are examples of whole numbers. Because they involve fractions or decimals, 3.68, 2½, and 6.67 are examples of numbers that are not whole numbers.

Some tips may be helpful in rekindling your knowledge of fractions. Multiplication of fractions is straightforward. One simply multiplies the numerator of one fraction by that of the other and does the same with the denominators:

$$\frac{1}{4} \times \frac{3}{8} = \frac{3}{32}$$

To divide one fraction by another, invert (flip) the second fraction and multiply:

$$\frac{1}{4} \div \frac{3}{8} = \frac{1}{4} \times \frac{8}{3} = \frac{8}{12}$$

The denominator of any whole number is always one. For instance, $6 = 6/1$. To solve the problem $5 \times 2/3 = ?$, one may find it convenient to express 5 as 5/1:

$$\frac{5}{1} \times \frac{2}{3} = \frac{10}{3}$$

When possible, fractions should be **reduced,** that is, expressed with the lowest possible denominator. To reduce a fraction, find a number that divides evenly ("goes into") both the numerator and denominator. For instance, 4 divides evenly into both the numerator and denominator of 8/12. Hence, 8/12 can be reduced to 2/3. Stated as an equation: $8/12 = 2/3$.

To add and subtract fractions, one must find a **common denominator.** One way to do this is to multiply each fraction by the value 1, with 1 expressed using the denominator of the other fraction. For instance, consider the problem $1/3 + 2/5 = ?$. The fraction 1/3 can be multiplied by 5/5: $1/3 \times 5/5 = 5/15$ (5/5 equals 1, so multiplying by it does not change the value of the fraction). Similarly, 2/5 can be multiplied by 3/3 (3/3 equals 1): $2/5 \times 3/3 = 6/15$. Now, both fractions have a common denominator (15) and they can be summed:

$$\frac{5}{15} + \frac{6}{15} = \frac{11}{15}$$

The **reciprocal** of a number is calculated by dividing 1 by that number. For instance, the reciprocal of 4 is $1 \div 4 = 1/4$ (one-fourth). Any number multiplied by its reciprocal equals 1. For instance:

$$4 \times \frac{1}{4} = \frac{4}{1} \times \frac{1}{4} = \frac{4}{4} = \frac{1}{1} = 1$$

B.7 ALGEBRA

To solve simple algebra problems, carry out the same operations on both sides of the equals sign. For instance, the following problem is solved by adding 5 to both sides:

$$X - 5 = 2$$
$$X - 5 + 5 = 2 + 5$$
$$X = 7$$

The next problem requires both addition and multiplication on both sides:

$$5X - 3 = 12$$
$$5X - 3 + 3 = 12 + 3$$
$$5X = 15$$
$$5X \div 5 = 15 \div 5$$
$$X = 3$$

B.8 ROUNDING AND OTHER TOPICS

It will be helpful to introduce some guidelines for **rounding.** Suppose that we have the number 518.42875432. For most purposes, this number has far more precision than is needed. We may wish to round it to, say, three decimal places. To see how to round, direct your attention to the number in the decimal place following the place to which you wish to round. If this number is 5 or greater, round upward; if it is 4 or lower, round downward. For our example, the number in the fourth decimal place is 7. Seven is greater than 5. Therefore, we round upward to 518.429. As another example, to round 29.53468 to two decimal places, focus on the number in the third decimal place; 4 is less than 5, so we round downward to 29.53.[2]

Whenever rounding is carried out, some **round-off error** is introduced into the answer. With calcuators and computers this is much less of a problem than it was when calculations were done by hand. The following guideline reduces (but does not eliminate) round-off error: In all calculations, round to at least one more decimal place than you will use to express your answer. For instance, suppose that you need to multiply 8.45419 by 3.539682 and want to express your answer (product) with two decimal places. According to the guideline, each number should be rounded to three decimal places (2 + 1 = 3). Hence you would multiply 8.454

(note that we rounded downward) by 3.540 (note that the third number, 9, rounded up to 10), which results in 29.92716. Rounding this product to two decimal places, the answer is 29.93.

B.9   VISUAL DISPLAYS

This text has many visual displays, that is, figures. The horizontal and vertical lines in figures such as Figure B.1 are termed **axes.** The vertical line is termed the **vertical axis** and the horizontal line is termed the **horizontal axis.** Another name for the vertical axis is the **Y axis,** and another name for the horizontal axis is the **X axis.** As Figure B.1 demonstrates, numbers always increase as one goes up the Y axis (for instance, numbers in the figure increase from 10 to 20) and as one goes from left to right across the X axis (here, numbers increase from 0 to 50).

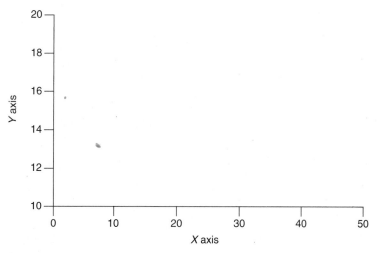

FIGURE **B.1**
GRAPH WITH X AND Y AXES

MATH REVIEW PROBLEMS

1. The result of addition is termed a _____; that of subtraction is a _____; that of multiplication is a _____; that of division is a _____.

2. What does each symbol convey?   ≥ _____
   ≈ _____   ± _____

3. What is Σ (4, 7, 2, 3, 3)? What is Σ (4, 4, 5, 0, 2)?

4. $(9 - 2) \times (3/4) = ?$
   $10 \times [(2 + 6)/(3 \times 8)] = ?$

5. $8 - (-3) + (-2) = ?$
   $5 + (-3) - (-2) + 7 = ?$

6. $|-7| = ?$ $|12| = ?$

7. $5^2 = ?$ $\sqrt{49} = ?$ $3^3 = ?$

8. In the expression 2^4, the number 2 is raised to the fourth _____. The 4 in this expression is termed an _____. $2^4 = ?$

9. Express in standard format: 6.83×10^{-5} _____; 3.3×10^4 _____

10. $\dfrac{2}{1} \div \dfrac{3}{2} = ?$ $\dfrac{7}{4} \times \dfrac{5}{12} = ?$

11. $\dfrac{8}{3} - \dfrac{3}{9} = ?$ $\dfrac{2}{5} + \dfrac{3}{4} = ?$

12. What is the reciprocal of 2.5? Of 0.40?

13. Solve each for X: $X + (7 - 2) = 2X + 4$; $(10X)/5 = 20$.

14. Round 3.42671 to two decimal places. Round it to four decimal places.

15. Another name for the horizontal axis is the _____ axis. Another name for the vertical axis is the _____ axis.

ANSWERS

1. sum; difference; product; quotient
2. $\geq$ greater than or equal to; $\approx$ approximately equal to; $\pm$ add and subtract
3. 19; 15
4. $5\frac{1}{4} = 5.25$; $3\frac{1}{3} = 3.33$
5. 9; 11
6. $|-7| = 7$; $|12| = 12$
7. $5^2 = 25$; $\sqrt{49} = 7$; $3^3 = 27$
8. power; exponent; $2^4 = 16$
9. $6.83 \times 10^{-5} = 0.0000683$; $3.3 \times 10^4 = 33,000$
10. $4/3 = 1.33$; $35/48 = 0.73$
11. $7/3 = 2.33$; $23/20 = 1.15$
12. $1/(2.50) = 0.40$; $1/(0.40) = 2.50$
13. $X = 1$; $X = 10$
14. 3.43; 3.4267
15. X axis; Y axis

NOTES

1. Formally speaking, positive numbers have two square roots, one a positive number and the other a negative. For instance, as presented in the text, one square root of 36 is 6 ($6^2 = 36$). A second square root of 36 is -6 ($-6^2 = 36$). In common usage and as used in this text, square roots are always positive numbers.

2. When the number in the decimal place that follows the place to which we wish to round is 5 and this 5 is followed by an unending string of zeros, special rules for rounding are required. For instance, consider the numbers 25.85000000000000 . . . and 25.7500000000000 . . . . In these numbers, the ellipsis dots (. . .) convey that the string of zeros continues infinitely. Suppose we wish to round these numbers to one (the first) decimal place. Both numbers meet the described condition (i.e., for both numbers, the number in the first decimal place is followed by 5 and an unending string of zeros). When this condition is met, the following rules apply: (1) if the number in the decimal place to which we wish to round is even, round downward, and (2) if this number is an odd number, round upward. In the number 25.850000000000000 . . . , the number in the decimal place to which we wish to round is even (8). Hence, we round downward to 25.8. In 25.750000000000 . . . , this number is odd (7). As such, we round upward, again to 25.8.

Introductory Computer Exercise for SPSS for Windows 10.0

Before you start the tutorial and exercise, consider finding a partner. The exercise goes quicker with one partner reading instructions aloud and the other carrying them out. (In order to carry out the tutorial and exercise, SPSS for Windows Version 10.0 must be installed on your computer. To start SPSS for Windows, click the Start button at the lower left corner of your screen and choose "SPSS for Windows" from the Programs list.)

THE SPSS TUTORIAL

SPSS for Windows Version 10.0 is an excellent and straightforward tool for data analysis. (SPSS used to stand for Statistical Package for the Social Sciences, but the program now seems to identify itself simply by its initials.) The tutorial included with the SPSS software introduces program features. Our exercise here builds on material from the tutorial, so before you proceed you may want to complete the sections of the tutorial marked with an asterisk (*) in the following outline of the tutorial:

    *Before You Start the Tutorial
    Overview
        *Flow chart of basic steps in analysis
        *Windows and Menus
        *Toolbars
        *Dialog boxes
    Getting Data
        *Basic structure of an SPSS data file
        Using the Data Editor
            *Entering numeric data
            *Entering non-numeric data

°Defining data
°Using value labels for data entry
°Copying and pasting variable attributes
°Transforming data values
Creating Tables and Calculating Statistics
°Select a procedure from the menus
°Select variables and options from dialog boxes
°Dialog box recall
°Creating Tables and Calculating Statistics
Working with Output
°Using the Viewer

This outline is from the tutorial's Contents list. You should complete the section marked with asterisks (°). Headings without asterisks are listed to guide you to the sections that you do complete. As the full tutorial covers many key features not presented in the outline above, at some point you may want to complete the tutorial in its entirety. To start the tutorial, choose "Tutorial" from the "Help" menu of SPSS. After starting the tutorial, you will want to click/choose "Contents" within the tutorial and then "expand" all of the headings listed above that do not have asterisks. (To expand a heading, double-click its "book.") To start a tutorial section, double-click its question mark icon. As you proceed through the tutorial, the section that you are working on is presented in the upper left corner of the window/screen. (Sometimes these section names differ slightly from headings used in the Contents.) If you find that you are doing a section not called for above, go to Contents and choose an appropriate section. The marked tutorial sections take about 30 minutes to complete.

An Exercise with SPSS

The exercise in this appendix demonstrates how to enter data and set up a data file for statistical analysis. It also demonstrates how to transform variables, that is, how to modify the values of existing variables and/or create new ones. The exercise takes about 90 minutes to complete. The following conventions are used:

Anything to be typed is **bold and underlined;** notice that the end of the underline here indicates that the punctuation following the phrase is not part of what you type.

Anything to be chosen or clicked is in *italics.* For instance, *OK* signals you to click the box entitled "OK."

Where multiple choices should be made sequentially, the "greater than" symbol (>) indicates this. For instance:

Analyze > Descriptive Statistics > Frequencies

instructs you to choose/click "Analyze," then "Descriptive Statistics," and then "Frequencies."

BACKGROUND AND DEFINING OF DATA

Presume that a questionnaire was administered to eight students, all of whom are either social work or psychology majors. The accompanying questionnaire shows the responses of the first student, Sally.

If the SPSS for Windows program is not open, click its icon to open it or locate it by clicking the "Start" button, choosing "Programs," and finding and clicking SPSS. To begin the exercise, you should be in the SPSS Data Editor window; look at the upper left corner to see if you are in this window. It may be that you are in a box asking you: "What would you like to do?" If so, click the button next to the "Type in data" choice and click *OK* to take you to the Data Editor. If you are somewhere else in the program, click in the toolbar on the Data Editor icon—it looks like a spreadsheet or grid—to go to the Data Editor window.

The exercise will be easier if you do the following: From the menus at the top, click/choose *Edit > Options*. If the "General" tab is not already selected, select it by clicking it. In the right upper space of the dialog box in the "Variable lists" area, look to see that the "Display names" and "Alphabetical" buttons are marked. If so, click *OK*. If not: (1) click as needed so that both of these are marked and (2) click *OK*, (3) observe that the program prompts you that these changes take effect the next time a data file is opened (click *OK* to any such prompts), and (4) in the menus at the top, click/choose *File > New > Data*. (In particular, the "Display names" choice makes the lists of variables that are displayed less cluttered and easier to use.)

The first big step in the exercise is to define the variables that will be entered. This is accomplished in the Variable View window of the Data Editor. So, click the "Variable View" tab to go to that view. The first variable in the survey pertains to the student's name. We need to enter a variety of defining information for that variable.

Name: <u>Sally</u>

Q1. What is your gender?   1 ___ male   2 _✓_ female

Q2. How old are you?   _2_ _7_ years

Q3. What is your major?   1 _✓_ social work   2 ___ psychology

For each of the next three questions, check a response:

	Strongly agree (4)	Agree (3)	Disagree (2)	Strongly disagree (1)
I am stressed to the max.	_____	_____	__✓__	_____
I feel cool as a cucumber.	_____	__✓__	_____	_____
I am totally frazzled.	_____	_____	_____	__✓__

First, we need to give it a "name." In SPSS jargon, a variable's name is termed a "Variable Name." Variable names may be up to eight characters in length, must begin with a letter, and may not have blank spaces in them. With respect to variable names, SPSS does not recognize differences between lowercase and capitalized letters. I have capitalized variable names in this exercise to make them stand out. You may enter variable names in either small or capital letters. SPSS may well change any capital letters that you enter to small letters; don't be concerned if this occurs.

To name the first variable, in the upper left white cell (directly under "Name"), type **STUNAME** and hit the enter key. Often the variable name gives a clue as to what the variable measures or records. In this case, STUNAME is short for "Student's name."

When you entered STUNAME, the SPSS program filled the STUNAME row with various pieces of information called *variable definition attributes.* The variable attributes filled in for STUNAME represent the SPSS program's default values, the values it uses unless instructed otherwise. (Some of these default values can be changed by choosing *Edit > Options > Data,* but we will not do so now.) STUNAME is not a numeric variable (one consisting of numbers) but a nonnumeric one (one with some nonnumeric symbols). The second column, entitled "Type," lets us set STUNAME's "variable type" appropriately. To do so, click the grayed (shaded) space in the cell directly under "Type" to open the "Variable Type" dialog box.

Next, click the button next to "String," which is the SPSS term for a variable composed predominantly of letters. Type **10** in the box next to "Characters," making sure to delete the 8 that is likely in the box. Having entered 10, you may specify student names up to 10 letters long. Click *OK* to exit the dialog box. Since you have set "Characters" to 10, you probably also want to set the number of characters displayed in the Data View to 10. Go over to the first cell in the "Columns" column. Click the cell. Click the up arrow at the right until 10 is displayed, and hit the enter key.

Let's go on to the next variable. The first survey question asks about gender. This will become the second variable in the data set. In the "Name" column in the second row, type **GENDER.** Refer back to Sally's questionnaire and note that for Q1 (the gender question), the numeric code 1 is next to male and the code 2 is next to female. Hence, whenever a respondent is male, a 1 will be entered, and whenever a respondent is female, a 2 will be entered. Given that numbers will be entered, GENDER is a numeric variable. Note that by default the "Type" column correctly displays that GENDER is numeric. Hence, no change is needed. Observe that no decimals will be entered for GENDER. (For instance, for a respondent who is female, you will simply type in 2, not 2.00 or 2.36.) Go to the appropriate cell in the "Decimals" column, click the cell, and click the down arrow at the cell's right until the value in the cell changes to 0. Next, go back to the "Width" column. Given that we will enter only a single digit (a single character), a "variable width" of one is all that is needed. Click the cell and then click the down arrow at the cell's right until the value is set to 1 and then hit the enter key.

Let's give GENDER a variable label by going to the "Labels" column, clicking the appropriate cell, and typing **Student's Gender.** It will also be convenient to have "Value Labels" for GENDER, that is, labels to remind us what the 1s and 2s to be entered represent. Go to the "Values" cell, click the cell, and click the grayed area at its right to open the "Value Labels" dialog box. In the space next to "Value" type **1.** In the space next to "Value Label:" type **male** and click *Add.* In the space next to "Value" type **2.** In the space next to "Value Label:" type **female,** click *Add > OK.* As you will see, these value labels will make reading your output easier and can also help with data entry.

SPSS allows one to specify whether a given variable is nominal, ordinal, or scale in terms of its measurement level. (The "scale" choice corresponds to what this text terms the "interval/ratio level or almost so.") GENDER is a nominal-level variable. Go to the "Measures" column at the far right of the window, click the cell, click the grayed area at the cell's right, select and click *Nominal,* and hit the enter key.

The next survey question pertains to age. We will simply name this variable AGE. So, in the third row in the "Name" column, type **AGE** and hit the enter key. Note that when AGE is entered, the SPSS program fills in the default variable definition attributes for AGE in the AGE row. To keep things simple and to enhance learning as we enter data and examine output, we will not make changes to any of AGE's attributes. Consider, for instance, that a variable label is not needed, as the variable name AGE is self-explanatory. Further, we don't need value labels. The value 2 that will be entered for GENDER has no inherent meaning—without the value label "female," one doesn't know what the 2 conveys. On the other hand, for AGE, values do have inherent meaning. For instance, 23 conveys 23 years and 32 conveys 32 years; we don't need labels to tell us this. Observe the "Measure" column, to see that by default AGE has been correctly designated as a "scale" variable. Note that the "Width" column is set to 8, although a width of 2 would be adequate because only two digits will be entered—32 is the highest age. Extra column width typically causes no problems. Also, note that no decimal places are needed because age is entered only to the year; see the questionnaire. Even so, we will leave the decimal places set at 2.

The next survey question pertains to the student's major. In the fourth row of the "Name" column, type **MAJOR** and hit the enter key. In the "Decimals" column, click the cell and then click the down arrow to set the decimal places to 0. In the appropriate cell in the "Labels" column, type **Student's Major** and hit the enter key. In the "Values" column, click the far right side of the appropriate cell (clicking where the gray area is located saves one click) to open the "Value Labels" dialog box. In the space next to "Value" type **1;** in the space next to "Value label" type **social work,** and click *Add.* In the space next to "Value" type **2,** in the space next to "Value label" type **psychology,** click *Add*, click *OK*. In the "Measures" column, set the measurement type to nominal. (I am presuming that you can do this without specific "clicking" instructions.)

The next three variables are the three items on different aspects of stress. Give the first item a variable name by typing **STRESS** in the appropriate cell and hitting the enter key. To save time, let's not bother to adjust either the variable's width or its decimal places. Similarly, let's not bother to give it a variable label, so leave the cell in the "Labels" column blank. And let's not give it any value labels, so leave the cell in the "Values" column blank. Go to the "Measures" column and set the measurement to "Ordinal."

The second stress-related item states: "I feel cool as a cucumber." Name this variable CUCUMBER by typing **CUCUMBER** in the appropriate cell and hitting the enter key. Go to the "Decimals" column and set decimal places to 0. Go to the width column and set the variable width to 1. Go to the "Measures" column and set the measurement level to "Ordinal." (I am presuming you know how to do all of these without "click-by-click" instruction.) Go to the "Labels" column and type in **Cool as a cucumber** and hit the enter key. Next, go to the "Values" column, click the cell, and then click the grayed area to open the "Value Labels" dialog box. Take a look at Sally's questionnaire to see which values (numbers) go with which value labels. In the space next to "Value" type **1,** in the space next to "Value Label" type **Strongly disagree,** then click *Add*. Using what you have learned so far, you should be able to enter the appropriate value labels for the values 2, 3, and 4. Do so now (check the questionnaire to see which value labels go with which values), and when you have finished, click *OK* to exit the "Value Labels" dialog box.

Now to save some time. Go to the far left column in the sixth row (not counting the row of titles) of the spreadsheet. If you have followed all steps so far, this is the cell with a 6 in it that is just to the left of the cell in which you typed CUCUMBER. Click this cell. When you do so, the entire CUCUMBER row will be highlighted. From menu choices at the top of the window (with the row still highlighted), click *Edit > Copy*. Now go to the cell directly below the just-described cell (to the cell at the far left with a 7) and click this cell to highlight the row. Now go to the menus above and click *Edit > Paste*. This pastes the variable definition attributes of CUCUMBER to a new variable, which SPSS names var00001. You want to give this new variable a more descriptive name than var00001, so click the cell with var00001 in it (clicking it outlines the cell with a thick line). Next, type in **FRAZZLED** and hit the enter key. Also, you do not want to simply use the variable label that has been copied from CUCUMBER, so highlight the appropriate cell in the "Labels" column, delete "Cool as a cucumber," and type in **totally frazzled** and hit the enter key. The other variable attributes, however, do not need to be changed, so you have saved a good deal of time.

You have finished defining your data. To examine your data definitions: From the menus above, choose *Utilities > File Info* and scroll through the output, which is displayed in the SPSS Viewer.

SAVING A FILE

Though you have not yet entered data, you have nevertheless put in a lot of work and might want to save your data file. Having just run the File Info procedure, you are at the Viewer window. It is easiest to save the data file from the Data Editor window. The easiest way to get to this window is to go to the top toolbar and click the Data Editor icon (the icon that looks like a spreadsheet or grid). (Another way to get to the Data Editor is to click the "Untitled - SPSS Data Editor" or similarly named button at the bottom of your screen.) From the Data Entry window, click the Save File icon (the picture of a diskette). You are taken to a "Save Data" dialog box. I recommend naming the file with your initials. Type your initials (or another name) in the space next to "File name" and click *Save*. The data file is saved with the name you gave it. (Or, if you want to save your file on a floppy disk in the A drive and your initials are, for instance, JAR, you would type A:JAR.)

ENTERING DATA

(If you are not in the Data Editor window, go there by clicking the Data Editor icon.) To see another way to get the same information as with File Info, click the Variables icon/button (the one with the question mark symbol), highlight some different variables, and click "Close" to close the dialog box. To enter data, you need to be in the Data View rather than the Variable View. If you are not in the Data View, click the "Data View" tab. For this exercise, data entry will be easiest if the Value Labels icon/button on the toolbar is not pushed in. This is the icon that looks like a diagonal luggage tag. (Click this icon once so that you can determine whether it is pushed in or not. If necessary, click it again so that it is not pushed in.) To enter data for the first case (Sally):

> Place the cursor in the first cell in the STUNAME column and type **Sally,** hit the right arrow key ($\rightarrow$; from here on the text uses this symbol to tell you to hit the right arrow key) so that the cursor moves to the first cell under GENDER, type **2** (to signify female). Now to enter Sally's age: Hit $\rightarrow$ to move to the first cell under AGE and type **27.** To enter Sally's major: Hit $\rightarrow$ (to move to the MAJOR column) and type **1** (to signify social work). Finally, to enter her responses to the three stress-related questions: Hit $\rightarrow$ (to move to the STRESS column) and type **2;** hit $\rightarrow$ (to move to the CUCUMBER column) and type **3;** hit $\rightarrow$ (to move to the FRAZZLED column), type **1** and hit $\rightarrow$. You have finished entering the data for the first case.

Now we are ready for the second student's responses, shown in the accompanying questionnaire for Juan. Position your cursor in the STUNAME column in the row directly underneath that in which you entered the data for the first case. Do the following to begin to enter the data for the second case:

> Type **Juan,** hit $\rightarrow$, type **1,** hit $\rightarrow$, type **20,** hit $\rightarrow$, type **2,** hit $\rightarrow$, type **4,** hit $\rightarrow$

Name: _Juan_

Q1. What is your gender?   1 _✓_ male   2 ___ female

Q2. How old are you?   _2_ _0_ years

Q3. What is your major?   1 ___ social work   2 _✓_ psychology

For each of the next four questions, check a response:

	Strongly agree (4)	Agree (3)	Disagree (2)	Strongly disagree (1)
I am stressed to the max.	✓	___	___	___
I feel cool as a cucumber.	___	___	___	___
I am totally frazzled.	✓	___	___	___

You are now ready to enter the data for CUCUMBER. Observe that, for whatever reason, the respondent (Juan) left this question/item blank. In such an instance, the best approach is usually to enter no data for the given question/item. This can be accomplished by hitting the right arrow (or a tab). So, hit →. Note that the SPSS program inserts a dot, or period, that being the code for "no data." (In the language of SPSS, the variable CUCUMBER is said to be "system missing" for Juan's case.) You are now ready for FRAZZLED: type **4** and then hit →.

Space constraints do not permit display of the questionnaires for the next six students in the data set. Table C.1 displays responses for the two students for whom data has already been entered and for the next six. Your task is to use what you already know to enter the data for the remaining six. Do so now.

Having entered your data, notice that for variables for which you set the number of decimal places to 0, no decimal places are displayed, and for those you left at 2 (the default), two places are displayed. Having the two extra places

---

TABLE C.1

STUNAME	GENDER	AGE	MAJOR	STRESS	CUCUMBER	FRAZZLED
Sally	2	27	1	2	3	1
Juan	1	20	2	4		4
Alberta	2	19	2	2	3	2
Tam	1	33	1	3	2	3
Justin	1	21	2	4	1	4
Shawna	2	19	1	1	3	1
Wayne	1	34	2	3	1	4
Maria	2	22	1	2	4	2

where they are not needed is a minor nuisance but does not affect calculations in any way.

A Clever Way to Enter Data

Just when you thought you were done entering data, you find a questionnaire for a student named Dana, as shown in the accompanying form.

On the toolbar at the top, click the Value Labels icon/button (it looks like a slanted luggage tag). Note that for variables for which value labels were entered, the labels rather than values (numbers) are displayed.

We need to enter Dana's data, so type **Dana** in the appropriate cell and then click the right arrow to move to the GENDER column. Notice that a gray button appears at the right of the cell. Click this button. As Dana is female, highlight and click the "Female" choice to enter this value. Move to the AGE column. No value labels were entered for age, so you must type **26** to enter her age. Move to the MAJOR column. The gray button appears at the right of the cell. Click the button; make sure that "social work" is highlighted and click to enter this value. Move to the STRESS column. We did not define labels for STRESS. So type **4** and move to the CUCUMBER column. Click the button at the right, and highlight and click the "Disagree" choice. Finally, click the far right side of the FRAZZLED cell (note that clicking the cell's far right saves one click) and choose the "Strongly agree" choice. Now you really are done entering data. Click the Value Labels icon a couple of times so that you can observe once again how it affects the display of data.

Having entered your data, you might want to save your data file again. After making sure that you are in the Data Editor window (go there if you are not), go to the toolbar and click the Save File icon (the floppy diskette symbol).

Name: Dana_____

Q1. What is your gender? 1 ___ male   2 _✓_ female

Q2. How old are you? _2_ _6_ years

Q3. What is your major? 1 _✓_ social work   2 ___ psychology

For each of the next four questions, check a response:

	Strongly agree (4)	Agree (3)	Disagree (2)	Strongly disagree (1)
I am stressed to the max.	✓	___	___	___
I feel cool as a cucumber.	___	___	✓	___
I am totally frazzled.	✓	___	___	___

GETTING A FIRST LOOK AT THE DATA

With your data entered, you are ready to analyze it. The basic, workhorse procedure in SPSS for getting an initial look at data is termed "Frequencies," which is selected by choosing *Analyze > Descriptive Statistics > Frequencies*. Having worked your way through the just-listed menu choices, place the cursor on top of the top variable (in most cases, this variable is AGE) in the list of variables in the left part of the dialog box. Depress the clicker and (with the clicker still depressed) move the cursor down through the list to the bottom variable so that all variables are highlighted. Click the right-pointing arrow to move the variables to the "Variables" box on the right side of the dialog box. Click *OK*. SPSS takes you automatically to the Viewer, which presents output. Find the Frequencies table. A first step in assessing one's data is to look for any "bad" values. For instance, if you observed the value 3 in the table for GENDER you would know something was amiss because only 1 (for males) and 2 (for females) are valid. In such a situation, you would return to the data and enter a correct value for the offending case.

Observe that the frequencies tables display the frequency of each response as well as percentages. Labels (such as male/female) rather than values (such as 1, 2) are probably displayed. (Hint you can use later: To change the SPSS default setting so that values (or both labels and values) are displayed, choose *Edit > Options > Output Labels* and make the changes in the "Pivot Tables" area of the dialog box.)

Here are some things to notice:

1. Recall that we did not bother to enter a variable label for AGE. Observe the frequency table for AGE. Note that, in contrast to most of the other frequency tables, this table lists a variable name (AGE) rather than a variable label at the top of the table. Variable labels are optional. Their key purpose is to facilitate interpretation of the output. Also, a variable label often enhances a printed table.

2. Observe the output for the variables AGE and STRESS. No value labels were entered for either of these, so values (numbers) rather than value labels are displayed. Value labels are optional; their main purpose is to facilitate interpretation of the output. Note again that no value labels are needed for AGE because the values are self-explanatory (each value represents age in years). On the other hand, value labels would have simplified interpretation of the STRESS table. (To add value labels for STRESS, you could simply copy and paste those from another variable, for instance, from CUCUMBER.) Value labels also simplify data entry and improve the appearance of tables.

3. Presuming that the SPSS program's defaults have not been reset, observe that the values displayed for AGE and STRESS have two decimal places. Recall that we set "Decimal Places" to 0 for most other variables. To improve the appearance of the output, you might want to do the same for AGE and STRESS. For numeric values, the number of decimal places does not affect the actual values of data but only how they are displayed

in the Data Editor and Viewer windows. (Hint for the future: Choosing *Edit > Options > Data* takes you to a dialog box where you can set the default to 0.)

4. Recall that for the second questionnaire, the variable CUCUMBER was left blank. Observe the frequency table for this variable and note that one case has a "system-missing" value (listed in the "Missing System" row). The SPSS program automatically enters a system-missing value when a field is left blank. A system-missing value is, in essence, the same thing as no value at all. On the other hand, "user-missing" values allow one to indicate that specific values convey missing data. For instance, the value 8 might convey "no opinion" and 9 "not applicable." User-missing values are designated in the "missing" column in the Variable View of the Data Editor.

DATA TRANSFORMATIONS

Most of the prior discussion has addressed data definition and its effect on the output that is generated. Data transformation typically (1) changes the values of existing variables or (2) uses existing variables to create new variables. For instance, AGE is presently a variable at the interval/ratio level (called a scale variable in SPSS). We might wish to display age in a different way, perhaps showing the numbers of students in their teens, 20s, and 30s. This can be accomplished via the "Recode into" procedure:

Make sure that you are in the Data Entry window and then choose *Transform > Recode > Into Different Variables,* highlight AGE, and click it over using the arrow. In the space under "Name," type **AGE3** (this will be the variable name for the newly created variable). In the space under "Label," type **age in three categories** (this is the variable label for AGE3); click *Old and New Values.* On the left side of the "Old and New Values" dialog box, click the button next to the second (middle) listing of "Range" and type **19** in the nearby space. In the space at the upper right corner of the dialog box (making sure that "Value" just to the left of this space is selected), type **1.** Next, click *Add.* You have just instructed the SPSS program to take all values of AGE that are 19 or below and assign to them the new value 1 for the newly created variable AGE3. Next, on the left side of the dialog box, click the button next to the first (top) "Range," and type **20** in the space just to the left of "through" and **29** in the space just to the right. In the upper right side of the box next to "Value," type **2;** click *Add.* You have just assigned the value 2 to ages 20–29. Finally, click the button next to the bottom "Range"; type **30** in the space just below; in the space at the upper right side, type **3,** and click *Add.* All ages 30 and above have now been assigned the value 3. Click *Continue,* click *Change,* click *OK.* The new variable AGE3 has now been added to the data file.

To see the results of your work: Choose *Analyze* > *Descriptive Statistics* > *Frequencies*. Click *Reset* (to clear previous variables away), click AGE3 over into the "Variables" space, click *OK*. Observe results in the Viewer to see that the newly created variable AGE3 takes on the values 1, 2, and 3. Clearly, value labels would help in interpreting the output.

Return to the Data Editor window by clicking the Data Editor icon in the toolbar. If necessary, click the "Variable View" tab. Find the appropriate cell in the "Values" column. Click the cell, then click the grayed area at the cell's right to open the "Value Labels" dialog box. To enter the first value label, type **1** in the space next to "Value," type **16 to 19 years** in the space next to "Value Label," and click *Add*. See if you can enter the value labels for the values 2 and 3. The label for 2 should read something like "20 to 29 years" and that for 3 something like "30 years and older." Exit the "Value Labels" dialog box by clicking *OK*. Go to the "Measures" column and set the measurement level to ordinal. (I presume that you know how to do so.) To see the results of having added the value labels, click the Dialog Recall icon/button on the toolbar (it is just to the right of the printer symbol and has a small triangular red arrow pointing downward at its lower right corner). Having clicked the icon/button, click the *Frequencies* choice that was generated below the icon. This brings up the prior "Frequencies" dialog box as it was used in the previous Frequencies procedure. (The Dialog Recall icon is a shortcut to avoid going through a longer series of menu choices.) With the "Frequencies" dialog box open, click *OK* to run the procedure. Observe that value labels appear in the Viewer output.

The final three items on the questionnaire all pertain to stress/tension. You will use these to build a three-item scale measuring stress/tension. A problem in doing so is that the second item of the three (CUCUMBER) is reverse-scored relative to the first and third items (STRESS and FRAZZLED). That is, the response "strongly agree" (the value 4) conveys high levels of stress/tension for STRESS and FRAZZLED but low levels for CUCUMBER. A first step in building a scale is to reverse the scoring for CUCUMBER so that high scores convey stress/tension rather than relaxation. So, return to the Data Editor and choose *Transform* > *Recode* > *Into Different Variables* to open the "Recode into Different Variables" dialog box. Click *Reset* to clear the dialog box. Click over CUCUMBER using the right-pointing arrow, and click *Old and New Values* to open the "Old and New Values" dialog box. At the top of the left side of the dialog box in the space next to "Value," type **1**; at the top of the right side of the box in the space next to "Value," type **4**, click *Add*. This has recoded all 1s entered for CUCUMBER as 4s. Now you need to repeat the recoding process for the other three values:

> In top left space, type **2**; in top right, type **3**, click *Add*.
> In top left space, type **3**; in top right, type **2**, click *Add*.
> In top left space, type **4**; in top right, type **1**, click *Add*.

Next, click *Continue*. To give the newly created variable a name, type **CUCUMRE** in the space under "Name." To give it a variable label, type **cucumber reverse coded** in the space under "Label." Click *Change* and then click *OK*. You have created a new variable, CUCUMRE, with values that are reverse-scored relative to CUCUMBER. To observe the results of your work, choose *Analyze* >

Descriptive Statistics > Frequencies. (If necessary, click *Reset* to clear variables.) Click over CUCUMRE; click *OK*. Observe that only eight of the nine cases have valid (nonmissing) values for CUCUMRE. This is because CUCUMBER, which was used to create CUCUMRE, had only eight valid values (recall that CUCUM-BER was missing for Juan's case).

The "Recode into Different Variables" is a key data transformation that SPSS provides to create new variables. Another important tool is the "Compute" facility. Given that the "cucumber question" has been recoded, Compute can be used to build a three-item scale. Click the Data Editor icon to go to the Data Editor window. From the menus, choose/click *Transform > Compute* to bring up the "Compute Variable" dialog box. To give the new variable (your three-item scale) a name, type **STRSCALE** in the space under "Target Variable:". Next, (1) highlight STRESS, use the arrow to click it over into the space below "Numeric Expression:", and click the + (plus) symbol on the calculator pad; (2) highlight FRAZ-ZLED, click it over, and click the + symbol; and (3) highlight CUCUMRE and click it over. Read the numeric expression that you have created. It instructs the SPSS program to create a new variable named STRSCAL, the value for which will be calculated (for each case) by summing the values for STRESS, FRAZZLED, and CUCUMRE. Click the "Type and Label" box, type **Stress scale score** in the space next to "Label," and click *Continue* to return to the "Compute Variable" dialog box. Click *OK*. To see the results of your work, run a Frequencies procedure for STRSCALE. (If you need help in running Frequencies, see the instructions in the prior paragraph for doing so with CUCUMRE. You will probably want to click the "Reset" button to clear prior variables from the right side of the dialog box.)

You might note that even though nine cases are in the data set, only eight have valid values for STRSCALE. This is because CUCUMBRE, one of the variables used to create STRSCALE, had only eight such values. (Tracing back to the source, CUCUMRE had only eight valid values because CUCUMBER, used to create CUCUMRE, had only eight.)

SPSS provides many other ways to transform data; check out SPSS "Functions" sometime to learn other methods. (One way to learn about Functions is to right-click some of the functions that appear in the lower right corner of the "Compute Variable" dialog box, the box that you just opened to create STRSCALE.)

Because you have created several new variables, you may want to save the data file again. Return to the Data Editor window by clicking the Data Editor icon, and then click the Save File icon (the diskette). Your updated file, including the new variables created via the data transformations, has been saved.

SELECTING SUBSETS OF CASES FOR ANALYSIS

Another useful feature is "Select Cases," which limits the analysis to cases that possess a given characteristic. For instance, perhaps you are interested in knowing the mean score on STRSCALE of social work majors only. To make this limitation: (1) (if necessary) click the Data Editor icon to return to the Data Editor window, (2) choose/click *Data > Select Cases*, (3) click the button next to "If condition is satisfied" and click *If*, (3) click over MAJOR, click the = sign on the calculator pad, click 1 on the pad. (Pause for a moment and read the expression that you have typed.) Click *Continue*, and (4) verify that under "Unselected Cases Are" the "Filtered" choice is selected and click *OK*. (The choice of "Filtered" rather than "Deleted" makes the Select Cases procedure a temporary rather than a permanent one, a distinct advantage, particularly as one becomes familiar with using SPSS.) Through the Select Cases procedure, you have instructed the computer program to restrict any subsequent analyses to cases where MAJOR equals 1. Recall that the value 1 for MAJOR conveys social work. Go to the Data Entry window, (if necessary) click the "Data View" tab to bring up the Data View, and observe the diagonal slashes in the leftmost column of the Data Editor window. These slashes convey cases that do not meet the Select Cases criteria and thus are excluded from analyses. (In our example, each slash indicates a case where the student is a psychology major.) To see the effect of the Select Cases filter, run a Frequencies procedure for STRSCALE. Results for only five cases appear in the output. These are the cases where MAJOR equals 1, that is, social work students.

Examining Relationships Between Variables

Perhaps now your interest shifts to which student group, psychology majors or social work majors, encounters higher stress levels. Such an analysis requires all cases in the data set. This being the case, you need to turn off the Select Cases facility. Go to the Data Editor window by clicking the Data Entry icon. Choose *Data > Select Cases*. Click the button next to select "All Cases" and click *OK*. Observe that the diagonal slashes are gone. Now all cases are available for analysis. To examine which student group experiences greater stress:

> Choose/click *Analyze > Compare Means > Means;* select STRSCALE and click it over to the space beneath "Dependent List"; select MAJOR and click it over to space beneath "Independent List:"; click *OK*.

The output/viewer window presents mean scores and standard deviations on STRSCALE for social work and psychology majors.

This concludes the introductory exercise. If you want to, you may print your output by (1) verifying that you are indeed in the Viewer (output) window and (2) choosing *File > Print*. To save your output: Make sure that you are in the Viewer window, click the Save File icon, type in a name for your output (for instance, your initials and other brief identifying info), and click *Save*.

Sometime in the future you will want to learn how to fine-tune the tables that SPSS produces and also how to work with Charts. The tutorial sections titled "Using the pivot table editor" (located within the "Working with output" section) and "Creating and editing charts" introduce these skills. By default, most SPSS programs print tables with variable labels rather than variable names and with value labels rather than values in tables. If you want to see both labels and values/names in your output, choose/click *Edit > Options > Output Labels* and in the "Pivot Table Labeling Area" choose/click "Names and Labels."

Description of Variables in Data Set for End-of-Chapter Computer Exercises

Variable Name	Level of Measurement	Description
AGECHIY	Interval/ratio	Child's age at time of survey accurate to the month (with number of months broken down into proportion of a year; for instance: 5 years and 9 months = 5.75)
AGEHOM3	Ordinal	Child's age at entry into adoptive home coded into three categories: 1 = 0 to 3 years, 2 = 4 to 7 years, 3 = 8 to 16 years
AGEHOMEY	Interval/ratio	Child's age in years at entry into adoptive home accurate to the month (with number of months given as proportion of a year; for instance, 4 years and 3 months = 4.25)
AGEHOMYT	Interval/ratio	Child's age in years at entry into adoptive home truncated to prior birthday (e.g., if entered home at $3\frac{1}{2}$, value is 3)
BEHAVTOT	Interval/ratio or almost so[a]	Score on the Child Behavior Checklist (CBCL) of behavior problems, as developed by Achenbach (1991)
BEHCLIN	Nominal	Coded as 1 if BEHAVTOT indicates level of problems in "clinical range" on CBCL, and as 0 if it does not
CHIETH	Nominal	Child's ethnicity coded into one of six categories
EDUCMOM	Ordinal	Adoptive mother's educational level on a 5-point scale where 5 represents highest level of education
EDUCRESP	Ordinal	Respondent's educational level on a 5-point scale where 5 represents highest level of education
ENJOYSCH	Ordinal	Parent's perception of child's opinion regarding school on a 3-point scale (1 = "enjoys," 2 = "neutral," 3 = "dislikes")
EXTERNAL	Interval/ratio or almost so[a]	A scale adapted from CBCL for study that conveys degree of external behavior problems (acting out, aggression, etc.; score conveys mean response to behavior problem questions on which 0 = "not true," 1 = "somewhat or sometimes true," and 2 = "very true or often true")

(continued)

(continued)

Variable Name	Level of Measurement	Description
FADA	Interval/ratio or almost so[a]	FACES III adaptability score (Olson et al., 1985): the higher the score, the greater the perceived flexibility of the family system
FAMETH	Nominal	"Family ethnicity" coded as 1 if minority parents adopt same-race child, 2 if white parents adopt same-race child, 3 if transracial adoption
FAMETH2	Nominal	Same as FAMETH except that transracial adoptions are coded as "missing"
FCOH	Interval/ratio or almost so[a]	FACES III cohesion score (Olson et al., 1985): the higher the score, the greater the perceived closeness of the family
FCOH4	Ordinal	FACES III cohesion score (Olson et al., 1985) coded into 4 categories (1 = disengaged, 2 = separated, 3 = connected, 4 = enmeshed)
FEELCLOS	Ordinal	Parent response on 4-point scale regarding whether they feel close to child (4 = "yes, very much" . . . 1 = "no")
FOSTER	Nominal	Coded as 1 if child was adopted by prior foster parents and as 0 if this was not the case
GENDER	Nominal	Coded 0 if adopted child is male and 1 if female
GETALONG	Ordinal	Parent perception on 4-point scale of how well parent and child get along (4 = "very well" . . . 1 = "very poorly")
HANDICAP	Nominal	Child's vision, hearing, or physical impairment or serious medical condition or mental retardation as reported by parent (1 = handicap, 0 = no handicap)
IMPACT	Ordinal	Parent perception of impact of child's adoption on family on 5-point scale where 5 is most positive response and 1 is least positive
IMPACTD	Nominal	Coded 1 if respondent answered "very positive" regarding impact of child's adoption on family; coded 0 if any other response
INCOMEK	Interval/ratio	Yearly family income at time of survey measured in 1000s of dollars (e.g., $42,000 coded as 42)
INTERNAL	Interval/ratio or almost so[a]	Same as EXTERNAL but measures internal behavior problems (withdrawn, anxious, depressed, etc.)
MINORCHI	Nominal	Coded 0 if child is white, 1 if any other ethnicity (including biracial)
ONEORTWO	Nominal	Coded as 0 if two-parent family at time of adoption and as 1 if a one-parent family at that time
RELSCALE	Interval/ratio or almost so[a]	Score ranging from lowest possible of 1.0 to highest possible of 4.0 on a scale composed of 5 questions pertaining to quality/closeness of parent-child relationship (each question had 4-point response scale, with 4 representing most positive and 1 least so; score on RELSCALE conveys the mean response to each of these 5 questions)

[a]Measurement is close enough to being at the interval/ratio level so that statistics appropriate for this level may be used.

Appropriate Measures for Different Situations

TABLE E.1   **SELECTED UNIVARIATE MEASURES AND BIVARIATE MEASURES OF ASSOCIATION**

BIVARIATE MEASURES OF ASSOCIATION BY TYPE OF SECOND VARIABLE

First Variable Type	Univariate Measures	Dichotomous	Nominal: 3 or More Categories	Ordinal	Interval/Ratio
Dichotomous	Proportion (p) Percentage (%) Ratio Frequency Mode Standard deviation of dichotomous variable (s_{dich})[a] 95% and 99% confidence intervals of the proportion	Difference in percentages ($D\%$) Ratio of percentages ($R\%$) Odds ratio (OR) Phi (r_{phi}) Lambda (λ)[a]	Cramer's V Phi Lambda (λ)[a]	Same procedures apply as in ordinal/ordinal cell below	Standardized difference between means (SDM) Eta (η) Eta squared (η^2) Point-biserial correlation r_{pb}[a]
Nominal: 3 or more categories	Same as above but s_{dich}[a] does not apply	—	Cramer's V Lambda (λ)[a]	Cramer's V Lambda (λ)[a]	Eta (η) Eta squared (η^2)
Ordinal	Same as above and also: Cumulative frequency Cumulative percentage Percentile rank Median	—	—	If relationship is directional: Spearman's r (r_{ranks}) Kendall's tau$_b$ (τ_b) Kendall's tau$_c$ (τ_c) Gamma (γ) Somer's d If nondirectional: Cramer's V Lambda (λ)[a]	No measures presented for this combination. Measures in cell directly above sometimes best choice; those in cell below sometimes best choice.
Interval/ratio	Same as above and: Mean ($\overline{X}$) Mean deviation Standard deviation (s) Variance (s^2) Range Interquartile range 95% and 99% confidence intervals of the mean	—	—	—	Pearson's r (r) (in bivariate situation, r is the standardized regression coefficient) Standardized regression coefficient (β) Unstandardized regression coefficient (B) Coefficient of determination (r^2)

[a] Procedure discussed only briefly in this text.

480

BIVARIATE TESTS BY TYPE OF SECOND VARIABLE

First Variable Type	Univariate Tests	Dichotomous	Nominal: 3 or More Categories	Ordinal	Interval/Ratio
Dichotomous	One-sample test of the proportion (p) Binomial test[a] (One-variable χ^2 test is an alternative to one-sample test of p)	Chi-square (χ^2) test of independence Fisher's exact test[a] z test of a difference in proportions[a]	Chi-square (χ^2) test of independence	Independent samples: Mann-Whitney U test Kolmogorov-Smirnov test Dependent samples: Sign test Wilcoxon test Tests in ordinal/ordinal cell below	Independent samples t test (or ANOVA) Dependent samples t test
Nominal: 3 or more categories	One-variable chi-square (χ^2) test	—	Chi-square (χ^2) test of independence	Kruskal-Wallis test (independent samples) Friedman test (dependent samples) χ^2 test of independence	Analysis of variance (ANOVA) Multiple comparison procedures
Ordinal	None presented One-variable χ^2 test can be appropriate	—	—	Directional relationship: test of: Spearman's r (r_{ranks}) Kendall's tau$_b$ (τ_b) Kendall's tau$_c$ (τ_c) Gamma (γ) Somer's d Nondirectional relationship: χ^2 test of independence	ANOVA is often appropriate (in particular, with linear polynomial contrast[a])
Interval/ratio	Large sample test of the mean ($\overline{X}$) One-sample t test	—	—	—	Pearson's r (r) In multiple regression analysis, tests of unstandardized (B) and standardized (β) coefficients

[a]Procedure discussed only briefly in this text.

Answers to End-of-Chapter Problems and Questions

Chapter 1

1. theory, research
2. data
3. quantitative, qualitative
4. numerical summary
5. F
6. case
7. variables
8. values
9. female and male
10. constants
11. concepts, variables
12. quantitative, qualitative
13. quantitative
14. qualitative
15. categorical
16. discrete
17. continuous
18. a. continuous   b. discrete   c. discrete
    d. discrete   e. continuous
19. dichotomous
20. nominal, ordinal, interval, ratio
21. classify/group, order, differences/intervals, ratios
22. ordinal
23. true, absence
24. You cannot form ratios ("twice as . . .") with a scale whose zero point does not convey the absence of the quantity being measured.

25. a. interval   b. ordinal   c. ratio   d. nominal
    e. ordinal   f. nominal
26. highest
27. T
28. F
29. F
30. T
31. univariate, bivariate, multivariate
32. vary, differ, change
33. association, associated
34. size, strength
35. causal
36. confounding
37. For instance, suppose that kids placed in group homes are less likely than kids placed in family foster homes to return to their birth homes. This may be so not because group homes are less effective than foster homes but instead because kids placed in group homes tend to have more difficult problems than those placed in foster homes.
38. experiments, surveys
39. intervention or treatment
40. population, sample, some, all
41. probability, nonprobability
42. random
43. a. probability   b. nonprobability   c. nonprobability

44. Social workers may well tend to remember clients who do particularly well in services. Hence, client opinions in the sample would tend to be more positive than those in the full population that received services.
45. biased
46. small
47. descriptive, inferential
48. estimates, decisions
49. random assignment or randomization
50. T
51. F
52. F
53. T
54. how likely it is that a study result is due simply to chance
55. T
56. the degree to which similar results are expected in a different setting or context

Chapter 2

1. a. $N = 120$ b. $f = 40$ c. $n = 40$ d. $p = .33$ e. 33% f. 8 to 5 or 1.6 to 1 g. 5 to 8 or .625 to 1
2. distribution, empirical, theoretical
3.

Concentration	f	%
Children and family	25	21
Mental health	40	33
Health	20	17
Community development	35	29

4. a. 9 b. 45 c. 12 d. 60
5. A case that has no value for the variable in question
6. Percentages in Percentage column are based on all cases; those in Valid Percentage column are based only on nonmissing cases.
7.

Stem	Leaf
4	2448
5	125556
6	489
7	12

8. a. 10.4 b. 10.4 or, rounded, 10 c. 10.4 or, rounded, 10 d. 742
9. 62.7 or 63
10. a. 37 b. 41 c. 44

11. tables, figures
12. line, bar
13. a. nominal b. bar chart c. No. There is no ordering to the values, and having the bars not touching reinforces the separateness of the values.
14. a. ordinal b. histogram c. Yes. Values naturally "flow" into each other.
16. T
17. A histogram is preferred when the number of different values is limited (say, seven or fewer). A frequency polygon is preferred when many different values must be presented.
18. a. 28%, 50%, and 22% b. 28%
19. a.

CONCENTRATION CHOICES

Concentration	WOMEN f	WOMEN %	MEN f	MEN %
Children and family	20	25	5	12
Mental health	25	31	15	38
Health	15	19	5	12
Community development	20	25	15	38

b. No, women are more likely than men to select children and family services and health services. Men are more likely than women to select the other two.
c. Yes, they are related. The percentages selecting the various concentrations differ for men and women (differ according to categories of gender).
20. Tinker with frequencies/percentages presented in (usually) the vertical axis. Change ratio of horizontal axis to vertical axis.
21. F
22. When relatively small differences are deemed important and would be obscured if 0 and 100 were used
23. 4 to 3

Chapter 3

1. central tendency, variability, shape of distribution
2. typical, cluster/converge, dispersed/spread out, pattern
3. mode, median, mean

4. frequency, greater/higher, less/lower, sum, number
5. a. mode = 2   b. median = 4   c. $\bar{X}$ = 7
6. bimodal
7. at all levels
8. ordinal
9. With nominal-level measurement, there is no median value.
10. a. 4, 6, 7, 8, 9   b. 7   c. 7
11. a. 8, 9, 11, 14, 15, 16   b. 11, 14   c. 12.5
    d. 12.5
12. a. 53.4   b. 41   c. 41
13. a. poor, 9; fair, 30; good, 73; excellent, 100
    b. 73   c. good   d. good
14. a. −2   b. 3   c. 0   d. 2.5
15. sum, absolute
16. mean
17. F
18. interval/ratio
19. mean
20. squared
21. 21.4
22. mean
23. a. outlier or extreme value   b. median   c. median = 11.5   d. positive/upward   e. 23 is not a typical and common value.
24. T
25. very easy to interpret and understand
26. Particularly for small samples it tends to jump around due to luck.
27. upward/higher/in a positive direction; downward/lower/in a negative direction

Chapter 4

1. spread/dispersion
2. central tendency
3. Set a (the first set) has greater variability.
4. F
5. Sample A
6. Gender has the same degree of variability in each sample.
7. F
8. Sample A
9. Difference between the highest value and the lowest
10. 7
11. increase
12. F

13. measure of the difference between the score at the 25th percentile and that at the 75th percentile
14. Subtract the mean from each score. Take the absolute values. Sum. Divide by N.
15. mean deviation = 2.67
16. F
17. T
18. Subtract the mean from each score. Square. Sum. Divide by $N - 1$. Take the square root.
19. a. underestimate
20. biased
21. s = 3.00
22. s = 3.29
23. the formula with $N - 1$ in the denominator
24. c. negligible bias
25. has no effect on standard deviation
26. s = 1.58
27. s = 1.58
28. s = 1.58 × 4 = 6.32
29. s of 11, 11.5, 12, 12.5, 13 is 0.79
30. s = 2.29
31. the average squared deviation score around the sample mean
32. square root
33. squared
34. underestimate
35. unbiased
36. s^2 = 2.5
37. s^2 = 5.25
38. a. s_{samp} b. s c. s^2_{samp} d. s^2
39. T
40. minimum (lowest) score, score at about 25th percentile, median, score at about 75th percentile, maximum (highest) score
42. whiskers
43. F

Chapter 5

1. pattern
2. F
3. T
4. F
5. bell
6. F (It has an infinite number.)
7. F (They have identical values.)
8. 68%

9. symmetrical or symmetric
10. 95%
11. about 0.25%
12. 95%
13. normality
14. tails
15. lower or negative
16. symmetry
17. b. upper (positive)
18. right/positive/upper
19. T
20. positively
21. negative
22. outlier
23. mean
24. F
25. negative/leftward
26. T
27. peakedness
28. T
29. b. platykurtic
30. T
31. b. platykurtic (Frequencies of age are likely to be distributed quite evenly as fairly equal numbers of students are likely in each grade.)
32. Perhaps scores on a math test that requires one to master a single key concept. Those who do master the concept get good scores (a "high" mode). Those who don't get poor scores ("low" mode).
33. a. 34%   b. 34%   c. 47.7%   d. 49.87%
34. a. 16   b. 84   c. 2   d. 99.9
35. a. 84   b. 16   c. 2
36. a. 4.6   b. 32   c. 0.26
37. Cannot be determined. With the information provided in the text, percentages can only be determined for the normal distribution.
38. standard
39. The number of standard deviation units a score is above or below the mean.
40. Subtract the mean from a score and then divide by the standard deviation.
41. $z = -1.5$
42. T
43. $\bar{X} = 0.00$
44. $s = 1.00$
45. $z = 0.30$

46. a. Ann, $z = 2.0$ b. Shawn, $z = 0.0$ c. Ramon, $z = 0.33$ d. Alice, $z = -0.75$
47. raw
48. F (shape stays the same)
49. Test 2
50. Test 1, $z = -0.5$; Test 2, $z = 0.2$
51. F, may be calculated on any variable that is at the interval/ratio level of measurement
52. a. .14   b. .38   c. .46
53. a. 50   b. 99   c. 21
54. .21
55. .42
56. a. below the mean
57. The raw scores of tangible, familiar variables make intuitive sense to us. This is not the case for most intangible, abstract variables. Once one comes to understand z scores, then the size of a given z score for an abstract variable takes on intuitive meaning.

Chapter 6

1. related/associated
2. a. R   b. R   c. R   d. U   e. R   f. I   g. I   h. R   i. U   j. R
3. T
4. F
5. F
6. readmitted vs. not readmitted
7. Program 1 vs. Program 2
8. Program 1 vs. Program 2
9. 160
10. 100
11. 60
12. cells
13. margins
14. 20
15. T
16. 33%
17. 40%
18. F
19. T
20. T
21. F
22. T
23. Those in Program 2 are less likely to be readmitted than those in Program 1. Those in 1 are more likely to be readmitted than those in 2.

Those in 1 are less likely not to be readmitted than those in 2. Those in 2 are more likely not to be readmitted than those in 1.

24. T
25. F (Whenever column percentages differ, so will row percentages.)
26. F
27. T
28. The degree to which values of two variables vary or change together
29. $D\% = 25\%$
30. F
31. T
32. $D\% = 7\%$
33. T
34. $D\% = 31\%$
35. F
36. T
37. F
38. a. small/weak
39. F (Most would characterize this as a very strong association.)
40. T
41. $R\% = 4.0$, or 4 to 1
42. $R\% = 2.5$, or 2.5 to 1
43. F (It is preferred where percentages are reasonably close to 0%.)
44. No, percentages are not close to 0 or to 100.
45. No, one should use those percentages close to 0 rather than those close to 100. So one should examine unsuccessful rather than successful outcomes in calculating $R\%$.
46. $R\% = 2.0$
47. T (Because it is calculated using percentages that are close to 0 rather than those close to 100, and because the result is greater than 1.0)

Chapter 7

1. odds are 3.00, or 3 to 1
2. odds are 0.33, or 1 to 3
3. cannot be calculated; need odds for two groups to be able to calculate an odds ratio
4. odds = 1.00
5. positive infinity
6. 0.00
7. odds = 0.33, or 1 to 3
8. odds = 5 to 3, or 1.67

9. $OR = 5.00$
10. five times greater
11. Those with high skills are five times more likely to find jobs than are those with low skills.
12. $OR = 0.2$
13. Those with high skills are one-fifth as likely to find jobs as are those with low skills. Or one could say: Those with low skills are five times less likely to find jobs than are those with high skills.
14. They are reciprocals.
15. $OR = 3.00$
16. $OR = 0.29$
17. $OR = 3.50$
18. a. reciprocal of 4 = 0.25   b. reciprocal of 0.25 = 4   c. reciprocal of 8 = 0.125   d. reciprocal of 0.125 = 8
19. Each conveys the same strength of association.
20. T
21. A calculation error was made; the odds ratio must be 0.00 or greater.
22. F
23. T
24. a. 12, very large   b. 0.20, large   c. 5, large   d. 0.70, small   e. 0.08, very large   f. 2.5, medium
25. F
26. d, may be applied in all of the above
27. F
28. T
29. collapsed
30. F
31. T
32. T
33. direction
34. ordinal
35. associated
36. yes
37. directional
38. positive [As political self-characterization increases (changes from conservative to moderate to liberal), degree of support for legislation Q also increases.]
39. F (It is the preferred measure for categorical variables that do not have a directional relationship.)
40. F

Chapter 8

1. linear
2. F
3. Pearson, r
4. positively
5. negatively
6. negatively
7. T
8. Multiply the z scores for each case together, sum, and divide by $N - 1$.
9. negatively
10. (Answers to a to c are listed in order that students are presented in table.)
    a. $-0.112, 1.006, -0.671, 1.006, -1.230$
    b. $-0.614, 0.153, 0.920, 0.920, -1.381$
    c. $0.07, 0.15, -0.62, 0.93, 1.70$
    d. 2.23
    e. $r = .56$
11. -1.00 to 1.00
12. perfect
13. straight line
14. random scattering, not unlike "buckshot" pattern from a shotgun
15. F (The statement is not always true; for instance, an r of $-.2$ is greater than an r of $-.4$ but conveys a weaker association.)
16. T
17. F
18. a. $.66$ b. $.66$ c. $-.7$ d. $-.92$
19. a. $r = .47$, strong or large   b. $r = -.32$, moderate or medium   c. $r = .82$, very strong or very large   d. $r = -.11$, weak or small
20. trick question; can be no such correlation
21. standardized
22. Predicted z score on Y equals z score on X times the correlation between X and Y.
23. decrease, $.7$
24. a. $z_y = .12$ b. $z_y = -.12$ c. $z_y = 2.00$
25. $-.30$
26. F
27. a. $r^2 = .16$ b. $r^2 = .01$ c. $r^2 = .49$ d. $r^2 = .25$
28. determination
29. variance, dependent, explained, independent
30. 25%
31. F
32. T

33. F (Consider the possibility of curvilinear association.)
34. F
35. T
36. T
37. F
38. reduces
39. b, Greater than $.10$
40. constant, or Y intercept
41. B is an unstandardized coefficient; r is a standardized coefficient
42. B is the predicted change in Y as X increases by one; or, alternatively, it is the slope of the regression line.
43. least-squares, best fit
44. sum of squares
45. a. $A = 3$ b. $B = 2.5$ c. slope $= 2.5$
    d. $\hat{Y}$ increases by 2.5 e. $\hat{Y} = 13$ f. $\hat{Y} = 3$
    g. $\hat{Y} = -7$ h. $\hat{Y} = -7$ i. 12.5 points higher
46. Regression coefficients allow direct interpretation of familiar variables. With intangible variables, correlation allows interpretation with reference to standard deviations; without such reference, any semblance of real-world meaning is difficult to derive.
47. T
48. phi (r_{phi})
49. F
50. Spearman's r, r_{ranks}

Chapter 9

1. Subtract the mean of the second group from that of the first and then divide by the standard deviation.
2. a. $SDM = -2.0$ b. $SDM = 2.0$ c. $SDM = -1.0$ d. $SDM = -3.0$
3. a. large/strong   b. large/strong   c. very large/very strong   d. between weak and moderate   e. medium or moderate
4. T
5. F
6. 90%
7. F
8. No, the standard deviations differ too greatly.
9. a. $s_{wg} \approx 10.00$ b. $s_{wg} \approx 11.00$ c. $s_{wg} \approx 7.00$
10. $SDM \approx 0.73$
11. $s_{wg} \approx 9.263$, $SDM \approx 0.65$

12. F

13. variance

14. 0.00 to 1.00

15. a. strong   b. moderate   c. moderate to strong
    d. weak   e. no such η^2; trick question

16. T

17. b, size of directional association

18. −1.00, 1.00

19. F

20. a. very strong, positive   b. weak, negative
    c. moderate, negative

Chapter 10

1. to affect, influence, lead to, explain, etc.

2. F

3. F

4. a. T   b. T   c. T

5. lurking variable, extraneous variable, control
   variable, nuisance variable

6. manipulates, controls

7. T

8. random assignment/randomization

9. quasi

10. a. No   b. Yes   c. No   d. Yes

11. F

12. T

13. T

14. causal model or path diagram

15. that one variable (directly) affects another

16. that two variables are related but that the cause
    of their relationship is unclear

17. direct

18. antecedent

19. F

20. F

21.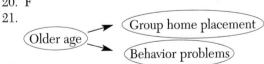

22. intervening

23. F

24. T

25. F

26. F

27. T

28. F

29. T

30. general confounding variable

31. F

32. F

33. Do not know; may or may not be the case.

34. Do not know; may or may not be the case.

35. A causes B; B causes A; an antecedent (unpictured) variable affects both A and B.

36. Depression causes people to seek therapy.

37. feedback model

38. (More than one answer and model can be correct for these.)

a. Presumably those with academic or social problems are more likely to be assigned mentors than are those without such problems. These same problems presumably lead also to lower graduation rates. An antecedent variable model with academic/social problems as an antecedent variable leading to both lower graduation rates and mentoring could explain the observed results.

b. Presumably highly intelligent kids are attracted to playing chess. An antecedent variable model with intelligence as an antecedent variable that leads to both chess playing and higher test scores could explain the observed results.

c. In the absence of random assignment, it may simply be the case that those served in the community program had less serious problems than did those served in the transition house. A general confounding variable model could be used to explain these results. Such a model would connect "fewer problems" and "community program" via a curved arrow and would have a straight arrow (direct effect) from "fewer problems" to "lower recidivism."

d. In the absence of random assignment, it may simply be the case that children placed via Program B have more traumatic backgrounds. One could build an antecedent variable model in which "traumatic background" is an antecedent variable with direct effects on both program placed in (A versus B) and risk for disruption.

Chapter 11

1. constant
2. F
3. constant
4. T
5. d, All of the above
6. disappeared
7. c, Disappears
8. T
9. antecedent
10. disappear
11. spurious
12. e, All of the above
13. intervening
14. disappear
15. c, A has an indirect effect on C
16. a, no direct effect of A on B or B on A
17. F
18. T
19. T
20. *Study 1:* No.   *Study 2:* Yes. Among men, readmission rate higher in traditional treatment than in community treatment. Among women, readmission rate higher in community treatment than in traditional treatment.   *Study 3:* No.   *Study 4:* Yes. For men, readmission rate is equal for both treatments. For women, readmission rate is higher in traditional treatment.

Chapter 12

1. populations, samples, randomly, populations
2. formal, chance
3. a. No   b. No   c. Yes   d. Yes
4. T
5. The selection of each case should be independent from that of each other case.
6. a. Yes   b. No   c. No
7. Characteristics of a sample are similar to those of the population.
8. F
9. F (The correct answer of false presumes that all persons randomly selected to participate in the study do indeed participate. Stated differently, it assumes a 100% response rate. See Chapter 13, Section 13.4, for discussion of how nonresponse can affect representativeness.)

10. b, There is often reason to suspect bias.
11. Probably not representative though one can't be positive; presumably the members of the sample (Young Republicans) as a group are less supportive of public welfare programs than is the full university population.
12. c, May not be representative due to the luck of the draw
13. Cases do not share a common, unmeasured factor that makes their scores similar.
14. dependent, dependency
15. Possible answer: Cliques of therapy group members spend extensive time together and thereby become more similar in areas that are being studied.
16. Possible answer: Students copy answers from one another.
17. statistics, parameters
18. estimator, inferential statistic
19. Roman, Greek
20. efficiency, unbiasedness
21. minimum
22. overestimate, underestimate
23. a. $\overline{X}$ and μ b. s and σ c. s^2 and σ^2 d. p and π
24. a. $\overline{X}$ is unbiased   b. s is biased   c. s^2 is unbiased   d. p is unbiased
25. $\mu = 10$, $\sigma = 6$
26. $\mu = 10$, $\sigma = 6$
27. trick question; cannot estimate characteristics of a population based on a sample selected from a different population
28. $\pi = .28$
29. $\pi = .25$
30. point estimate
31. interval estimate
32. sampling error
33. 2
34. Distribution of a statistic that results from selecting a random sample of fixed size an infinite number of times.
35. statistics
36. A frequency distribution of the mean of an infinite number of samples (all of the same size), all randomly selected from the same population.

37. Mean = mean in population. Standard deviation = standard deviation in population divided by $\sqrt{N}$. Approaches normality as sample size increases.
38. standard error of the mean, $\sigma_{\bar{X}}$
39. normal
40. Example 1: $\bar{X} = 25$, $\sigma_{\bar{X}} = 1.0$, close to normal
    Example 2: $\bar{X} = 25$, $\sigma_{\bar{X}} = 0.5$, close to normal
    Example 3: $\bar{X} = 25$, $\sigma_{\bar{X}} = 2.5$, cannot be sure; cannot be assumed to be close to normal as sample size is less than 100
    Example 4: $\bar{X} = 25$, $\sigma_{\bar{X}} = 2.5$, close to normal
    Example 5: $\bar{X} = 40$, $\sigma_{\bar{X}} = 1.0$, close to normal
41. a. 68   b. 95   c. 99.74
42. decreases
43. T
44. F

Chapter 13

1. confidence interval
2. range within which one is confident that the population parameter is located
3. 95% confidence interval, confident
4. F (not always)
5. T
6. F (not always)
7. T
8. T
9. 95% confidence interval of the mean
10. s
11. $s_{\bar{X}} = s/\sqrt{N}$
12. Take standard deviation in sample and divide by $\sqrt{N}$. Multiply by about 2. Add and subtract from the sample mean.
13. 1.96
14. #1, 48.04 to 51.96;   #2, 46.08 to 53.92; #3, 48.04 to 51.96;   #4, 49.02 to 50.98; #5, sample size too small for accurate calculation with the provided formulas
15. decreases
16. 95%
17. 99% confidence interval, confident
18. #2, 44.84 to 55.16,   #3, 47.42 to 52.58, #4, 48.71 to 51.29
19. narrower
20. wider
21. 99%

22. Mean is population proportion, π. Standard deviation, σ_p, is $\sqrt{\pi(1 - \pi)/N}$. Shape approaches normality as sample size increases.
23. Multiply population proportion by $(1 - $ population proportion$)$. Divide by N. Take the square root.
24. a. 180   b. 1200   c. 13   d. 60   e. 440
25. a. $\sigma_p = .069$ b. $\sigma_p = .069$ c. $\sigma_p = .049$
26. p, sample
27. s_p
28. a. $s_p = .069$ b. $s_p = .069$ c. $s_p = .049$
29. Yes in all three situations
30. a. .264 to .536   b. .464 to .736   c. .504 to .696
31. a. .221 to .579   b. .421 to .779   c. .474 to .726
32. F
33. T
34. F

Chapter 14

1. hypothesis test
2. number of events with characteristic divided by total number of events
3. 0.00 to 1.00
4. .40
5. Probability is symbolized by p, and proportion is symbolized by p.
6. a. .50   b. .68   c. .16
7. null, research, alternative, opposite
8. hypothesis pair
9. F
10. F
11. percentages
12. means
13. correlation, 0.00
14. false
15. F
16. equal, not equal
17. directional, greater than, less than
18. a. directional   b. nondirectional c. nondirectional   d. directional
19. (Answers will vary.)
20. (Answers will vary.)
21. (Answers will vary.)
22. T

23. research, null
24. T
25. F
26. sampling error (or, one may say, chance)
27. association
28. F
29. T
30. rejects, null, research
31. null, rejects, research
32. null
33. rejected, accepted
34. statistical significance level
35. alpha, α
36. $\alpha = .05$ when .05 level is used, $\alpha = .01$ when .01 level is used
37. .05, less than, equal to .05
38. d
39. .01, less than, equal to .01
40. F
41. statistically significant
42. F
43. Yes
44. No
45. 95, 99
46. sampling error; chance; null; true
47. F
48. T
49. a. F   b. T   c. F   d. F   e. T   f. T   g. T   h. T   i. T [Given a true null, the probability that chance alone could be the explanation for the study result is .48 (48 in 100). Hence, chance is a plausible explanation.]   j. F (Since chance is a plausible explanation for the result, one cannot be confident that the null is false.)
50. a. T   b. F   c. T   d. T   e. F   f. T   g. T   h. T   i. F [Given a true null, the probability that these results are due to chance alone is .002 (2 in 1000). Hence, chance alone is a highly unlikely explanation for the study result.]   j. T (As chance alone is a highly unlikely explanation, one can be confident that the null is false.)
51. null
52. T
53. F
54. T

55. fail to reject the null
56. a. not valid   b. valid   c. not valid   d. valid   e. not valid

Chapter 15

1. State hypothesis pair. Choose significance level. Carry out test. Make decision.
2. A requirement that must be met for a significance test to yield precisely accurate results
3. robust
4. Normal distribution (normality) in the population, and that the population standard deviation is known
5. robust
6. random sampling, independence of observations
7. H_0, H_1
8. $\mu = 10$, $s_{\bar{X}} = 0.5$, shape is close to normal
9. a. $p = .5$ b. $p = .16$ c. $p = .16$ d. $p = .32$
10. Yes. When the null is true, and considering both sides of the sampling distribution, results this extreme occur about 32% of the time.
11. No. This sample mean is three standard deviations above the mean of the sampling distribution. Given a true null, chances of obtaining such a mean are extremely small.
12. probability, extreme, extreme
13. 17%
14. two
15. F
16. directional, research
17. rejection or critical
18. $p = .05, p = .01$
19. two
20. alpha, or stated differently, to the probability associated with the chosen significance level
21. reject, accept
22. fail to reject, accept, reject
23. a. nondirectional   b. $\bar{X} = 25$, s is extremely close to 1.00, shape is extremely close to normal   c. $z = -1.60$ d. $p = .055$ e. $p = .11$ f. two-tailed   g. $p = .11$ h. greater than   i. .025 in each area   j. no   k. accept (fail to reject) the null, reject the research   l. $p = .11$

24. Fail to reject (accept) null when absolute value of obtained z is <1.96. Reject null when this is ≥ 1.96.
25. test statistic, or obtained statistic
26. T
27. Mean is 0.00, standard deviation is 1.00, shape is extremely close to normal (When the population is normally distributed, the shape of the sampling distribution would be precisely normal.)
28. critical
29. sampling error, or chance
30. F
31. F
32. T
33. a. two b. 2.64 c. reject the null d. reject the null e. F
34. a. T b. T
35. type I, false
36. α, the probability associated with the significance level
37. 10 errors
38. F
39. T
40. null, false
41. beta, β
42. T
43. T
44. F
45. fail to reject (accept) the null if $z < 1.645$; reject the null if $z \geq 1.645$
46. $p = .05$
47. a. directional b. one c. Yes d. $z = 1.70$ e. proportion is .044 f. $p = .044$ g. reject the null, accept the research h. accept (fail to reject) the null, reject the research i. accept (fail to reject) the null, reject the research
48. a. $z = -3.00$ b. .0013 c. .0026 d. one-tailed e. upper f. unexpected g. accept (fail to reject) the null h. When the result is in the unexpected direction (the direction in the null), one does not reject the null even when the study result is located in the extreme tail of the sampling distribution. Had the test been two-tailed, the null would have been soundly rejected. From a commonsense perspective, it is clear that $\mu \neq 50$.

Chapter 16

1. probability, false null, true research
2. 1.00
3. .70
4. type II
5. T
6. sample size
7. low/poor, high/good
8. decreases
9. a. $s_{\overline{X}} = 4$, about 8 b. $s_{\overline{X}} = 2$, about 4 c. $s_{\overline{X}} = 1$, about 2
10. T
11. T
12. F
13. T
14. T
15. F
16. F
17. B; low variability of dependent variable in A will almost certainly result in low power
18. T
19. F
20. .80
21. 80%
22. a. low/poor b. fair/moderate c. exceptional/extremely high d. excellent/very high
23. F
24. T
25. T
26. The probability resulting from the test. More specifically, (1) the probability of obtaining the study sample result given a true null and (2) the probability that the study sample result is due to chance alone.
27. Yes
28. No
29. a. F b. F c. F d. F
30. fail to reject the null
31. F

Chapter 17

1. F
2. greater, leptokurtic or peaked, thick/heavy, elongated
3. F
4. T
5. t score

6. F
7. T
8. number of independent values after mathematical restrictions have been applied
9. $N - 1$
10. $df = 49$
11. family
12. a. F b. F c. T d. T e. F f. T g. T
13. a. Assume a true null, pick an infinite number of random samples from population and, for each, carry out the formula for t and record t.
    b. F c. T d. T e. moderate skew, about 15; strong skew, about 30
14. t, normal
15. a. $df = 48$, $s_{\overline{X}} = 3$, 95%CI of $\mu = 33.94$ to 46.06
    b. $df = 24$, $s_{\overline{X}} = 6$, 95%CI of $\mu = 47.62$ to 72.38
    c. $df = 8$, $s_{\overline{X}} = 7$, sample size not adequate for accurate calculation of confidence interval
16. 99%CI of $\mu = 43.22$ to 76.78
17. normally, robust
18. F
19. T
20. F
21. a. The population mean does not equal 80.0.
    b. one-sample t test c. yes d. nondirectional e. two-tailed f. $df = 35$ g. 2.030 and -2.030 h. $s_{\overline{X}} = 3$ i. $t = 3.00$ j. reject the null, accept the alternative/research k. no l. T m. yes n. greater than
22. a. The population mean is less than 60.0.
    b. one-sample t test c. yes d. directional e. one-tailed f. $df = 63$ g. -1.671 h. $s_{\overline{X}} = 2.00$, i. $t = -1.50$ j. fail to reject (accept) the null, reject the research k. One cannot say that it is likely that null is true; one can say that this is plausible or, alternatively, that this is not unlikely. l. F m. no n. You were not asked to respond to question n because it has not been covered explicitly and because it is a tricky one. Formally, the correct answer would be "less than," because the study sample mean provides the best estimate of the population mean. On the other hand, as the null is accepted, the data do not provide sufficient reason for concluding that μ does not

equal the value stated in the null (60). Viewed from this perspective, the best answer would probably be "neither."
23. F

Chapter 18

1. difference, means
2. Randomly select a sample of a given size from a first population and compute $\overline{X}$. Do the same for a second population. Subtract $\overline{X}_2$ from $\overline{X}_2$. Repeat an infinite number of times, each time recording the difference.
3. $\sigma_{\overline{X}_1 - \overline{X}_2}$
4. a. $\mu_1 - \mu_2 = \mu = -10$ b. $\sigma_{\overline{X}_1 - \overline{X}_2} = 2.83$
    c. shape is approximately normal
5. T
6. $\mu_1 = \mu_2$
7. normally, robust
8. F
9. T
10. equal/the same, unequal
11. F
12. equality of variances test (or homogeneity of variances test)
13. $\sigma_1^2 = \sigma_2^2$
14. unequal
15. F
16. when sample sizes are both small and unequal and sample variances differ more than modestly
17. F
18. F
19. a. independent samples t test b. Means are equal in the populations from which samples were randomly selected. c. yes d. In effect they are neither but instead are the full population of 50 clients who are identified for the study. In a sense, there was no sampling process. e. imaginary f. T g. Random assignment in effect eliminates confounding variables and thus greatly enhances our confidence that study results are causal (rather than due to confounding variables). h. SDM is about 1.0 i. Technically the equal variances formula should be used but, given that sample sizes are equal, the two formulas result in identical values of t. Because it simplifies calculation, the unequal variances formula is

preferred if one is calculating t by hand. j. $s_{\bar{X}_1-\bar{X}_2} = 3.12$ k. $t = -3.52$ l. equal variances formula   m. $df = n_1 + n_2 - 2$; $df = 48$ n. 2.021 and -2.021 o. ≤ -2.021 or ≥ 2.021 p. reject the null; accept the research   q. unlikely   r. T   s. T; technically this conclusion is correct   t. Most would say no as the described population is abstract/imaginary. u. T   v. Most would say yes, because it applies to the study sample which is indeed composed of real people.   w. F (The random assignment process enables us to be confident that a confounding variable is not the cause of the result.)

20. a. Yes. The mean for Group 1 is lower than for Group 2.   b. H_0: $\mu_1 \geq \mu_2$ c. yes   d. unequal variances formula   e. $s_{\bar{X}_1-\bar{X}_2} = 3.93$ f. $t = -1.27$ g. -1.690; reject null for all values ≤ -1.690 h. accept (fail to reject) the null, reject the research   i. yes   j. F

21. a. $s_1^2 = 100$, $s_2^2 = 225$ b. Statistical power of the equality of variances test is quite low due to the small sample sizes.   c. Unequal variances formula. The equal variances formula yields inaccurate results when population variances are unequal and sample sizes differ. Sample sizes do indeed differ, and considering the large difference in sample variances and the low power of the equality of variances test, it may well be that $\sigma_1^2 \neq \sigma_2^2$.

22. $df = 70$ (this presumes equal variances formula is used), $s_{\bar{X}_1-\bar{X}_2} = 3.66$ $t = 1.37$, accept the null

23. pretest, posttest

24. dependent or matched

25. paired or dependent (or correlated, related, matched)

26. a. dependent   b. independent   c. paired   d. dependent   e. independent

27. smaller, larger

28. decreases

29. greater/higher

30. number of pairs minus 1

31. T

32. -5

33. 2.2

34. The mean of the difference scores is 0.00, or $\mu_{\text{dif}} = 0$

35. T

36. a. dependent samples t test   b. yes   c. $\bar{X}_1 - \bar{X}_2 = 5.0$ d. 5.0   e. 36   f. $s_{\bar{X}dif} = 2.0$ g. $t = 2.5$ h. $df = 35$ i. two-tailed   j. 2.030 and -2.030 k. reject the null; accept the research   l. no   m. yes

37. normally, robust

Chapter 19

1. T

2. z statistic

3. a. one-sample test of p b. H_0: $\pi = .15$, H_1: $\pi \neq .15$ (In words: Null: Proportion in population is .15. Research: Proportion in population is not .15.)   c. $\pi = .15$ should be used   d. yes   e. $\sigma_p = .0226$ f. $z = 4.42$ g. reject the null, accept the research   h. less than .05   i. less than .05

4. a. H_0: $\pi = .80$, H_1: $\pi \neq .80$ b. $\pi = .80$ c. yes   d. $\sigma_p = .040$ e. $z = 2.50$ f. reject the null, accept the research   g. less than .05   h. yes, it is statistically significant at the .05 level (two-tailed test)   i. Yes, you can be 95% confident that this is the case.

5. family, degrees of freedom

6. $\mu = 6$

7. positively, decreases

8. false

9. one, upper/positive

10. null, expected frequency

11. observed proportion, observed frequency

12. average, four

13. F

14. T

15 a. one-variable χ^2 test   b. 10   c. yes   d. For Hispanics $\pi = .35$, for Asian Americans $\pi = .25$, for Native Americans $\pi = .20$, for African Americans $\pi = .10$, for whites $\pi = .10$ e. Hispanic, .35; Asian American, .25; Native American, .20; African American, .10; white, .10   f. Hispanic, 17.5; Asian American, 12.5; Native American, 10; African American, 5; white, 5   g. Hispanic, .24; Asian American, .20; Native American, .14; African American, .16; white, .26   h. Hispanic, 12; Asian American, 10; Native American, 7; African American, 8; white, 13   i. $\chi^2 = 17.73$ j. $df = 4$ k. 13.28   l. reject the null, accept the re-

search   m. yes   n. No (this probability is <.01)

16. a. yes   b. 20 for each category   c. $\chi^2 = 4.30$
d. $df = 3$ e. 7.81   f. accept the null
g. greater than .05   h. No.   i. Yes. (Or, to be more precise, results are not sufficiently inconsistent with the null for it to be rejected.)

17. a. Yes   b. 20   c. $\chi^2 = 8.70$ d. $df = 3$
e. 7.81   f. reject the null   g. less than .05
h. No. Indeed, it is likely that the null is false. (We can be 95% confident that such is the case.)   i. No, it is inconsistent.

Chapter 20

1. average, six; minimum, three
2. F
3. unassociated/independent
4. nondirectional
5. a. $df = 6$ b. $df = 4$ c. $df = 15$ d. $df = 1$
6. a. In the population from which the study sample was randomly selected, workshop attendance and opinion are unassociated. Or, more simply: Workshop attendance and opinion are unassociated.   b. Equal percentages of workshop attendees and nonattendees agree with the statement.   c. Attend/agree, 36; attend/not agree, 14; not attend/agree, 36; not attend/not agree, 14.   d. Yes; the average expected frequency is greater than six: $100/4 = 25$. The minimum expected frequency is greater than one: $(50 \times 28)/100 = 14$.   e. For those who attended: agree, .80; disagree, .20. For those who did not attend: agree, .64; disagree, .36.   f. associated   g. For those who attended: agree, 72%; disagree, 28%. For those who did not attend: agree, 72%; disagree, 28%.   h. No   i. $\chi^2 = 3.175$ j. $df = 1$ k. 3.84
l. $\chi^2 (1, N = 100) = 3.175, p > .05$ m. accept (fail to reject) the null; reject the research   n. F   o. No; as there was no random assignment to groups, one should be alert to possible influence from confounding variables.
7. a. $\chi^2 = 6.35$ b. yes   c. reject the null; accept the research   d. yes   e. No. As there was no random assignment to groups, results may reflect the influence of confounding variables.

8. a. Children and family, 80%; mental health, 68%; health, 75%; community practice, 77%
b. .75, .25   c. yes   d. small/weak or very small/very weak   e. $\chi^2 = 2.06$ f. $df = 3$
g. 7.81   h. accept the null; reject the research   i. No   j. $\chi^2 (3, N = 200) = 2.06$, $p > .05$ k. Yes. (The probability that association is due solely to sampling error exceeds .05.)
9. F
10. F
11. increases

Chapter 21

1. T
2. $\sigma_{\bar{X}}^2 = \sigma^2/N$
3. normally, equal
4. Populations from which samples have been (randomly) selected have equal means.
5. $\mu_1 = \mu_2 = \ldots = \mu_J$
6. variance
7. variance, equal
8. groups, mean square within
9. average, within
10. between, mean square between
11. sampling distribution of $\bar{X}$
12. means, n (sample size of each group)
13. within, between
14. F (One expects approximately equal values.)
15. spread, sampling error/chance
16. between, within
17. F, F ratio
18. 1.00, larger
19. T
20. positively
21. T
22. F
23. T
24. nondirectional
25. one
26. F
27. For each group: find the mean, compute deviation scores, square deviation scores, sum. Finally, sum the results for each group.
28. degrees of freedom, $N - J$
29. For each group: subtract group mean from grand mean, square, multiply by n. Finally, sum results for each group.

30. degrees of freedom, $J - 1$
31. $F = MS_B/MS_W$
32. a. $df = 4, 35$ b. $df = 2, 97$ c. $df = 3, 24$
33. a. 8.0 b. 8.0 c. $MS_W = 8.0$ d. $df = 27$
34. a. $F = 1.5$ b. $F = 3.0$ c. $F = 0.75$
    d. $F = 4.0$
35. a. reject at both levels b. reject at .05 level; accept (fail to reject) at .01 level c. fail to reject at both levels
36. a. Between groups: $df = 4$, $MS_B = 90$. Within groups: $df = 100$, $MS_W = 45$. The F ratio is 2.00. b. $F = 2.46$ c. No d. Yes e. Fail to reject f. Yes
37. a. 4 b. $n = 25$ c. $MS_B = 100.0$, $MS_W = 10.0$, $F = 10.0$ d. 4.05 (When the exact df for MS_W is not given in Table A.4, one uses the closest lower number.) e. Reject f. No, it is not plausible; it is very unlikely.
38. α, the probability associated with the selected significance level
39. greater (than) α
40. greater (than) .05
41. multiple comparison procedures
42. T
43. T
44. F
45. Exploring your data may reveal interesting and important relationships that would otherwise have been overlooked.

Chapter 22

1. T
2. T
3. H_0: $\rho = 0.00$ H_1: $\rho \neq 0.00$
4. decreases
5. absolute, decreases
6. a. positive b. H_0: $\rho = 0.00$; H_1: $\rho \neq 0.00$ c. $df = 100$ d. $-.254$ and $.254$ e. $\leq -.254$ or $\geq .254$ f. reject the null g. 99% confident h. No, this is very unlikely; chance of this is less than 1 in 100 i. Probably not a good conclusion. A better one: increased health problems lead to increased visiting.
7. #1. a. $r \geq 0.00$ b. $df = 50$ c. $-.322$ d. fail to reject the null
   #2. a. $r \geq 0.00$ b. $df = 50$ c. $-.231$ d. reject the null

#3. a. $r = 0.00$ b. $df = 50$ c. .273 and $-.273$ d. fail to reject the null
#4. a. $r = 0.00$ b. $df = 70$ c. .232 and $-.232$ d. reject the null
#5. a. $r = 0.00$ b. $df = 70$ c. .302 and $-.302$ d. fail to reject the null

8. F
9. T
10. T
11. F
12. F
13. Very strong skew in one or both variables makes the test of Pearson's r suspect. A good alternative is to transform scores to ranks and test via r_{ranks}.
14. One must interpret results in terms of ranks rather than original scores.
15. T
16. $tau_b = 0.00$
17. that there is no directional association in the population from which the sample has been randomly selected
18. T
19. F
20. F
21. (In the populations from which samples were randomly selected) (1) mean ranks are equal or (2) medians are equal.
22. Kruskal-Wallis test
23. categorical
24. with dependent samples
25. that in the population from which the sample was randomly selected, 50% of (nontied) scores are higher in each group
26. the size of differences
27. dependent, ordinal
28. dependent samples t test
29. dependent/paired
30. T
31. a. independent samples, may not use b. paired samples, may use c. paired samples, may use d. independent samples, may not use
32. Well known. Easy to use. Extend easily to more advanced procedures. For the most part, highly robust to assumptions. Greater statistical power than nonparametric tests.

33. Will be inaccurate to at least some degree when assumptions are violated.
34. Where assumptions of parametric test are violated, nonparametric test is presumably more accurate than parametric test.
35. Not that well known. Do not set the stage for more complex (multivariate) analyses. Generally have less statistical power than do parametric tests.
36. F
37. The predicted change in the dependent variable (in original measurement units) as the predictor increases by 1.00, controlling for other predictors in the equation
38. The predicted change in standard deviation units in the dependent variable as the predictor increases by one (1.00) standard deviation, controlling for other predictors in the equation
39. T
40. F

Chapter 23

1. context
2. The degree to which similar results are expected in a different setting/context
3. T
4. F
5. T
6. Although one should not use inferential statistical procedures to do this, there are times when other tools may, cautiously and appropriately, be used for this purpose.
7. similarity
8. T
9. T
10. F
11. T
12. F
13. F
14. T
15. clinical significance
16. Yes
17. statistical significance, size of association, causality, generalizability, importance
18. statistical significance
19. F

20. F
21. say, a study that focuses on how to teach kids to blow big bubbles with their bubble gum
22. a. No association in study population between type of program and psychiatric hospitalization (or lack thereof). Or, alternatively, percentages who require hospitalization in A and B are equal. b. good/high c. yes, significant at .05 level d. $p \leq .05$ e. $p \leq .05$ f. yes, can be 95% confident g. reject the null; accept the alternative (research) h. medium/moderate i. May not be causal. No random assignment. Perhaps different client characteristics, not differences in program, explain the difference in outcomes. j. No mention of probability sampling from any wider population was made, so the answer is no. k. Presumably reasonably similar results would be obtained from similar programs in urban environments in the northeastern United States. (Questions pertaining to nonstatistical generalizability always involve considerable uncertainty.) l. perhaps clients with nonchronic problems in a different area of the country m. Yes, presumably so. An effective program for those with chronic serious mental health problems is indeed important.
23. a. Mean scores on the Rainbow Inventory are equal for those in A and B. b. fair/moderate c. yes, significant at .05 level d. $p \leq .05$ e. $p \leq .05$ f. yes, can be 95% confident g. reject null; accept research h. medium/moderate i. Presumably yes, due to random assignment. j. No, as no such population is mentioned. k. Cautiously, to other upscale clinics serving similar populations l. Public clinic in different part of country serving clients with different problems m. Presumably, yes; mental health treatment is an important field.
24. a. That the same percentages in each approach find jobs b. exceptional, or even better than this c. yes, significant at .05 level d. $p \leq .05$ e. $p \leq .05$ f. yes, can be 95% confident g. Reject null, accept alternative h. extremely small/extremely weak i. yes, due to the randomization j. No, the 8000 participants were not selected from any

wider population   k. Results should generalize reasonably well to states with populations with similar characteristics   l. Perhaps to a highly urbanized, northeastern state   m. Neither approach works much better than the other. Difficult to say if these results are important without substantial knowledge in area of welfare reform; if one approach is markedly less expensive than the other, results would seem to argue for that approach.

25. a. Palm and joystick controls are equally effective and realistic.   b. Power is excellent.   c. significant at .01 level   d. $p \leq .01$ e. $p \leq .01$ f. can be 99% confident   g. reject null; accept alternative   h. very large/very strong   i. Yes, due to the random assignment.   j. Yes, results may be generalized with known and considerable confidence to the full population of eleven-year-old boys in the six-state region. (One may be confident null is false for this population.)   k. Nonstatistical generalizability questions call, ultimately, for judgment. I suspect these results would generalize well to boys of similar ages across the United States and probably to similar-aged boys in many other developed countries as well.   l. Boys and/or girls in a nondeveloped country who had not had prior experience with video games.   m. Ultimately, the question is importance to whom. There is not much apparent significance for human services practice; though perhaps if the goal is to enhance a youth's sense of mastery one should secure a palm controller. Results would seem to have considerable importance to those who manufacture video games and components.

26. a. Same percentage of youth who receive intervention and youth who do not have used marijuana in the past six months.   b. power is excellent/very high   c. not significant at .05 level   d. $p > .05$ e. $p > .05$ f. No, can be less than 95% confident.   g. fail to reject null, reject research   h. exceedingly weak   i. Though randomization rules out confounding factors, the fact that the relationship in the study sample is not statistically significant indicates that it may be due simply to chance/sam-

pling error. Hence, one should not conclude that the relationship is causal. (Size of relationship is so small that it could be characterized as trivial; doesn't make much sense to think about the cause of a trivial-sized relationship.)   j. No, there is no larger population to which statistical generalizations may be made.   k. Presumably these results should generalize well to other medium-size Midwestern towns with similar characteristics; may also generalize well to other settings (hard to say)   l. very large urban center and/or extremely rural setting   m. Even though association does not achieve significance, result may well be important. Considerable costs are involved in the described intervention. If the intervention is not effective, knowing this is important. Given this knowledge, resources can be directed elsewhere.

27. a. Equal percentages in home-based and placement-based services commit offences.   b. power is exceptional/extremely high   c. significant at .01 level   d. $p \leq .01$ e. $p \leq .01$ f. can be 99% confident   g. reject null, accept alternative   h. moderately strong to strong   i. No, assignment to home-based versus placement-based service was nonrandom (when no mention of random assignment is made, one assumes that assignment is nonrandom). Differences in client characteristics, not home-based vs. placement-based services, may explain the differing outcomes.   j. No, presumably the full population of youth served by the agency composed the study sample.   k. Presumably, similar results would be obtained in states with similar programs and similar youth populations.   l. The less similar the setting to which generalization is contemplated, the less the expected generalizability. Perhaps results would not generalize well to a state with a very large urban population.   m. Question of importance is complicated by the fact that the relationship may well not be causal. Even so, knowing that fewer youth in home-based services commit new offenses strikes me as important information that could be useful in program planning.

Symbols in the Text

Greek Letters	Description
α	Alpha, probability connected with selected statistical significance level and probability of type I error
β	Beta, probability of type II error (pronounced "bait-ah")
β	Beta, standardized regression coefficient (same symbol as for probability of type II error)
η	Eta, measure of size/strength of association (pronounced "ate-ah")
η^2	Eta squared (correlation ratio), measure of size/strength of association
μ	Mu, population mean (pronounced "mew")
π	Pi, population proportion (pronounced "pie")
ρ	Rho, population correlation (pronounced "row")
Σ	Sigma (capital letter), summation sign
σ	Sigma ("small" letter), population standard deviation
σ^2	Population variance
σ_p	Standard error of the proportion
$\sigma_{\bar{X}}$	Standard error of the mean
$\sigma_{\bar{X}_1 - \bar{X}_2}$	Standard error of the difference between means
χ^2	Chi-square statistic as used in both chi-square tests (pronounced "ki" as in "kite")

English Letters	Description
A	Constant in regression equation (also the Y intercept)
B	Unstandardized regression coefficient
95%CI of μ	95% Confidence interval of the mean
99%CI of μ	99% Confidence interval of the mean
95%CI of π	95% Confidence interval of the proportion
99%CI of π	99% Confidence interval of the proportion
$D\%$	Difference in percentages (percentage difference)
df	Degrees of freedom
F	F ratio in analysis of variance
f	Frequency
H_0	Null hypothesis
H_1	Research (alternative) hypothesis
IQR	Interquartile range (midrange)
M	Sample mean (this text more often uses $\overline{X}$)
MS_B	Mean square between (in ANOVA)
MS_W	Mean square within (in ANOVA)
N	Number of cases in study sample
n	Number of cases in a group or "subsample" (also alternative symbol for frequency)
OR	Odds ratio
p	Proportion in sample
p	Probability (including probability resulting from statistical significance test)
$R\%$	Ratio of percentages
r	Pearson correlation coefficient
r_{phi}	Correlation between two dichotomous variables (phi is pronounced as in "five")
r_{ranks}	Spearman correlation coefficient
r^2	Coefficient of determination (percentage of shared or explained variance)
s	Sample standard deviation (preferred formula)
s_{samp}	Sample standard deviation (less preferred formula)
s^2	Sample variance (preferred formula)
s_{samp}^2	Sample variance (less preferred formula)
s_p	Estimate of standard error of the proportion
$s_{\overline{X}}$	Estimate of standard error of the mean
$s_{\overline{X}_1 - \overline{X}_2}$	Estimate of the standard error of the difference between means
t	Test statistic for t tests
X	Value of an individual case (raw score)
$\overline{X}$	Sample mean
$\overline{X}_{grand}$	In ANOVA, the mean of the full sample
$\hat{Y}$	Predicted value of Y (dependent variable) in unstandardized regression equation
z	z score (standard score) and test statistic for large sample test of $\overline{X}$
$\hat{z}_y$	Predicted z score of Y in standardized regression equation

Formulas in the Text

Proportion	$p = \dfrac{\text{number with given characteristic}}{\text{total number}}$	(2.1)
Proportion	$p = \dfrac{\text{frequency}}{\text{sample size}} = \dfrac{f}{N}$	(2.2)
Percentage	$\% = \dfrac{\text{number with a given characteristic}}{\text{total number}} \times 100$	(2.3)
Percentage	$\% = \dfrac{\text{frequency}}{\text{sample size}} \times 100 = \dfrac{f}{N} \times 100$	(2.4)
Ratio	$\text{Ratio} = \dfrac{\text{number (frequency) in first group}}{\text{number (frequency) in second group}}$	(2.5)
Cumulative percentage	$\text{Cumulative \%} = \dfrac{\text{cumulative frequency}}{\text{sample size}} \times 100$	(2.6)
Sample mean	$\overline{X} = \dfrac{\Sigma X}{N}$	(3.1)
Range	$\text{Range} = X_{\text{highest}} - X_{\text{lowest}}$	(4.1)
Interquartile range	$IQR = X_{75\%} - X_{25\%}$	(4.2)
Mean deviation	$MD = \dfrac{\Sigma |X - \overline{X}|}{N}$	(4.3)
Standard deviation (nonpreferred formula)	$s_{\text{samp}} = \sqrt{\dfrac{\Sigma(X - \overline{X})^2}{N}}$	(4.4)
Standard deviation (preferred formula)	$s = \sqrt{\dfrac{\Sigma(X - \overline{X})^2}{N - 1}}$	(4.5)
Variance (nonpreferred formula)	$s_{\text{samp}}^2 = \dfrac{\Sigma(X - \overline{X})^2}{N}$	(4.6)

Variance (preferred formula)	$s^2 = \dfrac{\Sigma(X - \overline{X})^2}{N - 1}$	(4.7)
z Score (standard score)	$z = \dfrac{X - \overline{X}}{s}$	(5.1)
Difference in percentages	$D\% = \%_1 - \%_2$	(6.1)
Ratio of percentages	$R\% = \dfrac{\%_1}{\%_2}$	(6.2)
Odds	$\text{Odds} = \dfrac{\text{number that experience event}}{\text{number that do not experience}} = \dfrac{n_e}{n_{ne}}$	(7.1)
Odds	$\text{Odds} = \dfrac{\text{proportion that experience event}}{\text{proportion that do not experience event}} = \dfrac{p_e}{p_{ne}}$	(7.2)
Odds ratio	$OR = \dfrac{\text{odds for first group}}{\text{odds for second group}} = \dfrac{\text{odds}_1}{\text{odds}_2}$	(7.3)
Pearson's r (correlation coefficient)	$r = \dfrac{\Sigma(z_x z_y)}{N - 1}$	(8.1)
Standardized regression equation (predicted z score on variable Y)	$z_y = r_{xy} z_x$	(8.2)
Unstandardized regression equation (predicted raw score on variable Y)	$Y = A + BX$	(8.3)
Standardized difference between means	$SDM = \dfrac{\overline{X}_1 - \overline{X}_2}{s_{wg}}$	(9.1)
Estimate of standard deviation within groups (equal sample sizes)	$s_{wg} \approx \dfrac{s_1 + s_2}{2}$	(9.2)
Estimate of standard deviation within groups (unequal sample sizes)	$s_{wg} \approx \dfrac{n_1 s_1 + n_2 s_2}{n_1 + n_2}$	(9.3)
z Score in a population	$z = \dfrac{X - \mu}{\sigma}$	(12.1)
Sampling error	$\text{Sampling error} = \text{sample statistic} - \text{population parameter}$	(12.2)
Standard error of the mean	$\sigma_{\overline{X}} = \dfrac{\sigma}{\sqrt{N}}$	(12.3)
Estimate of standard error of the mean	$s_{\overline{X}} = \dfrac{s}{\sqrt{N}}$	(13.1)

95% Confidence interval of the mean	$95\% \, CI \text{ of } \mu = \overline{X} \pm 1.96\left(\dfrac{s}{\sqrt{N}}\right)$	(13.2)
95% Confidence interval of the mean	$95\% \, CI \text{ of } \mu = \overline{X} \pm 1.96(s_{\overline{X}})$	(13.3)
99% Confidence interval of the mean	$99\% \, CI \text{ of } \mu = \overline{X} \pm 2.58\left(\dfrac{s}{\sqrt{N}}\right)$	(13.4)
99% Confidence interval of the mean	$99\% \, CI \text{ of } \mu = \overline{X} \pm 2.58(s_{\overline{X}})$	(13.5)
Standard error of the proportion	$\sigma_p = \sqrt{\dfrac{\pi(1-\pi)}{N}}$	(13.6)
Estimate of standard error of the proportion	$s_p = \sqrt{\dfrac{p(1-p)}{N}}$	(13.7)
95% Confidence interval of the proportion	$95\% \, CI \text{ of } \pi = p \pm 1.96\sqrt{\dfrac{p(1-p)}{N}}$	(13.8)
95% Confidence interval of the proportion	$95\% \, CI \text{ of } \pi = p \pm 1.96(s_p)$	(13.9)
99% Confidence interval of the proportion	$99\% \, CI \text{ of } \pi = p \pm 2.58\sqrt{\dfrac{p(1-p)}{N}}$	(13.10)
99% Confidence interval of the proportion	$99\% \, CI \text{ of } \pi = p \pm 2.58(s_p)$	(13.11)
Probability of event with given characteristic	$p = \dfrac{\text{number of events with characteristic}}{\text{total number of events}}$	(14.1)
Probability of event with given characteristic	$p = \text{Proportion of events with characteristic}$	(14.2)
Large sample test of $\overline{X}$ formula	$z \approx \dfrac{\overline{X} - \mu}{\left(\dfrac{s}{\sqrt{N}}\right)}$	(15.1)
Large sample test of $\overline{X}$ formula	$z \approx \dfrac{\overline{X} - \mu}{s_{\overline{X}}}$	(15.2)
Power	$\text{Power} = 1 - \beta$	(16.1)
Beta	$\beta = 1 - \text{power}$	(16.2)
One-sample t test formula	$t = \dfrac{\overline{X} - \mu}{s_{\overline{X}}}$	(17.1)
One-sample t test formula	$t = \dfrac{\overline{X} - \mu}{s/\sqrt{N}}$	(17.2)

Confidence interval of the mean	$CI \text{ of } \mu = \overline{X} \pm t(s/\sqrt{N})$	(17.3)
Confidence interval of the mean	$CI \text{ of } \mu = \overline{X} \pm t(s_{\overline{X}})$	(17.4)
Standard error of the difference between means	$\sigma_{\overline{X}_1 - \overline{X}_2} = \sqrt{\dfrac{\sigma_1^2}{N_1} + \dfrac{\sigma_2^2}{N_2}}$	(18.1)
General formula for the independent samples t test	$t = \dfrac{\overline{X}_1 - \overline{X}_2}{s_{\overline{X}_1 - \overline{X}_2}}$	(18.2)
Estimate of the standard error of the difference between means (for unequal variances formula)	$s_{\overline{X}_1 - \overline{X}_2} = \sqrt{\dfrac{s_1^2}{n_1} + \dfrac{s_2^2}{n_2}}$	(18.3)
Independent samples t test (unequal variances formula)	$t = \dfrac{\overline{X}_1 - \overline{X}_2}{\sqrt{\dfrac{s_1^2}{n_1} + \dfrac{s_2^2}{n_2}}}$	(18.4)
Estimate of the standard error of the difference between means (for equal variances formula)	$s_{\overline{X}_1 - \overline{X}_2} = \sqrt{\left(\dfrac{(n_1 - 1)s_1^2 + (n_2 - 1)s_2^2}{n_1 + n_2 - 2}\right)\left(\dfrac{1}{n_1} + \dfrac{1}{n_2}\right)}$	(18.5)
Independent samples t test (equal variances formula)	$t = \dfrac{\overline{X}_1 - \overline{X}_2}{\sqrt{\left(\dfrac{(n_1 - 1)s_1^2 + (n_2 - 1)s_2^2}{n_1 + n_2 - 2}\right)\left(\dfrac{1}{n_1} + \dfrac{1}{n_2}\right)}}$	(18.6)
Degrees of freedom for independent samples t test (unequal variances formula)	$df = \dfrac{\left(\dfrac{s_1^2}{n_1} + \dfrac{s_2^2}{n_2}\right)^2}{\dfrac{1}{n_1 - 1}\left(\dfrac{s_1^2}{n_1}\right)^2 + \dfrac{1}{n_2 - 1}\left(\dfrac{s_2^2}{n_2}\right)^2}$	(18.7)
Dependent samples t test (first formula presented)	$t = \dfrac{\overline{X}_1 - \overline{X}_2}{\sqrt{\dfrac{s_1^2}{N} + \dfrac{s_2^2}{N} - 2\,r_{12}\,(s_1/\sqrt{N})(s_2/\sqrt{N})}}$	(18.8)
Dependent samples t test (difference score formula)	$t = \dfrac{\overline{X}_{dif}}{s_{dif}/\sqrt{N}}$	(18.9)
Dependent samples t test (difference score formula)	$t = \dfrac{\overline{X}_{dif}}{s_{\overline{X}_{dif}}}$	(18.10)
One-sample test of a proportion	$z = \dfrac{p - \pi}{\sqrt{\pi(1 - \pi)/N}}$	(19.1)
One-sample test of a proportion	$z = \dfrac{p - \pi}{\sigma_p}$	(19.2)

One-variable chi-square test (formula using proportions)	$\chi^2 = N\left(\Sigma \dfrac{(p_o - p_e)^2}{p_e}\right)$	(19.3)
One-variable chi-square test (formula using frequencies)	$\chi^2 = \Sigma \dfrac{(f_o - f_e)^2}{f_e}$	(19.4)
Degrees of freedom for chi-square test of independence	$df = (R - 1)(C - 1)$	(20.1)
Expected column proportion	$p_e = \text{(row margin total)}/N$	(20.2)
Expected row proportion	$p_e = \text{(column margin total)}/N$	(20.3)
Expected frequency	$f_e = \dfrac{\text{(row margin total)} \times \text{(column margin total)}}{N}$	(20.4)
F ratio	$F = \dfrac{MS_B}{MS_W}$	(21.1)
Mean square within (only when sample sizes are equal)	$MS_W = \dfrac{s_1^2 + s_2^2 + \cdots + s_J^2}{J}$	(21.2)
Mean square within	$MS_W = \dfrac{SS_W}{df \text{ for } MS_W}$	(21.3)
Sum of squares within	$SS_W = \Sigma (X_1 - \overline{X}_1)^2 + \Sigma (X_2 - \overline{X}_2)^2 + \cdots + \Sigma (X_J - \overline{X}_J)^2$	(21.4)
Mean square between	$MS_B = \dfrac{SS_B}{df \text{ for } MS_B}$	(21.5)
Sums of squares between	$SS_B = n_1(\overline{X}_1 - \overline{X}_{\text{grand}})^2 + n_2(\overline{X}_2 - \overline{X}_{\text{grand}})^2 + \cdots + n_J(X_J - \overline{X}_{\text{grand}})^2$	(21.6)

References

Achenbach, T. M. (1991). *Manual for the child behavior checklist 4/18 and 1991 profile.* Burlington, VT: Department of Psychiatry, University of Vermont.

American Psychological Association. (1994). *Publication manual of the American Psychological Association* (4th ed.). Washington, DC: Author.

Aron, A., & Aron, E. N. (1997). *Statistics for the behavioral and social sciences: A brief course.* Upper Saddle River, NJ: Prentice-Hall.

Babbie, E., Halley, F., & Zaino, J. (2000). *Adventures in social research: Data analysis using SPSS for Windows 95/98.* Thousand Oaks, CA: Pine Forge Press.

Blalock, H. M., Jr. (1979). *Social Statistics* (2nd ed.). New York: McGraw-Hill.

Bloom, M., Fischer, J., & Orme, J. G. (1995). *Evaluating practice: Guidelines for the accountable professional* (2nd ed.). Boston: Allyn & Bacon.

Camilli, G., & Hopkins, K. D. (1978). Applicability of chi-square 2×2 contingency tables with small expected frequencies. *Psychological Bulletin, 85,* 163–167.

Camilli, G., & Hopkins, K. D. (1979). Testing for association in 2×2 contingency tables with very small samples. *Psychological Bulletin, 86,* 1011–1014.

Campbell, D. T. (1986). Relabeling internal and external validity for applied social scientists. In W. M. K. Trochim (Ed.), *Advances in quasi-experimental design analysis: New directions for program evaluation, Vol. 31.* San Francisco: Jossey-Bass.

Cohen, J. (1988). *Statistical power analysis for the social sciences.* Hillsdale, NJ: Erlbaum.

Cohen, J., & Cohen, P. (1983). *Applied multiple regression/correlation analysis for the behavioral sciences* (2nd ed.). Hillsdale, NJ: Erlbaum.

Comstock, G., & Strasburger, V. (1990). Deceptive appearances: Television violence and aggressive behavior. *Journal of Adolescent Health Care, 11,* 31–44.

Conover, W. J. (1971). *Practical nonparameteric statistics.* New York: John Wiley.

Conover, W. J. (1980). *Practical nonparameteric statistics* (2nd ed.). New York: John Wiley.

Davis, R. M., & Bouck, P. (1955). Crucial importance of adoption home study. *Child Welfare, 34,* 20–21.

Elifson, K. W., Runyon, R. P., & Haber, A. (1982). *Fundamentals of social statistics.* Reading, MA: Addison-Wesley.

Fleiss, J. L. (1994). Measures of effect size for categorical data. In H. Cooper & L. V. Hedges (Eds.), *The handbook of research synthesis* (pp. 245–260). New York: Russell Sage Foundation.

Glass, G. V., & Hopkins, K. D. (1996). *Statistical methods in education and psychology* (3rd ed.). Boston: Allyn and Bacon.

Green, S. B., Salkind, N. J., & Akey, T. M. (2000). *Using SPSS for Windows: Analyzing and understanding data* (2nd ed.). Upper Saddle River, NJ: Prentice-Hall.

Gupta, V. (1999). *SPSS for Beginners* [On-line and print]. Available Web: www.spss.org; or e-mail: vgupta1000@aol.com

Hopkins, K. D., & Glass, G. V. (1978). *Basic statistics for the behavioral sciences.* Englewood Cliffs, NJ: Prentice-Hall.

Hudson, W. W. (1992). *The WALMYR assessment scales scoring manual.* Tempe, AZ: WALMYR Publishing.

Jaffee, B., & Fanshel, D. (1970). *How they fared in adoption.* New York: Columbia University Press.

Kish, L. (1965). *Survey sampling.* New York: John Wiley.

Koehler, K. J., & Larantz, K. (1980). An empirical investigation of goodness-of-fit for sparse multinomials. *Journal of the American Statistical Association, 75*(370) 336–344.

Lazar, B. A. (1994). Why social work should care: Television violence and children. *Child and Adolescent Social Work Journal, 11,* 3–19.

McWhinnie, A. M. (1967). *Adopted children: How they grow up.* London: Routledge Kegan Paul.

Moore, D. S. (1997). *Statistics: Concepts and controversies* (4th ed.). New York: W. H. Freeman.

Moore, D. S., & McCabe, G. P. (1993). *Introduction to the practice of statistics* (2nd ed.). New York: W. H. Freeman.

Norusis, M. J. (1993). *SPSS\PC+ guide to data analysis.* Chicago: SPSS.

Norusis, M. J. (1997). *SPSS 7.5 guide to data analysis.* Upper Saddle River, NJ: Prentice-Hall.

Norusis, M. J. (2000). *SPSS 10.0 guide to data analysis.* Upper Saddle River, NJ: Prentice-Hall.

Olson, D. H., McCubbin, H. I., Larsen, A., Muxen, M., & Wilson, M. (1985). *Family inventories.* St. Paul, MN: Family Social Science, University of Minnesota.

Pilcher, D. M. (1990). *Data analysis for the helping professions: A practical guide.* Newbury Park, CA: Sage Publications.

Ripple, L. (1968). A follow-up study of adopted children. *Social Service Review, 42,* 479–497.

Roscoe, J. T., & Byars, J. A. (1971). An investigation of the restraints with respect to sample size commonly imposed on the use of the chi-square statistic. *Journal of the American Statistical Association, 66,* 755–759.

Rosenthal, J. A. (1988). Patterns of reported child abuse and neglect. *Child Abuse & Neglect, 12,* 263–271.

Rosenthal, J. A. (1996). Qualitative descriptors of strength of association and effect size. *Journal of Social Service Research, 21*(4), 37–59.

Rosenthal, J. A. (1997). Pragmatic concepts and tools for data interpretation: A balanced model. *Journal of Teaching in Social Work, 15*(1/2), 113–130.

Rosenthal, J. A., & Groze, V. K. (1992). *Special-needs adoption: A study of intact families.* New York: Praeger.

Rosenthal, J. A., & Groze, V. K. (1994). A longitudinal study of special-needs adoptive families. *Child Welfare, 73*(6), 689–706.

Rosenthal, R. (1994). Parameteric measures of effect size. In H. Cooper & L. V. Hedges (Eds.), *The handbook of research synthesis* (pp. 231–244). New York: Russell Sage Foundation.

Rubin, A., & Babbie, E. (1997). *Research methods for social work* (3rd ed.). Pacific Grove, CA: Brooks/Cole.

Samuels, M. L., & Lu, T. C. (1992). Sample size requirements for the back-of-the-envelope binomial confidence interval. *American Statistician, 46*(3), 228–231.

Siegel, S. (1956). *Nonparametric statistics for the behavioral sciences.* New York: McGraw-Hill.

Siegel, S., & Castellan, N. J. (1988). *Nonparametric statistics for the behavioral sciences* (2nd ed.). New York: McGraw-Hill.

SPSS Inc. (1999). *SPSS Base 10.0 Applications Guide.* Chicago: Author.

SPSS Inc. (1999). *SPSS Base 10.0 User's Guide.* Chicago: Author.

SPSS Inc. (1999). SPSS Graduate Pack 10.0 for Windows [Computer software]. Chicago: Author.

SPSS (2000). SPSS Student Version 10.0 for Windows [Computer software]. Chicago: Author.

Tatara, M. (1988). *Characteristics of children in substitute and adoptive care in FY 1985.* Washington, DC: American Public Welfare Association.

Toothaker, L. E. (1986). *Introductory statistics for the behavioral sciences.* New York: McGraw-Hill.

Toothaker, L. E., & Miller, L. (1996). *Introductory statistics for the behavioral sciences* (2nd ed.). Pacific Grove, CA: Brooks/Cole.

Tukey, J. W. (1977). *Exploratory data analysis.* Reading, MA: Addison-Wesley.

Zwimpfer, D. M. (1983). Indicators of adoption breakdown. *Social Casework: The Journal of Contempoarary Social Work, 64,* 169–177.

Index

TO THE OWNER OF THIS BOOK:

I hope that you have found *Statistics and Data Interpretation for the Helping Professions* useful. So that this book can be improved in a future edition, would you take the time to complete this sheet and return it? Thank you.

School and address: _____

_____

Department: _____

Instructor's name: _____

1. What I like most about this book is:_____

_____

_____

2. What I like least about this book is: _____

_____

_____

3. My general reaction to this book is: _____

_____

_____

4. The name of the course in which I used this book is: _____

_____

5. Were all of the chapters of the book assigned for you to read? _____

   If not, which ones weren't? _____

6. In the space below, or on a separate sheet of paper, please write specific suggestions for improving this book and anything else you'd care to share about your experience in using this book.

_____

_____

_____

OPTIONAL:

Your name: _____ Date: _____

May we quote you, either in promotion for *Statistics and Data Interpretation for the Helping Professions* or in future publishing ventures?

Yes: _____ No: _____

Sincerely yours,

James A. Rosenthal